The Silent Cry
Dealing with Subtracters in Work and Life

Verna Cornelia Price, Ph.D.

JCAMA Publishers©

The Silent Cry
Dealing with Subtracters in Work and Life

©2008 by Verna Cornelia Price, Ph.D.

Published by JCAMA Publishers

Editor: C. C. Strom
Transcriber: Patricia Hensler
Original Cover Art Work: Tee Simmons
Cover Design: Anna Fabian
Graphic Design: ✕ deanna moore
Photographer: Ann Marsden
Printer: Nystrom Publishing

JCAMA Publishers
Robbinsdale, MN 55422
www.jcama.com
jcameron@jcama.com

Price, Verna Cornelia, 2008
The Silent Cry: *Dealing with Subtracters in Work and Life*

LCCN 2008922404
ISBN 0-9717765-3-1
Printed in U.S.A. on acid-free paper
Distributed by JCAMA Publishers

**"Our Deepest Fear
is not
that we are inadequate.
Our deepest fear
is that
we are POWERFUL beyond measure"**

- Nelson Mandela[1]

---

1 Mandela, N. (1994). [A 1994 inaugural speech, written by Marianne Williamson]. Http://www.lightshift.com/inspiration/mandela.html

TABLE OF CONTENTS

THOUGHTS FOR READERS

As a young child, growing up on a small island in the Bahamas, my grandmother taught me and all her grandchildren how to be Adders. We learned how to give, to serve and be kind. We learned how to be people of integrity who added to each other and our community. But my life has taken many twists and turns since then and by my early twenties I was a Socialized Subtracter. I had become a needy person whose life was full of chaos and drama and loaded with Subtracters. I had learned how to manipulate, control and take from people. Like most people, however, I didn't understand the impact of personal power. I knew nothing about the power to add or subtract from myself and others. It took years, many mistakes, heartaches and much pain before I began to understand that everyone, including me, has the power to change. In my late twenties, I made a decision to change my life and become a positive influence in the lives of others. In the process, I had to deal with the Subtracter in me and the Subtracters in my life. I had to manage my "Just Is" family relationships, move people out of my circle of influence, by changing friends, letting people go, and suffering the consequences. It was a hard and painful journey to look in the mirror and see a Subtracter looking back at me. It almost broke my heart to realize that some of the people who I adored and looked up to were Subtracters. My decision to change my life by letting go of my Subtracters and becoming an Adder was one of the hardest but most rewarding things I have ever done. Why do I tell you this story? Because at some point in our lives, we have all been Subtracters or had to deal with a Subtracter. You are not alone.

My first book, *The Power of People, Four Kinds of People Who Can Change Your Life,* was divinely inspired. I had no intellectual knowledge about the four kinds of powerful people; I only knew that, as I began to write the book, wisdom and revelation unfolded in my spirit. Some people describe the book as a "simple but extraordinary and profound philosophy" that can change your life. I had no idea that people all over the world would not only read my first book, but actually use it as a guide for their lives. The book has been so successful that I have come to call it, "the little purple book that did." Its success stands as an incredible testimony to what happens when you say yes to a vision, dream, and find your purpose. When I was inspired to write my first book, somehow I found the power to say yes and the results have been amazing! The book has been used as a study guide, textbook, coaching tool, and training module for corporate executives, principals, teachers, community organizations, teenagers, offenders, and families struggling to get off of welfare. Regardless of the audience, people who have applied the core principles from the book have created positive changes in their life. Corporate executives have learned how to lead and manage more effectively, teachers have helped more students achieve academically, offenders have learned how to avoid re-offending, teenagers have discovered their power to be successful in school and life, women have used their personal power to escape domestic abuse and on and on. *The Power of People* has been a tool for people from every level and walk of life to begin to change their lives.

As I began to teach about personal power and the power of people, my ears, eyes and heart were opened to a cry from people who were struggling with the Subtracters in their lives. I recognized the cry because I had once suffered from the same cry. I didn't know what to do, but I knew that I was unhappy and my life was a wreck! So when people began to ask me what to do about their Subtracters, I immediately understood that they were asking for wisdom, revelation and strategies on how to continue to change their lives. *The Silent Cry* emerged from the voices of people who realized that they were giving away their power and allowing Subtracters to pull them back to past failures, derail their success and devalue their lives. After reading my first book and learning that they had the power to change their life, their immediate response was "how do I deal with my Subtracters"?

I do this work because I believe that you were created to be a phenomenal and extraordinary person with the power to change your life and world. I believe that you can become your most excellent self. The question is, are you ready to make that decision and to do the work? I made a decision that I would not be just an ordinary person who existed and let my life happen. I decided to **MAKE** a powerful, productive, excellent and fun life. Has it taken work? Yes. Has it been hard at times? Yes. Has it been painful at times? Yes. Is it a journey I would take again? Yes!

As you read this book you will find yourself challenged, angry, sad, happy and disgusted. You will laugh and cry. You will also find the courage to face yourself and deal with the reality of who you really are. You will learn how to stop using your power to subtract, and discover the power to add and attract Adders. You will also find the power, courage and confidence to move Subtracters out of your inner circle and, when necessary, out of your life. Will it take hard work? Yes. Do I expect you to do the work? Yes. Why? Because no one can do your work for you. In the process, you will discover core principles that show you how to stop giving away your personal power and become your most excellent self.

Chapter 1

The Silent Cry

One morning my seven-year-old son and I went for breakfast at a well-known local restaurant. It was very full that morning, so we sat at the breakfast bar, laughing and talking while we waited for our food. A woman kept looking at my son and me, so I politely smiled at her. Several minutes later, she leaned over to me and said, "You have such a nice son." Flattered, I smiled and said, "Well, thank you very much."

As we exchanged our greetings, I could hear a silent cry coming from her. I could hear this woman's pain. I didn't know what it was, but I could hear it. Almost immediately she began sharing her story with me. The woman had just returned from the hospital where she was visiting her father who was dying from cancer. As she talked, the silent cry grew louder. Then the moment of truth came when she said, "You know, I cannot remember my father ever saying anything nice to me. He always told me I would be nothing and go nowhere. He has never, ever been kind to me." Courageously, she continued with tears in her eyes, "So here I am at the hospital with my father who is dying and I am trying really hard to be nice to him. On his death bed, he is still talking me down and telling me what I can't be in life. I don't know what to do with that."

I knew at that moment this woman was dealing with a Subtracter, who happened to be her parent. A father who had taken away her dreams, vision, goals, courage and confidence to be successful in life. At 45 years old, she was still suffering from the impact, influence and power of a Subtracter, a father who had damaged her self-esteem and derailed her potential to be excellent.

> *People may never shed a physical tear, but watch their attitudes, behavior, and interactions with other people. Listen to their self-talk and you will hear the silent cry.*

Who is a Subtracter? Do Subtracters know they are Subtracters? Are they mean and vicious people? Do they understand what they are doing? This woman needed to understand who she was dealing with, even though it happened to be a parent, and how to deal with this Subtracter so she could begin to live a happy life. This woman deserved a life of confidence and fulfillment. She didn't deserve to carry around this cry in the depths of her bones for the rest of her life.

For many of us, there is a silent cry in our hearts and minds about the *why* in life. Many of us are secretly asking ourselves, "Why am I not where I should be in life?" "Why am I not happy?" "Why do I constantly doubt myself?" "Why do I have so much chaos in my life?" "Why do things always seem to go wrong for me?" "Why can't I get that promotion?"

Listen hard enough and you, too, will hear the silent cry at work, at home, at the mall, at school, everywhere you may work, travel or live. People may never shed a physical tear, but watch their attitudes, behavior, and interactions with other people. Listen to their self-talk and you will hear the silent cry.

I discovered the silent cry when I began conducting seminars and executive coaching based on my first book, *The Power of People, Four Kinds of People Who Can Change Your Life*. This book describes four core principles. First, you were born with power. It doesn't matter what color you are, what ethnicity you are, what gender, nationality or religion you are. It doesn't matter if your parents were wealthy or poor. It doesn't matter what circumstances you were born into. The fact that you were born means that you were born powerful. You were born with something in you — power! Power is an internal spiritual force that gives you what you need to create changes in your life and your world. Everyone has it. No matter who you are, you have power.

Second, no one else has more power than you have. You no longer have to be intimidated by people, or be moved by what they say or how they act. The fact is, no matter what someone else has accomplished, they still have no more power than you do.

The third thing you have to understand about your power is that no one can take it from you, but you can give it away. Your power belongs to you. The only way it can be used or abused is when you give it away. What does it mean

> *When you understand your power and begin to use it, your power begins to multiply. The more you use your power, the more you are able to use it.*

to give away your power? It means you give away your options to choose for yourself. When you let other people take away your option to choose, you surrender your power. In my workshops and seminars, I began to see how people reacted to learning these lessons about their personal power. Many would begin to cry because for so many years, they had given up their power. They were crying because they didn't understand how powerful they were and now wanted to stop giving away their power.

The fourth core principle about power is that when you understand your power and begin to use it, your power begins to multiply. The more you use your power, the more you are able to use it. As I began giving seminars and talking with people about their situations and their personal power, they began telling me about the powerful people in their lives.

In my first book I described four kinds of powerful people; Adders, Subtracters, Multipliers and Dividers. An Adder brings increased value to your life. An Adder is someone who works with you on your ability to improve your life in four dimensions, time, words, knowledge and vision. First, an Adder brings positive value in your use of time. Adders challenge you to use your time effectively because they know that how you use your time forms habits in your life, and those habits create the quality of your life.

Time = Habits = Life

An Adder says, "I want to bring increased value, positive value to the quality of your life, so I will challenge you to use your time wisely." For example, an Adder will say that, if you use your time watching television, then the quality of your life is going to become unproductive because television viewing is unproductive. Adders want to increase your productivity, and they challenge you to use your time to accomplish goals that will increase the quality of your life.

Second, an Adder wants to bring positive value to your words. An Adder realizes that whatever you speak, the words that come out of your mouth will take on a life of their own and will begin to live in you.

Words > Life

It's amazing to hear people speak. Some will say, "I am going to get sick," and without exception they will get sick within days. The reason why is because they have told themselves, "I am going to get sick." The power of words is a principle. Everything you say takes on a life of its own. That is why an Adder warns you to be careful of the words you choose. Be careful what you say. Be careful about what comes out of your mouth. Also, be careful what you think, because your thoughts form the words that you speak, which create the life that you live.

Third, Adders are committed to increasing your knowledge. You must learn more, know more, and grow more. You must increase your information. An Adder realizes you cannot grow beyond your knowledge. You cannot grow beyond how much you know. If you want to grow in your business, you have to learn more about business. If you want to grow in your relationships, learn more about relationships. If you want to grow in your finances, learn more about finances.

Fourth, Adders are also committed to bringing increased value in your vision and goals. An Adder will always challenge you to have clear goals and a powerful vision statement for your life. They realize that when you get to the place where you understand that your personal power and purpose are bigger than you are, you can then create positive change in your world. It is not just about feeling powerful. It is about how to bring positive value and changes in your life and your world. An Adder realizes that creating change might start with you and your children. It might start with your co-worker. It might start in your neighborhood around the block. Because Adders realize this, they encourage you to create a vision statement about bringing increased value to your world. What do Adders really want? They want you to become an Adder to yourself, the people in your life, your community, and your world. To make that happen, an Adder realizes you must have clear goals that are realistic, attainable and measurable. You must have goals in your personal and professional lives.

As I teach about Adders in my seminars and workshops I see hope in the eyes of the audience. I see them discovering their personal power. I see them realizing what they can do. Many have new revelations and begin to think new thoughts about their potential for excellence in life.

Then I begin to teach about Subtracters. Unlike Adders, the only thing Subtracters care about is themselves. They go about crashing people's lives. They take from people. They will take your energy, your time, your resources and your influence. Subtracters will steal your confidence and anything of value. Subtracters are energy suckers who get stuck in "drama." They know how to draw you into their drama cycle, taking everything you've worked so hard for. They get you to the place where you no longer have the confidence to take an action step to create change in your life. In your soul and spirit, you carry Subtracters on your back every day as they slowly take everything and anything of value out of your life. One day, you realize it has been fifteen years since you had any sense of fulfillment or happiness, or any positive change in your life because you are surrounded by a group of Subtracters who have drained you of your potential for success and happiness in life.

As I began to talk about Subtracters some people would begin to physically weep. Some would get mad and upset and others would have great revelations. But through it all I began to hear the silent cry. It would come up in all types of groups. Sometimes it was corporate executives with big titles wearing designer suits. Sometimes it was a mother on welfare. I would see the silent cry in their eyes. I would see it in their faces. I would see it in their posture. I would hear it. I would actually hear the silent cry from people who have lived with Subtracters for so long. They have allowed Subtracters to keep them from attaining anything of value in their lives, because they had given their lives to the Subtracters. They have been giving away their power to Subtracters for years.

At the end of the seminars, people come up to talk with me. Regardless of who they were or what they looked like, regardless of how much money they made or didn't make, they would all say the same thing. "Please help me deal with my Subtracters. I need help. My boss is a Subtracter. My mother is a Subtracter. My children are Subtracters. My best friend, my boyfriend, my girlfriend, what do I do?" After literally thousands of people asked, *The Silent Cry* emerged in my spirit as an answer to the call to help people. This book was created because thousands of people want to learn how to deal with Subtracters in work and life.

This book is designed to be a holistic view on how to deal with Subtracters. It will challenge you and give you specific techniques that will keep Subtracters from derailing and devaluing your life. It will provide you with strategies and tools for dealing with a Subtracter boss or co-worker. It will also give you tips and methods for dealing with a Subtracter parent or child. Let me warn you, however, this book will not help you if you are not ready to do the work. You must be ready to ask yourself the hard questions. You must be prepared to be honest with yourself. If you are not ready, this book will simply frustrate and offend you and be just another book on your shelf.

My goal is for you to understand that you have a birthright. You were born with a right to feel valuable. You were born with a right to feel important. You were born with a right to be loved and be powerful. In your life you cannot exercise your rights until you come to this place where you are honest with yourself and acknowledge your silent cry. I will give you strategies so that you will cry no more and that you will realize your full potential for excellence in work and life. You can realize your power and begin to use it to bring value to your life and to your world.

Chapter 2

Who is a Subtracter? Am *I* a Subtracter?

Let's start by defining a Subtracter. One of the first lessons you learn in elementary school is that two minus one is one. This begins our basic understanding that the most common definition of *subtraction* is to take something away. People become Subtracters when they use their personal power to take valuable things out of your life. Subtracters do the exact opposite of Adders who use their power to increase your value. Subtracters will take anything you give them or allow them to have. They will take your self-esteem, confidence, courage. They might take your money, your networks and your time. They can take your emotional stability. If you let them, a Subtracter will strip your life of anything that adds to it, leaving it fragmented and lacking. The bottom line is that a Subtracter decreases anything valuable in your life. When you have a Subtracter in your life, you will know it because your life will begin to literally fall apart. Think about your life right now. Are you whole or is your life fragmented? Do you feel like something important is missing from your life? Every so often in my seminars, someone will proudly announce to the whole group, "I don't have any Subtracters in my life." This is interesting to me because the reality is that we ALL have at least one Subtracter somewhere in our life and the question is: "Are we courageous enough to identify them and begin to deal with them?"

I once coached a woman who was smart, educated, and had a heart for helping others, but something was missing; her confidence was gone. I asked her, "Who took your confidence? Where did you leave it?" She was speechless. She had never considered the fact that her life was beginning to fall apart because her confidence was gone. Every time she wanted to try something new in her life, she would walk away from it because she no longer believed in herself. Somewhere in her life's journey, she had given away so much of her confidence that eventually she had forgotten the fact that we all have the power to create change in our lives. Her confidence was gone and my work was to help her figure out *WHO* she gave it to, and where she left it. If there is something missing or lacking in your life, it is never a *WHAT* that took it away. On the contrary, it is <u>always</u> a question of *WHO* took it?

People often complain about what their companies have done to them: "The company laid me off," "The system is smothering my career growth." Think about it, your company is made up of people, so it is not really the company taking anything from you, it is the people you work with or report to. It is never a *WHAT* that is taking things out of your life. It is *WHO*. What is missing in your life right now? Is it joy? Peace? Financial success? Your confidence? As we begin this conversation about Subtracters, it is critical that you identify what is missing in your life. Why? Because it is the first step in learning how to identify the Subtracters in our lives. When you begin to understand what is missing, then you will begin to think about where those things went and who you gave them to. Take a moment now to think about what is missing in your life. Be honest with yourself. Even if it's something painful like your confidence or self-esteem, write it down!

Everything that is missing in your life can be traced back to Subtracters. So, who are Subtracters? What are their core characteristics? How do they use their personal power in your life? What is their role in your life? If you were building a house, you

---

What is missing in your life?

_____

_____

_____

_____

_____

_____

_____

---

would have to start with strong a foundation. We all have foundations in our lives and it is important to understand what makes up our foundations. A Subtracter's foundation consists of three core ingredients. First, their foundation is built on their past failures. Most Subtracters base their lives on what didn't happen and what hasn't worked in their lives. Try having a conversation with a Subtracter and you will quickly realize that they are stuck in "failure mode." Time and time again, a subtracter will retell stories about what "almost did" or "almost won" or "almost accomplished." For many Subtracters, failure has become a way of life.

The second ingredient in a Subtracter's foundation is "fear of success." Most Subtracters are afraid of achieving goals or succeeding in life. It took me years to realize that Subtracters work hard to derail your success because they are afraid of their own success. They are literally afraid that they might succeed in life. Why is that? Because after so many years of focusing on their past failures, they are afraid that if they try, they might fail again, so why try?

I've met many people who refuse to write down their life goals. Why? They are afraid they won't be successful and will be even more disappointed in themselves, or they are afraid of what people will say about them. An Adder's approach to life is, "The only thing that can make me fail is to not try." A Subtracter says: "If I try again, I might fail, so why try?" The Subtracters in your life will use your successes to feel good about themselves. Why? Because they are afraid of attaining their own success!

The third and most complex ingredient in a Subtracter's foundation is that they are socialized to take. Somewhere in life, usually at a very young age, a parent, guardian, family member, teacher or friend, taught them how to use their power to devalue and take things out of people's lives. Consciously or subconsciously, Subtracters were taught to take whatever they can, as much as they can, whenever they can, from others. They have practiced the power of Subtraction for years and have become very skillful at it. Subtracters may not need anything from you, but the fact is that they will find ways to take anything you let them remove out of your life. What is the complexity of this ingredient? Subtracters can be smart, nice, accomplished people who consistently but unconsciously devalue your life. This is called the "clueless" factor. A Subtracter who has been socialized to subtract from others is often "clueless" about their role, impact or influence in your life. They are just doing what they know to do; Subtract!

Attitudes of Subtracters

Subtracters tend to be needy. They want others to solve their problems. They want you to answer their questions instead of learning things for themselves. They could attend the seminar and learn something new, but instead they refuse to participate. However, the moment you return from attending the seminar, they want you to tell them everything you learned. In an era of technology there is always some new computer program or new strategy, technique or tool to learn about. Instead of reading the manual and learning about the program, a Subtracter will run into your office time and time again to ask for help. Subtracters live an "I need" life. Many of them are in a perpetual state of "needing" something. How many times will a Subtracter need your financial help to rescue them out of debt, or come to your office to "talk" about their personal issues, or to babysit their children, or to borrow your car again? Do they want to find solutions to eliminating their "needs?" No, they simply want you to continue to rescue them and in the process they will take your energy, money, time, resources and anything else you will give them.

Subtracters are negative. They live in a world where something always goes wrong and nothing works. Their lens on life is clouded with pessimism. A Subtracter stays on the look-out for what will go wrong. I recently had a Subtracter tell me that I couldn't start a new project because I was already so busy that it just wouldn't work! Realizing that I was dealing with a Subtracter, I simply said, "Yes, I do have a full life and for that I am very thankful because I could have a life where I had *NOTHING* to do!"

The Subtracter cleared his throat and said, "I guess that's one way to look at it." I smiled and walked away. How can you tell that you are dealing with a Subtracter? Their pessimistic, can't do, will never work, attitude about life will begin to slowly drain you of your positive goals and aspirations.

A Subtracter's negative attitude is infectious and contagious. It is like catching a cold. If you are around someone who is coughing and sneezing frequently, sooner or later you will catch their cold. If you work with Subtracters every day, and they are sneezing out their negative energy, you have to distance yourself from these people because their germs are looking to re-create themselves. You! Be careful not to allow yourself to be pulled into this negative, unhealthy environment. One of my Subtracter family members who has perfected the art of negativity is so powerful that I can literally only talk to them or be around them for a very short time. As our conversation begins, I can feel the negative pull, like a force field, and over the years have learned how to escape! Why? Because, you can never be totally successful in life if you are negative. Negative people live lives of regret, not progress.

Subtracters can be very emotional. They use their emotions as a tool to manipulate others. When things go wrong for Subtracters they will not hesitate to use their emotions to make you feel bad. Subtracter want to make you feel as though it is your job to solve their problems. They have no plan of solving their own problems yet; they get energized by telling you about their problems as their way of getting you emotionally involved. A common tactic for Subtracters is to use their emotional outbursts to manipulate you into helping them, or solving their issues. The end result however is always the same: Subtracters are not ready to take responsibility and be accountable for their actions and, when things do not go their way, they will always blame the very person who has been trying to "help" them. Subtracters are socialized to manipulate your emotions and, in the process, they will drain you of your positive attitude and energy.

Words

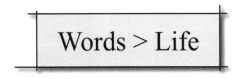

Words are very powerful. Why? Because words create life and life is created through our words. One of the greatest principles of success is that, whatever you want in your life, you must first think it, then speak it. For Subtracters, their use of words is one of their most powerful tools. Their words founded on negativity are designed to discourage, manipulate and annihilate your confidence. They use words to create doubts about your vision and goals. Whenever you begin to talk about your goals and visions, or any positive events in your life, Subtracters will immediately use their words to put you down, or belittle what you want in life. Their words can sabotage your self-esteem, leaving you feeling unqualified, unworthy or even incompetent. If you let them, Subtracters will use their words to rob you of your courage to take action — whether making a phone call, changing jobs, or ending a relationship — in every area of your life.

Years ago, I had a senior-year student in my leadership course at the university. She was pretty, smart, and the head of her class. This young woman was also engaged, about to graduate, and had a promising future. One day, I noticed

> *If you let them, Subtracters will use their words to rob you of your courage to take action – whether making a phone call, changing jobs, or ending a relationship – in every area of your life.*

she was crying in class so I asked her to stay after. I was shocked by her emotional outburst and knew that something was very wrong in her life. The story she shared with me was about her father who told her when she was ten years old that she would never be anything in life. This father will probably never know how much of a Subtracter he had been in his daughter's life. Here she was, about to graduate from college with excellent grades, engaged to be married to a very nice man, yet buried deep inside her soul were the words put there by her father: "You will never be anything in life." Even though she was outwardly succeeding, inwardly she suffered from the silent cry which took her confidence and destroyed her self-esteem. On the verge of success, she doubted herself, feared success, and was inwardly convinced that she couldn't succeed. Subtracters use their words to keep you focused on your past failures, creating self-doubt and insecurity in your life. How can you possibly be successful if you are constantly reminded of your past mistakes and failures?

I once worked with a very large organization on a leadership development project. The president of the organization was committed to promoting more women and people of color into prominent management positions. One day, as the senior level staff met to discuss candidates for a new high level executive position, the president recommended a woman she thought would be excellent. To her surprise, one of her staff members quickly replied that the woman shouldn't be promoted because of a past incident. Puzzled about her team's response to her recommendation, the president decided to ask the woman about the situation. As it turns out, the incident happened five years earlier and the woman's work record had been nothing short of excellent since then. While the president could look past the woman's mistake and focus on her excellence, the Subtracters on her team were stuck in their perception about this woman's potential and unwilling to move beyond her past mistake. If the Subtracters had their way, this woman would never be promoted because they refused to give her an opportunity to show her excellence.

Sarcasm is one of the Subtracters' secret weapons. What is sarcasm? "A cutting, often ironic remark intended to wound. A form of wit that is marked by the use of sarcastic language and is intended to make its victim the butt of contempt or ridicule."[2] After attending one of my seminars, a gentleman asked me if I knew his brother who worked at the same university where I taught. I said, "No, I don't know him." The man responded jokingly, "Oh, I was hoping you did know him because I wanted you to tell him that his brother said that he was a _____," and used a very derogatory term. After getting over the shock of the man's remarks, I firmly looked at him and said, "Sir, I could never say that to anybody much less to your very own brother!" The gentleman was surprised at my tone and response and asked, "why not?" I said, "Because then I would be acting like and talking like a Subtracter." Embarrassed, he made another sarcastic remark and walked away. This Subtracter was clueless to the fact that he was using sarcasm to devalue his brother. Whether we realize it or not, our words are very powerful and we must pay attention to what we say and to whom we listen.

Think about the people in your life right now. Who puts you down regularly? Who consistently reminds you of what you can't do? Who constantly rehearses your past failures and mistakes? Listen to

---

2   The American Heritage® Dictionary of the English Language, Fourth Edition. From Dictionary.com website: http://dictionary.reference.com/browse/sarcasm

them. What are they saying about you? What are your Subtracters
taking out of your life through their words? Take a moment and write
down *WHO* the Subtracters are and *HOW* they are using their negative
words in your life:

Who?

_____

How?

_____

_____

_____

_____

_____

_____

_____

Energy

Energy is a fascinating element in life. It gives us the drive,
passion, and intensity that provides us with the life and spirit we need
to make things happen. No energy, no passion. No energy, no drive. No
energy, no accomplishments. No energy, no success. You must have
energy to make things happen, and positive energy always multiplies
your personal power. When you have positive energy, things begin to
happen in your life. You begin to laugh more. You become happier.
You begin to feel more fulfilled. You begin to accomplish more in

your life. Energy is also very complex because it is a living dynamic force that is transferable from person to person. Have you ever

> *You must have energy to make things happen, and positive energy always multiplies your personal power.*

walked into someone's office and felt the negative energy? No one said anything. No one talked to you. You just *felt* it. You felt a negative force that immediately impacted your physical self. Sometimes, you can get an instant headache or break out into a sweat or get that strange feeling in your stomach. Instinctively, you feel like running away from that office, that space, that energy. Why? Because energy is transferable. You can't see it, but you know it's there because you can feel it in your bones. If you are paying close attention, you will know exactly when something is right or wrong because you can *feel* the energy.

No Energy = No Accomplishments

Subtracters specialize in negative energy. They are official carriers of negative energy. If you are experiencing an energy shift in your life in which you are thinking, feeling, or talking more negatively, it is your first clear signal that Subtracters are influencing your life. The way you see your world, and the way you deal with people will begin to take on a negative tone.

Recently, a very eager sales person from the Kirby Vacuum Company came to my home to demonstrate the latest and greatest in Kirby technology. As the salesperson began his demonstration, he asked me to show him carpet in my home that I thought was already clean. Then he turned on his high-powered vacuum and began cleaning the carpet. His machine was so powerful that it sucked up dirt that I didn't even know was still there! This machine reminded me of Subtracters who are like high-powered energy sucking machines that are after *ANY* positive energy that you may have. Even if you are normally a positive, optimistic person, when Subtracters are finished with you, you will be left with nothing but negative energy. Like the Kirby, they will use their high-powered sources of negative energy to suck out every bit of your positive energy, leaving you feeling empty and purposeless. And when there is emptiness, negativity grows. When negativity grows, your progress and productivity will decrease.

While training a group of managers for a large government social service agency, I encountered a Subtracter who was loaded with negative energy. The managers were required to attend the training to learn about how to create a culture of Adders, instead of Subtracters. Why? Because Subtracters who work with tough social issues only intensify the situation, creating more struggles and negativity rather than solutions that can help people. The Subtracter manager was obviously uninterested and tried her very best to distract everyone around her from focusing and benefiting from the training. She was clearly working overtime to drain the positive energy from her peers and replace it with her negative energy. Little by little, she began to turn up her negativity machine, but I knew exactly what she was doing so I quickly turned up my own personal power and positive energy. At one point, I literally stood right behind her chair and trained from that spot for about ten minutes. I could feel her discomfort and irritation because I refused to be pulled into her negative energy zone. When she realized that none of her peers were being side-tracked by her negative energy, she began looking for an opportunity to leave and did so when we took a break. The most amazing thing was that everyone knew a Subtracter had left the room. We could feel it; the room felt different. The other managers began to participate more, interact more, be more open with their responses and shared some good laughs during the training. As trainers, why did we not try to convince the Subtracter to stay? Because, our goal was to help this organization build a culture of Adders and you cannot do that if you are surrounded by negative energy. There are going to be times when a Subtracter in your life threatens to leave if you don't surrender to their negative energy and way. Don't chase after Subtracters. ***Let Them GO!***

Time

What is another clear signal that a Subtracter is in your life? You will find yourself wasting time. Are you frustrated right now? Are you not getting enough done? Do you feel like you can never reach your goals? If that is the case, it is because there is a Subtracter in your life. A neighbor once asked me how I was able to get so much accomplished. I thought about it for a moment and came to the realization that everyone has 24 hours every day, and the question is who will use their 24 hours most effectively? Subtracters are master time wasters. They work overtime to decrease your productivity and prevent you from accomplishing your own work, goals, and vision.

What are their strategies? First, Subtracters distract you with their own drama. Most Subtracters live lives filled with drama and chaos. They constantly have a problem that needs your attention. In the process, they consume your time and drain your positive energy. While most people want to minimize problems or dramatic situations,

Subtracters do just the opposite. They attract drama because it gives them something to do. The fact is that, for many Subtracters, drama actually gives them a false sense of worthiness and relevance in life. When a Subtracter comes into your life, they absorb your time leaving you feeling unproductive and going nowhere in life. The more time Subtracters take, the less time you have for creating success in your own life. The more time they take, the more frustration you experience.

Think about your days at work. During your typical day, how much time do you spend doing your work versus the amount of time you commit to helping out Subtracters? Are you more focused on your projects or on the Subtracter's responsibilities? Subtracters are amazing because they are not only time wasters but also expert time manipulators. A Subtracter will find creative ways to get you to use your time to work on their project or agenda. How do you know when a Subtracter is taking or manipulating your time?

1. Do you spend hours talking with them on the telephone? How often do they call you while you are at work?

2. Do they stop at your desk and talk about their personal problems and issues?

3. Do they complain to you about why they just can't get their work done and then ask you to stop what you are doing and help them do their work?

4. Do they constantly persuade you to use your personal time to "help them out" and do them a favor? The classic example is the Subtracter who doesn't have a car and has asked if you will pick them up for work. You arrive on time to pick them up and they are not ready. You waste 20 minutes waiting for them,

becoming more frustrated by the minute, because you have a meeting that morning and you need some time to prepare.

It's time for a personal reality check. Who is taking up your time? How are they taking up your time? Time is a key factor to your success in life and work. No time, no productivity, no accomplishments, no success. Take a moment and write down the names of those people *WHO* are wasting or manipulating your time. Then write down *HOW* they are doing this.

WHO is taking your time?

_____

HOW are they taking your time?

_____

_____

_____

_____

_____

Power Hungry

Ultimately, Subtracters want your personal power. The reality, however, is that no one can take your power unless you give it away. Why do Subtracters want your personal power? So they can control four areas in your life.

1. Control your time — what you do and when you do it.
2. Control your emotions. If they can manipulate your feelings

through guilt then they can leave you emotionally frustrated and vulnerable.

3. Control your resources. That means that, whatever you have, whether money, networks or experience, a Subtracter wants to control it. Subtracters will try to tell you how to use your money or interact with colleagues or treat your friends.

4. Control your information. If you let them, Subtracters will control what you say, when you say it, what you think and what you do.

Dream Blocking

Dream blocking is one of the most common techniques used by Subtracters to take your power. Because the life of the typical Subtracter is built on failure and fear of success, they have no interest in you achieving your dreams and goals. Think about some of your life goals. Have you been able to achieve them? The question is not why you haven't been able to achieve them. The question is: *who* has kept you from achieving them? Who in your life has been blocking your vision and goals? Who is taking your confidence so that you don't go after your goals? A Subtracter is a dream blocker. You cannot share your dreams and goals with Subtracters. Why? Because they will sow seeds of doubt in you about why you cannot, will not, and should not reach for that dream. Even worse, they will publicize your dream and increase the possibility of someone else stealing your dream before you have the chance to even pursue it! Some Subtracters will voice their concerns about your capacity to make that dream a reality. They will question your skills, your education and your expertise. Some Subtracters will appeal to your emotions, convincing you that they care so much about you that they are afraid you will only be disappointed if you try to accomplish your dreams.

The most fascinating thing about Subtracters is that most of them are clueless about being Dream Blockers or about their need to take your personal power. As we will explore in the next chapter, most Subtracters are unconscious about who they are and what they are doing in the lives of others. This is important because the reality is that we are all subject to using our personal power to subtract from others.

Chapter 3

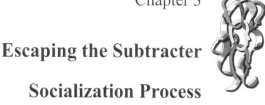

Escaping the Subtracter

Socialization Process

Are Subtracters born or made? This is a critical question, because, if a person were born a Subtracter, then there would be no hope for change. It would also mean that they were born with only one source of power. As I described in my first book,[3] people are born with power and they choose to use their power in four ways. You can use your power to become an Adder, Subtracter, Divider or Multiplier. Because everyone is born with all four power sources, then everyone has the potential to become a Subtracter. Think about your life. Have you ever been a Subtracter to yourself or others? You don't have to feel bad about that because at some point all of us, regardless of ethnicity, gender, socioeconomic status or religion, have used our power to subtract. The question here is how do we learn to become Subtracters? The simple answer is that, at some point in our lives, someone or a group of people taught us how to use our power to subtract. In other words, you can be socialized to be a Subtracter.

How does the Subtracter socialization process work? How do you know when you have been socialized to subtract? Can you change how you use your power even if you have been a Subtracter most of your life? How can you escape this socialization process? To understand the socialization process, we must understand the two ways in which people are taught to live life. First, we are taught implicitly

---

3   Price, Verna C. (2002) The Power of People: Four Kinds of People Who Can Change Your Life. JCAMA Publishers. Minneapolis, MN

how to think, what to value, how to treat others and how to conduct our lives. Implicit lessons are experienced and understood but rarely articulated directly through verbal communication. For example, while growing up you watched your parents live their life using certain rules and guidelines. They might have never articulated exactly what those rules were or why they were important to follow. The implicit message to you, however, was that you should also follow those rules. Your parents didn't sit you down one day at the kitchen table and say, "Today we are going to teach you how to be a Subtracter." Instead, they demonstrated through their actions how to be a Subtracter. The parents who only call their neighbors when they need help with the family but would otherwise not even speak to them, much less offer assistance to them were teaching you how to subtract. The teacher who treated her students like they were dumb and couldn't learn was teaching you how to subtract. The pastor who favored certain people in the church while ignoring others was teaching you to subtract. The boss who disrespected and treated you like you were incompetent was demonstrating the power of subtraction. Small children will watch their peers subtracting from others and will immediately imitate that behavior. As a college student studying education, I was taught that teachers teach the way they were taught. If you were taught primarily through lectures, then you will lecture to your students. If you were taught using hands-on methods, then you will engage your students in interactive learning.

What makes implicit socialization so important is that you were given an unspoken set of rules that taught you that subtracting is "normal." When being a Subtracter becomes an unquestioned norm, then it's very difficult for you to see why you should change.

Subconsciously, subtracting will become a way of life, and your life will reflect the consequences of consistently using this power source. A community member who works with families challenged with criminal behavior shared with a group that his family raised him to be a criminal. It was an unspoken rule but a demonstrated behavior that everyone in that family would and should participate in criminal activity. His family taught him implicitly that being a criminal was "normal." What was the consequence of living out this implicit message? Ultimately, this man became a criminal and was incarcerated for his actions. It wasn't until his early forties that he began to understand how the implicit messages from his family influenced him to pursue a life of crime, becoming a Subtracter to himself and his community. You might say that this is an extreme case, but think about how families teach their children to live. Some children are taught to disrespect others. Others are taught to discriminate based on race or religion. Children will naturally treat others the way they were treated by their family. When I think about my own children, I am challenged to think about what I am implicitly teaching them. In other words, what am I teaching them through my actions, attitudes, communication style, values, leadership? Am I teaching them to use their power to add or subtract? Children take their signals from parents and family members on how to use their power. We were all taught implicitly about how to use our power. The question is, were you taught to be an Adder or Subtracter?

The second way we learn to use our power to subtract is through explicit life lessons. An explicit life lesson is not only demonstrated but clearly articulated. Remembering explicit lessons about being taught how to be a Subtracter can be very painful. If your parents told you that certain people were "bad" or inferior to you because of their culture, color, ethnicity or religion, then it might be painful to admit that you were taught these lessons. There are some families that intentionally teach their children to steal, lie, abuse drugs, abuse others. Some children are instructed to fight if someone even looks at them too long! I remember a girl in my high school whose father was a drug dealer; he sent her to school with a briefcase full of drugs with specific instructions on how to sell them.

Explicit lessons can also be taught to adults. What happens when you are told by your supervisor or boss not to tell the whole truth about a situation in your company? Or asked to give a report that exaggerates the progress of the team? What if someone instructs you to tell lies about your competitors? There are many ways to explicitly teach someone to be a Subtracter. However, most people are taught to subtract not explicitly but implicitly. It is rare to find a family that will explicitly teach children to be Subtracters. Instead, most people are socialized to subtract implicitly and learn to unconsciously use this power in every aspect of their life. The result is that your life becomes a pattern of continued chaos and drama in which you spend your energy and time trying to take things from people instead of dealing with the truth and reality that you were socialized to subtract.

In life, there are also two types of people who will teach you how to subtract: "Just Is" and "Choice" people. How we deal with them and their roles in teaching us and socializing us to be Subtracters is very important. "Just Is" people are your family members. They are parents, children, siblings, blood relatives, spouses, and ex-spouses. You cannot change who your family members are, they "Just Is." Whether you like it or not, your family will be your family for life! "Just Is"

Subtracters are more complex to deal with than anyone else you will encounter. Why? Because they know you, know your weaknesses, know your history, and you cannot just cut them off. If you have an aunt, a Subtracter, who has never liked you, then she might find ways to create chaos and "drama" in your life subtracting from you and your children. Can you just cut her off or let her go? No, because she is your aunt and will always be a part of your life.

The mother of one of my coaching clients is a severe Subtracter and has been subtracting from her daughter for years. Her mother talks down to her, creating worry and chaos in her life. She uses

> *One of the main goals of this book is to teach you how to manage your "Just Is" Subtracter relationships without becoming a Subtracter yourself!*

up her daughter's resources and energy. This mother is a classic "Just Is" Subtracter. By the time I began coaching the daughter, she was in her late forties. Her confidence was all but gone. Her self-esteem was so low she barely knew it existed. She was afraid to make decisions on her own because her mother had convinced her that she was not capable or smart enough. The reality was that she was intimidated and afraid of her mother. Her life was severely and negatively influenced by this "Just Is" Subtracter. The daughter's lack of confidence and self-esteem led her to a life of drugs, alcohol, and unhealthy relationships. The silent cry in this woman's life was loud and painful to see and hear. So why did she keep the mother in her life? Because it was too painful to deal with the reality of this powerful "Just Is" Subtracter. She couldn't just cut off contact with her mother, so what was she to do? Ultimately, she had to learn how to manage her relationship with her mother and avoid her negative influence while still keeping her in her life.

One of the main goals of this book is to teach you how to manage your "Just Is" Subtracter relationships without becoming a Subtracter yourself! When a family member implicitly teaches you how to subtract, it is harder to question these lessons because we all want to think that our family should teach us to do the right thing. It's very hard to admit that a family member modeled how to be a Subtracter. Why? Because in our hearts, we all want to believe that our parents, or relatives taught us to add, not subtract. I can always tell when someone is dealing with a "Just Is" Subtracter because they are always torn with a sense of guilt about facing up to the realities, the truth about the power lessons they were taught. You can learn to manage your relationships with the "Just-Is" Subtracters in your life, but it might be difficult because some "Just Is" Subtracters believe they are entitled to control and devalue your life.

The second category of people is called "Choice" people. These might be friends, colleagues, neighbors or members of your religious community. When a "Choice" person becomes a Subtracter in your life, it's easier to deal with them because you have the option of "choosing" to omit them from your life. This element of "Choice" is important to understand because most Subtracters want you to believe that you have no choice and that they will be in your life forever! "Choice" people in the workplace are your colleagues or team members. It's liberating when you realize that you do not have to be a "friend" to your co-workers. As a matter of fact, you don't even have to like them. You must, however, respect them and work hard to be an Adder in the workplace.

Ironically, "Just Is" Subtracters will try to convince you that they are "Choice" people whom you have chosen into your life. In the workplace, this can be quite challenging because the people you report to become your "Just Is" people in the workplace. There is nothing you can do about the executive vice president you report to because of their position of power and authority in that company. If that person is a "Just Is" workplace Subtracter, then you must learn how to deal with them without jeopardizing your career. I once worked with a female supervisor who was a "Just Is" Subtracter in the workplace, but she worked really hard to make our team feel as though we chose her into our work life. The fact was that none of us chose her, but we all had to figure out ways to manage our relationship with her so that we could still be effective but not be infected by her Subtracter behavior and attitude. Like your family members, you must learn how to work with and interact with work "Just Is" Subtracters. This can be challenging, but you will find many strategies in this book to help you.

The socialization process happens at all levels and in all areas of work and life. During the process, the turning point in becoming a Subtracter is when you begin to believe that using your power to subtract is normal. Unfortunately, as long as you are a Subtracter, you cannot get to your next level of excellence in a holistic way. For example, some Subtracters may have gotten to where they are by cheating, lying and back-stabbing. But sooner or later, that very same Subtracter will experience trouble and pain in their life. You cannot spend a life planting seeds of pain, chaos and subtraction and expect to receive a life of joy. Socialized Subtracters have to learn that, if they do not take a very close look at themselves and decide to use their power to add, they will never experience excellence and fulfillment in a holistic way. What does that mean? Holistic fulfillment means that you experience excellence in your job, family, relationships, psychological life, spiritual life and your financial life. You are experiencing excellence in every area of your life. You are also happy and you have a sense of purpose and fulfillment. You have strong, healthy relationships. You have become an amazing Adder to yourself, your family, your friends, your community and your world. You cannot get to a level of attaining holistic excellence by being a Subtracter.

When I first discovered Subtracters and began to write about them, I was very hard and judgmental on those family members who taught me to subtract. I have learned, however, that people only know what they know. People live their lives based on what they know to be normal. If your mother, boss or best friend was taught to see subtracting as a normal way of life, then that's exactly what they will do to your life; subtract. Were you socialized to be a Subtracter? If so, who socialized you to subtract? Were you socialized to subtract by family members or your "Choice" people? Often in my seminars, when faced with this direct question, the silent cry will become so evident that people will often begin to weep. Why? Because it is a painful moment to deal with the reality that you were socialized to subtract, and that the very people in your life who should have been teaching you to add were consciously or unconsciously teaching you to subtract.

Take a moment to think and write about who socialized you to be a Subtracter. How did they socialize you? How did this socialization impact your life? It might be painful, but be honest.

Teaching college students is very interesting because I can always tell when they connect with other students who were Subtracters. Suddenly, they get pulled into a cycle, a vortex of Subtracter socialization. Before long, these students are infected with what I called the "Subtracter Syndrome." How do you know if this is happening to you? What are the symptoms of the "Subtracter Syndrome?"

1. People who are infected with the "Subtracter Syndrome" blame others for their mistakes and failures instead of being accountable and taking responsibility. It becomes someone else's fault.

2. Your perspective on life becomes increasingly negative.

3. You drive away the Adders from your inner circle and invite in a new group of people, Subtracters.

4. You begin to operate like a Subtracter, manipulating people, trying to take their power, friends or resources. Being infected with the "Subtracter Syndrome" can happen to anyone, anywhere.

> *The "Subtracter Syndrome" is not a permanent condition. You can change it because you have the power to change your life!*

How can you escape the "Subtracter Syndrome?" First you must face up to the fact that you have been infected. Then you must critically look at what it has done in your life. Third, you must immediately let go of <u>any</u> "Choice" Subtracters (including boyfriends or girlfriends) in your inner circle. Finally, you must reclaim your power to add and begin to use that power in every aspect of your life. The "Subtracter Syndrome" is not a permanent condition. You can change it because you have the power to change your life! You can choose to use your power to be an Adder and avoid being a Subtracter. You can escape the Subtracter socialization process, but it will take hardcore honesty, courage and work to relearn how to redirect your power source to become an extraordinary Adder. If you believe you can change, then you will, because God has already given you the power needed to change your life: personal power.

Chapter 4

Subtracter Personalities

Do Subtracters realize who they are and what they are doing in your life? The answer is simple; at least 85% of all Subtracters are unconscious of how they are using their power. As a result, most people have no idea how they are impacting your life. It would even be much easier if all Subtracters were mean and terrible people. The fact is that many Subtracters are not necessarily vindictive, cruel or even blatant. However, Subtracters do have distinct personalities, and how they influence and impact your inner circle and life depends on their personality type.

There are seven Subtracter personalities. Learning about these personalities will clarify what your Subtracters are doing in your life, and in some cases, why they continue to subtract from you. As you learn about these Subtracter personalities, you must also challenge yourself to be honest about who you are being. You must ask yourself the question: Who am I being? Have I subconsciously taken on a Subtracter personality?

Identifying a Subtracter's personality takes knowledge and skill because you have to know what you are looking for. The key is to carefully observe their actions, listen to their words and observe their attitudes. It's also important to see what kind of results their lives have produced. Consistently using the power of a Subtracter will produce negative consequences in our lives. Each Subtracter personality is distinct and unique. It can be challenging, to identify them because a Subtracter could have one or two personalities, or could have all of them.

The Smiler

The first Subtracter personality is the *Smiler*. These Subtracters are the hardest to identify because they come across as being nice, kind and wonderful people. However, over time, you will notice that *Smilers* use their "niceness" to take things out of your life. Because *Smilers* are such nice people, your first reaction is to help them out, but the reality is that if you look at their actions and listen to their words, you will begin to see the pattern of *Smilers*. With a smile they will take up your time telling you about their chaotic life. They will use up your resources to rescue themselves from their recurring issues. They will take your positive energy and, little by little, your life will decrease in value because *Smilers* are taking everything and anything you give them.

A social worker once had a client who was a *Smiler*. Over time, the social worker realized that the *Smiler* continued to have the same pattern of problems and nothing seemed to change, except for the fact that they were always so nice and gracious during the social worker visits. The *Smiler* would be wrapped up in the same "drama" month to month. They never had enough money, something was always going on with the children, and on and on. The social worker would have the best visits with the *Smiler,* who would promise to be accountable and responsible. The social worker would emphasize the importance of the *Smiler* taking responsibility, and the *Smiler* would apologize for not getting anything done the month before and promise with a smile to do better this month. But two weeks later, the *Smiler* would call the social worker with another problem, nicely asking for help again. The social worker would return to the *Smiler's* home only to find that nothing had been done! What was happening? The social worker was giving her time, resources and energy to the *Smiler* to the point of feeling exhausted and drained. It is hard to say "no" to *Smilers* because on the surface they are polite and considerate. The reality, however, is that *Smilers* will not take responsibility for their own actions, and gradually will entangle you in their "drama," while taking everything they possibly can out of your life.

I can remember having a *Smiler* in my life who was so nice and wonderful but every time she called, she wanted something. She was constantly involved in chaos and drama. Every time the *Smiler* called I knew that I would have to give up my time, money, resources or emotional energy to help her. It became clear that, even though she was the nicest person, she was not at all interested in avoiding drama or solving it. The *Smiler* is going to continue to be nice, sweet, and kind, but they are also going to totally depend on you to help them solve their problems while taking no accountability for their life. It's hard to get mad at *Smilers* because they are sincerely nice people who were socialized to be "needy."

The best thing about *Smilers* are that they are one of the easier Subtracters to deal with largely because most of them have no idea that they are subtracting from others. *Smilers* is not trying to harm you or be mean to you. *Smilers* have been socialized to get "help" from people, so they spend their lives asking for help instead of helping themselves. The first step in dealing with a *Smiler* is to start holding that person accountable for their actions. Stop rescuing the *Smiler*! If you must, let that person fall and fail. As you start holding them accountable, *Smiles* will begin to realize how they have been socialized to subtract and they will begin to change. *Smilers* can still be hard to deal with because they are so nice that you might feel guilty setting boundaries that keep them from taking your power. When you decide to deal with the *Smiler*, it might be very tough on them because at their core they really are nice people who were taught to live chaotic lives. The bottom line, however, is that a *Smiler* will nicely take your power, and it might be years before you realize just how much they have devalued and decreased your life.

The Shamer

The *Shamer* is the total opposite of the *Smiler*. The *Smiler* would never try to shame you publicly. The goal of the *Shamer*, in contrast, is to make you feel like you're not good enough or that you have done something wrong. A *Shamer* can be very vicious with their words and accusations. *Shamers* wait for strategic moments to devalue you in public places around other people. *Shamers* constantly remind you of your past failures. One of their favorite things to do is to make you feel as though you don't keep your word and that you are not who you say you are. They take your power by discrediting you publicly and raising questions about your integrity and character.

Shamers show up in all parts of our lives. Think about the boss who looks for public opportunities to put down his team. Or the husband who thinks it's funny to share his wife's faults when her girlfriends are visiting. Or the mother who waits until her children are in public to talk about what they "can't do." Teachers can be very dangerous *Shamers* because of the negative impact they have on young people when they put them down in front of their peers.

Sarcasm is one of the *Shamers'* favorite tools. *Shamers* will wait for just the right moment during a big meeting or in front of a customer to make a sarcastic comment about what you are not good at. *Shamers* are very hard to deal with because many of them believe it is their job to remind you of your mistakes and "keep you in check." Many think they are keeping you honest. When you finally confront *Shamers*, some take great offense because they believed they were helping you by doing you a favor. I had a friend who was a *Shamer*. Every time we were in public, my friend would shame me in a joking manner. It occurred to me that this *Shamer* used this Subtracter tactic because she was actually intimidated by me, so shaming was her way of making herself look good. Often *Shamers* in the workplace and life are secretly intimidated by your success and progress. The bottom line is that, if *Shamers* can't stop you from being a powerful positive person, they will certainly work to slow down your success.

What happens when you are shamed by a Subtracter? What happens to your confidence? What happens to your self esteem? What happens to your courage? What happens to your sense of power? The goal of a *Shamer* is to take your power by taking your confidence. The first signal that you have a *Shamer* Subtracter in your life is self doubt; you will begin to second guess yourself. Another signal is that you will stop speaking up for yourself. A *Shamer* wants to take your voice and your leadership capacity. In time, your personal power will decrease and you will lose the confidence to make critical decisions about your life. Think about it; you are not going to apply for a new position or be an effective leader for your team if a *Shamer* is continually humiliating you by reminding you of your failures. A *Shamer* counts on the fact that they can shame you into a place of non-action.

Shamers are very difficult to deal with but you cannot continue to ignore them or discount the damage they are doing in your life. Why? Because *Shamers* get their sense of power and recognition by shaming you. The more you ignore them, the more powerful they become, and the more damaging they are to your life. So, what if you are a *Shamer*? Can you change? Yes you can, because you have the power to be an Adder or Subtracter. You can relearn how to use your power, and become an Adder who encourages others instead of putting them down. There is always hope!

The Snipper-Nipper

Words are very important, and the *Snipper-Nipper* Subtracter is a master at using negative words. A *Snipper-Nipper* is a fault finder who is on the lookout for any and everything wrong, or that could go wrong, in your life. If you can imagine a giant pair of scissors, that constantly snips and nips away at your life, then you are on your way to identifying a *Snipper-Nipper*.

> *Snipper-Nippers are difficult to have in your life and you cannot begin to deal with them without rediscovering your personal power. Just as you were born with power, you were also born with a right to be valued by others.*

Using their words, they slowly cut away at your life, eventually leaving you feeling empty, frustrated and powerless. They snip and nip at your confidence by constantly reminding you of your weaknesses. They snip and nip at your appearance, making you self-conscious and uncomfortable in your own skin. They snip and nip at your work experience, producing self doubt about your success. They snip and nip at your choice of relationships, which results in you second guessing who is in your life. *Snipper-Nippers* will go after anything and anyone in your life. They will snip and nip about your children, spouse, house, clothes, furniture, car, hairstyle, shoes, professional success or promotion!

They will snip at how you talk, how you act, what you wear, what you write, how you manage. If they are your friends, they will snip at your personal life, at how you raise your family, at the car you drive, and at your house. They will visit your home, snipping about your furniture and your kitchen while they eat your food and enjoy your hospitality. Their slight little comments cut like scissors and at times they are unrelenting and uncaring. They snip and nip until you no longer have any energy, drive or confidence. As time goes on, a *Snipper-Nipper* will wear you down and wear you out! Eventually, *Snipper-Nippers* will devalue you to the point where you will wake up one morning and wonder what happened to you, your confidence, your power, your success? The question is not *what* happened to your confidence; it is *who* took your confidence. Who has been snipping and nipping at you?

Snipper-Nippers are close cousins to the *Shamer.* However, *Snipper-Nippers* do not have any motive to shame, and don't wait for an audience to subtract from you. What makes the *Snipper-Nippers* difficult to deal with is that they are usually your "Just-Is" people. *Snipper-Nippers* are usually family members who are clueless about what they are doing to you! *Snipper-Nipper* family members know your history, so they use your past and present experiences as subtracting opportunities. They get a sense of satisfaction from telling you what you are not doing right and how you should be acting. Many "Just-Is" *Snipper-Nippers* consider themselves to be helping you as they remind you of all your past failures and second guess your abilities to be successful in life. Many see themselves as your advice givers who are there to help you. In the workplace, the *Snipper-Nipper* is the person who comes into your office and questions everything that you do, points out every mistake you made on a report, and critiques every comment you made in a meeting. Some snip and nip about how you run your team, who you hired or even how you dress.

Snipper-Nippers are difficult to have in your life and you cannot begin to deal with them without rediscovering your personal power. Just as you were born with power, you were also born with a right to be valued by others. You were born with a destiny in you. You were born with a purpose, and the goal of the *Snipper-Nippers* is to use a tidal wave of negative words to create self doubt and uncertainty in your life. *Snipper-Nippers* are not interested in constructive criticism, or critical dialogue about their actions. You cannot argue with or convince *Snipper-Nippers* that they are wrong about you. However, when you understand that you have the power to change your life, you **CAN** do something about the *Snipper-Nippers*. Will it be easy? No! However, as you will learn from this book, it is possible to constructively deal with a *Snipper-Nipper* in work and life.

The Gamer

Of all the Subtracter personalities, *Gamers* are the hardest to identify because they can trick you into thinking that they are Adders in your life. What distinguishes them from any other personality is that they are very strategic and knowledgeable about how they are influencing your life. *Gamers* always enters your life looking like Adders. *Gamers* pay close attention to your likes, and dislikes. They may give you gifts or invite you to be a part of projects on which they are working on. They may even help you get a promotion. The *Gamer* can become your advisor, someone you trust and with whom you share your hard realities. They often learn very intimate and confidential things about your life. Watch out, however, because *Gamers* keep score. They calculate everything they do for you and tally up the favors you owe them. The *Gamer* observes how you respond to issues and challenges. Soon you will find yourself depending on the *Gamer* for advice and emotional support.

Watch for clues, however, because eventually, the *Gamer* will begin showing their other side - the controlling, manipulating Subtracter. Ultimately, the *Gamer's* goal is to manipulate your emotional state, leaving you feeling vulnerable, upset and emotionally unstable. Within moments, a *Gamer* can switch from complimenting and encouraging you to demeaning and devaluing you. All in the same breath. The *Gamer* is deliberate about manipulating your emotions and chooses strategic moments in your conversations or interactions to play mind games with you. *Gamers* are typically very intelligent people who know exactly what to say or do, to throw you into an emotional spin in which you feel out of control. *Gamers* want to twist your emotions so much that you will not look at the reality of what they are doing in your life. Many people, simply want to run away from *Gamers* instead of dealing with them. *Gamers* throw emotional tantrums and outbursts designed to scare and intimidate you. They take your personal power by convincing you that you are not who you think you are. They want you to think that something is wrong with you and that you do not have what it takes to make good decisions in your life.

I knew a *Gamer* who happened to be a boss that would conduct performance evaluations with her entire staff when she was upset with something one of them did. Instead of dealing with the one person and confronting the issue directly, she would bring her entire staff into her office one by one and yell at each of them. She would throw temper tantrums, banging on the table and swearing. Many of her employees would leave her office crying. Others would leave angry or disillusioned, but all of them suffered from the games played with their emotions by the *Gamer*. Her staff was not only intimidated by her, but ultimately afraid of upsetting her. Like children with abusive parents, they learned to be very cautious around her and avoided her at all costs, to keep their jobs.

The mistake most people make with *Gamers* is to try to reason with them. You cannot reason with Subtracters who are *Gamers* because they are all about playing mind games and manipulating your emotions. Trying to reason with them or getting your viewpoint across is like saying, "Let the games begin!" The bottom line is that the *Gamer* wants to intimidate you and leave you emotionally unstable and unbalanced to the point where you feel like you cannot make a clear decision about your life. In many ways, *Gamers* can be really dangerous because they will play with your emotions until you get to the place where you question whether you can handle the issues in your life. The ultimate trick that *Gamers* play is convincing you that you are not capable of making decisions in life, so they will have to make them for you! This is the danger zone because *Gamers* have the capacity of take over your life, if you let them.

The Dreamer

Dreamers are fascinating Subtracters because they are typically interesting, smart and innovative people with tremendous potential. *Dreamers* have no intention to subtract from others, however, they were never taught how to complete anything or authentically give to others. *Dreamers* are the people who live in the world of "if only" — if only I could have, if only I should have, if only I would have. They never quite complete anything, but have learned how to use their charms and talents to draw you into their "Wouldn't it be great if we could..." cycle. They were socialized to waste your time, and to convince you that their 'great idea' is exactly what you need to be successful in life. They are fascinating people who could easily be Adders. But *Dreamers* have never been taught how to use their powers to add, only to unconsciously subtract as a strategy for getting their dreams fulfilled. Because *Dreamers* are also likeable people with good social skills, they know how to find people who will help them fulfill their dreams. The reality, however, is that they won't ever fulfill their dreams because they are missing key components in their life.

One of my former clients was married to an entrepreneur whose goal was to build a solid business. He was young and smart, with lots of energy and a commitment to succeeding, but frequently found himself partnering with *Dreamers*. The entrepreneur poured money, time and his creativity into making deals work, but his *Dreamer* partners would always fail to do their part. The *Dreamers* always started out the partnership with energy and passion for making the deal work. They would tell everyone about their new business but that's all they ever did - talk. They would convince the entrepreneur into thinking that the business deals were on track and going great, but in reality, the *Dreamers* lacked the skills, experience and/or talents needed to do their parts. Eventually, the deals fell apart and the entrepreneur would be left "holding the bag" – that is, left with the bad debt, bad reputation, old product, etc.

Dreamers will lead you into a whirlwind process where you find yourself giving everything you have to make their dreams a reality. The fascinating thing about *Dreamers* is that, when you first start working with them, they are very energetic people with great ideas. But, you must listen carefully to them for clues about their success records. Yes, *Dreamers* might have started amazing projects but did they finish them? How did they finish them? Listen to *Dreamers* language and watch for phrases like: *I really should have, I really could have, if only I would have.* *Dreamers* experience many near-successes and have a pattern of engaging others in conversation about how they "almost did it." *Dreamers* fail because they are not honest about their capacity and are not committed to doing the work it takes to complete projects. Even though you may be attracted to their dreams, be careful, because *Dreamers* will ultimately take your time, resources, and energy, and you will be left disappointed, frustrated and in maybe even broke!

If you decide to work with a *Dreamer,* you must be prepared to hold them accountable so that they don't become a Subtracter to you. As you will learn, *Dreamers* can become Adders. However, a *Dreamer* who is never instructed or confronted about their impact in your life will use their big dreams to severely subtract from your life. Every dream requires human capital, social capital and economic capital. And, the *Dreamer* has no problem taking it all from you!

The Blamer

Blamers are one of the easiest Subtracters to identify because they do not take any responsibility for their own actions. What does it mean to blame? "To blame is to hold another person or group responsible for perceived faults, be those faults real, imagined, or merely invented for pejorative purposes. Blame is an act of censure, reproach, and often cases outright condemnation."[4] *Blamers* operate on the assumption that you are the reason they have not succeeded in life. They work hard to draw you into their drama cycle by blaming

---

4   en.wikipedia.org/wiki/Blame

you for everything that has gone wrong in their life. They are not willing to be accountable or responsible for their words, actions and attitudes. *Blamers* can live their entire lives blaming others for their failures. *Blamers* are blatant and very vocal. They will blame you publicly or privately. *Blamers* are known for seeking your advice then blaming you when something goes wrong, even though they never followed your advice. Never give *Blamers* advice. If they ask, simply say; " Let me think about it," then change the subject! Why? Because somewhere in a *Blamer's* mind they believe that other people are responsible for their success or failure. In other words, someone else has the power to change their life.

If you have a boss who is a *Blamer*, you will find that when something goes wrong in the department, or on your project team, he/she will immediately point fingers. *Blamers* refuse to look at their own actions and take responsibility. Their first response is always to look for someone to blame. *Blamers* make poor leaders who spend their energy putting down, instead of building up, their teams. The *Blamer* boss says, "This department is not successful because we don't have the right people, or they don't know what they are doing, or they are always making me look bad…." Instead of looking at the core issues and ways to solve problems in the department, a *Blamer* will resort to firing people. They think that firing their employees is the solution, but the reality is that the real problem is the *Blamer* boss who refuses to admit that as the positional leader, the overall lack of success in the department is their fault. They do not understand how their blaming results in low productivity and morale in the office.

Blamers think they are increasing their power when they point fingers and find fault in others. Many think they are coming across as smart and assertive, but what they are actually doing is hiding their own insecurities. *Blamers* are the most blatant Subtracter personalities and, just like *Gamers*, you cannot argue with them. The *Blamer* who is a "Just Is" family member lives to tell others that you are the reason they have not been successful in life. *Blamer* family members take every opportunity to tell you and others how you ruined their life. Whether the accusations are true or false, the mistake we make is trying to correct, explain or prove ourselves to a *Blamer*. Why is this a mistake? Because the *Blamer* has already decided that you are the reason for their failure and nothing you say or do can change that decision. As a matter of fact, when you try to prove yourself to a *Blamer*, you are giving them even more of your time, emotional energy and new information they can use to continue blaming you. The most that you can do with a *Blamer* is to strategically monitor and record your own actions and successes so, when a *Blamer* points their finger at you, you know in your heart that it's not your fault.

The Worrier

Worriers are the least harmful and assertive of the Subtracter personalities. They would never think of being mean, or hurtful to anyone. A *Worrier* is often their own biggest Subtracters. *Worriers* don't work on solving problems, they just worry about them. Having a conversation with *Worriers* is very frustrating because they might act like they want solutions, but will then question every possible solution by creating excuses and reasons why it wouldn't work. *Worriers* fear the possibility of failure. As a result, many *Worriers* miss great opportunities to expand and increase their lives. *Worriers* can spend years worrying if they should do something new, find a new job, or change a relationship. Their worry results in non-action, which then leads to a lack of confidence and courage to try anything new. Eventually, many *Worriers* find themselves stuck in a place where their minds are caught up in cycles of negative emotions and pessimism.

What happens when you have *Worriers* in your life? First, they will share all of the reasons why they haven't been successful. *Worriers* will tell you their stories of failures and give you reasons why

> *Remember, Worriers don't want to create solutions; they simply want to worry about the problem. In the process, they take your energy, time, enthusiasm, resources, confidence and potential for success.*

they can't try again. Even though they might have the skills, talents and abilities, *Worriers* will refuse to try again because they are afraid to fail. Most *Worriers* cannot see how they are subtracting from others, but the reality is that as they constantly engage you in their conversations of worry, you will begin to connect with their drama cycles of self doubt and disbelief. The more you listen, the deeper you will go into the *Worrier's* drama cycle. Soon, the *Worrier* will begin worrying about your life and why you should or should not try new things. They will begin to question your actions and second guess your decisions. Keep in mind that a *Worrier* does not mean you any harm, nor are they conscious of how they are subtracting from you. Worrying is simply a habit. It's automatic. If you are not careful, a *Worrier* will get you trapped in their worrying patterns and, before you know it, you too will begin to spend your time worrying, instead of making life happen.

A typical scenario of a *Worrier* in the workplace looks like this: You go to work one morning, and one of your colleagues, who is a *Worrier*, has a project due. However, the *Worrier* is too busy spending time anticipating that someone won't like the project, instead of spending their creative energy working on a solution. In your meetings, the *Worrier* spends their time questioning everything, putting down every possible idea and reminding the team about what happened last time. As a result, the team is stuck because the *Worrier* has thrown everyone into a drama cycle of worry and frustration. Team members will waste their time discussing the same problems and issues over and over, but without any solutions. Before long, the entire team has fallen apart and everyone is frustrated and feeling stuck. Unless someone confronts the *Worrier*, your team will spend endless unproductive hours trying to solve a problem that the *Worrier* is afraid to solve. Remember, *Worriers* don't want to create solutions; they simply want to worry about the problem. In the process, they take your energy, time, enthusiasm, resources, confidence and potential for success.

Worriers have a pattern. Listen carefully and you will discover that all of their worrying can be traced back to specific unresolved issues in their lives. Usually, it is an issue related to low self-esteem or confidence, or past failures. Many *Worriers* struggle with their self-esteem. Somewhere in life, Subtracters significantly impacted them and many *Worriers* never recovered. A director of a school came for a coaching session and spent almost her entire session verbalizing her worry about losing her job. She was consumed with worry about what might go wrong. Unfortunately, within months, she did lose her job. This incident was so damaging to the *Worrier* that she struggled for years finding a new job, and at one point admitted that she did not know how to rebound from this setback in her life. As a *Worrier*, her first response was not to find a new job but to spend months worrying about what would happen if she tried to find a new job. Instead of asking herself what she could learn from her setback, she subtracted from herself and others by worrying about it. She allowed that one situation to put her into a drama cycle from which it took her almost two years to recover.

Worriers are very complex Subtracters because on one level, they want your help but at the same time, they are

> *You cannot and will not change until you deal with the reality of who you are and how you are using your personal power.*

so stuck in their past failures that it is very painful for them to stop worrying and take action. They have the habit of approaching every new opportunity with a "what if it doesn't work" attitude. *Worriers* are socialized Subtracters who use worry as a tool for dealing with life. Unfortunately, the core principle of words – you become what you think about and say – is so powerful, that *Worriers* can unknowingly use their worry to create negative outcomes for their lives. Why? The more they think and talk about what could go wrong, the more failure they will experience. Can *Worriers* become Adders? Yes, if they make a conscious decision to change how they think about life. When *Worriers* decide to readjust their questions and thinking from "what if I fail" to "what if I succeed", then anything becomes possible and they can stop subtracting and begin to add to themselves and others.

Having learned about the seven personalities, take a moment to think about the Subtracters in your life. Is there *Smiler* who is always nice and sweet, but at the same time pulls you into an amazing drama cycle? Is there a *Snipper-Nipper* who is continually cutting away at your confidence? Is there a Gamer, who knows how to manipulate your emotions and throw you into an emotional spin? Is there a *Dreamer*, who takes you to a place where you think you can accomplish something, when they have absolutely no intention of following through? Is there a *Shamer,* who makes you feel unworthy? Is there a *Blamer*, who sees you as the reason for their issues in life? Or a *Worrier* who keeps you in a place of constantly questioning and doubting if you can be successful? Who are these people? Take a moment to think about who they are, what their personality types are and how they are influencing your life. This book offers you many strategies for dealing with each personality, but you first must identify who they are. Be honest; if you are one of your own Subtracters, write it down. Why? You cannot and will not change until you deal with the reality of who you are and how you are using your personal power. (Create a chart below)

Subtracters in your Life	Personality Type	Impact/Influence

Who is in Your Inner Circle?

Every person, whether they know ten or 10,000 people, has an inner circle. The first step in dealing with your Subtracters is to assess your inner circle. An inner circle is a small group of people to whom you look for advice, counsel, leadership, mentorship and guidance. Your inner circle directly influences what you say, what you do, your attitude, how you think and the major decisions you make in life. They are very important and powerful people in our lives. In your work situation, for example, you may have a team member to whom you look up, from whom you seek guidance, and whom you see as a mentor. When you have a major issue at your job, you will seek out that team member for advice and counsel. If they are in your inner circle, you will find yourself not only listening to them, but taking action based on their insight and suggestions. That is the power of your inner circle. When people are in your inner circle, whoever they are, whatever they say, whatever their attitude and actions, they will directly influence you. There is a direct correlation between who is in your inner circle and your progress in life. This is critical to know because, if your inner circle is full of Subtracters, then every decision you make will be influenced by the attitudes, actions, and power of those Subtracters.

I once coached a woman in her forties whose mother was an important part of her inner circle. This was a huge challenge because her mother was a *Snipper-Nipper* and *Gamer* who constantly put her down and played with her emotions. This woman was emotionally unstable, frustrated and afraid to make her own decisions. She was stuck! It took months of coaching before she could deal with the reality that her mother was a severe Subtracter who needed to be moved out of her inner circle. This woman had to learn how to keep her mother in her life but out of her inner circle. She had to learn to manage her mother's power and role in her life.

If your inner circle is full of Subtracters, then every decision you make will be influenced by the attitudes, actions, and power of those Subtracters.

Any success or failure in your life can be traced back to your inner circle. I guarantee that if you have found success in life and work, it is because your inner circle is filled with mostly Adders who are positively increasing your value and influencing you to create positive changes. If you feel stuck, like you don't know where you are going, or you live in a world of self doubt and you are struggling to find success in work and life, then more than likely your inner circle is full of Subtracters who have been decreasing your value and negatively influencing your life. That is the power of your inner circle.

Before we can talk about the keys to creating an inner circle that can positively influence your life, you must first identify who is currently in your inner circle. Who is directly influencing how you think, how you act and what you say? Who is influencing your overall perspective and outlook on life? Who is influencing the major decisions you have or will make in your life? Make a list of the people (from work and/or life) in your inner circle.

Your Inner Circle

1. _____

2. _____

3. _____

4. _____

5. _____

6. _____

7. _____

Keys to Your Inner Circle

The first key to your inner circle is that it must be a circle of people you have chosen. Unfortunately, most people live with inner circles that have chosen them. People, especially family members, have a habit of putting themselves in your inner circle. Some family members think that they are entitled to be there. I am not suggesting that you push your family members out of your life, but it is important to choose whether to include them in your inner circle. One of my goals in life is to be a part of my adult children's inner circles. But I also realize that my children have to choose me. I can't just decide to be in their circles! You choose who will be in your inner circle.

The second key to your inner circle is that it should be a circle of Adders- powerful people who bring increased positive value to your life. Adders will challenge you to think differently, change your attitude, increase your knowledge and create manageable goals for your life. They add to your life not for self-gratification, self-promotion or to use you, but because they authentically care about you as a person and are committed to empowering you to reach your fullest potential. Adders positively influence your life without attaching strings, and they have a heart for seeing you become a positive, powerful person.[5]

The third key is that your inner circle must be flexible and fluid. That is, your inner circle is not constant; it can and will change. Your inner circle has seasons during which you move people in and out of it. The number one myth of inner circles is that, if someone has been in your inner circle for a long time, then they should stay in your inner circle for life. If your friend who has been in your inner circle since kindergarten is a Subtracter, then you have to move them out! If someone has been in your inner circle for years but you finally realize that you never chose them in the first place, then you have to move them out. Only you know when it's time to reconstruct your inner circle. This may sound simple, but it's very hard to do, especially when you have to move out an Adder whose season is finished in your life. When I completed graduate school and entered into a new season in my life, it was clear that it was time to reconstruct my inner circle. I remember having to move out one particular professor, a mentor, from my inner circle. It was not easy to do, but necessary for me to move on with my life. Was the professor still in my life? Absolutely. Reconstructing your inner circle does not mean dismissing people from your life, only decreasing their levels of impact and influence. Your inner circle can and will change, and that is not only okay, but imperative for your continued success in life.

An effective inner circle consists of five people. Having more

---

5   Price, Verna C. (2002) The Power of People: Four Kinds of People Who Can Change Your Life. JCAMA Publishers. Minneapolis, MN. Pp 25.

than five creates the potential for confusion and chaos. Typically these five people will have specific roles in your life. The first role is the purpose person. This person's influence in your life relates to deciding where you are going, what you want to accomplish and how you want to change your world. They really believe that you have a purpose in life. Without a purpose person, you will find yourself searching for and/or questioning your overall reason for living and your vision in life.

Second, your inner circle should always have a person who is proven.[6] This person has proven in their own life and profession that they know how to be successful. Sometimes, a proven person could be a *Multiplier, a* miraculous mentor who can help you enlarge, magnify, amplify, expand and increase your life![7] You cannot be successful in your marriage, work, finances, relationships, family or career without having at least one proven person in your inner circle. These are people who have already accomplished what you want to do, been where you want to go and achieved what you are now only dreaming about. The proven person plays a key role in your inner circle because they will connect you to new opportunities, advise you on how best to get things done and increase your network and net worth.

The third role in your inner circle is the productive person. This is the "work it out" person in your circle who knows how to make things happen. They have not yet reached the proven level but they are obviously on a success track and are prepared to work hard to reach their goals. The productive person will help you create and

---

6   Maxwell, John C. (2007) The 21 Irrefutable Laws of Leadership. Thomas Nelson Publishers, Nashville, TN

7   Price, Verna C. (2002) The Power of People: Four Kinds of People Who Can Change Your Life. JCAMA Publishers. Minneapolis, MN. Pp. 87-88

sustain momentum in your life. They are the people with a strategy and are prepared to take action. What makes them unique is that they will work with you to make your goals a reality. They believe in being productive and celebrating the small milestones of accomplishment in your life. The productive people will not just listen to you talk about your purpose and plans, they will want to know how you will make it happen. Many people confuse their proven with their productive person. How can you tell the difference?

A potential person in your inner circle is someone who is going to challenge you to that next level, to truly discover your potential, to create change in your life and world.

The proven person is someone who has already been there, accomplished tasks, and knows how success feels and is willing to coach and mentor you on how to get there. The productive person will work with you to actually get it done. Productive people don't want to talk about it, they are ready to take action and work beside you to do it! The purpose person helps you define your vision, the proven person connects you with the networks and resources needed to achieve your purpose, and the productive person says, "Now let's do something about the purpose, vision, goal. Let's create a plan and start." Every inner circle must have one productive person. They are the people who keep you going, keep you thinking and keep you pursuing. The productive person will not settle for anything less than getting things done.

The fourth type of person is the potential person. This is the person who challenges your potential. This is the person who continually asks where you are going and how you will get there. They continually see your potential, and their task is to get you to think about your potential, discover it, believe in it, focus on it, and understand it. No matter what you have achieved, the potential person will always ask you about the next level and challenge you to achieve it. Potential people will never settle for your current successes; they are always interested in what else you can accomplish.

I recently had a conversation with my thirteen-year-old son who came home and reported he got a B on his science test. "Well," I said, "That is a good thing. But, did you really study or did you get a B because you are a naturally smart, talented person who happens to like science?" I looked him in the eye and continued. "Now, if that is the case, it means that you didn't really get a B. It means you barely passed the test because, if you really studied, and gave this some effort, you would have gotten an A." Taking on the role of a potential person in my son's inner circle, I wanted to challenge him to not settle for the B, but to study more and pursue a better grade. A potential person in your inner circle is someone who is going to challenge you to that next level, to truly discover your potential, to create change in your life and world. The mistake we make is thinking that our potential people can mentor us on how to get to our next level. Their role is not to help you figure out how to get there, but to raise the challenging questions needed to keep you from becoming stuck in your life.

The final role is your <u>people</u> person. This is someone you just like talking to. They might never give you solutions, or raise critical questions or share ideas with you, but they like care about you as a person and know how to engage you in fun-filled, interesting conversations. They know how to listen to you. As they listen, you will often find yourself creating your own solutions simply because someone has given you the space and opportunity to just talk, laugh and clear your mind. They are the people who call you once a week just to check in and see how you are doing. The people person is a member of your personal fan club. They are going to make sure that they keep you encouraged and motivated, but they will also help you find ways to relax and have fun. The role of the people person is critical to your inner circle, but loading up your inner circle with people persons can be a problem. Why? Because you will get into the habit of just talking about your life instead of taking the actions necessary to create the productive, proven, purposeful, powerful life that you want.

Analyzing Your Inner Circle

Who is in your inner circle? What are their roles? How are they using their personal power in your life? Are they Adders or Subtracters? Analyzing your inner circle is not a one-time event, it's ongoing. Your life's work is to structure and restructure your inner circle. What changes do you want to see in your life? Are there people in your inner circle who can help you create that change? Is your inner circle clogged up with people from your past and/or family members whom you never chose to be there? Do you have too many people in your inner circle? Think about how your current inner circle has directly impacted your life. How have they impacted your life's dreams, vision and/or goals? How have they influenced your happiness, confidence and self-esteem? How have they affected your professional success? It is critical to understand what your current inner circle has produced in your life.

In recent years, I have been interviewed about helping people create New Year's resolutions. My response to the interviewer is always that I don't believe in resolutions, but I do believe in life vision and goals. I also believe that we have the power to create the lives we want. Where do you start in creating the life you want? By doing a New Year's inner circle assessment. Look at who influenced your life last year. How did they influence you? Was your life helped, hindered or hurt by their influence? Does this mean that you can blame your lack of success, or your failure, on your inner circle? Absolutely not! You are a powerful person who is ultimately responsible for the success or failure in your life. Remember that your power is your ability to do something about your life by taking action steps. You are the only person who can take the action steps necessary to change your life. However, your inner circle directly and indirectly influences which action steps you decide to take. I have seen people in top executive positions make wrong decisions because their inner circle consisted of Subtracters. I have also seen people with little material resources achieve great things in life because they had strategically created an inner circle of Adders and Multipliers. Recreating and restructuring your inner circle is one of the hardest things you will ever do in your life, because moving someone out of your inner circle can be difficult and painful. It requires personal power, courage, confidence, clear goals and a personal strategic plan.

Let's start the analysis process. Take a moment and think about your inner circle. In the diagram that follows, write your name in the middle. Around your name, write the names of those people in your inner circle. Next to their names, indicate if they are adding or subtracting from your life. If someone is a Subtracter, then indicate their personality type. Finally, indicate the role of each person in your circle and how they have impacted and influenced your life. Now, take some time to think about what you wrote, study it, and be honest about steps you will take to begin restructuring your inner circle.

Inner Circle Diagram

Let's start the analysis process. Take a moment and think about your inner circle. In the diagram that follows, write your name in the middle. Around your name write the names of those people in your inner circle. Next to their name, indicate if they are adding or subtracting from your life. If they are a Subtracter then indicate their personality type. Finally, indicate the role of each person in your circle and how they have impacted and influenced your life.

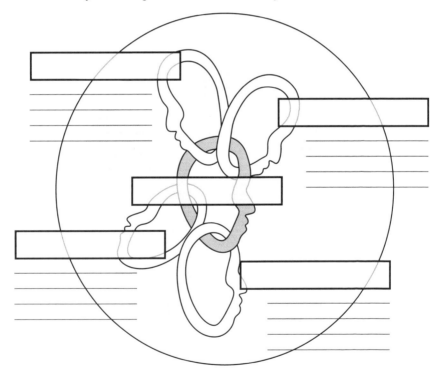

Now take some time and think about what you wrote, study it, and be honest about steps you will take to begin restructuring your inner circle.

What if Your Boss is a Subtracter?

A well-educated young professional who had worked hard to build a great team and earn respect from her colleagues requested a coaching session with me. I saw this young woman as an aspiring leader, so I was somewhat surprised by her urgency. Even though she had accomplished amazing things for her company, she was struggling with a major dilemma; her boss was a Subtracter. When we began our coaching session, it was clear that this seemingly confident leader was quietly suffering and suffocating under the pressure of having to deal with a Subtracter boss. Her silent cry filled my office as she told the story of her daily struggle to do her job, be a leader and keep her sanity! She was beginning to lose her confidence and had become intimidated by the Subtracter boss to the point where she was ready to walk away from her position. There was no other person for her to report to in the company, and her boss had worked hard to dismantle this woman's confidence, accomplishments and character. He tried to sabotage her meetings, kept her out of the information loop and regularly denied her requests to attend important conferences that would further her professional development. She was passed over for promotions, even though her record clearly demonstrated she was the most qualified candidate. The young professional felt belittled, frustrated and confused. How did her boss become a Subtracter? Was he aware of how he was using his power? What could she do? What should she do? Should she just stop looking for answers and quit her job, losing everything she had worked so hard for?

What if your boss is a Subtracter? Many people don't like the word "boss" but whether you call them supervisors or managers, these are the people in your company to whom you report. Whatever

> *Subtracters are very powerful people, but they can only be as powerful as you let them be in your life. You have to make a commitment to yourself that you will refuse to run.*

you call them, if they are Subtracters, then you have an issue! Unfortunately, many people just suffer silently, shut down completely or quit their jobs, instead of dealing with the Subtracter boss. If your boss is a Subtracter, you must **make a decision now not to let them chase you away from your position.** First read, study and apply the strategies shared in this chapter. If, after you have tried everything you can, you decide that you cannot work with your Subtracter boss, then make a plan to resign but don't just quit! I have seen people give up all they have built and worked for because of one Subtracter boss. Subtracters are very powerful people, but they can only be as powerful as you let them be in your life. You have to make a commitment to yourself that you will refuse to run. Instead, decide to learn what it takes to deal with this person while maintaining your character and giving yourself time to create a plan of action.

The Professional "Just Is" Person

In the workplace, a boss is your "Just Is" person. In your personal life, "Just Is" people are your family members, children, blood relatives, spouses or former spouses. You can never get them out of your life, but you can learn to manage their impact on you. Professionally, your "Just Is" people are the ones to whom you report, typically called your bosses. Very few people can do anything about their professional "Just Is person." Your boss comes along with your professional package, she "Just Is." What does this mean for you?

1. Whether you like, dislike, respect or disrespect them, you are assigned to report to them.

2. You must find strategies to best deal with your boss while still maintaining your productivity, morale, character and personal power.

3. You cannot just dismiss your boss from your work life and refuse to work with them; you must find ways to work with them so that can keep your job.

4. You must learn to manage your "Just Is" boss so that you are not giving away your power and left feeling powerless and helpless.

I worked for an organization in which the "Just Is" person, the president of the organization, was a Subtracter. This person was a *Gamer, Shamer* and *Blamer*. None of the staff knew anything about the "Just Is" principle and, as a result, many of us ended up fired or nearly being fired from the organization. What we did not understand was that our boss was a "Just Is" person who was not going anywhere anytime soon. We either had to learn to deal with him or leave the organization. I did not have any skills or strategies to deal with this person. After much frustration and painful confrontations which almost cost me my job, I faced up to the reality of my "Just Is" Subtracter boss, took a deep breath, and decided to start looking for another position.

Personal vs. Positional Leadership

Dealing with a Subtracter boss requires understanding the dynamics and difference between Personal and Positional leadership. Many people are confused about how these two forms of leadership impact the workplace. What is the difference? A Personal leader may not have the highest position in an organization, but they demonstrate a strong set of values and a work ethic that others admire and respect. Personal leaders authentically care about others and know how to partner and collaborate with others to get things done. They trust their own judgment and understand how to lead. Personal leaders know who they are, why they are there, and where they want to go. They

> *Leadership is 99% about people and 1% about position.*

usually have a personal vision and life plan. They do not chase after promotions or positions yet they are confident in their skills, talents and abilities. People naturally respect, follow and seek out the advice and counsel of Personal leaders in the workplace. Unfortunately, Personal leaders are rarely the people in the "boss" positions. Having a boss who is both a Positional and Personal leader is a blessing!

Positional leaders are people with significant positions or titles. Their positions give them a certain level of authority and control in the organization. Positional leaders can mandate that people follow policies and procedures, and can reprimand employees who fail to do so. These people are usually considered the "bosses" and are responsible for holding others accountable. Effective Positional leaders are important to the success of an organization. So what happens when Positional leaders are not Personal leaders? When they don't have a strong set of values or work ethic? What if they don't know how to work with people and build good relationships? What if they use their position to dictate what you will and won't do? Can you be an effective Positional leader without being a Personal leader?

There is an old saying that states, "People don't care how

much you know until they know how much you care." Authentic leadership is about people and you cannot lead if no one is following you. Leadership is 99% about people and 1% about position. When a Positional leader lacks Personal leadership skills, they will demand respect instead of earning it.

A Subtracter boss is someone who has attained a high level of Positional leadership without having strong Personal leadership skills. A core leadership principle is that high levels of Positional leadership can never compensate for low levels of personal power and Personal leadership. That is why it's important to know what type of leader you are dealing with. Do you have a boss who is first and foremost a strong and positive Personal leader, or one who relies only on their position? How can you tell the difference? You have to do your research. Study the person and observe them over time to see what they really believe in and stand for. Pay attention to how they relate to, work with and manage people. Watch how they demonstrate and live out their values in the workplace. The bottom line is that most Subtracter bosses have a position but no Personal leadership.

Is Your Boss A Subtracter?

To know if your boss is really a Subtracter, take the time to conduct a *Subtracter Boss Assessment*. The assessment consists of six key areas in which you will study and observe your boss. This assessment will clearly indicate if your boss is a Subtracter, or if you are simply operating at two different levels of assumptions and perspective about your roles and responsibilities.

Why is the *Subtracter Boss Assessment* so important? It allows

Subtractor Boss Assessment

1. Assess their words.
    How do they talk? What do they say? How do they
    communicate?

    _____

    _____

    _____

    _____

    _____

    _____

    _____

2. Assess the energy they bring to the workplace.
    Do they bring positive or negative energy?
    How does this energy affect the overall work environment and
    culture?

    _____

    _____

    _____

    _____

    _____

    _____

    _____

3. Assess their emotions.
   How do they use their emotions in the workplace? What kind of emotional response are they trying to evoke? Are they trying to manipulate people? Are they trying to make people feel emotionally unstable?

   _____

   _____

   _____

   _____

   _____

   _____

   _____

4. Assess their personal resources.
   What kind of resources do they bring to their team? Do they offer resources to your team? Do they offer resources to you?

   _____

   _____

   _____

   _____

   _____

   _____

5. Assess their personal power.
   How do they use their personal power? Do they increase or decrease the value of their team? Do they empower or disempower others? Do they value and encourage the team members to use their personal power?

   _____

   _____

   _____

   _____

   _____

   _____

   _____

6. Assess their leadership.
   How well do they lead? What kind of leaders are they? Are they leaders who embrace change? Do they invite their team into critical conversations? Are they leaders who dictate? How do they treat people?

   _____

   _____

   _____

   _____

   _____

   _____

you to avoid making assumptions about your boss. In his well-known book called *The Four Agreements,*[8] Don Miguel Ruiz explains that we make agreements with people about how we should be treated and how they should treat us. One of the agreements that you must make with yourself is that you will not make assumptions. The *Subtracter Boss Assessment* helps you avoid assumptions and provides you with real information about your boss and how they are using their power.

After completing the assessment, compare your responses to the definition of a Subtracter and the seven Subtracter personalities. If you have evidence that your boss is truly a Subtracter, then finish this chapter. But, if your boss is not a Subtracter, create a plan to begin readjusting how you interact with them. Schedule a meeting to discuss ways to better work together.

Where to Start in Dealing with a Subtracter Boss?

Know Your Strengths

The first place to start, of course, is with you. You cannot deal with a Subtracter boss unless you have a clear understanding about your own leadership strengths. When the young leader came into my office to talk about her Subtracter boss, the first task was to ask some critical questions: Who are you? What do you bring to your team? What do you bring to your organization? What are your strengths? What are your professional goals? What is your vision? What do you want to change or enhance in your organization?

The young leader felt oppressed by her Subtracter boss. She felt as though she were being squashed and stepped on. When you have worked for a Subtracter boss for a long period of time, you

---

8   Ruiz, Miguel Angel, M.D. (1997). The Four Agreements: A Practical Guide to Personal Freedom. Amber-Allen Publishing, San Rafael, CA

cannot begin to deal with that person until you rediscover yourself. This woman had to remember who she was when she arrived at the organization. She had to remember the strengths, skills and competencies that earned her the position. She had to recall why she chose to work for the organization and what she had hoped to accomplish.

Dealing with a Subtracter boss requires preparation. You must strengthen your confidence and reclaim your courage. Why? Because your Subtracter boss knows how to intimidate you, derail your confidence, and send you into an emotional spin of self doubt. If you are unprepared, you will find yourself being even more unproductive, becoming increasingly negative, and being driven away from your original purpose and vision for joining to the organization.

One of the most common strategies used by a Subtracter boss is to exaggerate your weaknesses. Knowing your leadership strengths is critical. There are existing tools, like the book *Now Discover Your Strengths,*[9] that provides an assessment to help you identify and better understand your strengths so that you can lead from a place of strength, not weakness. As you become clear about what makes you a strong Personal leader, you will regain your confidence and courage to deal with your boss. A Subtracter cannot negatively influence and impact your life unless you continue to let them. However, you cannot stop the negative influence if you are not clear about your personal power and Personal leadership. You can only deal with a Subtracter boss from a place of strength. Understanding who you are and what makes you a strong Personal leader is imperative as you begin the

---

9   Buckingham, M. and Clifton, D. O. (2001). Now Discover Your Strengths. Simon & Schuster, Inc. Publisher, New York, New York

process of dealing with a Subtracter boss.

Take a moment to create your profile of leadership strengths. Think about who you are as a Personal leader in your organization. What you are really good at? What do you do well? What are your leadership strengths? Are you a good communicator? Do you demonstrate integrity? Are you a great listener? Do you have great interpersonal skills? What are you known for making happen?

Next, think about how you know you are good in those areas. What evidence do you have that you are a Personal leader? What do others who respect you say about your leadership? What do people compliment you on? What evidence do you have that you are a person of integrity? How do you know that your leadership strengths are really your strengths? You must have evidence. Why? Because a Subtracter boss wants you to prove yourself. If you haven't thought about and prepared for this pressure you will fall apart and become emotionally unstable, angry and out of control. Eventually, you will say or do something that gives your Subtracter boss justifiable reasons to fire or demote you. Knowing your leadership strengths and gathering your evidence prepares you for dealing with your Subtracter boss.

What are your Personal leadership strengths?

_____

_____

_____

_____

_____

_____

_____

_____

_____

What evidence do you have? How do you know you have these strengths?

_____

_____

_____

_____

_____

_____

_____

_____

_____

Know Your Values

We all have values, those intangible core principles, beliefs and convictions which guide our behavior, decisions and attitudes in work and life. Values are non-negotiable. If honesty is a value, then telling a lie about someone in your office is unacceptable. I will never forget a man in a high-level position at a noted university coming into my office and quietly saying, "My integrity is in jeopardy." He went on to explain how he was one step away from crossing that line of doing something his boss had asked of him to meet the goals of the university, but which would ultimately sacrifice his integrity. He said, "I needed to tell someone that I am unwilling to sacrifice my integrity for position or money. I have decided that I have to give up the position because there is no way I can do this job without losing my integrity." Within two weeks he resigned. He didn't have another job or know exactly what he was going to do, but he did know that his values of integrity and honesty were non-negotiables. When you deal with a Subtracter boss, you have to know your values. You must have clear boundaries between what you will and will not do or say.

Another coaching client, a young mother who was a rising star in her company, wanted more work-life balance because of her value of family. She was married with young children but she worked for a female boss who was single and without children. Her boss did not understand how important family was to her employee, and constantly gave her a workload that required long hours and extensive traveling. My client felt stuck and frustrated because her value of family meant spending more time at home and creating a better work-life balance. She enjoyed her job, but not to the point of neglecting her family. My client decided to meet with her Subtracter boss to discuss restructuring her job so she could still have time for her family. This was a risky move because the young mother had no idea how her boss would respond to this values discussion. However, she was prepared to take a demotion or even walk away from the organization because her family was a non-negotiable.

What are your values? You cannot effectively deal with a Subtracter boss if you are unclear or unsure of your values. Why? Because a Subtracter boss will intentionally put you in situations that will challenge your values. Most people have a handful of, about five, core values that guide and direct their life. Reflecting on and identifying your core values is another step in preparing to deal with your Subtracter boss. For example, if respect is a core value, then being disrespected by your boss is a non-negotiable. But if you don't know and understand your personal core values, then you will allow a Subtracter boss to say and do whatever they want to you.

Take a moment to write down your core values, those non-negotiables that will guide how you live your life and interact with others, particularly your Subtracter boss.

_____

_____

_____

_____

_____

_____

Know Your Partners, Collaborators and Networks

You cannot deal with a Subtracter boss alone. You need a network of people, partners, and collaborators both within and outside of your company-who know you, know your work, and respect your accomplishments. Your partners are people in other departments or companies, with whom you work closely on a variety of projects. Collaborations are groups of people or organizations who have committed their time, energy and resources to completing a joint project. Dealing with a Subtracter boss may require the support of your network. For example, what if your boss avoids making decisions and refuses to take action, which results in your missing important project timelines? This makes it seem as if you are not doing your job, when you really are. What can you do? If you have good networks and partnerships in the organization, then you can ask them for advice and help in dealing with your boss. In the process, your networks will also protect your credibility and integrity. Your networks could also approach your boss regarding their concerns about project turn-around and completions. If necessary, your networks could find ways to help you work around your boss so that you could still meet project timelines without sacrificing your position. You cannot operate in isolation when working with a Subtracter boss. You need your trusted networks to understand what you are going through and to be prepared to stand up on your behalf. When your Subtracter boss realizes that you have strong connections within and outside of the company, they are less likely to sabotage you. However, the opposite is also true. If you do not have a network then it becomes easier for your boss to continue as a Subtracter.

Do you have a strong professional network both within and

outside of your company? If so, take a moment and list those people and their roles in your professional life. If not, then take your first step in building a strong network. Begin looking around your company for potential people you admire or respect and would like to be in your network.

Your Current Network

_____

_____

_____

_____

_____

_____

_____

Your Potential Network

_____

_____

_____

_____

_____

_____

_____

Identifying your networks is critical because, as a Personal Leader, you must know who is in your inner circle within the workplace. The next step is to assess the strength of your networks, your professional inner circle. How strong are they? Are these people you can trust? Can you be honest with them? Do they listen to you? When you decide to have some level of confrontation with your Subtracter boss, are these people willing to stand up for you or speak on your behalf? Does your network have the courage to bring up the issues to your boss? It's important to know if your network is strong or weak. If it is a weak network or one you do not trust, you want to keep them out of the plan for dealing with your Subtracter boss. As a matter of fact, if your network is weak, or if there is a Subtracter in it, you want to avoid telling them anything about your Subtracter boss. Only a strong, trusted network will support you in the process and help you think critically about creative strategies for dealing with a Subtracter boss.

Know Your Agreements

One of the most critical components of dealing with a Subtracter boss is being honest about the agreements you have made with that person. Agreements[10] include those non-verbal messages we give to others through our body language, voice tones, and/or actions that give them clues and signals about how they should treat us, talk to us or even think about us. We make agreements with others every day. Some of these agreements help others respect our personal power, character or accomplishments. Other agreements teach people how to take our personal power and subtract from us. If your boss is a

---

10 Ruiz, Miguel Angel, M.D. (1997). The Four Agreements: A Practical Guide to Personal Freedom. Amber-Allen Publishing: San Rafael, CA

Subtracter, more than likely you made an agreement(s) with them that gave them not only the permission but also ideas on how to devalue you in the workplace.

In a coaching session I asked a client who was a director, for her area to think about agreements she had made with her team. She was the boss, but had a Subtracter on her team. After learning about the role of agreements in the workplace, she realized that she had

> *You cannot break an old agreement without verbally addressing the existence and impact of that agreement.*

unknowingly made an agreement with the manager that they could complain to her about other staff members. This agreement was made when that manager, during her weekly meetings with the director, began to consistently complain about other team members. Could the director have stopped this agreement from forming? Yes, by directly addressing the manager's actions the first time she started to complain about her team. Instead, the director continued to let this manager complain, and it wasn't long before the team members began complaining about one another. The director needed to break the old agreement and create a new one with the manager. You cannot break an old agreement without verbally addressing the existence and impact of that agreement. You must know what agreement you made, how the agreement was made and how it has impacted your interactions with your boss.

According to Don Miguel Ruiz, author of *The Four Agreements*, we live our lives based on four agreements. One of the most common is: Don't Take Things Personally. Ruiz says that, when someone says something to you and you take it personally, then you are admitting that the person is correct. If you refuse to take it personally, you are refusing to admit to that statement in your life.

Now think about it. What agreements have you made with your Subtracter boss? What agreement do you have with your boss about how he/she should treat you? Typically, there are one or two negative agreements operating in your relationship with your Subtracter boss that support their subtracting behavior. What role did you play in forming this negative agreement? Do you remember when the agreement was originally formed? For example, the first time your Subtracter boss referred to you in a negative manner, what did you do? Did you just laugh it off? Did you ask them what they meant by that statement? Did you ignore them and walk away? Agreements are critical because they are an invisible force that fuels you to use your personal power to add or subtract. Knowing and understanding the agreements you have made with your Subtracter boss is critical to dealing with them.

A chemist worked in an environment where an agreement was made that employees did not need encouragement or compliments from the boss. It was a very scientific environment where everyone did their own thing. However, this woman valued interpersonal interactions and thought it was inconsiderate for her boss to just ignore the team and not even say *"good morning"*. On one occasion, she was out of the office for a week and when she returned, it was as if the boss hadn't even noticed she was gone. It was a non-interactive, non-interpersonal working environment. She was so discouraged and frustrated that she was close to quitting her job. She felt undervalued and disconnected. What she needed to understand was that the interaction her boss had with her and the entire team was based on some core agreement. He was a scientist who was socialized to be isolated and introverted. His agreement was that he should stay to himself and get his work done and his team should do the same. The chemist wanted a new agreement that their workplace should have basic levels of civility, cordiality and professionalism. However, no one had ever pointed out to the boss that it would be appreciated if he would simply greet or acknowledge people on his team.

Take a moment and think about the agreements you have made with your Subtracter boss. Those agreements could relate to how they treat you, respect you or interact with you. This is not an easy exercise, and at times could be painful, because you have to honestly face the reality of your role in creating agreements that could be negatively impacting you in the workplace.

Agreements Made with Your Subtracter Boss

_____

_____

_____

_____

How Have These Agreements Impacted You?

_____

_____

_____

_____

**New Agreements You Would Like to Make with Your
Subtracter Boss**

_____

_____

_____

_____

_____

Five Core Strategies for Dealing with the Subtracter Boss

Strategy One: Manage Your Time

Is your Subtracter boss consuming, infringing on or wasting your
time? The first and most common thing a Subtracter boss takes from
you is your time. When you think about your eight-to-ten-hour work
day, how much time are you giving to your Subtracter boss? Naturally,
in every work situation it is imperative to set aside some time to be
cordial, get caught up with co-workers, talk about what's going on
in the office, attend meetings and collaborate on projects. That is all
necessary to create a productive and professional work environment.
This is known as productive time. In the workplace, productive time
is any time connected to your ability to produce or perform your job.
Unproductive time focuses on non-work issues, or the dramas that
have nothing to do with your job.

I talked with a small business owner whose intention was not
to be a Subtracter to her team members but she usually had bursts of
energy and creativity toward the end of the work day when her team
was getting ready to go home. Her administrative assistant was a
committed team member but needed to leave work at a certain time to

pick up her son from child care. The administrative assistant's routine also included stopping at the post office to handle the office mail for the day. The entrepreneur paid good salaries, offered great working conditions and had good relationships with her team, so she couldn't figure out why her administrative assistant was getting more frustrated by the day. The entrepreneur finally asked about her frustration and unhappiness. The entrepreneur was very surprised to discover that her late afternoon creative bursts usually resulted in her assistant having to quickly readjust her work plans, leaving little time to complete her afternoon responsibilities. The assistant just needed earlier notice about new projects so she could make the necessary adjustments and be on time for her child.

A common time waster in organizations is meetings. The Subtracter boss who calls a meeting every week, with little or no agenda is taking your productive time. What can you do? Stay away from these meetings by finding ways to be excused for work on other projects. Or look for productive things you can work on during the meeting, for example, creating a plan of action for your week, making a list of clients with whom you need to follow up with, making a list of your successes and challenges from last week, drafting a letter for your clients. If during the meeting you are scheduled to present a report on your project, then ask your boss prior to the meeting if you could be excused after giving your report.

Another common way to waste time is returning and creating personal e-mails. Productive e-mail time is spent responding to work-related inquiries, and getting things done. Then there are unproductive e-mails which clog up your computer and your life! Do your e-mails line up with your main job description? Do they connect with the projects or work plan for which you are responsible? If you respond to non-productive e-mails from your Subtracter boss, then he/she will send you more and soon expect you to respond to them all.

Subtracters are professional time wasters. Why do they waste your time? Because, you let them! When dealing with a Subtracter boss, you must balance the use of productive and unproductive time. For example, does your Subtracter boss think it is okay to drop into your office to just chat about things that are totally unrelated to your job or work load? Do they waste hours of your time complaining about the company and/or their personal life? The moment that your boss sits down to talk, you must consciously focus your conversation on work, and not their drama! In other words, you must decide only to engage in discussions about your projects, productivity or job description.

So how do you get your time back? Where do you start?

1. Do a short study of how and when your Subtracter boss is wasting your time.
2. Take a week or so to study the pattern.
3. Do your own analysis.
   + What time of day does your boss typically waste your time? (e.g. morning, afternoon, or right before you go home?)
   + How is your boss taking your time? (e.g. complaining, retelling the drama from their weekend)
   + What is their main topics? (e.g. family, colleagues, team, the company)

After the analysis, begin predicting when your boss is coming into your office. The key is to prevent them from coming into your office or space. If they manage to get in, you must learn how to politely get them out as soon as possible. Here is a process to use when you see your boss coming toward your office:

✦ Immediately get up from your desk.

✦ Go to the door and greet them.

✦ Simply say, "Is there something I can help you with?"

✦ Take the lead in initiating and leading the conversation.

✦ Do not respond or give feedback to any unproductive conversation.

✦ Redirect the conversation back to what they wanted help with.

✦ Give your response to the issue at hand.

✦ If they have a question, answer it quickly.

✦ Then thank them for coming and walk back to your desk.

✦ Do not look back at them.

✦ Get to your desk, and immediately start doing something.

✦ Look busy and do not look up at your Subtracter boss!

The first time you try this approach, your Subtracter boss will be surprised and might try to move you back into your office or encourage you to sit down in your chair. Politely stick with your script and soon your Subtracter boss will decrease their visits to your office. What you are really doing is creating a new agreement with your boss about how to respect you and your office space. One manager always wanted to check in on her team to know what they were doing. She had a certain time in the afternoon when she would stroll the hallways, peeking into offices. The offices had glass windows so her team members knew exactly when she was coming and what she was doing. The manager would look in, but her team members would always look away and try to ignore the spectator manager. One of the team members finally got tired of feeling like a caged zoo animal and decided to do something about it. One day, as the manager walked by looking in the offices, the employee stood up from her desk, looked the manager directly in the eyes and said "hello!" The manager became visibly nervous and quickly walked away without responding. The team member continued greeting the manager for the next couple of days and soon the manager stopped walking by her office.

What if your boss looks for opportunities to stop you in the hall and waste your time? What should you do? Do your analysis. Study when you know they are going to stop you, and where it will occur. Then, change your pattern as to when you are in the hallways and your walking route. If you have to walk by your boss's office, make sure that you walk quickly. Do not look in; keep walking like you are on a mission! If you have to make eye contact, quickly greet your boss and keep going! If at all possible, do not stop or start up a conversation with them. If you meet your boss in the hallway, immediately initiate the conversation with a "hello" and keep going. If your boss asks you a question, answer if you can, or let them know you will get back to them. Excuse yourself from the conversation and get back to work.

You cannot continue to let a Subtracter boss take your productive time. You must learn to manage how much time you spend with your boss, and you must also manage the spaces where you interact with your boss. Can you take your time back without getting fired? Absolutely, but the key is to become conscious of how you are using your time and to whom you are giving your time. Taking back your time is not about being rude, but rather about strategically using your power to reshape how you use your time to be more productive and effective in the workplace. Manage your time with your Subtracter boss with civility, remembering that even Subtracters need to be respected and valued in the workplace.

Take a moment and think about how you use your time at work. Document how you are giving away your time, to whom you are giving your time and how your lack of time is impacting your productivity and effectiveness.

How much of your work day is spent using "productive time?"

_____

_____

_____

How do you know you are being productive? How do you feel when you are being productive?

_____

_____

_____

How much of your work day is spent using "unproductive time?"

_____

_____

_____

How is your Subtracter Boss wasting your time?

_____

_____

_____

Strategy Two: Manage Your Words

Subtracters thrive on words. Your words give them the strategies needed to effectively subtract from you. Watch what you say and learn how to listen and breathe before you respond to Subtracters. Your words are critical. Why? Because words create your reality; they create life. You will become whatever you say on a regular basis. A Subtracter boss uses any and all information against you. Watch your words. The ones you speak, what you write, your e-mails, even your non-verbal communication and your interactions with others. All of your words spoken or unspoken matter to a Subtracter boss.

Dealing with a Subtracter boss requires that you take certain words out of your vocabulary. One of my coaching clients, a very talented engineer, thought it was funny to call herself "The Pest." The first few times she did this, people responded with laughter and commented on how silly she was being. Remember though, that words create life. So if you do not want to do something, be something or become something, don't say it. You should only speak what you want created in your life. This woman had created a reality of being a pest, and soon her boss began to treat her like a pest. Little by little, she lost respect from her boss and co-workers.

What should you stop saying? Any words that make it seem as though you are unsure of your gifts, talents, abilities and competencies. Never diminish or devalue your work or skills in front of your Subtracter boss. Avoid saying statements like: "I don't know," "I'm not sure I can do this," "I'm so stupid," " I never get it right," and so on. You must be very careful about what you are saying about yourself because your words will teach others how to interact with you. Your words create the perception others have about you, and perception is reality for most people.

Second, never share any personal information with a subtracter boss. Remember, the more you share, the more ammunition the Subtracter boss has to use against you. An aspiring corporate attorney made a huge mistake when she began sharing her personal struggles with her Subtracter boss. She thought that the boss was listening because they cared, but she later found out that her own information was used against her to devalue and question whether she was fit to do her job. Be careful. A Subtracter boss files away your personal stories in their mind and conveniently uses them to take away your personal power and devalue you in the workplace.

Third, refuse to repeat or rehearse your failures. A Subtracter boss is looking for opportunities to dismantle your integrity and success record. Do not be an accomplice to your own sabotage. We all make mistakes, but it doesn't mean that you have to bring yours up in every meeting.

Fourth, refuse to publicly put down or complain about your boss, co-workers or the company. Elders in the African American community often tell young people that, if you can't say something good about someone, don't say anything at all. Your Subtracter boss is looking for opportunities to accuse you of being negative and not a "team player." It is also a reality that our words become seeds that we plant into our lives. Sooner or later, those seeds are going to produce some harvest. You can only produce what you planted. If you plant complaining, negativity and back-biting behavior, then that is exactly what will happen to you.

Fifth, refuse to engage in office politics or your Subtracter boss's personal drama. Avoid listening to your boss complain about the team and refuse to be drawn into any personal issues and drama. Do not get comfortable hearing complaints about your co-workers. Remember that the goal of most Subtracters is for you to also become a Subtracter. Decide to use your power to Add and not subtract from others.

Your words are a critical factor when dealing with a Subtracter boss. Decide to only speak those things that will create a productive, effective and collegial work environment. Only speak what you want for your life and nothing else!

Stay Positive

I recently called one of our consultants to check on her project. The moment she answered the phone I could tell that she was struggling. She is usually a very positive person but she had let her Subtracter boss get the best of her. She was swearing, yelling and on the verge of tears. She had allowed the pressure from her Subtracter boss to take away her positive outlook on life. I commented on her disposition and encouraged her to regain her positive energy and hope for her situation. Your Subtracter boss is counting on the fact that, sooner or later, you will give in to negativity. That is the goal. Refuse to be negative and decide to stay positive no matter what! Become a positive thinker and refuse to give in to negative words, emotions, attitudes or behaviors.

We host an annual Power of People conference designed to empower people to excellence through understanding their personal power and leadership. The day-long event is planned and implemented by a team of staff, consultants and volunteers. During one of our planning meetings, a team member commented that she didn't think we would make our conference goals. I immediately sensed the impact that this negative statement had on the team. There was no way I could let that statement go without correcting her. I know that having a positive perspective and attitude about your goals is critical to your success. If you doubt your goals, then why should anyone else believe you can do it? As an Adder, you become a possibility thinker. You become a possibility person. In other words, you always think of what positive things could happen. You must not only believe that you can do it, but that you *will* do it!

Do not give in to negative talk, behavior, attitudes or interactions. Your words create your life. What do you do when a negative statement is made and you don't agree with it? If the statement refers specifically to you, then you must counter it with a positive response. If the statement is not about you and will not impact you, then you have to leave it alone. One of the great mistakes I have made in my life is to take things on that did not belong to me. If your Subtracter boss says something negative about someone or something that is totally unrelated to you, refuse to engage in that conversation. If something is put on the table and it doesn't belong to you, leave it there. So often, we take on issues or agendas that are not our own because we feel obligated or guilty. This is a huge mistake. If there is an issue on the table and it is not your issue, leave it on the table. Take a deep breath, sit back, be comfortable with the silence and leave it there! When your Subtracter boss throws issues and agendas on the table that don't belong to you, refuse to touch them and you will find that someone else will. Do not pick up what is not yours. If you don't own it, don't pick it up. If it is yours, then pick it up immediately, and refuse to let others, especially your Subtracter boss, pick up what is yours.

The biggest mistake that women typically make is that, if no one else picks up the issue, the woman at the table will usually do so. Why? Because women tend to have a nurturing part of them that wants to take care of others. Many want to keep peace and avoid confrontations. Being a nurturing person is great, however, it doesn't work when it comes to taking on agendas and responsibilities that do not belong to you. Stay positive, operate from a place of positive possibilities, and refuse to take on what is not yours.

Don't Participate in Drama

When I taught fifth and sixth grades, one of the tenured teachers loved drama. She loved to talk about and complain about students. Her favorite activity was lunchtime in the teacher's lounge, because she had an audience to listen to her complain and share negative things about her students and their families. I was a new teacher and I simply refused to listen to her or participate in her conversations. One day, she asked me about my students and I knew that she just wanted to create negative drama. Somehow I knew that if I shared anything about my students with her that she would see it as an agreement being made between us to share negative information about students. I could not let this happen, so I simply responded that I believed students were amazing people and that it was an honor to teach them. I explained that I believed that I was hired to help my students reach their potential and to inspire them to become their most excellent in school and life. I also made it clear to her that I would not share confidential information about my students unless it were necessary for their academic success or safety. It was obvious that this tenured teacher was asking me to gossip about and devalue my students in the teacher's lounge. She wanted me to engage in her drama and chaos. I refused to do it! Did I suffer some consequences from this tenured teacher? Yes. The teacher said to me, in front of all the other teachers, "Who do you think you are? Do you think you are better than the rest of us?" She accused me of being stuck up and a "know it all." That was very painful and shaming to hear. However, when I think about it now, I know I am better than those other teachers. The reason I know I am better is because I chose to be a consistent Adder to my students-not just to their faces, but even when they were not there to defend themselves. I was mildly offended for a moment, but quickly recovered because I knew that I was doing the right thing by Adding and not Subtracting from my students.

All drama begins with negative words and conversations. If your boss likes to create drama, work hard not to participate at any level. That means not listening, commenting or discussing it. Also, avoid the temptation to share your boss's drama with others in your office. I pride myself on my ability to maintain confidentiality with my team members. They know that whatever they say to me is confidential. I believe that this is also one of the reasons people in influential positions share confidential issues and ideas with me. I have earned their respect because they know that I will not share their information with others. Staying out of the drama is not always easy because sharing drama can appear to be fun and interesting. It gives people something to talk about. The reality is that drama creates a cycle that is waiting to get you so involved and interconnected that you will soon find yourself trapped in it. Avoid participating in, sharing or encouraging drama in any way or form!

Don't Take it Personally

The final strategy with regard to words is to simply not take anything personally. For a Subtracter boss, words are one of the primary strategies used to bring down your confidence and create self doubt. When a Subtracter boss says something about you that is not true, you must not take it personally. Remember that, when you take something personally, you are admitting to the other person that they are correct.

How do you show that you are not taking something personally? Teach yourself to not show *any* reaction. Like a duck in water, just let the statement slide off your back. Do not argue or try to defend yourself, even if your heart is beating fast, you can feel your body temperature increasing, and you want to scream. Resist the urge to get mad or upset. Once you've gotten your emotions under control, make a simple correcting comment that clears the record as to who you really are. Do not stay for a discussion about why you want to defend yourself. Your attempt will only give your Subtracter boss more ammunition to continue their sabotage of your character. Is this hard to do? Yes. It is very difficult to listen to your boss say false statements about you. However, you will find that, the less you react, the more power and confidence you will gain. Your Subtracter boss feels powerful when you stop using your personal power and start losing your confidence.

When you don't take things personally, you give a clear signal to your Subtracter boss that you are powerful and prepared to deal with them. In the meantime, look to the Adders in your life to help you stay encouraged, empowered and confident. You cannot depend on a Subtracter boss to help you feel as though you are important, valuable, cared for or powerful. You will not get these things from a Subtracter because many suffer from feeling inadequate, helpless, hopeless and powerless. A Subtracter cannot give you something they don't have. It's hard and painful work, but refuse to take things personally.

Strategy Three: Build Your Knowledge Base

Success in work and life is intricately linked to your level of knowledge and skill. You cannot deal with a Subtracter boss without a broad understanding and knowledge of yourself, your boss and your organization. Knowing as much as possible about all aspects of your position, team, boss and organization is key. Have you done your homework? Do you know the history of your team, or your Subtracter boss? Young children are so interesting because they believe that life began when they were born! More than likely, your company did not begin when you became an employee. Learning about the overall culture of the organization before you arrived is critical. Your boss was already an Adder or Subtracter before you were hired. Getting a broad perspective on their history and why they might be a Subtracter is key. Could it be that your boss has been socialized to be a Subtracter by their work history or their own boss? Many people are absolutely clueless of their actions, who they are being and why they do what they do. Study the history of your organization and get the facts. Get to know those unspoken, invisible processes and paradigms that create the culture of your organization. Learn as much as possible about the spoken and unspoken rules, responsibilities and expectations associated with your job. Be patient; it will take some time, but do your research so that you avoid obvious pitfalls and painful situations with your Subtracter boss. Be eager to learn new approaches and technologies that will help you become more effective. Seek out as many professional development opportunities as possible. The more you know, the more effective you will be in dealing with your

Subtracter boss.

Relying on someone else's knowledge base is dangerous because people tend to only tell you what they want you to know. Do the work it takes to build your own knowledge base. Creating collaborations, networks and partnerships is key to broadening your knowledge base. Many Subtracter bosses intentionally withhold information from you. It is one of their core strategies of derailing your success and keeping you stuck. Why? Because the typical Subtracter boss believes that information is power. So, the less information you have, the less power you have in the organization. If this is the case, then you must work overtime to listen, observe and learn everything you can to be effective in your position.

The movie *A Night at the Museum* is the story of Larry, a man who really needs a job and is hired to be the night guard at the Museum of Natural History in New York. Larry is hired to replace three older gentlemen who were being let go to trim the budget. On his first night, the three gentlemen gave Larry his instructions and quickly leave. The written directions are worn and hardly legible, leaving Larry without much guidance when all the museum artifacts come alive that night. Larry is in such shock that he loses the worn directions and calls the former night guards for help. After a short, unhelpful conversation with the men, Larry knows that he has been set up for failure and that the former guards are simply going to sit back and watch him fail. These men have the knowledge for dealing with the museum at night but refuse to share it. Larry takes his success in his own hands and begins to study everything he can find about the artifacts. Larry decides to build his own knowledge base. The three former guards later attempt to steal a valuable Egyptian artifact but, because Larry has obtained his own knowledge, he knows exactly what to do. Larry is able to not only save the artifact, but also to assist in the capturing and arrest of the three men.

What was the key? If Larry had not gotten his own knowledge base, he would have lost his job and the rare piece would have been stolen. The entire museum would have been destroyed if he had not obtained his own knowledge base. Those three men who were being Subtracters were not interested in Larry learning for himself. They were counting on their assumption that he would not seek out his own knowledge and would remain ignorant.

You cannot rely on the knowledge base of a Subtracter boss. You must get the information yourself. If you know that new research has emerged about your product line or a new sales training is being offered, you must take the initiative to obtain knowledge. You cannot depend on your boss to suggest opportunities for your professional development. If you learn about an important sales meeting or conference, then let your boss know that you are planning to attend. What if your boss will not send you? If it's important to you, then use vacation time and attend anyway!

A key strategy to dealing with your Subtracter boss is to become as knowledgeable as possible about every aspect of your job and company. Be open to learning as much as you can as often as you can. Get to the point where you know as much, if not more than, your boss. The more you know, the more effectively you can deal with your Subtracter boss.

Strategy Four: Managing Emotions and Energy

A Subtracter boss can drain you of all your energy and leave you an emotional wreck! Managing your emotions and energy is critical.

How much time do you spend thinking about what your boss is doing or did to you? How quickly can your boss get you upset to the point where you can no longer think straight? What kind of energy are you exchanging with your boss? Are you stressing about the fact that your boss is unkind or mean to you? How much do you tell others about your boss? Are you waiting for your boss to see you as a successful person who has something to offer? Are you working overtime to prove yourself to your Subtracter boss? How do you manage your emotions and energy when your boss is a Subtracter?

Don't look to your boss for affirmations

A Subtracter boss will not affirm you in your work, so stop expecting or wishing for that! Instead, look to your inner circle for your " I believe in you," "good job" and "way to go." Your Subtracter boss may not even know how to affirm or compliment you. Unfortunately, most Subtracters are so busy trying to find your faults that they cannot even acknowledge your accomplishments. The problem is that most people have a high need to be liked, so they unconsciously look to their bosses for affirmation. Remember the Subtracter boss who calls her team members into her office every week and yells at them? The reality is that she is not going to suddenly change and start affirming them. Instead of becoming emotionally upset, angry and frustrated, those team members need to collectively confront their boss about her behavior. The team has to make it very clear, both verbally and in writing, that being treated with disrespect is unacceptable.

Identify Your Emotional Triggers

We all have things that trigger our emotional reactions. Subtracter bosses will often study your emotional triggers. Why? So that they can use them to manipulate and control you in the workplace. Emotional triggers are things that people say or do which influence your emotional state. Sometimes, a person can use a look or a tone of voice to trigger an emotional response. A key to dealing with a Subtracter is being aware and conscious of your emotional triggers. Study the what, why, where, when and how of your emotional triggers. Do you become emotionally unraveled because you want your boss to accept you? Or do you want someone to notice you are doing a good job? Or do you want to look good in front of people? Are you intimidated? Do you not feel good enough? What is it? Your boss is looking for your triggers and will use them as tools for subtracting from you.

Understanding what your emotional triggers are, why you have them, and how to adjust those triggers so you can become objective is critical. Think about your emotional state in the workplace. What are your triggers? In other words, what throws you into an emotional spin or leaves you feeling emotionally unbalanced? Why do you have those triggers? If you have a Subtracter boss, how are they using those triggers to devalue and derail your success? What are you going to do to start managing those triggers?

Your Emotional Triggers:
Why do you have them? How will you manage them?

_____

_____

_____

_____

_____

_____

_____

_____

There are five ways to manage your emotions when dealing with a Subtracter boss.

1. **Manage your reactions to what is being said.** Do not react immediately. Instead, take a deep breath and think about the validity of their statement. Just take a moment and think critically about how and if you want to respond.

2. **Ask power questions.** These are questions that address the underlying power dynamics that exist between you and your boss. Power questions address the reality of the issues on the table. Directly address how the issues impact you, and your job, productivity, effectiveness or reputation in the company. These are hard questions to ask but necessary to uncovering the real agenda. Power questions get you to the center of the core issues. What is really going on? Why is it going

on? What have you done to create the issue? How was the issue created? What was the role of your Subtracter boss? Know that when you ask power questions, the response from your Subtracter boss might be confrontational, emotional, dismissive or ignore you. Your role is to ask the questions, but you have no control over your boss's response.

3. **Know when to be silent.** If you are in a meeting with your Subtracter boss and they make an accusation, try to put you down, or unjustly blame you for something, do not respond or take it personally. Don't even try to defend yourself. Just be silent, take a deep breath and continue on with the next item on your meeting agenda.

4. **Choose your moment to speak.** Then speak with confidence and passion. Speak clearly and directly without apologizing. Speak with conviction. Be honest but kind. Directly address the core issues, even the hard ones. Speak like an Adder bringing increased value to the situation at hand.

5. **Know when to end the conversation.** Managing your emotions also means knowing when to leave. There are times when you simply have to get up and exit out of the conversation. A common Subtracter strategy is to slowly pull you deeper and deeper into an emotional conversation. When you find that your positive energy is being drained and you can no longer maintain your emotional balance, it's time to leave. A Subtracter boss wants you to argue, scream, curse or even cry. Why? If they can push you over your emotional edge, then they can better control and manipulate you. You will find yourself agreeing to take on jobs that are not yours, taking the

blame for problems you did not cause, and jeopardizing your future in the organization. Only you know when it's time to leave. Don't hesitate or apologize, just excuse yourself and leave!

Strategy Five: Be Clear About Your Goals

The fifth core strategy in dealing with a Subtracter is being clear about your personal and professional goals. What do you want to accomplish professionally? What are your personal goals? How will you measure your success in life? Do you know what you want? Having goals and a plan for your life is critical because, without them, you will feel stuck, helpless, powerless and hopeless. A Subtracter boss plays on your past failures and lack of personal direction. They are counting on the fact that you don't know where you are going. They manipulate the fact that you are frozen by fear of your future - afraid to go forward, to try again, to succeed. The only way to get beyond this fear is to develop a vision for who you want to be, where you want to go, what you want to do. Your vision and goals give you hope and direction for your life.

My coaching client who felt stuck and fearful about her future in the company needed to develop written goals for her life. She needed a new picture of who she wanted to be. As she took on the challenge to create her vision and goals, her perspective about her job began to change. She could no longer be emotionally manipulated by her boss or pushed out of the company. Her goals gave her clarity and focus about her personal and professional life.

Living life without goals is like walking around underneath a big cloud with no hope of sunshine. You cannot see anything clearly, so you just stumble through life searching for a path to follow. You move around but make no real movement. A Subtracter boss wants to keep you in the clouds. They do not want you to discover your full potential or get to your next level of success.

A young banker who had a Subtracter boss was stuck and going nowhere in the company. She didn't know what to do, but she also didn't have a plan. She didn't have a goal statement. She didn't have a vision statement. I asked her to go home and write the description of the job she wanted. Her next step was to assess her networks, partnerships and collaborations. Then she was to share her job description with her Adders and Multipliers. I knew that within months she would be offered a new position similar to her written description of her new job. She needed to stop looking for a new job and start writing her personal vision and goals so that her new position could start looking for her.

Now think about your life. Have you written your personal and professional goals? Professionally, who do you want to be in your company? What do you want to accomplish? Do you want to stay with your company? What types of positions do you want to attain? Do you have a plan for your professional career within that company? What kind of impact do you want to have? What type of leader do you want to be? What legacy do you want to leave? A Subtracter boss cannot handle a person with a clear vision and goals. Why? Because your vision and goals increase your personal power. A Subtracter boss has to work twice as hard to take your personal power and subtract from you. Take some time to think and write about who you really want to be.

What are your personal goals?

_____

_____

_____

_____

_____

What are your professional goals?

_____

_____

_____

_____

_____

Who do you want to be in your company? What do you want to accomplish?

_____

_____

_____

_____

_____

Dealing With the Seven Subtracter Personalities

These five core strategies can be used to deal with any of the seven Subtracter personalities. However, there are some very specific concepts to keep in mind when dealing with the specific personalities. This segment is designed to give you some very short strategies to use with particular personalities.

The Smiler

Whenever the *Smiler* promises anything, get it in writing. Do not trust the *Smiler* to keep their word, get it done, or follow through to make it happen. Use e-mail as a tool to track your discussions with the *Smiler.* Document roles and responsibilities and work hard not to do the *Smiler's* job. Do not complete the *Smiler* part of the project even if it means not meeting project timelines. The more you cover for the *Smiler*, the more of their work you will do.

The Blamer

Remember that the *Blamer* is determined to make everything your fault. Record and track everything the *Blamer* says. Do not argue with them publicly. Schedule a private meeting with the *Blamer* and confront them privately about their comments and behavior. Do your homework and be prepared to ask power questions that force the *Blamer* to look at the real issues. Be sure you have a strong network to share information about your interactions with, and your plan to, confront the *Blamer*. A *Blamer* might retaliate, so you need to have good records, a strong network, and the power, confidence and courage to confront them.

The Shamer

Break any old agreements with the *Shamer* that gave them the right to shame you. The next time a *Shamer* tries to shame you publicly, you must immediately speak up to correct them. Let them know that their accusation is not true and that you neither appreciate, nor will you tolerate, them sharing inaccurate information about you with others. You must respond to a *Shamer* immediately. Some *Shamers* find it humorous to share negative stories about you. You cannot let a *Shamer* think that shaming you is acceptable. Confront them immediately and make a note of the conversation for future reference.

The Gamer

Gamers are difficult so be prepared to ask power questions. Refrain from reacting to them. Refuse to get caught up in their emotional manipulation. Avoid having private conversations with them. Resist the temptation to defend yourself or argue with the *Gamer*. Do not share any personal stories or professional struggles with them. Get out of the conversation as soon as possible. Prepare a script before meeting with them, invite another colleague or someone from your network and know what you want to accomplish. Limit your interactions with the *Gamer*. Do not give them your emotional energy. Whenever you feel that the energy is getting negative, leave.

The Snipper-Nipper

Avoid spending time with the *Snipper-Nipper*. Do not give them any unnecessary information about your life or work. Refuse to tell them about your failures or mistakes. Immediately correct them about false accusations or statements. Do not share your dreams, goals or vision with the *Snipper-Nipper.* Severely limit your conversation with them.

The Dreamer

If possible, avoid working on projects with a *Dreamer*. Keep good records. Document what the *Dreamer* promised to do. Track their outcomes or just refuse to do a *Dreamer's* job, even if it means the project might fail. Dare to let the *Dreamer* fail. Clarify roles and responsibilities so that you can document the outcomes and hold the *Dreamer* accountable.

The Worrier

Manage and limit the amount of time you spend with the *Worrier*. Stop listening to the *Worrier's* stories, complaints and doubts. Do not ask a *Worrier* questions about their concerns about life or work. Refuse to get caught in the *Worrier's* drama cycle by immediately excusing yourself from the conversation. Ask critical questions about the real issues that cause them to worry. Break old agreements with *Worriers* that resulted in supporting their behavior. Challenge *Worrier's* to use their personal power to create change in their life.

Your Plan for Your Subtracter Boss

Reading this chapter does not make you an overnight expert on dealing with your Subtracter boss, however, it has given you many strategies to try. The next step is to use these strategies to create a customized plan for your situation. Your plan will be unique to you, your boss and your situation. Where do you begin?

1. **Be realistic; reflect on whether you are being a Subtracter to your boss.**

   _____

   _____

   _____

   _____

   _____

   _____

   _____

   _____

   _____

2. **Create a vision statement for who you want to be in your company.**

   _____

   _____

   _____

   _____

   _____

   _____

   _____

   _____

3. Assess the personality type of your Subtracter boss.

_____

_____

_____

_____

_____

_____

_____

_____

_____

4. Choose at least five strategies you are going to use.

_____

_____

_____

_____

_____

_____

_____

_____

_____

_____

5. **Create a time line for implementing your plan.**

6. **Implement a strategy and discuss the outcomes and lessons learned with someone in your trusted network.**

Chapter 7

The Subtracter Co-Worker

Walk through any corporation or organization and you will hear the silent cry. It doesn't matter if the organization is governmental, corporate, educational, nonprofit or faith-based. Listen carefully and you will hear the silent cry in the conversations and see it in the body language of the employees. The stories people share about their work environments and cultures are disheartening. Many people are just hanging on and barely making it through each work day. The reality is that many people are suffering in their workplaces and much of their silent cry is connected to having Subtracter co-workers. You cannot get away from them or fire them; you must work with them. Having co-worker Subtracters drains your energy, decreases your productivity and stresses you out! So what can you do? How do you deal with them?

After a large, state-wide social services conference, a woman patiently waited until everyone had gone through the book signing line then asked if she could tell me a workplace Subtracter story. She shared how she had changed jobs within her company, just to realize that her new department was full of Subtracter co-workers. She had really enjoyed going to work and doing her job, but that all changed with her new role. She left work each day with a slight headache and upset stomach. Much of her stress had to do with one particular Subtracter co-worker. This co-worker had worked really hard to create a negative, dysfunctional work environment. Everything changed when this particular co-worker attended one of my *Power of People* seminars. Without anyone knowing it, she purchased and read my first book, *The Power of People: Four Kinds of People Who Can Change*

Your Life, and discovered that she was a Subtracter! She learned how her negative energy, communication style, and use of personal power were negatively impacting her department. The Subtracter co-worker had a revelation that she was using her power to subtract from, instead of adding to, her co-workers. To the surprise of her colleagues, she came to a department meeting and shared how she had read a book that revolutionized how she thought about herself and others. She shared how she realized that she was a Subtracter and that she had made a decision to change. Then she recommended that everyone in the office read my book. It wasn't long before their work environment was noticeably different and the negative energy and interactions disappeared. The woman shared that she regained her sense of passion and commitment and is once again enjoying her colleagues and work.

Dealing with Subtracter co-workers are pivotal to creating a positive workplace and a culture of Adders. The story was encouraging because the co-worker learned how to be an Adder instead of a Subtracter and decided to change. That, however, is not the typical workplace scenario. Unfortunately, most Subtracter co-workers are clueless about who they are and how they are affecting others. Typically, they have no idea how they are negatively using their personal power to impact the workplace. They are clueless about their role in the workplace and how much they are taking from others.

Another woman attending one of my workshops approached me during our break to tell me about one of her co-worker Subtracters. My first question to her was if she had ever had a meaningful conversation with the person about their role and impact in the workplace. To my surprise, she had only had one direct interaction with the co-worker and hadn't talked to her since! She had based her assumption of the person on one incident that happened between them during her first week on the job. She had allowed one event to dictate her future interactions with the co-worker. People make mistakes and poor judgment, but that doesn't make them Subtracters. About 85% of people are clueless about how they come across to others or how others perceive them, much less about being Subtracters. How often do your co-workers honestly communicate with you about how you come across? Most people want to be liked so they avoid talking about hard issues.

How can you tell if you or a co-worker is a Subtracter? The first step is to take the *Personal Power Assessment*. As you do the assessment, consider your attitudes, perceptions, communication and use of personal power. Are you being a Subtracter in the workplace? Or is your co-worker? Conduct the assessment on yourself then your co-workers. The key is to rule yourself out as being a workplace Subtracter. Why? Because Subtracters think that everyone else is the problem. They struggle with critically looking at themselves and are afraid to ask the hard questions: "Do these issues exist because of me? Am I the problem?" Subtracters like company and work hard to bring others into their drama cycles. Take a moment to complete the personal power assessment.

Personal Power Assessment

How do you use your personal power?
To find out, answer yes or no to the questions below:

1. I believe in possibilities.   ___Yes ___No

2. I tend to second guess myself.   ___Yes ___No

3. I think that most people are "needy."   ___Yes ___No

4. I have written goals for my life.   ___Yes ___No

5. I think that people "should" help me out.   ___Yes ___No

6. I look for the good in life.   ___Yes ___No

7. I think that people are full of potential.   ___Yes ___No

8. I think that success only happens   ___Yes ___No
    to some people.

9. I like learning new things.   ___Yes ___No

10. I tend to put off getting things done.   ___Yes ___No

Answer Key:
- If you answered Yes to Questions 1, 4, 6, 7, 9 – You have
  the potential of using your personal power to be an Adder to
  yourself and others.
- If you answered Yes to Questions 2, 3, 5, 8, 10 – You have the
  potential of using your personal power to be a Subtracter to
  yourself and others.

Three Types of Subtracter Co-Workers

Most of your co-workers are professional "Just Is" people because they are a part of the landscape and fabric of the organization. You didn't hire them and you cannot fire them. The "just is!" Subtracter co-workers come in three types. First, most of them are *Socialized Subtracters* who were taught since childhood how to subtract from others. Being a Subtracter is normal to them. Using their power to subtract is how they operate at work and in life. *Socialized Subtracters* unconsciously subtract from others and have no idea how they are taking from and devaluing their co-workers. They think it's humorous to shame or blame others. Gossiping and back-biting is their way of making the workplace interesting. They boldly bring their personal drama to work. Professionalism to *Socialized Subtracters* means that you will repeatedly take on their responsibilities. The best thing about *Socialized Subtracters i*s that when they discover how they have been using their personal power, they usually change to become Adders in the workplace.

The *Situational Subtracter* is someone who is typically an Adder but, for multiple reasons, will choose to be a Subtracter in specific situations and to certain people. These Subtracters consciously choose to subtract based on personal reasons that others may not understand or be aware of. There was a woman who thought her co-worker was a Subtracter because of a comment made years ago. This woman was typically an Adder to her team members but would noticeably change her use of personal power when the supposed Subtracter co-worker was around. She thought her co-worker disliked her. As a result, the woman ignored her co-worker and refused to speak to her. For years, the woman would walk by the co-worker's office without saying anything. The woman attended one of my *Power of People* seminars and approached me about what to do with her Subtracter. My first question was, "How do you know that your co-worker is a Subtracter?" This woman told me about the statement that person made about her years ago. I asked the woman if she had ever considered the fact that her co-worker might not have meant her any harm. I also asked her if she had ever attempted to discuss the incident with the co-worker. Finally, I asked if she had considered the possibility that she was the one being a Subtracter to the co-worker. Of course, the woman had never thought about these questions and was really surprised to learn that she was being a *Situational Subtracter* to her co-worker. Over the years, both women had become *Situational Subtracters* to each other.

> *Situational Subtracters can change once they understand the core issues that have been the catalyst for negatively using their personal power to subtract from their co-workers.*

Situational Subtracters can be very simple to deal with if they are willing to do the work of discovering why they choose to subtract. This might sound simple to do but it can be very painful and complex to deal with the emotional hurt. You have to be ready to address the core issues and, in some cases, forgive the other person. *Situational Subtracters* can change once they understand the core issues that have been the catalyst for negatively using their personal power to subtract from their co-workers.

The third type of co-worker is the *Chronic Subtracter*. These are tricky people because they are not only aware of using their personal power to subtract but also see their behavior as interesting, fun, a strategy for getting attention or a survival tool in the workplace.

Because many *Chronic Subtracters* suffer from low self-esteem and confidence, they learn how to thrive on the negative attention which gives them a false sense of importance, power and value. Many pride themselves on creating negative drama that drains their co-workers of positive energy. Why are *Chronic Subtracters* so difficult to deal with? Because they know exactly what they are doing and are not interested in changing. *Chronic Subtracters* think that their ability to subtract is what gives them power. They reason that if they cannot get attention with their skills, productivity or competence, they will get it by being negative, sarcastic, pessimistic, dominant, controlling or manipulative.

Think about your co-worker Subtracters. Are they *Socialized, Situational* or *Chronic*? Then reflect on why you would describe them as that type of Subtracter.

Who?	What Type?	Why?

"Just Is" and "Choice" Co-Workers

Even though your co-worker is a "Just Is" person, they can also be a "Choice" person. For example, every morning a co-worker comes to your office, sits down at your desk, and slowly drinks their coffee as they tell you about their personal drama and gossips about everyone in the office. You always listen to them and occasionally offer your thoughts and respond to their comments. If you are honest, however, most times when they leave your office you feel drained, stressed out and unproductive. Your co-worker has created a pattern of subtracting from you and thinks it is absolutely acceptable to waste your time, drain your energy and immerse you in their drama.

Co-workers in your professional inner circle significantly impact your career development and overall work experience. These are the work place "Choice" people who you choose to listen to, share your personal stories with. They mentor and coach you about major decisions and influence how you think about your professional life. If these co-workers are Subtracters, not only will your reputation and work history become limited these people, but your opportunities for promotion may also be limited.

Subtracter co-workers plant seeds of negativity, pessimism, drama and self doubt in your professional life. Spending too much time with them will leave you feeling unproductive, ineffective and stressed. Regardless of your job title or level in the company, having a professional inner circle of Subtracter co-workers will only bring you misery, strife and frustration. Whether you are the CEO of your company or an administrative assistant who has chosen a Subtracter co-worker into your inner circle, sooner or later you will be devalued and negatively influenced. If you find yourself in constant negative conflict with others, or feeling isolated and marginalized by other co-workers, check your professional inner circle for a Subtracter. More than likely, you have allowed your workplace Subtracters to negatively influence your interactions with others and your overall perspectives about work.

So the question is: Have you chosen Subtracter co-workers into your professional inner circle? If so, why did you choose them and what is your plan for dealing with them or moving them out?

Where to Start

History and Patterns

More than likely, your Subtracter co-workers have been a part of your professional life for some time and you have history with them. During this time, you have created patterns of behavior and interactions that are based on specific, but unspoken agreements. A psychologist who uses my first book as a tool for working with his clients told me about a Fifty-five year-old man who, after reading the book, realized that one of his co-workers, a member of his weekly card group, was a major Subtracter. Every Friday evening for Fifteen years, this particular Subtracter would spend the entire time taking the man's personal power, positive attitude, confidence and money. He would shame and snip and nip at the client, leaving him exhausted and exasperated from the negativity. The client would then take his frustration and feelings of powerlessness out on his family. It wasn't until the client learned about the impact of Subtracters that he finally began confronting his Friday night Subtracter co-worker. After the client began studying his history and pattern of interactions with the co-worker, he decided to make a drastic change and discontinued his affiliation with the Friday night group so that he could move the

Subtracter out of his life.

How do you start dealing with your Subtracter co-worker? By taking a critical look at your history with them. When did you choose them into your professional inner circle? Did you choose them or did they choose you? What are they subtracting from you? When do they subtract from you? How have they impacted your professional career and development? Why have you kept them in your inner circle? Next you must discover the agreements[11] you have made with your Subtracter co-worker. At some point in your relationship, you made specific agreements with your co-worker about how they should treat, talk to, interact with, and work with you. For example, some Subtracter co-workers refuse to explore professional development opportunities but expect you to attend and then report to them what you learned. Why? Because at some point you made an unspoken agreement that you will give them your knowledge. If you come back from the seminar pumped up and energized, then your Subtracter co-worker will quickly drain you of it by reminding you of office politics or other negative situations. The bottom line is that they do not want you to be or feel successful or experience professional success at any level in your career. Why? Because many Subtracter co-workers are intimidated by your success. Agreements with Subtracter co-workers are typically based on six things:

1. **How they treat you**
2. **How they communicate with you**
3. **What attitudes they have about you**
4. **What they tell others about you**

---

11 Ruiz, Miguel Angel, M.D. (1997). The Four Agreements: A Practical Guide to Personal Freedom. Amber-Allen Publishing: San Rafael, CA

5. **What they ask of you**

6. **What they take from you.**

You cannot reshape your relationship and create new agreements with your Subtracter co-worker until you are honest and clear about your existing agreements. Take a moment and use the following six questions to reflect on your agreements with your Subtracter co-worker. Then create new agreements you would like to make with them.

Stop Giving Up Your Power

Existing Agreements with Your Subtracter Co-worker

_____

_____

_____

_____

_____

_____

New Agreements You Will Make with Your Subtracter Co-worker

_____

_____

_____

_____

_____

_____

Subtracters are looking for ways to feel important, valuable, loved and powerful. Most have been socialized to think that whatever you have is theirs. A true Subtracter co-worker will take anything you give them. Subtracters thrive on other people's power because their life is built on fear and failure. Many of them feel powerless and unconsciously look for others who will give away their personal power. What does it mean to give away your personal power? It means that you give away your options to choose your destiny. Your success in life is directly related to how you use your personal power. If you give it to a Subtracter, then you will hinder your progress and decrease your possibilities for success.

Sharing your personal and professional information with a Subtracter co-worker is like giving them keys to accessing and unlocking your personal power and most valuable possessions. Telling a Subtracter about your family issues, emotional struggles, finances, dreams, professional goals and fears is a mistake. Subtracters thrive on the information you share with them. The more they know, the more personal power they can take. You can deal with a Subtracter co-worker today by limiting what you share with them. Remember that, if something is important to you, don't tell your Subtracters!

The second way we give up our personal power is by failing to make our own decisions. Your Subtracter co-worker wants to speak for you, tell your success stories and make decisions for you. They want you to release your decisions to them so that they can choose your destiny. Your Subtracter co-worker will talk you out of attending important company meetings where decisions are being made about your professional future. They will convince you that those meetings are meaningless and a waste of time. Some co-worker Subtracters will discourage you from attending company functions by planting seeds of fear about not being accepted or welcomed. When a Subtracter co-worker makes your decisions, or talks you out of making important decisions, they are decreasing your options for professional success.

Third, have you missed out on opportunities because of your Subtracter co-workers? It happens all of the time because most of us want to share our progress and exciting news with someone so we make the mistake of telling our Subtracters. Most Subtracter co-workers are intimidated by your potential for promotion. One day, I received an e-mail from someone inquiring about a consulting opportunity with my company. I was curious about this request because we had already decided to pick a particular consultant for the project. I couldn't imagine how the gentleman sending the e-mail knew about the project. As it turns out, one of our consultants already working on the project had shared the opportunity with the gentleman's wife. The wife, who was supposedly a friend of the consultant, immediately took the information and used it to sabotage his opportunity by telling her husband to compete for the project. Sharing your professional growth possibilities and opportunities with Subtracters is like giving them permission to sabotage your future. Subtracters will take your information and use it to their own advantage and self-promotion.

The fourth way to stop giving up your power is to simply stop introducing your co-worker Subtracters to people you know. Connecting your Subtracter co-workers with your professional networks always produces negative results. Subtracters will use up your networks, subtract from them or try to take them. They will use your name to deepen their relationships with your networks and leave you isolated. They will benefit from your networks without ever acknowledging or thanking you. They will destroy the trust you have built with your networks without apology.

Subtracter co-workers are after your personal power - that internal spiritual force you were born with that gives you the power to create change in your life. They want to derail your destiny and decrease your value and professional success. You can stop giving up your personal power by limiting the information you share about your personal life, your career opportunities and networks. Do not share your plans with Subtracters. When a co-worker Subtracter asks how you are doing, always respond with a short positive statement: "I'm doing great!" If a Subtracter co-worker asks about your network, respond by saying, "Let me think about who might be interested in that!" When a Subtracter asks about your future plans reply, "I'm still working on it!" Keep your statements, comments and conversation short and your attitude positive. The key is to consciously refuse to give your personal power to your Subtracter co-workers.

Take Back Your Time

Subtracters are after your time. Think about it. No matter what time you come into your office, within moments your Subtracter co-worker will come and find you. Subtracters are socialized to waste time. Time can be your friend or enemy depending on how you use it. You cannot be effective, productive or position yourself for a promotion unless you learn to manage your time. If a Subtracter co-worker can take your time, they can limit your effectiveness and overall success in the workplace. When a Subtracter comes into your office first thing in the morning and sips their coffee while telling you about their drama, what are they really doing? Taking your time and pulling you into their drama cycle! How do you prevent a Subtracter from consuming and wasting your time?

1. Restructure your day

If a Subtracter is used to you coming to work at 8:00, then change your pattern and come at 7:45 instead. If a Subtracter is used to you having your door open, then close your door. Restructure your day to change your time patterns. If your Subtracter typically wants to go to lunch with you so they can immerse you in their personal drama, drain your energy and gossip about your coworkers, then change your lunch time and schedule lunch with an Adder in your office. Begin creating new patterns for your day and eliminate time spent with your Subtracter co-workers.

2. Create new work habits

Restructure and re-create how you think about your work day. When are you in your office? How long are you in your office? When are you at your computer? How much time are you spending in the hallways? Do you attend meetings with your Subtracter co-workers? Who do you sit next to during meetings? How much time do you spend responding to e-mails from your Subtracter co-workers? Re-creating your work habits cannot be done just by thinking about it. You have to create a written plan for strategically decreasing the amount of time you spend with Subtracter co-workers. When you must meet with your Subtracter co-workers, meet in a neutral space and create an agenda to keep you on task and prevent you from being sidetracked. When your meeting is finished, do not stay to chat. Immediately leave and go back to your office. The mistake that most people make with Subtracter co-workers is to abandon the agenda and let the Subtracter take over. Remember that your Subtracter co-worker's agenda always includes strategies for distracting you from your core responsibilities, wasting your time and leaving you frustrated and unproductive. Subtracters are counting on the fact that they can keep you from getting your work done and will often manipulate you into helping them get their own work done.

For example, your Subtracter co-worker, the *Smiler*, calls your office three times a day nicely asking you to help them problem-solve something that they should already know. Every call takes at least 30 minutes of your time. What can you do? Simply tell the *Smiler* you would really like to help, but have a project to get done. Stay engaged with your own work. Stay focused and take care of your own responsibilities. The *Smiler* might get offended but will eventually stop wasting your time with phone calls. Reclaim your time and you will rediscover your productivity and potential for excellence.

Protect Your Emotional Energy

Negative energy is prevalent and pervasive in many workplaces. People are negative about their company, bosses, managers and each other. This negative energy is directly linked to the volume of the silent cry in these organizations. Sometimes you can feel the negative energy in the halls as if it is waiting to jump on anyone who comes near it. Negative energy is emotionally draining and at times damaging. Subtracter co-workers specialize in and thrive on negative energy. So how do you protect your emotional energy from being negatively influenced by Subtracter co-workers?

1. Pay close attention to clues you are receiving from your own physical body

If you are listening, your body will tell you when a Subtracter is trying to take away your positive emotional energy. You might feel slightly sick in the stomach, or get a headache. You might get flustered and find your heart beating fast. You might begin sweating and developing blotches on your skin. Or you might lose your ability to focus and present your ideas clearly. Your body knows when you are being emotionally drained. When a Subtracter co-worker takes your positive emotional energy, it is a signal that they are after your confidence and sense of well-being. Once you detect these energy-draining signals, immediately begin to move yourself out of the physical space of a Subtracter. Get up, go back to your office, go for a walk or take a break. If possible, get away from your Subtracter as soon as possible.

2. Watch for and stay away from complaining

Many Subtracter co-workers think that complaining is not only normal but necessary for survival in the work place. They constantly complain about anything and anyone in the company. They complain about coming to work, being at work and getting their work done. Subtracter co-workers are not interested in solutions, only complaining about the real or perceived problems. A classic example is the Subtracter co-worker who complains about the latest computer program and how it never works. But the truth is that they refused to attend the training on the new program and now complain every time they run into a problem. If you decide to listen to and help them, then you are actually supporting their complaining and allowing them to take your emotional energy. Zig Ziglar[12], a prominent business leader, consultant and motivational speaker, put it this way, **"Don't be distracted by criticism. Remember the only taste of success some people have is when they take a bite out of you."**

12 Ziglar, Zig. (2008) - www.ZigZiglar.com Weekly Ezine

Complaining is a vehicle for infusing negative energy and drama into the workplace. If you stay around a complainer long enough, you will develop a pessimistic perspective on life. You will also close the door to your potential and possible opportunities. If a Subtracter co-worker from your professional inner circle is complaining, interrupt them and ask them to think about solutions to the problems and people they are complaining about. If the Subtracter is not in your inner circle, do not comment on anything they say and look for the appropriate time to respectfully leave the conversation.

3. Avoid work place drama

Gamer, *Blamer* and *Shamer* co-workers thrive on drama. They know how to start, maintain and increase drama in the work place. Subtracter co-workers typically share drama from their family life with anyone who will listen. However, the other type of drama that drains your emotional energy is known as office politics. Subtracter co-workers create drama by gossiping, backbiting, and spreading rumors. Office politics is usually damaging to your reputation and distracts you from focusing on the mission and vision of the company. It wraps you up in negative energy and decreases your creativity and productivity. Beware of office politics. Avoid it like a plague. If your Subtracter co-worker wants to get you involved, refuse to participate. Don't listen to it, repeat it or make decisions based on it. Protect your positive emotional energy and decline any spoken or unspoken offers to participate in office politics.

4. Manage your reactions

The final way to protect your emotional energy from a Subtracter co-worker is to be consciously aware of your reactions. Your reactions encourage or discourage Subtracters from draining you emotionally.

Reacting emotionally to something a Subtracter co-worker says or does is the beginning stage of giving away your power. When you laugh at the inappropriate jokes, listen to gossip, repeat a rumor or discuss office politics, you are in danger of being pulled into the Subtracter drama cycle. The more you react to a Subtracter, the more emotionally drained you will become. The key is to get to a point at which your response is neutral. What if you are running a meeting and your Subtracter co-worker decides to derail the agenda? Do you visibly show your frustration? No, you stay emotionally neutral, wait for the Subtracter to finish, thank them for their comment, then redirect the meeting back to the agenda. Why not ignore them? Because Subtracters will interpret this as an emotional response and will continue to push you further into their drama cycle. Do not hesitate. Keep your meeting moving and stick with your agenda.

5. Talk Less and Think More

Your Subtracter co-worker has one bottom-line goal. They want you to become a Subtracter, just like them. Ultimately, Subtracters want you to talk and act like them. So pay close attention to your conversations and interactions. Don't just watch what you're saying, watch how you're saying it. Monitor how much time you spend listening and responding to them. Subtracters negatively impact your career because they distract you from doing your job and focusing on the organization's vision and mission. Your productivity, success, and excellence are directly connected to your ability to stay focused. Talk less to your Subtracters and think more about their influence and impact on your career. Listen intently and strategically for the key issues, concerns or problems being raised by your Subtracters. Are they saying that they don't believe in you and your abilities? Are they

> *When you consistently listen to your Subtracter co-workers complain, gossip, put you down, lie and spread rumors, you are unconsciously supporting and affirming their behaviors.*

expressing their own lack of confidence or self-esteem? Are they intimidated by you? Are they afraid of failure? Do they feel incompetent?

Understanding what your Subtracter co-workers are really saying is a key to effectively dealing with them.

6. Ask Critical Questions

When you consistently listen to your Subtracter co-workers complain, gossip, put you down, lie and spread rumors, you are unconsciously supporting and affirming their behaviors. You are making an agreement that their subtracting behavior is not only acceptable but welcomed! How do you signal to a Subtracter that you can no longer support their negativity? Learn how to ask critical questions that challenge their intellect and promote positive dialogue. There are three levels of questions[13] to use when dealing with a Subtracter co-worker. The first level is *WHAT?* questions. These questions help the Subtracter describe what they see as the core issues. Ask your Subtracter co-worker:

✦ **What happened?**

✦ **What are the real issues?**

✦ **What changes do you want to see?**

The second level of critical questions is *SO WHAT?* Most Subtracters operate life on automatic subtracting mode and rarely stop to think about why they act the way they do. Subtracting has become

---

13 Anderson, L.W., Krathwohl, D. R.(Eds.) (2000). Adapted from Bloom's
Taxonomy of Learning. Allyn & Bacon Publishers. Boston, MA

a way of life. When Subtracters understand the *WHAT* and *WHY* they subtract, they can gain a new perspective on life. Questions at this level include:

- ✦ **Why are you concerned about this issue?**
- ✦ **Why is this issue important to you and your job?**
- ✦ **Why is this issue important to the organization?**

The highest level of critical thinking is stimulated by *NOW WHAT?* questions. Finding fault is easy, but creating solutions requires you to think differently about who you are and how you can help. At this level, the goal is to encourage and challenge the Subtracter co-worker to focus on finding solutions to the issues they consistently complain about. These questions are necessary because they offer an opportunity and avenue for Subtracters to change their thoughts, words, attitudes and behavior. It is a catalyst for Subtracters to become Adders. Ask your Subtracter:

- ✦ **What do you see as the solution?**
- ✦ **What can you do to solve the problem?**
- ✦ **What can you do to create new attitudes and perspectives about the issue?**
- ✦ **How can you help create the change?**
- ✦ **What do you think you can do differently?**
- ✦ **How can you prevent this issue from happening again?**

Ultimately, critical questions give your Subtracter co-workers the tools and strategies needed to rediscover and restructure how they use their personal power.

Reframing and Redirecting

Reframing keeps you from getting offended, angry or frustrated and from reacting immediately. It helps you look at the Subtracter's actions or attitudes from a different perspective. It redirects emotional energy and reduces psychological stress. Reframing also gives you time to think about what your Subtracter co-worker is really saying and paves the pathway for asking critical questions. Seven common reframing questions are:

1. **How else can I look at this?**
2. **How can I put this in a different perspective?**
3. **Are there any positives or benefits to this situation?**
4. **How can these issues impact my career?**
5. **Have I done or said something to prompt this?**
6. **How can I change my response?**
7. **What lesson can I learn from this?**

Reframing can be as simple as rephrasing what you heard and asking the Subtracter if your interpretation is correct. It also gives you an opportunity to redirect the conversation back to something constructive and work related. For example, a co-worker Subtracter complains to you about a new employee they think is unqualified and shouldn't have been hired. As you listen carefully to the Subtracter, it is clear that there is a deeper issue. What you hear the Subtracter saying is: "I am intimidated by the new employee because they might have more skills than me, and I am afraid of losing my job to them. So instead of giving the new person a chance to be successful on our team, I have decided to take away their power by creating drama, chaos and office politics about who they are and why they were hired."

What could you do to use the reframing technique and redirect the Subtracter's complaining?

1. **Ask if they have actually met the new employee and talked with them one-on-one.**

2. **Ask them if the person did something to offend them.**

3. **Ask them about their main concern.**

4. **Ask them to think about the team and how this employee can be an asset.**

5. **Ask them to think back on when they were first hired and what it was like to get adjusted to a new company and team of co-workers.**

6. **Ask them to consider setting up a meeting with the new employee to discuss roles and responsibilities – who does what and why.**

7. **Unless they are a Chronic Subtracter, ask them to consider being a mentor to the new employee to help them get adjusted.**

Beware that when you consistently reframe, some Subtracters will get offended and accuse you of not being "real" or thinking that you are better or smarter than they are. Some might become sarcastic and call you names. Most Subtracters, however, will either stop being negative or at least stop talking to you!

Professionalism without Disrespect

Have you ever gotten a rude, mean or disrespectful e-mail from a Subtracter? How did you respond? While teaching at a large university, I worked on a project with a Subtracter who was very critical and belittling. After a particular team meeting, the Subtracter sent me a nasty e-mail criticizing me and the project. This took me by surprise because the Subtracter, who was typically outspoken and negative, was quiet and cordial during the meeting. I was still new and considered to be one of the junior leaders, so the Subtracter must have reasoned that he could send me a disrespectful e-mail without any consequences.

As I read the e-mail and my emotions intensified, I had to breathe deeply, calm down, think about the core issues, and plan a response. The Subtracter was shocked that instead of ignoring him or responding with a negative e-mail, I picked up the phone and called him! Using a calm but assertive tone, I made it very clear that his e-mail was inappropriate, unprofessional and disrespectful. I also informed him that, in the future, I would prefer a face-to-face conversation about issues instead of nasty e-mails behind my back. The Subtracter was nothing short of terrified. His voice shook and he could barely speak. He could not believe that I called him immediately and confronted him about his actions. Even though I was a new leader in the organization, I needed to make it clear that being disrespectful and unprofessional toward me would not be tolerated. This senior level leader thought he could get away with pretending to publicly agree, then privately use e-mail to belittle and criticize me. I could not allow that!

Was that bold and risky? Of course! Did it take confidence and courage? Yes, lots of it! Think about how many people just sit and suffer with this type of workplace behavior. Sadly, many people were never taught how to treat others in a civil, kind, cordial and respectful way. Professionalism is determined by how you talk to, treat and respond to your colleagues. With professionalism, "you leave out the outbursts and emotional thralls that accompany stressful situations and success. You maintain focus, with a sense of urgency, and accept responsibility on a path toward a specific goal. In the process, you maintain respect for your superiors, peers, and subordinates as well as respect them as human beings."[14]

---

14 **Toupin, Edward B.(2008).** *"Professionalism ... How do I get one?"* http://www.selfgrowth.com/articles/Toupin14.html

Being unprofessional is a form of subtracting. People who are socialized Subtracters use the power of subtracting as their "default power mechanism." When something doesn't go their way or they want something, they automatically turn on this power. Subtracters use their power to get immediate negative results. It is like going through the drive-thru at a fast food restaurant. There is no waiting or processing time. The food is already made and ready for you. Subtracter co-workers use unprofessional behavior to achieve immediate negative results. Their power is used to frustrate, belittle, disrespect and discourage you while creating chaos and confusion in the workplace. Over time, however, being unprofessional always leads to more failure for the Subtracter.

On the other hand, being cordial, thoughtful, kind and professional is like planting good seeds into your career. Over time, you will benefit from a harvest of respect and trust from your colleagues. I had a co-worker who never responded when I greeted him each morning with a "hello" or "good morning." Instead, he would turn his back on me and start working or pretend to work on his computer. I decided that I would not be discouraged by his unprofessional behavior and kept greeting him and everyone else in the office. This went on for a year. Then one day as I walked by his office to say "good morning," he turned around and replied, "Good morning, how are you?" I was surprised by his response but took the opportunity to have a short conversation with him. As it turns out, he was a very influential senior level manager in the organization. Some months later, I was working on a project that needed support from a senior level leader and, to my surprise, this man stepped up and gave me and my team the support needed to move the project forward.

Being cordial and professional doesn't always get immediate positive results, but in the end you will attract Adders and your career will benefit.

Protect Your Knowledge

Are you giving away your knowledge, information, tools or techniques to your co-worker Subtracters? Many people do not want to do the work it takes to increase their knowledge base but will work hard to take your knowledge and use it to their advantage. You made a choice to use your time, energy and power to learn new things. You took the initiative to attend the seminars, or complete the certification. So why give away your knowledge so quickly and easily to your Subtracters when you know they will use it to better their own career options or even try to take your position?

For example, your whole team is required to attend a training to learn a new software program that will change your project management process. Instead of attending all of the training sessions, your Subtracter co-worker hangs out, goes to bars and refuses to study the new material. When the new software gets implemented, the Subtracter is confused and needs your assistance. The Subtracter wasn't interested in learning the new program but was quick to call you for help. So what should you do? The first time they call for help, give them limited advice and encourage them to review their program manual for further questions. Let them know that your schedule and work load will not allow you the time to teach them the software and suggest they take a refresher course.

Stop teaching Subtracters how to do their job. Their job is their job, and it is their responsibility to learn it and to do it well. However, if you become their unofficial technical assistance resource then you are socializing them to take your knowledge.

Refuse to do your Subtracter's job. Don't just stop teaching them how to do their jobs, stop doing their jobs for them. Many of my coaching clients complain about their boss or co-worker who doesn't know what they are doing and relies on them to do their job. This problem is not the boss's or the co-worker's, it's my client's problem! Why? Because the more you do for your Subtracter co-worker, the more they want you to do. It is simply time to stop doing your co-worker's job. Some Subtracters are used to being enabled. They are used to someone else doing their work and not taking responsibility. Subtracters know how to find people who will enable them. What if you refuse to do your co-worker's job and they fail? Let them! Their job is not your responsibility and it's time for you to focus on your own productivity and progress. In general, should you be helpful to your co-workers? Absolutely! Should you allow a Subtracter co-worker to socialize, intimidate or guilt you into doing their job? Never.

Don't give the knowledge you worked so hard to attain to a Subtracter co-worker! Why? Because Subtracters will use up your time and energy to get their questions answered and leave you unthanked, unproductive and frustrated.

Stop Connecting Co-worker Subtracters to Your Networks

Many Subtracters are like "network leeches." They probe to find out who you know, then latch onto them and act as if your networks belonged to them first. Subtracters will not only take and use up your networks but also destroy the trust relationships you worked so hard to build. They will also undermine the influence you have established with your networks. Connecting co-worker Subtracters to your personal and professional networks is a common mistake. So how do you stop this from happening?

First, guard the access to your networks. When a Subtracter asks if you know someone who can help them, you don't have to feel obligated to offer up your networks. You can suggest a well-known resource, Web site or professional association. If you do suggest someone in your network, do not give the Subtracter the direct contact information. Instead, let them know that you will contact your network first about the Subtracter and give them the option of contacting the Subtracter.

Second, if a Subtracter co-worker asks to join you for an event where people from your network will be attending, should you introduce them to members of your network? This all depends on the personality of the Subtracter. If you are dealing with a *Gamer* Subtracter, keep them away from your networks. If you are dealing with a *Smiler*, briefly introduce them to your networks but keep the conversation specific and short. Be careful not to engage your Subtracters in discussions about the details of how you are connected to your networks. Avoid discussions with your Subtracter about how your networks have benefited you.

Third, if you decide to connect your Subtracter co-worker to your network, first do your homework. Contact your network immediately and give them some background about your Subtracter. Share your experiences with your Subtracter and the challenges you have had with them. Be honest with your networks about your Subtracter. Be careful not to set up your networks for failure, confusion or frustration. The strength of your networks is very important to your career advancement. The people in your networks trust you and will directly associate whoever you refer to them with who you are. If you send them Subtracters then, sooner or later, they will see you as a Subtracter.

Fourth, recommending a Subtracter co-worker to your networks as a potential hire is risky and harmful to your reputation. If a Subtracter asks you for a reference letter, be honest and decline the offer. Why? Because we are aligned with the people who recommend us for promotion in life. If you recommend a Subtracter co-worker who ultimately becomes a "problem employee," your network will hold you responsible and your integrity will be questioned.

Think about it. Have you ever connected a Subtracter co-worker to your networks? What happened? What lessons did you learn? Take a moment to write about this experience.

Document Your Interactions

Co-workers, especially those who are *Chronic Subtracters,* can create a difficult work environment for you and your team. They constantly look for ways to devalue you and your good intentions. *Chronic Subtracter* co-workers can sabotage your hard work and set you up for failure. They cannot be trusted, so you must document your interactions with them. If you are working on a project with a *Chronic*

Subtracter, consistently document your role and accomplishments. Send simple but assertive (to the point, factual and informational) e-mails that explain what you did and your results. Avoid using emotional or negative words or statements to describe you, the Subtracter or the project. Be cordial and professional. A sample assertive e-mail might read:

> *"Thank you for working with me on the _____ project. I just completed the items for which I was responsible. The results are:_ _____. Additional information is attached. Let me know if there is anything else I can do to make this project more effective and successful. I appreciate you taking the time to review and respond with any questions/thoughts. Have a good day."*

Copy an Adder on your team who is familiar with the project and the *Chronic Subtracter*. Also send a copy to your supervisor and yourself. It is not necessary to blind copy others, which is actually a Subtracter sabotage technique. Be open and honest about the fact that you are sharing the information with others. Demonstrating your willingness to positively involve others in your dealings with *Chronic Subtracters* is a strategy for stabilizing the negative impact they can have on your career.

If you like to journal, keep notes on your daily interactions with your *Chronic Subtracter*. These notes should be dated and legible in the event that you ever need to use them to support a dispute between you and the *Chronic Subtracter*. If a Subtracter publicly confronts you and says you have never done this or that, you will have evidence. *Chronic Subtracters* will twist the facts or blatantly lie, so taking extra time and effort to maintain written documentation is essential.

Create a Plan

If your co-worker is a Subtracter, then you have to deal with them. So where do you start? What will you do? When will you do it? What will you say? Many strategies were shared in this chapter but each Subtracter is different and requires a unique plan for dealing with them. Not all strategies work for every Subtracter, so you have to take a close look at your Subtracter co-worker and then create a plan. Before you begin working your plan, reflect on and write on the following:

Who is your co-worker Subtracter? Are they in your professional inner circle?

What is their Subtracter personality?

What is your history with this person?

What agreements have you made with this person?

Now it's time to create a detailed plan that includes the strategies you are going to use and your implementation plan. This plan will help you reduce or eliminate the impact of Subtracter co-workers in your life.

Strategy	**Implementation Plan**
Example: *Stop giving away* *my knowledge.*	*Starting today,* *Stop answering questions about* *the Subtracter's job.*
1.	
2.	
3.	
4.	
5.	

Chapter 8

The Subtracter Friend

When he was a middle school student, my son had a Subtracter friend. The friend called my son constantly about every little thing and wanted to come to our house almost daily. He was often bossy and acted as if my son belonged to him. Initially my son enjoyed the friendship because they were both skateboarders. But the friend soon changed from being a really fun person to being controlling and at times manipulative. If he couldn't have his way, the friend would get mad, pout, and even throw temper tantrums. Sometimes, his negative attitude and behavior were almost intolerable. My son felt stuck because he liked his friend and enjoyed skating with him but did not know what to do about his subtracting behavior. I finally had to step in and tell the boy that his behavior was unacceptable. I even had a conversation with the boy's parents about his behavior. When the friend was not being a Subtracter, he was a really nice person who was very smart and fun to be around. As I observed him, I realized that the boy wanted to be a good friend to my son but he had already been socialized to use his power to subtract. It was also clear that his parents tolerated his subtracting behavior.

My first reaction was to simply tell my son that his friend was a Subtracter and that he should quickly get him out of his life! But it was clear that my son wanted to make the friendship work so I decided to teach the boy how to be an Adder. I let him know that I liked him as a person but would not tolerate his negative behavior. I encouraged him to be positive. I gave him clear expectations about his attitude and behavior. I challenged him with the fact that he could not and would

We tend to attract people who are like us so, if your life is loaded with Subtracter friends, then it might be time for you to take a serious look at your own use of personal power.

not always get his way. I also limited the amount of time he spent with my son. Thankfully, over the years, the friend has become an Adder, but there are still times when that subtracting power reappears and we have to address it.

While this example is about children, these same patterns carry over into adulthood. Is your friend a Subtracter? How can you be sure? What if you are a Subtracter and your friend is just reacting to you? We tend to attract people who are like us so, if your life is loaded with Subtracter friends, then it might be time for you to take a serious look at your own use of personal power. However, this is not always the case. Most people have had Subtracter friends since childhood and have struggled with them but never knew what to do about them.

Is your friend a Subtracter? How do you know?

The first step in identifying a Subtracter friend is to look at the **history** you have developed with them. Understanding what has happened in your friendship over time is critical. You must take a long and realistic look at what your friends add or subtract from your life. You cannot change your relationship with a Subtracter friend until you understand their impact in your life. Keep in mind that it doesn't matter how long you've known your friend, how much you care about them, or what you have shared with them. If they are a Subtracter, they will decrease and devalue your life, ultimately stripping you of your personal power. Without personal power, you will never take an action step toward excellence. If a Subtracter can take your power, they can take your joy, confidence and chance for a fulfilled life.

Take a moment to recall your **history** with your Subtracter friend.

When did you first meet them? How did you meet them? How long have you known them? Describe your relationship. What important memories have you shared together?

The second question is **how** does your friend subtract from you? What is their Subtracter personality? Are they a *Smiler, Snipper-Nipper, Blamer, Gamer, Shamer, Dreamer* or *Worrier*? How do you know they are subtracting from you? What behaviors, actions or words do they use to subtract? For example, I had a Subtracter friend who would only come around me when she needed something. She knew that I was resourceful and productive. Being a *Smiler*, she had a way of making me feel important as I continually bailed her out of her drama. In reality, she was taking anything and everything she could out of my life.

Think about your Subtracter friend(s). Write down **how** they are subtracting from you. Be honest even if it hurts!

Third, **when** does your friend subtract from you? Subtracters tend to have a specific schedule and cycle. If your friend is a *Shamer*, they will find pivotal public moments at which to devalue and criticize you. They will wait until you are at dinner with other friends, or are at an important meeting, to begin announcing your faults, failures and mistakes. Or they will wait until your entire family is listening, then make a sarcastic joke about you. A *Dreamer* will wait until you have come into some level of prominence or financial success then show up with another good idea. The *Worrier* will call you every evening at the same time then keep you on the phone for hours with their drama. Your Subtracter friend has a pattern. The key is to learn their pattern so that you can anticipate their subtracting behavior and have time to create a plan for dealing with them.

Think about **when** your friend subtracts from your life. Be specific about the time, seasons and situations.

Over the years - whether two or twenty - **what** has the Subtracter friend taken out of your life? Have they taken your money, time, positive energy, confidence, self-esteem, resources, networks? If they are a Subtracter, then you have given them valuable parts of yourself and your life. So what have they taken? This might be a painful question to think about and document but the bottom line is that when you are clear about what your friend has subtracted from you then you can begin to create a plan to get it back!

I was at the mall shopping with my son for baseball hats when I overheard two men talking. I immediately recognized that one of the two men was a Subtracter. He was loud, talkative and constantly making sarcastic comments and jokes about his friend. The friend just put up with the Subtracter and pretended to laugh at some of his jokes. But the friend was visually becoming frustrated and tried ignoring the Subtracter. They finally got to the register and, of course, the Subtracter did not have any money, so he turned to his friend and asked him to pay for his hat just this once. The friend stopped, looked at the Subtracter and commented, "You said that last time!" Then he proceeded to pay for the Subtracter's hat. I could tell that this was a pattern in their friendship and that the Subtracter had taken not only money but confidence and self-worth from his friend.

Over the lifetime of your friendship with a Subtracter, what have you given up and what have they taken? Can you live a whole life if you have given up your power and confidence to a Subtracter friend? Absolutely not! If your life feels like it's missing something, then you've probably given pieces of your life to Subtracters.

Think about **what** your Subtracter friend has taken out of your life. Think about all aspects of your life (emotional, physical, spiritual, financial, social, professional, etc.). Be honest and specific.

The most challenging question you must ask yourself is: "**Why** is this person still in my life?" Why are you still in this relationship? Is there something you love or appreciate about this person that keeps you in the relationship with them? Friends are "Choice" people and you have the power to choose them or dismiss them from your life. So why did you originally choose them, and why do you continue to choose them? You must have a reason for keeping your Subtracter friend(s) in your life.

Take a moment to think about **why** you continue to choose your Subtracter friend(s). Be specific about your reasons, even if they are selfish ones.

```
_____

_____

_____

_____
```

Subtracter Doors

Your life is like a house with multiple entrances. Subtracter friends enter your life through a variety of doors and it's important to know which door(s) they are using to access your life. Friendships are initiated through pain or pleasure. How did the friend enter your life? Was it through the door of pain, grief, career, family, marriage, religion, education, motherhood or struggle? How a Subtracter enters your life has everything to do with how much you allow them to take from you. Unlike co-workers or bosses, friends are not limited to a time and space. They have access to your entire life, which means that their ability to subtract from you is much more comprehensive and complex. So what are Subtracter friends taking from you?

> *How a Subtracter enters your life has everything to do with how much you allow them to take from you.*

Space Invaders

Subtracter friends can smother you and leave you feeling like you are suffocating. Every time you turn around, your Subtracter friend is there. They are like leeches that refuse to let go! They want to be involved in every part of your life. They constantly want your attention and get upset if you don't include them in everything you do. Subtracter friends are *Space Invaders* who leave you gasping for air. They take away your power by limiting access to your own life. They clog up your life with their issues, drama and activities. Subtracter friends keep you distracted and busy with their drama. Soon, you will begin neglecting your own life. As the Subtracter takes up more and more of your emotional and physical space, your life will begin to slowly fall apart.

Time Guzzlers

Subtracter friends are notorious for wasting your time. They have 24-hour access to you and they will use as much of that time as possible. Think about your Subtracter friend who comes to your house uninvited and sits at your kitchen table, eats your food and spends hours complaining, gossiping and putting you down. They never offer to help you with the dishes or with the kids. They just invade your space, sit, talk and waste your time. Your Subtracter friend convinces you to go shopping or to a ball game when you really don't have the time, but guilt drives you to accept their invitation. The reality is that you have many chores, errands or projects that need your attention at home, but week after week you give into your Subtracter.

Female Subtracter friends are good for talking you into "Going shopping!" The problem is that your friend rarely has any money and relies on you to buy their treats or lunch while they window shop. You walk around the mall for hours with your Subtracter friend, thinking the whole time about what you should be doing to improve your life. Working out at the gym, I overheard a woman complaining to another woman about a Subtracter friend. The woman said she was busy trying to clean her house when her friend called and asked her for help with a project. The woman had no idea what the project entailed but agreed to help her friend. As it turns out, the friend first needed a ride to a home improvement store to buy a bookcase. Then she needed help getting it into the house and then she asked for help to put it together. Before the woman knew it, she had spent her entire day helping her friend, while her own home project was left undone. Subtracter friends have one agenda only: their own. And they expect you to stop what you are doing and use your time to help them. The more you let them, the more time Subtracter friends will take and waste!

Subtracters maximize technology in wasting your time. They have access to your cell, home, and work phones. They call, e-mail or text message you about every little thing. They use technology to stay connected while they wrap you up in their drama 24 hours a day. As Subtracter friends use up your time, they take away your options and opportunities to strategically address the priorities in your own life. How can you possibly achieve excellence in life without time for yourself?

Energy Suckers

Other than your family members, Subtracter friends have the most influence on your emotional stability and energy level. They know how to manipulate your social, psychological, spiritual and professional self because, over the years, you have taught them how to do it! They bring dump trucks of negative energy and chaos into your life. They believe that your work in life is to make their life better, but they still blame you anytime something goes wrong. Subtracter friends play with your emotions to take away your power, waste your time and suffocate your life. If a Subtracter friend entered your life through the emotional door, they know how to make you feel guilty, hurt or offended. They use their emotional outburst to create doubt and fear in your life. A Subtracter friend who says "Oh, I wouldn't try that because I tried once and failed" is manipulating you to walk away from your success potential. Subtracter friends take your positive energy and socialize you to become negative and pessimistic.

Money Vacuums

How often does your Subtracter friend ask you to help them out financially? What about using your resources? Do they borrow your car and return it on empty? Do they ask you to baby-sit free of charge, but never return the favor? How often do they borrow your tools? When a Subtracter friend borrows your books or movies, do they come back? The classic situation is when your Subtracter friend invites you to lunch but doesn't have any money so you end up paying again! Or the friend who suggests a movie or play but can't afford the ticket, so who pays? You! Some Subtracter friends are bold enough to ask you to purchase something for them on your credit card. Subtracter friends are known for consuming your money and resources. Think about it. How much money and what resources have you given to your Subtracter friend?

Opportunity Blockers

Who do you know? Your Subtracter friend wants to know because they want to leverage your networks and opportunities. Your gossiping girlfriend tells everyone about your newest opportunity or idea. It makes her feel informed and important. One day you make the mistake of telling her about a new job for which you are applying. She immediately starts telling her other friends and co-workers about

Practice the art of silence!

it. You don't get the job, but later learn that another person became your competitor after they heard about the job from your gossiping girlfriend. Sharing opportunities with a Subtracter friend is always a mistake. Why? Because they will find ways to limit and eliminate your chances for success.

Dream Stealers

The sad reality is that many of your Subtracter friends are intimidated by you. Their foundation of fear and failure prevents them from celebrating your success. Even though they may say they want the best for you, their actions and attitudes are all designed to leave you questioning and doubting your vision, goals and dreams. Because they are takers, Subtracter friends devalue, and will potentially steal, your aspirations and dreams. Subtracters who come into your life through the door of vision and dreams can severely decrease your options to choose your destiny because they will either talk you out of your dreams or take them. Some Subtracters will reframe, restructure and repackage your dream to make it their own. Some are even bold enough to then convince you that you should get involved with it! If you have a good idea or a dream, don't share it with your Subtracter friend. Practice the art of silence!

Confidence Annihilators

Personal power was given to you at birth, but confidence must be learned and practiced. Subtracters are habitual confidence destroyers. Subtracter friends are experts at making you doubt yourself. They know special techniques for sarcastically putting you down. They pride themselves on telling others about your faults. They rehearse your weaknesses and convince you not to try again. Often in church, people who are struggling with life's challenges will ask another church member to pray for them. This is fine, except when the person to whom you reveal your struggle is a Subtracter who uses prayer as a gossiping technique. As they "share" your prayer request, they are really telling others about your weaknesses. What should have been prayer turns into a spiritual gossiping session. In the process, your confidence is damaged and your trust in God and the church diminishes. Confidence is a critical component of personal power because it gives you the drive, energy and passion to take action steps needed to change your life. No confidence, no personal power, no action step, no change, no success!

Think about it. What have your Subtracter friends taken from you? What impact have they had on your life? How do you know they have had this impact? As you reflect and write about these questions, be honest. It might be painful, but the end result will give you the evidence needed to make an informed decision about keeping them in your life or letting them go!

The Decision

Now that you know about the many doors your friends can enter and use to subtract from you, it's time to make a decision about whether or not you will keep them in your inner circle or life. No one knows you like you do. No one knows and understands the relationship between you and your Subtracter friend like you do, so only you can make the decision. However, once you decide, quickly take action to change the relationship. Whether you decide to keep the Subtracter in your inner circle, to move them out of the inner circle but still keep them in your life, or to completely let them go, you must create a plan of action.

Moving Subtracter Friends Out of Your Inner Circle

Five steps are necessary for moving Subtracter friends out of your inner circle, while keeping them in your life.

Step #1

Starting today, significantly reduce the amount of time you spend with your Subtracter friend. If they call, immediately find something else to do, gracefully excuse yourself and get off the phone! A Subtracter's opening question is usually "Hi, what are you doing?" Your response has to be, "I'm working on a project and can't talk right now." Click! Do not give your Subtracter time to ask follow-up questions or start a conversation. If they come to your house, look busy and do not engage them in a conversation. Ask them for help with a project. When your Subtracter friend discovers that you want them to work, they will find an excuse to leave. You can also let them know that you have to leave in a few minutes. I remember having to literally walk a Subtracter friend to the front door and telling them that is was time for them to go. You may not have to go to that extreme, but you must reduce the amount of time your Subtracters take. If they call and ask you to go somewhere, say "no" without apologizing or offering an excuse.

Step #2

Stop talking to your Subtracter friend about critical issues or challenges in your life. Resist the temptation to share the details of your life (children, spouse or job). You cannot change how much your Subtracter friend already knows, but you can change your communication pattern and limit the amount of new information you share. When a Subtracter friend asks "How are you doing?" respond with a simple but pleasant, "Fine, I'm doing great!" Then stop talking! Keep your conversations brief and basic. Stay away from discussing anything of value or importance.

Step #3

Do not react or try to defend yourself when your Subtracter friend tries to blame you or put you down. Refuse to get involved in their drama. Practice managing your emotional reactions to them. Don't give away your personal power by becoming frustrated or emotional. Avoid conversations and topics that typically lead you to feeling emotionally frustrated, vulnerable or powerless.

Step #4

Limit the amount of resources you give to your Subtracter friend. This includes money, food, clothes, transportation or a place to stay. Should you help them out of desperate situations? Yes, if the situation is a first time occurrence. However, if it is a recurring pattern due to their failure to take responsibility, then say "no." The first time you refuse to help, your friend will be surprised, hurt or even offended.

Get ready for their response, stand your ground and refuse to give into their emotional tantrum.

Step #5

Stop trying to be an Adder to a Subtracter friend. You cannot add to a Subtracter because they will interpret this as you giving them your power. Subtracter friends will continually take and use your power, positive energy, time, resources and networks to their advantage. Your Subtracter friends will not add to you and will rarely say thank you. They will take until you have nothing else to give.

Implementing these five steps will help you restructure the relationship and change the paradigm of your friendship. You will move your friend out of your inner circle without them even knowing it. You can also use these steps to continually manage the relationship. Your life will no longer be dictated or negatively influenced by your Subtracter friend. You will reclaim the power to decide how much information, time, and resources you want to give to a Subtracter.

Letting Your Subtracter Friend Go!

In my seminars and workshops, people get excited when they hear me say, "It's time to let that Subtracter go!" People are empowered and motivated by these words but the reality is that it's easier to say than do. The fact is that people find it very hard to move friends totally out of their lives. However, there are times when this is not only appropriate but absolutely necessary. I remember a woman whose life was so negatively impacted and influenced by a Subtracter friend that she found herself becoming a Subtracter. This woman was so caught up in the drama and negative energy of her Subtracter friend that she found herself feeling stuck and unfocused. She felt like her whole life was about to fall apart and that she could no longer manage the relationship. The woman had to immediately let go of her Subtracter friend.

The five steps for letting go of a Subtracter friend are very simple and to the point, but not easy to do.

1. **Immediately stop spending any time with them.**
2. **Stop giving them any space in your life.**
3. **Stop talking to them. Check your caller ID and don't take their call.**
4. **Stop offering any help. Of course you must use wise judgment to make a decision about life threatening situations, but short of a major tragedy do not offer to help.**
5. **Refuse to give them access to any of your resources.**

Unless you are unsure about letting go of your Subtracter friend, do not attempt to engage them in a conversation about ending the relationship. Just follow the five steps and move on with your life. Create a plan for implementing these steps and start. For example, you might use a vacation as a way to stop spending any time with your Subtracter friend and then continue to implement the other steps when you return home.

Do these steps work for Chronic Subtracter friends who have strategically taken away your power and slowly devalued your life? Yes, but you have to be more persistent and courageous because a Chronic Subtracter friend will not just go away. They will find innovative ways to spend time with you or create excuses for needing to talk. They will guilt you into giving up your resources. They will find new ways to manipulate your emotions and keep you in their drama cycle. Why? Because Chronic Subtracter friends think that they have earned the right to be a "Just Is" person in your life. They have already decided to stay in your life no matter what. Moving a Chronic Subtracter out of your life takes longer so be patient and stick with your plan. You must be committed to really letting them go even if it means some hardship and pain. The key is to decrease the amount of time and information you give to the Chronic Subtracter until they are totally out of your life. This process will take time and commitment. If a Chronic Subtracter has been in your life for 20 years, they will not just leave your life. So get ready to work your plan until your Chronic Subtracter friend is gone. In the process of moving them out, focus on becoming an Adder to others in your inner circle so that you can begin attracting new Adders. The more Adders you attract, the less influence a Chronic Subtracter will have in your life.

Keeping Your Friend in Your Inner Circle

Deciding to keep a Subtracter friend in your inner circle will take work, time, emotions and a lot of energy. Why? Because you must change the overall paradigm of your relationship and their power influence in your life. The formula for keeping a Subtracter friend in your inner circle is called *S.T.O.P.* It only works for mild or moderately socialized Subtracters who are clueless about how they use their power in your life. The *S.T.O.P.* formula is designed to be implemented during casual conversations with your Subtracter friend.

The "S" in *S.T.O.P.* stands for *Signals*. Every Subtracter has certain signals that alert you to their subtracting behavior. Begin studying your Subtracter friend. What are their signals? When, what, and how do they subtract? Understanding their signals prepares you for responding appropriately to them. For example, most Subtracters use certain words, or conversations as signals. If your Subtracter friend likes to involve you in their family drama, then pay close attention when they begin talking about their family and quickly redirect the conversation. If your friend is a Shamer, then look for signals when you are in public with them and get ready to take action. Take a moment to think about your Subtracter friend. What are their subtracting signals? How do you know when they are about to subtract from you? These signals could consist of words, actions, attitudes or behaviors.

Signal #1

Signal #2

Signal #3

"**T**" in the *S.T.O.P.* formula stands for *Truth*. Find out the truth about your Subtracter friend's reality. What is really going on with them? What is the real problem and what are the facts? Why do they subtract from you? People rarely have honest conversations about the important things that matter in life. Most often we talk about surface issues while avoiding topics that require us to honestly look at the condition of our lives. Getting to the truths that drive the relationship between you and your Subtracter friend is crucial. It will take courage, confidence, multiple conversations and a lot of time. The key is to come to the point at which you can truthfully address the Subtracter's role in your life. What are the core issues related to the Subtracter's behavior? Are they insecure, suffering from low self-esteem, lacking goals, feeling stuck, hurt or offended? For example, if your friend is a *Snipper-Nipper* who constantly talks you down, is the core issue jealously, fear of success or intimidation? You cannot keep a Subtracter in your inner circle if you are not willing to deal with the truth underlying their use of power in your life. Learning the truth about your Subtracter can also be painful because it might reveal how your role in the friendship has encouraged them to be a Subtracter. So where do you begin? Start by using the WHAT, SO WHAT, NOW WHAT critical questions process described earlier[15]. Ultimately, going through the truth process will open up the eyes of your Subtracter friend to how they have been using their power and give them an opportunity to become an Adder in your life. As you both discover the truth, you can both begin to reframe and restructure your relationship.

  "O" in the *S.T.O.P.* formula stands for ***Options***. Now that you have gone through the Truth process with your Subtracter, it's time to rethink your options for keeping them in your inner circle. For example, I knew a man who thought that his father was a great Subtracter. As a child, he saw his father as uncaring and distant. But, when he grew up, the man learned that his father had to work three jobs just to make ends meet and provide for his family. As a child, he

---

15 Price, Verna C. (2008). The Silent Cry: Dealing with Subtracters in Work and
    Life. Chapter 7, Pp. 130-131.

had no access to all of this information nor did he understand the role of poverty in his family. He only looked at the obvious which was that his father was often absent. When he finally understood the truth of his life, he reconsidered his options and decided to think about, and interact with, his father differently. Knowing the truth gives you new options for your relationship with your Subtracter. For example, if your Subtracter has been intimidated by you since childhood and continues to blame you for their failure in life, then your options might be to move them out of your inner circle but still keep them in your life. However, if your friend is a Worrier who constantly pulls you into their drama cycle and, in the truth process, you learn that they are simply afraid of success because of something that happened early in their career, then your option might be to keep them in your inner circle but consciously find ways to mentor and coach them to take advantage of new opportunities. Understanding and exercising your options helps you reclaim your personal power.

"**P**" in the ***S.T.O.P.*** formula stands for ***Plan***. Changing the relationship with your Subtracter friend will require a plan. Begin by having a discussion about the meaning of personal power. It is important to talk about the difference between using your power to add versus subtract. The fact is that the word *friend* does not belong in the same sentence with *Subtracter,* so it is important to teach your friend how to add to your life. You must also be patient as your friend learns how to use their power to add. This will take time, but stick with the process and you will not only keep a friend for life, but also earn a new level of respect from them.

The second step in the Plan is to identify your Subtracter friends' behavior patterns and decide which ones you will address or ignore.

For example if your friend has a habit of asking to borrow money at a certain time each month, then you might want to have an honest discussion with them about money management. Do not give them any more money but offer to help them change this negative pattern. If your friend is a time waster, you might refuse to attend an outing or event but explain your reasons. If your friend is pessimistic and negative, have a discussion about why this is unacceptable. Stay away from trying to address all of your friend's subtracting behaviors at once. Make a list, then prioritize the list based on the overall impact on your friendship. Begin working on those subtracting behaviors that currently have the biggest negative impact.

The third step is to engage your friend in an accountability

Subtracting Behavior	Impact	Plan for Addressing It
1.		
2.		
3.		
4.		

conversation. In other words, what are you and your friend willing to do to make the relationship more positive and effective? Nothing changes in relationships without reciprocity. Until both parties are giving and receiving, neither can be fulfilled in the relationship. If you are the only giver, then sooner or later the relationship will fail. During an accountability conversation, both parties must answer the questions: How can I be a better friend? What can I do to change? How can I be an Adder? These conversations will clarify your values and beliefs about the relationship and demonstrate your commitment to your friend. Take a moment to reflect on these questions. Be honest. This exercise will prepare you for this conversation.

The Private Snatching

How can I be a better friend?

_____

_____

_____

_____

What can I do to change?

_____

_____

_____

_____

How can I be an Adder?

_____

_____

_____

_____

The ***S.T.O.P.*** formula works well with most Subtracter friends but not with severe Subtracters. These are friends who have been in your life for years and you want them to stay, but they are such severe Subtracters that they have almost become Chronic. You care about them and cherish your friendship but they are literally wearing you out! You feel drained and exhausted from having to deal with them. You don't want to let them go but you are beginning to feel like you have no other choice. The most intense intervention process for dealing with a Subtracter friend is called a Private Snatching. The process involves engaging your friend in a private, face-to-face, intense conversation about their impact in your life and why the relationship must change today.

A Private Snatching requires preparation and thoughtfulness. It is not about "telling someone off," giving someone a "piece of your mind" or throwing an emotional temper tantrum. No, it is a strategic process that intensely addresses Subtracter behaviors that can potentially destroy your friendships. Some years ago I confronted a woman publicly when I should have done a private snatching. I knew that I needed to have a private intense conversation with her, but instead I spontaneously confronted her in an emotional outburst. What I said to her was honest and factual but my approach was totally inappropriate. Instead of strengthening the relationship, I ended up hurting the woman's feelings, damaging my own character and losing her trust. In an attempt to "be real" with her, I instead used my power to publicly shame and devalue her integrity. I knew I was acting like a Subtracter. After several days, I wrote a formal apology letter to the woman.

Preparing for a *Private Snatching* is as important as

implementing the process. Attempting to conduct a private snatching when you are mad, angry, or upset is a mistake. You cannot have a private snatching if your emotions are out of control. To get the positive results you want for your friendship, you must wait until you are prepared and emotionally stable. So how do you prepare? Begin with the following:

1. Request a formal meeting with your friend.
2. Let them know that you need to have a very serious and hard conversation with them about the state of your friendship.
3. Reassure them that you care about them and will continue to do so regardless of the outcome of the conversation.
4. Reassure them that you value the friendship.
5. Let them know that you think some immediate and drastic changes are needed in the relationship.

Rules for a Private Snatching

A Private Snatching done correctly can strengthen the friendship by directly confronting the Subtracter power being used by your friend. However, there are certain rules to follow so that the conversation doesn't turn into a blaming bash against your friend. These rules are designed to help you communicate assertively, openly, positively and honestly about how your friend has subtracted from your life. In the process, you will not only confront your friend's negative behavior but give them the opportunity to change.

Rule #1 - Schedule a Specific Time and Place for the Private Snatching

Do not have a private snatching based on an emotional reaction. Take the time to calm your emotions, gather important information and plan out the conversation. A Private Snatching cannot be effective if it is unplanned or uncontrolled. When it is done well, it will result in positive solutions. When it is done poorly, it will create new offenses, hurt, guilt and resentment. Do not feel forced into having the conversation before you are ready. A Private Snatching will require you to be courageous, confident and informed. What if your friend is so anxious about the conversation that they cannot wait for the scheduled time and demands to talk right away? Do not give in to the pressure and stick with the agreed-on schedule.

Rule #2 – Know the Facts

Do your homework. Write out specific incidents, experiences and stories that illustrate how your friend is subtracting from your life. Because 85% of Subtracters are socialized, their first response will be to deny anything and everything you are telling them. Relying just on your feelings will not work in a Private Snatching. You must base your conversation on the facts, even if they are painful.

Rule #3 – Know Your Outcome

Have a clear understanding about your desired outcome for the Private Snatching. What are the specific changes you are seeking from yourself and your friend? How do you want the relationship to change? Be very specific and strategic about the issues you want to address and stick with your agenda. Do not get caught up in an emotional tennis match with your Subtracter friend. State the facts; identify the changes you want to see; and stay focused.

Rule #4 – See the Innocence

Enter the *Private Snatching* with a commitment to see the innocence[16] in your friend's behavior. Is it possible that your friend

---

16 Carlson, Richard (1997). Don't Sweat the Small Stuff--and it's all small stuff. Hyperion Books, New York, NY

has no idea how they are using their power to subtract? What if they simply don't know how to be a positive friend? Be prepared to see and accept their innocence then offer them every opportunity to explain themselves and change.

Rule #5 – Forgive your Friend before the Private Snatching

Have your friend's actions, behaviors or words hurt you? How long have you been wounded? Have you forgiven them? I am amazed by how many people harbor unforgiveness in their hearts. What is forgiveness? Forgiveness is choosing to release your friend from anything they might have done consciously or unconsciously to hurt you. It's very important to forgive your friend before the Private Snatching. You cannot be an Adder if you can't forgive. Clear your heart and mind of any resentment, unforgiveness or offense. Why? Because unforgiveness blocks positive progress in relationships. Forgiving prior to the Private Snatching, opens up your heart and mind to new possibilities for growth and change in the friendship.

Finally, you must be willing to accept the fact that a Private Snatching can either strengthen or end the friendship. Sometimes, a friend might not have the emotional energy and desire required to change who they are in the relationship. Despite your friend's reaction, if you know you've followed the rules, done your research, focused on the core issues, and approached the process with openness and honesty, then you can walk away from the relationship with a clear conscience.

Planning Your Private Snatching

Take a moment and create your plan. Be sure to write about all aspects of the plan.

When will it happen? Where will it happen?

\
\
\

How will you prepare?

\
\
\
\
\

How will you begin the conversation? What core issues will you address?

\
\
\
\
\

What do you want for a solution?

_____

_____

_____

_____

_____

The "Just Is" Subtracters – Your Family

The most difficult group of Subtracters you will ever have to manage is your family members. What makes them so difficult? It is because you did not choose them, they "Just Is." You did not choose your mother, father or siblings. While you did choose your spouse, the moment you married, them they became a "Just Is" person. You didn't choose your children unless you adopted them, and then they became "Just Is" people, as well. You have to live with whoever is in your family. And because family is so important and critical to our success or failure, their role as a Subtracter can devastate our lives.

Some family members believe they have an absolute right to create chaos, havoc and drama in your life. They think they have a right to immerse you in their own chaos, drama and crisis. While friends may only have access to, and come into your life through, a particular door, your family members don't need a door. They have total access to your life. In some cultures, you are not only obligated to take care of family, but expected to be constantly involved in each other's lives. There is nothing wrong with a collective perspective about family. However, when your family members become Subtracters, then you must learn how to manage their power and negative impact in your life. As long as you live, your family will be your family. But that doesn't mean they have to be in your personal inner circle or that you have to put up with or tolerate their Subtracter behavior.

I remember working with a woman leader who had been in a place of confusion, crisis and chaos with her mother for a long time.

During one session I said that, if your mother is a Subtracter, you have to get her out of your inner circle. This woman became very confused by my statement and began to cry silently. She asked how she could move her mother out of her inner circle. My response was very simple. She didn't have to move her mother out of her life, only out of her inner circle of influence. As long as you live and have breath in your body, your mother will be in your life, but that doesn't mean that you have to accept her negative influence. If your mother has used her power to subtract from you, then you must learn strategies to manage her impact in your life.

If you look just under the crisis and chaos associated with Subtracter family members, you will find that their core issues always point to the fact that they don't fully understand who they are.

Every person in your family has the very same needs. They need to know that they were born with power and that they can change their lives by taking an action step. They all need to know that they were born to be valuable, important, powerful and lovable. I like to say that they were born to be a loved VIP. If you look just under the crisis and chaos associated with Subtracter family members, you will find that their core issues always point to the fact that they don't fully understand who they are. They do not know what it means to live like someone who is powerful, important and valuable. Many of them have never felt as though they were loved for who they are.

I received a letter from a woman whose stepfather was a huge Subtracter in her life. She was in her mid-forties, but still severely impacted by her Subtracter. Her stepfather had taken away her confidence, sense of well-being and self-esteem. The woman had been damaged for life. Another young woman confessed to having a family full of Subtracters. Her boss sent her to me for executive coaching, but her primary issue was not the workplace but the impact of her subtracting family. We may think that we can leave our lives at the door of our workplaces, but we cannot. When you walk into your office you bring your history and family with you. Workplaces are filled with people who are unproductive and ineffective because of the chaos in their subtracting families. Many people will never deal with their Subtracter family members because it is too painful and the consequences are unpredictable. You must be prepared to suffer the consequences of dealing with a Subtracter family member - which could include being isolated, marginalized, talked about and emotionally hurt. As you begin this work, be ready for emotional and psychological pain. Get ready to have your character and integrity tested. And finally, be patient with the process. Your family member did not become a Subtracter in a day and it will take time, energy and persistence to deal with them.

Where to Start?

The first step is to take a long look at your family members. Is there a particular family member who has been a Subtracter in your life? Is that member a *Situational*, *Socialized* or *Chronic* Subtracter? What is their personality? Why have you identified them as a Subtracter in your life?

Family Member(s)	Type	Personality	Why Did You Identify Them?
1.			
2.			
3.			
4.			
5.			

How have they subtracted from your life?

Identifying a family member Subtracter is an "ah-ha" experience. It's as if a light goes on in your heart and mind and you can finally see the family member for who they have been in your life. It is often a painful but liberating experience. However, it's not enough to acknowledge certain family members as Subtracters. You must also be "real" about how they are subtracting from your life. You cannot change their negative influence and impact in your life if you are not willing to think long and hard about their roles in your life. Take a moment to reflect on how a family member has subtracted from your life. Be real. Be honest!

1. How do they talk to you? Do they talk to you in a condescending way? Are they sarcastic? Are they talking

down to you? Are they mean to you? Are they swearing at
you? Do they talk to you as if you are a child?

---

2. How do they treat you? Do they treat you as if you are
   someone important? Do they treat you as if you are a nobody?
   When you come into the room, do they even say hello? Do
   they acknowledge you? How do they treat you in public? How
   do they treat you in private?

---

3. How do they feel about you? You can tell from family member's actions and attitude how they feel about you. The uncle who doesn't speak to you at family events or only has something negative to say is using his actions to tell you how he feels. The father who finds every opportunity to make fun of you, to remind you of your past failures or makes you feel as though you don't belong or are not good enough is also sharing his thoughts.

_____

_____

_____

_____

_____

4. What do they believe about your future? What do they believe that you can and cannot do? When you bring up an idea, what do they say? Do they encourage you? Do they try to keep you from pursuing your goals? Do they discourage you?

_____

_____

_____

_____

_____

5. What do they tell their friends about you? How do they talk
   about you to other people?

_____

_____

_____

_____

_____

_____

6. What are they taking from you? Are they taking your integrity,
   faith, sense of humor? Are they taking material objects or
   money?

_____

_____

_____

_____

_____

_____

Blatant versus Subtle Subtracters

Your family Subtracters can be blatant or subtle. Blatant
Subtracters are *Snipper-Nippers*, *Shamers*, *Gamers*, and *Blamers*. They
shame and blame you in front of other family members. They talk
about you, talk you down and play emotional games with you. Blatant
Subtracters keep you emotionally unstable and unsure about your life.
They thrive on your co-dependency and inability to make decisions.

The classic example is the daughter in her thirties who cannot make a decision without seeking her mother's opinion. She is co-dependent, and continually enabled by her Subtracter mother. Then there is the Subtracter who only calls when they are in trouble, needs money or wants to get you caught up in their drama. Blatant Subtracters are obvious and typically known by the whole family but they are rarely confronted.

Subtle Subtracters are the *Smilers, Worriers* and *Dreamers*. These family members may even appear to be adding to you, but are really taking your confidence and creating self doubt. Little by little, they pick you apart, by questioning your goals, dreams and vision. *Subtle Subtracters* play games with your sense of self by saying things like, "I told you that you shouldn't have done that" or "what makes you think that you can do that?" They use passive-aggressive approaches to get back at you, share your mistakes, and gossip about you. The *Subtle Subtracter* creates no-win financial situations and relies on you to bail them out. For example, maybe your *Smiler Subtracter* aunt, has gotten involved in another multi-level home party sales business and wants you to access your networks and resources to help her host her first party. This is not the first venture in which she has nicely asked you to participate. The only problem is that you usually get stuck with providing all of the responsibility and resources for the party.

Emotional Traps

Because of the important place "Just Is" Subtracters can have in our lives, it's easy for them to trap us emotionally and take our power. With one statement, action or attitude, a "Just Is" Subtracter can leave you feeling emotionally paralyzed, psychologically immobile and confused. You experience an emotional override and lose all objectivity. Before you can strategically

> *If you think that you need someone else to change your life, you will be trapped for life!*

manage your Subtracter family member, you must understand the most common "Just Is" emotional traps and learn how to avoid them.

"You Owe Me"

Subtracter family members feel entitled to everything you have because of what they have done for you. They will use the "you owe me" trap to access whatever you have - time, money, positive energy and resources. When you finally decide to deal with your Subtracter mother by having a hard conversation about her negative actions, she will make you feel guilty by reminding you of how much she has done for you. The Subtracters goal is to short circuit your attempt to deal with their Subtracter behavior.

"You Need Me"

This emotional trap questions your value and importance. The core message is that you are not whole without your Subtracter family member. The Subtracter wife who says to her husband "You are not going to be anybody without me because you need me," is playing on his need for love and acceptance. If a Subtracter can convince you that no matter how negative they are, you still need them, then they can take your power and subtract from you at will. Why is this emotional trap so serious? Because it is deeply connected to our sense of belonging and self-esteem. It also defies the very definition of personal power: *My ability to think a thought and do something about my life by taking an action step.* It is your ability to change your life - not the ability of your family member. If you think that you need someone else to change your life, you will be trapped for life!

"You Hurt My Feelings"

This is the most common trap used to stop you from dealing with the reality of what Subtracters are taking from your life. It doesn't matter if you hurt them yesterday or fifteen years ago, a Subtracter family member feels as though they have earned the right to subtract from you because of this hurt. I recently coached an elderly gentleman who confessed that his wife was being a Subtracter because of something he had done thirty years ago. She had never forgotten or forgiven him, and now uses that hurt as her excuse for devaluing and belittling him. The Subtracter family member uses this hurt as their excuse for not feeling loved, important and valuable. They hold you in an emotional prison of trying to fill this void in their self-esteem. The reality, of course, is that no one can truly take or give you back your value, importance, love or power. It is already in you, and you just have to realize and use it.

"You Should Be Thankful"

Obligation is one of the most common reasons for dysfunctional behavior in families. Even the most obvious Subtracter family members will remind you that you should be thankful for that one thing they did for you ten years ago. They feel entitled to subtract from you because you should just be thankful. The abusive father thinks that you should be thankful because he has kept a job and provided for his family. After all, you had a house to live in, food on the table, and college tuition. They use this emotional trap of gratitude to justify their negative actions. Subtracter family members will trap you into feeling obligated to them for life. Getting out will take persistence, courage and confidence.

"That's Just the Way our Family Is."

This trap tricks you into accepting your Subtracter family member's behavior as normal. I will never forget being in a professional meeting with a woman who swore like it was the most natural thing to do. I was both surprised and disappointed by her words. The first time it happened, I thought she might apologize and correct herself. When I realized that she was totally unaware of what she was doing, I decided to address it. To my surprise, she said, "Well, that is just the way our family is. My mother swears, I swear and my kids swear. We just swear in our family." Following our conversation, I had to make it clear that I could not accept swearing as a part of our professional relationship and that I needed her to make a conscious effort to stop. Swearing had become so normal to this woman that she had to stop and think about why her actions were unacceptable. If a family member can convince you that subtracting is normal, then you will never challenge them. At some point, you have to take a hard look at subtracting behavior and its negative impact on your life.

Dr. Na'im Akbar[17] is a well-known scholar, whose research on the five parts of self helps describes "that's just the way my family is" trap. Dr. Akbar found that every person is raised in a particular type of environmental box which teaches them what life is all about. In their environmental box, people learn about what is "normal". These norms can either help or hinder your life. What is interesting about the environmental box is that most people never question the norms they were raised with; they just accept them. So, if your environmental box taught you to be a Subtracter, then you can spend your entire life thinking it is normal to take from others. So the question is, are

---

17 Akbar, Na'im, Hilliard III, Asa G. (1998). Know Thy Self. Mind Productions & Associates, Inc: Tallahassee, FL

you comfortable with the norms in your life? If a family member's words and actions consistently result in your feeling less valuable, less important, less lovable and less powerful, then they are being Subtracters! You can no longer accept your environmental box. You must challenge the negative norms and change them.

"Why Can't You Be Like Someone Else?"

Comparing you with other family members, is a "Just Is" Subtracter's way of making you doubt yourself and keeping you in your place. A parent will tell one child, "Why can't you be like your brother?" The fact is that you have never been and never will be your brother. You don't have the same gifts, talents, abilities, goals and dreams. You are who you are. Maybe your sister is tall and graceful but you are athletic, humorous, or intelligent. The goal of your Subtracter family member is to convince you that you are not good enough just being you. You get trapped into thinking that you cannot be successful unless you are trying to be like another family member. People spend a lifetime wishing they were like someone else and, in the process, fail to ever become their most powerful excellent self.

"What Will People Say?"

Are you a public success but a private failure? Does your family look and act as if they have it all together, but when the doors are closed and no one else is watching, you live in constant chaos and crisis? Have you spent your life protecting a public image that is really a facade of private pain and struggle? Often this happens in families with dysfunctions related to all types of abuse - physical, alcohol, emotional and drug. Publicly, the family seems healthy and happy but, privately, the power of subtraction is pervasive. People fake happiness, when in fact, their lives are being destroyed by

Subtracter family members. This trap is prevalent in our society because no one wants to look bad in front of others. We are afraid that if other people know our real pain, they would reject us. So we live in the trap of "what will people say?"

I have come to the place in my life where I have simply decided to be a private success even if it means looking like a public failure. What does it mean to be a private success? It is understanding how to become your most excellent self by being clear about who you are, why you are, what you will do, what you won't do, where you are going and how to add to your life, family and world.

Have you been caught in a Subtracter family member's emotional trap? Which trap? How long have you been trapped? Who has trapped you? How have those traps impacted your life? What will you do to escape the trap? Take a moment to study your list of "Just Is" Subtracters. Then write about the traps they have used to subtract from your life. As you do this work, you will find yourself getting back to understanding the core issues concerning your "Just Is" Subtracters. In doing this work you may find out that there are some things you have to change about yourself. Beware that the core reality of why you are trapped may be very painful, but don't let the pain stop you. There is a saying that people who are successful learn how to play with pain. You cannot get your power back without experiencing emotional pain. Decide to free yourself from emotional traps, no matter how painful it may be!

Family Member	Empotional Trap	How Will You Escape?

Break Old Agreements that Strengthen Your "Just Is"

Subtracters

Every family has agreements that govern how they operate as a unit. These are unspoken contracts created between individual family members about how to treat and interact with each other. Agreements dictate how much a Subtracter family member takes from you. They give you invisible boundaries about what you should or should not say and do. In marriage, your agreement to allow your spouse to yell at you or sarcastically put you down determines how much you are willing to challenge him or her. Some couples have an agreement to play emotional tennis - one person says something critical, then the other sends back the critical remark with more intensity, and thus the game begins. The agreement is to keep this emotional match going until someone loses. In the meantime, the couple walks away from the game feeling emotionally broken and stripped of their power, confidence, and self-esteem. Do you have to continue living with negative agreements between you and your Subtracter family member?

No. So how do you break old agreements and create new ones?

Step 1 – Articulate the agreement

You cannot break an old agreement without first saying what it is. For most people, this is the hardest but most critical step in breaking agreements between you and your Subtracter family member. Identifying a family member as a Subtracter is easy, but it's much harder to say why you have allowed them to continue subtracting from you. In my coaching practice, people will weep as they verbalize the agreements that have kept them from dealing with their "Just Is" Subtracters.

Step 2 – Get to the root of how the agreement was initially created

Was the agreement made through simple positioning in the family? (E.g., your mom can say or do whatever she wants because she's the mother)? Was the agreement made out of habit? (E.g., your mom visits each child's home whenever she wants to, says whatever she wants to, and stays as long as she likes)? Was it instigated by a specific incident? (E.g. your sister got a divorce and now expects you to pick up the pieces of her life and regularly babysit her kids)? Is it a family pattern? (E.g. your dad was an alcoholic, now your brother is drinking heavily and depending on you to bail them out of their chaos and drama)? Was it created out of fear? (E.g. you are afraid of losing a relationship so you accept subtracting behavior instead of challenging it)? Was it the result of your own lack of self-esteem? (E.g. you think your sister is better than you so you let her talk you down)?

Step 3 – Take action to break the agreement

Agreements cannot be broken unless you know what they are and are willing to do something about them. For example, if a "Just Is" Subtracter repeatedly calls you "stupid," and you do not say

When you learn how to stop giving them your power, you can also decrease their negative impact in your life.

anything to them, your brain will process it as a truth and soon you will believe it. If a parent repeatedly tells a child that they will not be anything in life, then sooner or later that child will internalize that message. The key to breaking an agreement is that you must say or do something to directly address it. You must use your words and actions. Ignoring an agreement only strengthens it. If your spouse plays emotional tennis with you, then you must decide to put down your tennis racket and walk away from the conversation. Refuse to return that negative comment and tell your spouse that you cannot talk with them until they are ready to be positive and respectful.

For many people, taking an action step to break an old agreement might be the hardest thing you have ever done. It takes courage, confidence and personal power to speak up and challenge your Subtracter family member. Many people spend a lifetime quietly dealing with negative agreements. But in their hearts there is unforgiveness, resentment, pain and offense. Take a moment and think about your "Just Is" Subtracters. What agreements have you made with them? If you don't know the agreement or if it doesn't come to you right away, start thinking about how they talk to you, how they treat you, how they make you feel, and what they believe about you. Breaking old agreements is the first major step in dealing with the "Just Is" Subtracters in your life.

Family Member	Agreements	Action Steps to Break Them?

Stop Giving Up Your Power

Your "Just Is" Subtracters can impact your life because they have learned how to take away your personal power. When you learn how to stop giving them your power, you can also decrease their negative impact in your life. It's time to take back your power. What does that mean? It means choosing your own destiny and no longer allowing your Subtracter family members to dictate your life. That sounds good, but where do you start?

1. Stop giving your Subtracter family members the road map to your emotions.

Have you taught them how to make you feel guilty, afraid, worried or intimidated? Have you shown them your emotional hot buttons? How do you stop giving away your positive emotional energy? Change your responses or reactions to them. For example, when your brother calls at 10:00 p.m. because he has been arrested for driving under the influence again, don't go and rescue him! Tell him that you cannot bail him out again. Of course your brother will throw an emotional temper tantrum. He might swear and accuse you of not caring and trying to judge him. He will try to manipulate and control your emotional energy and leave you feeling guilty for not coming to his rescue. His goal is to interrupt your life, change your plans and dictate your resources. You can stop giving away your power by changing your emotional response.

2. Protect your time. Refuse to have your time wasted.

Stop giving away your time to your Subtracter family members. Your sister who only calls when she has an emergency and needs help with her kids will continue this pattern until you finally tell her "No, I cannot take care of your kids today." When your mother calls for the tenth time, don't answer the call. One woman with a Subtracter mother literally stopped answering her door and acted as though she was not even home because she knew her mother was coming by to waste her time and put her down. She finally changed her work schedule because her mother knew exactly when she was going to be home. The woman decided to restructure her relationship with her mother by limiting the amount of time with her mother. When your daughter wants to come to your house again so that she can complain about her husband and children, let her know that you have other plans and will not be at home.

What if your "Just Is" Subtracter is an adult child who has asked to live with you because they are unemployed. Maybe, they are not interested in finding employment, only in wasting your time complaining about how hard life is and how they lost their job. In the meantime, you spend your time trying to connect them to resources and people. You find yourself looking through newspaper ads and employment sites on the Internet, while your adult child sleeps late, hangs out, eats your food, watches television and uses your cell telephone minutes.

On a recent flight home, I sat next to a woman who allowed her 30-year-old daughter to move back home because she was single, unemployed and trying to get her life back together again. Her daughter was supposed to be finding employment but instead spent her time socializing with her mother, hanging out with her boyfriend and making excuses for why she couldn't find a job. The woman asked me what she should do. I looked at the woman and calmly said, "Give your daughter three months to get a job and her life together and, if she is not employed and contributing to your household by that time, put her out!" The woman's eyes widened and, choking back her tears, she said, "I don't think I can do that." This woman's daughter was invading her life, controlling her time and consuming her resources. Does this mean that you should not spend time with your family? Absolutely not. As a matter of fact, when you decide to take your power back you will find yourself spending more quality time with your family members and feeling more powerful and positive.

3. Stop telling "Just Is" Subtracters your business.

Subtracters have a "need to know" what is going on in your life. They are like trained attorneys who know how to cross examine you until you expose your entire life to them. Information is power to Subtracter family members. The more they know, the more of your power they can take. First they gather your information, then they put a spin on it, and use it to take your power. They manipulate your information to control, blame, shame and game you. If you are experiencing difficulty in your marriage, at work or with your children, do not tell your Subtracter aunt, the family gossip, who has never liked you, but who loves to pretend like she really cares so that she can gather your information and spread it to your family members.

Do not tell your Subtracter family member anything about your vision, goals, dreams or future plans. Why? Because they will find a way to sabotage you. Remember that a Subtracter's life is built on fear and failure and they are very intimidated by your success. If you share your plan for success with a Subtracter, you can be sure that they will create road blocks for you. Your Subtracter family member cannot celebrate your success so stop looking to them for encouragement and motivation. On the contrary they will look for opportunities to minimize your success. In my seminars I teach people that when a "Just Is" Subtracter asks you how you are doing, your response should be a simple, "I am doing great!" Don't give Subtracters any signals that you are doing anything other than fine. Don't say another word, just look at them and smile. If you want to get your power back from a Subtracter family member, stop telling them anything significant about your life.

4. Stop giving your Subtracter family members your money or resources.

What are you giving to your Subtracter family members? Do you give them money, clothes, food, temporary housing? Are you lending them your car, bus pass, frequent flyer miles? Are you letting them use your credit card? It's time to stop giving your Subtracter any money or resources. You cannot take back your power from a Subtracter if you are not willing to stop giving them your money and resources. If your Subtracter family member needs money again, then you must be willing to say "No, I cannot give you any money." Do not apologize or explain why you cannot give them the money, just say "no!" If your Subtracter cousin asks to borrow your car, tell them "no." It's your car and you have the right to decide who will drive it. If your children have a pattern of being financially irresponsible and asking you for money to get them out of crisis, you must say "no", even though it might be the hardest thing you will ever do. The first time you say no, they will press your emotional buttons and make you feel guilty. Some Subtracters will even demand that you explain yourself. But take your power back by saying no and soon your Subtracters will stop asking you.

5. Don't recommend your trusted networks to Subtracter family members.

The easiest way to damage your reputation and integrity is to refer a Subtracter family member to your trusted networks. If you know that your sister has a habit of not paying her bills, don't put your reputation on the line by recommending friends to do contracting work on her house. When she doesn't pay, you will get stuck with the bill. When a "Just Is" Subtracter asks for your help in finding a service or resource, be careful not to connect them with your personal networks because they could ruin your relationships. Instead, suggest they look in the phone book or on the Internet.

Do not recommend anyone from your personal network.

Seven Strategies for Getting Your Power Back

Now that you have stopped giving away your power to your "Just Is" Subtracters, it's time to get it back. There are seven strategies to getting your power back.

Strategy #1 – See the innocence

Step back, think about your "Just Is" Subtracters and ask yourself the question, "Do they know what they are doing?" Give yourself the opportunity to see the innocence in your Subtracter family members. Could it be that they are clueless about how they are using their power to subtract?

Strategy #2 – Get to the real issue

Find out why your family member are Subtracters. Get to the real issues and reasons behind their actions. Think about their patterns of behavior and begin a critical dialogue with them about why they do what they do.

Strategy #3 – Reframe the issue

Once you have gotten to the core issue, reframe it to see their innocence. Reframe how you deal with the Subtracter. That means rethinking your interactions and trying new approaches. For example, instead of ignoring them, you might try to be cordial. Practice being neutral instead of becoming emotional. Offer to help them learn to better manage their money instead of bailing them out. Reframing helps you look at the whole picture while reassessing your role in the relationship.

Strategy #4 – Set new boundaries

Subtracters need boundaries and limitations. There should be a boundary for every aspect of your relationship (e.g. emotion, time, physical space, finances, words). Boundaries help you manage and define the expectations for your relationship. Your new boundary might be to only talk on the phone for ten minutes at a time and not take any phone calls after 8:00 p.m. If your "Just Is" Subtracter is a very negative person, your new boundary might be to make it very clear that you excuse yourself from the conversation if it starts getting negative. Articulate these boundaries to your Subtracters so that they are clear about your expectations and not surprised by your actions.

Strategy #5 – Clarify your role as an Adder

Most Subtracter family members simply want to know that someone cares about them, and thinks that they are important. When you clarify your role as an Adder, you demonstrate that you are committed to increasing the quality of life for your family members. It means that you are committed to being a positive person who will encourage, inspire and create positive changes in your family and your world. You make a commitment to add, but also create an expectation for your Subtracter family member that you expect them to discontinue their subtracting. Remind them that your goal is for them to achieve their potential and to become positive, powerful people. This is tricky because this strategy can only work if your Subtracter family member is ready to become an Adder. Why? Because you cannot add to a Subtracter. You might think you are being an Adder by lending them money, but that is not how the Subtracter sees it. A Subtracter simply thinks they are taking away your power and resources.

Strategy #6 – Forgive and Forget

Look in your heart and forgive your Subtracter for any and everything they have done to you. Refuse to be offended and decide to put all of their subtracting behavior in the past. Even if you decide to move your Subtracter family member out of your inner circle, still release them from everything they did to hurt you. Refuse to be held prisoner by your pain. Free yourself from the power of your Subtracter by forgiving them and moving on with your life. Get to the place where you can treat your Subtracter family member with civility without giving them your power. Forgiveness is one of the most powerful tools you were given to increase your personal power. Is it easy? No. Is it doable? Absolutely.

One day as I sat working on this book in a local park, an elderly man, about 85- years-old, sat on a bench and said hello. I returned his greeting. After a brief casual conversation, he began to tell me about his two brothers who were Subtracters. He didn't know they were Subtracters, but as he talked about them it was obvious to me. These men felt they were obligated and entitled to things. They sued their own 101-year-old mother because they wanted to make sure that they got their part of her estate. Sadly, this woman was in a nursing home where her estate was paying for her care. The man's brothers were not willing to take care of her, but wanted to "protect" their inheritance. The mother was deeply hurt by her two sons turned on her so they could collect an early inheritance.

No words could really describe the pain this brother felt watching his brothers betray his mother. I could see the silent cry and pain in his eyes. But the most painful part for me was seeing the unforgiveness that this man had for his brothers. I knew in my heart that he would go to his death bed trapped in this prison of unforgiveness.

If you are serious about getting your personal power back, then you must forgive your Subtracter family member. Whether you have to meditate on it, ask God for help, journal or even see a counselor or therapist, do the work it takes to forgive. Deal with the pain, push through the pain and choose to forgive.

Strategy #7 – Make a Decision and Take Action

Subtracter family members don't just go away and leave you alone. On the contrary, the longer you allow them to subtract, the more they will seek to take out of your life. My pastor[18] often says "<u>You will never</u> change what you are willing to tolerate." Like *Fannie*

18 Morrison, Randy, Pastor, Speak the Word Church International, Golden Valley, MN

Lou Hamer[19], the notable American voting rights activist and civil rights leader said, you have to get *"sick and tired of being sick and tired"* before you decide to do whatever it takes to create change in your life and world. You must get to the place where you are "sick and tired" of Subtracter family members devaluing your life, and taking your power. Make a decision <u>today</u> to deal with them, then create a plan to start the process.

The Most Difficult "Just Is" Subtracters

Mothers, Spouses and Children

One of the most painful realities in life is dealing with the fact that your mother, spouse or child is a Subtracter. Why is this so difficult? Because all of us want to believe in our heart of hearts that these people love us and want the best for us. Many of us are afraid that if we challenge or confront these particular family members, they will reject us. Secretly, we are afraid of being unloved and alone. So what do we do? We tolerate them as Subtracters in our lives and suffer silently. Isn't it time to do something about your Subtracter husband, wife, mother or child? Life is very rewarding when you realize your ability to make changes that can positively influence your life, family and world. But making changes can also be incredibly frightening and intimidating. Many people choose to live with pain and dysfunction and settle for a life of powerlessness and hopelessness, because they are afraid to change. The fact is that no one can change your life but you. God cannot even change your life until you decide that you want to change. God has already given you the power to change your life so now it's up to you!

---

19 Mills, Kay. (1994) This Little Light of Mine: The Life of Fannie Lou Hamer. Plume Publisher, Santa Cruz, CA

Of all the strategies presented in this book, the one that works most effectively with the most difficult Subtracter family members is the *Private Snatching*. This level of *private snatching* with a family member is different than the one you might have with your best friend or co-worker. Conducting a *Private Snatching* should be the last resort, not your first course of action. Why? Because it will take more research, time and risk. First, you must be prepared to be totally honest and vulnerable. Second, you must intentionally address those emotional traps a family member has used to subtract from you. Third, you must be comfortable with the outcome whether it is good, bad, ugly or indifferent. Fourth, you must be ready to forgive, forget and move on. Fifth, you must be willing to deal with the pain.

So where do you start?

1. Take the time to plan the *Private Snatching*. The more you prepare, the better the outcome. This is not a casual conversation. Anticipate the *private snatching* from every angle. Do your research. Know what you want and why you are doing it.

> *Example:* Write out the plan – include major issues you want to address, and your desired outcome. Invite your mother out to dinner and conduct the *private snatching* during dessert.

2. Begin your conversation by addressing the old agreement and state your intention for creating a new agreement.

Example: Reassure your husband of your love and commitment, then share the old agreement and how his subtracting has impacted you over the years. Then tell him how you expect to be treated from now on.

3. Guarantee confidentiality and finality. Keep in mind that the most difficult "Just Is" Subtracters are very powerful people in your life and, even though you are committed to confidentiality, it doesn't mean that they are willing to do the same. However, when you keep their confidence, over time they will come to respect you.

Example: Reassure your mother that you will not share this conversation with anyone else in the family and that once the conversation is finished you will not reference it again.

4. Admit to giving away your power.

Example: Explain to your mother how you have allowed her to take your power and why you have decided to take your power back. Focus on your reasons on changing your life and going on to your next level of excellence.

5. Articulate the core reasons for giving up your power.

Example: Explain to your wife why you have allowed her to devalue your life and take your power. Be totally honest – you were afraid she might leave you, you didn't want to be rejected, you were intimidated.

6.   Commit to being an Adder.

Example: Reassure your child that you want to add to their life but you have non-negotiable expectations for them. Clearly state your expectations.

7.   Stay with the tension and it will get intense! Prepare for the moments when you will want to hold them responsible for your pain. Stay with the tension but resist those moments when you feel like becoming emotionally unstable and unbalanced.

Example: Resist the temptation to blame, shame, game, lose your temper, or have an emotional temper tantrum. Pause for ten seconds, take a breath, calm your mind, be present and listen with your heart, soul and spirit.

8.   Stay focused on the core issues. Don't let go of the core truths that you want to address. Refuse to be taken as an emotional hostage. Take a deep breath. Review your plan and desired outcome. Remember to listen and think critically about what you want and why.

Example: Take a moment to review your notes and bring the dialog back to your goals for the conversation.

9. Bring closure to the conversation and be prepared for the
    consequences.

    Example: Accept your mother's reaction and thank her for the
    conversation. Reassure her of your confidentiality. Review
    the reasons why you wanted to have the conversation. Review
    the outcomes and the change you are prepared to make in the
    relationship.

Create your Private Snatching Plan

1. What research do you have to do before starting the process?

2. What core issues do you want to address?

3. What evidence do you have that those issues exist?

4. How have you given away your power?

_____

_____

_____

_____

5. Why have you given away your power?

_____

_____

_____

_____

6. What do you want to accomplish?

_____

_____

_____

_____

7. What are you willing to change about you?

_____

_____

_____

_____

8. How could it help or hurt your relationship?

_____

_____

_____

_____

9. When and where will you conduct the Private Snatching?

_____

_____

_____

_____

10. What are the possible outcomes? How will you deal with them?

_____

_____

_____

_____

My goal is for you to realize your personal power, and to use your personal power to positively change your life and become your most excellent self. This cannot happen if your "Just Is" Subtracters continue to take your power, devalue your life and decrease your options to choose a positive destiny. You cannot get to your next level of excellence without understanding your Birth Right and personal power. You must claim your right to be valuable, important, lovable and powerful. Managing your "Just Is" Subtracters will take time, thought, heart and power. Begin by studying this chapter and doing the exercises. Then take the time to create your plan and begin implementing it one strategy at a time. As you begin taking action, your personal power will increase and you will gain the courage and confidence to use more strategies. Be patient and little by little you will regain and reclaim your personal power from your "Just Is" Subtracters. Don't wait to change your life. Start today by dealing with your Subtracter family members.

Now What Will You Do?

This book was created by the voices of people of every color, culture, ethnicity, religion and gender who all suffered from the silent cry, "What can I do about my Subtracters?" The question is: How long will you suffer from the silent cry? Isn't it time to release your life from the power of Subtracters? There is a verse in the *Holy Bible* that says "weeping may endure for a night, but joy comes in the morning."[20] What does that mean? It's time to stop crying and take a long hard look at the realities of what Subtracters are doing in and to your life. It's time to use your personal power to deal with your Subtracters and change your life! Those days of suffering silently are over! It's not too late. You can recover from the pain and damage caused by your Subtracters. It's time to get your smile, joy, peace and success back. It's time to get your power and life back! I believe that every person was born to be powerful, successful and happy. Days before completing this book, a woman sent me an e-mail expressing her gratitude for a presentation I had given about the four types of powerful people, and shared her story about a long time Subtracter friend. After many years and attempts to add to her friend, she realized that you cannot add to a Subtracter. She went on to share that letting go of her Subtracter was like moving out of the clouds and seeing sunshine again.

A Moment to Stand Alone

A natural consequence of dealing with your Subtracters is that for a moment you might feel like you are all alone. You might feel

---

20   *Holy Bible* - New International Version. Psalm 30:5

as though you no longer have people with whom to talk or spend time. This is the place where most people give in and go back to their Subtracters. Resist the emotions that draw you back into the drama cycle and chaos of your Subtracters. Why? Because the fact is that you had given up your power and potential for a fulfilled life to Subtracters for too long. You had become comfortable with the silent cry. You had given away your potential for success and happiness and settled for just getting by. It takes time and space to regain your power and restructure your life. Enduring this moment requires courage and confidence. In the process, remind yourself of who you are - lovable, valuable, important and powerful. Instead of dreading this moment of aloneness, embrace it as an opportunity to reignite your positive energy, power and fire for life!

Stay with the Tension

Changing your life is not easy but it is doable! Expect and accept the tension that comes along with dealing with Subtracters or moving them out of your life. Maybe you only had one mild Subtracter and immediately understood how to deal with them from reading this book. But what if your entire life was clogged with Subtracters? Then you will experience more tension and a greater sense of loneliness. Do not rush the moment or run away from the tension. Simply take time to breathe, reflect and redesign your life. Your moment might last for a week or two years. Accept this moment of tension as a blessing and space for creating a power paradigm shift in your life from subtracting to the power of adding. However long, stay with the tension and dare to change your life!

Become a Severe Adder

How do you live a long, productive, healthy and happy life? In a recent book, entitled "The Blue Zone," the author/researcher Dan Buettner writes about his world-wide research on people who have lived the longest. What were some of the lessons he learned? First, the things that give you extra quality years and make you look and feel younger are easy and don't cost anything. Second, you have to be very careful about who is in your life. Third, you must have a sense of purpose. People who live long, healthy lives are connected to their religion and volunteer regularly.[21] Why is this study important? Because it clearly points out how critical it is to navigate the power of people in your life and the importance of using your personal power to add to your community. The most effective way to deal with feeling alone and with that moment of tension is to reclaim your personal power to add. Look around your neighborhood, community or religious organizations and you will find endless opportunities to be an Adder. Become a mentor to a younger person; volunteer with a nonprofit; get involved in your church, mosque or synagogue; volunteer with your workplace to support a local school or community organization. Becoming a severe Adder means that you are intentionally, actively and consistently adding to others. And what is the secret? As you stop giving away your power to Subtracters and begin to add to your community, you will plant the seeds of adding in your life. As you continue to add, the law of seed-time-harvest will take effect in your life. You will shift the power paradigm and begin attracting Adders into your life.

21 Buettner, Dan (2008). The Blue Zone: Lessons for Living Longer From the People Who've Lived the Longest. National Geographic. Article in the Minneapolis Star Tribune – April 1, 2008 – "Live & Learn" by Randy A. Salas

Create a Vision Plan for Your Life

Who do you want to be? What do you want in life? What do you want from life?

What do you want your life to accomplish? In 2005, the principal from a local high school asked me to help him keep girls from fighting, being suspended, joining gangs and failing in school. They literally had "girl fights" every week, sometimes everyday. To help solve his problem, I founded an organization called *Girls in Action™*. Saying "yes" to the principal was a life-changing experience for me because it gave me an amazing opportunity to become a severe Adder to my community. After working with one hundred girls, in the first year of the program, I learned three important lessons. First, most of our girls had friends who were Subtracters. Second, most of the girls had never had a female role model or mentor who consistently taught them how to be powerful, productive, positive and successful young women. Third, most of our girls had no vision or plan for their future. I realized once again that Subtracters are a powerful force who decrease your pathways to success in life. I also profoundly understood the phenomenon that you cannot be what you cannot see. Our girls had to see successful female Adders before they could see themselves being that. And I understood in my bones that "without a vision, people do perish." [22] Our girls were preparing to leave high school with no vision and no plan for their futures. This was critical because, without a plan for your future, you will return to a life loaded with Subtracters. The combination of feeling lonely with having no Adders, no vision and no plan leaves an open door for your Subtracters. Don't look back or go back. Move forward in your life, even if it's hard and painful!

---

22 Holy Bible - New International Version. Proverbs 29:18

How do you avoid going back to your past? Create a vision for your future. Remember that vision calls you into the future and towards your most excellent self.

Your life might be busy, but I encourage you to make and take the time to create your plan. Be honest and give yourself the freedom to think, dream and hope. A plan is an excellent way to use your personal power to add to yourself and your world.

Your Personal Vision

What do you want to do, be, or become? What change do you want to make in your life, community and world? How do you want to impact your family, community and world? How do you want to help others? What do you want to be known for? What legacy do you want to leave? Write your vision statement. Do not limit yourself by what others have said about you. You have the power to create the life you want!

Your Inner Circle

You might not have the exact names, but list the types of people you want in your inner circle. Do you want an Adder? Do you want a personable or productive person? Are there some Adders you let go of because of Subtracters? Invite them back into your inner circle. Restructure your inner circle to include at least five Adders. They should have different purposes and different roles, but they should all have a goal of adding to your life.

_____

_____

_____

_____

_____

_____

_____

_____

Your Role as an Adder

How will you be an Adder at work and in your personal life? What kind of Adder do you want to be to your co-workers? What kind of Adder do you want to be to your friends and family? One of my personal goals is to have my children choose me even though I am a "Just Is" person. I want to add to the lives of my children, not because they are my "Just Is" people, but because I think that they are phenomenal people whom I love with all my heart and soul. Who do you want to be as an Adder? What do you want to bring into people's lives? How will you avoid being a Subtracter at work and home?

Share Your Lessons Learned

Having read this book, what lessons will you share or teach to someone else? What strategies did you use in dealing with your Subtracters? What strategies will you share with others?

Write Your Goals

What are your short and long term goals for your personal and professional life? What do you want to accomplish in your life? How will you know you have accomplished your goals?

Short Term Goals (one minute to two years)

Long Term Goals (three to five years)

Benchmarks of Success

You cannot get to your future by focusing on your past. Your past will never change but your future can. Now that you have taken back your power and know how to deal with the Subtracters in your life, how will you know that you are a powerful, successful person who is valuable, important and lovable? How will you know that you have achieved success in your life? How will you know that you have become your most excellent self? What will be the benchmarks for your success?

```
_____

_____

_____

_____

_____

_____
```

My Hope for You

Why do I do my work? Because I believe in my bones that God made us all to be productive, powerful, prosperous, successful and happy people. We were not created to simply struggle in life, then die! No, we were born to live, learn, lead and positively change our life and world. We were born with power and my hope is that you will avoid using your power to Subtract and will commit to being an Adder to yourself, family, workplace and world. You do not have to suffer with the silent cry. You can free yourself from the power of Subtracters so why not do it!

My hope is that you have learned how to escape the Subtracter socialization process and avoid being a Subtracter. My goal is that you have gained the strategies and now have the courage and confidence to effectively deal with Subtracters in the workplace, and manage the "Just Is" Subtracters in your life.

I hope that you will change your life, then help someone else do the same. I hope that you will give attention to the silent cry in your family, community and workplace and have the courage to share the strategies learned from this book. Do not keep this information to yourself. Share it through your actions and words with those in your circle of influence.

No matter what has happened in your life-good, bad, ugly or indifferent- remember that you have everything that you need to change your life. Changing your life does not require money, status or material goods. You simply need to decide to use your personal power to positively change your life and world. My hope is that you have the faith and determination to put the strategies from this book into action, and you will not give in to your Subtracters but will stay with the tension and take back your power! My hope is that you will regain your personal power and reclaim your most excellent self.

Acknowledgements

I thank God for loving me, for giving me His wisdom, and for giving me His Son, Jesus Christ. I am humbled that God would use me to write, teach and mentor others. I thank God for my husband, mentor, and friend, Shane Martin Price, a true Adder and Multiplier who loves, supports, challenges, and encourages me. I thank God for my children Justice Cameron, and twins, Cornelius Scott and Ktyal Liberty Amani who have taught me love, compassion, determination, and a severe respect for humanity. I give honor to God for blessing us with the little one in my womb who slowed me down enough to complete this project.

I thank God for my J. Cameron & Associates team who gave me the space and time to complete this book while patiently supporting me throughout the process. Thanks to the many readers who completed my first book and encouraged me to write this one.

A special thanks to my publishing team, Pat Hensler, my transcriber; C.C. Strom, my editor who spent numerous hours transforming the transcriptions of my spoken word into a working written format; Deanna Moore my desktop publisher; Tee Simmons, the artist who created the original art work for the book cover; Anna Fabian, my graphic designer who created the book cover; and, Gerry Nystrom and his team from Nystrom Publishing, my printer and a supporter and partner in this work.

My sincere and humble thanks for the many people who have supported, prayed for, encouraged and challenged me throughout this process. Thanks to my mentors, Alice Journey, M.A., L.P., Dr. Pamela Toole, Dr. Marilyn Weldin and Wokie Weah for their words of wisdom, encouragement and expertise. Special thanks to my *Girls in Action*™ team of women leaders who continue to inspire and motivate me to pursue excellence in every area of my life. Special thanks to Coffee on Broadway owners, Tom and Barb Richardson, who willingly offered up their coffee shop as a quiet place to write, and provided me with great food and a tasty chai tea. And special thanks to the readers who took the time to review this book and give me their constructive feedback, praise and encouragement.

Verna Cornelia Price, Ph.D.
2008

About the Author

Verna Cornelia Price, Ph.D., is the founder, president and principal consultant of J. Cameron & Associates, an organization committed to empowering and motivating people to realize and positively use their personal power. Dr. Verna is an author, organizational consultant, motivational speaker, executive coach, and educator. Her professional experience includes teaching preschool through 6th grade and working as a program director, senior marketing manager, assistant dean of women, director of leadership programs and college professor. In 2002, she created the *Power of People Professional Development Process™* which equips businesses with tools and strategies to empower their employees to new levels of excellence through personal power and leadership. In 2005, Dr. Verna founded *Girls in Action™*, a leadership empowerment project for which she was honored in 2006 with an Ann Bancroft Leadership Award. In 2007, Dr. Verna and her husband co-founded *The Power of People Leadership Institute™*, a nonprofit organization committed to helping people overcome life's obstacles while finding success in every area of life through personal power and leadership. She is the author of numerous research and educational articles and chapters, and the best-selling motivational book, *The Power of People: Four Kinds of People Who Can Change Your Life*. Dr. Verna is a Leadership Institute faculty member at The College of St. Catherine in St. Paul, Minnesota. She received her Ph.D. in Educational Policy and Administration from the University of Minnesota. She is married to Shane Martin Price and is blessed to be the mother of Justice Cameron and twins, Cornelius Scott and Ktyal Liberty Amani.

Dedication

This Bible is given to

Brooke Secreto

by

Teachers Pat & Julie

VMPS   June 10, 2008

on this day of

Since this is **your** Bible now,
go ahead and trace your handprint on the page!

Then start reading to **experience** God's Word!

THE NEW TESTAMENT

Group

Loveland, Colorado

New Living
Translation®

SECOND EDITION

TYNDALE

TYNDALE

Acknowledgments

The following people contributed to the *Hands-On Bible*:

Group Publishing, Inc., editorial team:
Joani Schultz, Sue Geiman, Karl Leuthauser, Jan Kershner, Lyndsay E. Gerwing, Alison Imbriaco

Tyndale House Publishers, Inc., editorial team:
Tim Willms, Betty Free Swanberg, Pat LaCosse, Leanne Roberts, Anisa Baker, Gwen Elliott

Writers:
Linda Anderson, Gwyn Borcherding, Teryl Cartwright, Nancy Wendland Feehrer, Jane Fries, Jennifer Hooks, Allison Hummel, Mikal Keefer, Scott M. Kinner, Gina Leuthauser, Carolyn Luengen, Nappaland Communications, Beth Robinson, Larry Shallenberger, Amy Simpson, Bonnie Temple, Helen Turnbull, Paul Woods

Designers and artists:
Sharon Anderson, Nancy Serbus, Allen Tefft, Stephen Beer, Jeff Spencer, Jacqueline L. Noe, Toolbox Creative

Other artists include Mitch Mortimer, Joe Stites, Vlasta van Kampen, and Matt Wood

THE NEW TESTAMENT

Alphabetical Book Listing

Other Cool Stuff

What's special about the HANDS-ON BIBLE

INTRODUCTIONS

make you want to read *every* book in the Bible!

Check out why the *Hands-On Bible* is the book you can't put down.

These quick, funny overviews are written in a style you can relate to.

COOL Facts!

VALUABLE INFO!

Sends you straight into the BIBLE!

WHAT ELSE?

Every introduction includes a **TIMELINE** to show you when the action took place. Dates from world history add to the fun!

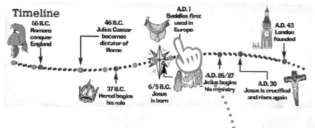

Do you know when the first saddle was used? • Now you do!

A7

39 HANDS-ON BIBLE EXPERIENCES

This Bible will excite, ignite, and invite you to experience the Bible as you read it. **Science experiments, crafts, journals, snacks—** you'll *do* the Bible, which means you'll *learn* the Bible and *remember* the Bible!

Here's what the *Hands-On Bible* offers!

REAL BIBLE LEARNING!

ACTIVE LEARNING!

BUILDS RELATIONSHIPS!

LIFE APPLICATION!

You *love* mysteries and challenges, right? That's why we've included **SECRET MESSAGES** throughout the Bible that send you searching for *other* places in the Bible. Think of it as a Bible treasure hunt! You'll explore the Bible like never before and discover that God's Word is an amazing whole, not just disconnected books under one cover.

Can you find the secret message in this activity?

Grab your magnifying glass and start searching!

L♥ve All Ar♥und

YOU KNOW WHAT A DICTIONARY'S FOR, **RIGHT?**

IT GIVES YOU **DEFINITIONS** OF WORDS.

Well, there's a cool definition in the Bible, too! **Read 1 CORINTHIANS 13:4-7.**
To help you remember everything that love is, make this rolling reminder.

FIRST GATHER

- glue
- cup
- water
- paintbrush
- magazines
- permanent markers
- inexpensive ball (the bigger the better, like a soccer ball).

① In a cup, add a little water to some white glue.

② Look through old magazines, and tear out words that remind you of what the Bible says love is. Use the paintbrush and glue mixture to attach the words to the ball, and paint a little of the mixture over the words so they're smooth.

③ Set the ball on an empty aluminum can to dry.

Find a friend, and bounce the ball to each other. Whatever words your hands land on when you catch the ball, ask yourselves, **"Is this how I treat others?"**

NOW TRY THIS!

BIBLE HERO BIOGRAPHIES

talk straight to you, heart-to-heart. These heroes admit mistakes, joke around, confess when they're scared, and marvel at how God used them. Real people. Real heroes. *Real Bible learning.* And every biography contains a life-application activity!

BIBLE BIOS
Hear From the Heroes

Hi, my name is
SAUL *(religious leader)*

Oh, the stories I could tell! First, you need to know who I really am. (I'm not King Saul of the Old Testament.) I'm sometimes known as Saul of Tarsus, since Tarsus is where I came from. But after I became a follower of Jesus, I became known as Paul. Before I met Jesus, I thought Christians were trying to change our Jewish faith with wrong teachings. So I was all about trying to stop them.

But Jesus stopped me in my tracks—literally! I was on my way to Damascus to nab some more Christians, when Jesus stopped me. A light from heaven shone down on me, and I heard a man's voice but couldn't see anyone! The voice said, "I am Jesus, the one you are persecuting." He told me to go into the city and wait.

When I stood up, I was blind! My friends led me into town, and I stayed there blind for three days. Then God sent a man named Ananias, a believer in Jesus, to restore my sight and get me started on the right path of telling others about Jesus.

God is amazing! Even though I had once tried to stop Christians, God changed my life and used me to spread the truth about Jesus. During my life I went on three big missionary trips. At God's direction and with his inspiration, I wrote a whole bunch of letters to people and churches, many of which are in this very Bible you're reading. I realized that nothing was more important than believing in Jesus!

> For the whole startling story of Saul becoming a Christian, read ACTS 9:1-22.

Key Verse "Do to others whatever you would like them to do to you."—MATTHEW 7:12a
Mirror Image

Read MATTHEW 7:12a out loud with a friend. Say it together a few times.

Place your palms near your friend's palms, about an inch apart. Slowly move your hands while your friend tries to follow your motions. Then switch roles.

You tried to mirror your friend's motions.

Jesus wants us to treat other people exactly how we'd like to be treated—to be a mirror image of how we'd like to be treated! Write this verse on a sticky note on your bathroom mirror to remind you to be a mirror image!

32 KEY VERSE ACTIVITIES

help you learn, understand, and remember important Bible verses. Plus, 63 more great verses are highlighted!

THE JESUS CONNECTION

We want you to grow in your friendship with Jesus—it's our main goal. That's why we've included a feature called THE JESUS CONNECTION in every book introduction and on every Bible Bonanza page. We show you how the focus of the Bible is Jesus!

The book of Matthew is *all* about Jesus. It's one of the four Gospels, the books that tell us about Jesus' life. We get to follow Jesus from birth to death, to his resurrection, and into the clouds as he ascended to heaven. **Thanks to the Gospel writers, we understand who Jesus is—God's Son!—and what his life on earth was all about—reaching out to people with God's gift of love.**

FUN fact

Pack It Up

If you were a Bible-times traveler, you might have carried a **hollowed-out gourd** weighted with a stone for drawing water from wells. You might also have carried a **stick** and a **money belt.** You may not have to travel to tell others about Jesus but you can still be prepared just the same!

What three items can you carry with you to tell others about Jesus?
Maybe you can keep a pocket Bible in your backpack. Or maybe you can write invitations to your church and keep them with you. Write your ideas below.

1. _____
2. _____
3. _____

Then start telling others about Jesus!

LOTS OF FUN FACTS

These FUN FACTS help you understand Bible-times culture, Bible story details, and key biblical concepts. Each Fun Fact helps you see the Bible as true and amazing.

The facts are fun, true, and—yup—hands-on!

How to Know Jesus as Your Personal Savior

God loves us so much that he sent his Son, Jesus, to die on the cross for us. Why would he do that? Here's why!

You've probably figured out by now that you're a sinner. We all are. Jesus died on the cross to take the punishment for our sins. Then he rose again so we could be forgiven for all those wrong things we do. Jesus wants to be our forever friend. If we ask him, Jesus will come into our lives. He will always be with us and help us to make the right choices. If we believe in Jesus, someday we'll live with him forever in heaven.

IT'S SO SIMPLE

The only way to heaven is through faith in Jesus. That's it. It really is that simple. If you think you're ready to invite Jesus into your life, you could pray a prayer similar to this one:

God, I'm sorry for all my sins. Thank you for sending your Son, Jesus, to die on the cross for my sins. Jesus, please come into my heart and guide me to do what's right. Help me to follow you as Lord and Savior, all my life.

Thank you for forgiving me and accepting me right now.

In Jesus' name, amen.

NOW WHAT?

You just made the most important decision of your life. Way to go!

But now what? First, go share the news of your decision with your parents, teacher, or another Christian! Then get ready to grow!

Being a Christian means that we live our lives each day in a way that honors Jesus. When you believe in Jesus, the Holy Spirit comes and changes your heart so that living for God is something you just *want* to do!

Sure, you'll mess up sometimes. But Jesus will always be there to help you back on the right path. Remember, you're never alone. Jesus promises to always be with you. He loves you. He died for you. Now he lives in you. There's nothing better than that!

A great way to get to know Jesus better is by reading your Bible! Here are a few Scriptures to get you started:

- **John 3:16**
- **Romans 5:8-11**
- **Romans 6:23**
- **Ephesians 2:4-8**

What's The 1 Thing?

In Luke, chapter 10, Jesus visits the home of Mary and Martha. As Martha worries about preparing dinner and being a busy servant, she gets upset because Mary isn't helping. But Jesus tells her, "There is only **one thing** worth being concerned about. Mary has discovered it, and it will not be taken away from her."

Martha was doing good work. In fact, she was serving the Lord. But Jesus made it clear what his priority is for us. Even more than serving him, he wants to have a loving relationship with us.

What's the "One Thing"? Many might say it's Jesus. But no, it's a **growing relationship with Jesus**. Martha would have identified serving Jesus as the "One Thing." But Mary better understood the real "One Thing."

A "One Thing" relationship with Jesus resembles in many ways a human-to-human relationship—a friendship. The process of attraction, getting acquainted, enjoying each other's company, having fun, growing closer, and forming a bond of love and devotion is a natural one that lends clues to how a "One Thing" relationship may form.

That's what the *Hands-On Bible* is all about—helping you grow your friendship with Jesus. This Bible lets you do the things you would do with your friends. As you read the Scripture and do the activities, you're building your relationship with Jesus in a real and relevant way.

The Bible comes in several different translations. The one you're holding, the New Living Translation, is accurate, easy-to-read, and friendly. Want to know more? Read on!

The *Holy Bible*, New Living Translation, was first published in 1996. It quickly became one of the most popular Bible translations in the English-speaking world. While the NLT's influence was rapidly growing, the Bible Translation Committee determined that an additional investment in scholarly review and text refinement could make it even better. So shortly after its initial publication, the committee began an eight-year process with the purpose of increasing the level of the NLT's precision without sacrificing its easy-to-understand quality. This second-generation text was completed in 2004 and is reflected in this edition of the New Living Translation.

The goal of any Bible translation is to convey the meaning and content of the ancient Hebrew, Aramaic, and Greek texts as accurately as possible to contemporary readers. The challenge for our translators was to create a text that would communicate as clearly and powerfully to today's readers as the original texts did to readers and listeners in the ancient biblical world. The resulting translation is easy to read and understand, while also accurately communicating the meaning and content of the original biblical texts. The NLT is a general-purpose text especially good for study, devotional reading, and reading aloud in worship services.

We believe that the New Living Translation—which combines the latest biblical scholarship with a clear, dynamic writing style—will communicate God's Word powerfully to all who read it. We publish it with the prayer that God will use it to speak his timeless truth to the church and the world in a fresh, new way.

The Publishers
July 2004

It takes a lot of smart people to make sure that a translation of the Bible is right! Here are the people who worked on the New Living Translation. Hey, great job, everyone!

BIBLE TRANSLATION TEAM
HOLY BIBLE, NEW LIVING TRANSLATION

■ **PENTATEUCH**
Daniel I. Block, Senior Translator
The Southern Baptist Theological Seminary

GENESIS
Allen Ross, *Beeson Divinity School, Samford University*
Gordon Wenham, *University of Gloucester*

EXODUS
Robert Bergen, *Hannibal-LaGrange College*
Daniel I. Block, *The Southern Baptist Theological Seminary*
Eugene Carpenter, *Bethel College, Mishawaka, Indiana*

LEVITICUS
David Baker, *Ashland Theological Seminary*
Victor Hamilton, *Asbury College*
Kenneth Mathews, *Beeson Divinity School, Samford University*

NUMBERS
Dale A. Brueggemann, *Assemblies of God Division of Foreign Missions*
R. K. Harrison (deceased), *Wycliffe College*
Paul R. House, *Wheaton College*
Gerald L. Mattingly, *Johnson Bible College*

DEUTERONOMY
J. Gordon McConville, *University of Gloucester*
Eugene H. Merrill, *Dallas Theological Seminary*
John A. Thompson (deceased), *University of Melbourne*

■ **HISTORICAL BOOKS**
Barry J. Beitzel, Senior Translator
Trinity Evangelical Divinity School

JOSHUA, JUDGES
Carl E. Armerding, *Schloss Mittersill Study Centre*
Barry J. Beitzel, *Trinity Evangelical Divinity School*
Lawson Stone, *Asbury Theological Seminary*

1 & 2 SAMUEL
Robert Gordon, *Cambridge University*
V. Philips Long, *Regent College*
J. Robert Vannoy, *Biblical Theological Seminary*

1 & 2 KINGS
Bill T. Arnold, *Asbury Theological Seminary*
William H. Barnes, *North Central University*
Frederic W. Bush, *Fuller Theological Seminary*

1 & 2 CHRONICLES
Raymond B. Dillard (deceased), *Westminster Theological Seminary*
David A. Dorsey, *Evangelical School of Theology*
Terry Eves, *Erskine College*

RUTH, EZRA—ESTHER
William C. Williams, *Vanguard University*
H. G. M. Williamson, *Oxford University*

■ **WISDOM BOOKS**
Tremper Longman III, Senior Translator
Westmont College

JOB
August Konkel, *Providence Theological Seminary*
Tremper Longman III, *Westmont College*
Al Wolters, *Redeemer College*

PSALMS 1–75
Mark D. Futato, *Reformed Theological Seminary*
Douglas Green, *Westminster Theological Seminary*
Richard Pratt, *Reformed Theological Seminary*

PSALMS 76–150
David M. Howard Jr., *Bethel Theological Seminary*
Raymond C. Ortlund Jr., *Trinity Evangelical Divinity School*
Willem VanGemeren, *Trinity Evangelical Divinity School*

PROVERBS
Ted Hildebrandt, *Gordon College*
Richard Schultz, *Wheaton College*
Raymond C. Van Leeuwen, *Eastern College*

ECCLESIASTES, SONG OF SONGS
Daniel C. Fredericks, *Belhaven College*
David Hubbard (deceased), *Fuller Theological Seminary*
Tremper Longman III, *Westmont College*

■ **PROPHETS**
John N. Oswalt, Senior Translator
Wesley Biblical Seminary

ISAIAH
John N. Oswalt, *Wesley Biblical Seminary*
Gary Smith, *Midwestern Baptist Theological Seminary*
John Walton, *Wheaton College*

JEREMIAH, LAMENTATIONS
G. Herbert Livingston, *Asbury Theological Seminary*
Elmer A. Martens, *Mennonite Brethren Biblical Seminary*

EZEKIEL
Daniel I. Block, *The Southern Baptist Theological Seminary*
David H. Engelhard, *Calvin Theological Seminary*
David Thompson, *Asbury Theological Seminary*

DANIEL, HAGGAI—MALACHI

Joyce Baldwin Caine (deceased), *Trinity College, Bristol*
Douglas Gropp, *Catholic University of America*
Roy Hayden, *Oral Roberts School of Theology*
Andrew Hill, *Wheaton College*
Tremper Longman III, *Westmont College*

HOSEA—ZEPHANIAH

Joseph Coleson, *Nazarene Theological Seminary*
Roy Hayden, *Oral Roberts School of Theology*
Andrew Hill, *Wheaton College*
Richard Patterson, *Liberty University*

■ GOSPELS AND ACTS

Grant R. Osborne, Senior Translator
Trinity Evangelical Divinity School

MATTHEW

Craig Blomberg, *Denver Seminary*
Donald A. Hagner, *Fuller Theological Seminary*
David Turner, *Grand Rapids Baptist Seminary*

MARK

Robert Guelich (deceased), *Fuller Theological Seminary*
George Guthrie, *Union University*
Grant R. Osborne, *Trinity Evangelical Divinity School*

LUKE

Darrell Bock, *Dallas Theological Seminary*
Scot McKnight, *North Park University*
Robert Stein, *The Southern Baptist Theological Seminary*

JOHN

Gary M. Burge, *Wheaton College*
Philip W. Comfort, *Coastal Carolina University*
Marianne Meye Thompson, *Fuller Theological Seminary*

ACTS

D. A. Carson, *Trinity Evangelical Divinity School*
William J. Larkin, *Columbia International University*
Roger Mohrlang, *Whitworth College*

■ LETTERS AND REVELATION

Norman R. Ericson, Senior Translator
Wheaton College

ROMANS, GALATIANS

Gerald Borchert, *Northern Baptist Theological Seminary*
Douglas J. Moo, *Wheaton College*
Thomas R. Schreiner, *The Southern Baptist Theological Seminary*

1 & 2 CORINTHIANS

Joseph Alexanian, *Trinity International University*
Linda Belleville, *North Park Theological Seminary*
Douglas A. Oss, *Central Bible College*
Robert Sloan, *Baylor University*

EPHESIANS—PHILEMON
Harold W. Hoehner, *Dallas Theological Seminary*
Moises Silva, *Gordon-Conwell Theological Seminary*
Klyne Snodgrass, *North Park Theological Seminary*

HEBREWS, JAMES, 1 & 2 PETER, JUDE
Peter Davids, *Schloss Mittersill Study Centre*
Norman R. Ericson, *Wheaton College*
William Lane (deceased), *Seattle Pacific University*
J. Ramsey Michaels, *S. W. Missouri State University*

1—3 JOHN, REVELATION
Greg Beale, *Wheaton College*
Robert Mounce, *Whitworth College*
M. Robert Mulholland Jr., *Asbury Theological Seminary*

■ **SPECIAL REVIEWERS**
F. F. Bruce (deceased), *University of Manchester*
Kenneth N. Taylor (deceased), *Translator*, The Living Bible

■ **COORDINATING TEAM**
Mark D. Taylor, *Director and Chief Stylist*
Ronald A. Beers, *Executive Director and Stylist*
Mark R. Norton, *Managing Editor and O.T. Coordinating Editor*
Philip W. Comfort, *N.T. Coordinating Editor*
Daniel W. Taylor, *Bethel University, Senior Stylist*

OK, you're ready!

You've got the world's coolest Bible in your hands, so where do you start?

Anywhere! Any page you open this Bible to will be a good place to start. God's Word is great, from the first page to the last. Every word is true, inspired by God, and written for you!

Of course, if you want a little more direction, go to the Reading Plan found on page 363. It'll give you tips on how to make your *own* plan to read all of God's personal message to you.

If you've opened this Bible, you've probably noticed all the fun activities inside. Good! Here are a few tips about them, too!

Before you start any activity in this Bible, always check with a parent or teacher first. Here's why:

- **Some activities require adult help or supervision. An adult may know some safety precautions you haven't thought of.**

- **Sometimes it'll be easier to have an adult get the supplies you need.**

- **Some people have food allergies that can be dangerous. So before you do a snack activity, an adult can help you carefully read food labels to check for hidden ingredients that can cause allergy-related problems.**

So, are you ready to get started? Good for you! Remember, this is *your* Bible.

**Read it.
Remember it.
Write in it.
Share it.
Measure it.
Treasure it.
Live it!**

There's only one last rule— have FUN with it!

Here Are the Basics . . . about using the Bible, that is!

The book you're holding is very special—it's God's Word, written to YOU!

How is the Bible put together? LET'S SEE!

You might hear several names for this book: the Bible, the Holy Bible, Scripture, God's Word. But they all mean the same thing: the Bible. The Bible comes from God, who inspired people to write exactly what he wanted them to write. (For more about why and how the Bible was written, turn to the Frequently Asked Questions About the Bible section, starting on page 337.)

The Old and New Testaments

The Bible is one book, but it's made up of 66 smaller books. Those 66 books are grouped into two main sections called the Old Testament and the New Testament. Let's look at each.

The Old Testament has 39 of the books, from Genesis to Malachi.

The Old Testament covers a lot of ground, from the creation of the world through the time of the prophets. It covers everything up to the time right before Jesus was born. You'd find the Old Testament in the complete *Hands-On Bible* (or any complete Bible).

The New Testament contains the other 27 books of the Bible, from Matthew to Revelation.

You're holding the New Testament right now. Find the beginning of Matthew and the end of Revelation to see how many pages that is. The New Testament tells about Jesus' life, his death and resurrection, and the early church (plus some stuff that hasn't even happened yet!).

How to Find Your Way Around the Bible

Finding your way around the Bible is easy!

The first thing is finding the book you want. Just go to "The Books of the Bible" page in the beginning of this Bible, and look for the name of the book. That'll tell you what page to turn to. (If you already know the order of the books, look it up that way. If not, look up the name in the "Alphabetical Book Listing.")

Next, you'll want to find a certain chapter in that book. Each book of the Bible is divided into chapters and verses, and each chapter and verse has a number. The bigger numbers on the pages are the chapter numbers. You can also find the chapter numbers at the top of every page. The smaller numbers on the pages are the verse numbers.

Here's how a Bible verse is usually written. Let's say you want to find a verse in the Bible. It would be written like this: Luke 2:7. Here's what that means!

LUKE 2:7

1
OK, first you find the
BOOK OF LUKE.

Remember how? You got it! Look it up in "The Books of the Bible." (The more you read your Bible, the more you'll get to know the books. Pretty soon you won't even have to look at the list. Really!)

2
Next, you need to find
CHAPTER 2.

Just look for the bigger numbers.

3
Finally, look in
CHAPTER 2 for the little number 7—
that's VERSE 7.

Now read it! See? You just found a verse that tells a very important part of the history of the world. Way to go!

Now that you have the hang of it, try looking these up on your own! After you read each verse, write it in your own words, OK? Ready, set, start!

JOHN 3:16

Here's what I think this verse means:

. . . .

. . . .

. . . .

. . . .

LUKE 1:37

Here's what I think this verse means:

. . . .

. . . .

. . . .

. . . .

1 CORINTHIANS 13:13

Here's what I think this verse means:

. . . .

. . . .

. . . .

. . . .

1 PETER 5:7

Here's what I think this verse means:

. . . .

. . . .

. . . .

. . . .

MATTHEW 28:5-7

Ha! Here's a tricky one! When there's a short line between the verse numbers, it means to read more than one verse. So here it means: Read verses 5 through 7.

Here's what I think these verses mean:. . . . .

. . . .

. . . .

MARK 2:23-3:6

Another tricky one? Yup—one more. You're getting good at this! You can do it! When you see a longer line between numbers, that means you should read from one chapter into another. So in this next one, you go from the book of Mark, chapter 2, verse 23, all the way to Mark, chapter 3, verse 6. Try it!

Here's what I think these verses mean:. . . . .

. . . .

. . . .

Great job!

Soon you'll be sailing around the Bible! The more you practice, the easier it gets.

SO KEEP READING!

About the New Testament Books

The GOSPELS

The first four books of the New Testament are called the Gospels. And here's something you might not know—*Gospel* means "Good News." Guess what good news the Gospels tell. Did you guess the good news about Jesus? You're right!

All four Gospels tell about the life of Jesus. But that's not all; they tell about his death and resurrection too! The writers of the Gospels were Matthew, Mark, Luke, and John. Each of the four writers tried to reach a different audience, so each book contains slightly different details. Matthew wrote mostly to the Jews, Mark wrote to the Christians in Rome, Luke tried to reach the Gentile Christians, and John wrote to new Christians. But God inspired all four Gospel writers, and what they wrote long ago was written for us, too!

HISTORY

Acts, the next book in the New Testament, tells the history of the early Christian church. This book is sometimes called the Acts of the Apostles because it tells how the apostles spread the good news about Jesus after his death and resurrection.

EPISTLES

The rest of the New Testament (all except for the last book) consists of the epistles, or letters. The Apostle Paul wrote thirteen of the letters. Most of Paul's letters were written to give advice and encouragement to new churches. The rest of the letters are more general in nature. But *all* of the epistles, just like all of the other books in the Bible, are important for us today as well!

REVELATION

The last book of the Bible is the book of Revelation. It's an apocalyptic book of prophecy, meaning it uses powerful images to tell how the whole story ends! And here's how it ends: God wins, and anyone who believes in Jesus will live with him forever in a new heaven and new earth.

THE NEW TESTAMENT

Just when you thought it couldn't get any more exciting . . .

IT DOES!

Angels. Water into wine. Walking on water. Earthquakes. Prison escapes. Shipwrecks.

And the greatest miracle of all—A SAVIOR WHO CAME JUST FOR YOU!

What are you waiting for? Start reading!

MATTHEW
The Messiah Is Here!

Look for **3** hidden messages in Matthew!

Matthew wrote his book of the Bible to prove that Jesus is the Messiah. Look for these events in Jesus' life:

- **BIRTH AS A BABY**
- **MANHOOD MIRACLES**
- **POWERFUL PARABLES**
- **SUFFERING SERVANTHOOD**
- **CRUCIFIXION ON THE CROSS**
- **RESURRECTION AS THE RISEN SAVIOR!**

...49, 50!

Messiah Makes Waves— and Calms Them Too!

Jesus made lots of waves with his words and actions. Not only did he make waves, he *talked* to waves. Want to know more? Read the stormy story in Matthew 8:23-27.

Sports Report— Getting Warmed Up

Jesus put himself through some pretty rough workouts as he "warmed up" for his ministry. Read more about Jesus' warm-up for the big job ahead in Matthew 3:1–4:11.

Show Us the King!

I'M the Man!

A group of wise men came all the way to Jerusalem to see the new king. That was quite a surprise to Herod, who thought *he* was the only king around. Read all about it in Matthew 2:1-12.

HEY! Have You Heard?

Everyone was talking about him! Some said good things, some said bad. But *everyone* had an opinion. Who were they talking about, and what did they say? Read Matthew 4:23-25 (for some good reactions) and Matthew 12:9-14 (for some bad ones).

Jesus Shocks — Religious Community

Pharisees Up In Arms

Who is Jesus — And Why Is He Saying Those Things?

Tell Us More!

Jesus had a way of talking about God so that everyone could understand. Read a few of his stories (actually they're called parables) in Matthew 13:1-52!

A Verrry Long Week

It may have seemed like the longest week in history. It started with a parade, but went downhill fast from there. Read about the high and low points in Matthew 21:1-11 and Matthew 27:26-50.

Sneak Preview

Storms were on the horizon and growing closer. Jesus knew exactly what was going to happen, and he gave his disciples a shocking sneak preview. Read what he said in Matthew 20:17-19.

WANTED

FOR LOVING EVERYONE

Oh Happy Day!

Jesus had died. He had been crucified. His body had been placed in a guarded tomb. So why were his followers so happy? Find out the amazing reason for yourself in Matthew 28:1-10!

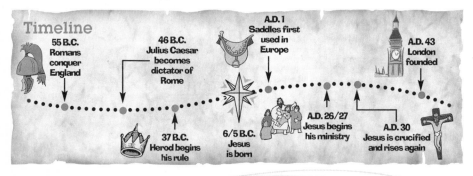

Timeline

55 B.C. Romans conquer England

46 B.C. Julius Caesar becomes dictator of Rome

37 B.C. Herod begins his rule

A.D. 1 Saddles first used in Europe

6/5 B.C. Jesus is born

A.D. 26/27 Jesus begins his ministry

A.D. 30 Jesus is crucified and rises again

A.D. 43 London founded

The JESUS CONNECTION

The book of Matthew is *all* about Jesus. It's one of the four Gospels, the books that tell us about Jesus' life. We get to follow Jesus from birth to death, to his resurrection, and into the clouds as he ascended to heaven. Thanks to the Gospel writers, we understand who Jesus is—God's Son!—and what his life on earth was all about—reaching out to people with God's gift of love.

CHAPTER **1**
The Ancestors of Jesus the Messiah

This is a record of the ancestors of Jesus the Messiah, a descendant of David and of Abraham:

2 Abraham was the father of Isaac.
Isaac was the father of Jacob.
Jacob was the father of Judah and his brothers.
3 Judah was the father of Perez and Zerah (whose mother was Tamar).
Perez was the father of Hezron.
Hezron was the father of Ram.
4 Ram was the father of Amminadab.
Amminadab was the father of Nahshon.
Nahshon was the father of Salmon.
5 Salmon was the father of Boaz (whose mother was Rahab).
Boaz was the father of Obed (whose mother was Ruth).
Obed was the father of Jesse.
6 Jesse was the father of King David.
David was the father of Solomon (whose mother was Bathsheba, the widow of Uriah).
7 Solomon was the father of Rehoboam.
Rehoboam was the father of Abijah.
Abijah was the father of Asa.
8 Asa was the father of Jehoshaphat.
Jehoshaphat was the father of Jehoram.
Jehoram was the father of Uzziah.
9 Uzziah was the father of Jotham.
Jotham was the father of Ahaz.
Ahaz was the father of Hezekiah.
10 Hezekiah was the father of Manasseh.
Manasseh was the father of Amon.
Amon was the father of Josiah.
11 Josiah was the father of Jehoiachin and his brothers (born at the time of the exile to Babylon).
12 After the Babylonian exile:
Jehoiachin was the father of Shealtiel.
Shealtiel was the father of Zerubbabel.
13 Zerubbabel was the father of Abiud.
Abiud was the father of Eliakim.
Eliakim was the father of Azor.
14 Azor was the father of Zadok.
Zadok was the father of Akim.
Akim was the father of Eliud.
15 Eliud was the father of Eleazar.
Eleazar was the father of Matthan.
Matthan was the father of Jacob.
16 Jacob was the father of Joseph, the husband of Mary.

Mary gave birth to Jesus, who is called the Messiah.

17 All those listed above include fourteen generations from Abraham to David, fourteen from David to the Babylonian exile, and fourteen from the Babylonian exile to the Messiah.

The Birth of Jesus the Messiah

18 This is how Jesus the Messiah was born. His mother, Mary, was engaged to be married to Joseph. But before the marriage took place, while she was still a virgin, she became pregnant through the power of the Holy Spirit. 19 Joseph, her fiancé, was a good man and did not want to disgrace her publicly, so he decided to break the engagement quietly.

20 As he considered this, an angel of the Lord appeared to him in a dream. "Joseph, son of David," the angel said, "do not be afraid to take Mary as your wife. For the child within her was conceived by the Holy Spirit. 21 And she will have a son, and you are to name him Jesus, for he will save his people from their sins."

22 All of this occurred to fulfill the Lord's message through his prophet:

23 "Look! The virgin will conceive a child!
She will give birth to a son,
and they will call him Immanuel,
which means 'God is with us.'"

24 When Joseph woke up, he did as the angel of the Lord commanded and took Mary as his wife. 25 But he did not have sexual relations with her until her son was born. And Joseph named him Jesus.

CHAPTER **2**
Visitors from the East

Jesus was born in Bethlehem in Judea, during the reign of King Herod. About that time some wise men from eastern lands arrived in Jerusalem, asking, 2 "Where is the newborn king of the Jews? We saw his star as it rose, and we have come to worship him."

3 King Herod was deeply disturbed when he heard this, as was everyone in Jerusalem. 4 He called a meeting of the leading priests and teachers of religious law and asked, "Where is the Messiah supposed to be born?"

5 "In Bethlehem in Judea," they said, "for this is what the prophet wrote:

6 'And you, O Bethlehem in the land of Judah,
are not least among the ruling cities of Judah,

for a ruler will come from you
who will be the shepherd for my
people Israel.'"

7Then Herod called for a private meeting with the wise men, and he learned from them the time when the star first appeared. 8Then he told them, "Go to Bethlehem and search carefully for the child. And when you find him, come back and tell me so that I can go and worship him, too!"

9After this interview the wise men went their way. And the star they had seen in the east guided them to Bethlehem. It went ahead of them and stopped over the place where the child was. 10When they saw the star, they were filled with joy! 11They entered the house and saw the child with his mother, Mary, and they bowed down and worshiped him. Then they opened their treasure chests and gave him gifts of gold, frankincense, and myrrh.

12When it was time to leave, they returned to their own country by another route, for God had warned them in a dream not to return to Herod.

The Escape to Egypt

13After the wise men were gone, an angel of the Lord appeared to Joseph in a dream. "Get up! Flee to Egypt with the child and his mother," the angel said. "Stay there until I tell you to return, because Herod is going to search for the child to kill him."

14That night Joseph left for Egypt with the child and Mary, his mother, 15and they stayed there until Herod's death. This fulfilled what the Lord had spoken through the prophet: "I called my Son out of Egypt."

16Herod was furious when he realized that the wise men had outwitted him. He sent soldiers to kill all the boys in and around Bethlehem who were two years old and under, based on the wise men's report of the star's first appearance. 17Herod's brutal action fulfilled what God had spoken through the prophet Jeremiah:

18 "A cry was heard in Ramah—
weeping and great mourning.
Rachel weeps for her children,
refusing to be comforted,
for they are dead."

The Return to Nazareth

19When Herod died, an angel of the Lord appeared in a dream to Joseph in Egypt. 20"Get up!" the angel said. "Take the child and his mother back to the land of Israel, because those who were trying to kill the child are dead."

21So Joseph got up and returned to the land of Israel with Jesus and his mother. 22But when he learned that the new ruler of Judea was Herod's son Archelaus, he was afraid to go there. Then, after being warned in a dream, he left for the region of Galilee. 23So the family went and lived in a town called Nazareth. This fulfilled what the prophets had said: "He will be called a Nazarene."

CHAPTER **3**
John the Baptist Prepares the Way

In those days John the Baptist came to the Judean wilderness and began preaching. His message was, 2"Repent of your sins and turn to God, for the Kingdom of Heaven is near." 3The prophet Isaiah was speaking about John when he said,

"He is a voice shouting in the wilderness,
'Prepare the way for the Lord's coming!
Clear the road for him!'"

4John's clothes were woven from coarse camel hair, and he wore a leather belt around his waist. For food he ate locusts and wild honey. 5People from Jerusalem and from all of Judea and all over the Jordan Valley went out to see and hear John. 6And when they confessed their sins, he baptized them in the Jordan River.

7But when he saw many Pharisees and Sadducees coming to watch him baptize, he denounced them. "You brood of snakes!" he exclaimed. "Who warned you to flee God's coming wrath? 8Prove by the way you live that you have repented of your sins and turned to God. 9Don't just say to each other, 'We're safe, for we are descendants of Abraham.' That means nothing, for I tell you, God can create children of Abraham from these very stones. 10Even now the ax of God's judgment is poised, ready to sever the roots of the trees. Yes, every tree that does not produce good fruit will be chopped down and thrown into the fire.

11"I baptize with water those who repent of their sins and turn to God. But someone is coming soon who is greater than I am—so much greater that I'm not worthy even to be his slave and carry his sandals. He will baptize you with the Holy Spirit and with fire. 12He is ready to separate the chaff from the wheat with his winnowing fork. Then he will clean up the threshing area, gathering the wheat into his barn but burning the chaff with never-ending fire."

The Baptism of Jesus

13Then Jesus went from Galilee to the Jordan River to be baptized by John. 14But John tried to

Disappearing Act

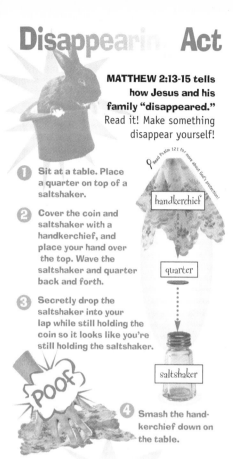

MATTHEW 2:13-15 tells how Jesus and his family "disappeared." Read it! Make something disappear yourself!

1. Sit at a table. Place a quarter on top of a saltshaker.

2. Cover the coin and saltshaker with a handkerchief, and place your hand over the top. Wave the saltshaker and quarter back and forth.

3. Secretly drop the saltshaker into your lap while still holding the coin so it looks like you're still holding the saltshaker.

Read Psalm 121 for more about God's protection!

handkerchief

quarter

POOF!

saltshaker

4. Smash the handkerchief down on the table.

YOU MADE THE SALTSHAKER DISAPPEAR!
(Not really, but it was a pretty good trick.)
God helped Jesus and his family "disappear" when Jesus was in danger, and that was *no* trick!

talk him out of it. "I am the one who needs to be baptized by you," he said, "so why are you coming to me?"

15 But Jesus said, "It should be done, for we must carry out all that God requires." So John agreed to baptize him.

16 After his baptism, as Jesus came up out of the water, the heavens were opened and he saw the Spirit of God descending like a dove and settling on him. 17 And a voice from heaven said, "This is my dearly loved Son, who brings me great joy."

CHAPTER **4**
The Temptation of Jesus
Then Jesus was led by the Spirit into the wilderness to be tempted there by the devil. 2 For forty days and forty nights he fasted and became very hungry.

3 During that time the devil came and said to him, "If you are the Son of God, tell these stones to become loaves of bread."

4 But Jesus told him, "No! The Scriptures say,

'People do not live by bread alone,
  but by every word that comes from the
    mouth of God.'"

5 Then the devil took him to the holy city, Jerusalem, to the highest point of the Temple, 6 and said, "If you are the Son of God, jump off! For the Scriptures say,

'He will order his angels to protect you.
And they will hold you up with their hands
  so you won't even hurt your foot
    on a stone.'"

7 Jesus responded, "The Scriptures also say, 'You must not test the LORD your God.'"

8 Next the devil took him to the peak of a very high mountain and showed him all the kingdoms of the world and their glory. 9 "I will give it all to you," he said, "if you will kneel down and worship me."

10 "Get out of here, Satan," Jesus told him. "For the Scriptures say,

'You must worship the LORD your God
  and serve only him.'"

11 Then the devil went away, and angels came and took care of Jesus.

The Ministry of Jesus Begins
12 When Jesus heard that John had been arrested, he left Judea and returned to Galilee. 13 He went first to Nazareth, then left there and moved to Capernaum, beside the Sea of Galilee, in the region of Zebulun and Naphtali. 14 This fulfilled what God said through the prophet Isaiah:

15 "In the land of Zebulun and of Naphtali,
    beside the sea, beyond the Jordan River,
    in Galilee where so many Gentiles live,
16 the people who sat in darkness
    have seen a great light.
And for those who lived in the land where
      death casts its shadow,
    a light has shined."

17 From then on Jesus began to preach, "Repent of your sins and turn to God, for the Kingdom of Heaven is near."

The First Disciples

[18] One day as Jesus was walking along the shore of the Sea of Galilee, he saw two brothers—Simon, also called Peter, and Andrew—throwing a net into the water, for they fished for a living. [19] Jesus called out to them, "Come, follow me, and I will show you how to fish for people!" [20] And they left their nets at once and followed him.

[21] A little farther up the shore he saw two other brothers, James and John, sitting in a boat with their father, Zebedee, repairing their nets. And he called them to come, too. [22] They immediately followed him, leaving the boat and their father behind.

Crowds Follow Jesus

[23] Jesus traveled throughout the region of Galilee, teaching in the synagogues and announcing the Good News about the Kingdom. And he healed every kind of disease and illness. [24] News about him spread as far as Syria, and people soon began bringing to him all who were sick. And whatever their sickness or disease, or if they were demon possessed or epileptic or paralyzed—he healed them all. [25] Large crowds followed him wherever he went—people from Galilee, the Ten Towns, Jerusalem, from all over Judea, and from east of the Jordan River.

CHAPTER **5**

The Sermon on the Mount

One day as he saw the crowds gathering, Jesus went up on the mountainside and sat down. His disciples gathered around him, [2] and he began to teach them.

The Beatitudes

[3] "God blesses those who are poor and
 realize their need for him,
 for the Kingdom of Heaven is theirs.
[4] God blesses those who mourn,
 for they will be comforted.
[5] God blesses those who are humble,
 for they will inherit the whole earth.
[6] God blesses those who hunger and thirst
 for justice,
 for they will be satisfied.
[7] God blesses those who are merciful,
 for they will be shown mercy.
[8] God blesses those whose hearts
 are pure,
 for they will see God.
[9] God blesses those who work for peace,
 for they will be called the children
 of God.
[10] God blesses those who are persecuted
 for doing right,
 for the Kingdom of Heaven
 is theirs.

[11] "God blesses you when people mock you and persecute you and lie about you and say all sorts of evil things against you because you are my followers. [12] Be happy about it! Be very glad!

STANDING FIRM

Even Jesus was tempted to sin. But he didn't give in! **Read MATTHEW 4:1-11 to see how Jesus stood firm.** Then try this experiment!

1 Use five toothpicks to connect five gumdrops in a circle.

2 Take two more toothpicks and one more gumdrop, and make a stand-up triangle using two of the bottom gumdrops as a base.

3 Keep making triangles until you have five triangles sticking up from the base.

Make as many structures as you want, and let them dry overnight. Then see how many books you can stack on top!

As the gumdrops got harder, they became stronger.

SCRIPTURE HELPS US STAND STRONG.

Cut three small paper flags. On each flag write a Scripture verse that will help you stand firm against temptation. Attach the flags to toothpicks, and stick each flag in a gumdrop. Keep them by your bed to remind you that Jesus taught us how to resist temptation!

worship only God

For a great reward awaits you in heaven. And remember, the ancient prophets were persecuted in the same way.

Teaching about Salt and Light

13 "You are the salt of the earth. But what good is salt if it has lost its flavor? Can you make it salty again? It will be thrown out and trampled underfoot as worthless.

14 "You are the light of the world—like a city on a hilltop that cannot be hidden. 15 No one lights a lamp and then puts it under a basket. Instead, a lamp is placed on a stand, where it gives light to everyone in the house. 16 In the same way, let your good deeds shine out for all to see, so that everyone will praise your heavenly Father.

Teaching about the Law

17 "Don't misunderstand why I have come. I did not come to abolish the law of Moses or the writings of the prophets. No, I came to accomplish their purpose. 18 I tell you the truth, until heaven and earth disappear, not even the smallest detail of God's law will disappear until its purpose is achieved. 19 So if you ignore the least commandment and teach others to do the same, you will be called the least in the Kingdom of Heaven. But anyone who obeys God's laws and teaches them will be called great in the Kingdom of Heaven.

20 "But I warn you—unless your righteousness is better than the righteousness of the teachers of religious law and the Pharisees, you will never enter the Kingdom of Heaven!

Teaching about Anger

21 "You have heard that our ancestors were told, 'You must not murder. If you commit murder, you are subject to judgment.' 22 But I say, if you are even angry with someone, you are subject to judgment! If you call someone an idiot, you are in danger of being brought before the court. And if you curse someone, you are in danger of the fires of hell.

23 "So if you are presenting a sacrifice at the altar in the Temple and you suddenly remember that someone has something against you, 24 leave your sacrifice there at the altar. Go and be reconciled to that person. Then come and offer your sacrifice to God.

25 "When you are on the way to court with your adversary, settle your differences quickly. Otherwise, your accuser may hand you over to the judge, who will hand you over to an officer, and you will be thrown into prison. 26 And if that happens, you surely won't be free again until you have paid the last penny.

Teaching about Adultery

27 "You have heard the commandment that says, 'You must not commit adultery.' 28 But I say, anyone who even looks at a woman with lust has already committed adultery with her in his heart. 29 So if your eye—even your good eye—causes you to lust, gouge it out and throw it away. It is better for you to lose one part of your body than for your whole body to be thrown into hell. 30 And if your hand—even your stronger hand—causes you to sin, cut it off and throw it away. It is better for you to lose one part of your body than for your whole body to be thrown into hell.

Teaching about Divorce

31 "You have heard the law that says, 'A man can divorce his wife by merely giving her a written notice of divorce.' 32 But I say that a man who divorces his wife, unless she has been unfaithful, causes her to commit adultery. And anyone who marries a divorced woman also commits adultery.

Teaching about Vows

33 "You have also heard that our ancestors were told, 'You must not break your vows; you must carry out the vows you make to the Lord.' 34 But I say, do not make any vows! Do not say, 'By heaven!' because heaven is God's throne. 35 And do not say, 'By the earth!' because the earth is his footstool. And do not say, 'By Jerusalem!' for Jerusalem is the city of the great King. 36 Do not even say, 'By my head!' for you can't turn one hair white or black. 37 Just say a simple, 'Yes, I will,' or 'No, I won't.' Anything beyond this is from the evil one.

Teaching about Revenge

38 "You have heard the law that says the punishment must match the injury: 'An eye for an eye, and a tooth for a tooth.' 39 But I say, do not resist an evil person! If someone slaps you on the right cheek, offer the other cheek also. 40 If you are sued in court and your shirt is taken from you, give your coat, too. 41 If a soldier demands that you carry his gear for a mile, carry it two miles. 42 Give to those who ask, and don't turn away from those who want to borrow.

Teaching about Love for Enemies

43 "You have heard the law that says, 'Love your neighbor' and hate your enemy. **44But I say, love your enemies!* Pray for those who persecute you!** 45 In that way, you will be acting as true children of your Father in heaven. For he gives his sunlight to both the evil and the good, and he sends rain on the just and the unjust alike. 46 If you love only those who love you, what reward is there for that? Even corrupt tax collectors do that much. 47 If you are kind only to your friends, how are you different from anyone else? Even pagans do that. 48 But you are to be perfect, even as your Father in heaven is perfect.

CHAPTER **6**

Teaching about Giving to the Needy

"Watch out! Don't do your good deeds publicly, to be admired by others, for you will lose the reward from your Father in heaven. 2 When you give to someone in need, don't do as the hypocrites do—blowing trumpets in the synagogues and streets to call attention to their acts of charity! I tell you the truth, they have received all the reward they will ever get. 3 But when you give to someone in need, don't let your left hand know what your right hand is doing. 4 Give your gifts in private, and your Father, who sees everything, will reward you.

Teaching about Prayer and Fasting

5 "When you pray, don't be like the hypocrites who love to pray publicly on street corners and in the synagogues where everyone can see them. I tell you the truth, that is all the reward they will ever get. 6 But when you pray, go away by yourself, shut the door behind you, and pray to your Father in private. Then your Father, who sees everything, will reward you.

7 "When you pray, don't babble on and on as people of other religions do. They think their prayers are answered merely by repeating their words again and again. 8 Don't be like them, for your Father knows exactly what you need even before you ask him! 9 Pray like this:

Our Father in heaven,
  may your name be kept holy.
10 May your Kingdom come soon.
May your will be done on earth,
  as it is in heaven.
11 Give us today the food we need,
12 and forgive us our sins,
  as we have forgiven those who sin
    against us.
13 And don't let us yield to temptation,
  but rescue us from the evil one.*

14 "If you forgive those who sin against you, your heavenly Father will forgive you. 15 But if you refuse to forgive others, your Father will not forgive your sins.

16 "And when you fast, don't make it obvious, as the hypocrites do, for they try to look miserable and disheveled so people will admire them for their fasting. I tell you the truth, that is the only reward they will ever get. 17 But when you fast, comb your hair and wash your face. 18 Then no one will notice that you are fasting, except your Father, who knows what you do in private. And your Father, who sees everything, will reward you.

Teaching about Money and Possessions

19 "Don't store up treasures here on earth, where moths eat them and rust destroys them, and where thieves break in and steal. 20 Store your treasures in heaven, where moths and rust cannot destroy, and thieves do not break in and steal. 21 Wherever your treasure is, there the desires of your heart will also be.

22 "Your eye is a lamp that provides light for your body. When your eye is good, your whole body is filled with light. 23 But when your eye is bad, your whole body is filled with darkness. And if the light you think you have is actually darkness, how deep that darkness is!

24 "No one can serve two masters. For you will hate one and love the other; you will be devoted to one and despise the other. You cannot serve both God and money.

25 "That is why I tell you not to worry about everyday life—whether you have enough food and drink, or enough clothes to wear. Isn't life more than food, and your body more than clothing? 26 Look at the birds. They don't plant or harvest or store food in barns, for your heavenly Father feeds them. And aren't you far more valuable to him than they are? 27 Can all your worries add a single moment to your life?

28 "And why worry about your clothing? Look at the lilies of the field and how they grow. They

5:44 Some manuscripts add *Bless those who curse you. Do good to those who hate you.* Compare Luke 6:27-28. 6:13 Some manuscripts add *For yours is the kingdom and the power and the glory forever. Amen.*

don't work or make their clothing, 29yet Solomon in all his glory was not dressed as beautifully as they are. 30And if God cares so wonderfully for wildflowers that are here today and thrown into the fire tomorrow, he will certainly care for you. Why do you have so little faith?

31"So don't worry about these things, saying, 'What will we eat? What will we drink? What will we wear?' 32These things dominate the thoughts of unbelievers, but your heavenly Father already knows all your needs. 33Seek the Kingdom of God above all else, and live righteously, and he will give you everything you need.

34"So don't worry about tomorrow, for tomorrow will bring its own worries. Today's trouble is enough for today.

CHAPTER 7
Do Not Judge Others

"Do not judge others, and you will not be judged. 2For you will be treated as you treat others. The standard you use in judging is the standard by which you will be judged.

3"And why worry about a speck in your friend's eye when you have a log in your own? 4How can you think of saying to your friend, 'Let me help you get rid of that speck in your eye,' when you can't see past the log in your own eye? 5Hypocrite! First get rid of the log in your own eye; then you will see well enough to deal with the speck in your friend's eye.

6"Don't waste what is holy on people who are unholy. Don't throw your pearls to pigs! They will trample the pearls, then turn and attack you.

Effective Prayer

7"Keep on asking, and you will receive what you ask for. Keep on seeking, and you will find. Keep on knocking, and the door will be opened to you. 8For everyone who asks, receives. Everyone who seeks, finds. And to everyone who knocks, the door will be opened.

9"You parents—if your children ask for a loaf of bread, do you give them a stone instead? 10Or if they ask for a fish, do you give them a snake? Of course not! 11So if you sinful people know how to give good gifts to your children, how much more will your heavenly Father give good gifts to those who ask him.

The Golden Rule

12"**Do to others whatever you would like them to do to you. This is the essence of all that is taught in the law and the prophets.**

The Way to Pray

Jesus taught us the best way to pray. Read his recipe for prayer in MATTHEW 6:9-13.

THEN MAKE YOUR OWN RECIPE.

1. Gather five trail mix ingredients in separate bowls.

2. Put a small handful of each ingredient in a small plastic bag. Then zip the bag shut. Keep making bags.

3. Use a fine-tipped permanent marker to write, "MATTHEW 6:9-13: The Recipe for Prayer" on each bag.

The **five ingredients** in your trail mix can remind you of **five ingredients** in the Lord's Prayer:

♦ **Praise** *(honoring God)*

♦ **Purpose** *(wanting God's will, not our own)*

♦ **Provision** *(trusting God to take care of us)*

♦ **Pardon** *(forgiveness from God and for others)*

♦ **Protection** *(from temptation and evil)*

GIVE YOUR BAGS AWAY TO FAMILY MEMBERS AND FRIENDS. TELL THEM TO READ THE LORD'S PRAYER TO LEARN THE WAY TO PRAY!

The Narrow Gate

13"You can enter God's Kingdom only through the narrow gate. The highway to hell is broad, and its gate is wide for the many who choose that way. 14But the gateway to life is very narrow and the road is difficult, and only a few ever find it.

The Tree and Its Fruit

15"Beware of false prophets who come disguised as harmless sheep but are really vicious wolves. 16You can identify them by their fruit, that is, by the way they act. Can you pick grapes from thornbushes, or figs from thistles? 17A good tree produces good fruit, and a bad tree produces bad fruit. 18A good tree can't produce bad fruit, and a bad tree can't produce good fruit. 19So every tree that does not produce good fruit is chopped down and thrown into the fire. 20 Yes, just as you can identify a tree by its fruit, so you can identify people by their actions.

True Disciples

21 "Not everyone who calls out to me, 'Lord! Lord!' will enter the Kingdom of Heaven. Only those who actually do the will of my Father in heaven will enter. 22 On judgment day many will say to me, 'Lord! Lord! We prophesied in your name and cast out demons in your name and performed many miracles in your name.' 23 But I will reply, 'I never knew you. Get away from me, you who break God's laws.'

Building on a Solid Foundation

24 "Anyone who listens to my teaching and follows it is wise, like a person who builds a house on solid rock. 25 Though the rain comes in torrents and the floodwaters rise and the winds beat against that house, it won't collapse because it is built on bedrock. 26 But anyone who hears my teaching and doesn't obey it is foolish, like a person who builds a house on sand. 27 When the rains and floods come and the winds beat against that house, it will collapse with a mighty crash."

28 When Jesus had finished saying these things, the crowds were amazed at his teaching, 29 for he taught with real authority—quite unlike their teachers of religious law.

CHAPTER **8**

Jesus Heals a Man with Leprosy

Large crowds followed Jesus as he came down the mountainside. 2 Suddenly, a man with leprosy approached him and knelt before him. "Lord," the man said, "if you are willing, you can heal me and make me clean."

3 Jesus reached out and touched him. "I am willing," he said. "Be healed!" And instantly the leprosy disappeared. 4 Then Jesus said to him, "Don't tell anyone about this. Instead, go to the priest and let him examine you. Take along the offering required in the law of Moses for those who have been healed of leprosy. This will be a public testimony that you have been cleansed."

The Faith of a Roman Officer

5 When Jesus returned to Capernaum, a Roman officer came and pleaded with him, 6 "Lord, my young servant lies in bed, paralyzed and in terrible pain."

7 Jesus said, "I will come and heal him."

8 But the officer said, "Lord, I am not worthy to have you come into my home. Just say the word from where you are, and my servant will be healed. 9 I know this because I am under the authority of my superior officers, and I have authority over my soldiers. I only need to say, 'Go,' and they go, or 'Come,' and they come. And if I say to my slaves, 'Do this,' they do it."

10 When Jesus heard this, he was amazed. Turning to those who were following him, he said, "I tell you the truth, I haven't seen faith like this in all Israel! 11 And I tell you this, that many Gentiles will come from all over the world—from east and west—and sit down with Abraham, Isaac, and Jacob at the feast in the Kingdom of Heaven. 12 But many Israelites—those for whom the Kingdom was prepared—will be thrown into outer darkness, where there will be weeping and gnashing of teeth."

13 Then Jesus said to the Roman officer, "Go back home. Because you believed, it has happened." And the young servant was healed that same hour.

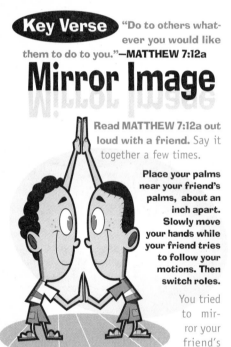

Key Verse "Do to others whatever you would like them to do to you."—MATTHEW 7:12a

Mirror Image

Read MATTHEW 7:12a out loud with a friend. Say it together a few times.

Place your palms near your friend's palms, about an inch apart. Slowly move your hands while your friend tries to follow your motions. Then switch roles.

You tried to mirror your friend's motions.

Jesus wants us to treat other people exactly how we'd like to be treated—to be a mirror image of how we'd like to be treated! Write this verse on a sticky note on your bathroom mirror to remind you to be a mirror image!

Jesus Heals Many People

¹⁴When Jesus arrived at Peter's house, Peter's mother-in-law was sick in bed with a high fever. ¹⁵But when Jesus touched her hand, the fever left her. Then she got up and prepared a meal for him.

¹⁶That evening many demon-possessed people were brought to Jesus. He cast out the evil spirits with a simple command, and he healed all the sick. ¹⁷This fulfilled the word of the Lord through the prophet Isaiah, who said,

"He took our sicknesses
and removed our diseases."

The Cost of Following Jesus

¹⁸When Jesus saw the crowd around him, he instructed his disciples to cross to the other side of the lake.

¹⁹Then one of the teachers of religious law said to him, "Teacher, I will follow you wherever you go."

²⁰But Jesus replied, "Foxes have dens to live in, and birds have nests, but the Son of Man has no place even to lay his head."

²¹Another of his disciples said, "Lord, first let me return home and bury my father."

²²But Jesus told him, "Follow me now. Let the spiritually dead bury their own dead."

Jesus Calms the Storm

²³Then Jesus got into the boat and started across the lake with his disciples. ²⁴Suddenly, a fierce storm struck the lake, with waves breaking into the boat. But Jesus was sleeping. ²⁵The disciples went and woke him up, shouting, "Lord, save us! We're going to drown!"

²⁶Jesus responded, "Why are you afraid? You have so little faith!" Then he got up and rebuked the wind and waves, and suddenly there was a great calm.

²⁷The disciples were amazed. "Who is this man?" they asked. "Even the winds and waves obey him!"

Jesus Heals Two Demon-Possessed Men

²⁸When Jesus arrived on the other side of the lake, in the region of the Gadarenes, two men who were possessed by demons met him. They lived in a cemetery and were so violent that no one could go through that area.

²⁹They began screaming at him, "Why are you interfering with us, Son of God? Have you come here to torture us before God's appointed time?"

³⁰There happened to be a large herd of pigs feeding in the distance. ³¹So the demons begged, "If you cast us out, send us into that herd of pigs."

³²"All right, go!" Jesus commanded them. So the demons came out of the men and entered

COMPLETE CONTROL

Do *you* get scared in storms? **Read about a stormy situation in MATTHEW 8:23-27.** The next time you're scared, remember that Jesus is in complete control. **HERE'S A REMINDER.**

1 Draw the outline of a cross on a plastic lid. Use fine-tipped markers to decorate your cross everywhere but in the center.

2 Add food coloring to a little water. Use an eye dropper to put a drop of the colored water in the center of the cross.

3 Cover the cross and drop of water with clear packing tape, pressing around, but not on top of, the droplet.

4 Trim around the cross. Poke a hole in the top of the cross, and add yarn to make a necklace.

The drop of water in the center of your necklace can remind you that Jesus was in control in the center of the storm.

REMEMBER THAT JESUS IS IN CONTROL OF EVERYTHING IN YOUR LIFE TOO!

the pigs, and the whole herd plunged down the steep hillside into the lake and drowned in the water.

33 The herdsmen fled to the nearby town, telling everyone what happened to the demon-possessed men. 34 Then the entire town came out to meet Jesus, but they begged him to go away and leave them alone.

CHAPTER **9**

Jesus Heals a Paralyzed Man

Jesus climbed into a boat and went back across the lake to his own town. 2 Some people brought to him a paralyzed man on a mat. Seeing their faith, Jesus said to the paralyzed man, "Be encouraged, my child! Your sins are forgiven."

3 But some of the teachers of religious law said to themselves, "That's blasphemy! Does he think he's God?"

4 Jesus knew what they were thinking, so he asked them, "Why do you have such evil thoughts in your hearts? 5 Is it easier to say 'Your sins are forgiven,' or 'Stand up and walk'? 6 So I will prove to you that the Son of Man has the authority on earth to forgive sins." Then Jesus turned to the paralyzed man and said, "Stand up, pick up your mat, and go home!"

7 And the man jumped up and went home! 8 Fear swept through the crowd as they saw this happen. And they praised God for sending a man with such great authority.

Jesus Calls Matthew

9 As Jesus was walking along, he saw a man named Matthew sitting at his tax collector's booth. "Follow me and be my disciple," Jesus said to him. So Matthew got up and followed him.

10 Later, Matthew invited Jesus and his disciples to his home as dinner guests, along with many tax collectors and other disreputable sinners. 11 But when the Pharisees saw this, they asked his disciples, "Why does your teacher eat with such scum?"

12 When Jesus heard this, he said, "Healthy people don't need a doctor—sick people do." 13 Then he added, "Now go and learn the meaning of this Scripture: 'I want you to show mercy, not offer sacrifices.' For I have come to call not those who think they are righteous, but those who know they are sinners."

A Discussion about Fasting

14 One day the disciples of John the Baptist came to Jesus and asked him, "Why don't your disciples fast like we do and the Pharisees do?"

15 Jesus replied, "Do wedding guests mourn while celebrating with the groom? Of course not. But someday the groom will be taken away from them, and then they will fast.

16 "Besides, who would patch old clothing with new cloth? For the new patch would shrink and rip away from the old cloth, leaving an even bigger tear than before.

17 "And no one puts new wine into old wineskins. For the old skins would burst from the pressure, spilling the wine and ruining the skins. New wine is stored in new wineskins so that both are preserved."

Jesus Heals in Response to Faith

18 As Jesus was saying this, the leader of a synagogue came and knelt before him. "My daughter has just died," he said, "but you can bring her back to life again if you just come and lay your hand on her."

19 So Jesus and his disciples got up and went with him. 20 Just then a woman who had suffered for twelve years with constant bleeding came up behind him. She touched the fringe of his robe, 21 for she thought, "If I can just touch his robe, I will be healed."

22 Jesus turned around, and when he saw her he said, "Daughter, be encouraged! Your faith has made you well." And the woman was healed at that moment.

23 When Jesus arrived at the official's home, he saw the noisy crowd and heard the funeral music. 24 "Get out!" he told them. "The girl isn't dead; she's only asleep." But the crowd laughed at him. 25 After the crowd was put outside, however, Jesus went in and took the girl by the hand, and she stood up! 26 The report of this miracle swept through the entire countryside.

Jesus Heals the Blind

27 After Jesus left the girl's home, two blind men followed along behind him, shouting, "Son of David, have mercy on us!"

28 They went right into the house where he was staying, and Jesus asked them, "Do you believe I can make you see?"

"Yes, Lord," they told him, "we do."

29 Then he touched their eyes and said, "Because of your faith, it will happen." 30 Then their eyes were opened, and they could see! Jesus sternly warned them, "Don't tell anyone about this." 31 But instead, they went out and spread his fame all over the region.

32 When they left, a demon-possessed man

who couldn't speak was brought to Jesus. ³³So Jesus cast out the demon, and then the man began to speak. The crowds were amazed. "Nothing like this has ever happened in Israel!" they exclaimed.

³⁴But the Pharisees said, "He can cast out demons because he is empowered by the prince of demons."

The Need for Workers

³⁵Jesus traveled through all the towns and villages of that area, teaching in the synagogues and announcing the Good News about the Kingdom. And he healed every kind of disease and illness. ³⁶When he saw the crowds, he had compassion on them because they were confused and helpless, like sheep without a shepherd. ³⁷He said to his disciples, "The harvest is great, but the workers are few. ³⁸So pray to the Lord who is in charge of the harvest; ask him to send more workers into his fields."

CHAPTER 10

Jesus Sends Out the Twelve Apostles

Jesus called his twelve disciples together and gave them authority to cast out evil spirits and to heal every kind of disease and illness. ²Here are the names of the twelve apostles:

first, Simon (also called Peter),
then Andrew (Peter's brother),
James (son of Zebedee),
John (James's brother),
³ Philip,
Bartholomew,
Thomas,
Matthew (the tax collector),
James (son of Alphaeus),
Thaddaeus,
⁴ Simon (the zealot),
Judas Iscariot (who later betrayed him).

⁵Jesus sent out the twelve apostles with these instructions: "Don't go to the Gentiles or the Samaritans, ⁶but only to the people of Israel—God's lost sheep. ⁷Go and announce to them that the Kingdom of Heaven is near. ⁸Heal the sick, raise the dead, cure those with leprosy, and cast out demons. Give as freely as you have received!

⁹"Don't take any money in your money belts—no gold, silver, or even copper coins. ¹⁰Don't carry a traveler's bag with a change of clothes and sandals or even a walking stick. Don't hesitate to accept hospitality, because those who work deserve to be fed.

¹¹"Whenever you enter a city or village, search for a worthy person and stay in his home until you leave town. ¹²When you enter the home, give it your blessing. ¹³If it turns out to be a worthy home, let your blessing stand; if it is not, take back the blessing. ¹⁴If any household or town refuses to welcome you or listen to your message, shake its dust from your feet as you leave. ¹⁵I tell you the truth, the wicked cities of Sodom and Gomorrah will be better off than such a town on the judgment day.

¹⁶"Look, I am sending you out as sheep among wolves. So be as shrewd as snakes and harmless as doves. ¹⁷But beware! For you will be handed over to the courts and will be flogged with whips in the synagogues. ¹⁸You will stand trial before governors and kings because you are my followers. But this will be your opportunity to tell the rulers and other unbelievers about me. ¹⁹When you are arrested, don't worry about how to respond or what to say. God will give you the right words at the right time. ²⁰For it is not you who will be speaking—it will be the Spirit of your Father speaking through you.

²¹"A brother will betray his brother to death, a father will betray his own child, and children will rebel against their parents and cause them to be killed. ²²And all nations will hate you because you are my followers. But everyone who endures to the end will be saved. ²³When you are persecuted in one town, flee to the next. I tell you the truth, the Son of Man will return before you have reached all the towns of Israel.

²⁴"Students are not greater than their teacher, and slaves are not greater than their master. ²⁵Students are to be like their teacher, and slaves are to be like their master. And since I, the master of the household, have been called the prince of demons, the members of my household will be called by even worse names!

²⁶"But don't be afraid of those who threaten you. For the time is coming when everything that is covered will be revealed, and all that is secret will be made known to all. ²⁷What I tell you now in the darkness, shout abroad when daybreak comes. What I whisper in your ear, shout from the housetops for all to hear!

²⁸"Don't be afraid of those who want to kill your body; they cannot touch your soul. Fear only God, who can destroy both soul and body in hell. ²⁹What is the price of two sparrows—one copper coin? But not a single sparrow can fall to the ground without your Father knowing it. ³⁰And the very hairs on your head are all numbered. ³¹So don't be afraid; you are more valuable to God than a whole flock of sparrows.

32"Everyone who acknowledges me publicly here on earth, I will also acknowledge before my Father in heaven. 33 But everyone who denies me here on earth, I will also deny before my Father in heaven.

34"Don't imagine that I came to bring peace to the earth! I came not to bring peace, but a sword.

35 'I have come to set a man against his father,
   a daughter against her mother,
   and a daughter-in-law against her mother-in-law.
36   Your enemies will be right in your own household!'

37"If you love your father or mother more than you love me, you are not worthy of being mine; or if you love your son or daughter more than me, you are not worthy of being mine. 38 If you refuse to take up your cross and follow me, you are not worthy of being mine. 39 If you cling to your life, you will lose it; but if you give up your life for me, you will find it.

40"Anyone who receives you receives me, and anyone who receives me receives the Father who sent me. 41 If you receive a prophet as one who speaks for God, you will be given the same reward as a prophet. And if you receive righteous people because of their righteousness, you will be given a reward like theirs. 42 And if you give even a cup of cold water to one of the least of my followers, you will surely be rewarded."

CHAPTER **11**
Jesus and John the Baptist

When Jesus had finished giving these instructions to his twelve disciples, he went out to teach and preach in towns throughout the region.

2 John the Baptist, who was in prison, heard about all the things the Messiah was doing. So he sent his disciples to ask Jesus, 3 "Are you the Messiah we've been expecting, or should we keep looking for someone else?"

4 Jesus told them, "Go back to John and tell him what you have heard and seen—5 the blind see, the lame walk, the lepers are cured, the deaf hear, the dead are raised to life, and the Good News is being preached to the poor. 6 And tell him, 'God blesses those who do not turn away because of me.'"

7 As John's disciples were leaving, Jesus began talking about him to the crowds. "What kind of man did you go into the wilderness to see? Was he a weak reed, swayed by every breath of wind? 8 Or were you expecting to see a man dressed in expensive clothes? No, people with expensive

Key Verse "Come to me, all of you who are weary and carry heavy burdens, and I will give you rest."—**MATTHEW 11:28**

Jesus Attraction

Read MATTHEW 11:28 out loud until you can say it by yourself. Jesus wants us to come to him. Here's an experiment to show what that's like.

1 Tie several O-shaped cereal pieces to the end of a piece of string.

2 Rub a plastic comb on a wool sweater or your hair so the comb's full of static electricity.

3 Carefully move the comb toward the cereal.

What happens? The cereal comes toward the comb, just like Jesus wants us to come to him!

Glue pieces of cereal to a sheet of construction paper so they spell a reminder of this verse. (You might write, "Jesus" or "Come to me.") Spray the sheet with hair spray, and hang it in your kitchen to remind you that Jesus wants you to come to him!

clothes live in palaces. 9 Were you looking for a prophet? Yes, and he is more than a prophet. 10 John is the man to whom the Scriptures refer when they say,

'Look, I am sending my messenger ahead of you,
   and he will prepare your way before you.'

11"I tell you the truth, of all who have ever lived, none is greater than John the Baptist. Yet even the least person in the Kingdom of Heaven is greater than he is! 12 And from the time John the Baptist began preaching until now, the Kingdom of Heaven has been forcefully advancing, and violent people are attacking it. 13For before John came, all the prophets and the law of Moses looked forward to this present time. 14And if you are willing to accept what I say, he is Elijah, the one the prophets said would come. 15Anyone with ears to hear should listen and understand!

16"To what can I compare this generation? It is like children playing a game in the public square. They complain to their friends,

17 'We played wedding songs,
and you didn't dance,
so we played funeral songs,
and you didn't mourn.'

18For John didn't spend his time eating and drinking, and you say, 'He's possessed by a demon.' 19The Son of Man, on the other hand, feasts and drinks, and you say, 'He's a glutton and a drunkard, and a friend of tax collectors and other sinners!' But wisdom is shown to be right by its results."

Judgment for the Unbelievers

20Then Jesus began to denounce the towns where he had done so many of his miracles, because they hadn't repented of their sins and turned to God. 21"What sorrow awaits you, Korazin and Bethsaida! For if the miracles I did in you had been done in wicked Tyre and Sidon, their people would have repented of their sins long ago, clothing themselves in burlap and throwing ashes on their heads to show their remorse. 22I tell you, Tyre and Sidon will be better off on judgment day than you.

23"And you people of Capernaum, will you be honored in heaven? No, you will go down to the place of the dead. For if the miracles I did for you had been done in wicked Sodom, it would still be here today. 24I tell you, even Sodom will be better off on judgment day than you."

Jesus' Prayer of Thanksgiving

25At that time Jesus prayed this prayer: "O Father, Lord of heaven and earth, thank you for hiding these things from those who think themselves wise and clever, and for revealing them to the childlike. 26Yes, Father, it pleased you to do it this way!

27"My Father has entrusted everything to me. No one truly knows the Son except the Father, and no one truly knows the Father except the Son and those to whom the Son chooses to reveal him."

28Then Jesus said, "Come to me, all of you who are weary and carry heavy burdens, and I will give you rest. 29Take my yoke upon you. Let me teach you, because I am humble and gentle at heart, and you will find rest for your souls. 30For my yoke is easy to bear, and the burden I give you is light."

CHAPTER **12**
A Discussion about the Sabbath

At about that time Jesus was walking through some grainfields on the Sabbath. His disciples were hungry, so they began breaking off some heads of grain and eating them. 2But some Pharisees saw them do it and protested, "Look, your disciples are breaking the law by harvesting grain on the Sabbath."

3Jesus said to them, "Haven't you read in the Scriptures what David did when he and his companions were hungry? 4He went into the house of God, and he and his companions broke the law by eating the sacred loaves of bread that only the priests are allowed to eat. 5And haven't you read in the law of Moses that the priests on duty in the Temple may work on the Sabbath? 6I tell you, there is one here who is even greater than the Temple! 7But you would not have condemned my innocent disciples if you knew the meaning of this Scripture: 'I want you to show mercy, not offer sacrifices.' 8For the Son of Man is Lord, even over the Sabbath!"

Jesus Heals on the Sabbath

9Then Jesus went over to their synagogue, 10where he noticed a man with a deformed hand. The Pharisees asked Jesus, "Does the law permit a person to work by healing on the Sabbath?" (They were hoping he would say yes, so they could bring charges against him.)

11And he answered, "If you had a sheep that fell into a well on the Sabbath, wouldn't you work to pull it out? Of course you would. 12And how much more valuable is a person than a sheep! Yes, the law permits a person to do good on the Sabbath."

13Then he said to the man, "Hold out your hand." So the man held out his hand, and it was restored, just like the other one! 14Then the Pharisees called a meeting to plot how to kill Jesus.

Jesus, God's Chosen Servant

15But Jesus knew what they were planning. So he left that area, and many people followed him. He healed all the sick among them, 16but he warned them not to reveal who he was. [17]This fulfilled the prophecy of Isaiah concerning him:

[18] "Look at my Servant, whom I have chosen.
   He is my Beloved, who pleases me.
 I will put my Spirit upon him,
   and he will proclaim justice to the nations.
[19] He will not fight or shout
   or raise his voice in public.
[20] He will not crush the weakest reed
   or put out a flickering candle.
   Finally he will cause justice to be
     victorious.
[21] And his name will be the hope
   of all the world."

Jesus and the Prince of Demons

[22]Then a demon-possessed man, who was blind and couldn't speak, was brought to Jesus. He healed the man so that he could both speak and see. [23]The crowd was amazed and asked, "Could it be that Jesus is the Son of David, the Messiah?"

[24]But when the Pharisees heard about the miracle, they said, "No wonder he can cast out demons. He gets his power from Satan, the prince of demons."

[25]Jesus knew their thoughts and replied, "Any kingdom divided by civil war is doomed. A town or family splintered by feuding will fall apart. [26]And if Satan is casting out Satan, he is divided and fighting against himself. His own kingdom will not survive. [27]And if I am empowered by Satan, what about your own exorcists? They cast out demons, too, so they will condemn you for what you have said. [28]But if I am casting out demons by the Spirit of God, then the Kingdom of God has arrived among you. [29]For who is powerful enough to enter the house of a strong man like Satan and plunder his goods? Only someone even stronger—someone who could tie him up and then plunder his house.

[30]"Anyone who isn't with me opposes me, and anyone who isn't working with me is actually working against me.

[31]"So I tell you, every sin and blasphemy can be forgiven—except blasphemy against the Holy Spirit, which will never be forgiven. [32]Anyone who speaks against the Son of Man can be forgiven, but anyone who speaks against the Holy Spirit will never be forgiven, either in this world or in the world to come.

[33]"A tree is identified by its fruit. If a tree is good, its fruit will be good. If a tree is bad, its fruit will be bad. [34]You brood of snakes! How could evil men like you speak what is good and right? For whatever is in your heart determines what you say. [35]A good person produces good things from the treasury of a good heart, and an evil person produces evil things from the treasury of an evil heart. [36]And I tell you this, you must give an account on judgment day for every idle word you speak. [37]The words you say will either acquit you or condemn you."

The Sign of Jonah

[38]One day some teachers of religious law and Pharisees came to Jesus and said, "Teacher, we want you to show us a miraculous sign to prove your authority."

[39]But Jesus replied, "Only an evil, adulterous generation would demand a miraculous sign; but the only sign I will give them is the sign of the prophet Jonah. [40]For as Jonah was in the belly of the great fish for three days and three nights, so will the Son of Man be in the heart of the earth for three days and three nights.

[41]"The people of Nineveh will stand up against this generation on judgment day and condemn it, for they repented of their sins at the preaching of Jonah. Now someone greater than Jonah is here—but you refuse to repent. [42]The queen of Sheba will also stand up against this generation on judgment day and condemn it, for she came from a distant land to hear the wisdom of Solomon. Now someone greater than Solomon is here—but you refuse to listen.

[43]"When an evil spirit leaves a person, it goes into the desert, seeking rest but finding none. [44]Then it says, 'I will return to the person I came from.' So it returns and finds its former home empty, swept, and in order. [45]Then the spirit finds seven other spirits more evil than itself, and they all enter the person and live there. And so that person is worse off than before. That will be the experience of this evil generation."

The True Family of Jesus

[46]As Jesus was speaking to the crowd, his mother and brothers stood outside, asking to speak to him. [47]Someone told Jesus, "Your mother and your brothers are outside, and they want to speak to you."

[48]Jesus asked, "Who is my mother? Who are my brothers?" [49]Then he pointed to his disciples and said, "Look, these are my mother and brothers. [50]Anyone who does the will of my Father in heaven is my brother and sister and mother!"

CHAPTER **13**

Parable of the Farmer Scattering Seed

Later that same day Jesus left the house and sat beside the lake. 2A large crowd soon gathered around him, so he got into a boat. Then he sat there and taught as the people stood on the shore. 3He told many stories in the form of parables, such as this one:

"Listen! A farmer went out to plant some seeds. 4As he scattered them across his field, some seeds fell on a footpath, and the birds came and ate them. 5Other seeds fell on shallow soil with underlying rock. The seeds sprouted quickly because the soil was shallow. 6But the plants soon wilted under the hot sun, and since they didn't have deep roots, they died. 7Other seeds fell among thorns that grew up and choked out the tender plants. 8Still other seeds fell on fertile soil, and they produced a crop that was thirty, sixty, and even a hundred times as much as had been planted! 9Anyone with ears to hear should listen and understand."

10His disciples came and asked him, "Why do you use parables when you talk to the people?"

11He replied, "You are permitted to understand the secrets of the Kingdom of Heaven, but others are not. 12To those who listen to my teaching, more understanding will be given, and they will have an abundance of knowledge. But for those who are not listening, even what little understanding they have will be taken away from them. 13That is why I use these parables,

For they look, but they don't really see.
They hear, but they don't really listen
    or understand.

14This fulfills the prophecy of Isaiah that says,

'When you hear what I say,
    you will not understand.
When you see what I do,
    you will not comprehend.
15 For the hearts of these people are hardened,
    and their ears cannot hear,
and they have closed their eyes—
    so their eyes cannot see,
and their ears cannot hear,
    and their hearts cannot understand,
and they cannot turn to me
    and let me heal them.'

16"But blessed are your eyes, because they see; and your ears, because they hear. 17I tell you the truth, many prophets and righteous people longed to see what you see, but they didn't see it.

And they longed to hear what you hear, but they didn't hear it.

18"Now listen to the explanation of the parable about the farmer planting seeds: 19The seed that fell on the footpath represents those who hear the message about the Kingdom and don't understand it. Then the evil one comes and snatches away the seed that was planted in their hearts. 20The seed on the rocky soil represents those who hear the message and immediately receive it with joy. 21But since they don't have deep roots, they don't last long. They fall away as soon as they have problems or are persecuted for believing God's word. 22The seed that fell among the thorns represents those who hear God's word, but all too quickly the message is crowded out by the worries of this life and the lure of wealth, so no fruit is produced. 23The seed that fell on good soil represents those who truly hear and understand God's word and produce a harvest of thirty, sixty, or even a hundred times as much as had been planted!"

Parable of the Wheat and Weeds

24Here is another story Jesus told: "The Kingdom of Heaven is like a farmer who planted good seed in his field. 25But that night as the workers slept, his enemy came and planted weeds among the wheat, then slipped away. 26When the crop began to grow and produce grain, the weeds also grew.

27"The farmer's workers went to him and said, 'Sir, the field where you planted that good seed is full of weeds! Where did they come from?'

28"'An enemy has done this!' the farmer exclaimed.

"'Should we pull out the weeds?' they asked.

29"'No,' he replied, 'you'll uproot the wheat if you do. 30Let both grow together until the harvest. Then I will tell the harvesters to sort out the weeds, tie them into bundles, and burn them, and to put the wheat in the barn.'"

Parable of the Mustard Seed

31Here is another illustration Jesus used: "The Kingdom of Heaven is like a mustard seed planted in a field. 32It is the smallest of all seeds, but it becomes the largest of garden plants; it grows into a tree, and birds come and make nests in its branches."

Parable of the Yeast

33Jesus also used this illustration: "The Kingdom of Heaven is like the yeast a woman used in making bread. Even though she put only a little yeast in three measures of flour, it permeated every part of the dough."

34Jesus always used stories and illustrations like these when speaking to the crowds. In fact, he never spoke to them without using such parables. 35This fulfilled what God had spoken through the prophet:

"I will speak to you in parables.
  I will explain things hidden since the
    creation of the world."

Parable of the Wheat and Weeds Explained

36Then, leaving the crowds outside, Jesus went into the house. His disciples said, "Please explain to us the story of the weeds in the field."

37Jesus replied, "The Son of Man is the farmer who plants the good seed. 38The field is the world, and the good seed represents the people of the Kingdom. The weeds are the people who belong to the evil one. 39The enemy who planted the weeds among the wheat is the devil. The harvest is the end of the world, and the harvesters are the angels.

40"Just as the weeds are sorted out and burned in the fire, so it will be at the end of the world. 41The Son of Man will send his angels, and they will remove from his Kingdom everything that causes sin and all who do evil. 42And the angels will throw them into the fiery furnace, where there will be weeping and gnashing of teeth. 43Then the righteous will shine like the sun in their Father's Kingdom. Anyone with ears to hear should listen and understand!

Parables of the Hidden Treasure and the Pearl

44"The Kingdom of Heaven is like a treasure that a man discovered hidden in a field. In his excitement, he hid it again and sold everything he owned to get enough money to buy the field.

45"Again, the Kingdom of Heaven is like a merchant on the lookout for choice pearls. 46When he discovered a pearl of great value, he sold everything he owned and bought it!

Parable of the Fishing Net

47"Again, the Kingdom of Heaven is like a fishing net that was thrown into the water and caught fish of every kind. 48When the net was full, they dragged it up onto the shore, sat down, and sorted the good fish into crates, but threw the bad ones away. 49That is the way it will be at the end of the world. The angels will come and separate the wicked people from the righteous, 50throwing the wicked into the fiery furnace, where there will be weeping and gnashing of teeth. 51Do you understand all these things?"

"Yes," they said, "we do."

52Then he added, "Every teacher of religious law who becomes a disciple in the Kingdom of Heaven is like a homeowner who brings from his storeroom new gems of truth as well as old."

Jesus Rejected at Nazareth

53When Jesus had finished telling these stories and illustrations, he left that part of the country. 54He returned to Nazareth, his hometown. When he taught there in the synagogue, everyone was amazed and said, "Where does he get this wisdom and the power to do miracles?" 55Then they scoffed, "He's just the carpenter's son, and we know Mary, his mother, and his brothers—James, Joseph, Simon, and Judas. 56All his sisters live right here among us. Where did he learn all these things?" 57And they were deeply offended and refused to believe in him.

Then Jesus told them, "A prophet is honored everywhere except in his own hometown and among his own family." 58And so he did only a few miracles there because of their unbelief.

CHAPTER **14**
The Death of John the Baptist

When Herod Antipas, the ruler of Galilee, heard about Jesus, 2he said to his advisers, "This must be John the Baptist raised from the dead! That is why he can do such miracles."

3For Herod had arrested and imprisoned John as a favor to his wife Herodias (the former wife of Herod's brother Philip). 4John had been telling Herod, "It is against God's law for you to marry her." 5Herod wanted to kill John, but he was afraid of a riot, because all the people believed John was a prophet.

6But at a birthday party for Herod, Herodias's daughter performed a dance that greatly pleased him, 7so he promised with a vow to give her anything she wanted. 8At her mother's urging, the girl said, "I want the head of John the Baptist on a tray!" 9Then the king regretted what he had said; but because of the vow he had made in front of his guests, he issued the necessary orders. 10So John was beheaded in the prison, 11and his head was brought on a tray and given to the girl, who took it to her mother. 12Later, John's disciples came for his body and buried it. Then they went and told Jesus what had happened.

Jesus Feeds Five Thousand

13 As soon as Jesus heard the news, he left in a boat to a remote area to be alone. But the crowds heard where he was headed and followed on foot from many towns. 14 Jesus saw the huge crowd as he stepped from the boat, and he had compassion on them and healed their sick.

15 That evening the disciples came to him and said, "This is a remote place, and it's already getting late. Send the crowds away so they can go to the villages and buy food for themselves."

16 But Jesus said, "That isn't necessary—you feed them."

17 "But we have only five loaves of bread and two fish!" they answered.

18 "Bring them here," he said. 19 Then he told the people to sit down on the grass. Jesus took the five loaves and two fish, looked up toward heaven, and blessed them. Then, breaking the loaves into pieces, he gave the bread to the disciples, who distributed it to the people. 20 They all ate as much as they wanted, and afterward, the disciples picked up twelve baskets of leftovers. 21 About 5,000 men were fed that day, in addition to all the women and children!

Jesus Walks on Water

22 Immediately after this, Jesus insisted that his disciples get back into the boat and cross to the other side of the lake, while he sent the people home. 23 After sending them home, he went up into the hills by himself to pray. Night fell while he was there alone.

24 Meanwhile, the disciples were in trouble far away from land, for a strong wind had risen, and they were fighting heavy waves. 25 About three o'clock in the morning Jesus came toward them, walking on the water. 26 When the disciples saw him walking on the water, they were terrified. In their fear, they cried out, "It's a ghost!"

27 But Jesus spoke to them at once. "Don't be afraid," he said. "Take courage. I am here!"

28 Then Peter called to him, "Lord, if it's really you, tell me to come to you, walking on the water."

29 "Yes, come," Jesus said.

So Peter went over the side of the boat and walked on the water toward Jesus. 30 But when he saw the strong wind and the waves, he was terrified and began to sink. "Save me, Lord!" he shouted.

31 Jesus immediately reached out and grabbed him. "You have so little faith," Jesus said. "Why did you doubt me?"

32 When they climbed back into the boat, the wind stopped. 33 Then the disciples worshiped him. "You really are the Son of God!" they exclaimed.

34 After they had crossed the lake, they landed at Gennesaret. 35 When the people recognized Jesus, the news of his arrival spread quickly throughout the whole area, and soon people were bringing all their sick to be healed. 36 They begged him to let the sick touch at least the fringe of his robe, and all who touched him were healed.

CHAPTER **15**

Jesus Teaches about Inner Purity

Some Pharisees and teachers of religious law now arrived from Jerusalem to see Jesus. They asked him, 2 "Why do your disciples disobey our age-old tradition? For they ignore our tradition of ceremonial hand washing before they eat."

3 Jesus replied, "And why do you, by your traditions, violate the direct commandments of God? 4 For instance, God says, 'Honor your father and mother,' and 'Anyone who speaks disrespectfully of father or mother must be put to death.' 5 But you say it is all right for people to say to their parents, 'Sorry, I can't help you. For I have vowed to give to God what I would have given to you.' 6 In this way, you say they don't need to honor their parents. And so you cancel the word of God for the sake of your own tradition. 7 You hypocrites! Isaiah was right when he prophesied about you, for he wrote,

8 'These people honor me with their lips,
　　but their hearts are far from me.
9 Their worship is a farce,
　　for they teach man-made ideas as
　　　commands from God.'"

10 Then Jesus called to the crowd to come and hear. "Listen," he said, "and try to understand. 11 It's not what goes into your mouth that defiles you; you are defiled by the words that come out of your mouth."

12 Then the disciples came to him and asked, "Do you realize you offended the Pharisees by what you just said?"

13 Jesus replied, "Every plant not planted by my heavenly Father will be uprooted, 14 so ignore them. They are blind guides leading the blind, and if one blind person guides another, they will both fall into a ditch."

15 Then Peter said to Jesus, "Explain to us the parable that says people aren't defiled by what they eat."

16"Don't you understand yet?" Jesus asked. 17"Anything you eat passes through the stomach and then goes into the sewer. 18But the words you speak come from the heart—that's what defiles you. 19For from the heart come evil thoughts, murder, adultery, all sexual immorality, theft, lying, and slander. 20These are what defile you. Eating with unwashed hands will never defile you."

The Faith of a Gentile Woman

21Then Jesus left Galilee and went north to the region of Tyre and Sidon. 22A Gentile woman who lived there came to him, pleading, "Have mercy on me, O Lord, Son of David! For my daughter is possessed by a demon that torments her severely."

23But Jesus gave her no reply, not even a word. Then his disciples urged him to send her away. "Tell her to go away," they said. "She is bothering us with all her begging."

24Then Jesus said to the woman, "I was sent only to help God's lost sheep—the people of Israel."

25But she came and worshiped him, pleading again, "Lord, help me!"

26Jesus responded, "It isn't right to take food from the children and throw it to the dogs."

27She replied, "That's true, Lord, but even dogs are allowed to eat the scraps that fall beneath their masters' table."

28"Dear woman," Jesus said to her, "your faith is great. Your request is granted." And her daughter was instantly healed.

Jesus Heals Many People

29Jesus returned to the Sea of Galilee and climbed a hill and sat down. 30A vast crowd brought to him people who were lame, blind, crippled, those who couldn't speak, and many others. They laid them before Jesus, and he healed them all. 31The crowd was amazed! Those who hadn't been able to speak were talking, the crippled were made well, the lame were walking, and the blind could see again! And they praised the God of Israel.

Jesus Feeds Four Thousand

32Then Jesus called his disciples and told them, "I feel sorry for these people. They have been here with me for three days, and they have nothing left to eat. I don't want to send them away hungry, or they will faint along the way."

33The disciples replied, "Where would we get enough food here in the wilderness for such a huge crowd?"

34Jesus asked, "How much bread do you have?"

They replied, "Seven loaves, and a few small fish."

35So Jesus told all the people to sit down on the ground. 36Then he took the seven loaves and the fish, thanked God for them, and broke them into pieces. He gave them to the disciples, who distributed the food to the crowd.

37They all ate as much as they wanted. Afterward, the disciples picked up seven large baskets of leftover food. 38There were 4,000 men who were fed that day, in addition to all the women and children. 39Then Jesus sent the people home, and he got into a boat and crossed over to the region of Magadan.

CHAPTER **16**

Leaders Demand a Miraculous Sign

One day the Pharisees and Sadducees came to test Jesus, demanding that he show them a miraculous sign from heaven to prove his authority.

2He replied, "You know the saying, 'Red sky at night means fair weather tomorrow; 3red sky in the morning means foul weather all day.' You know how to interpret the weather signs in the sky, but you don't know how to interpret the signs of the times! 4Only an evil, adulterous generation would demand a miraculous sign, but the only sign I will give them is the sign of the prophet Jonah." Then Jesus left them and went away.

Yeast of the Pharisees and Sadducees

5Later, after they crossed to the other side of the lake, the disciples discovered they had forgotten to bring any bread. 6"Watch out!" Jesus warned them. "Beware of the yeast of the Pharisees and Sadducees."

7At this they began to argue with each other because they hadn't brought any bread. 8Jesus knew what they were saying, so he said, "You have so little faith! Why are you arguing with each other about having no bread? 9Don't you understand even yet? Don't you remember the 5,000 I fed with five loaves, and the baskets of leftovers you picked up? 10Or the 4,000 I fed with seven loaves, and the large baskets of leftovers you picked up? 11Why can't you understand that I'm not talking about bread? So again I say, 'Beware of the yeast of the Pharisees and Sadducees.'"

12Then at last they understood that he wasn't speaking about the yeast in bread, but about the deceptive teaching of the Pharisees and Sadducees.

Peter's Declaration about Jesus

13When Jesus came to the region of Caesarea Philippi, he asked his disciples, "Who do people say that the Son of Man is?"

14"Well," they replied, "some say John the Baptist, some say Elijah, and others say Jeremiah or one of the other prophets."

15Then he asked them, "But who do you say I am?"

16Simon Peter answered, "You are the Messiah, the Son of the living God."

17Jesus replied, "You are blessed, Simon son of John, because my Father in heaven has revealed this to you. You did not learn this from any human being. 18Now I say to you that you are Peter (which means 'rock'), and upon this rock I will build my church, and all the powers of hell will not conquer it. 19And I will give you the keys of the Kingdom of Heaven. Whatever you forbid on earth will be forbidden in heaven, and whatever you permit on earth will be permitted in heaven."

20Then he sternly warned the disciples not to tell anyone that he was the Messiah.

Jesus Predicts His Death

21From then on Jesus began to tell his disciples plainly that it was necessary for him to go to Jerusalem, and that he would suffer many terrible things at the hands of the elders, the leading priests, and the teachers of religious law. He would be killed, but on the third day he would be raised from the dead.

22But Peter took him aside and began to reprimand him for saying such things. "Heaven forbid, Lord," he said. "This will never happen to you!"

23Jesus turned to Peter and said, "Get away from me, Satan! You are a dangerous trap to me. You are seeing things merely from a human point of view, not from God's."

24Then Jesus said to his disciples, "If any of you wants to be my follower, you must turn from your selfish ways, take up your cross, and follow me. 25If you try to hang on to your life, you will lose it. But if you give up your life for my sake, you will save it. 26And what do you benefit if you gain the whole world but lose your own soul? Is anything worth more than your soul? 27For the Son of Man will come with his angels in the glory of his Father and will judge all people according to their deeds. 28And I tell you the truth, some standing here right now will not die before they see the Son of Man coming in his Kingdom."

CHAPTER **17**

The Transfiguration

Six days later Jesus took Peter and the two brothers, James and John, and led them up a high mountain to be alone. 2As the men watched, Jesus' appearance was transformed so that his face shone like the sun, and his clothes became as white as light. 3Suddenly, Moses and Elijah appeared and began talking with Jesus.

4Peter exclaimed, "Lord, it's wonderful for us to be here! If you want, I'll make three shelters as memorials—one for you, one for Moses, and one for Elijah."

5But even as he spoke, a bright cloud overshadowed them, and a voice from the cloud said, "This is my dearly loved Son, who brings me great joy. Listen to him." 6The disciples were terrified and fell face down on the ground.

7Then Jesus came over and touched them. "Get up," he said. "Don't be afraid." 8And when they looked up, Moses and Elijah were gone, and they saw only Jesus.

9As they went back down the mountain, Jesus commanded them, "Don't tell anyone what you have seen until the Son of Man has been raised from the dead."

10Then his disciples asked him, "Why do the teachers of religious law insist that Elijah must return before the Messiah comes?"

11Jesus replied, "Elijah is indeed coming first to get everything ready. 12But I tell you, Elijah has already come, but he wasn't recognized, and they chose to abuse him. And in the same way they will also make the Son of Man suffer." 13Then the disciples realized he was talking about John the Baptist.

Jesus Heals a Demon-Possessed Boy

14At the foot of the mountain, a large crowd was waiting for them. A man came and knelt before Jesus and said, 15"Lord, have mercy on my son. He has seizures and suffers terribly. He often falls into the fire or into the water. 16So I brought him to your disciples, but they couldn't heal him."

17Jesus said, "You faithless and corrupt people! How long must I be with you? How long must I put up with you? Bring the boy here to me." 18Then Jesus rebuked the demon in the boy, and it left him. From that moment the boy was well.

19Afterward the disciples asked Jesus privately, "Why couldn't we cast out that demon?"

20"You don't have enough faith," Jesus told them. "I tell you the truth, if you had faith even as small as a mustard seed, you could say to this mountain, 'Move from here to there,' and it would move. Nothing would be impossible.*"

Jesus Again Predicts His Death

22After they gathered again in Galilee, Jesus told them, "The Son of Man is going to be betrayed into the hands of his enemies. 23He will be killed, but on the third day he will be raised from the dead." And the disciples were filled with grief.

Payment of the Temple Tax

24On their arrival in Capernaum, the collectors of the Temple tax came to Peter and asked him, "Doesn't your teacher pay the Temple tax?"

25"Yes, he does," Peter replied. Then he went into the house.

But before he had a chance to speak, Jesus asked him, "What do you think, Peter? Do kings tax their own people or the people they have conquered?"

26"They tax the people they have conquered," Peter replied.

"Well, then," Jesus said, "the citizens are free! 27However, we don't want to offend them, so go down to the lake and throw in a line. Open the mouth of the first fish you catch, and you will find a large silver coin. Take it and pay the tax for both of us."

CHAPTER **18**
The Greatest in the Kingdom

About that time the disciples came to Jesus and asked, "Who is greatest in the Kingdom of Heaven?"

2Jesus called a little child to him and put the child among them. 3Then he said, "I tell you the truth, unless you turn from your sins and become like little children, you will never get into the Kingdom of Heaven. 4So anyone who becomes as humble as this little child is the greatest in the Kingdom of Heaven.

5"And anyone who welcomes a little child like this on my behalf is welcoming me. 6But if you cause one of these little ones who trusts in me to fall into sin, it would be better for you to have a large millstone tied around your neck and be drowned in the depths of the sea.

7"What sorrow awaits the world, because it tempts people to sin. Temptations are inevitable, but what sorrow awaits the person who does the tempting. 8So if your hand or foot causes you to sin, cut it off and throw it away. It's better to enter eternal life with only one hand or one foot than to be thrown into eternal fire with both of your hands and feet. 9And if your eye causes you to sin, gouge it out and throw it away. It's better to enter eternal life with only one eye than to have two eyes and be thrown into the fire of hell.

10"Beware that you don't look down on any of these little ones. For I tell you that in heaven their angels are always in the presence of my heavenly Father.*

Parable of the Lost Sheep

12"If a man has a hundred sheep and one of them wanders away, what will he do? Won't he leave the ninety-nine others on the hills and go out to search for the one that is lost? 13And if he finds it, I tell you the truth, he will rejoice over it more than over the ninety-nine that didn't wander away! 14In the same way, it is not my heavenly Father's will that even one of these little ones should perish.

Correcting Another Believer

15"If another believer sins against you, go privately and point out the offense. If the other person listens and confesses it, you have won that person back. 16But if you are unsuccessful, take one or two others with you and go back again, so that everything you say may be confirmed by two or three witnesses. 17If the person still refuses to listen, take your case to the church. Then if he or she won't accept the church's decision, treat that person as a pagan or a corrupt tax collector.

18"I tell you the truth, whatever you forbid on earth will be forbidden in heaven, and whatever you permit on earth will be permitted in heaven.

19"I also tell you this: If two of you agree here on earth concerning anything you ask, my Father in heaven will do it for you. **20For where two or three gather together as my followers, I am there among them.**"

Parable of the Unforgiving Debtor

21Then Peter came to him and asked, "Lord, how often should I forgive someone who sins against me? Seven times?"

22"No, not seven times," Jesus replied, "but seventy times seven!

17:20 Some manuscripts add verse 21, *But this kind of demon won't leave except by prayer and fasting.* Compare Mark 9:29.
18:10 Some manuscripts add verse 11, *And the Son of Man came to save those who are lost.* Compare Luke 19:10.

23"Therefore, the Kingdom of Heaven can be compared to a king who decided to bring his accounts up to date with servants who had borrowed money from him. 24In the process, one of his debtors was brought in who owed him millions of dollars. 25He couldn't pay, so his master ordered that he be sold—along with his wife, his children, and everything he owned—to pay the debt.

26"But the man fell down before his master and begged him, 'Please, be patient with me, and I will pay it all.' 27Then his master was filled with pity for him, and he released him and forgave his debt.

28"But when the man left the king, he went to a fellow servant who owed him a few thousand dollars. He grabbed him by the throat and demanded instant payment.

29"His fellow servant fell down before him and begged for a little more time. 'Be patient with me, and I will pay it,' he pleaded. 30But his creditor wouldn't wait. He had the man arrested and put in prison until the debt could be paid in full.

31"When some of the other servants saw this, they were very upset. They went to the king and told him everything that had happened. 32Then the king called in the man he had forgiven and said, 'You evil servant! I forgave you that tremendous debt because you pleaded with me. 33Shouldn't you have mercy on your fellow servant, just as I had mercy on you?' 34Then the angry king sent the man to prison to be tortured until he had paid his entire debt.

35"That's what my heavenly Father will do to you if you refuse to forgive your brothers and sisters from your heart."

CHAPTER **19**
Discussion about Divorce and Marriage

When Jesus had finished saying these things, he left Galilee and went down to the region of Judea east of the Jordan River. 2Large crowds followed him there, and he healed their sick.

3Some Pharisees came and tried to trap him with this question: "Should a man be allowed to divorce his wife for just any reason?"

4"Haven't you read the Scriptures?" Jesus replied. "They record that from the beginning 'God made them male and female.' 5And he said, 'This explains why a man leaves his father and mother and is joined to his wife, and the two are united into one.' 6Since they are no longer two

Key Verse

"For where two or three gather together as my followers, I am there among them."—MATTHEW 18:20

Find a friend or two, and read MATTHEW 18:20 out loud. Then think about this.

A Real Reaction!

In science, a chemical reaction can happen when you put two things together. When two or more Christians gather together, a spiritual reaction happens!

TRY THIS!

Read about a cool spiritual reaction in Acts 21-4!

1 Pour cranberry juice into several clear plastic cups.

2 Add a teaspoon of baking soda to each cup.

BAKING SODA

3 Add other liquids, like lemon juice or cola, to the cups. See if you can make the juice turn back to its original color.

Adding two or three ingredients together caused chemical reactions in this experiment. **How can you and your friends cause a spiritual reaction?** Pray and ask God the best way to serve him this week!

but one, let no one split apart what God has joined together."

7"Then why did Moses say in the law that a man could give his wife a written notice of divorce and send her away?" they asked.

8Jesus replied, "Moses permitted divorce only as a concession to your hard hearts, but it was not what God had originally intended. 9And I tell you this, whoever divorces his wife and marries someone else commits adultery—unless his wife has been unfaithful.*"

10Jesus' disciples then said to him, "If this is the case, it is better not to marry!"

11"Not everyone can accept this statement," Jesus said. "Only those whom God helps. 12Some are born as eunuchs, some have been made eunuchs by others, and some choose not to marry for the sake of the Kingdom of Heaven. Let anyone accept this who can."

Jesus Blesses the Children

13One day some parents brought their children to Jesus so he could lay his hands on them and pray for them. But the disciples scolded the parents for bothering him.

14But Jesus said, "Let the children come to me. Don't stop them! For the Kingdom of Heaven belongs to those who are like these children." 15And he placed his hands on their heads and blessed them before he left.

The Rich Man

16Someone came to Jesus with this question: "Teacher, what good deed must I do to have eternal life?"

17"Why ask me about what is good?" Jesus replied. "There is only One who is good. But to answer your question—if you want to receive eternal life, keep the commandments."

18"Which ones?" the man asked.

And Jesus replied: "'You must not murder. You must not commit adultery. You must not steal. You must not testify falsely. 19Honor your father and mother. Love your neighbor as yourself.'"

20"I've obeyed all these commandments," the young man replied. "What else must I do?"

21Jesus told him, "If you want to be perfect, go and sell all your possessions and give the money to the poor, and you will have treasure in heaven. Then come, follow me."

22But when the young man heard this, he went away sad, for he had many possessions.

23Then Jesus said to his disciples, "I tell you the truth, it is very hard for a rich person to enter the Kingdom of Heaven. 24I'll say it again—it is easier for a camel to go through the eye of a needle than for a rich person to enter the Kingdom of God!"

25The disciples were astounded. "Then who in the world can be saved?" they asked.

26Jesus looked at them intently and said, "Humanly speaking, it is impossible. But with God everything is possible."

27Then Peter said to him, "We've given up everything to follow you. What will we get?"

28Jesus replied, "I assure you that when the world is made new and the Son of Man sits upon his glorious throne, you who have been my followers will also sit on twelve thrones, judging the twelve tribes of Israel. 29And everyone who has given up houses or brothers or sisters or father or mother or children or property, for my sake, will receive a hundred times as much in return and will inherit eternal life. 30But many who are the greatest now will be least important then, and those who seem least important now will be the greatest then.

CHAPTER **20**

Parable of the Vineyard Workers

"For the Kingdom of Heaven is like the landowner who went out early one morning to hire workers for his vineyard. 2He agreed to pay the normal daily wage and sent them out to work.

3"At nine o'clock in the morning he was passing through the marketplace and saw some people standing around doing nothing. 4So he hired them, telling them he would pay them whatever was right at the end of the day. 5So they went to work in the vineyard. At noon and again at three o'clock he did the same thing.

6"At five o'clock that afternoon he was in town again and saw some more people standing around. He asked them, 'Why haven't you been working today?'

7"They replied, 'Because no one hired us.'

"The landowner told them, 'Then go out and join the others in my vineyard.'

8"That evening he told the foreman to call the workers in and pay them, beginning with the last workers first. 9When those hired at five o'clock were paid, each received a full day's wage. 10When those hired first came to get their pay, they assumed they would receive more. But they, too, were paid a day's wage. 11When they received their pay, they protested to the owner, 12'Those people worked only one hour, and yet you've paid them just as much as you paid us who worked all day in the scorching heat.'

13"He answered one of them, 'Friend, I haven't been unfair! Didn't you agree to work all day for the usual wage? 14Take your money and go. I wanted to pay this last worker the same as you. 15Is it against the law for me to do what I want with my money? Should you be jealous because I am kind to others?'

19:9 Some manuscripts add *And anyone who marries a divorced woman commits adultery.* Compare Matt 5:32.

16"So those who are last now will be first then, and those who are first will be last."

Jesus Again Predicts His Death

17As Jesus was going up to Jerusalem, he took the twelve disciples aside privately and told them what was going to happen to him. 18"Listen," he said, "we're going up to Jerusalem, where the Son of Man will be betrayed to the leading priests and the teachers of religious law. They will sentence him to die. 19Then they will hand him over to the Romans to be mocked, flogged with a whip, and crucified. But on the third day he will be raised from the dead."

Jesus Teaches about Serving Others

20Then the mother of James and John, the sons of Zebedee, came to Jesus with her sons. She knelt respectfully to ask a favor. 21"What is your request?" he asked.

She replied, "In your Kingdom, please let my two sons sit in places of honor next to you, one on your right and the other on your left."

22But Jesus answered by saying to them, "You don't know what you are asking! Are you able to drink from the bitter cup of suffering I am about to drink?"

"Oh yes," they replied, "we are able!"

23Jesus told them, "You will indeed drink from my bitter cup. But I have no right to say who will sit on my right or my left. My Father has prepared those places for the ones he has chosen."

24When the ten other disciples heard what James and John had asked, they were indignant. 25But Jesus called them together and said, "You know that the rulers in this world lord it over their people, and officials flaunt their authority over those under them. 26But among you it will be different. Whoever wants to be a leader among you must be your servant, 27and whoever wants to be first among you must become your slave. 28For even the Son of Man came not to be served but to serve others and to give his life as a ransom for many."

Jesus Heals Two Blind Men

29As Jesus and the disciples left the town of Jericho, a large crowd followed behind. 30Two blind men were sitting beside the road. When they heard that Jesus was coming that way, they began shouting, "Lord, Son of David, have mercy on us!"

31"Be quiet!" the crowd yelled at them.

But they only shouted louder, "Lord, Son of David, have mercy on us!"

32When Jesus heard them, he stopped and called, "What do you want me to do for you?"

33"Lord," they said, "we want to see!" 34Jesus felt sorry for them and touched their eyes. Instantly they could see! Then they followed him.

CHAPTER **21**
Jesus' Triumphant Entry

As Jesus and the disciples approached Jerusalem, they came to the town of Bethphage on the Mount of Olives. Jesus sent two of them on ahead. 2"Go into the village over there," he said. "As soon as you enter it, you will see a donkey tied there, with its colt beside it. Untie them and bring them to me. 3If anyone asks what you are doing, just say, 'The Lord needs them,' and he will immediately let you take them."

4This took place to fulfill the prophecy that said,

5 "Tell the people of Israel,
  'Look, your King is coming to you.
 He is humble, riding on a donkey—
  riding on a donkey's colt.'"

6The two disciples did as Jesus commanded. 7They brought the donkey and the colt to him and threw their garments over the colt, and he sat on it.

8Most of the crowd spread their garments on the road ahead of him, and others cut branches from the trees and spread them on the road. 9Jesus was in the center of the procession, and the people all around him were shouting,

"Praise God for the Son of David!
  Blessings on the one who comes in the
   name of the LORD!
  Praise God in highest heaven!"

10The entire city of Jerusalem was in an uproar as he entered. "Who is this?" they asked.

11And the crowds replied, "It's Jesus, the prophet from Nazareth in Galilee."

Jesus Clears the Temple

12Jesus entered the Temple and began to drive out all the people buying and selling animals for sacrifice. He knocked over the tables of the money changers and the chairs of those selling doves. 13He said to them, "The Scriptures declare, 'My Temple will be called a house of prayer,' but you have turned it into a den of thieves!"

14The blind and the lame came to him in the Temple, and he healed them. 15The leading

PARADE of Praise

Everyone loves a parade! **Read MATTHEW 21:1-11 to learn about a special parade!**

The people in Jerusalem had a parade-like gathering to honor Jesus. What can *you* do to honor Jesus? **THINK OF A FEW WAYS, AND WRITE THEM HERE.**

_____

_____

_____

The people cheered Jesus. They laid their coats in the road and shouted praises. Think of ways *you* can praise Jesus. **WRITE YOUR IDEAS HERE.**

_____

_____

_____

NOW THAT YOU'VE MADE A PLAN, GET GOING! Show Jesus that he's more important than anything else in your life.

priests and the teachers of religious law saw these wonderful miracles and heard even the children in the Temple shouting, "Praise God for the Son of David."

But the leaders were indignant. 16 They asked Jesus, "Do you hear what these children are saying?"

"Yes," Jesus replied. "Haven't you ever read the Scriptures? For they say, 'You have taught children and infants to give you praise.'" 17 Then he returned to Bethany, where he stayed overnight.

Jesus Curses the Fig Tree

18 In the morning, as Jesus was returning to Jerusalem, he was hungry, 19 and he noticed a fig tree beside the road. He went over to see if there were any figs, but there were only leaves. Then he said to it, "May you never bear fruit again!" And immediately the fig tree withered up.

20 The disciples were amazed when they saw this and asked, "How did the fig tree wither so quickly?"

21 Then Jesus told them, "I tell you the truth, if you have faith and don't doubt, you can do things like this and much more. You can even say to this mountain, 'May you be lifted up and thrown into the sea,' and it will happen. 22 You can pray for anything, and if you have faith, you will receive it."

The Authority of Jesus Challenged

23 When Jesus returned to the Temple and began teaching, the leading priests and elders came up to him. They demanded, "By what authority are you doing all these things? Who gave you the right?"

24 "I'll tell you by what authority I do these things if you answer one question," Jesus replied. 25 "Did John's authority to baptize come from heaven, or was it merely human?"

They talked it over among themselves. "If we say it was from heaven, he will ask us why we didn't believe John. 26 But if we say it was merely human, we'll be mobbed because the people believe John was a prophet." 27 So they finally replied, "We don't know."

And Jesus responded, "Then I won't tell you by what authority I do these things.

Parable of the Two Sons

28 "But what do you think about this? A man with two sons told the older boy, 'Son, go out and work in the vineyard today.' 29 The son answered, 'No, I won't go,' but later he changed his mind and

went anyway. ³⁰Then the father told the other son, 'You go,' and he said, 'Yes, sir, I will.' But he didn't go.

³¹"Which of the two obeyed his father?"

They replied, "The first."

Then Jesus explained his meaning: "I tell you the truth, corrupt tax collectors and prostitutes will get into the Kingdom of God before you do. ³²For John the Baptist came and showed you the right way to live, but you didn't believe him, while tax collectors and prostitutes did. And even when you saw this happening, you refused to believe him and repent of your sins.

Parable of the Evil Farmers

³³"Now listen to another story. A certain landowner planted a vineyard, built a wall around it, dug a pit for pressing out the grape juice, and built a lookout tower. Then he leased the vineyard to tenant farmers and moved to another country. ³⁴At the time of the grape harvest, he sent his servants to collect his share of the crop. ³⁵But the farmers grabbed his servants, beat one, killed one, and stoned another. ³⁶So the landowner sent a larger group of his servants to collect for him, but the results were the same.

³⁷"Finally, the owner sent his son, thinking, 'Surely they will respect my son.'

³⁸"But when the tenant farmers saw his son coming, they said to one another, 'Here comes the heir to this estate. Come on, let's kill him and get the estate for ourselves!' ³⁹So they grabbed him, dragged him out of the vineyard, and murdered him.

⁴⁰"When the owner of the vineyard returns," Jesus asked, "what do you think he will do to those farmers?"

⁴¹The religious leaders replied, "He will put the wicked men to a horrible death and lease the vineyard to others who will give him his share of the crop after each harvest."

⁴²Then Jesus asked them, "Didn't you ever read this in the Scriptures?

'The stone that the builders rejected
  has now become the cornerstone.
This is the LORD's doing,
  and it is wonderful to see.'

⁴³I tell you, the Kingdom of God will be taken away from you and given to a nation that will produce the proper fruit. ⁴⁴Anyone who stumbles over that stone will be broken to pieces, and it will crush anyone it falls on."

⁴⁵When the leading priests and Pharisees heard this parable, they realized he was telling the story against them—they were the wicked farmers. ⁴⁶They wanted to arrest him, but they were afraid of the crowds, who considered Jesus to be a prophet.

CHAPTER **22**

Parable of the Great Feast

Jesus also told them other parables. He said, ²"The Kingdom of Heaven can be illustrated by the story of a king who prepared a great wedding feast for his son. ³When the banquet was ready, he sent his servants to notify those who were invited. But they all refused to come!

⁴"So he sent other servants to tell them, 'The feast has been prepared. The bulls and fattened cattle have been killed, and everything is ready. Come to the banquet!' ⁵But the guests he had invited ignored them and went their own way, one to his farm, another to his business. ⁶Others seized his messengers and insulted them and killed them.

⁷"The king was furious, and he sent out his army to destroy the murderers and burn their town. ⁸And he said to his servants, 'The wedding feast is ready, and the guests I invited aren't worthy of the honor. ⁹Now go out to the street corners and invite everyone you see.' ¹⁰So the servants brought in everyone they could find, good and bad alike, and the banquet hall was filled with guests.

¹¹"But when the king came in to meet the guests, he noticed a man who wasn't wearing the proper clothes for a wedding. ¹²'Friend,' he asked, 'how is it that you are here without wedding clothes?' But the man had no reply. ¹³Then the king said to his aides, 'Bind his hands and feet and throw him into the outer darkness, where there will be weeping and gnashing of teeth.'

¹⁴"For many are called, but few are chosen."

Taxes for Caesar

¹⁵Then the Pharisees met together to plot how to trap Jesus into saying something for which he could be arrested. ¹⁶They sent some of their disciples, along with the supporters of Herod, to meet with him. "Teacher," they said, "we know how honest you are. You teach the way of God truthfully. You are impartial and don't play favorites. ¹⁷Now tell us what you think about this: Is it right to pay taxes to Caesar or not?"

¹⁸But Jesus knew their evil motives. "You hypocrites!" he said. "Why are you trying to trap me? ¹⁹Here, show me the coin used for the tax." When they handed him a Roman coin, ²⁰he asked, "Whose picture and title are stamped on it?"

21"Caesar's," they replied.

"Well, then," he said, "give to Caesar what belongs to Caesar, and give to God what belongs to God."

22His reply amazed them, and they went away.

Discussion about Resurrection

23That same day Jesus was approached by some Sadducees—religious leaders who say there is no resurrection from the dead. They posed this question: 24"Teacher, Moses said, 'If a man dies without children, his brother should marry the widow and have a child who will carry on the brother's name.' 25Well, suppose there were seven brothers. The oldest one married and then died without children, so his brother married the widow. 26But the second brother also died, and the third brother married her. This continued with all seven of them. 27Last of all, the woman also died. 28So tell us, whose wife will she be in the resurrection? For all seven were married to her."

29Jesus replied, "Your mistake is that you don't know the Scriptures, and you don't know the power of God. 30For when the dead rise, they will neither marry nor be given in marriage. In this respect they will be like the angels in heaven. 31"But now, as to whether there will be a resurrection of the dead—haven't you ever read about this in the Scriptures? Long after Abraham, Isaac, and Jacob had died, God said, 32'I am the God of Abraham, the God of Isaac, and the God of Jacob.' So he is the God of the living, not the dead."

33When the crowds heard him, they were astounded at his teaching.

The Most Important Commandment

34But when the Pharisees heard that he had silenced the Sadducees with his reply, they met together to question him again. 35One of them, an expert in religious law, tried to trap him with this question: 36"Teacher, which is the most important commandment in the law of Moses?"

37Jesus replied, "'You must love the LORD your God with all your heart, all your soul, and all your mind.' 38This is the first and greatest commandment. 39A second is equally important: 'Love your neighbor as yourself.' 40The entire law and all the demands of the prophets are based on these two commandments."

Whose Son Is the Messiah?

41Then, surrounded by the Pharisees, Jesus asked them a question: 42"What do you think about the Messiah? Whose son is he?"

They replied, "He is the son of David."

43Jesus responded, "Then why does David, speaking under the inspiration of the Spirit, call the Messiah 'my Lord'? For David said,

44 'The LORD said to my Lord,
 Sit in the place of honor at my right hand
  until I humble your enemies beneath
  your feet.'

45Since David called the Messiah 'my Lord,' how can the Messiah be his son?"

46No one could answer him. And after that, no one dared to ask him any more questions.

CHAPTER **23**
Jesus Criticizes the Religious Leaders

Then Jesus said to the crowds and to his disciples, 2"The teachers of religious law and the Pharisees are the official interpreters of the law of Moses. 3So practice and obey whatever they tell you, but don't follow their example. For they don't practice what they teach. 4They crush people with unbearable religious demands and never lift a finger to ease the burden.

5"Everything they do is for show. On their arms they wear extra wide prayer boxes with Scripture verses inside, and they wear robes with extra long tassels. 6And they love to sit at the head table at banquets and in the seats of honor in the synagogues. 7They love to receive respectful greetings as they walk in the marketplaces, and to be called 'Rabbi.'

8"Don't let anyone call you 'Rabbi,' for you have only one teacher, and all of you are equal as brothers and sisters. 9And don't address anyone here on earth as 'Father,' for only God in heaven is your spiritual Father. 10And don't let anyone call you 'Teacher,' for you have only one teacher, the Messiah. 11The greatest among you must be a servant. 12But those who exalt themselves will be humbled, and those who humble themselves will be exalted.

13"What sorrow awaits you teachers of religious law and you Pharisees. Hypocrites! For you shut the door of the Kingdom of Heaven in people's faces. You won't go in yourselves, and you don't let others enter either.*

15"What sorrow awaits you teachers of reli-

23:13 Some manuscripts add verse 14, *What sorrow awaits you teachers of religious law and you Pharisees. Hypocrites! You shamelessly cheat widows out of their property and then pretend to be pious by making long prayers in public. Because of this, you will be severely punished.* Compare Mark 12:40 and Luke 20:47.

gious law and you Pharisees. Hypocrites! For you cross land and sea to make one convert, and then you turn that person into twice the child of hell you yourselves are!

16"Blind guides! What sorrow awaits you! For you say that it means nothing to swear 'by God's Temple,' but that it is binding to swear 'by the gold in the Temple.' 17Blind fools! Which is more important—the gold or the Temple that makes the gold sacred? 18And you say that to swear 'by the altar' is not binding, but to swear 'by the gifts on the altar' is binding. 19How blind! For which is more important—the gift on the altar or the altar that makes the gift sacred? 20When you swear 'by the altar,' you are swearing by it and by everything on it. 21And when you swear 'by the Temple,' you are swearing by it and by God, who lives in it. 22And when you swear 'by heaven,' you are swearing by the throne of God and by God, who sits on the throne.

23"What sorrow awaits you teachers of religious law and you Pharisees. Hypocrites! For you are careful to tithe even the tiniest income from your herb gardens, but you ignore the more important aspects of the law—justice, mercy, and faith. You should tithe, yes, but do not neglect the more important things. 24Blind guides! You strain your water so you won't accidentally swallow a gnat, but you swallow a camel!

25"What sorrow awaits you teachers of religious law and you Pharisees. Hypocrites! For you are so careful to clean the outside of the cup and the dish, but inside you are filthy—full of greed and self-indulgence! 26You blind Pharisee! First wash the inside of the cup and the dish, and then the outside will become clean, too.

27"What sorrow awaits you teachers of religious law and you Pharisees. Hypocrites! For you are like whitewashed tombs—beautiful on the outside but filled on the inside with dead people's bones and all sorts of impurity. 28Outwardly you look like righteous people, but inwardly your hearts are filled with hypocrisy and lawlessness.

29"What sorrow awaits you teachers of religious law and you Pharisees. Hypocrites! For you build tombs for the prophets your ancestors killed, and you decorate the monuments of the godly people your ancestors destroyed. 30Then you say, 'If we had lived in the days of our ancestors, we would never have joined them in killing the prophets.'

31"But in saying that, you testify against yourselves that you are indeed the descendants of those who murdered the prophets. 32Go ahead and finish what your ancestors started. 33Snakes! Sons of vipers! How will you escape the judgment of hell?

34"Therefore, I am sending you prophets and wise men and teachers of religious law. But you will kill some by crucifixion, and you will flog others with whips in your synagogues, chasing them from city to city. 35As a result, you will be held responsible for the murder of all godly people of all time—from the murder of righteous Abel to the murder of Zechariah son of Barachiah, whom you killed in the Temple between the sanctuary and the altar. 36I tell you the truth, this judgment will fall on this very generation.

Jesus Grieves over Jerusalem

37"O Jerusalem, Jerusalem, the city that kills the prophets and stones God's messengers! How often I have wanted to gather your children together as a hen protects her chicks beneath her wings, but you wouldn't let me. 38And now, look, your house is abandoned and desolate. 39For I tell you this, you will never see me again until you say, 'Blessings on the one who comes in the name of the LORD!'"

CHAPTER **24**
Jesus Foretells the Future

As Jesus was leaving the Temple grounds, his disciples pointed out to him the various Temple buildings. 2But he responded, "Do you see all these buildings? I tell you the truth, they will be completely demolished. Not one stone will be left on top of another!"

3Later, Jesus sat on the Mount of Olives. His disciples came to him privately and said, "Tell us, when will all this happen? What sign will signal your return and the end of the world?"

4Jesus told them, "Don't let anyone mislead you, 5for many will come in my name, claiming, 'I am the Messiah.' They will deceive many. 6And you will hear of wars and threats of wars, but don't panic. Yes, these things must take place, but the end won't follow immediately. 7Nation will go to war against nation, and kingdom against kingdom. There will be famines and earthquakes in many parts of the world. 8But all this is only the first of the birth pains, with more to come.

9"Then you will be arrested, persecuted, and killed. You will be hated all over the world because you are my followers. 10And many will turn away from me and betray and hate each other. 11And many false prophets will appear and will deceive many people. 12Sin will be rampant everywhere, and the love of many will grow cold. ¹³But the one who endures to the end will be saved. ¹⁴And the Good News about the Kingdom will be preached throughout the whole world, so that all nations will hear it; and then the end will come.

¹⁵"The day is coming when you will see what Daniel the prophet spoke about—the sacrilegious object that causes desecration standing in the Holy Place." (Reader, pay attention!) ¹⁶"Then those in Judea must flee to the hills. ¹⁷A person out on the deck of a roof must not go down into the house to pack. ¹⁸A person out in the field must not return even to get a coat. ¹⁹How terrible it will be for pregnant women and for nursing mothers in those days. ²⁰And pray that your flight will not be in winter or on the Sabbath. ²¹For there will be greater anguish than at any time since the world began. And it will never be so great again. ²²In fact, unless that time of calamity is shortened, not a single person will survive. But it will be shortened for the sake of God's chosen ones.

²³"Then if anyone tells you, 'Look, here is the Messiah,' or 'There he is,' don't believe it. ²⁴For false messiahs and false prophets will rise up and perform great signs and wonders so as to deceive, if possible, even God's chosen ones. ²⁵See, I have warned you about this ahead of time.

²⁶"So if someone tells you, 'Look, the Messiah is out in the desert,' don't bother to go and look. Or, 'Look, he is hiding here,' don't believe it! ²⁷For as the lightning flashes in the east and shines to the west, so it will be when the Son of Man comes. ²⁸Just as the gathering of vultures shows there is a carcass nearby, so these signs indicate that the end is near.

²⁹"Immediately after the anguish of those days,

the sun will be darkened,
    the moon will give no light,
the stars will fall from the sky,
    and the powers in the heavens will be
        shaken.

³⁰And then at last, the sign that the Son of Man is coming will appear in the heavens, and there will be deep mourning among all the peoples of the earth. And they will see the Son of Man coming on the clouds of heaven with power and great glory. ³¹And he will send out his angels with the mighty blast of a trumpet, and they will gather his chosen ones from all over the world—from the farthest ends of the earth and heaven.

³²"Now learn a lesson from the fig tree. When its branches bud and its leaves begin to sprout, you know that summer is near. ³³In the same way, when you see all these things, you can know his return is very near, right at the door. ³⁴I tell you the truth, this generation will not pass from the scene until all these things take place. ³⁵Heaven and earth will disappear, but my words will never disappear.

³⁶"However, no one knows the day or hour when these things will happen, not even the angels in heaven or the Son himself. Only the Father knows.

³⁷"When the Son of Man returns, it will be like it was in Noah's day. ³⁸In those days before the flood, the people were enjoying banquets and parties and weddings right up to the time Noah entered his boat. ³⁹People didn't realize what was going to happen until the flood came and swept them all away. That is the way it will be when the Son of Man comes.

⁴⁰"Two men will be working together in the field; one will be taken, the other left. ⁴¹Two women will be grinding flour at the mill; one will be taken, the other left.

⁴²"So you, too, must keep watch! For you don't know what day your Lord is coming. ⁴³Understand this: If a homeowner knew exactly when a burglar was coming, he would keep watch and not permit his house to be broken into. ⁴⁴You also must be ready all the time, for the Son of Man will come when least expected.

⁴⁵"A faithful, sensible servant is one to whom the master can give the responsibility of managing his other household servants and feeding them. ⁴⁶If the master returns and finds that the servant has done a good job, there will be a reward. ⁴⁷I tell you the truth, the master will put that servant in charge of all he owns. ⁴⁸But what if the servant is evil and thinks, 'My master won't be back for a while,' ⁴⁹and he begins beating the other servants, partying, and getting drunk? ⁵⁰The master will return unannounced and unexpected, ⁵¹and he will cut the servant to pieces and assign him a place with the hypocrites. In that place there will be weeping and gnashing of teeth.

CHAPTER **25**

Parable of the Ten Bridesmaids

"Then the Kingdom of Heaven will be like ten bridesmaids who took their lamps and went to meet the bridegroom. ²Five of them were foolish, and five were wise. ³The five who were foolish didn't take enough olive oil for their lamps, ⁴but the other five were wise enough to take along extra oil. 5When the bridegroom was delayed, they all became drowsy and fell asleep.

6"At midnight they were roused by the shout, 'Look, the bridegroom is coming! Come out and meet him!'

7"All the bridesmaids got up and prepared their lamps. 8Then the five foolish ones asked the others, 'Please give us some of your oil because our lamps are going out.'

9"But the others replied, 'We don't have enough for all of us. Go to a shop and buy some for yourselves.'

10"But while they were gone to buy oil, the bridegroom came. Then those who were ready went in with him to the marriage feast, and the door was locked. 11Later, when the other five bridesmaids returned, they stood outside, calling, 'Lord! Lord! Open the door for us!'

12"But he called back, 'Believe me, I don't know you!'

13"So you, too, must keep watch! For you do not know the day or hour of my return.

Parable of the Three Servants

14"Again, the Kingdom of Heaven can be illustrated by the story of a man going on a long trip. He called together his servants and entrusted his money to them while he was gone. 15He gave five bags of silver to one, two bags of silver to another, and one bag of silver to the last—dividing it in proportion to their abilities. He then left on his trip.

16"The servant who received the five bags of silver began to invest the money and earned five more. 17The servant with two bags of silver also went to work and earned two more. 18But the servant who received the one bag of silver dug a hole in the ground and hid the master's money.

19"After a long time their master returned from his trip and called them to give an account of how they had used his money. 20The servant to whom he had entrusted the five bags of silver came forward with five more and said, 'Master, you gave me five bags of silver to invest, and I have earned five more.'

21"The master was full of praise. 'Well done, my good and faithful servant. You have been faithful in handling this small amount, so now I will give you many more responsibilities. Let's celebrate together!'

22"The servant who had received the two bags of silver came forward and said, 'Master, you gave me two bags of silver to invest, and I have earned two more.'

23"The master said, 'Well done, my good and faithful servant. You have been faithful in handling this small amount, so now I will give you many more responsibilities. Let's celebrate together!'

24"Then the servant with the one bag of silver came and said, 'Master, I knew you were a harsh man, harvesting crops you didn't plant and gathering crops you didn't cultivate. 25I was afraid I would lose your money, so I hid it in the earth. Look, here is your money back.'

26"But the master replied, 'You wicked and lazy servant! If you knew I harvested crops I didn't plant and gathered crops I didn't cultivate, 27why didn't you deposit my money in the bank? At least I could have gotten some interest on it.'

28"Then he ordered, 'Take the money from this servant, and give it to the one with the ten bags of silver. 29To those who use well what they are given, even more will be given, and they will have an abundance. But from those who do nothing, even what little they have will be taken away. 30Now throw this useless servant into outer darkness, where there will be weeping and gnashing of teeth.'

The Final Judgment

31"But when the Son of Man comes in his glory, and all the angels with him, then he will sit upon his glorious throne. 32All the nations will be gathered in his presence, and he will separate the people as a shepherd separates the sheep from the goats. 33He will place the sheep at his right hand and the goats at his left.

34"Then the King will say to those on his right, 'Come, you who are blessed by my Father, inherit the Kingdom prepared for you from the creation of the world. 35For I was hungry, and you fed me. I was thirsty, and you gave me a drink. I was a stranger, and you invited me into your home. 36I was naked, and you gave me clothing. I was sick, and you cared for me. I was in prison, and you visited me.'

37"Then these righteous ones will reply, 'Lord, when did we ever see you hungry and feed you? Or thirsty and give you something to drink? 38Or a stranger and show you hospitality? Or naked and give you clothing? 39When did we ever see you sick or in prison and visit you?'

40"And the King will say, 'I tell you the truth, when you did it to one of the least of these my brothers and sisters, you were doing it to me!'

41"Then the King will turn to those on the left and say, 'Away with you, you cursed ones, into the eternal fire prepared for the devil and his demons. **42**For I was hungry, and you didn't feed me. I was thirsty, and you didn't give me a drink. **43**I was a stranger, and you didn't invite me into your home. I was naked, and you didn't give me clothing. I was sick and in prison, and you didn't visit me.'

44"Then they will reply, 'Lord, when did we ever see you hungry or thirsty or a stranger or naked or sick or in prison, and not help you?'

45"And he will answer, 'I tell you the truth, when you refused to help the least of these my brothers and sisters, you were refusing to help me.'

46"And they will go away into eternal punishment, but the righteous will go into eternal life."

CHAPTER **26**
The Plot to Kill Jesus

When Jesus had finished saying all these things, he said to his disciples, **2**"As you know, Passover begins in two days, and the Son of Man will be handed over to be crucified."

3At that same time the leading priests and elders were meeting at the residence of Caiaphas, the high priest, **4**plotting how to capture Jesus secretly and kill him. **5**"But not during the Passover celebration," they agreed, "or the people may riot."

Jesus Anointed at Bethany

6Meanwhile, Jesus was in Bethany at the home of Simon, a man who had previously had leprosy. **7**While he was eating, a woman came in with a beautiful alabaster jar of expensive perfume and poured it over his head.

8The disciples were indignant when they saw this. "What a waste!" they said. **9**"It could have been sold for a high price and the money given to the poor."

10But Jesus, aware of this, replied, "Why criticize this woman for doing such a good thing to me? **11**You will always have the poor among you, but you will not always have me. **12**She has poured this perfume on me to prepare my body for burial. **13**I tell you the truth, wherever the Good News is preached throughout the world, this woman's deed will be remembered and discussed."

Judas Agrees to Betray Jesus

14Then Judas Iscariot, one of the twelve disciples, went to the leading priests **15**and asked, "How much will you pay me to betray Jesus to you?" And they gave him thirty pieces of silver. **16**From that time on, Judas began looking for an opportunity to betray Jesus.

The Last Supper

17On the first day of the Festival of Unleavened Bread, the disciples came to Jesus and asked, "Where do you want us to prepare the Passover meal for you?"

18"As you go into the city," he told them, "you will see a certain man. Tell him, 'The Teacher says: My time has come, and I will eat the Passover meal with my disciples at your house.'" **19**So the disciples did as Jesus told them and prepared the Passover meal there.

20When it was evening, Jesus sat down at the table with the twelve disciples. **21**While they were eating, he said, "I tell you the truth, one of you will betray me."

22Greatly distressed, each one asked in turn, "Am I the one, Lord?"

23He replied, "One of you who has just eaten from this bowl with me will betray me. **24**For the Son of Man must die, as the Scriptures declared long ago. But how terrible it will be for the one who betrays him. It would be far better for that man if he had never been born!"

25Judas, the one who would betray him, also asked, "Rabbi, am I the one?"

And Jesus told him, "You have said it."

26As they were eating, Jesus took some bread and blessed it. Then he broke it in pieces and gave it to the disciples, saying, "Take this and eat it, for this is my body."

27And he took a cup of wine and gave thanks to God for it. He gave it to them and said, "Each of you drink from it, **28**for this is my blood, which confirms the covenant between God and his people. It is poured out as a sacrifice to forgive the sins of many. **29**Mark my words—I will not drink wine again until the day I drink it new with you in my Father's Kingdom."

30Then they sang a hymn and went out to the Mount of Olives.

Jesus Predicts Peter's Denial

31On the way, Jesus told them, "Tonight all of you will desert me. For the Scriptures say,

'God will strike the Shepherd,
and the sheep of the flock will be scattered.'

32But after I have been raised from the dead, I will go ahead of you to Galilee and meet you there."

33Peter declared, "Even if everyone else deserts you, I will never desert you."

34Jesus replied, "I tell you the truth, Peter—

this very night, before the rooster crows, you will deny three times that you even know me."

35"No!" Peter insisted. "Even if I have to die with you, I will never deny you!" And all the other disciples vowed the same.

Jesus Prays in Gethsemane

36Then Jesus went with them to the olive grove called Gethsemane, and he said, "Sit here while I go over there to pray." 37He took Peter and Zebedee's two sons, James and John, and he became anguished and distressed. 38He told them, "My soul is crushed with grief to the point of death. Stay here and keep watch with me."

39He went on a little farther and bowed with his face to the ground, praying, "My Father! If it is possible, let this cup of suffering be taken away from me. Yet I want your will to be done, not mine."

40Then he returned to the disciples and found them asleep. He said to Peter, "Couldn't you watch with me even one hour? 41Keep watch and pray, so that you will not give in to temptation. For the spirit is willing, but the body is weak!"

42Then Jesus left them a second time and prayed, "My Father! If this cup cannot be taken away unless I drink it, your will be done." 43When he returned to them again, he found them sleeping, for they couldn't keep their eyes open.

44So he went to pray a third time, saying the same things again. 45Then he came to the disciples and said, "Go ahead and sleep. Have your rest. But look—the time has come. The Son of Man is betrayed into the hands of sinners. 46Up, let's be going. Look, my betrayer is here!"

Jesus Is Betrayed and Arrested

47And even as Jesus said this, Judas, one of the twelve disciples, arrived with a crowd of men armed with swords and clubs. They had been sent by the leading priests and elders of the people. 48The traitor, Judas, had given them a prearranged signal: "You will know which one to arrest when I greet him with a kiss." 49So Judas came straight to Jesus. "Greetings, Rabbi!" he exclaimed and gave him the kiss.

50Jesus said, "My friend, go ahead and do what you have come for."

Then the others grabbed Jesus and arrested him. 51But one of the men with Jesus pulled out his sword and struck the high priest's slave, slashing off his ear.

52"Put away your sword," Jesus told him. "Those who use the sword will die by the sword. 53Don't you realize that I could ask my Father for thousands of angels to protect us, and he would send them instantly? 54But if I did, how would the Scriptures be fulfilled that describe what must happen now?"

55Then Jesus said to the crowd, "Am I some dangerous revolutionary, that you come with swords and clubs to arrest me? Why didn't you arrest me in the Temple? I was there teaching every day. 56But this is all happening to fulfill the words of the prophets as recorded in the Scriptures." At that point, all the disciples deserted him and fled.

Jesus before the Council

57Then the people who had arrested Jesus led him to the home of Caiaphas, the high priest, where the teachers of religious law and the elders had gathered. 58Meanwhile, Peter followed him at a distance and came to the high priest's courtyard. He went in and sat with the guards and waited to see how it would all end.

59Inside, the leading priests and the entire high council were trying to find witnesses who would lie about Jesus, so they could put him to death. 60But even though they found many who agreed to give false witness, they could not use anyone's testimony. Finally, two men came forward 61who declared, "This man said, 'I am able to destroy the Temple of God and rebuild it in three days.'"

62Then the high priest stood up and said to Jesus, "Well, aren't you going to answer these charges? What do you have to say for yourself?" 63But Jesus remained silent. Then the high priest said to him, "I demand in the name of the living God—tell us if you are the Messiah, the Son of God."

64Jesus replied, "You have said it. And in the future you will see the Son of Man seated in the place of power at God's right hand and coming on the clouds of heaven."

65Then the high priest tore his clothing to show his horror and said, "Blasphemy! Why do we need other witnesses? You have all heard his blasphemy. 66What is your verdict?"

"Guilty!" they shouted. "He deserves to die!"

67Then they began to spit in Jesus' face and beat him with their fists. And some slapped him, 68jeering, "Prophesy to us, you Messiah! Who hit you that time?"

Peter Denies Jesus

69Meanwhile, Peter was sitting outside in the courtyard. A servant girl came over and said to him, "You were one of those with Jesus the Galilean."

70But Peter denied it in front of everyone. "I don't know what you're talking about," he said.

71Later, out by the gate, another servant girl noticed him and said to those standing around, "This man was with Jesus of Nazareth."

72Again Peter denied it, this time with an oath. "I don't even know the man," he said.

73A little later some of the other bystanders came over to Peter and said, "You must be one of them; we can tell by your Galilean accent."

74Peter swore, "A curse on me if I'm lying— I don't know the man!" And immediately the rooster crowed.

75Suddenly, Jesus' words flashed through Peter's mind: "Before the rooster crows, you will deny three times that you even know me." And he went away, weeping bitterly.

CHAPTER **27**

Judas Hangs Himself

Very early in the morning the leading priests and the elders met again to lay plans for putting Jesus to death. 2Then they bound him, led him away, and took him to Pilate, the Roman governor.

3When Judas, who had betrayed him, realized that Jesus had been condemned to die, he was filled with remorse. So he took the thirty pieces of silver back to the leading priests and the elders. 4"I have sinned," he declared, "for I have betrayed an innocent man."

"What do we care?" they retorted. "That's your problem."

5Then Judas threw the silver coins down in the Temple and went out and hanged himself.

6The leading priests picked up the coins. "It wouldn't be right to put this money in the Temple treasury," they said, "since it was payment for murder." 7After some discussion they finally decided to buy the potter's field, and they made it into a cemetery for foreigners. 8That is why the field is still called the Field of Blood. 9This fulfilled the prophecy of Jeremiah that says,

"They took the thirty pieces of silver—
the price at which he was valued by the
people of Israel,
10 and purchased the potter's field,
as the LORD directed."

Jesus' Trial before Pilate

11Now Jesus was standing before Pilate, the Roman governor. "Are you the king of the Jews?" the governor asked him.

Jesus replied, "You have said it."

12But when the leading priests and the elders made their accusations against him, Jesus remained silent. 13"Don't you hear all these charges they are bringing against you?" Pilate demanded. 14But Jesus made no response to any of the charges, much to the governor's surprise.

15Now it was the governor's custom each year during the Passover celebration to release one prisoner to the crowd—anyone they wanted. 16This year there was a notorious prisoner, a man named Barabbas. 17As the crowds gathered before Pilate's house that morning, he asked them, "Which one do you want me to release to you—Barabbas, or Jesus who is called the Messiah?" 18(He knew very well that the religious leaders had arrested Jesus out of envy.)

19Just then, as Pilate was sitting on the judgment seat, his wife sent him this message: "Leave that innocent man alone. I suffered through a terrible nightmare about him last night."

20Meanwhile, the leading priests and the elders persuaded the crowd to ask for Barabbas to be released and for Jesus to be put to death. 21So the governor asked again, "Which of these two do you want me to release to you?"

The crowd shouted back, "Barabbas!"

22Pilate responded, "Then what should I do with Jesus who is called the Messiah?"

They shouted back, "Crucify him!"

23"Why?" Pilate demanded. "What crime has he committed?"

But the mob roared even louder, "Crucify him!"

24Pilate saw that he wasn't getting anywhere and that a riot was developing. So he sent for a bowl of water and washed his hands before the crowd, saying, "I am innocent of this man's blood. The responsibility is yours!"

25And all the people yelled back, "We will take responsibility for his death—we and our children!"

26So Pilate released Barabbas to them. He ordered Jesus flogged with a lead-tipped whip, then turned him over to the Roman soldiers to be crucified.

The Soldiers Mock Jesus

27Some of the governor's soldiers took Jesus into their headquarters and called out the entire regiment. 28They stripped him and put a scarlet robe on him. 29They wove thorn branches into a crown and put it on his head, and they placed a reed stick in his right hand as a scepter. Then they knelt before him in mockery and taunted, "Hail! King of the Jews!" 30And they spit on him and grabbed the stick and struck him on the head with it. 31When they were finally tired of mocking him, they took off the robe and put his own clothes on him again. Then they led him away to be crucified.

The Crucifixion

32Along the way, they came across a man named Simon, who was from Cyrene, and the soldiers forced him to carry Jesus' cross. 33And they went out to a place called Golgotha (which means "Place of the Skull"). 34The soldiers gave him wine mixed with bitter gall, but when he had tasted it, he refused to drink it.

35After they had nailed him to the cross, the soldiers gambled for his clothes by throwing dice.* 36Then they sat around and kept guard as he hung there. 37A sign was fastened to the cross above Jesus' head, announcing the charge against him. It read: "This is Jesus, the King of the Jews." 38Two revolutionaries were crucified with him, one on his right and one on his left.

39The people passing by shouted abuse, shaking their heads in mockery. 40"Look at you now!" they yelled at him. "You said you were going to destroy the Temple and rebuild it in three days. Well then, if you are the Son of God, save yourself and come down from the cross!"

41The leading priests, the teachers of religious law, and the elders also mocked Jesus. 42"He saved others," they scoffed, "but he can't save himself! So he is the King of Israel, is he? Let him come down from the cross right now, and we will believe in him! 43He trusted God, so let God rescue him now if he wants him! For he said, 'I am the Son of God.'" 44Even the revolutionaries who were crucified with him ridiculed him in the same way.

The Death of Jesus

45At noon, darkness fell across the whole land until three o'clock. 46At about three o'clock, Jesus called out with a loud voice, *"Eli, Eli, lema sabachthani?"* which means "My God, my God, why have you abandoned me?"

47Some of the bystanders misunderstood and thought he was calling for the prophet Elijah. 48One of them ran and filled a sponge with sour wine, holding it up to him on a reed stick so he could drink. 49But the rest said, "Wait! Let's see whether Elijah comes to save him."*

50Then Jesus shouted out again, and he released his spirit. 51At that moment the curtain in

Worth the Effort

It's not always easy to tell others about Jesus. Sometimes it's kind of like this!

1 Find a friend, two wrapped pieces of gum, and four socks.

2 Put the socks over your hands.

3 See who can unwrap the gum first!

What was it like to unwrap the gum wearing socks on your hands?

Sometimes we may feel like we're "all thumbs" when we share our faith. **Read MATTHEW 28:18-20 with your friend.** Jesus promises to be with us as we tell others about him. We don't have to feel nervous because he'll help us say the right thing. Say a quick prayer with your friend, asking for opportunities to share your faith in Jesus!

the sanctuary of the Temple was torn in two, from top to bottom. The earth shook, rocks split apart, 52and tombs opened. The bodies of many godly men and women who had died were raised from the dead. 53They left the cemetery after Jesus' resurrection, went into the holy city of Jerusalem, and appeared to many people.

54The Roman officer and the other soldiers at the crucifixion were terrified by the earthquake and all that had happened. They said, "This man truly was the Son of God!"

55And many women who had come from

27:35 Greek *by casting lots.* A few late manuscripts add *This fulfilled the word of the prophet: "They divided my garments among themselves and cast lots for my robe."* See Ps 22:18.   27:49 Some manuscripts add *And another took a spear and pierced his side, and out flowed water and blood.* Compare John 19:34.

Galilee with Jesus to care for him were watching from a distance. 56 Among them were Mary Magdalene, Mary (the mother of James and Joseph), and the mother of James and John, the sons of Zebedee.

The Burial of Jesus

57 As evening approached, Joseph, a rich man from Arimathea who had become a follower of Jesus, 58 went to Pilate and asked for Jesus' body. And Pilate issued an order to release it to him. 59 Joseph took the body and wrapped it in a long sheet of clean linen cloth. 60 He placed it in his own new tomb, which had been carved out of the rock. Then he rolled a great stone across the entrance and left. 61 Both Mary Magdalene and the other Mary were sitting across from the tomb and watching.

The Guard at the Tomb

62 The next day, on the Sabbath, the leading priests and Pharisees went to see Pilate. 63 They told him, "Sir, we remember what that deceiver once said while he was still alive: 'After three days I will rise from the dead.' 64 So we request that you seal the tomb until the third day. This will prevent his disciples from coming and stealing his body and then telling everyone he was raised from the dead! If that happens, we'll be worse off than we were at first."

65 Pilate replied, "Take guards and secure it the best you can." 66 So they sealed the tomb and posted guards to protect it.

CHAPTER **28**
The Resurrection

Early on Sunday morning, as the new day was dawning, Mary Magdalene and the other Mary went out to visit the tomb.

2 Suddenly there was a great earthquake! For an angel of the Lord came down from heaven, rolled aside the stone, and sat on it. 3 His face shone like lightning, and his clothing was as white as snow. 4 The guards shook with fear when they saw him, and they fell into a dead faint.

5 Then the angel spoke to the women. "Don't be afraid!" he said. "I know you are looking for Jesus, who was crucified. 6 He isn't here! He is risen from the dead, just as he said would happen. Come, see where his body was lying. 7 And now, go quickly and tell his disciples that he has risen from the dead, and he is going ahead of you to Galilee. You will see him there. Remember what I have told you."

8 The women ran quickly from the tomb. They were very frightened but also filled with great joy, and they rushed to give the disciples the angel's message. 9 And as they went, Jesus met them and greeted them. And they ran to him, grasped his feet, and worshiped him. 10 Then Jesus said to them, "Don't be afraid! Go tell my brothers to leave for Galilee, and they will see me there."

The Report of the Guard

11 As the women were on their way, some of the guards went into the city and told the leading priests what had happened. 12 A meeting with the elders was called, and they decided to give the soldiers a large bribe. 13 They told the soldiers, "You must say, 'Jesus' disciples came during the night while we were sleeping, and they stole his body.' 14 If the governor hears about it, we'll stand up for you so you won't get in trouble." 15 So the guards accepted the bribe and said what they were told to say. Their story spread widely among the Jews, and they still tell it today.

The Great Commission

16 Then the eleven disciples left for Galilee, going to the mountain where Jesus had told them to go. 17 When they saw him, they worshiped him—but some of them doubted! 18 Jesus came and told his disciples, "I have been given all authority in heaven and on earth. **19 Therefore, go and make disciples of all the nations, baptizing them in the name of the Father and the Son and the Holy Spirit. 20 Teach these new disciples to obey all the commands I have given you. And be sure of this: I am with you always, even to the end of the age."**

MARK The Messiah in Motion

Look for ② hidden messages in Mark!

Mark gives us pictures of what Jesus did during his ministry—one right after another. Look for the Messiah (that's Jesus!)

- **TEACHING**
- **HEALING**
- **SERVING**
- **SAVING**
- **PREACHING**
- **FEEDING**
- **SACRIFICING**

Is there a doctor in the house?

ER

He wasn't a doctor, but he performed heart surgery. He never used medicine, but he healed tons of people. **Read about one of his famous patients in Mark 2:1-12.**

Digging Deeper

Boy, you'd think Jesus was a farmer, the way he talked about seeds and soil so much. He *wasn't* a farmer, but he knew a lot about planting seeds. **Dig into Mark 4:1-34 to hear from the Master Gardener himself!**

Did You Hear That?

John the Baptist hung out in the wilderness, telling people to confess their sins and be baptized. When John baptized Jesus, even though he had never sinned, something *incredible* happened. **Discover what it was in Mark 1:9-11!**

Gone Fishing

"Put down your fishing gear. You won't need it anymore."

"Huh? But I thought we were goin' fishin'!"

Hmm...this story sounds a little fishy. **Better read it for yourself in Mark 1:16-20!**

How'd He Do That?

Inflatable shoes? Water wings? An invisible raft? How *else* could Jesus walk on water? Guess what—Jesus didn't need any of those things! **Get the details in Mark 6:45-52!**

Food for Thought

"It was 4,000 people!"

"The crowd *I* saw was 5,000. Get your numbers straight!"

Want to settle the argument? Read Mark 6:30-44 and Mark 8:1-10. (Altogether, how many people did Jesus really feed?)

A Dark Day—for Real!

Darkness at noon? *Staying* dark for three hours?

You could say it was truly the world's darkest day. Find out why in Mark 15:33-41.

Everyone Loves a Parade

This may have been the most important parade in history! There weren't floats or giant cartoon balloons, but there was plenty of celebrating. Read Mark 11:1-11 to see where— and why— this amazing parade took place.

Sonrise!

An amazing thing happened at *Sonrise* three days after Jesus was crucified. Read Mark 16:1-6 to see if you can guess what this strange spelling means!

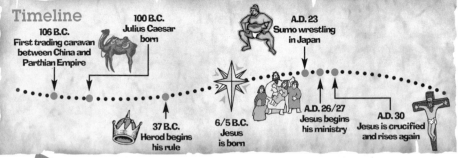

Timeline

106 B.C.
First trading caravan between China and Parthian Empire

100 B.C.
Julius Caesar born

37 B.C.
Herod begins his rule

6/5 B.C.
Jesus is born

A.D. 23
Sumo wrestling in Japan

A.D. 26/27
Jesus begins his ministry

A.D. 30
Jesus is crucified and rises again

The JESUS CONNECTION

Mark's focus for this Gospel is simple: to show Jesus in action. Think about it! The Son of God, the King of the universe, came to serve others! How? Tons of ways! But the most important was when he died on the cross for our sins. Three days later, he rose from the dead and lives forever! If you believe in Jesus, your sins are forgiven. He'll live in your heart here on earth, and later you can live with him forever in heaven.

CHAPTER **1**

John the Baptist Prepares the Way

This is the Good News about Jesus the Messiah, the Son of God. It began ²just as the prophet Isaiah had written:

"Look, I am sending my messenger ahead
of you,
and he will prepare your way.
³ He is a voice shouting in the wilderness,
'Prepare the way for the LORD's coming!
Clear the road for him!'"

⁴This messenger was John the Baptist. He was in the wilderness and preached that people should be baptized to show that they had repented of their sins and turned to God to be forgiven. ⁵All of Judea, including all the people of Jerusalem, went out to see and hear John. And when they confessed their sins, he baptized them in the Jordan River. ⁶His clothes were woven from coarse camel hair, and he wore a leather belt around his waist. For food he ate locusts and wild honey.

⁷John announced: "Someone is coming soon who is greater than I am—so much greater that I'm not even worthy to stoop down like a slave and untie the straps of his sandals. ⁸I baptize you with water, but he will baptize you with the Holy Spirit!"

The Baptism and Temptation of Jesus

⁹One day Jesus came from Nazareth in Galilee, and John baptized him in the Jordan River. ¹⁰As Jesus came up out of the water, he saw the heavens splitting apart and the Holy Spirit descending on him like a dove. ¹¹And a voice from heaven said, "You are my dearly loved Son, and you bring me great joy."

¹²The Spirit then compelled Jesus to go into the wilderness, ¹³where he was tempted by Satan for forty days. He was out among the wild animals, and angels took care of him.

¹⁴Later on, after John was arrested, Jesus went into Galilee, where he preached God's Good News. ¹⁵"The time promised by God has come at last!" he announced. "The Kingdom of God is near! Repent of your sins and believe the Good News!"

The First Disciples

¹⁶One day as Jesus was walking along the shore of the Sea of Galilee, he saw Simon and his brother Andrew throwing a net into the water, for they fished for a living. ¹⁷Jesus called out to them, "Come, follow me, and I will show you how to fish for people!" ¹⁸And they left their nets at once and followed him.

¹⁹A little farther up the shore Jesus saw Zebedee's sons, James and John, in a boat repairing their nets. ²⁰He called them at once, and they also followed him, leaving their father, Zebedee, in the boat with the hired men.

Jesus Casts Out an Evil Spirit

²¹Jesus and his companions went to the town of Capernaum. When the Sabbath day came, he went into the synagogue and began to teach. ²²The people were amazed at his teaching, for he taught with real authority—quite unlike the teachers of religious law.

²³Suddenly, a man in the synagogue who was possessed by an evil spirit began shouting, ²⁴"Why are you interfering with us, Jesus of Nazareth? Have you come to destroy us? I know who you are—the Holy One sent from God!"

²⁵Jesus cut him short. "Be quiet! Come out of the man," he ordered. ²⁶At that, the evil spirit screamed, threw the man into a convulsion, and then came out of him.

²⁷Amazement gripped the audience, and they began to discuss what had happened. "What sort of new teaching is this?" they asked excitedly. "It has such authority! Even evil spirits obey his orders!" ²⁸The news about Jesus spread quickly throughout the entire region of Galilee.

Jesus Heals Many People

²⁹After Jesus left the synagogue with James and John, they went to Simon and Andrew's home. ³⁰Now Simon's mother-in-law was sick in bed with a high fever. They told Jesus about her right away. ³¹So he went to her bedside, took her by the hand, and helped her sit up. Then the fever left her, and she prepared a meal for them.

³²That evening after sunset, many sick and demon-possessed people were brought to Jesus. ³³The whole town gathered at the door to watch. ³⁴So Jesus healed many people who were sick with various diseases, and he cast out many demons. But because the demons knew who he was, he did not allow them to speak.

Jesus Preaches in Galilee

³⁵Before daybreak the next morning, Jesus got up and went out to an isolated place to pray. ³⁶Later Simon and the others went out to find

him. ³⁷When they found him, they said, "Everyone is looking for you."

³⁸But Jesus replied, "We must go on to other towns as well, and I will preach to them, too. That is why I came." ³⁹So he traveled throughout the region of Galilee, preaching in the synagogues and casting out demons.

Jesus Heals a Man with Leprosy

⁴⁰A man with leprosy came and knelt in front of Jesus, begging to be healed. "If you are willing, you can heal me and make me clean," he said.

⁴¹Moved with compassion, Jesus reached out and touched him. "I am willing," he said. "Be healed!" ⁴²Instantly the leprosy disappeared, and the man was healed. ⁴³Then Jesus sent him on his way with a stern warning: ⁴⁴"Don't tell anyone about this. Instead, go to the priest and let him examine you. Take along the offering required in the law of Moses for those who have been healed of leprosy. This will be a public testimony that you have been cleansed."

⁴⁵But the man went and spread the word, proclaiming to everyone what had happened. As a result, large crowds soon surrounded Jesus, and he couldn't publicly enter a town anywhere. He had to stay out in the secluded places, but people from everywhere kept coming to him.

CHAPTER 2
Jesus Heals a Paralyzed Man

When Jesus returned to Capernaum several days later, the news spread quickly that he was back home. ²Soon the house where he was staying was so packed with visitors that there was no more room, even outside the door. While he was preaching God's word to them, ³four men arrived carrying a paralyzed man on a mat. ⁴They couldn't bring him to Jesus because of the crowd, so they dug a hole through the roof above his head. Then they lowered the man on his mat, right down in front of Jesus. ⁵Seeing their faith, Jesus said to the paralyzed man, "My child, your sins are forgiven."

⁶But some of the teachers of religious law who were sitting there thought to themselves, ⁷"What is he saying? This is blasphemy! Only God can forgive sins!"

⁸Jesus knew immediately what they were thinking, so he asked them, "Why do you question this in your hearts? ⁹Is it easier to say to the paralyzed man 'Your sins are forgiven,' or 'Stand up, pick up your mat, and walk'? ¹⁰So I will prove to you that the Son of Man has the authority on earth to forgive sins." Then Jesus turned to the paralyzed man and said, ¹¹"Stand up, pick up your mat, and go home!"

¹²And the man jumped up, grabbed his mat, and walked out through the stunned onlookers. They were all amazed and praised God, exclaiming, "We've never seen anything like this before!"

Jesus Calls Levi (Matthew)

¹³Then Jesus went out to the lakeshore again and taught the crowds that were coming to him. ¹⁴As he walked along, he saw Levi son of Alphaeus sitting at his tax collector's booth. "Follow me and be my disciple," Jesus said to him. So Levi got up and followed him.

¹⁵Later, Levi invited Jesus and his disciples to his home as dinner guests, along with many tax collectors and other disreputable sinners. (There were many people of this kind among Jesus' followers.) ¹⁶But when the teachers of religious law who were Pharisees saw him eating with tax collectors and other sinners, they asked his disciples, "Why does he eat with such scum?"

¹⁷When Jesus heard this, he told them, "Healthy people don't need a doctor—sick people do. I have come to call not those who think they are righteous, but those who know they are sinners."

A Discussion about Fasting

¹⁸Once when John's disciples and the Pharisees were fasting, some people came to Jesus and asked, "Why don't your disciples fast like John's disciples and the Pharisees do?"

¹⁹Jesus replied, "Do wedding guests fast while celebrating with the groom? Of course not. They can't fast while the groom is with them. ²⁰But someday the groom will be taken away from them, and then they will fast.

²¹"Besides, who would patch old clothing with new cloth? For the new patch would shrink and rip away from the old cloth, leaving an even bigger tear than before.

²²"And no one puts new wine into old wineskins. For the wine would burst the wineskins, and the wine and the skins would both be lost. New wine calls for new wineskins."

A Discussion about the Sabbath

²³One Sabbath day as Jesus was walking through some grainfields, his disciples began breaking off heads of grain to eat. ²⁴But the Pharisees said to Jesus, "Look, why are they breaking the law by harvesting grain on the Sabbath?"

²⁵Jesus said to them, "Haven't you ever read in

the Scriptures what David did when he and his companions were hungry? 26He went into the house of God (during the days when Abiathar was high priest) and broke the law by eating the sacred loaves of bread that only the priests are allowed to eat. He also gave some to his companions."

27Then Jesus said to them, "The Sabbath was made to meet the needs of people, and not people to meet the requirements of the Sabbath. 28So the Son of Man is Lord, even over the Sabbath!"

CHAPTER **3**
Jesus Heals on the Sabbath
Jesus went into the synagogue again and noticed a man with a deformed hand. 2Since it was the Sabbath, Jesus' enemies watched him closely. If he healed the man's hand, they planned to accuse him of working on the Sabbath.

3Jesus said to the man with the deformed hand, "Come and stand in front of everyone." 4Then he turned to his critics and asked, "Does the law permit good deeds on the Sabbath, or is it a day for doing evil? Is this a day to save life or to destroy it?" But they wouldn't answer him.

5He looked around at them angrily and was deeply saddened by their hard hearts. Then he said to the man, "Hold out your hand." So the man held out his hand, and it was restored! 6At once the Pharisees went away and met with the supporters of Herod to plot how to kill Jesus.

Crowds Follow Jesus
7Jesus went out to the lake with his disciples, and a large crowd followed him. They came from all over Galilee, Judea, 8Jerusalem, Idumea, from east of the Jordan River, and even from as far north as Tyre and Sidon. The news about his miracles had spread far and wide, and vast numbers of people came to see him.

9Jesus instructed his disciples to have a boat ready so the crowd would not crush him. 10He had healed many people that day, so all the sick people eagerly pushed forward to touch him. 11And whenever those possessed by evil spirits caught sight of him, the spirits would throw them to the ground in front of him shrieking, "You are the Son of God!" 12But Jesus sternly commanded the spirits not to reveal who he was.

Jesus Chooses the Twelve Apostles
13Afterward Jesus went up on a mountain and called out the ones he wanted to go with him.

And they came to him. 14Then he appointed twelve of them and called them his apostles. They were to accompany him, and he would send them out to preach, 15giving them authority to cast out demons. 16These are the twelve he chose:

Simon (whom he named Peter),
17 James and John (the sons of Zebedee, but Jesus nicknamed them "Sons of Thunder"),
18 Andrew,
Philip,
Bartholomew,
Matthew,
Thomas,
James (son of Alphaeus),
Thaddaeus,
Simon (the zealot),
19 Judas Iscariot (who later betrayed him).

Jesus and the Prince of Demons
20One time Jesus entered a house, and the crowds began to gather again. Soon he and his disciples couldn't even find time to eat. 21When his family heard what was happening, they tried to take him away. "He's out of his mind," they said.

22But the teachers of religious law who had arrived from Jerusalem said, "He's possessed by Satan, the prince of demons. That's where he gets the power to cast out demons."

23Jesus called them over and responded with an illustration. "How can Satan cast out Satan?" he asked. 24"A kingdom divided by civil war will collapse. 25Similarly, a family splintered by feuding will fall apart. 26And if Satan is divided and fights against himself, how can he stand? He would never survive. 27Let me illustrate this further. Who is powerful enough to enter the house of a strong man like Satan and plunder his goods? Only someone even stronger—someone who could tie him up and then plunder his house.

28"I tell you the truth, all sin and blasphemy can be forgiven, 29but anyone who blasphemes the Holy Spirit will never be forgiven. This is a sin with eternal consequences." 30He told them this because they were saying, "He's possessed by an evil spirit."

The True Family of Jesus
31Then Jesus' mother and brothers came to see him. They stood outside and sent word for him to come out and talk with them. 32There was a

crowd sitting around Jesus, and someone said, "Your mother and your brothers are outside asking for you."

³³Jesus replied, "Who is my mother? Who are my brothers?" ³⁴Then he looked at those around him and said, "Look, these are my mother and brothers. ³⁵Anyone who does God's will is my brother and sister and mother."

CHAPTER **4**

Parable of the Farmer Scattering Seed

Once again Jesus began teaching by the lakeshore. A very large crowd soon gathered around him, so he got into a boat. Then he sat in the boat while all the people remained on the shore. ²He taught them by telling many stories in the form of parables, such as this one:

³"Listen! A farmer went out to plant some seed. ⁴As he scattered it across his field, some of the seed fell on a footpath, and the birds came and ate it. ⁵Other seed fell on shallow soil with underlying rock. The seed sprouted quickly because the soil was shallow. ⁶But the plant soon wilted under the hot sun, and since it didn't have deep roots, it died. ⁷Other seed fell among thorns that grew up and choked out the tender plants so they produced no grain. ⁸Still other seeds fell on fertile soil, and they sprouted, grew, and produced a crop that was thirty, sixty, and even a hundred times as much as had been planted!" ⁹Then he said, "Anyone with ears to hear should listen and understand."

¹⁰Later, when Jesus was alone with the twelve disciples and with the others who were gathered around, they asked him what the parables meant.

¹¹He replied, "You are permitted to understand the secret of the Kingdom of God. But I use parables for everything I say to outsiders, ¹²so that the Scriptures might be fulfilled:

'When they see what I do,
    they will learn nothing.
When they hear what I say,
    they will not understand.
Otherwise, they will turn to me
    and be forgiven.'"

¹³Then Jesus said to them, "If you can't understand the meaning of this parable, how will you understand all the other parables? ¹⁴The farmer plants seed by taking God's word to others. ¹⁵The seed that fell on the footpath represents those who hear the message, only to have Satan come at once and take it away. ¹⁶The seed on the rocky

Do you have a green thumb? To find out collect four small flower pots and a packet of seeds. **Read Jesus' parable of the four soils in MARK 4:1-20.**

1 Fill your first pot with flat stones, and plant a few seeds in it. **Read MARK 4:15 again.**

2 Fill your second pot with pebbles, and plant a few seeds in it. **Read MARK 4:16-17 again.**

3 Fill your third pot with sticks, and plant a few seeds in it. **Read MARK 4:18-19.**

4 Fill your fourth pot with good potting soil, and plant a few seeds in it. Keep it lightly watered. **Read MARK 4:20 again.**

WHICH SOIL WILL BE BEST?

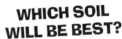

Paint, **"What kind of soil am I?"** on the fourth pot. Every time you water your seedling, ask God to help you be good soil.

Read Mark 4:30-34 to see what else Jesus said about seeds!

soil represents those who hear the message and immediately receive it with joy. 17But since they don't have deep roots, they don't last long. They fall away as soon as they have problems or are persecuted for believing God's word. 18The seed that fell among the thorns represents others who hear God's word, 19but all too quickly the message is crowded out by the worries of this life, the lure of wealth, and the desire for other things, so no fruit is produced. 20And the seed that fell on good soil represents those who hear and accept God's word and produce a harvest of thirty, sixty, or even a hundred times as much as had been planted!"

Parable of the Lamp

21Then Jesus asked them, "Would anyone light a lamp and then put it under a basket or under a bed? Of course not! A lamp is placed on a stand, where its light will shine. 22For everything that is hidden will eventually be brought into the open, and every secret will be brought to light. 23Anyone with ears to hear should listen and understand."

24Then he added, "Pay close attention to what you hear. The closer you listen, the more understanding you will be given—and you will receive even more. 25To those who listen to my teaching, more understanding will be given. But for those who are not listening, even what little understanding they have will be taken away from them."

Parable of the Growing Seed

26Jesus also said, "The Kingdom of God is like a farmer who scatters seed on the ground. 27Night and day, while he's asleep or awake, the seed sprouts and grows, but he does not understand how it happens. 28The earth produces the crops on its own. First a leaf blade pushes through, then the heads of wheat are formed, and finally the grain ripens. 29And as soon as the grain is ready, the farmer comes and harvests it with a sickle, for the harvest time has come."

Parable of the Mustard Seed

30Jesus said, "How can I describe the Kingdom of God? What story should I use to illustrate it? 31It is like a mustard seed planted in the ground. It is the smallest of all seeds, 32but it becomes the largest of all garden plants; it grows long branches, and birds can make nests in its shade."

33Jesus used many similar stories and illustrations to teach the people as much as they could understand. 34In fact, in his public ministry he never taught without using parables; but afterward, when he was alone with his disciples, he explained everything to them.

Jesus Calms the Storm

35As evening came, Jesus said to his disciples, "Let's cross to the other side of the lake." 36So they took Jesus in the boat and started out, leaving the crowds behind (although other boats followed). 37But soon a fierce storm came up. High waves were breaking into the boat, and it began to fill with water.

38Jesus was sleeping at the back of the boat with his head on a cushion. The disciples woke him up, shouting, "Teacher, don't you care that we're going to drown?"

39When Jesus woke up, he rebuked the wind and said to the waves, "Silence! Be still!" Suddenly the wind stopped, and there was a great calm. 40Then he asked them, "Why are you afraid? Do you still have no faith?"

41The disciples were absolutely terrified. "Who is this man?" they asked each other. "Even the wind and waves obey him!"

CHAPTER **5**
Jesus Heals a Demon-Possessed Man

So they arrived at the other side of the lake, in the region of the Gerasenes. 2When Jesus climbed out of the boat, a man possessed by an evil spirit came out from a cemetery to meet him. 3This man lived among the burial caves and could no longer be restrained, even with a chain. 4Whenever he was put into chains and shackles—as he often was—he snapped the chains from his wrists and smashed the shackles. No one was strong enough to subdue him. 5Day and night he wandered among the burial caves and in the hills, howling and cutting himself with sharp stones.

6When Jesus was still some distance away, the man saw him, ran to meet him, and bowed low before him. 7With a shriek, he screamed, "Why are you interfering with me, Jesus, Son of the Most High God? In the name of God, I beg you, don't torture me!" 8For Jesus had already said to the spirit, "Come out of the man, you evil spirit."

9Then Jesus demanded, "What is your name?"

And he replied, "My name is Legion, because there are many of us inside this man." 10Then the evil spirits begged him again and again not to send them to some distant place.

11There happened to be a large herd of pigs

feeding on the hillside nearby. [12]"Send us into those pigs," the spirits begged. "Let us enter them."

[13]So Jesus gave them permission. The evil spirits came out of the man and entered the pigs, and the entire herd of 2,000 pigs plunged down the steep hillside into the lake and drowned in the water.

[14]The herdsmen fled to the nearby town and the surrounding countryside, spreading the news as they ran. People rushed out to see what had happened. [15]A crowd soon gathered around Jesus, and they saw the man who had been possessed by the legion of demons. He was sitting there fully clothed and perfectly sane, and they were all afraid. [16]Then those who had seen what happened told the others about the demon-possessed man and the pigs. [17]And the crowd began pleading with Jesus to go away and leave them alone.

[18]As Jesus was getting into the boat, the man who had been demon possessed begged to go with him. [19]But Jesus said, "No, go home to your family, and tell them everything the Lord has done for you and how merciful he has been." [20]So the man started off to visit the Ten Towns of that region and began to proclaim the great things Jesus had done for him; and everyone was amazed at what he told them.

Jesus Heals in Response to Faith

[21]Jesus got into the boat again and went back to the other side of the lake, where a large crowd gathered around him on the shore. [22]Then a leader of the local synagogue, whose name was Jairus, arrived. When he saw Jesus, he fell at his feet, [23]pleading fervently with him. "My little daughter is dying," he said. "Please come and lay your hands on her; heal her so she can live."

[24]Jesus went with him, and all the people followed, crowding around him. [25]A woman had suffered for twelve years with constant bleeding. [26]She had suffered a great deal from many doctors, and over the years she had spent everything she had to pay them, but she had gotten no better. In fact, she had gotten worse. [27]She had heard about Jesus, so she came up behind him through the crowd and touched his robe. [28]For she thought to herself, "If I can just touch his robe, I will be healed." [29]Immediately the bleeding stopped, and she could feel in her body that she had been healed of her terrible condition.

[30]Jesus realized at once that healing power had gone out from him, so he turned around in the crowd and asked, "Who touched my robe?"

[31]His disciples said to him, "Look at this crowd pressing around you. How can you ask, 'Who touched me?'"

[32]But he kept on looking around to see who had done it. [33]Then the frightened woman, trembling at the realization of what had happened to her, came and fell to her knees in front of him and told him what she had done. [34]And he said to her, "Daughter, your faith has made you well. Go in peace. Your suffering is over."

[35]While he was still speaking to her, messengers arrived from the home of Jairus, the leader of the synagogue. They told him, "Your daughter is dead. There's no use troubling the Teacher now."

[36]But Jesus overheard them and said to Jairus, "Don't be afraid. Just have faith."

[37]Then Jesus stopped the crowd and wouldn't let anyone go with him except Peter, James, and John (the brother of James). [38]When they came to the home of the synagogue leader, Jesus saw much commotion and weeping and wailing. [39]He went inside and asked, "Why all this commotion and weeping? The child isn't dead; she's only asleep."

[40]The crowd laughed at him. But he made them all leave, and he took the girl's father and mother and his three disciples into the room where the girl was lying. [41]Holding her hand, he said to her, *"Talitha koum,"* which means "Little girl, get up!" [42]And the girl, who was twelve years old, immediately stood up and walked around! They were overwhelmed and totally amazed. [43]Jesus gave them strict orders not to tell anyone what had happened, and then he told them to give her something to eat.

CHAPTER **6**
Jesus Rejected at Nazareth

Jesus left that part of the country and returned with his disciples to Nazareth, his hometown. [2]The next Sabbath he began teaching in the synagogue, and many who heard him were amazed. They asked, "Where did he get all this wisdom and the power to perform such miracles?" [3]Then they scoffed, "He's just a carpenter, the son of Mary and the brother of James, Joseph, Judas, and Simon. And his sisters live right here among us." They were deeply offended and refused to believe in him.

[4]Then Jesus told them, "A prophet is honored everywhere except in his own hometown and among his relatives and his own family." [5]And

because of their unbelief, he couldn't do any miracles among them except to place his hands on a few sick people and heal them. 6And he was amazed at their unbelief.

Jesus Sends Out the Twelve Disciples

Then Jesus went from village to village, teaching the people. 7And he called his twelve disciples together and began sending them out two by two, giving them authority to cast out evil spirits. 8He told them to take nothing for their journey except a walking stick—no food, no traveler's bag, no money. 9He allowed them to wear sandals but not to take a change of clothes.

10"Wherever you go," he said, "stay in the same house until you leave town. 11But if any place refuses to welcome you or listen to you, shake its dust from your feet as you leave to show that you have abandoned those people to their fate."

12So the disciples went out, telling everyone they met to repent of their sins and turn to God. 13And they cast out many demons and healed many sick people, anointing them with olive oil.

The Death of John the Baptist

14Herod Antipas, the king, soon heard about Jesus, because everyone was talking about him. Some were saying, "This must be John the Baptist raised from the dead. That is why he can do such miracles." 15Others said, "He's the prophet Elijah." Still others said, "He's a prophet like the other great prophets of the past."

16When Herod heard about Jesus, he said, "John, the man I beheaded, has come back from the dead."

17For Herod had sent soldiers to arrest and imprison John as a favor to Herodias. She had been his brother Philip's wife, but Herod had married her. 18John had been telling Herod, "It is against God's law for you to marry your brother's wife." 19So Herodias bore a grudge against John and wanted to kill him. But without Herod's approval she was powerless, 20for Herod respected John; and knowing that he was a good and holy man, he protected him. Herod was greatly disturbed whenever he talked with John, but even so, he liked to listen to him.

21Herodias's chance finally came on Herod's birthday. He gave a party for his high government officials, army officers, and the leading citizens of Galilee. 22Then his daughter, also named Herodias, came in and performed a dance that greatly pleased Herod and his guests.

"Ask me for anything you like," the king said to the girl, "and I will give it to you." 23He even vowed, "I will give you whatever you ask, up to half my kingdom!"

24She went out and asked her mother, "What should I ask for?"

Her mother told her, "Ask for the head of John the Baptist!"

25So the girl hurried back to the king and told him, "I want the head of John the Baptist, right now, on a tray!"

26Then the king deeply regretted what he had said; but because of the vows he had made in front of his guests, he couldn't refuse her. 27So

Walk on water? Can't be done, right? **WRONG! Read MARK 6:45-52 for** the world's first—and only—account of a man able to walk on water! Then try this experiment.

1 Grab two pieces of clay of equal size. Roll one into a ball. Pat the other into a flat "raft" shape. Fill a cup with water.

2 Place the ball of clay on the water. Then try the flat piece. What happened?

The flat piece floated and the ball sank. Why? The flat piece had more surface for the water to push against.

There's no way, according to science, that a man should be able to walk on water. Unless the man is Jesus! Make a list of Jesus' other miracles. Keep the list by your bed. Remember—**Jesus isn't limited by the laws of science—he can do anything.**

Trust him whenever you get a "sinking" feeling, and let him keep you afloat!

he immediately sent an executioner to the prison to cut off John's head and bring it to him. The soldier beheaded John in the prison, 28brought his head on a tray, and gave it to the girl, who took it to her mother. 29When John's disciples heard what had happened, they came to get his body and buried it in a tomb.

Jesus Feeds Five Thousand

30The apostles returned to Jesus from their ministry tour and told him all they had done and taught. 31Then Jesus said, "Let's go off by ourselves to a quiet place and rest awhile." He said this because there were so many people coming and going that Jesus and his apostles didn't even have time to eat.

32So they left by boat for a quiet place, where they could be alone. 33But many people recognized them and saw them leaving, and people from many towns ran ahead along the shore and got there ahead of them. 34Jesus saw the huge crowd as he stepped from the boat, and he had compassion on them because they were like sheep without a shepherd. So he began teaching them many things.

35Late in the afternoon his disciples came to him and said, "This is a remote place, and it's already getting late. 36Send the crowds away so they can go to the nearby farms and villages and buy something to eat."

37But Jesus said, "You feed them."

"With what?" they asked. "We'd have to work for months to earn enough money to buy food for all these people!"

38"How much bread do you have?" he asked. "Go and find out."

They came back and reported, "We have five loaves of bread and two fish."

39Then Jesus told the disciples to have the people sit down in groups on the green grass. 40So they sat down in groups of fifty or a hundred. 41Jesus took the five loaves and two fish, looked up toward heaven, and blessed them. Then, breaking the loaves into pieces, he kept giving the bread to the disciples so they could distribute it to the people. He also divided the fish for everyone to share. 42They all ate as much as they wanted, 43and afterward, the disciples picked up twelve baskets of leftover bread and fish. 44A total of 5,000 men and their families were fed from those loaves!

Jesus Walks on Water

45Immediately after this, Jesus insisted that his disciples get back into the boat and head across the lake to Bethsaida, while he sent the people home. 46After telling everyone good-bye, he went up into the hills by himself to pray.

47Late that night, the disciples were in their boat in the middle of the lake, and Jesus was alone on land. 48He saw that they were in serious trouble, rowing hard and struggling against the wind and waves. About three o'clock in the morning Jesus came toward them, walking on the water. He intended to go past them, 49but when they saw him walking on the water, they cried out in terror, thinking he was a ghost. 50They were all terrified when they saw him.

But Jesus spoke to them at once. "Don't be afraid," he said. "Take courage! I am here!" 51Then he climbed into the boat, and the wind stopped. They were totally amazed, 52for they still didn't understand the significance of the miracle of the loaves. Their hearts were too hard to take it in.

53After they had crossed the lake, they landed at Gennesaret. They brought the boat to shore 54and climbed out. The people recognized Jesus at once, 55and they ran throughout the whole area, carrying sick people on mats to wherever they heard he was. 56Wherever he went—in villages, cities, or the countryside—they brought the sick out to the marketplaces. They begged him to let the sick touch at least the fringe of his robe, and all who touched him were healed.

CHAPTER **7**

Jesus Teaches about Inner Purity

One day some Pharisees and teachers of religious law arrived from Jerusalem to see Jesus. 2They noticed that some of his disciples failed to follow the Jewish ritual of hand washing before eating. 3(The Jews, especially the Pharisees, do not eat until they have poured water over their cupped hands, as required by their ancient traditions. 4Similarly, they don't eat anything from the market until they immerse their hands in water. This is but one of many traditions they have clung to—such as their ceremonial washing of cups, pitchers, and kettles.)

5So the Pharisees and teachers of religious law asked him, "Why don't your disciples follow our age-old tradition? They eat without first performing the hand-washing ceremony."

6Jesus replied, "You hypocrites! Isaiah was right when he prophesied about you, for he wrote,

'These people honor me with their lips,
  but their hearts are far from me.

7 Their worship is a farce,
  for they teach man-made ideas as
    commands from God.'

8 For you ignore God's law and substitute your own tradition." 9 Then he said, "You skillfully sidestep God's law in order to hold on to your own tradition. 10 For instance, Moses gave you this law from God: 'Honor your father and mother,' and 'Anyone who speaks disrespectfully of father or mother must be put to death.' 11 But you say it is all right for people to say to their parents, 'Sorry, I can't help you. For I have vowed to give to God what I would have given to you.' 12 In this way, you let them disregard their needy parents. 13 And so you cancel the word of God in order to hand down your own tradition. And this is only one example among many others."

14 Then Jesus called to the crowd to come and hear. "All of you listen," he said, "and try to understand. 15 It's not what goes into your body that defiles you; you are defiled by what comes from your heart.*"

17 Then Jesus went into a house to get away from the crowd, and his disciples asked him what he meant by the parable he had just used. 18 "Don't you understand either?" he asked. "Can't you see that the food you put into your body cannot defile you? 19 Food doesn't go into your heart, but only passes through the stomach and then goes into the sewer." (By saying this, he declared that every kind of food is acceptable in God's eyes.)

20 And then he added, "It is what comes from inside that defiles you. 21 For from within, out of a person's heart, come evil thoughts, sexual immorality, theft, murder, 22 adultery, greed, wickedness, deceit, lustful desires, envy, slander, pride, and foolishness. 23 All these vile things come from within; they are what defile you."

The Faith of a Gentile Woman

24 Then Jesus left Galilee and went north to the region of Tyre. He didn't want anyone to know which house he was staying in, but he couldn't keep it a secret. 25 Right away a woman who had heard about him came and fell at his feet. Her little girl was possessed by an evil spirit, 26 and she begged him to cast out the demon from her daughter.

Since she was a Gentile, born in Syrian Phoenicia, 27 Jesus told her, "First I should feed the children—my own family, the Jews. It isn't right to take food from the children and throw it to the dogs."

28 She replied, "That's true, Lord, but even the dogs under the table are allowed to eat the scraps from the children's plates."

29 "Good answer!" he said. "Now go home, for the demon has left your daughter." 30 And when she arrived home, she found her little girl lying quietly in bed, and the demon was gone.

Jesus Heals a Deaf Man

31 Jesus left Tyre and went up to Sidon before going back to the Sea of Galilee and the region of the Ten Towns. 32 A deaf man with a speech impediment was brought to him, and the people begged Jesus to lay his hands on the man to heal him.

33 Jesus led him away from the crowd so they could be alone. He put his fingers into the man's ears. Then, spitting on his own fingers, he touched the man's tongue. 34 Looking up to heaven, he sighed and said, *"Ephphatha,"* which means, "Be opened!" 35 Instantly the man could hear perfectly, and his tongue was freed so he could speak plainly!

36 Jesus told the crowd not to tell anyone, but the more he told them not to, the more they spread the news. 37 They were completely amazed and said again and again, "Everything he does is wonderful. He even makes the deaf to hear and gives speech to those who cannot speak."

CHAPTER **8**
Jesus Feeds Four Thousand

About this time another large crowd had gathered, and the people ran out of food again. Jesus called his disciples and told them, 2 "I feel sorry for these people. They have been here with me for three days, and they have nothing left to eat. 3 If I send them home hungry, they will faint along the way. For some of them have come a long distance."

4 His disciples replied, "How are we supposed to find enough food to feed them out here in the wilderness?"

5 Jesus asked, "How much bread do you have?"

"Seven loaves," they replied.

6 So Jesus told all the people to sit down on the ground. Then he took the seven loaves, thanked God for them, and broke them into pieces. He gave them to his disciples, who distributed the bread to the crowd. 7 A few small fish were found, too, so Jesus also blessed these and told the disciples to distribute them.

7:15 Some manuscripts add verse 16, *Anyone with ears to hear should listen and understand.* Compare 4:9, 23.

8They ate as much as they wanted. Afterward, the disciples picked up seven large baskets of leftover food. 9There were about 4,000 people in the crowd that day, and Jesus sent them home after they had eaten. 10Immediately after this, he got into a boat with his disciples and crossed over to the region of Dalmanutha.

Pharisees Demand a Miraculous Sign

11When the Pharisees heard that Jesus had arrived, they came and started to argue with him. Testing him, they demanded that he show them a miraculous sign from heaven to prove his authority.

12When he heard this, he sighed deeply in his spirit and said, "Why do these people keep demanding a miraculous sign? I tell you the truth, I will not give this generation any such sign." 13So he got back into the boat and left them, and he crossed to the other side of the lake.

Yeast of the Pharisees and Herod

14But the disciples had forgotten to bring any food. They had only one loaf of bread with them in the boat. 15As they were crossing the lake, Jesus warned them, "Watch out! Beware of the yeast of the Pharisees and of Herod."

16At this they began to argue with each other because they hadn't brought any bread. 17Jesus knew what they were saying, so he said, "Why are you arguing about having no bread? Don't you know or understand even yet? Are your hearts too hard to take it in? 18'You have eyes—can't you see? You have ears—can't you hear?' Don't you remember anything at all? 19When I fed the 5,000 with five loaves of bread, how many baskets of leftovers did you pick up afterward?"

"Twelve," they said.

20"And when I fed the 4,000 with seven loaves, how many large baskets of leftovers did you pick up?"

"Seven," they said.

21"Don't you understand yet?" he asked them.

Jesus Heals a Blind Man

22When they arrived at Bethsaida, some people brought a blind man to Jesus, and they begged him to touch the man and heal him. 23Jesus took the blind man by the hand and led him out of the village. Then, spitting on the man's eyes, he laid his hands on him and asked, "Can you see anything now?"

24The man looked around. "Yes," he said, "I see people, but I can't see them very clearly. They look like trees walking around."

25Then Jesus placed his hands on the man's eyes again, and his eyes were opened. His sight was completely restored, and he could see everything clearly. 26Jesus sent him away, saying, "Don't go back into the village on your way home."

Peter's Declaration about Jesus

27Jesus and his disciples left Galilee and went up to the villages near Caesarea Philippi. As they were walking along, he asked them, "Who do people say I am?"

28"Well," they replied, "some say John the Baptist, some say Elijah, and others say you are one of the other prophets."

29Then he asked them, "But who do you say I am?"

Peter replied, "You are the Messiah."

30But Jesus warned them not to tell anyone about him.

Jesus Predicts His Death

31Then Jesus began to tell them that the Son of Man must suffer many terrible things and be rejected by the elders, the leading priests, and the teachers of religious law. He would be killed, but three days later he would rise from the dead. 32As he talked about this openly with his disciples, Peter took him aside and began to reprimand him for saying such things.

33Jesus turned around and looked at his disciples, then reprimanded Peter. "Get away from me, Satan!" he said. "You are seeing things merely from a human point of view, not from God's."

34Then, calling the crowd to join his disciples, he said, "If any of you wants to be my follower, you must turn from your selfish ways, take up your cross, and follow me. 35If you try to hang on to your life, you will lose it. But if you give up your life for my sake and for the sake of the Good News, you will save it. 36And what do you benefit if you gain the whole world but lose your own soul? 37Is anything worth more than your soul? 38If anyone is ashamed of me and my message in these adulterous and sinful days, the Son of Man will be ashamed of that person when he returns in the glory of his Father with the holy angels."

CHAPTER 9

Jesus went on to say, "I tell you the truth, some standing here right now will not die before they see the Kingdom of God arrive in great power!"

The Transfiguration

²Six days later Jesus took Peter, James, and John, and led them up a high mountain to be alone. As the men watched, Jesus' appearance was transformed, ³and his clothes became dazzling white, far whiter than any earthly bleach could ever make them. ⁴Then Elijah and Moses appeared and began talking with Jesus.

⁵Peter exclaimed, "Rabbi, it's wonderful for us to be here! Let's make three shelters as memorials—one for you, one for Moses, and one for Elijah." ⁶He said this because he didn't really know what else to say, for they were all terrified.

⁷Then a cloud overshadowed them, and a voice from the cloud said, "This is my dearly loved Son. Listen to him." ⁸Suddenly, when they looked around, Moses and Elijah were gone, and they saw only Jesus with them.

⁹As they went back down the mountain, he told them not to tell anyone what they had seen until the Son of Man had risen from the dead. ¹⁰So they kept it to themselves, but they often asked each other what he meant by "rising from the dead."

¹¹Then they asked him, "Why do the teachers of religious law insist that Elijah must return before the Messiah comes?"

¹²Jesus responded, "Elijah is indeed coming first to get everything ready. Yet why do the Scriptures say that the Son of Man must suffer greatly and be treated with utter contempt? ¹³But I tell you, Elijah has already come, and they chose to abuse him, just as the Scriptures predicted."

Jesus Heals a Demon-Possessed Boy

¹⁴When they returned to the other disciples, they saw a large crowd surrounding them, and some teachers of religious law were arguing with them. ¹⁵When the crowd saw Jesus, they were overwhelmed with awe, and they ran to greet him.

¹⁶"What is all this arguing about?" Jesus asked.

¹⁷One of the men in the crowd spoke up and said, "Teacher, I brought my son so you could heal him. He is possessed by an evil spirit that won't let him talk. ¹⁸And whenever this spirit seizes him, it throws him violently to the ground. Then he foams at the mouth and grinds his teeth and becomes rigid. So I asked your disciples to cast out the evil spirit, but they couldn't do it."

¹⁹Jesus said to them, "You faithless people! How long must I be with you? How long must I put up with you? Bring the boy to me."

Key Verse

"Whoever wants to be first must take last place and be the servant of everyone else."—MARK 9:35b

Read MARK 9:35b out loud a few times so it sticks. Then try this challenge. For one whole day, do what this verse says—put others first. How? Here are a few ideas:

Let everyone go in front of you in line!

Let others be the first to be served food or drinks.

Let others choose what movie to watch or game to play.

Open doors for others.

AT THE END OF THE DAY, write in this space what it was like to be last at things and to put others first.

It may have felt a little weird at first, but putting others first is what Jesus wants us to do. AFTER ALL, THAT'S WHAT HE DID FOR US!

20So they brought the boy. But when the evil spirit saw Jesus, it threw the child into a violent convulsion, and he fell to the ground, writhing and foaming at the mouth.

21"How long has this been happening?" Jesus asked the boy's father.

He replied, "Since he was a little boy. 22The spirit often throws him into the fire or into water, trying to kill him. Have mercy on us and help us, if you can."

23"What do you mean, 'If I can'?" Jesus asked. "Anything is possible if a person believes."

24The father instantly cried out, "I do believe, but help me overcome my unbelief!"

25When Jesus saw that the crowd of onlookers was growing, he rebuked the evil spirit. "Listen, you spirit that makes this boy unable to hear and speak," he said. "I command you to come out of this child and never enter him again!"

26Then the spirit screamed and threw the boy into another violent convulsion and left him. The boy appeared to be dead. A murmur ran through the crowd as people said, "He's dead." 27But Jesus took him by the hand and helped him to his feet, and he stood up.

28Afterward, when Jesus was alone in the house with his disciples, they asked him, "Why couldn't we cast out that evil spirit?"

29Jesus replied, "This kind can be cast out only by prayer."

Jesus Again Predicts His Death

30Leaving that region, they traveled through Galilee. Jesus didn't want anyone to know he was there, 31for he wanted to spend more time with his disciples and teach them. He said to them, "The Son of Man is going to be betrayed into the hands of his enemies. He will be killed, but three days later he will rise from the dead." 32They didn't understand what he was saying, however, and they were afraid to ask him what he meant.

The Greatest in the Kingdom

33After they arrived at Capernaum and settled in a house, Jesus asked his disciples, "What were you discussing out on the road?" 34But they didn't answer, because they had been arguing about which of them was the greatest. **35He sat down, called the twelve disciples over to him, and said, "Whoever wants to be first must take last place and be the servant of everyone else."**

36Then he put a little child among them. Taking the child in his arms, he said to them, 37"Anyone who welcomes a little child like this on my behalf welcomes me, and anyone who welcomes me welcomes not only me but also my Father who sent me."

Using the Name of Jesus

38John said to Jesus, "Teacher, we saw someone using your name to cast out demons, but we told him to stop because he wasn't in our group."

39"Don't stop him!" Jesus said. "No one who performs a miracle in my name will soon be able to speak evil of me. 40Anyone who is not against us is for us. 41If anyone gives you even a cup of water because you belong to the Messiah, I tell you the truth, that person will surely be rewarded.

42"But if you cause one of these little ones who trusts in me to fall into sin, it would be better for you to be thrown into the sea with a large millstone hung around your neck. 43If your hand causes you to sin, cut it off. It's better to enter eternal life with only one hand than to go into the unquenchable fires of hell with two hands.* 45If your foot causes you to sin, cut it off. It's better to enter eternal life with only one foot than to be thrown into hell with two feet.* 47And if your eye causes you to sin, gouge it out. It's better to enter the Kingdom of God with only one eye than to have two eyes and be thrown into hell, 48'where the maggots never die and the fire never goes out.'

49"For everyone will be tested with fire. 50Salt is good for seasoning. But if it loses its flavor, how do you make it salty again? You must have the qualities of salt among yourselves and live in peace with each other."

CHAPTER **10**
Discussion about Divorce and Marriage

Then Jesus left Capernaum and went down to the region of Judea and into the area east of the Jordan River. Once again crowds gathered around him, and as usual he was teaching them.

2Some Pharisees came and tried to trap him with this question: "Should a man be allowed to divorce his wife?"

3Jesus answered them with a question: "What did Moses say in the law about divorce?"

4"Well, he permitted it," they replied. "He said a man can give his wife a written notice of divorce and send her away."

9:43 Some manuscripts add verse 44, *'where the maggots never die and the fire never goes out.'* See 9:48.   9:45 Some manuscripts add verse 46, *'where the maggots never die and the fire never goes out.'* See 9:48.

5But Jesus responded, "He wrote this commandment only as a concession to your hard hearts. 6But 'God made them male and female' from the beginning of creation. 7'This explains why a man leaves his father and mother and is joined to his wife, 8and the two are united into one.' Since they are no longer two but one, 9let no one split apart what God has joined together."

10Later, when he was alone with his disciples in the house, they brought up the subject again. 11He told them, "Whoever divorces his wife and marries someone else commits adultery against her. 12And if a woman divorces her husband and marries someone else, she commits adultery."

Jesus Blesses the Children

13One day some parents brought their children to Jesus so he could touch and bless them. But the disciples scolded the parents for bothering him.

14When Jesus saw what was happening, he was angry with his disciples. He said to them, "Let the children come to me. Don't stop them! For the Kingdom of God belongs to those who are like these children. 15I tell you the truth, anyone who doesn't receive the Kingdom of God like a child will never enter it." 16Then he took the children in his arms and placed his hands on their heads and blessed them.

The Rich Man

17As Jesus was starting out on his way to Jerusalem, a man came running up to him, knelt down, and asked, "Good Teacher, what must I do to inherit eternal life?"

18"Why do you call me good?" Jesus asked. "Only God is truly good. 19But to answer your question, you know the commandments: 'You must not murder. You must not commit adultery. You must not steal. You must not testify falsely. You must not cheat anyone. Honor your father and mother.'"

20"Teacher," the man replied, "I've obeyed all these commandments since I was young."

21Looking at the man, Jesus felt genuine love for him. "There is still one thing you haven't done," he told him. "Go and sell all your possessions and give the money to the poor, and you will have treasure in heaven. Then come, follow me."

22At this the man's face fell, and he went away sad, for he had many possessions.

23Jesus looked around and said to his disciples, "How hard it is for the rich to enter the Kingdom of God!" 24This amazed them. But Jesus said again, "Dear children, it is very hard to enter the Kingdom of God. 25In fact, it is easier for a camel to go through the eye of a needle than for a rich person to enter the Kingdom of God!"

26The disciples were astounded. "Then who in the world can be saved?" they asked.

27Jesus looked at them intently and said, "Humanly speaking, it is impossible. But not with God. Everything is possible with God."

28Then Peter began to speak up. "We've given up everything to follow you," he said.

29"Yes," Jesus replied, "and I assure you that everyone who has given up house or brothers or sisters or mother or father or children or property, for my sake and for the Good News, 30will receive now in return a hundred times as many houses, brothers, sisters, mothers, children, and property—along with persecution. And in the world to come that person will have eternal life. 31But many who are the greatest now will be least important then, and those who seem least important now will be the greatest then."

Jesus Again Predicts His Death

32They were now on the way up to Jerusalem, and Jesus was walking ahead of them. The disciples were filled with awe, and the people following behind were overwhelmed with fear. Taking the twelve disciples aside, Jesus once more began to describe everything that was about to happen to him. 33"Listen," he said, "we're going up to Jerusalem, where the Son of Man will be betrayed to the leading priests and the teachers of religious law. They will sentence him to die and hand him over to the Romans. 34They will mock him, spit on him, flog him with a whip, and kill him, but after three days he will rise again."

Jesus Teaches about Serving Others

35Then James and John, the sons of Zebedee, came over and spoke to him. "Teacher," they said, "we want you to do us a favor."

36"What is your request?" he asked.

37They replied, "When you sit on your glorious throne, we want to sit in places of honor next to you, one on your right and the other on your left."

38But Jesus said to them, "You don't know

what you are asking! Are you able to drink from the bitter cup of suffering I am about to drink? Are you able to be baptized with the baptism of suffering I must be baptized with?"

39 "Oh yes," they replied, "we are able!"

Then Jesus told them, "You will indeed drink from my bitter cup and be baptized with my baptism of suffering. 40 But I have no right to say who will sit on my right or my left. God has prepared those places for the ones he has chosen."

41 When the ten other disciples heard what James and John had asked, they were indignant.

Find a friend and a Bible. **Read MARK 10:46-52 together.** Then try this activity.

Try to do these tasks wearing a blindfold: Tie your shoes, write your name, and do your math homework. Then switch roles.

Discuss these questions together.

What was it like trying to do things while you were blindfolded?

What do you think it would have been like to be blind in Bible times? (How would it be different from today?)

The blind man must have been thankful. **Be thankful yourself!**

Write today's date here

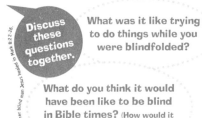

From this day on, try to be aware of your amazing senses and abilities.

Thank God for blessing you so richly when you use your hands, feet, eyes, ears, nose, mouth, arms, or legs!

42 So Jesus called them together and said, "You know that the rulers in this world lord it over their people, and officials flaunt their authority over those under them. 43 But among you it will be different. Whoever wants to be a leader among you must be your servant, 44 and whoever wants to be first among you must be the slave of everyone else. 45 For even the Son of Man came not to be served but to serve others and to give his life as a ransom for many."

Jesus Heals Blind Bartimaeus

46 Then they reached Jericho, and as Jesus and his disciples left town, a large crowd followed him. A blind beggar named Bartimaeus (son of Timaeus) was sitting beside the road. 47 When Bartimaeus heard that Jesus of Nazareth was nearby, he began to shout, "Jesus, Son of David, have mercy on me!"

48 "Be quiet!" many of the people yelled at him. But he only shouted louder, "Son of David, have mercy on me!"

49 When Jesus heard him, he stopped and said, "Tell him to come here."

So they called the blind man. "Cheer up," they said. "Come on, he's calling you!" 50 Bartimaeus threw aside his coat, jumped up, and came to Jesus.

51 "What do you want me to do for you?" Jesus asked.

"My rabbi," the blind man said, "I want to see!"

52 And Jesus said to him, "Go, for your faith has healed you." Instantly the man could see, and he followed Jesus down the road.

CHAPTER **11**
Jesus' Triumphant Entry

As Jesus and his disciples approached Jerusalem, they came to the towns of Bethphage and Bethany on the Mount of Olives. Jesus sent two of them on ahead. 2 "Go into that village over there," he told them. "As soon as you enter it, you will see a young donkey tied there that no one has ever ridden. Untie it and bring it here. 3 If anyone asks, 'What are you doing?' just say, 'The Lord needs it and will return it soon.'"

4 The two disciples left and found the colt standing in the street, tied outside the front door. 5 As they were untying it, some bystanders demanded, "What are you doing, untying that colt?" 6 They said what Jesus had told them to say, and they were permitted to take it. 7 Then they brought the colt to Jesus and threw their garments over it, and he sat on it.

8 Many in the crowd spread their garments on the road ahead of him, and others spread leafy branches they had cut in the fields. 9 Jesus was in the center of the procession, and the people all around him were shouting,

"Praise God!
  Blessings on the one who comes in the
    name of the LORD!
10 Blessings on the coming Kingdom of our
    ancestor David!
  Praise God in highest heaven!"

11 So Jesus came to Jerusalem and went into the Temple. After looking around carefully at everything, he left because it was late in the afternoon. Then he returned to Bethany with the twelve disciples.

Jesus Curses the Fig Tree

12 The next morning as they were leaving Bethany, Jesus was hungry. 13 He noticed a fig tree in full leaf a little way off, so he went over to see if he could find any figs. But there were only leaves because it was too early in the season for fruit. 14 Then Jesus said to the tree, "May no one ever eat your fruit again!" And the disciples heard him say it.

Jesus Clears the Temple

15 When they arrived back in Jerusalem, Jesus entered the Temple and began to drive out the people buying and selling animals for sacrifices. He knocked over the tables of the money changers and the chairs of those selling doves, 16 and he stopped everyone from using the Temple as a marketplace. 17 He said to them, "The Scriptures declare, 'My Temple will be called a house of prayer for all nations,' but you have turned it into a den of thieves."

18 When the leading priests and teachers of religious law heard what Jesus had done, they began planning how to kill him. But they were afraid of him because the people were so amazed at his teaching.

19 That evening Jesus and the disciples left the city.

20 The next morning as they passed by the fig tree he had cursed, the disciples noticed it had withered from the roots up. 21 Peter remembered what Jesus had said to the tree on the previous day and exclaimed, "Look, Rabbi! The fig tree you cursed has withered and died!"

22 Then Jesus said to the disciples, "Have faith in God. 23 I tell you the truth, you can say to this mountain, 'May you be lifted up and thrown into the sea,' and it will happen. But you must really believe it will happen and have no doubt in your heart. 24 I tell you, you can pray for anything, and if you believe that you've received it, it will be yours. 25 But when you are praying, first forgive anyone you are holding a grudge against, so that your Father in heaven will forgive your sins, too.*"

The Authority of Jesus Challenged

27 Again they entered Jerusalem. As Jesus was walking through the Temple area, the leading priests, the teachers of religious law, and the elders came up to him. 28 They demanded, "By what authority are you doing all these things? Who gave you the right to do them?"

29 "I'll tell you by what authority I do these things if you answer one question," Jesus replied. 30 "Did John's authority to baptize come from heaven, or was it merely human? Answer me!"

31 They talked it over among themselves. "If we say it was from heaven, he will ask why we didn't believe John. 32 But do we dare say it was merely human?" For they were afraid of what the people would do, because everyone believed that John was a prophet. 33 So they finally replied, "We don't know."

And Jesus responded, "Then I won't tell you by what authority I do these things."

CHAPTER **12**
Parable of the Evil Farmers

Then Jesus began teaching them with stories: "A man planted a vineyard. He built a wall around it, dug a pit for pressing out the grape juice, and built a lookout tower. Then he leased the vineyard to tenant farmers and moved to another country. 2 At the time of the grape harvest, he sent one of his servants to collect his share of the crop. 3 But the farmers grabbed the servant, beat him up, and sent him back empty-handed. 4 The owner then sent another servant, but they insulted him and beat him over the head. 5 The next servant he sent was killed. Others were either beaten or killed, 6 until there was only one left—his son whom he loved dearly. The owner finally sent him, thinking, 'Surely they will respect my son.'

7 "But the tenant farmers said to one another, 'Here comes the heir to this estate. Let's kill him and get the estate for ourselves!' 8 So they

11:25 Some manuscripts add verse 26, *But if you refuse to forgive, your Father in heaven will not forgive your sins.* Compare Matt 6:15.

grabbed him and murdered him and threw his body out of the vineyard.

9"What do you suppose the owner of the vineyard will do?" Jesus asked. "I'll tell you—he will come and kill those farmers and lease the vineyard to others. 10Didn't you ever read this in the Scriptures?

'The stone that the builders rejected
     has now become the cornerstone.
11 This is the LORD's doing,
     and it is wonderful to see.'"

12The religious leaders wanted to arrest Jesus because they realized he was telling the story against them—they were the wicked farmers. But they were afraid of the crowd, so they left him and went away.

Taxes for Caesar

13Later the leaders sent some Pharisees and supporters of Herod to trap Jesus into saying something for which he could be arrested. 14"Teacher," they said, "we know how honest you are. You are impartial and don't play favorites. You teach the way of God truthfully. Now tell us—is it right to pay taxes to Caesar or not? 15Should we pay them, or shouldn't we?"

Jesus saw through their hypocrisy and said, "Why are you trying to trap me? Show me a Roman coin, and I'll tell you." 16When they handed it to him, he asked, "Whose picture and title are stamped on it?"

"Caesar's," they replied.

17"Well, then," Jesus said, "give to Caesar what belongs to Caesar, and give to God what belongs to God."

His reply completely amazed them.

Discussion about Resurrection

18Then Jesus was approached by some Sadducees—religious leaders who say there is no resurrection from the dead. They posed this question: 19"Teacher, Moses gave us a law that if a man dies, leaving a wife without children, his brother should marry the widow and have a child who will carry on the brother's name. 20Well, suppose there were seven brothers. The oldest one married and then died without children. 21So the second brother married the widow, but he also died without children. Then the third brother married her. 22This continued with all seven of them, and still there were no children. Last of all, the woman also died. 23So tell us, whose wife will she be in the resurrection? For all seven were married to her."

24Jesus replied, "Your mistake is that you don't know the Scriptures, and you don't know the power of God. 25For when the dead rise, they will neither marry nor be given in marriage. In this respect they will be like the angels in heaven.

26"But now, as to whether the dead will be raised—haven't you ever read about this in the writings of Moses, in the story of the burning bush? Long after Abraham, Isaac, and Jacob had died, God said to Moses, 'I am the God of Abraham, the God of Isaac, and the God of Jacob.' 27So he is the God of the living, not the dead. You have made a serious error."

The Most Important Commandment

28One of the teachers of religious law was standing there listening to the debate. He realized that Jesus had answered well, so he asked, "Of all the commandments, which is the most important?"

29Jesus replied, "The most important commandment is this: 'Listen, O Israel! The LORD our God is the one and only LORD. 30And you must love the LORD your God with all your heart, all your soul, all your mind, and all your strength.' 31The second is equally important: 'Love your neighbor as yourself.' No other commandment is greater than these."

32The teacher of religious law replied, "Well said, Teacher. You have spoken the truth by saying that there is only one God and no other. 33And I know it is important to love him with all my heart and all my understanding and all my strength, and to love my neighbor as myself. This is more important than to offer all of the burnt offerings and sacrifices required in the law."

34Realizing how much the man understood, Jesus said to him, "You are not far from the Kingdom of God." And after that, no one dared to ask him any more questions.

Whose Son Is the Messiah?

35Later, as Jesus was teaching the people in the Temple, he asked, "Why do the teachers of religious law claim that the Messiah is the son of David? 36For David himself, speaking under the inspiration of the Holy Spirit, said,

'The LORD said to my Lord,
Sit in the place of honor at my right hand
     until I humble your enemies beneath
       your feet.'

37Since David himself called the Messiah 'my Lord,' how can the Messiah be his son?" The large crowd listened to him with great delight.

³⁸Jesus also taught: "Beware of these teachers of religious law! For they like to parade around in flowing robes and receive respectful greetings as they walk in the marketplaces. ³⁹And how they love the seats of honor in the synagogues and the head table at banquets. ⁴⁰Yet they shamelessly cheat widows out of their property and then pretend to be pious by making long prayers in public. Because of this, they will be more severely punished."

The Widow's Offering

⁴¹Jesus sat down near the collection box in the Temple and watched as the crowds dropped in their money. Many rich people put in large amounts. ⁴²Then a poor widow came and dropped in two small coins.

⁴³Jesus called his disciples to him and said, "I tell you the truth, this poor widow has given more than all the others who are making contributions. ⁴⁴For they gave a tiny part of their surplus, but she, poor as she is, has given everything she had to live on."

CHAPTER **13**
Jesus Foretells the Future

As Jesus was leaving the Temple that day, one of his disciples said, "Teacher, look at these magnificent buildings! Look at the impressive stones in the walls."

²Jesus replied, "Yes, look at these great buildings. But they will be completely demolished. Not one stone will be left on top of another!"

³Later, Jesus sat on the Mount of Olives across the valley from the Temple. Peter, James, John, and Andrew came to him privately and asked him, ⁴"Tell us, when will all this happen? What sign will show us that these things are about to be fulfilled?"

⁵Jesus replied, "Don't let anyone mislead you, ⁶for many will come in my name, claiming, 'I am the Messiah.' They will deceive many. ⁷And you will hear of wars and threats of wars, but don't panic. Yes, these things must take place, but the end won't follow immediately. ⁸Nation will go to war against nation, and kingdom against kingdom. There will be earthquakes in many parts of the world, as well as famines. But this is only the first of the birth pains, with more to come.

⁹"When these things begin to happen, watch out! You will be handed over to the local councils and beaten in the synagogues. You will stand trial before governors and kings because you are my followers. But this will be your opportunity to tell them about me. ¹⁰For the Good News must first be preached to all nations. ¹¹But when you are arrested and stand trial, don't worry in advance about what to say. Just say what God tells

The **#1** COMMAND

Grab a friend, a pencil, some markers, and two big sheets of newsprint.

GET ARTISTIC!

1 Lie on your back on a sheet of newsprint.

If you don't have newsprint, just draw pictures of each other on regular paper.

2 Have your friend use the pencil to trace around your body outline. Do the same for your friend with the other paper.

3 Use markers to fill in facial features, hair, and clothing.

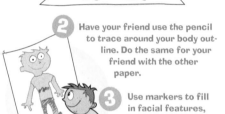

Then read MARK 12:28-31 together. Around your shape outline, write ways you can love God with all your heart, soul, mind, and strength.

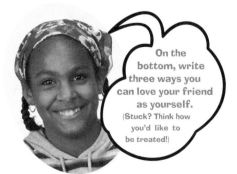

On the bottom, write three ways you can love your friend as yourself. (Stuck? Think how you'd like to be treated!)

you at that time, for it is not you who will be speaking, but the Holy Spirit.

12"A brother will betray his brother to death, a father will betray his own child, and children will rebel against their parents and cause them to be killed. 13And everyone will hate you because you are my followers. But the one who endures to the end will be saved.

14"The day is coming when you will see the sacrilegious object that causes desecration standing where he should not be." (Reader, pay attention!) "Then those in Judea must flee to the hills. 15A person out on the deck of a roof must not go down into the house to pack. 16A person out in the field must not return even to get a coat. 17How terrible it will be for pregnant women and for nursing mothers in those days. 18And pray that your flight will not be in winter. 19For there will be greater anguish in those days than at any time since God created the world. And it will never be so great again. 20In fact, unless the Lord shortens that time of calamity, not a single person will survive. But for the sake of his chosen ones he has shortened those days.

21"Then if anyone tells you, 'Look, here is the Messiah,' or 'There he is,' don't believe it. 22For false messiahs and false prophets will rise up and perform signs and wonders so as to deceive, if possible, even God's chosen ones. 23Watch out! I have warned you about this ahead of time!

24"At that time, after the anguish of those days,

the sun will be darkened,
the moon will give no light,
25 the stars will fall from the sky,
and the powers in the heavens will be
shaken.

26Then everyone will see the Son of Man coming on the clouds with great power and glory. 27And he will send out his angels to gather his chosen ones from all over the world—from the farthest ends of the earth and heaven.

28"Now learn a lesson from the fig tree. When its branches bud and its leaves begin to sprout, you know that summer is near. 29In the same way, when you see all these things taking place, you can know that his return is very near, right at the door. 30I tell you the truth, this generation will not pass from the scene before all these things take place. 31Heaven and earth will disappear, but my words will never disappear.

32"However, no one knows the day or hour when these things will happen, not even the angels in heaven or the Son himself. Only the Father knows. 33And since you don't know when that time will come, be on guard! Stay alert!

34"The coming of the Son of Man can be illustrated by the story of a man going on a long trip. When he left home, he gave each of his slaves instructions about the work they were to do, and he told the gatekeeper to watch for his return. 35You, too, must keep watch! For you don't know when the master of the household will return—in the evening, at midnight, before dawn, or at daybreak. 36Don't let him find you sleeping when he arrives without warning. 37I say to you what I say to everyone: Watch for him!"

CHAPTER **14**

Jesus Anointed at Bethany

It was now two days before Passover and the Festival of Unleavened Bread. The leading priests and the teachers of religious law were still looking for an opportunity to capture Jesus secretly and kill him. 2"But not during the Passover celebration," they agreed, "or the people may riot."

3Meanwhile, Jesus was in Bethany at the home of Simon, a man who had previously had leprosy. While he was eating, a woman came in with a beautiful alabaster jar of expensive perfume made from essence of nard. She broke open the jar and poured the perfume over his head.

4Some of those at the table were indignant. "Why waste such expensive perfume?" they asked. 5"It could have been sold for a year's wages and the money given to the poor!" So they scolded her harshly.

6But Jesus replied, "Leave her alone. Why criticize her for doing such a good thing to me? 7You will always have the poor among you, and you can help them whenever you want to. But you will not always have me. 8She has done what she could and has anointed my body for burial ahead of time. 9I tell you the truth, wherever the Good News is preached throughout the world, this woman's deed will be remembered and discussed."

Judas Agrees to Betray Jesus

10Then Judas Iscariot, one of the twelve disciples, went to the leading priests to arrange to betray Jesus to them. 11They were delighted when they heard why he had come, and they promised to give him money. So he began looking for an opportunity to betray Jesus.

The Last Supper

12On the first day of the Festival of Unleavened Bread, when the Passover lamb is sacrificed,

Jesus' disciples asked him, "Where do you want us to go to prepare the Passover meal for you?"

13 So Jesus sent two of them into Jerusalem with these instructions: "As you go into the city, a man carrying a pitcher of water will meet you. Follow him. 14 At the house he enters, say to the owner, 'The Teacher asks: Where is the guest room where I can eat the Passover meal with my disciples?' 15 He will take you upstairs to a large room that is already set up. That is where you should prepare our meal." 16 So the two disciples went into the city and found everything just as Jesus had said, and they prepared the Passover meal there.

17 In the evening Jesus arrived with the twelve disciples. 18 As they were at the table eating, Jesus said, "I tell you the truth, one of you eating with me here will betray me."

19 Greatly distressed, each one asked in turn, "Am I the one?"

20 He replied, "It is one of you twelve who is eating from this bowl with me. 21 For the Son of Man must die, as the Scriptures declared long ago. But how terrible it will be for the one who betrays him. It would be far better for that man if he had never been born!"

22 As they were eating, Jesus took some bread and blessed it. Then he broke it in pieces and gave it to the disciples, saying, "Take it, for this is my body."

23 And he took a cup of wine and gave thanks to God for it. He gave it to them, and they all drank from it. 24 And he said to them, "This is my blood, which confirms the covenant between God and his people. It is poured out as a sacrifice for many. 25 I tell you the truth, I will not drink wine again until the day I drink it new in the Kingdom of God."

26 Then they sang a hymn and went out to the Mount of Olives.

Jesus Predicts Peter's Denial

27 On the way, Jesus told them, "All of you will desert me. For the Scriptures say,

'God will strike the Shepherd,
    and the sheep will be scattered.'

28 But after I am raised from the dead, I will go ahead of you to Galilee and meet you there."

29 Peter said to him, "Even if everyone else deserts you, I never will."

30 Jesus replied, "I tell you the truth, Peter—this very night, before the rooster crows twice, you will deny three times that you even know me."

31 "No!" Peter declared emphatically. "Even if I

have to die with you, I will never deny you!" And all the others vowed the same.

Jesus Prays in Gethsemane

32 They went to the olive grove called Gethsemane, and Jesus said, "Sit here while I go and pray." 33 He took Peter, James, and John with him, and he became deeply troubled and distressed. 34 He told them, "My soul is crushed with grief to the point of death. Stay here and keep watch with me."

35 He went on a little farther and fell to the ground. He prayed that, if it were possible, the awful hour awaiting him might pass him by. 36 "Abba, Father," he cried out, "everything is possible for you. Please take this cup of suffering away from me. Yet I want your will to be done, not mine."

37 Then he returned and found the disciples asleep. He said to Peter, "Simon, are you asleep? Couldn't you watch with me even one hour? 38 Keep watch and pray, so that you will not give in to temptation. For the spirit is willing, but the body is weak."

39 Then Jesus left them again and prayed the same prayer as before. 40 When he returned to them again, he found them sleeping, for they couldn't keep their eyes open. And they didn't know what to say.

41 When he returned to them the third time, he said, "Go ahead and sleep. Have your rest. But no—the time has come. The Son of Man is betrayed into the hands of sinners. 42 Up, let's be going. Look, my betrayer is here!"

Jesus Is Betrayed and Arrested

43 And immediately, even as Jesus said this, Judas, one of the twelve disciples, arrived with a crowd of men armed with swords and clubs. They had been sent by the leading priests, the teachers of religious law, and the elders. 44 The traitor, Judas, had given them a prearranged signal: "You will know which one to arrest when I greet him with a kiss. Then you can take him away under guard." 45 As soon as they arrived, Judas walked up to Jesus. "Rabbi!" he exclaimed, and gave him the kiss.

46 Then the others grabbed Jesus and arrested him. 47 But one of the men with Jesus pulled out his sword and struck the high priest's slave, slashing off his ear.

48 Jesus asked them, "Am I some dangerous revolutionary, that you come with swords and clubs to arrest me? 49 Why didn't you arrest me in the Temple? I was there among you teaching

every day. But these things are happening to fulfill what the Scriptures say about me."

50Then all his disciples deserted him and ran away. 51One young man following behind was clothed only in a long linen shirt. When the mob tried to grab him, 52he slipped out of his shirt and ran away naked.

Jesus before the Council

53They took Jesus to the high priest's home where the leading priests, the elders, and the teachers of religious law had gathered. 54Meanwhile, Peter followed him at a distance and went right into the high priest's courtyard. There he sat with the guards, warming himself by the fire.

55Inside, the leading priests and the entire high council were trying to find evidence against Jesus, so they could put him to death. But they couldn't find any. 56Many false witnesses spoke against him, but they contradicted each other. 57Finally, some men stood up and gave this false testimony: 58"We heard him say, 'I will destroy this Temple made with human hands, and in three days I will build another, made without human hands.'" 59But even then they didn't get their stories straight!

60Then the high priest stood up before the others and asked Jesus, "Well, aren't you going to answer these charges? What do you have to say for yourself?" 61But Jesus was silent and made no reply. Then the high priest asked him, "Are you the Messiah, the Son of the Blessed One?"

62Jesus said, "I Am. And you will see the Son of Man seated in the place of power at God's right hand and coming on the clouds of heaven."

63Then the high priest tore his clothing to show his horror and said, "Why do we need other witnesses? 64You have all heard his blasphemy. What is your verdict?"

"Guilty!" they all cried. "He deserves to die!"

65Then some of them began to spit at him, and they blindfolded him and beat him with their fists. "Prophesy to us," they jeered. And the guards slapped him as they took him away.

Peter Denies Jesus

66Meanwhile, Peter was in the courtyard below. One of the servant girls who worked for the high priest came by 67and noticed Peter warming himself at the fire. She looked at him closely and said, "You were one of those with Jesus of Nazareth."

68But Peter denied it. "I don't know what you're talking about," he said, and he went out into the entryway. Just then, a rooster crowed.

69When the servant girl saw him standing there, she began telling the others, "This man is definitely one of them!" 70But Peter denied it again.

A little later some of the other bystanders confronted Peter and said, "You must be one of them, because you are a Galilean."

71Peter swore, "A curse on me if I'm lying—I don't know this man you're talking about!" 72And immediately the rooster crowed the second time.

Suddenly, Jesus' words flashed through Peter's mind: "Before the rooster crows twice, you will deny three times that you even know me." And he broke down and wept.

CHAPTER **15**

Jesus' Trial before Pilate

Very early in the morning the leading priests, the elders, and the teachers of religious law—the entire high council—met to discuss their next step. They bound Jesus, led him away, and took him to Pilate, the Roman governor.

FUN fact I Know I'm Fast, but Is That Fasting?

You may be really fast when you run in soccer, but is that what the Bible means when it talks about fasting? Nah! In the Bible, fasting means going without food for a certain length of time so you can pray and focus on God. **Jesus himself fasted for forty days when Satan was tempting him (MATTHEW 4:1-2).**

Try fasting through one meal (ask your parents for permission first, and don't pick the night you're having liver and onions!).

While others are eating, spend time praying, reading your Bible, and focusing on God.

2 Pilate asked Jesus, "Are you the king of the Jews?"

Jesus replied, "You have said it."

3 Then the leading priests kept accusing him of many crimes, 4 and Pilate asked him, "Aren't you going to answer them? What about all these charges they are bringing against you?" 5 But Jesus said nothing, much to Pilate's surprise.

6 Now it was the governor's custom each year during the Passover celebration to release one prisoner—anyone the people requested. 7 One of the prisoners at that time was Barabbas, a revolutionary who had committed murder in an uprising. 8 The crowd went to Pilate and asked him to release a prisoner as usual.

9 "Would you like me to release to you this 'King of the Jews'?" Pilate asked. 10 (For he realized by now that the leading priests had arrested Jesus out of envy.) 11 But at this point the leading priests stirred up the crowd to demand the release of Barabbas instead of Jesus. 12 Pilate asked them, "Then what should I do with this man you call the king of the Jews?"

13 They shouted back, "Crucify him!"

14 "Why?" Pilate demanded. "What crime has he committed?"

But the mob roared even louder, "Crucify him!"

15 So to pacify the crowd, Pilate released Barabbas to them. He ordered Jesus flogged with a lead-tipped whip, then turned him over to the Roman soldiers to be crucified.

The Soldiers Mock Jesus

16 The soldiers took Jesus into the courtyard of the governor's headquarters (called the Praetorium) and called out the entire regiment. 17 They dressed him in a purple robe, and they wove thorn branches into a crown and put it on his head. 18 Then they saluted him and taunted, "Hail! King of the Jews!" 19 And they struck him on the head with a reed stick, spit on him, and dropped to their knees in mock worship. 20 When they were finally tired of mocking him, they took off the purple robe and put his own clothes on him again. Then they led him away to be crucified.

The Crucifixion

21 A passerby named Simon, who was from Cyrene, was coming in from the countryside just then, and the soldiers forced him to carry Jesus' cross. (Simon was the father of Alexander and Rufus.) 22 And they brought Jesus to a place called Golgotha (which means "Place of the Skull"). 23 They offered him wine drugged with myrrh, but he refused it.

24 Then the soldiers nailed him to the cross. They divided his clothes and threw dice to decide who would get each piece. 25 It was nine o'clock in the morning when they crucified him. 26 A sign was fastened to the cross, announcing the charge against him. It read, "The King of the Jews." 27 Two revolutionaries were crucified with him, one on his right and one on his left.*

29 The people passing by shouted abuse, shaking their heads in mockery. "Ha! Look at you now!" they yelled at him. "You said you were going to destroy the Temple and rebuild it in three days. 30 Well then, save yourself and come down from the cross!"

31 The leading priests and teachers of religious law also mocked Jesus. "He saved others," they scoffed, "but he can't save himself! 32 Let this Messiah, this King of Israel, come down from the cross so we can see it and believe him!" Even the men who were crucified with Jesus ridiculed him.

The Death of Jesus

33 At noon, darkness fell across the whole land until three o'clock. 34 Then at three o'clock Jesus called out with a loud voice, *"Eloi, Eloi, lema sabachthani?"* which means "My God, my God, why have you abandoned me?"

35 Some of the bystanders misunderstood and thought he was calling for the prophet Elijah. 36 One of them ran and filled a sponge with sour wine, holding it up to him on a reed stick so he could drink. "Wait!" he said. "Let's see whether Elijah comes to take him down!"

37 Then Jesus uttered another loud cry and breathed his last. 38 And the curtain in the sanctuary of the Temple was torn in two, from top to bottom.

39 When the Roman officer who stood facing him saw how he had died, he exclaimed, "This man truly was the Son of God!"

40 Some women were there, watching from a distance, including Mary Magdalene, Mary (the mother of James the younger and of Joseph), and Salome. 41 They had been followers of Jesus and had cared for him while he was in Galilee. Many other women who had come with him to Jerusalem were also there.

The Burial of Jesus

42 This all happened on Friday, the day of preparation, the day before the Sabbath. As evening

15:27 Some manuscripts add verse 28, *And the Scripture was fulfilled that said, "He was counted among those who were rebels."* See Isa 53:12; also compare Luke 22:37.

approached, [43]Joseph of Arimathea took a risk and went to Pilate and asked for Jesus' body. (Joseph was an honored member of the high council, and he was waiting for the Kingdom of God to come.) [44]Pilate couldn't believe that Jesus was already dead, so he called for the Roman officer and asked if he had died yet. [45]The officer confirmed that Jesus was dead, so Pilate told Joseph he could have the body. [46]Joseph bought a long sheet of linen cloth. Then he took Jesus' body down from the cross, wrapped it in the cloth, and laid it in a tomb that had been carved out of the rock. Then he rolled a stone in front of the entrance. [47]Mary Magdalene and Mary the mother of Joseph saw where Jesus' body was laid.

CHAPTER **16**

The Resurrection

Saturday evening, when the Sabbath ended, Mary Magdalene, Mary the mother of James, and Salome went out and purchased burial spices so they could anoint Jesus' body. [2]Very early on Sunday morning, just at sunrise, they went to the tomb. [3]On the way they were asking each other, "Who will roll away the stone for us from the entrance to the tomb?" [4]But as they arrived, they looked up and saw that the stone, which was very large, had already been rolled aside.

[5]When they entered the tomb, they saw a young man clothed in a white robe sitting on the right side. The women were shocked, [6]but the angel said, "Don't be alarmed. You are looking for Jesus of Nazareth, who was crucified. He isn't here! He is risen from the dead! Look, this is where they laid his body. [7]Now go and tell his disciples, including Peter, that Jesus is going ahead of you to Galilee. You will see him there, just as he told you before he died."

[8]The women fled from the tomb, trembling and bewildered, and they said nothing to anyone because they were too frightened.

[Shorter Ending of Mark]

Then they briefly reported all this to Peter and his companions. Afterward Jesus himself sent them out from east to west with the sacred and unfailing message of salvation that gives eternal life. Amen.

[Longer Ending of Mark]

[9]After Jesus rose from the dead early on Sunday morning, the first person who saw him was Mary Magdalene, the woman from whom he had cast out seven demons. [10]She went to the disciples, who were grieving and weeping, and told them what had happened. [11]But when she told them that Jesus was alive and she had seen him, they didn't believe her.

[12]Afterward he appeared in a different form to two of his followers who were walking from Jerusalem into the country. [13]They rushed back to tell the others, but no one believed them.

[14]Still later he appeared to the eleven disciples as they were eating together. He rebuked them for their stubborn unbelief because they refused to believe those who had seen him after he had been raised from the dead.

[15]And then he told them, "Go into all the world and preach the Good News to everyone. [16]Anyone who believes and is baptized will be saved. But anyone who refuses to believe will be condemned. [17]These miraculous signs will accompany those who believe: They will cast out demons in my name, and they will speak in new languages. [18]They will be able to handle snakes with safety, and if they drink anything poisonous, it won't hurt them. They will be able to place their hands on the sick, and they will be healed."

[19]When the Lord Jesus had finished talking with them, he was taken up into heaven and sat down in the place of honor at God's right hand. [20]And the disciples went everywhere and preached, and the Lord worked through them, confirming what they said by many miraculous signs.

LUKE A Look at Jesus' Life

Look for **7** hidden messages in Luke!

Luke, a Greek doctor, gives a detailed account of Jesus' life. Look for
- **A SPECIAL BIRTHDAY**
- **PRAYERS AND PREACHING**
- **A CLIMB TO THE CROSS**
- **OUR RISEN SAVIOR**

"KNOCK, KNOCK."

"WHO'S THERE?"

"MARY AND JOSEPH."

GO AWAY. THERE'S NO ROOM.

Did you at least catch his name?

Is Anybody Home?

OK, so it isn't a very good joke. It was no joke for Mary and Joseph either. **Read Luke 2:1-7 to find out all about a special night and special birthday.**

A Night to Remember

What's that in the sky? A bird? A plane? It's...**Read Luke 2:8-20 to find out what some shepherds saw in a long-ago sky.**

What's in a Name?

Did you know that there are only two angels mentioned by name in the whole Bible? **Meet one of them in Luke 1:11-25.**

Instruction Manual

You know it's good to pray. But do you always know what to say? (Hey, a poem!) **Read Luke 11:1-13 for complete instructions!**

He's Back

Did you find out the name of that messenger who appeared to Zechariah?

Well, he came back with an even more amazing message. **Find out in Luke 1:26-38 what it was and who it was he gave it to.**

Why Worry?

Do you worry a lot? Well, knock it off! That's basically what Jesus says in Luke 12:22-34. Of course, Jesus says it a little better than that. Read his advice for yourself!

Dear Blabby,

Q: I'm a little guy with big bucks. But there's still one thing I want—to see Jesus. But I'll never be able to see over the crowd. I guess I'll just go climb a tree. A: Get a bird's-eye view of this story in Luke 19:1-10.

Not Guilty!

Three men were crucified. Two of them deserved to die. One didn't. Read Luke 23:32-49 for a complete account.

Lost: A wandering sheep, a shiny silver coin, an unwise young man.
Found: God's love and forgiveness. Feeling a little "lost"? Read Luke 15 to "find" out the whole story!

Lost & Found

Rock and Roll

You've heard of rock and roll. But have you ever heard of a rock rolling with no people to move it? Read Luke 24 for the most amazing, awesome, powerful, and beautiful story in the history of the world.

Timeline

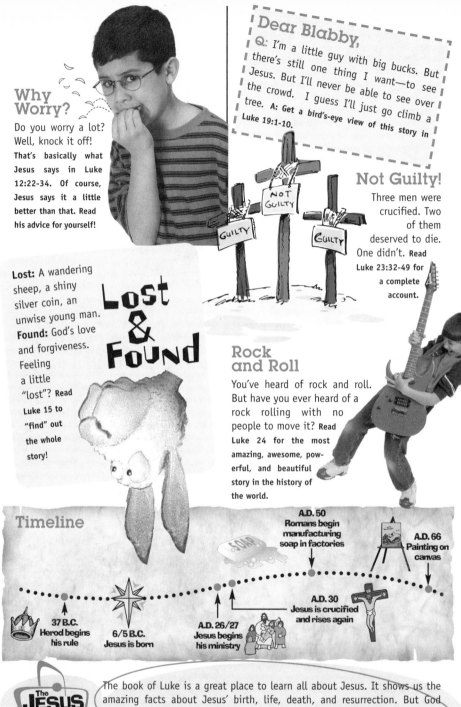

A.D. 50 Romans begin manufacturing soap in factories

A.D. 66 Painting on canvas

37 B.C. Herod begins his rule

6/5 B.C. Jesus is born

A.D. 26/27 Jesus begins his ministry

A.D. 30 Jesus is crucified and rises again

The book of Luke is a great place to learn all about Jesus. It shows us the amazing facts about Jesus' birth, life, death, and resurrection. But God wants you to do more than just learn *about* Jesus. He wants you to have a relationship *with* Jesus. So as you read the book of Luke, think of it as a way to get to know a friend—**the best friend you'll ever have!**

CHAPTER **1**
Introduction
Many people have set out to write accounts about the events that have been fulfilled among us. ²They used the eyewitness reports circulating among us from the early disciples. ³Having carefully investigated everything from the beginning, I also have decided to write a careful account for you, most honorable Theophilus, ⁴so you can be certain of the truth of everything you were taught.

The Birth of John the Baptist Foretold
⁵When Herod was king of Judea, there was a Jewish priest named Zechariah. He was a member of the priestly order of Abijah, and his wife, Elizabeth, was also from the priestly line of Aaron. ⁶Zechariah and Elizabeth were righteous in God's eyes, careful to obey all of the Lord's commandments and regulations. ⁷They had no children because Elizabeth was unable to conceive, and they were both very old.

⁸One day Zechariah was serving God in the Temple, for his order was on duty that week. ⁹As was the custom of the priests, he was chosen by lot to enter the sanctuary of the Lord and burn incense. ¹⁰While the incense was being burned, a great crowd stood outside, praying.

¹¹While Zechariah was in the sanctuary, an angel of the Lord appeared to him, standing to the right of the incense altar. ¹²Zechariah was shaken and overwhelmed with fear when he saw him. ¹³But the angel said, "Don't be afraid, Zechariah! God has heard your prayer. Your wife, Elizabeth, will give you a son, and you are to name him John. ¹⁴You will have great joy and gladness, and many will rejoice at his birth, ¹⁵for he will be great in the eyes of the Lord. He must never touch wine or other alcoholic drinks. He will be filled with the Holy Spirit, even before his birth. ¹⁶And he will turn many Israelites to the Lord their God. ¹⁷He will be a man with the spirit and power of Elijah. He will prepare the people for the coming of the Lord. He will turn the hearts of the fathers to their children, and he will cause those who are rebellious to accept the wisdom of the godly."

¹⁸Zechariah said to the angel, "How can I be sure this will happen? I'm an old man now, and my wife is also well along in years."

¹⁹Then the angel said, "I am Gabriel! I stand in the very presence of God. It was he who sent me to bring you this good news! ²⁰But now, since

1:28 Some manuscripts add *Blessed are you among women.*

you didn't believe what I said, you will be silent and unable to speak until the child is born. For my words will certainly be fulfilled at the proper time."

²¹Meanwhile, the people were waiting for Zechariah to come out of the sanctuary, wondering why he was taking so long. ²²When he finally did come out, he couldn't speak to them. Then they realized from his gestures and his silence that he must have seen a vision in the sanctuary.

²³When Zechariah's week of service in the Temple was over, he returned home. ²⁴Soon afterward his wife, Elizabeth, became pregnant and went into seclusion for five months. ²⁵"How kind the Lord is!" she exclaimed. "He has taken away my disgrace of having no children."

The Birth of Jesus Foretold
²⁶In the sixth month of Elizabeth's pregnancy, God sent the angel Gabriel to Nazareth, a village in Galilee, ²⁷to a virgin named Mary. She was engaged to be married to a man named Joseph, a descendant of King David. ²⁸Gabriel appeared to her and said, "Greetings, favored woman! The Lord is with you!*"

²⁹Confused and disturbed, Mary tried to think what the angel could mean. ³⁰"Don't be afraid, Mary," the angel told her, "for you have found favor with God! ³¹You will conceive and give birth to a son, and you will name him Jesus. ³²He will be very great and will be called the Son of the Most High. The Lord God will give him the throne of his ancestor David. ³³And he will reign over Israel forever; his Kingdom will never end!"

³⁴Mary asked the angel, "But how can this happen? I am a virgin."

³⁵The angel replied, "The Holy Spirit will come upon you, and the power of the Most High will overshadow you. So the baby to be born will be holy, and he will be called the Son of God. ³⁶What's more, your relative Elizabeth has become pregnant in her old age! People used to say she was barren, but she's now in her sixth month. ³⁷**For nothing is impossible with God.**"

³⁸Mary responded, "I am the Lord's servant. May everything you have said about me come true." And then the angel left her.

Mary Visits Elizabeth
³⁹A few days later Mary hurried to the hill country of Judea, to the town ⁴⁰where Zechariah lived. She entered the house and greeted Elizabeth. ⁴¹At the sound of Mary's greeting, Elizabeth's

Is That Possible?

God sent an angel to give an amazing message to a young woman named Mary. **Read LUKE 1:26-38 to see for yourself.** The message must have seemed impossible!

Try this "impossible" activity!

1 Fill a drinking glass *almost* to the top with water.

2 Drop a small cork into the glass, and make the cork float in the center of the water without touching the glass.

WHAT HAPPENS?

The cork keeps floating off to the side. It seems impossible to keep it in the center!

NOW TRY THIS!

Slowly pour water from another glass until the water rises just above the rim without spilling. The cork will move to where the water is the highest—the center. It wasn't impossible when you knew what to do.

With God, truly *nothing* is impossible!

---

child leaped within her, and Elizabeth was filled with the Holy Spirit.

42Elizabeth gave a glad cry and exclaimed to Mary, "God has blessed you above all women, and your child is blessed. 43Why am I so honored, that the mother of my Lord should visit me? 44When I heard your greeting, the baby in my womb jumped for joy. 45You are blessed because you believed that the Lord would do what he said."

The Magnificat: Mary's Song of Praise

46Mary responded,

"Oh, how my soul praises the Lord.
47 How my spirit rejoices in God my Savior!
48 For he took notice of his lowly servant girl,
   and from now on all generations will
      call me blessed.
49 For the Mighty One is holy,
   and he has done great things for me.
50 He shows mercy from generation to
      generation
   to all who fear him.
51 His mighty arm has done tremendous things!
   He has scattered the proud and
      haughty ones.
52 He has brought down princes from their
      thrones
   and exalted the humble.
53 He has filled the hungry with good things
   and sent the rich away with empty hands.
54 He has helped his servant Israel
   and remembered to be merciful.
55 For he made this promise to our ancestors,
   to Abraham and his children forever."

56Mary stayed with Elizabeth about three months and then went back to her own home.

The Birth of John the Baptist

57When it was time for Elizabeth's baby to be born, she gave birth to a son. 58And when her neighbors and relatives heard that the Lord had been very merciful to her, everyone rejoiced with her.

59When the baby was eight days old, they all came for the circumcision ceremony. They wanted to name him Zechariah, after his father. 60But Elizabeth said, "No! His name is John!"

61"What?" they exclaimed. "There is no one in all your family by that name." 62So they used gestures to ask the baby's father what he wanted to name him. 63He motioned for a writing tablet, and to everyone's surprise he wrote, "His name is

John." 64Instantly Zechariah could speak again, and he began praising God.

65Awe fell upon the whole neighborhood, and the news of what had happened spread throughout the Judean hills. 66Everyone who heard about it reflected on these events and asked, "What will this child turn out to be?" For the hand of the Lord was surely upon him in a special way.

Zechariah's Prophecy

67Then his father, Zechariah, was filled with the Holy Spirit and gave this prophecy:

68 "Praise the Lord, the God of Israel,
> because he has visited and redeemed
>> his people.
69 He has sent us a mighty Savior
> from the royal line of his servant David,
70 just as he promised
> through his holy prophets long ago.
71 Now we will be saved from our enemies
> and from all who hate us.
72 He has been merciful to our ancestors
> by remembering his sacred covenant—
73 the covenant he swore with an oath
> to our ancestor Abraham.
74 We have been rescued from our enemies
> so we can serve God without fear,
75 in holiness and righteousness
> for as long as we live.

76 "And you, my little son,
> will be called the prophet of the
>> Most High,
> because you will prepare the way for
>> the Lord.
77 You will tell his people how to find salvation
> through forgiveness of their sins.
78 Because of God's tender mercy,
> the morning light from heaven is about
>> to break upon us,
79 to give light to those who sit in darkness
> and in the shadow of death,
> and to guide us to the path of peace."

80John grew up and became strong in spirit. And he lived in the wilderness until he began his public ministry to Israel.

CHAPTER **2**
The Birth of Jesus

At that time the Roman emperor, Augustus, decreed that a census should be taken throughout the Roman Empire. 2(This was the first census taken when Quirinius was governor of Syria.) 3All returned to their own ancestral towns to register for this census. 4And because Joseph was a descendant of King David, he had to go to Bethlehem in Judea, David's ancient home. He traveled there from the village of Nazareth in Galilee. 5He took with him Mary, his fiancée, who was now obviously pregnant.

6And while they were there, the time came for her baby to be born. 7She gave birth to her first child, a son. She wrapped him snugly in strips of cloth and laid him in a manger, because there was no lodging available for them.

The Shepherds and Angels

8That night there were shepherds staying in the fields nearby, guarding their flocks of sheep. 9Suddenly, an angel of the Lord appeared among them, and the radiance of the Lord's glory surrounded them. They were terrified, 10but the angel reassured them. "Don't be afraid!" he said. "I bring you good news that will bring great joy to all people. 11The Savior—yes, the Messiah, the Lord—has been born today in Bethlehem, the city of David! 12And you will recognize him by this sign: You will find a baby wrapped snugly in strips of cloth, lying in a manger."

13Suddenly, the angel was joined by a vast host of others—the armies of heaven—praising God and saying,

14 "Glory to God in highest heaven,
> and peace on earth to those with whom
>> God is pleased."

15When the angels had returned to heaven, the shepherds said to each other, "Let's go to Bethlehem! Let's see this thing that has happened, which the Lord has told us about."

16They hurried to the village and found Mary and Joseph. And there was the baby, lying in the manger. 17After seeing him, the shepherds told everyone what had happened and what the angel had said to them about this child. 18All who heard the shepherds' story were astonished, 19but Mary kept all these things in her heart and thought about them often. 20The shepherds went back to their flocks, glorifying and praising God for all they had heard and seen. It was just as the angel had told them.

Jesus Is Presented in the Temple

21Eight days later, when the baby was circumcised, he was named Jesus, the name given him by the angel even before he was conceived.

22Then it was time for their purification offering, as required by the law of Moses after the birth of a child; so his parents took him to Jerusalem to present him to the Lord. 23 The law of the Lord says, "If a woman's first child is a boy, he must be dedicated to the LORD." 24 So they offered the sacrifice required in the law of the Lord—"either a pair of turtledoves or two young pigeons."

The Prophecy of Simeon

25 At that time there was a man in Jerusalem named Simeon. He was righteous and devout and was eagerly waiting for the Messiah to come and rescue Israel. The Holy Spirit was upon him 26 and had revealed to him that he would not die until he had seen the Lord's Messiah. 27 That day the Spirit led him to the Temple. So when Mary and Joseph came to present the baby Jesus to the Lord as the law required, 28 Simeon was there. He took the child in his arms and praised God, saying,

29 "Sovereign Lord, now let your servant die in
     peace,
   as you have promised.
30 I have seen your salvation,
31   which you have prepared for all people.
32 He is a light to reveal God to the nations,
     and he is the glory of your people Israel!"

33 Jesus' parents were amazed at what was being said about him. 34 Then Simeon blessed them, and he said to Mary, the baby's mother, "This child is destined to cause many in Israel to fall, but he will be a joy to many others. He has been sent as a sign from God, but many will oppose him. 35 As a result, the deepest thoughts of many hearts will be revealed. And a sword will pierce your very soul."

The Prophecy of Anna

36 Anna, a prophet, was also there in the Temple. She was the daughter of Phanuel from the tribe of Asher, and she was very old. Her husband died when they had been married only seven years. 37 Then she lived as a widow to the age of eighty-four. She never left the Temple but stayed there day and night, worshiping God with fasting and prayer. 38 She came along just as Simeon was talking with Mary and Joseph, and she began praising God. She talked about the child to everyone who had been waiting expectantly for God to rescue Jerusalem.

39 When Jesus' parents had fulfilled all the requirements of the law of the Lord, they returned home to Nazareth in Galilee. 40 There the child grew up healthy and strong. He was filled with wisdom, and God's favor was on him.

Armies of Heaven

HAVE YOU EVER SEEN AN ANGEL?

READ LUKE 2:13 to find out about the "armies of heaven," a whole bunch of angels who came to tell the shepherds about the birth of the Messiah. **Whoa! Angels everywhere!**

Use this idea to create an army of angels.

1. With a permanent marker, draw a face on the back of a plastic spoon.

2. Fold a piece of gold or silver foil back and forth like an accordion.

Read more about angels in Psalm 91:11.

3. Tape the foil to the handle of the spoon behind the angel's spoon face to remind you of the angel's radiance.

Make a bunch of these angels, and stick them in the ground outside your house. Or poke them in a flat piece of craft foam, and put them in your house. When visitors ask what they are, be sure to tell them the story from **LUKE 2:8-15**!

Jesus Speaks with the Teachers

41 Every year Jesus' parents went to Jerusalem for the Passover festival. 42 When Jesus was twelve years old, they attended the festival as usual. 43 After the celebration was over, they started home to Nazareth, but Jesus stayed behind in Jerusalem. His parents didn't miss him at first, 44 because they assumed he was among the other travelers. But when he didn't show up that

evening, they started looking for him among their relatives and friends.

⁴⁵When they couldn't find him, they went back to Jerusalem to search for him there. ⁴⁶Three days later they finally discovered him in the Temple, sitting among the religious teachers, listening to them and asking questions. ⁴⁷All who heard him were amazed at his understanding and his answers.

⁴⁸His parents didn't know what to think. "Son," his mother said to him, "why have you done this to us? Your father and I have been frantic, searching for you everywhere."

⁴⁹"But why did you need to search?" he asked. "Didn't you know that I must be in my Father's house?" ⁵⁰But they didn't understand what he meant.

⁵¹Then he returned to Nazareth with them and was obedient to them. And his mother stored all these things in her heart.

⁵²Jesus grew in wisdom and in stature and in favor with God and all the people.

CHAPTER **3**

John the Baptist Prepares the Way

It was now the fifteenth year of the reign of Tiberius, the Roman emperor. Pontius Pilate was governor over Judea; Herod Antipas was ruler over Galilee; his brother Philip was ruler over Iturea and Traconitis; Lysanias was ruler over Abilene. ²Annas and Caiaphas were the high priests. At this time a message from God came to John son of Zechariah, who was living in the wilderness. ³Then John went from place to place on both sides of the Jordan River, preaching that people should be baptized to show that they had repented of their sins and turned to God to be forgiven. ⁴Isaiah had spoken of John when he said,

"He is a voice shouting in the wilderness,
    'Prepare the way for the LORD's coming!
        Clear the road for him!
⁵ The valleys will be filled,
        and the mountains and hills made level.
    The curves will be straightened,
        and the rough places made smooth.
⁶ And then all people will see
        the salvation sent from God.'"

⁷When the crowds came to John for baptism, he said, "You brood of snakes! Who warned you to flee God's coming wrath? ⁸Prove by the way you live that you have repented of your sins and turned to God. Don't just say to each other, 'We're safe, for we are descendants of Abra-

ham.' That means nothing, for I tell you, God can create children of Abraham from these very stones. ⁹Even now the ax of God's judgment is poised, ready to sever the roots of the trees. Yes, every tree that does not produce good fruit will be chopped down and thrown into the fire."

¹⁰The crowds asked, "What should we do?"

¹¹John replied, "If you have two shirts, give one to the poor. If you have food, share it with those who are hungry."

¹²Even corrupt tax collectors came to be baptized and asked, "Teacher, what should we do?"

¹³He replied, "Collect no more taxes than the government requires."

¹⁴"What should we do?" asked some soldiers.

John replied, "Don't extort money or make false accusations. And be content with your pay."

¹⁵Everyone was expecting the Messiah to come soon, and they were eager to know whether John might be the Messiah. ¹⁶John answered their

Young and Old TOGETHER

When Jesus was twelve, he had quite a discussion about God with a group of adults. **Read what happened in LUKE 2:41-47.**

You can talk to adults about God too! Find two adults (or more!) to talk to about God—maybe parents, grandparents, teachers, or pastors. Talk together about your favorite Bible stories and how God answered your prayers.

Remember your talk by having the adults sign and date your Bible on the lines below. Then you sign too!

WE SHARED OUR FAITH TOGETHER...

_____

_____

_____

questions by saying, "I baptize you with water; but someone is coming soon who is greater than I am—so much greater that I'm not even worthy to be his slave and untie the straps of his sandals. He will baptize you with the Holy Spirit and with fire. 17He is ready to separate the chaff from the wheat with his winnowing fork. Then he will clean up the threshing area, gathering the wheat into his barn but burning the chaff with never-ending fire." 18John used many such warnings as he announced the Good News to the people.

19John also publicly criticized Herod Antipas, the ruler of Galilee, for marrying Herodias, his brother's wife, and for many other wrongs he had done. 20So Herod put John in prison, adding this sin to his many others.

The Baptism of Jesus

21One day when the crowds were being baptized, Jesus himself was baptized. As he was praying, the heavens opened, 22and the Holy Spirit, in bodily form, descended on him like a dove. And a voice from heaven said, "You are my dearly loved Son, and you bring me great joy."

The Ancestors of Jesus

23Jesus was about thirty years old when he began his public ministry.

Jesus was known as the son of Joseph.
Joseph was the son of Heli.
24 Heli was the son of Matthat.
Matthat was the son of Levi.
Levi was the son of Melki.
Melki was the son of Jannai.
Jannai was the son of Joseph.
25 Joseph was the son of Mattathias.
Mattathias was the son of Amos.
Amos was the son of Nahum.
Nahum was the son of Esli.
Esli was the son of Naggai.
26 Naggai was the son of Maath.
Maath was the son of Mattathias.
Mattathias was the son of Semein.
Semein was the son of Josech.
Josech was the son of Joda.
27 Joda was the son of Joanan.
Joanan was the son of Rhesa.
Rhesa was the son of Zerubbabel.
Zerubbabel was the son of Shealtiel.
Shealtiel was the son of Neri.
28 Neri was the son of Melki.
Melki was the son of Addi.
Addi was the son of Cosam.
Cosam was the son of Elmadam.
Elmadam was the son of Er.
29 Er was the son of Joshua.
Joshua was the son of Eliezer.
Eliezer was the son of Jorim.
Jorim was the son of Matthat.
Matthat was the son of Levi.
30 Levi was the son of Simeon.
Simeon was the son of Judah.
Judah was the son of Joseph.
Joseph was the son of Jonam.
Jonam was the son of Eliakim.
31 Eliakim was the son of Melea.
Melea was the son of Menna.
Menna was the son of Mattatha.
Mattatha was the son of Nathan.
Nathan was the son of David.
32 David was the son of Jesse.
Jesse was the son of Obed.
Obed was the son of Boaz.
Boaz was the son of Salmon.
Salmon was the son of Nahshon.
33 Nahshon was the son of Amminadab.
Amminadab was the son of Admin.
Admin was the son of Arni.
Arni was the son of Hezron.
Hezron was the son of Perez.
Perez was the son of Judah.
34 Judah was the son of Jacob.
Jacob was the son of Isaac.
Isaac was the son of Abraham.
Abraham was the son of Terah.
Terah was the son of Nahor.
35 Nahor was the son of Serug.
Serug was the son of Reu.
Reu was the son of Peleg.
Peleg was the son of Eber.
Eber was the son of Shelah.
36 Shelah was the son of Cainan.
Cainan was the son of Arphaxad.
Arphaxad was the son of Shem.
Shem was the son of Noah.
Noah was the son of Lamech.
37 Lamech was the son of Methuselah.
Methuselah was the son of Enoch.
Enoch was the son of Jared.
Jared was the son of Mahalalel.
Mahalalel was the son of Kenan.
38 Kenan was the son of Enosh.
Enosh was the son of Seth.
Seth was the son of Adam.
Adam was the son of God.

CHAPTER **4**

The Temptation of Jesus

Then Jesus, full of the Holy Spirit, returned from the Jordan River. He was led by the Spirit in the wilderness, 2where he was tempted by the devil for forty days. Jesus ate nothing all that time and became very hungry.

3Then the devil said to him, "If you are the Son of God, tell this stone to become a loaf of bread."

4But Jesus told him, "No! The Scriptures say, 'People do not live by bread alone.'"

5Then the devil took him up and revealed to him all the kingdoms of the world in a moment of time. 6"I will give you the glory of these kingdoms and authority over them," the devil said, "because they are mine to give to anyone I please. 7I will give it all to you if you will worship me."

8Jesus replied, "The Scriptures say,

'You must worship the LORD your God
and serve only him.'"

9Then the devil took him to Jerusalem, to the highest point of the Temple, and said, "If you are the Son of God, jump off! 10For the Scriptures say,

'He will order his angels to protect and
guard you.
11 And they will hold you up with their hands
so you won't even hurt your foot on
a stone.'"

12Jesus responded, "The Scriptures also say, 'You must not test the LORD your God.'"

13When the devil had finished tempting Jesus, he left him until the next opportunity came.

Jesus Rejected at Nazareth

14Then Jesus returned to Galilee, filled with the Holy Spirit's power. Reports about him spread quickly through the whole region. 15He taught regularly in their synagogues and was praised by everyone.

16When he came to the village of Nazareth, his boyhood home, he went as usual to the synagogue on the Sabbath and stood up to read the Scriptures. 17The scroll of Isaiah the prophet was handed to him. He unrolled the scroll and found the place where this was written:

18 "The Spirit of the LORD is upon me,
for he has anointed me to bring Good
News to the poor.
He has sent me to proclaim that captives
will be released,
that the blind will see,
that the oppressed will be set free,
19 and that the time of the LORD's favor
has come."

20He rolled up the scroll, handed it back to the attendant, and sat down. All eyes in the synagogue looked at him intently. 21Then he began to speak to them. "The Scripture you've just heard has been fulfilled this very day!"

22Everyone spoke well of him and was amazed by the gracious words that came from his lips. "How can this be?" they asked. "Isn't this Joseph's son?"

23Then he said, "You will undoubtedly quote me this proverb: 'Physician, heal yourself'— meaning, 'Do miracles here in your hometown like those you did in Capernaum.' 24But I tell you the truth, no prophet is accepted in his own hometown.

25"Certainly there were many needy widows in Israel in Elijah's time, when the heavens were closed for three and a half years, and a severe famine devastated the land. 26Yet Elijah was not sent to any of them. He was sent instead to a foreigner—a widow of Zarephath in the land of Sidon. 27And there were many lepers in Israel in the time of the prophet Elisha, but the only one healed was Naaman, a Syrian."

28When they heard this, the people in the synagogue were furious. 29Jumping up, they mobbed him and forced him to the edge of the hill on which the town was built. They intended to push him over the cliff, 30but he passed right through the crowd and went on his way.

Jesus Casts Out a Demon

31Then Jesus went to Capernaum, a town in Galilee, and taught there in the synagogue every Sabbath day. 32There, too, the people were amazed at his teaching, for he spoke with authority.

33Once when he was in the synagogue, a man possessed by a demon—an evil spirit—began shouting at Jesus, 34"Go away! Why are you interfering with us, Jesus of Nazareth? Have you come to destroy us? I know who you are—the Holy One sent from God!"

35Jesus cut him short. "Be quiet! Come out of the man," he ordered. At that, the demon threw the man to the floor as the crowd watched; then it came out of him without hurting him further.

36Amazed, the people exclaimed, "What authority and power this man's words possess! Even evil spirits obey him, and they flee at his command!" 37The news about Jesus spread through every village in the entire region.

Jesus Heals Many People

38After leaving the synagogue that day, Jesus went to Simon's home, where he found Simon's mother-in-law very sick with a high fever. "Please heal her," everyone begged. 39 Standing at her bedside, he rebuked the fever, and it left her. And she got up at once and prepared a meal for them.

40 As the sun went down that evening, people throughout the village brought sick family members to Jesus. No matter what their diseases were, the touch of his hand healed every one. 41 Many were possessed by demons; and the demons came out at his command, shouting, "You are the Son of God!" But because they knew he was the Messiah, he rebuked them and refused to let them speak.

Jesus Continues to Preach

42 Early the next morning Jesus went out to an isolated place. The crowds searched everywhere for him, and when they finally found him, they begged him not to leave them. 43 But he replied, "I must preach the Good News of the Kingdom of God in other towns, too, because that is why I was sent." 44 So he continued to travel around, preaching in synagogues throughout Judea.

CHAPTER **5**
The First Disciples

One day as Jesus was preaching on the shore of the Sea of Galilee, great crowds pressed in on him to listen to the word of God. 2 He noticed two empty boats at the water's edge, for the fishermen had left them and were washing their nets. 3 Stepping into one of the boats, Jesus asked Simon, its owner, to push it out into the water. So he sat in the boat and taught the crowds from there.

4 When he had finished speaking, he said to Simon, "Now go out where it is deeper, and let down your nets to catch some fish."

5 "Master," Simon replied, "we worked hard all last night and didn't catch a thing. But if you say so, I'll let the nets down again." 6 And this time their nets were so full of fish they began to tear! 7 A shout for help brought their partners in the other boat, and soon both boats were filled with fish and on the verge of sinking.

8 When Simon Peter realized what had happened, he fell to his knees before Jesus and said, "Oh, Lord, please leave me—I'm too much of a sinner to be around you." 9 For he was awestruck by the number of fish they had caught, as were the others with him. 10 His partners, James and John, the sons of Zebedee, were also amazed.

Jesus replied to Simon, "Don't be afraid! From now on you'll be fishing for people!" 11 And as soon as they landed, they left everything and followed Jesus.

Jesus Heals a Man with Leprosy

12 In one of the villages, Jesus met a man with an advanced case of leprosy. When the man saw Jesus, he bowed with his face to the ground, begging to be healed. "Lord," he said, "if you are willing, you can heal me and make me clean."

13 Jesus reached out and touched him. "I am willing," he said. "Be healed!" And instantly the leprosy disappeared. 14 Then Jesus instructed him not to tell anyone what had happened. He said, "Go to the priest and let him examine you. Take along the offering required in the law of Moses for those who have been healed of leprosy. This will be a public testimony that you have been cleansed."

15 But despite Jesus' instructions, the report of his power spread even faster, and vast crowds came to hear him preach and to be healed of their diseases. 16 But Jesus often withdrew to the wilderness for prayer.

Jesus Heals a Paralyzed Man

17 One day while Jesus was teaching, some Pharisees and teachers of religious law were sitting nearby. (It seemed that these men showed up from every village in all Galilee and Judea, as well as from Jerusalem.) And the Lord's healing power was strongly with Jesus.

18 Some men came carrying a paralyzed man on a sleeping mat. They tried to take him inside to Jesus, 19 but they couldn't reach him because of the crowd. So they went up to the roof and took off some tiles. Then they lowered the sick man on his mat down into the crowd, right in front of Jesus. 20 Seeing their faith, Jesus said to the man, "Young man, your sins are forgiven."

21 But the Pharisees and teachers of religious law said to themselves, "Who does he think he is? That's blasphemy! Only God can forgive sins!"

22 Jesus knew what they were thinking, so he asked them, "Why do you question this in your hearts? 23 Is it easier to say 'Your sins are forgiven,' or 'Stand up and walk'? 24 So I will prove to you that the Son of Man has the authority on earth to forgive sins." Then Jesus turned to the paralyzed man and said, "Stand up, pick up your mat, and go home!"

25 And immediately, as everyone watched, the man jumped up, picked up his mat, and went home praising God. 26 Everyone was gripped with great wonder and awe, and they praised God, exclaiming, "We have seen amazing things today!"

⚬⚬ Gone Fishin'

Have you ever caught a fish? **Read LUKE 5:1-11 to learn about an amazing fishing trip!**

Huh? Fishing for people? Yup! Think who you could tell about Jesus as you do this fishy experiment.

1 Tape a bar magnet to a table edge. The magnet should stick out over the edge.

2 Bend some paper clips open.

3 Touch the unbent end of a paper clip to the underside of the magnet, and let the other end hang down like a fish hook.

4 See how many other paper clips you can hang on the hook before the hook falls.

FISHING'S FUN! Especially when you fish for people, like Jesus said to do.

So start fishing!

God, these are people I want to "catch" for you:

Write those named on slips of paper, and "hook" them with a paper clip. Add more names as you tell more people about Jesus!

Jesus Calls Levi (Matthew)

27 Later, as Jesus left the town, he saw a tax collector named Levi sitting at his tax collector's booth. "Follow me and be my disciple," Jesus said to him. 28 So Levi got up, left everything, and followed him.

29 Later, Levi held a banquet in his home with Jesus as the guest of honor. Many of Levi's fellow tax collectors and other guests also ate with them. 30 But the Pharisees and their teachers of religious law complained bitterly to Jesus' disciples, "Why do you eat and drink with such scum?"

31 Jesus answered them, "Healthy people don't need a doctor—sick people do. 32 I have come to call not those who think they are righteous, but those who know they are sinners and need to repent."

A Discussion about Fasting

33 One day some people said to Jesus, "John the Baptist's disciples fast and pray regularly, and so do the disciples of the Pharisees. Why are your disciples always eating and drinking?"

34 Jesus responded, "Do wedding guests fast while celebrating with the groom? Of course not. 35 But someday the groom will be taken away from them, and then they will fast."

36 Then Jesus gave them this illustration: "No one tears a piece of cloth from a new garment and uses it to patch an old garment. For then the new garment would be ruined, and the new patch wouldn't even match the old garment.

37 "And no one puts new wine into old wineskins. For the new wine would burst the wineskins, spilling the wine and ruining the skins. 38 New wine must be stored in new wineskins. 39 But no one who drinks the old wine seems to want the new wine. 'The old is just fine,' they say."

CHAPTER **6**

A Discussion about the Sabbath

One Sabbath day as Jesus was walking through some grainfields, his disciples broke off heads of grain, rubbed off the husks in their hands, and ate the grain. 2 But some Pharisees said, "Why are you breaking the law by harvesting grain on the Sabbath?"

3 Jesus replied, "Haven't you read in the Scriptures what David did when he and his companions were hungry? 4 He went into the house of God and broke the law by eating the sacred loaves of bread that only the priests can eat. He also gave some to his companions." 5 And Jesus added, "The Son of Man is Lord, even over the Sabbath."

Anything Is Possible

Want to read about something that sounds impossible to do? Try LUKE 6:27-36!

Love your enemies? Sounds impossible. But as sure as there's a hole in your hand, you can do it!

What? There's no hole in your hand?

TRY THIS:

1 Stand by a white wall, and roll up a piece of paper. Look through it toward the wall with your left eye.

2 Hold your right hand up, close to the rolled paper. Keep both eyes open! Can you see the hole in your hand?

Actually, that hole is an optical illusion. But Jesus telling us to love our enemies is for real!

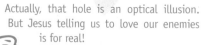

But don't worry—you don't have to do it by yourself! Ask God to help you love your enemies, and it won't be impossible at all!

Jesus Heals on the Sabbath

⁶On another Sabbath day, a man with a deformed right hand was in the synagogue while Jesus was teaching. ⁷The teachers of religious law and the Pharisees watched Jesus closely. If he healed the man's hand, they planned to accuse him of working on the Sabbath.

⁸But Jesus knew their thoughts. He said to the man with the deformed hand, "Come and stand in front of everyone." So the man came forward. ⁹Then Jesus said to his critics, "I have a question for you. Does the law permit good deeds on the Sabbath, or is it a day for doing evil? Is this a day to save life or to destroy it?"

¹⁰He looked around at them one by one and then said to the man, "Hold out your hand." So the man held out his hand, and it was restored! ¹¹At this, the enemies of Jesus were wild with rage and began to discuss what to do with him.

Jesus Chooses the Twelve Apostles

¹²One day soon afterward Jesus went up on a mountain to pray, and he prayed to God all night. ¹³At daybreak he called together all of his disciples and chose twelve of them to be apostles. Here are their names:

¹⁴ Simon (whom he named Peter),
   Andrew (Peter's brother),
   James,
   John,
   Philip,
   Bartholomew,
¹⁵ Matthew,
   Thomas,
   James (son of Alphaeus),
   Simon (who was called the zealot),
¹⁶ Judas (son of James),
   Judas Iscariot (who later betrayed him).

Crowds Follow Jesus

¹⁷When they came down from the mountain, the disciples stood with Jesus on a large, level area, surrounded by many of his followers and by the crowds. There were people from all over Judea and from Jerusalem and from as far north as the seacoasts of Tyre and Sidon. ¹⁸They had come to hear him and to be healed of their diseases; and those troubled by evil spirits were healed. ¹⁹Everyone tried to touch him, because healing power went out from him, and he healed everyone.

The Beatitudes

²⁰Then Jesus turned to his disciples and said,

"God blesses you who are poor,
   for the Kingdom of God is yours.
²¹ God blesses you who are hungry now,
   for you will be satisfied.
God blesses you who weep now,
   for in due time you will laugh.

²²What blessings await you when people hate you and exclude you and mock you and curse you as evil because you follow the Son of Man. ²³When that happens, be happy! Yes, leap for joy! For a great reward awaits you in heaven. And remember, their ancestors treated the ancient prophets that same way.

Sorrows Foretold

24 "What sorrow awaits you who are rich,
for you have your only happiness now.
25 What sorrow awaits you who are fat and
prosperous now,
for a time of awful hunger awaits you.
What sorrow awaits you who laugh now,
for your laughing will turn to mourning
and sorrow.
26 What sorrow awaits you who are praised
by the crowds,
for their ancestors also praised false
prophets.

Love for Enemies

27"But to you who are willing to listen, I say, love
your enemies! Do good to those who hate you.
28Bless those who curse you. Pray for those who
hurt you. 29If someone slaps you on one cheek,
offer the other cheek also. If someone demands
your coat, offer your shirt also. 30Give to anyone
who asks; and when things are taken away from
you, don't try to get them back. 31**Do to others
as you would like them to do to you.**

32"If you love only those who love you, why
should you get credit for that? Even sinners love
those who love them! 33And if you do good only
to those who do good to you, why should you get
credit? Even sinners do that much! 34And if you
lend money only to those who can repay you,
why should you get credit? Even sinners will lend
to other sinners for a full return.

35"Love your enemies! Do good to them. Lend
to them without expecting to be repaid. Then
your reward from heaven will be very great, and
you will truly be acting as children of the Most
High, for he is kind to those who are unthankful
and wicked. 36You must be compassionate, just
as your Father is compassionate.

Do Not Judge Others

37"Do not judge others, and you will not be
judged. Do not condemn others, or it will all
come back against you. Forgive others, and you
will be forgiven. 38Give, and you will receive.
Your gift will return to you in full—pressed
down, shaken together to make room for more,
running over, and poured into your lap. The
amount you give will determine the amount you
get back."

39Then Jesus gave the following illustration:
"Can one blind person lead another? Won't they
both fall into a ditch? 40Students are not greater
than their teacher. But the student who is fully
trained will become like the teacher.

41"And why worry about a speck in your
friend's eye when you have a log in your own?
42How can you think of saying, 'Friend, let me
help you get rid of that speck in your eye,' when
you can't see past the log in your own eye? Hypocrite! First get rid of the log in your own eye; then
you will see well enough to deal with the speck in
your friend's eye.

The Tree and Its Fruit

43"A good tree can't produce bad fruit, and a bad
tree can't produce good fruit. 44A tree is identified by its fruit. Figs are never gathered from
thornbushes, and grapes are not picked from
bramble bushes. 45A good person produces
good things from the treasury of a good heart,
and an evil person produces evil things from the
treasury of an evil heart. What you say flows
from what is in your heart.

Building on a Solid Foundation

46"So why do you keep calling me 'Lord, Lord!'
when you don't do what I say? 47I will show you
what it's like when someone comes to me, listens
to my teaching, and then follows it. 48It is like a
person building a house who digs deep and lays
the foundation on solid rock. When the floodwaters rise and break against that house, it
stands firm because it is well built. 49But anyone
who hears and doesn't obey is like a person who
builds a house without a foundation. When the
floods sweep down against that house, it will collapse into a heap of ruins."

CHAPTER **7**
The Faith of a Roman Officer

When Jesus had finished saying all this to the
people, he returned to Capernaum. 2At that time
the highly valued slave of a Roman officer was
sick and near death. 3When the officer heard
about Jesus, he sent some respected Jewish elders to ask him to come and heal his slave. 4So
they earnestly begged Jesus to help the man. "If
anyone deserves your help, he does," they said,
5"for he loves the Jewish people and even built a
synagogue for us."

6So Jesus went with them. But just before they
arrived at the house, the officer sent some friends
to say, "Lord, don't trouble yourself by coming to
my home, for I am not worthy of such an honor. 7I
am not even worthy to come and meet you. Just
say the word from where you are, and my servant
will be healed. 8I know this because I am under
the authority of my superior officers, and I have
authority over my soldiers. I only need to say, 'Go,'

and they go, or 'Come,' and they come. And if I say to my slaves, 'Do this,' they do it."

9 When Jesus heard this, he was amazed. Turning to the crowd that was following him, he said, "I tell you, I haven't seen faith like this in all Israel!" 10 And when the officer's friends returned to his house, they found the slave completely healed.

Jesus Raises a Widow's Son

11 Soon afterward Jesus went with his disciples to the village of Nain, and a large crowd followed him. 12 A funeral procession was coming out as he approached the village gate. The young man who had died was a widow's only son, and a large crowd from the village was with her. 13 When the Lord saw her, his heart overflowed with compassion. "Don't cry!" he said. 14 Then he walked over to the coffin and touched it, and the bearers stopped. "Young man," he said, "I tell you, get up." 15 Then the dead boy sat up and began to talk! And Jesus gave him back to his mother.

16 Great fear swept the crowd, and they praised God, saying, "A mighty prophet has risen among us," and "God has visited his people today." 17 And the news about Jesus spread throughout Judea and the surrounding countryside.

Jesus and John the Baptist

18 The disciples of John the Baptist told John about everything Jesus was doing. So John called for two of his disciples, 19 and he sent them to the Lord to ask him, "Are you the Messiah we've been expecting, or should we keep looking for someone else?"

20 John's two disciples found Jesus and said to him, "John the Baptist sent us to ask, 'Are you the Messiah we've been expecting, or should we keep looking for someone else?'"

21 At that very time, Jesus cured many people of their diseases, illnesses, and evil spirits, and he restored sight to many who were blind. 22 Then he told John's disciples, "Go back to John and tell him what you have seen and heard—the blind see, the lame walk, the lepers are cured, the deaf hear, the dead are raised to life, and the Good News is being preached to the poor. 23 And tell him, 'God blesses those who do not turn away because of me.'"

24 After John's disciples left, Jesus began talking about him to the crowds. "What kind of man did you go into the wilderness to see? Was he a weak reed, swayed by every breath of wind? 25 Or were you expecting to see a man dressed in expensive clothes? No, people who wear beautiful clothes and live in luxury are found in palaces. 26 Were you looking for a prophet? Yes, and he is more than a prophet. 27 John is the man to whom the Scriptures refer when they say,

'Look, I am sending my messenger ahead
   of you,
   and he will prepare your way before you.'

28 I tell you, of all who have ever lived, none is greater than John. Yet even the least person in the Kingdom of God is greater than he is!"

29 When they heard this, all the people—even the tax collectors—agreed that God's way was right, for they had been baptized by John. 30 But the Pharisees and experts in religious law rejected God's plan for them, for they had refused John's baptism.

31 "To what can I compare the people of this generation?" Jesus asked. "How can I describe them? 32 They are like children playing a game in the public square. They complain to their friends,

'We played wedding songs,
   and you didn't dance,
so we played funeral songs,
   and you didn't weep.'

33 For John the Baptist didn't spend his time eating bread or drinking wine, and you say, 'He's possessed by a demon.' 34 The Son of Man, on the other hand, feasts and drinks, and you say, 'He's a glutton and a drunkard, and a friend of tax collectors and other sinners!' 35 But wisdom is shown to be right by the lives of those who follow it."

Jesus Anointed by a Sinful Woman

36 One of the Pharisees asked Jesus to have dinner with him, so Jesus went to his home and sat down to eat. 37 When a certain immoral woman from that city heard he was eating there, she brought a beautiful alabaster jar filled with expensive perfume. 38 Then she knelt behind him at his feet, weeping. Her tears fell on his feet, and she wiped them off with her hair. Then she kept kissing his feet and putting perfume on them.

39 When the Pharisee who had invited him saw this, he said to himself, "If this man were a prophet, he would know what kind of woman is touching him. She's a sinner!"

40 Then Jesus answered his thoughts. "Simon," he said to the Pharisee, "I have something to say to you."

"Go ahead, Teacher," Simon replied.

41Then Jesus told him this story: "A man loaned money to two people—500 pieces of silver to one and 50 pieces to the other. 42But neither of them could repay him, so he kindly forgave them both, canceling their debts. Who do you suppose loved him more after that?"

43Simon answered, "I suppose the one for whom he canceled the larger debt."

"That's right," Jesus said. 44Then he turned to the woman and said to Simon, "Look at this woman kneeling here. When I entered your home, you didn't offer me water to wash the dust from my feet, but she has washed them with her tears and wiped them with her hair. 45You didn't greet me with a kiss, but from the time I first came in, she has not stopped kissing my feet. 46You neglected the courtesy of olive oil to anoint my head, but she has anointed my feet with rare perfume.

47"I tell you, her sins—and they are many—have been forgiven, so she has shown me much love. But a person who is forgiven little shows only little love." 48Then Jesus said to the woman, "Your sins are forgiven."

49The men at the table said among themselves, "Who is this man, that he goes around forgiving sins?"

50And Jesus said to the woman, "Your faith has saved you; go in peace."

CHAPTER **8**
Women Who Followed Jesus

Soon afterward Jesus began a tour of the nearby towns and villages, preaching and announcing the Good News about the Kingdom of God. He took his twelve disciples with him, 2along with some women who had been cured of evil spirits and diseases. Among them were Mary Magdalene, from whom he had cast out seven demons; 3Joanna, the wife of Chuza, Herod's business manager; Susanna; and many others who were contributing their own resources to support Jesus and his disciples.

Parable of the Farmer Scattering Seed

4One day Jesus told a story in the form of a parable to a large crowd that had gathered from many towns to hear him: 5"A farmer went out to plant his seed. As he scattered it across his field, some seed fell on a footpath, where it was stepped on, and the birds ate it. 6Other seed fell among rocks. It began to grow, but the plant soon wilted and died for lack of moisture. 7Other seed fell among thorns that grew up with it and choked out the tender plants. 8Still other seed fell on fertile soil. This seed grew and produced a crop that was a hundred times as much as had been planted!" When he had said this, he called out, "Anyone with ears to hear should listen and understand."

9His disciples asked him what this parable meant. 10He replied, "You are permitted to understand the secrets of the Kingdom of God. But I use parables to teach the others so that the Scriptures might be fulfilled:

'When they look, they won't really see.
    When they hear, they won't understand.'

11"This is the meaning of the parable: The seed is God's word. 12The seeds that fell on the footpath represent those who hear the message, only to have the devil come and take it away from their hearts and prevent them from believing and being saved. 13The seeds on the rocky soil represent those who hear the message and receive it with joy. But since they don't have deep roots, they believe for a while, then they fall away when they face temptation. 14The seeds that fell among the thorns represent those who hear the message, but all too quickly the message is crowded out by the cares and riches and pleasures of this life. And so they never grow into maturity. 15And the seeds that fell on the good soil represent honest, good-hearted people who hear God's word, cling to it, and patiently produce a huge harvest.

Parable of the Lamp

16"No one lights a lamp and then covers it with a bowl or hides it under a bed. A lamp is placed on a stand, where its light can be seen by all who enter the house. 17For all that is secret will eventually be brought into the open, and everything that is concealed will be brought to light and made known to all.

18"So pay attention to how you hear. To those who listen to my teaching, more understanding will be given. But for those who are not listening, even what they think they understand will be taken away from them."

The True Family of Jesus

19Then Jesus' mother and brothers came to see him, but they couldn't get to him because of the crowd. 20Someone told Jesus, "Your mother and your brothers are outside, and they want to see you."

21Jesus replied, "My mother and my brothers are all those who hear God's word and obey it."

Jesus Calms the Storm

22 One day Jesus said to his disciples, "Let's cross to the other side of the lake." So they got into a boat and started out. 23 As they sailed across, Jesus settled down for a nap. But soon a fierce storm came down on the lake. The boat was filling with water, and they were in real danger.

24 The disciples went and woke him up, shouting, "Master, Master, we're going to drown!"

When Jesus woke up, he rebuked the wind and the raging waves. Suddenly the storm stopped and all was calm. 25 Then he asked them, "Where is your faith?"

The disciples were terrified and amazed. "Who is this man?" they asked each other. "When he gives a command, even the wind and waves obey him!"

Jesus Heals a Demon-Possessed Man

26 So they arrived in the region of the Gerasenes, across the lake from Galilee. 27 As Jesus was climbing out of the boat, a man who was possessed by demons came out to meet him. For a long time he had been homeless and naked, living in a cemetery outside the town.

28 As soon as he saw Jesus, he shrieked and fell down in front of him. Then he screamed, "Why are you interfering with me, Jesus, Son of the Most High God? Please, I beg you, don't torture me!" 29 For Jesus had already commanded the evil spirit to come out of him. This spirit had often taken control of the man. Even when he was placed under guard and put in chains and shackles, he simply broke them and rushed out into the wilderness, completely under the demon's power.

30 Jesus demanded, "What is your name?"

"Legion," he replied, for he was filled with many demons. 31 The demons kept begging Jesus not to send them into the bottomless pit.

32 There happened to be a large herd of pigs feeding on the hillside nearby, and the demons begged him to let them enter into the pigs.

So Jesus gave them permission. 33 Then the demons came out of the man and entered the pigs, and the entire herd plunged down the steep hillside into the lake and drowned.

34 When the herdsmen saw it, they fled to the nearby town and the surrounding countryside, spreading the news as they ran. 35 People rushed out to see what had happened. A crowd soon gathered around Jesus, and they saw the man who had been freed from the demons. He was sitting at Jesus' feet, fully clothed and perfectly sane, and they were all afraid. 36 Then those who had seen what happened told the others how the demon-possessed man had been healed. 37 And all the people in the region of the Gerasenes begged Jesus to go away and leave them alone, for a great wave of fear swept over them.

So Jesus returned to the boat and left, crossing back to the other side of the lake. 38 The man who had been freed from the demons begged to go with him. But Jesus sent him home, saying, 39 "No, go back to your family, and tell them everything God has done for you." So he went all through the town proclaiming the great things Jesus had done for him.

Jesus Heals in Response to Faith

40 On the other side of the lake the crowds welcomed Jesus, because they had been waiting for him. 41 Then a man named Jairus, a leader of the local synagogue, came and fell at Jesus' feet, pleading with him to come home with him. 42 His only daughter, who was about twelve years old, was dying.

As Jesus went with him, he was surrounded by the crowds. 43 A woman in the crowd had suffered for twelve years with constant bleeding, and she could find no cure. 44 Coming up behind Jesus, she touched the fringe of his robe. Immediately, the bleeding stopped.

45 "Who touched me?" Jesus asked.

Everyone denied it, and Peter said, "Master, this whole crowd is pressing up against you."

46 But Jesus said, "Someone deliberately touched me, for I felt healing power go out from me." 47 When the woman realized that she could not stay hidden, she began to tremble and fell to her knees in front of him. The whole crowd heard her explain why she had touched him and that she had been immediately healed. 48 "Daughter," he said to her, "your faith has made you well. Go in peace."

49 While he was still speaking to her, a messenger arrived from the home of Jairus, the leader of the synagogue. He told him, "Your daughter is dead. There's no use troubling the Teacher now."

50 But when Jesus heard what had happened, he said to Jairus, "Don't be afraid. Just have faith, and she will be healed."

51 When they arrived at the house, Jesus wouldn't let anyone go in with him except Peter, John, James, and the little girl's father and mother. 52 The house was filled with people

weeping and wailing, but he said, "Stop the weeping! She isn't dead; she's only asleep."

⁵³But the crowd laughed at him because they all knew she had died. ⁵⁴Then Jesus took her by the hand and said in a loud voice, "My child, get up!" ⁵⁵And at that moment her life returned, and she immediately stood up! Then Jesus told them to give her something to eat. ⁵⁶Her parents were overwhelmed, but Jesus insisted that they not tell anyone what had happened.

Jesus Sends Out the Twelve Disciples

One day Jesus called together his twelve disciples and gave them power and authority to cast out all demons and to heal all diseases. ²Then he sent them out to tell everyone about the Kingdom of God and to heal the sick. ³"Take nothing for your journey," he instructed them. "Don't take a walking stick, a traveler's bag, food, money, or even a change of clothes. ⁴Wherever you go, stay in the same house until you leave town. ⁵And if a town refuses to welcome you, shake its dust from your feet as you leave to show that you have abandoned those people to their fate."

⁶So they began their circuit of the villages, preaching the Good News and healing the sick.

Herod's Confusion

⁷When Herod Antipas, the ruler of Galilee, heard about everything Jesus was doing, he was puzzled. Some were saying that John the Baptist had been raised from the dead. ⁸Others thought Jesus was Elijah or one of the other prophets risen from the dead.

⁹"I beheaded John," Herod said, "so who is this man about whom I hear such stories?" And he kept trying to see him.

Jesus Feeds Five Thousand

¹⁰When the apostles returned, they told Jesus everything they had done. Then he slipped quietly away with them toward the town of Bethsaida. ¹¹But the crowds found out where he was going, and they followed him. He welcomed them and taught them about the Kingdom of God, and he healed those who were sick.

¹²Late in the afternoon the twelve disciples came to him and said, "Send the crowds away to the nearby villages and farms, so they can find food and lodging for the night. There is nothing to eat here in this remote place."

¹³But Jesus said, "You feed them."

"But we have only five loaves of bread and two fish," they answered. "Or are you expecting us to go and buy enough food for this whole crowd?" ¹⁴For there were about 5,000 men there.

Jesus replied, "Tell them to sit down in groups of about fifty each." ¹⁵So the people all sat down. ¹⁶Jesus took the five loaves and two fish, looked up toward heaven, and blessed them. Then, breaking the loaves into pieces, he kept giving the bread and fish to the disciples so they could distribute it to the people. ¹⁷They all ate as much as they wanted, and afterward, the disciples picked up twelve baskets of leftovers!

Peter's Declaration about Jesus

¹⁸One day Jesus left the crowds to pray alone. Only his disciples were with him, and he asked them, "Who do people say I am?"

¹⁹"Well," they replied, "some say John the Baptist, some say Elijah, and others say you are one of the other ancient prophets risen from the dead."

²⁰Then he asked them, "But who do you say I am?"

Peter replied, "You are the Messiah sent from God!"

Jesus Predicts His Death

²¹Jesus warned his disciples not to tell anyone who he was. ²²"The Son of Man must suffer many terrible things," he said. "He will be rejected by the elders, the leading priests, and the teachers of religious law. He will be killed, but on the third day he will be raised from the dead."

²³Then he said to the crowd, "If any of you wants to be my follower, you must turn from your selfish ways, take up your cross daily, and follow me. ²⁴If you try to hang on to your life, you will lose it. But if you give up your life for my sake, you will save it. ²⁵And what do you benefit if you gain the whole world but are yourself lost or destroyed? ²⁶If anyone is ashamed of me and my message, the Son of Man will be ashamed of that person when he returns in his glory and in the glory of the Father and the holy angels. ²⁷I tell you the truth, some standing here right now will not die before they see the Kingdom of God."

The Transfiguration

²⁸About eight days later Jesus took Peter, John, and James up on a mountain to pray. ²⁹And as he was praying, the appearance of his face was transformed, and his clothes became dazzling white. ³⁰Suddenly, two men, Moses and Elijah, appeared and began talking with Jesus. ³¹They were glorious to see. And they were speaking

about his exodus from this world, which was about to be fulfilled in Jerusalem.

32 Peter and the others had fallen asleep. When they woke up, they saw Jesus' glory and the two men standing with him. 33 As Moses and Elijah were starting to leave, Peter, not even knowing what he was saying, blurted out, "Master, it's wonderful for us to be here! Let's make three shelters as memorials—one for you, one for Moses, and one for Elijah." 34 But even as he was saying this, a cloud overshadowed them, and terror gripped them as the cloud covered them.

35 Then a voice from the cloud said, "This is my Son, my Chosen One. Listen to him." 36 When the voice finished, Jesus was there alone. They didn't tell anyone at that time what they had seen.

Jesus Heals a Demon-Possessed Boy

37 The next day, after they had come down the mountain, a large crowd met Jesus. 38 A man in the crowd called out to him, "Teacher, I beg you to look at my son, my only child. 39 An evil spirit keeps seizing him, making him scream. It throws him into convulsions so that he foams at the mouth. It batters him and hardly ever leaves him alone. 40 I begged your disciples to cast out the spirit, but they couldn't do it."

41 Jesus said, "You faithless and corrupt people! How long must I be with you and put up with you?" Then he said to the man, "Bring your son here."

42 As the boy came forward, the demon knocked him to the ground and threw him into a violent convulsion. But Jesus rebuked the evil spirit and healed the boy. Then he gave him back to his father. 43 Awe gripped the people as they saw this majestic display of God's power.

Jesus Again Predicts His Death

While everyone was marveling at everything he was doing, Jesus said to his disciples, 44 "Listen to me and remember what I say. The Son of Man is going to be betrayed into the hands of his enemies." 45 But they didn't know what he meant. Its significance was hidden from them, so they couldn't understand it, and they were afraid to ask him about it.

The Greatest in the Kingdom

46 Then his disciples began arguing about which of them was the greatest. 47 But Jesus knew their thoughts, so he brought a little child to his side. 48 Then he said to them, "Anyone who welcomes a little child like this on my behalf welcomes me, and anyone who welcomes me also welcomes my Father who sent me. Whoever is the least among you is the greatest."

Using the Name of Jesus

49 John said to Jesus, "Master, we saw someone using your name to cast out demons, but we told him to stop because he isn't in our group."

50 But Jesus said, "Don't stop him! Anyone who is not against you is for you."

Opposition from Samaritans

51 As the time drew near for him to ascend to heaven, Jesus resolutely set out for Jerusalem. 52 He sent messengers ahead to a Samaritan village to prepare for his arrival. 53 But the people of the village did not welcome Jesus because he was on his way to Jerusalem. 54 When James and John saw this, they said to Jesus, "Lord, should we call down fire from heaven to burn them up?" 55 But Jesus turned and rebuked them.* 56 So they went on to another village.

The Cost of Following Jesus

57 As they were walking along, someone said to Jesus, "I will follow you wherever you go."

58 But Jesus replied, "Foxes have dens to live in, and birds have nests, but the Son of Man has no place even to lay his head."

59 He said to another person, "Come, follow me."

The man agreed, but he said, "Lord, first let me return home and bury my father."

60 But Jesus told him, "Let the spiritually dead bury their own dead! Your duty is to go and preach about the Kingdom of God."

61 Another said, "Yes, Lord, I will follow you, but first let me say good-bye to my family."

62 But Jesus told him, "Anyone who puts a hand to the plow and then looks back is not fit for the Kingdom of God."

CHAPTER 10

Jesus Sends Out His Disciples

The Lord now chose seventy-two other disciples and sent them ahead in pairs to all the towns and places he planned to visit. 2 These were his instructions to them: "The harvest is great, but the workers are few. So pray to the Lord who is in charge of the harvest; ask him to send more workers into his fields. 3 Now go, and remember

---

9:55 Some manuscripts add an expanded conclusion to verse 55 and an additional sentence in verse 56: *And he said, "You don't realize what your hearts are like.* 56 *For the Son of Man has not come to destroy people's lives, but to save them."*

THE ADVENTURES OF SUPER SAMARITAN!

If ever someone needed a super-hero, it was the guy Jesus told about in LUKE 10:25-37. Go read it.

Boy, that guy was like a superhero. Maybe we should call him Super Samaritan! You can be a Super Samaritan too!

1. Draw a large S on a stick-on name tag.

2. Decorate the rest of the sticker to look like your very own superhero logo.

3. Stick the tag to the inside of your shirt where no one else can see it.

Now ask God to help you be on the look-out for people to help. **Maybe you can even help someone you don't usually get along with!**

Don't pass them by! Instead, think,

"This is a job for Super Samaritan!"

Later, write here how you obeyed God and acted as a Super Samaritan!

that I am sending you out as lambs among wolves. 4Don't take any money with you, nor a traveler's bag, nor an extra pair of sandals. And don't stop to greet anyone on the road.

5"Whenever you enter someone's home, first say, 'May God's peace be on this house.' 6If those who live there are peaceful, the blessing will stand; if they are not, the blessing will return to you. 7Don't move around from home to home. Stay in one place, eating and drinking what they provide. Don't hesitate to accept hospitality, be-cause those who work deserve their pay.

8"If you enter a town and it welcomes you, eat whatever is set before you. 9Heal the sick, and tell them, 'The Kingdom of God is near you now.' 10But if a town refuses to welcome you, go out into its streets and say, 11'We wipe even the dust of your town from our feet to show that we have abandoned you to your fate. And know this—the Kingdom of God is near!' 12I assure you, even wicked Sodom will be better off than such a town on judgment day.

13"What sorrow awaits you, Korazin and Bethsaida! For if the miracles I did in you had been done in wicked Tyre and Sidon, their peo-ple would have repented of their sins long ago, clothing themselves in burlap and throwing ashes on their heads to show their remorse. 14Yes, Tyre and Sidon will be better off on judg-ment day than you. 15And you people of Caper-naum, will you be honored in heaven? No, you will go down to the place of the dead."

16Then he said to the disciples, "Anyone who accepts your message is also accepting me. And anyone who rejects you is rejecting me. And anyone who rejects me is rejecting God, who sent me."

17When the seventy-two disciples returned, they joyfully reported to him, "Lord, even the de-mons obey us when we use your name!"

18"Yes," he told them, "I saw Satan fall from heaven like lightning! 19Look, I have given you authority over all the power of the enemy, and you can walk among snakes and scorpions and crush them. Nothing will injure you. 20But don't rejoice because evil spirits obey you; rejoice be-cause your names are registered in heaven."

Jesus' Prayer of Thanksgiving

21At that same time Jesus was filled with the joy of the Holy Spirit, and he said, "O Father, Lord of heaven and earth, thank you for hiding these things from those who think themselves wise and clever, and for revealing them to the child-like. Yes, Father, it pleased you to do it this way.

22"My Father has entrusted everything to me. No one truly knows the Son except the Father, and no one truly knows the Father except the Son and those to whom the Son chooses to reveal him."

23Then when they were alone, he turned to the disciples and said, "Blessed are the eyes that see what you have seen. 24I tell you, many prophets and kings longed to see what you see, but they didn't see it. And they longed to hear what you hear, but they didn't hear it."

The Most Important Commandment

25One day an expert in religious law stood up to test Jesus by asking him this question: "Teacher, what should I do to inherit eternal life?"

26Jesus replied, "What does the law of Moses say? How do you read it?"

27The man answered, "'You must love the LORD your God with all your heart, all your soul, all your strength, and all your mind.' And, 'Love your neighbor as yourself.'"

28"Right!" Jesus told him. "Do this and you will live!"

29The man wanted to justify his actions, so he asked Jesus, "And who is my neighbor?"

Parable of the Good Samaritan

30Jesus replied with a story: "A Jewish man was traveling on a trip from Jerusalem to Jericho, and he was attacked by bandits. They stripped him of his clothes, beat him up, and left him half dead beside the road.

31"By chance a priest came along. But when he saw the man lying there, he crossed to the other side of the road and passed him by. 32A Temple assistant walked over and looked at him lying there, but he also passed by on the other side.

33"Then a despised Samaritan came along, and when he saw the man, he felt compassion for him. 34Going over to him, the Samaritan soothed his wounds with olive oil and wine and bandaged them. Then he put the man on his own donkey and took him to an inn, where he took care of him. 35The next day he handed the innkeeper two silver coins, telling him, 'Take care of this man. If his bill runs higher than this, I'll pay you the next time I'm here.'

36"Now which of these three would you say was a neighbor to the man who was attacked by bandits?" Jesus asked.

37The man replied, "The one who showed him mercy."

Then Jesus said, "Yes, now go and do the same."

Jesus Visits Martha and Mary

38As Jesus and the disciples continued on their way to Jerusalem, they came to a certain village where a woman named Martha welcomed him into her home. 39Her sister, Mary, sat at the Lord's feet, listening to what he taught. 40But Martha was distracted by the big dinner she was preparing. She came to Jesus and said, "Lord, doesn't it seem unfair to you that my sister just sits here while I do all the work? Tell her to come and help me."

41But the Lord said to her, "My dear Martha, you are worried and upset over all these details! 42There is only one thing worth being concerned about. Mary has discovered it, and it will not be taken away from her."

CHAPTER **11**

Teaching about Prayer

Once Jesus was in a certain place praying. As he finished, one of his disciples came to him and said, "Lord, teach us to pray, just as John taught his disciples."

2Jesus said, "This is how you should pray:

"Father, may your name be kept holy.
 May your Kingdom come soon.
3 Give us each day the food we need,
4 and forgive us our sins,
  as we forgive those who sin against us.
 And don't let us yield to temptation."

5Then, teaching them more about prayer, he used this story: "Suppose you went to a friend's house at midnight, wanting to borrow three loaves of bread. You say to him, 6'A friend of mine has just arrived for a visit, and I have nothing for him to eat.' 7And suppose he calls out from his bedroom, 'Don't bother me. The door is locked for the night, and my family and I are all in bed. I can't help you.' 8But I tell you this—though he won't do it for friendship's sake, if you keep knocking long enough, he will get up and give you whatever you need because of your shameless persistence.

9"**And so I tell you, keep on asking, and you will receive what you ask for. Keep on seeking, and you will find. Keep on knocking, and the door will be opened to you.** 10For everyone who asks, receives. Everyone who seeks, finds. And to everyone who knocks, the door will be opened.

11"You fathers—if your children ask for a fish, do you give them a snake instead? 12Or if they ask for an egg, do you give them a scorpion? Of course not! ¹³So if you sinful people know how to give good gifts to your children, how much more will your heavenly Father give the Holy Spirit to those who ask him."

Jesus and the Prince of Demons

¹⁴One day Jesus cast out a demon from a man who couldn't speak, and when the demon was gone, the man began to speak. The crowds were amazed, ¹⁵but some of them said, "No wonder he can cast out demons. He gets his power from Satan, the prince of demons." ¹⁶Others, trying to test Jesus, demanded that he show them a miraculous sign from heaven to prove his authority.

¹⁷He knew their thoughts, so he said, "Any kingdom divided by civil war is doomed. A family splintered by feuding will fall apart. ¹⁸You say I am empowered by Satan. But if Satan is divided and fighting against himself, how can his kingdom survive? ¹⁹And if I am empowered by Satan, what about your own exorcists? They cast out demons, too, so they will condemn you for what you have said. ²⁰But if I am casting out demons by the power of God, then the Kingdom of God has arrived among you. ²¹For when a strong man like Satan is fully armed and guards his palace, his possessions are safe—²²until someone even stronger attacks and overpowers him, strips him of his weapons, and carries off his belongings.

²³"Anyone who isn't with me opposes me, and anyone who isn't working with me is actually working against me.

²⁴"When an evil spirit leaves a person, it goes into the desert, searching for rest. But when it finds none, it says, 'I will return to the person I came from.' ²⁵So it returns and finds that its former home is all swept and in order. ²⁶Then the spirit finds seven other spirits more evil than itself, and they all enter the person and live there. And so that person is worse off than before."

²⁷As he was speaking, a woman in the crowd called out, "God bless your mother—the womb from which you came, and the breasts that nursed you!"

²⁸Jesus replied, "But even more blessed are all who hear the word of God and put it into practice."

The Sign of Jonah

²⁹As the crowd pressed in on Jesus, he said, "This evil generation keeps asking me to show them a miraculous sign. But the only sign I will give them is the sign of Jonah. ³⁰What happened to

Key Verse

"And so I tell you, keep on asking, and you will receive what you ask for. Keep on seeking, and you will find. Keep on knocking, and the door will be opened to you."—LUKE 11:9

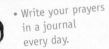
ASK, SEEK, KNOCK

God doesn't want you to close your eyes and make a wish. He wants you to pray. **Read LUKE 11:9 to find out why!**
And when you think you've prayed enough, pray some more! Use these ways to ask, seek, and knock:

KEEP ON ASKING

• Pray every 60 minutes for a whole day.

• Write your prayers in a journal every day.

• Ask a friend to pray for you or with you.

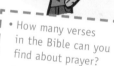

KEEP ON SEEKING

• How many verses in the Bible can you find about prayer?

• Look at something God made. Then say thanks to him!

• Seek people you can pray for.

KEEP ON KNOCKING

• Knock on the door of someone who really loves God. Ask how and when that person likes to pray.

• Knock a rhythm on your door as you sing a praise song.

• Knock on your parents' door. Ask them to pray with you.

him was a sign to the people of Nineveh that God had sent him. What happens to the Son of Man will be a sign to these people that he was sent by God.

31"The queen of Sheba will stand up against this generation on judgment day and condemn it, for she came from a distant land to hear the wisdom of Solomon. Now someone greater than Solomon is here—but you refuse to listen. 32The people of Nineveh will also stand up against this generation on judgment day and condemn it, for they repented of their sins at the preaching of Jonah. Now someone greater than Jonah is here—but you refuse to repent.

Receiving the Light

33"No one lights a lamp and then hides it or puts it under a basket. Instead, a lamp is placed on a stand, where its light can be seen by all who enter the house.

34"Your eye is a lamp that provides light for your body. When your eye is good, your whole body is filled with light. But when it is bad, your body is filled with darkness. 35Make sure that the light you think you have is not actually darkness. 36If you are filled with light, with no dark corners, then your whole life will be radiant, as though a floodlight were filling you with light."

Jesus Criticizes the Religious Leaders

37As Jesus was speaking, one of the Pharisees invited him home for a meal. So he went in and took his place at the table. 38His host was amazed to see that he sat down to eat without first performing the hand-washing ceremony required by Jewish custom. 39Then the Lord said to him, "You Pharisees are so careful to clean the outside of the cup and the dish, but inside you are filthy—full of greed and wickedness! 40Fools! Didn't God make the inside as well as the outside? 41So clean the inside by giving gifts to the poor, and you will be clean all over.

42"What sorrow awaits you Pharisees! For you are careful to tithe even the tiniest income from your herb gardens, but you ignore justice and the love of God. You should tithe, yes, but do not neglect the more important things.

43"What sorrow awaits you Pharisees! For you love to sit in the seats of honor in the synagogues and receive respectful greetings as you walk in the marketplaces. 44Yes, what sorrow awaits you! For you are like hidden graves in a field. People walk over them without knowing the corruption they are stepping on."

45"Teacher," said an expert in religious law, "you have insulted us, too, in what you just said."

46"Yes," said Jesus, "what sorrow also awaits you experts in religious law! For you crush people with unbearable religious demands, and you never lift a finger to ease the burden. 47What sorrow awaits you! For you build monuments for the prophets your own ancestors killed long ago. 48But in fact, you stand as witnesses who agree with what your ancestors did. They killed the prophets, and you join in their crime by building the monuments! 49This is what God in his wisdom said about you: 'I will send prophets and apostles to them, but they will kill some and persecute the others.'

50"As a result, this generation will be held responsible for the murder of all God's prophets from the creation of the world—51from the murder of Abel to the murder of Zechariah, who was killed between the altar and the sanctuary. Yes, it will certainly be charged against this generation.

52"What sorrow awaits you experts in religious law! For you remove the key to knowledge from the people. You don't enter the Kingdom yourselves, and you prevent others from entering."

53As Jesus was leaving, the teachers of religious law and the Pharisees became hostile and tried to provoke him with many questions. 54They wanted to trap him into saying something they could use against him.

CHAPTER **12**

A Warning against Hypocrisy

Meanwhile, the crowds grew until thousands were milling about and stepping on each other. Jesus turned first to his disciples and warned them, "Beware of the yeast of the Pharisees—their hypocrisy. 2The time is coming when everything that is covered up will be revealed, and all that is secret will be made known to all. 3Whatever you have said in the dark will be heard in the light, and what you have whispered behind closed doors will be shouted from the housetops for all to hear!

4"Dear friends, don't be afraid of those who want to kill your body; they cannot do any more to you after that. 5But I'll tell you whom to fear. Fear God, who has the power to kill you and then throw you into hell. Yes, he's the one to fear.

6"What is the price of five sparrows—two copper coins? Yet God does not forget a single one of them. 7And the very hairs on your head are all numbered. So don't be afraid; you are more valuable to God than a whole flock of sparrows.

8"I tell you the truth, everyone who acknowledges me publicly here on earth, the Son of Man will also acknowledge in the presence of God's angels. 9But anyone who denies me here on earth will be denied before God's angels. 10Anyone who speaks against the Son of Man can be forgiven, but anyone who blasphemes the Holy Spirit will not be forgiven.

11"And when you are brought to trial in the synagogues and before rulers and authorities, don't worry about how to defend yourself or what to say, 12for the Holy Spirit will teach you at that time what needs to be said."

Parable of the Rich Fool

13Then someone called from the crowd, "Teacher, please tell my brother to divide our father's estate with me."

14Jesus replied, "Friend, who made me a judge over you to decide such things as that?" 15Then he said, "Beware! Guard against every kind of greed. Life is not measured by how much you own."

16Then he told them a story: "A rich man had a fertile farm that produced fine crops. 17He said to himself, 'What should I do? I don't have room for all my crops.' 18Then he said, 'I know! I'll tear down my barns and build bigger ones. Then I'll have room enough to store all my wheat and other goods. 19And I'll sit back and say to myself, "My friend, you have enough stored away for years to come. Now take it easy! Eat, drink, and be merry!"'

20"But God said to him, 'You fool! You will die this very night. Then who will get everything you worked for?'

21"Yes, a person is a fool to store up earthly wealth but not have a rich relationship with God."

Teaching about Money and Possessions

22Then, turning to his disciples, Jesus said, "That is why I tell you not to worry about everyday life—whether you have enough food to eat or enough clothes to wear. 23For life is more than food, and your body more than clothing. 24Look at the ravens. They don't plant or harvest or store food in barns, for God feeds them. And you are far more valuable to him than any birds! 25Can all your worries add a single moment to your life? 26And if worry can't accomplish a little thing like that, what's the use of worrying over bigger things?

27"Look at the lilies and how they grow. They don't work or make their clothing, yet Solomon in all his glory was not dressed as beautifully as they are. 28And if God cares so wonderfully for flowers that are here today and thrown into the fire tomorrow, he will certainly care for you. Why do you have so little faith?

29"And don't be concerned about what to eat and what to drink. Don't worry about such things. 30These things dominate the thoughts of unbelievers all over the world, but your Father already knows your needs. 31Seek the Kingdom of God above all else, and he will give you everything you need.

32"So don't be afraid, little flock. For it gives your Father great happiness to give you the Kingdom.

33"Sell your possessions and give to those in need. This will store up treasure for you in heaven! And the purses of heaven never get old or develop holes. Your treasure will be safe; no thief can steal it and no moth can destroy it. 34Wherever your treasure is, there the desires of your heart will also be.

Be Ready for the Lord's Coming

35"Be dressed for service and keep your lamps burning, 36as though you were waiting for your master to return from the wedding feast. Then you will be ready to open the door and let him in the moment he arrives and knocks. 37The servants who are ready and waiting for his return will be rewarded. I tell you the truth, he himself will seat them, put on an apron, and serve them as they sit and eat! 38He may come in the middle of the night or just before dawn. But whenever he comes, he will reward the servants who are ready.

39"Understand this: If a homeowner knew exactly when a burglar was coming, he would not permit his house to be broken into. 40You also must be ready all the time, for the Son of Man will come when least expected."

41Peter asked, "Lord, is that illustration just for us or for everyone?"

42And the Lord replied, "A faithful, sensible servant is one to whom the master can give the responsibility of managing his other household servants and feeding them. 43If the master returns and finds that the servant has done a good job, there will be a reward. 44I tell you the truth, the master will put that servant in charge of all he owns. 45But what if the servant thinks, 'My master won't be back for a while,' and he begins beating the other servants, partying, and getting drunk? 46The master will return unannounced and unexpected, and he will cut the servant in pieces and banish him with the unfaithful.

47"And a servant who knows what the master wants, but isn't prepared and doesn't carry out those instructions, will be severely punished. 48But someone who does not know, and then does something wrong, will be punished only lightly. When someone has been given much, much will be required in return; and when someone has been entrusted with much, even more will be required.

Jesus Causes Division

49"I have come to set the world on fire, and I wish it were already burning! 50I have a terrible baptism of suffering ahead of me, and I am under a heavy burden until it is accomplished. 51Do you think I have come to bring peace to the earth? No, I have come to divide people against each other! 52From now on families will be split apart, three in favor of me, and two against—or two in favor and three against.

53 'Father will be divided against son
    and son against father;
mother against daughter
    and daughter against mother;
and mother-in-law against daughter-in-law
    and daughter-in-law against
        mother-in-law.'"

54Then Jesus turned to the crowd and said, "When you see clouds beginning to form in the west, you say, 'Here comes a shower.' And you are right. 55When the south wind blows, you say, 'Today will be a scorcher.' And it is. 56You fools! You know how to interpret the weather signs of the earth and sky, but you don't know how to interpret the present times.

57"Why can't you decide for yourselves what is right? 58When you are on the way to court with your accuser, try to settle the matter before you get there. Otherwise, your accuser may drag you before the judge, who will hand you over to an officer, who will throw you into prison. 59And if that happens, you won't be free again until you have paid the very last penny."

CHAPTER **13**
A Call to Repentance

About this time Jesus was informed that Pilate had murdered some people from Galilee as they were offering sacrifices at the Temple. 2"Do you think those Galileans were worse sinners than all the other people from Galilee?" Jesus asked. "Is that why they suffered? 3Not at all! And you will perish, too, unless you repent of your sins and turn to God. 4And what about the eighteen peo-

ple who died when the tower in Siloam fell on them? Were they the worst sinners in Jerusalem? 5No, and I tell you again that unless you repent, you will perish, too."

Parable of the Barren Fig Tree

6Then Jesus told this story: "A man planted a fig tree in his garden and came again and again to see if there was any fruit on it, but he was always disappointed. 7Finally, he said to his gardener, 'I've waited three years, and there hasn't been a single fig! Cut it down. It's just taking up space in the garden.'

8"The gardener answered, 'Sir, give it one more chance. Leave it another year, and I'll give it special attention and plenty of fertilizer. 9If we get figs next year, fine. If not, then you can cut it down.'"

Jesus Heals on the Sabbath

10One Sabbath day as Jesus was teaching in a synagogue, 11he saw a woman who had been

Everyone loves a winner, right? But in the Bible, the *losers* seem to end up winning.

Remember Zacchaeus? *Loser.* Everyone hated that cheat! (Everyone but Jesus, that is.) **Who did Jesus spend all his time with?** Poor people. Sick people. Lonely people. The people who everyone thought were losers. But it was the people who thought they knew it all and didn't need Jesus who were the *real* losers.

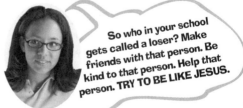

So who in your school gets called a loser? Make friends with that person. Be kind to that person. Help that person. TRY TO BE LIKE JESUS.

crippled by an evil spirit. She had been bent double for eighteen years and was unable to stand up straight. ¹²When Jesus saw her, he called her over and said, "Dear woman, you are healed of your sickness!" ¹³Then he touched her, and instantly she could stand straight. How she praised God!

¹⁴But the leader in charge of the synagogue was indignant that Jesus had healed her on the Sabbath day. "There are six days of the week for working," he said to the crowd. "Come on those days to be healed, not on the Sabbath."

¹⁵But the Lord replied, "You hypocrites! Each of you works on the Sabbath day! Don't you untie your ox or your donkey from its stall on the Sabbath and lead it out for water? ¹⁶This dear woman, a daughter of Abraham, has been held in bondage by Satan for eighteen years. Isn't it right that she be released, even on the Sabbath?"

¹⁷This shamed his enemies, but all the people rejoiced at the wonderful things he did.

Parable of the Mustard Seed

¹⁸Then Jesus said, "What is the Kingdom of God like? How can I illustrate it? ¹⁹It is like a tiny mustard seed that a man planted in a garden; it grows and becomes a tree, and the birds make nests in its branches."

Parable of the Yeast

²⁰He also asked, "What else is the Kingdom of God like? ²¹It is like the yeast a woman used in making bread. Even though she put only a little yeast in three measures of flour, it permeated every part of the dough."

The Narrow Door

²²Jesus went through the towns and villages, teaching as he went, always pressing on toward Jerusalem. ²³Someone asked him, "Lord, will only a few be saved?"

He replied, ²⁴"Work hard to enter the narrow door to God's Kingdom, for many will try to enter but will fail. ²⁵When the master of the house has locked the door, it will be too late. You will stand outside knocking and pleading, 'Lord, open the door for us!' But he will reply, 'I don't know you or where you come from.' ²⁶Then you will say, 'But we ate and drank with you, and you taught in our streets.' ²⁷And he will reply, 'I tell you, I don't know you or where you come from. Get away from me, all you who do evil.'

²⁸"There will be weeping and gnashing of teeth, for you will see Abraham, Isaac, Jacob, and all the prophets in the Kingdom of God, but you will be thrown out. ²⁹And people will come from all over the world—from east and west, north and south—to take their places in the Kingdom of God. ³⁰And note this: Some who seem least important now will be the greatest then, and some who are the greatest now will be least important then."

Jesus Grieves over Jerusalem

³¹At that time some Pharisees said to him, "Get away from here if you want to live! Herod Antipas wants to kill you!"

³²Jesus replied, "Go tell that fox that I will keep on casting out demons and healing people today and tomorrow; and the third day I will accomplish my purpose. ³³Yes, today, tomorrow, and the next day I must proceed on my way. For it wouldn't do for a prophet of God to be killed except in Jerusalem!

³⁴"O Jerusalem, Jerusalem, the city that kills the prophets and stones God's messengers! How often I have wanted to gather your children together as a hen protects her chicks beneath her wings, but you wouldn't let me. ³⁵And now, look, your house is abandoned. And you will never see me again until you say, 'Blessings on the one who comes in the name of the LORD!'"

CHAPTER **14**
Jesus Heals on the Sabbath

One Sabbath day Jesus went to eat dinner in the home of a leader of the Pharisees, and the people were watching him closely. ²There was a man there whose arms and legs were swollen. ³Jesus asked the Pharisees and experts in religious law, "Is it permitted in the law to heal people on the Sabbath day, or not?" ⁴When they refused to answer, Jesus touched the sick man and healed him and sent him away. ⁵Then he turned to them and said, "Which of you doesn't work on the Sabbath? If your son or your cow falls into a pit, don't you rush to get him out?" ⁶Again they could not answer.

Jesus Teaches about Humility

⁷When Jesus noticed that all who had come to the dinner were trying to sit in the seats of honor near the head of the table, he gave them this advice: ⁸"When you are invited to a wedding feast, don't sit in the seat of honor. What if someone who is more distinguished than you has also been invited? ⁹The host will come and say, 'Give this person your seat.' Then you will be embarrassed, and you will have to take whatever seat is left at the foot of the table!

10"Instead, take the lowest place at the foot of the table. Then when your host sees you, he will come and say, 'Friend, we have a better place for you!' Then you will be honored in front of all the other guests. 11For those who exalt themselves will be humbled, and those who humble themselves will be exalted."

12Then he turned to his host. "When you put on a luncheon or a banquet," he said, "don't invite your friends, brothers, relatives, and rich neighbors. For they will invite you back, and that will be your only reward. 13Instead, invite the poor, the crippled, the lame, and the blind. 14Then at the resurrection of the righteous, God will reward you for inviting those who could not repay you."

Parable of the Great Feast

15Hearing this, a man sitting at the table with Jesus exclaimed, "What a blessing it will be to attend a banquet in the Kingdom of God!"

16Jesus replied with this story: "A man prepared a great feast and sent out many invitations. 17When the banquet was ready, he sent his servant to tell the guests, 'Come, the banquet is ready.' 18But they all began making excuses. One said, 'I have just bought a field and must inspect it. Please excuse me.' 19Another said, 'I have just bought five pairs of oxen, and I want to try them out. Please excuse me.' 20Another said, 'I now have a wife, so I can't come.'

21"The servant returned and told his master what they had said. His master was furious and said, 'Go quickly into the streets and alleys of the town and invite the poor, the crippled, the blind, and the lame.' 22After the servant had done this, he reported, 'There is still room for more.' 23So his master said, 'Go out into the country lanes and behind the hedges and urge anyone you find to come, so that the house will be full. 24For none of those I first invited will get even the smallest taste of my banquet.'"

The Cost of Being a Disciple

25A large crowd was following Jesus. He turned around and said to them, 26"If you want to be my disciple, you must hate everyone else by comparison—your father and mother, wife and children, brothers and sisters—yes, even your own life. Otherwise, you cannot be my disciple. 27And if you do not carry your own cross and follow me, you cannot be my disciple.

28"But don't begin until you count the cost. For who would begin construction of a building without first calculating the cost to see if there is enough money to finish it? 29Otherwise, you might complete only the foundation before running out of money, and then everyone would laugh at you. 30They would say, 'There's the person who started that building and couldn't afford to finish it!'

31"Or what king would go to war against another king without first sitting down with his counselors to discuss whether his army of 10,000 could defeat the 20,000 soldiers marching against him? 32And if he can't, he will send a delegation to discuss terms of peace while the enemy is still far away. 33So you cannot become my disciple without giving up everything you own.

34"Salt is good for seasoning. But if it loses its flavor, how do you make it salty again? 35Flavorless salt is good neither for the soil nor for the manure pile. It is thrown away. Anyone with ears to hear should listen and understand!"

CHAPTER 15
Parable of the Lost Sheep

Tax collectors and other notorious sinners often came to listen to Jesus teach. 2This made the Pharisees and teachers of religious law complain that he was associating with such sinful people—even eating with them!

3So Jesus told them this story: 4"If a man has a hundred sheep and one of them gets lost, what will he do? Won't he leave the ninety-nine others in the wilderness and go to search for the one that is lost until he finds it? 5And when he has found it, he will joyfully carry it home on his shoulders. 6When he arrives, he will call together his friends and neighbors, saying, 'Rejoice with me because I have found my lost sheep.' 7In the same way, there is more joy in heaven over one lost sinner who repents and returns to God than over ninety-nine others who are righteous and haven't strayed away!

Parable of the Lost Coin

8"Or suppose a woman has ten silver coins and loses one. Won't she light a lamp and sweep the entire house and search carefully until she finds it? 9And when she finds it, she will call in her friends and neighbors and say, 'Rejoice with me because I have found my lost coin.' 10In the same way, there is joy in the presence of God's angels when even one sinner repents."

Parable of the Lost Son

11To illustrate the point further, Jesus told them this story: "A man had two sons. 12The younger son told his father, 'I want my share of your estate now before you die.' So his father agreed to divide his wealth between his sons.

¹³"A few days later this younger son packed all his belongings and moved to a distant land, and there he wasted all his money in wild living. ¹⁴About the time his money ran out, a great famine swept over the land, and he began to starve. ¹⁵He persuaded a local farmer to hire him, and the man sent him into his fields to feed the pigs. ¹⁶The young man became so hungry that even the pods he was feeding the pigs looked good to him. But no one gave him anything.

¹⁷"When he finally came to his senses, he said to himself, 'At home even the hired servants have food enough to spare, and here I am dying of hunger! ¹⁸I will go home to my father and say, "Father, I have sinned against both heaven and you, ¹⁹and I am no longer worthy of being called your son. Please take me on as a hired servant." '

²⁰"So he returned home to his father. And while he was still a long way off, his father saw him coming. Filled with love and compassion, he ran to his son, embraced him, and kissed him. ²¹His son said to him, 'Father, I have sinned against both heaven and you, and I am no longer worthy of being called your son.'

²²"But his father said to the servants, 'Quick! Bring the finest robe in the house and put it on him. Get a ring for his finger and sandals for his feet. ²³And kill the calf we have been fattening. We must celebrate with a feast, ²⁴for this son of mine was dead and has now returned to life. He was lost, but now he is found.' So the party began.

²⁵"Meanwhile, the older son was in the fields working. When he returned home, he heard music and dancing in the house, ²⁶and he asked one of the servants what was going on. ²⁷'Your brother is back,' he was told, 'and your father has killed the fattened calf. We are celebrating because of his safe return.'

²⁸"The older brother was angry and wouldn't go in. His father came out and begged him, ²⁹but he replied, 'All these years I've slaved for you and never once refused to do a single thing you told me to. And in all that time you never gave me even one young goat for a feast with my friends. ³⁰Yet when this son of yours comes back after squandering your money on prostitutes, you celebrate by killing the fattened calf!'

³¹"His father said to him, 'Look, dear son, you have always stayed by me, and everything I have is yours. ³²We had to celebrate this happy day. For your brother was dead and has come back to life! He was lost, but now he is found!'"

Parable of the Shrewd Manager

Jesus told this story to his disciples: "There was a certain rich man who had a manager handling his affairs. One day a report came that the manager was wasting his employer's money. ²So the employer called him in and said, 'What's this I hear about you? Get your report in order, because you are going to be fired.'

³"The manager thought to himself, 'Now what? My boss has fired me. I don't have the strength to dig ditches, and I'm too proud to beg. ⁴Ah, I know how to ensure that I'll have plenty of friends who will give me a home when I am fired.'

⁵"So he invited each person who owed money to his employer to come and discuss the situation. He asked the first one, 'How much do you owe him?' ⁶The man replied, 'I owe him 800 gallons of olive oil.' So the manager told him, 'Take the bill and quickly change it to 400 gallons.'

⁷"'And how much do you owe my employer?' he asked the next man. 'I owe him 1,000 bushels of wheat,' was the reply. 'Here,' the manager said, 'take the bill and change it to 800 bushels.'

⁸"The rich man had to admire the dishonest rascal for being so shrewd. And it is true that the children of this world are more shrewd in dealing with the world around them than are the children of the light. ⁹Here's the lesson: Use your worldly resources to benefit others and make friends. Then, when your earthly possessions are gone, they will welcome you to an eternal home.

¹⁰"If you are faithful in little things, you will be faithful in large ones. But if you are dishonest in little things, you won't be honest with greater responsibilities. ¹¹And if you are untrustworthy about worldly wealth, who will trust you with the true riches of heaven? ¹²And if you are not faithful with other people's things, why should you be trusted with things of your own?

¹³"No one can serve two masters. For you will hate one and love the other; you will be devoted to one and despise the other. You cannot serve both God and money."

¹⁴The Pharisees, who dearly loved their money, heard all this and scoffed at him. ¹⁵Then he said to them, "You like to appear righteous in public, but God knows your hearts. What this world honors is detestable in the sight of God.

¹⁶"Until John the Baptist, the law of Moses and the messages of the prophets were your guides. But now the Good News of the Kingdom of God is preached, and everyone is eager to get in. ¹⁷But that doesn't mean that the law has lost its force. It is easier for heaven and earth to disappear

than for the smallest point of God's law to be overturned.

18"For example, a man who divorces his wife and marries someone else commits adultery. And anyone who marries a woman divorced from her husband commits adultery."

Parable of the Rich Man and Lazarus

19Jesus said, "There was a certain rich man who was splendidly clothed in purple and fine linen and who lived each day in luxury. 20At his gate lay a poor man named Lazarus who was covered with sores. 21As Lazarus lay there longing for scraps from the rich man's table, the dogs would come and lick his open sores.

22"Finally, the poor man died and was carried by the angels to be with Abraham. The rich man also died and was buried, 23and his soul went to the place of the dead. There, in torment, he saw Abraham in the far distance with Lazarus at his side.

24"The rich man shouted, 'Father Abraham, have some pity! Send Lazarus over here to dip the tip of his finger in water and cool my tongue. I am in anguish in these flames.'

25"But Abraham said to him, 'Son, remember that during your lifetime you had everything you wanted, and Lazarus had nothing. So now he is here being comforted, and you are in anguish. 26And besides, there is a great chasm separating us. No one can cross over to you from here, and no one can cross over to us from there.'

27"Then the rich man said, 'Please, Father Abraham, at least send him to my father's home. 28For I have five brothers, and I want him to warn them so they don't end up in this place of torment.'

29"But Abraham said, 'Moses and the prophets have warned them. Your brothers can read what they wrote.'

30"The rich man replied, 'No, Father Abraham! But if someone is sent to them from the dead, then they will repent of their sins and turn to God.'

31"But Abraham said, 'If they won't listen to Moses and the prophets, they won't listen even if someone rises from the dead.'"

CHAPTER **17**
Teachings about Forgiveness and Faith

One day Jesus said to his disciples, "There will always be temptations to sin, but what sorrow awaits the person who does the tempting! 2It

would be better to be thrown into the sea with a millstone hung around your neck than to cause one of these little ones to fall into sin. 3So watch yourselves!

"If another believer sins, rebuke that person; then if there is repentance, forgive. 4Even if that person wrongs you seven times a day and each time turns again and asks forgiveness, you must forgive."

5The apostles said to the Lord, "Show us how to increase our faith."

6The Lord answered, "If you had faith even as small as a mustard seed, you could say to this mulberry tree, 'May you be uprooted and thrown into the sea,' and it would obey you!

7"When a servant comes in from plowing or taking care of sheep, does his master say, 'Come in and eat with me'? 8No, he says, 'Prepare my meal, put on your apron, and serve me while I eat. Then you can eat later.' 9And does the master thank the servant for doing what he was told to do? Of course not. 10In the same way, when you obey me you should say, 'We are unworthy servants who have simply done our duty.'"

Ten Healed of Leprosy

11As Jesus continued on toward Jerusalem, he reached the border between Galilee and Samaria. 12As he entered a village there, ten lepers stood at a distance, 13crying out, "Jesus, Master, have mercy on us!"

14He looked at them and said, "Go show yourselves to the priests." And as they went, they were cleansed of their leprosy.

15One of them, when he saw that he was healed, came back to Jesus, shouting, "Praise God!" 16He fell to the ground at Jesus' feet, thanking him for what he had done. This man was a Samaritan.

17Jesus asked, "Didn't I heal ten men? Where are the other nine? 18Has no one returned to give glory to God except this foreigner?" 19And Jesus said to the man, "Stand up and go. Your faith has healed you."

The Coming of the Kingdom

20One day the Pharisees asked Jesus, "When will the Kingdom of God come?"

Jesus replied, "The Kingdom of God can't be detected by visible signs. 21You won't be able to say, 'Here it is!' or 'It's over there!' For the Kingdom of God is already among you."

22Then he said to his disciples, "The time is coming when you will long to see the day when the Son of Man returns, but you won't see it.

23People will tell you, 'Look, there is the Son of Man,' or 'Here he is,' but don't go out and follow them. 24For as the lightning flashes and lights up the sky from one end to the other, so it will be on the day when the Son of Man comes. 25But first the Son of Man must suffer terribly and be rejected by this generation.

26"When the Son of Man returns, it will be like it was in Noah's day. 27In those days, the people enjoyed banquets and parties and weddings right up to the time Noah entered his boat and the flood came and destroyed them all.

28"And the world will be as it was in the days of Lot. People went about their daily business—eating and drinking, buying and selling, farming and building—29until the morning Lot left Sodom. Then fire and burning sulfur rained down from heaven and destroyed them all. 30Yes, it will be 'business as usual' right up to the day when the Son of Man is revealed. 31On that day a person out on the deck of a roof must not go down into the house to pack. A person out in the field must not return home. 32Remember what happened to Lot's wife! 33If you cling to your life, you will lose it, and if you let your life go, you will save it. 34That night two people will be asleep in one bed; one will be taken, the other left. 35Two women will be grinding flour together at the mill; one will be taken, the other left.*"

37"Where will this happen, Lord?" the disciples asked.

Jesus replied, "Just as the gathering of vultures shows there is a carcass nearby, so these signs indicate that the end is near."

CHAPTER **18**
Parable of the Persistent Widow

One day Jesus told his disciples a story to show that they should always pray and never give up. 2"There was a judge in a certain city," he said, "who neither feared God nor cared about people. 3A widow of that city came to him repeatedly, saying, 'Give me justice in this dispute with my enemy.' 4The judge ignored her for a while, but finally he said to himself, 'I don't fear God or care about people, 5but this woman is driving me crazy. I'm going to see that she gets justice, because she is wearing me out with her constant requests!'"

6Then the Lord said, "Learn a lesson from this unjust judge. 7Even he rendered a just decision

17:35 Some manuscripts add verse 36, *Two men will be working in the field; one will be taken, the other left.* Compare Matt 24:40.

When you were a little kid, did you ever take your parent's hand to cross the street? Little kids trust their parents. So what's that got to do with the Bible? **Read LUKE 18:15-17 to find out.** Jesus wants everyone (even grown-ups!) to have faith like little kids. We *all* need Jesus, *all* the time! Here's something to remind you that Jesus wants you to trust him the same way little kids trust their parents.

Read Romans 5:1-2 for more about faith!

1 Write "JESUS" in the middle of a sheet of construction paper. Draw a heart around his name.

2 Get a picture of yourself when you were little. Tape it to the left side of the paper.

3 Now get a recent picture of yourself. Tape it to the right side of the paper.

4 Decorate your paper any way you want.

Hang your paper in your room to remind you to have "little kid" faith in Jesus!

in the end. So don't you think God will surely give justice to his chosen people who cry out to him day and night? Will he keep putting them off? 8I tell you, he will grant justice to them quickly! But when the Son of Man returns, how many will he find on the earth who have faith?"

Parable of the Pharisee and Tax Collector

9Then Jesus told this story to some who had great confidence in their own righteousness and scorned everyone else: 10"Two men went to the Temple to pray. One was a Pharisee, and the other was a despised tax collector. 11The Pharisee stood by himself and prayed this prayer: 'I thank you, God, that I am not a sinner like everyone else. For I don't cheat, I don't sin, and I don't commit adultery. I'm certainly not like that tax collector! 12I fast twice a week, and I give you a tenth of my income.'

13"But the tax collector stood at a distance and dared not even lift his eyes to heaven as he prayed. Instead, he beat his chest in sorrow, saying, 'O God, be merciful to me, for I am a sinner.' 14I tell you, this sinner, not the Pharisee, returned home justified before God. For those who exalt themselves will be humbled, and those who humble themselves will be exalted."

Jesus Blesses the Children

15One day some parents brought their little children to Jesus so he could touch and bless them. But when the disciples saw this, they scolded the parents for bothering him.

16Then Jesus called for the children and said to the disciples, "Let the children come to me. Don't stop them! For the Kingdom of God belongs to those who are like these children. 17I tell you the truth, anyone who doesn't receive the Kingdom of God like a child will never enter it."

The Rich Man

18Once a religious leader asked Jesus this question: "Good Teacher, what should I do to inherit eternal life?"

19"Why do you call me good?" Jesus asked him. "Only God is truly good. 20But to answer your question, you know the commandments: 'You must not commit adultery. You must not murder. You must not steal. You must not testify falsely. Honor your father and mother.'"

21The man replied, "I've obeyed all these commandments since I was young."

22When Jesus heard his answer, he said, "There is still one thing you haven't done. Sell all your possessions and give the money to the poor, and you will have treasure in heaven. Then come, follow me."

23But when the man heard this he became very sad, for he was very rich.

24When Jesus saw this, he said, "How hard it is for the rich to enter the Kingdom of God! 25In fact, it is easier for a camel to go through the eye of a needle than for a rich person to enter the Kingdom of God!"

26Those who heard this said, "Then who in the world can be saved?"

27He replied, "What is impossible for people is possible with God."

28Peter said, "We've left our homes to follow you."

29"Yes," Jesus replied, "and I assure you that everyone who has given up house or wife or brothers or parents or children, for the sake of the Kingdom of God, 30will be repaid many times over in this life, and will have eternal life in the world to come."

Jesus Again Predicts His Death

31Taking the twelve disciples aside, Jesus said, "Listen, we're going up to Jerusalem, where all the predictions of the prophets concerning the Son of Man will come true. 32He will be handed over to the Romans, and he will be mocked, treated shamefully, and spit upon. 33They will flog him with a whip and kill him, but on the third day he will rise again."

34But they didn't understand any of this. The significance of his words was hidden from them, and they failed to grasp what he was talking about.

Jesus Heals a Blind Beggar

35As Jesus approached Jericho, a blind beggar was sitting beside the road. 36When he heard the noise of a crowd going past, he asked what was happening. 37They told him that Jesus the Nazarene was going by. 38So he began shouting, "Jesus, Son of David, have mercy on me!"

39"Be quiet!" the people in front yelled at him.

But he only shouted louder, "Son of David, have mercy on me!"

40When Jesus heard him, he stopped and ordered that the man be brought to him. As the man came near, Jesus asked him, 41"What do you want me to do for you?"

"Lord," he said, "I want to see!"

42And Jesus said, "All right, receive your sight! Your faith has healed you." 43Instantly the man could see, and he followed Jesus, praising God. And all who saw it praised God, too.

CHAPTER 19

Jesus and Zacchaeus

Jesus entered Jericho and made his way through the town. ²There was a man there named Zacchaeus. He was the chief tax collector in the region, and he had become very rich. ³He tried to get a look at Jesus, but he was too short to see over the crowd. ⁴So he ran ahead and climbed a sycamore-fig tree beside the road, for Jesus was going to pass that way.

⁵When Jesus came by, he looked up at Zacchaeus and called him by name. "Zacchaeus!" he said. "Quick, come down! I must be a guest in your home today."

⁶Zacchaeus quickly climbed down and took Jesus to his house in great excitement and joy. ⁷But the people were displeased. "He has gone to be the guest of a notorious sinner," they grumbled.

⁸Meanwhile, Zacchaeus stood before the Lord and said, "I will give half my wealth to the poor, Lord, and if I have cheated people on their taxes, I will give them back four times as much!"

⁹Jesus responded, "Salvation has come to this home today, for this man has shown himself to be a true son of Abraham. ¹⁰**For the Son of Man came to seek and save those who are lost.**"

Parable of the Ten Servants

¹¹The crowd was listening to everything Jesus said. And because he was nearing Jerusalem, he told them a story to correct the impression that the Kingdom of God would begin right away. ¹²He said, "A nobleman was called away to a distant empire to be crowned king and then return. ¹³Before he left, he called together ten of his servants and divided among them ten pounds of silver, saying, 'Invest this for me while I am gone.' ¹⁴But his people hated him and sent a delegation after him to say, 'We do not want him to be our king.'

¹⁵"After he was crowned king, he returned and called in the servants to whom he had given the money. He wanted to find out what their profits were. ¹⁶The first servant reported, 'Master, I invested your money and made ten times the original amount!'

¹⁷"'Well done!' the king exclaimed. 'You are a good servant. You have been faithful with the little I entrusted to you, so you will be governor of ten cities as your reward.'

¹⁸"The next servant reported, 'Master, I invested your money and made five times the original amount.'

¹⁹"'Well done!' the king said. 'You will be governor over five cities.'

²⁰"But the third servant brought back only the original amount of money and said, 'Master, I hid your money and kept it safe. ²¹I was afraid because you are a hard man to deal with, taking what isn't yours and harvesting crops you didn't plant.'

²²"'You wicked servant!' the king roared. 'Your own words condemn you. If you knew that I'm a hard man who takes what isn't mine and harvests crops I didn't plant, ²³why didn't you deposit my money in the bank? At least I could have gotten some interest on it.'

²⁴"Then, turning to the others standing nearby, the king ordered, 'Take the money from this servant, and give it to the one who has ten pounds.'

²⁵"'But, master,' they said, 'he already has ten pounds!'

²⁶"'Yes,' the king replied, 'and to those who use well what they are given, even more will be given. But from those who do nothing, even what little they have will be taken away. ²⁷And as for these enemies of mine who didn't want me to be their king—bring them in and execute them right here in front of me.'"

Jesus' Triumphant Entry

²⁸After telling this story, Jesus went on toward Jerusalem, walking ahead of his disciples. ²⁹As he came to the towns of Bethphage and Bethany on the Mount of Olives, he sent two disciples ahead. ³⁰"Go into that village over there," he told them. "As you enter it, you will see a young donkey tied there that no one has ever ridden. Untie it and bring it here. ³¹If anyone asks, 'Why are you untying that colt?' just say, 'The Lord needs it.'"

³²So they went and found the colt, just as Jesus had said. ³³And sure enough, as they were untying it, the owners asked them, "Why are you untying that colt?"

³⁴And the disciples simply replied, "The Lord needs it." ³⁵So they brought the colt to Jesus and threw their garments over it for him to ride on.

³⁶As he rode along, the crowds spread out their garments on the road ahead of him. ³⁷When he reached the place where the road started down the Mount of Olives, all of his followers began to shout and sing as they walked along, praising God for all the wonderful miracles they had seen.

38 "Blessings on the King who comes in the
name of the LORD!
Peace in heaven, and glory in highest
heaven!"

39 But some of the Pharisees among the crowd said, "Teacher, rebuke your followers for saying things like that!"

40 He replied, "If they kept quiet, the stones along the road would burst into cheers!"

Jesus Weeps over Jerusalem

41 But as he came closer to Jerusalem and saw the city ahead, he began to weep. 42 "How I wish today that you of all people would understand the way to peace. But now it is too late, and peace is hidden from your eyes. 43 Before long your enemies will build ramparts against your walls and encircle you and close in on you from every side. 44 They will crush you into the ground, and your children with you. Your enemies will not leave a single stone in place, because you did not accept your opportunity for salvation."

Jesus Clears the Temple

45 Then Jesus entered the Temple and began to drive out the people selling animals for sacrifices. 46 He said to them, "The Scriptures declare, 'My Temple will be a house of prayer,' but you have turned it into a den of thieves."

47 After that, he taught daily in the Temple, but the leading priests, the teachers of religious law, and the other leaders of the people began planning how to kill him. 48 But they could think of nothing, because all the people hung on every word he said.

CHAPTER 20
The Authority of Jesus Challenged

One day as Jesus was teaching the people and preaching the Good News in the Temple, the leading priests, the teachers of religious law, and the elders came up to him. 2 They demanded, "By what authority are you doing all these things? Who gave you the right?"

3 "Let me ask you a question first," he replied. 4 "Did John's authority to baptize come from heaven, or was it merely human?"

5 They talked it over among themselves. "If we say it was from heaven, he will ask why we didn't believe John. 6 But if we say it was merely human, the people will stone us because they are convinced John was a prophet." 7 So they finally replied that they didn't know.

CLEAN UP Your Act

Have you ever done something wrong? A guy named Zacchaeus had done a *lot* wrong. **Read LUKE 19:1-9 for details.**

Jesus didn't wait for Zacchaeus to stop sinning before he called to him. It's the same with us. We don't have to clean up our lives before we get to know Jesus.

JESUS CALLS TO US JUST THE WAY WE ARE.

1 Pour a cup of water into a glass. Add a few drops of red food coloring. This red water represents your sinful life.

2 Now use food coloring to make a glass of blue water. The blue water can represent Jesus.

3 Pour the blue water into the red water.

Read Romans 3:21-22 to read more about being made clean!

LOOK— A BIG CHANGE!

When we follow Jesus, he makes big changes in our lives.

Jesus changed Zacchaeus, and he can change you, too!

8 And Jesus responded, "Then I won't tell you by what authority I do these things."

Parable of the Evil Farmers

9 Now Jesus turned to the people again and told them this story: "A man planted a vineyard, leased it to tenant farmers, and moved to another country to live for several years. 10 At the time of the grape harvest, he sent one of his servants to collect his share of the crop. But the farmers attacked the servant, beat him up, and sent him back empty-handed. 11 So the owner sent another servant, but they also insulted him, beat him up, and sent him away empty-handed. 12 A third man was sent, and they wounded him and chased him away.

13 "'What will I do?' the owner asked himself.

'I know! I'll send my cherished son. Surely they will respect him.'

14"But when the tenant farmers saw his son, they said to each other, 'Here comes the heir to this estate. Let's kill him and get the estate for ourselves!' 15So they dragged him out of the vineyard and murdered him.

"What do you suppose the owner of the vineyard will do to them?" Jesus asked. 16"I'll tell you—he will come and kill those farmers and lease the vineyard to others."

"How terrible that such a thing should ever happen," his listeners protested.

17Jesus looked at them and said, "Then what does this Scripture mean?

'The stone that the builders rejected
    has now become the cornerstone.'

18Everyone who stumbles over that stone will be broken to pieces, and it will crush anyone it falls on."

19The teachers of religious law and the leading priests wanted to arrest Jesus immediately because they realized he was telling the story against them—they were the wicked farmers. But they were afraid of the people's reaction.

Taxes for Caesar

20Watching for their opportunity, the leaders sent spies pretending to be honest men. They tried to get Jesus to say something that could be reported to the Roman governor so he would arrest Jesus. 21"Teacher," they said, "we know that you speak and teach what is right and are not influenced by what others think. You teach the way of God truthfully. 22Now tell us—is it right for us to pay taxes to Caesar or not?"

23He saw through their trickery and said, 24"Show me a Roman coin. Whose picture and title are stamped on it?"

"Caesar's," they replied.

25"Well then," he said, "give to Caesar what belongs to Caesar, and give to God what belongs to God."

26So they failed to trap him by what he said in front of the people. Instead, they were amazed by his answer, and they became silent.

Discussion about Resurrection

27Then Jesus was approached by some Sadducees—religious leaders who say there is no resurrection from the dead. 28They posed this question: "Teacher, Moses gave us a law that if a man dies, leaving a wife but no children, his brother should marry the widow and have a child who will carry on the brother's name. 29Well, suppose there were seven brothers. The oldest one married and then died without children. 30So the second brother married the widow, but he also died. 31Then the third brother married her. This continued with all seven of them, who died without children. 32Finally, the woman also died. 33So tell us, whose wife will she be in the resurrection? For all seven were married to her!"

34Jesus replied, "Marriage is for people here on earth. 35But in the age to come, those worthy of being raised from the dead will neither marry nor be given in marriage. 36And they will never die again. In this respect they will be like angels. They are children of God and children of the resurrection.

37"But now, as to whether the dead will be raised—even Moses proved this when he wrote about the burning bush. Long after Abraham, Isaac, and Jacob had died, he referred to the Lord as 'the God of Abraham, the God of Isaac, and the God of Jacob.' 38So he is the God of the living, not the dead, for they are all alive to him."

39"Well said, Teacher!" remarked some of the teachers of religious law who were standing there. 40And then no one dared to ask him any more questions.

Whose Son Is the Messiah?

41Then Jesus presented them with a question. "Why is it," he asked, "that the Messiah is said to be the son of David? 42For David himself wrote in the book of Psalms:

'The LORD said to my Lord,
    Sit in the place of honor at my
        right hand
43 until I humble your enemies,
    making them a footstool under
        your feet.'

44Since David called the Messiah 'Lord,' how can the Messiah be his son?"

45Then, with the crowds listening, he turned to his disciples and said, 46"Beware of these teachers of religious law! For they like to parade around in flowing robes and love to receive respectful greetings as they walk in the marketplaces. And how they love the seats of honor in the synagogues and the head table at banquets. 47Yet they shamelessly cheat widows out of their property and then pretend to be pious by making long prayers in public. Because of this, they will be severely punished."

CHAPTER **21**

The Widow's Offering

While Jesus was in the Temple, he watched the rich people dropping their gifts in the collection box. ²Then a poor widow came by and dropped in two small coins.

³"I tell you the truth," Jesus said, "this poor widow has given more than all the rest of them. ⁴For they have given a tiny part of their surplus, but she, poor as she is, has given everything she has."

Jesus Foretells the Future

⁵Some of his disciples began talking about the majestic stonework of the Temple and the memorial decorations on the walls. But Jesus said, ⁶"The time is coming when all these things will be completely demolished. Not one stone will be left on top of another!"

⁷"Teacher," they asked, "when will all this happen? What sign will show us that these things are about to take place?"

⁸He replied, "Don't let anyone mislead you, for many will come in my name, claiming, 'I am the Messiah,' and saying, 'The time has come!' But don't believe them. ⁹And when you hear of wars and insurrections, don't panic. Yes, these things must take place first, but the end won't follow immediately." ¹⁰Then he added, "Nation will go to war against nation, and kingdom against kingdom. ¹¹There will be great earthquakes, and there will be famines and plagues in many lands, and there will be terrifying things and great miraculous signs from heaven.

¹²"But before all this occurs, there will be a time of great persecution. You will be dragged into synagogues and prisons, and you will stand trial before kings and governors because you are my followers. ¹³But this will be your opportunity to tell them about me. ¹⁴So don't worry in advance about how to answer the charges against you, ¹⁵for I will give you the right words and such wisdom that none of your opponents will be able to reply or refute you! ¹⁶Even those closest to you—your parents, brothers, relatives, and friends—will betray you. They will even kill some of you. ¹⁷And everyone will hate you because you are my followers. ¹⁸But not a hair of your head will perish! ¹⁹By standing firm, you will win your souls.

²⁰"And when you see Jerusalem surrounded by armies, then you will know that the time of its destruction has arrived. ²¹Then those in Judea must flee to the hills. Those in Jerusalem must get out, and those out in the country should not

return to the city. ²²For those will be days of God's vengeance, and the prophetic words of the Scriptures will be fulfilled. ²³How terrible it will be for pregnant women and for nursing mothers in those days. For there will be disaster in the land and great anger against this people. ²⁴They will be killed by the sword or sent away as captives to all the nations of the world. And Jerusalem will be trampled down by the Gentiles until the period of the Gentiles comes to an end.

²⁵"And there will be strange signs in the sun, moon, and stars. And here on earth the nations will be in turmoil, perplexed by the roaring seas and strange tides. ²⁶People will be terrified at what they see coming upon the earth, for the powers in the heavens will be shaken. ²⁷Then everyone will see the Son of Man coming on a cloud with power and great glory. ²⁸So when all these things begin to happen, stand and look up, for your salvation is near!"

²⁹Then he gave them this illustration: "Notice the fig tree, or any other tree. ³⁰When the leaves come out, you know without being told that summer is near. ³¹In the same way, when you see all these things taking place, you can know that the Kingdom of God is near. ³²I tell you the truth, this generation will not pass from the scene until all these things have taken place. ³³Heaven and earth will disappear, but my words will never disappear.

³⁴"Watch out! Don't let your hearts be dulled by carousing and drunkenness, and by the worries of this life. Don't let that day catch you unaware, ³⁵like a trap. For that day will come upon everyone living on the earth. ³⁶Keep alert at all times. And pray that you might be strong enough to escape these coming horrors and stand before the Son of Man."

³⁷Every day Jesus went to the Temple to teach, and each evening he returned to spend the night on the Mount of Olives. ³⁸The crowds gathered at the Temple early each morning to hear him.

CHAPTER **22**

Judas Agrees to Betray Jesus

The Festival of Unleavened Bread, which is also called Passover, was approaching. ²The leading priests and teachers of religious law were plotting how to kill Jesus, but they were afraid of the people's reaction.

³Then Satan entered into Judas Iscariot, who was one of the twelve disciples, ⁴and he went to the leading priests and captains of the Temple guard to discuss the best way to betray Jesus to them. ⁵They were delighted, and they promised

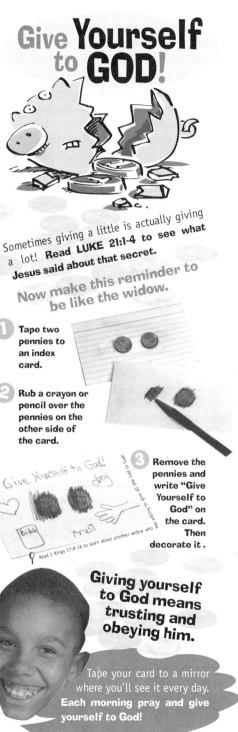

Give **Yourself**
to **GOD!**

Sometimes giving a little is actually giving a lot! **Read LUKE 21:1-4 to see what Jesus said about that secret.**

Now make this reminder to be like the widow.

1 Tape two pennies to an index card.

2 Rub a crayon or pencil over the pennies on the other side of the card.

3 Remove the pennies and write "Give Yourself to God" on the card. Then decorate it .

Give Yourself to God!
obey
Bible
trust

she had to live on. to God!

Read 1 Kings 17:8-16 to learn about another widow who

Giving yourself to God means trusting and obeying him.

Tape your card to a mirror where you'll see it every day. **Each morning pray and give yourself to God!**

to give him money. 6So he agreed and began looking for an opportunity to betray Jesus so they could arrest him when the crowds weren't around.

The Last Supper

7Now the Festival of Unleavened Bread arrived, when the Passover lamb is sacrificed. 8Jesus sent Peter and John ahead and said, "Go and prepare the Passover meal, so we can eat it together."

9"Where do you want us to prepare it?" they asked him.

10He replied, "As soon as you enter Jerusalem, a man carrying a pitcher of water will meet you. Follow him. At the house he enters, 11say to the owner, 'The Teacher asks: Where is the guest room where I can eat the Passover meal with my disciples?' 12He will take you upstairs to a large room that is already set up. That is where you should prepare our meal." 13They went off to the city and found everything just as Jesus had said, and they prepared the Passover meal there.

14When the time came, Jesus and the apostles sat down together at the table. 15Jesus said, "I have been very eager to eat this Passover meal with you before my suffering begins. 16For I tell you now that I won't eat this meal again until its meaning is fulfilled in the Kingdom of God."

17Then he took a cup of wine and gave thanks to God for it. Then he said, "Take this and share it among yourselves. 18For I will not drink wine again until the Kingdom of God has come."

19He took some bread and gave thanks to God for it. Then he broke it in pieces and gave it to the disciples, saying, "This is my body, which is given for you. Do this to remember me."

20After supper he took another cup of wine and said, "This cup is the new covenant between God and his people—an agreement confirmed with my blood, which is poured out as a sacrifice for you.

21"But here at this table, sitting among us as a friend, is the man who will betray me. 22For it has been determined that the Son of Man must die. But what sorrow awaits the one who betrays him." 23The disciples began to ask each other which of them would ever do such a thing.

24Then they began to argue among themselves about who would be the greatest among them. 25Jesus told them, "In this world the kings and great men lord it over their people, yet they are called 'friends of the people.' 26But among you it will be different. Those who are the greatest among you should take the lowest rank, and the leader should be like a servant. 27Who is more important, the one who sits at the table or the one who serves? The one who sits at the table, of course. But not here! For I am among you as one who serves.

28 "You have stayed with me in my time of trial. 29 And just as my Father has granted me a Kingdom, I now grant you the right 30 to eat and drink at my table in my Kingdom. And you will sit on thrones, judging the twelve tribes of Israel.

Jesus Predicts Peter's Denial

31 "Simon, Simon, Satan has asked to sift each of you like wheat. 32 But I have pleaded in prayer for you, Simon, that your faith should not fail. So when you have repented and turned to me again, strengthen your brothers."

33 Peter said, "Lord, I am ready to go to prison with you, and even to die with you."

34 But Jesus said, "Peter, let me tell you something. Before the rooster crows tomorrow morning, you will deny three times that you even know me."

35 Then Jesus asked them, "When I sent you out to preach the Good News and you did not have money, a traveler's bag, or extra clothing, did you need anything?"

"No," they replied.

36 "But now," he said, "take your money and a traveler's bag. And if you don't have a sword, sell your cloak and buy one! 37 For the time has come for this prophecy about me to be fulfilled: 'He was counted among the rebels.' Yes, everything written about me by the prophets will come true."

38 "Look, Lord," they replied, "we have two swords among us."

"That's enough," he said.

Jesus Prays on the Mount of Olives

39 Then, accompanied by the disciples, Jesus left the upstairs room and went as usual to the Mount of Olives. 40 There he told them, "Pray that you will not give in to temptation."

41 He walked away, about a stone's throw, and knelt down and prayed, 42 "Father, if you are willing, please take this cup of suffering away from me. Yet I want your will to be done, not mine." 43 Then an angel from heaven appeared and strengthened him. 44 He prayed more fervently, and he was in such agony of spirit that his sweat fell to the ground like great drops of blood.

45 At last he stood up again and returned to the disciples, only to find them asleep, exhausted from grief. 46 "Why are you sleeping?" he asked

them. "Get up and pray, so that you will not give in to temptation."

Jesus Is Betrayed and Arrested

47 But even as Jesus said this, a crowd approached, led by Judas, one of the twelve disciples. Judas walked over to Jesus to greet him with a kiss. 48 But Jesus said, "Judas, would you betray the Son of Man with a kiss?"

49 When the other disciples saw what was about to happen, they exclaimed, "Lord, should we fight? We brought the swords!" 50 And one of them struck at the high priest's slave, slashing off his right ear.

51 But Jesus said, "No more of this." And he touched the man's ear and healed him.

52 Then Jesus spoke to the leading priests, the captains of the Temple guard, and the elders who had come for him. "Am I some dangerous revolutionary," he asked, "that you come with swords and clubs to arrest me? 53 Why didn't you arrest me in the Temple? I was there every day. But this is your moment, the time when the power of darkness reigns."

Peter Denies Jesus

54 So they arrested him and led him to the high priest's home. And Peter followed at a distance. 55 The guards lit a fire in the middle of the courtyard and sat around it, and Peter joined them there. 56 A servant girl noticed him in the firelight and began staring at him. Finally she said, "This man was one of Jesus' followers!"

57 But Peter denied it. "Woman," he said, "I don't even know him!"

58 After a while someone else looked at him and said, "You must be one of them!"

"No, man, I'm not!" Peter retorted.

59 About an hour later someone else insisted, "This must be one of them, because he is a Galilean, too."

60 But Peter said, "Man, I don't know what you are talking about." And immediately, while he was still speaking, the rooster crowed.

61 At that moment the Lord turned and looked at Peter. Suddenly, the Lord's words flashed through Peter's mind: "Before the rooster crows tomorrow morning, you will deny three times that you even know me." 62 And Peter left the courtyard, weeping bitterly.

63 The guards in charge of Jesus began mocking and beating him. 64 They blindfolded him and said, "Prophesy to us! Who hit you that time?" 65 And they hurled all sorts of terrible insults at him.

Jesus before the Council

66At daybreak all the elders of the people assembled, including the leading priests and the teachers of religious law. Jesus was led before this high council, 67and they said, "Tell us, are you the Messiah?"

But he replied, "If I tell you, you won't believe me. 68And if I ask you a question, you won't answer. 69But from now on the Son of Man will be seated in the place of power at God's right hand."

70They all shouted, "So, are you claiming to be the Son of God?"

And he replied, "You say that I am."

71"Why do we need other witnesses?" they said. "We ourselves heard him say it."

CHAPTER **23**
Jesus' Trial before Pilate

Then the entire council took Jesus to Pilate, the Roman governor. 2They began to state their case: "This man has been leading our people astray by telling them not to pay their taxes to the Roman government and by claiming he is the Messiah, a king."

3So Pilate asked him, "Are you the king of the Jews?"

Jesus replied, "You have said it."

4Pilate turned to the leading priests and to the crowd and said, "I find nothing wrong with this man!"

5Then they became insistent. "But he is causing riots by his teaching wherever he goes—all over Judea, from Galilee to Jerusalem!"

6"Oh, is he a Galilean?" Pilate asked. 7When they said that he was, Pilate sent him to Herod Antipas, because Galilee was under Herod's jurisdiction, and Herod happened to be in Jerusalem at the time.

8Herod was delighted at the opportunity to see Jesus, because he had heard about him and had been hoping for a long time to see him perform a miracle. 9He asked Jesus question after question, but Jesus refused to answer. 10Meanwhile, the leading priests and the teachers of religious law stood there shouting their accusations. 11Then Herod and his soldiers began mocking and ridiculing Jesus. Finally, they put a royal robe on him and sent him back to Pilate. 12(Herod and Pilate, who had been enemies before, became friends that day.)

13Then Pilate called together the leading priests and other religious leaders, along with the people, 14and he announced his verdict. "You brought this man to me, accusing him of leading a revolt. I have examined him thoroughly on this point in your presence and find him innocent. 15Herod came to the same conclusion and sent him back to us. Nothing this man has done calls for the death penalty. 16So I will have him flogged, and then I will release him."*

18Then a mighty roar rose from the crowd, and with one voice they shouted, "Kill him, and release Barabbas to us!" 19(Barabbas was in prison for taking part in an insurrection in Jerusalem against the government, and for murder.) 20Pilate argued with them, because he wanted to release Jesus. 21But they kept shouting, "Crucify him! Crucify him!"

22For the third time he demanded, "Why? What crime has he committed? I have found no reason to sentence him to death. So I will have him flogged, and then I will release him."

23But the mob shouted louder and louder, demanding that Jesus be crucified, and their voices prevailed. 24So Pilate sentenced Jesus to die as they demanded. 25As they had requested, he released Barabbas, the man in prison for insurrection and murder. But he turned Jesus over to them to do as they wished.

The Crucifixion

26As they led Jesus away, a man named Simon, who was from Cyrene, happened to be coming in from the countryside. The soldiers seized him and put the cross on him and made him carry it behind Jesus. 27A large crowd trailed behind, including many grief-stricken women. 28But Jesus turned and said to them, "Daughters of Jerusalem, don't weep for me, but weep for yourselves and for your children. 29For the days are coming when they will say, 'Fortunate indeed are the women who are childless, the wombs that have not borne a child and the breasts that have never nursed.' 30People will beg the mountains, 'Fall on us,' and plead with the hills, 'Bury us.' 31For if these things are done when the tree is green, what will happen when it is dry?"

32Two others, both criminals, were led out to be executed with him. 33When they came to a place called The Skull, they nailed him to the cross. And the criminals were also crucified—one on his right and one on his left.

34Jesus said, "Father, forgive them, for they don't know what they are doing." And the soldiers gambled for his clothes by throwing dice.

35The crowd watched and the leaders scoffed.

23:16 Some manuscripts add verse 17, *Now it was necessary for him to release one prisoner to them during the Passover celebration.* Compare Matt 27:15; Mark 15:6; John 18:39.

"He saved others," they said, "let him save himself if he is really God's Messiah, the Chosen One." 36 The soldiers mocked him, too, by offering him a drink of sour wine. 37 They called out to him, "If you are the King of the Jews, save yourself!" 38 A sign was fastened to the cross above him with these words: "This is the King of the Jews."

39 One of the criminals hanging beside him scoffed, "So you're the Messiah, are you? Prove it by saving yourself—and us, too, while you're at it!"

40 But the other criminal protested, "Don't you fear God even when you have been sentenced to die? 41 We deserve to die for our crimes, but this man hasn't done anything wrong." 42 Then he said, "Jesus, remember me when you come into your Kingdom."

43 And Jesus replied, "I assure you, today you will be with me in paradise."

The Death of Jesus

44 By this time it was noon, and darkness fell across the whole land until three o'clock. 45 The light from the sun was gone. And suddenly, the curtain in the sanctuary of the Temple was torn down the middle. 46 Then Jesus shouted, "Father, I entrust my spirit into your hands!" And with those words he breathed his last.

47 When the Roman officer overseeing the execution saw what had happened, he worshiped God and said, "Surely this man was innocent." 48 And when all the crowd that came to see the crucifixion saw what had happened, they went home in deep sorrow. 49 But Jesus' friends, including the women who had followed him from Galilee, stood at a distance watching.

The Burial of Jesus

50 Now there was a good and righteous man named Joseph. He was a member of the Jewish high council, 51 but he had not agreed with the decision and actions of the other religious leaders. He was from the town of Arimathea in Judea, and he was waiting for the Kingdom of God to come. 52 He went to Pilate and asked for Jesus' body. 53 Then he took the body down from the cross and wrapped it in a long sheet of linen cloth and laid it in a new tomb that had been carved out of rock. 54 This was done late on Friday afternoon, the day of preparation, as the Sabbath was about to begin.

55 As his body was taken away, the women from Galilee followed and saw the tomb where his body was placed. 56 Then they went home and prepared spices and ointments to anoint his body. But by the time they were finished the Sabbath had begun, so they rested as required by the law.

CHAPTER 24

The Resurrection

But very early on Sunday morning the women went to the tomb, taking the spices they had prepared. 2 They found that the stone had been rolled away from the entrance. 3 So they went in, but they didn't find the body of the Lord Jesus. 4 As they stood there puzzled, two men suddenly appeared to them, clothed in dazzling robes.

5 The women were terrified and bowed with their faces to the ground. Then the men asked, "Why are you looking among the dead for someone who is alive? 6 He isn't here! He is risen from the dead! Remember what he told you back in Galilee, 7 that the Son of Man must be betrayed into the hands of sinful men and be crucified, and that he would rise again on the third day."

8 Then they remembered that he had said this. 9 So they rushed back from the tomb to tell his eleven disciples—and everyone else—what had happened. 10 It was Mary Magdalene, Joanna, Mary the mother of James, and several other women who told the apostles what had happened. 11 But the story sounded like nonsense to the men, so they didn't believe it. 12 However, Peter jumped up and ran to the tomb to look. Stooping, he peered in and saw the empty linen wrappings; then he went home again, wondering what had happened.

The Walk to Emmaus

13 That same day two of Jesus' followers were walking to the village of Emmaus, seven miles from Jerusalem. 14 As they walked along they were talking about everything that had happened. 15 As they talked and discussed these things, Jesus himself suddenly came and began walking with them. 16 But God kept them from recognizing him.

17 He asked them, "What are you discussing so intently as you walk along?"

They stopped short, sadness written across their faces. 18 Then one of them, Cleopas, replied, "You must be the only person in Jerusalem who hasn't heard about all the things that have happened there the last few days."

19 "What things?" Jesus asked.

"The things that happened to Jesus, the man from Nazareth," they said. "He was a prophet who did powerful miracles, and he was a mighty teacher in the eyes of God and all the people. [20]But our leading priests and other religious leaders handed him over to be condemned to death, and they crucified him. [21]We had hoped he was the Messiah who had come to rescue Israel. This all happened three days ago.

[22]"Then some women from our group of his followers were at his tomb early this morning, and they came back with an amazing report. [23]They said his body was missing, and they had seen angels who told them Jesus is alive! [24]Some of our men ran out to see, and sure enough, his body was gone, just as the women had said."

[25]Then Jesus said to them, "You foolish people! You find it so hard to believe all that the prophets wrote in the Scriptures. [26]Wasn't it clearly predicted that the Messiah would have to suffer all these things before entering his glory?" [27]Then Jesus took them through the writings of Moses and all the prophets, explaining from all the Scriptures the things concerning himself.

[28]By this time they were nearing Emmaus and the end of their journey. Jesus acted as if he were going on, [29]but they begged him, "Stay the night with us, since it is getting late." So he went home with them. [30]As they sat down to eat, he took the bread and blessed it. Then he broke it and gave it to them. [31]Suddenly, their eyes were opened, and they recognized him. And at that moment he disappeared!

[32]They said to each other, "Didn't our hearts burn within us as he talked with us on the road and explained the Scriptures to us?" [33]And within the hour they were on their way back to Jerusalem. There they found the eleven disciples and the others who had gathered with them, [34]who said, "The Lord has really risen! He appeared to Peter."

Jesus Appears to the Disciples

[35]Then the two from Emmaus told their story of how Jesus had appeared to them as they were walking along the road, and how they had recognized him as he was breaking the bread. [36]And just as they were telling about it, Jesus himself was suddenly standing there among them. "Peace be with you," he said. [37]But the whole group was startled and frightened, thinking they were seeing a ghost!

[38]"Why are you frightened?" he asked. "Why are your hearts filled with doubt? [39]Look at my hands. Look at my feet. You can see that it's really me. Touch me and make sure that I am not a ghost, because ghosts don't have bodies, as you see that I do." [40]As he spoke, he showed them his hands and his feet.

[41]Still they stood there in disbelief, filled with joy and wonder. Then he asked them, "Do you have anything here to eat?" [42]They gave him a piece of broiled fish, [43]and he ate it as they watched.

[44]Then he said, "When I was with you before, I told you that everything written about me in the law of Moses and the prophets and in the Psalms must be fulfilled." [45]Then he opened their minds to understand the Scriptures. [46]And he said, "Yes, it was written long ago that the Messiah would suffer and die and rise from the dead on the third day. [47]It was also written that this message would be proclaimed in the authority of his name to all the nations, beginning in Jerusalem: 'There is forgiveness of sins for all who repent.' [48]You are witnesses of all these things.

[49]"And now I will send the Holy Spirit, just as my Father promised. But stay here in the city until the Holy Spirit comes and fills you with power from heaven."

The Ascension

[50]Then Jesus led them to Bethany, and lifting his hands to heaven, he blessed them. [51]While he was blessing them, he left them and was taken up to heaven. [52]So they worshiped him and then returned to Jerusalem filled with great joy. [53]And they spent all of their time in the Temple, praising God.

JOHN
Jesus Is the Son of God!

Look for **3** hidden messages in John!

All of the Gospels reveal that Jesus is the Son of God. But the book of John really focuses on that fact. John also tells about some miracles Jesus did that the other Gospels don't mention. Look for

- **WATER TO WINE**
- **MUD IN YOUR EYE**
- **A SUPER SUPPER**
- **A FISHING FRENZY**
- **EMPTY TOMBS**

It's Not the Pots!

What's so special about these stone pots? Nothing!

But something special happened *in* the pots. **Find out what it was by reading John 2:1-11.**

Here's Mud in Your Eye

Take one blind man. Add one part dirt, two parts spit, and, oh yeah, the one and only Son of God, and what do you get? **Find out in John 9:1-12! (For the whole story, read the whole chapter.)**

This Says It All

Did you ever wish for a Bible verse that sums it all up for you?

Have you ever wanted to tell someone about your faith but didn't know quite what to say?

Does God have a verse for you! **Check it out in John 3:16!**

LAZARUS' TOMB

VACANCY

HEY, Wasn't This Guy Dead?

The obituary that said "Lazarus Dies" was wrong. Well, it was right for a while, because he *did* die. But he didn't *stay* dead. **Confused? You won't be after you read John 11:38-44!**

A Special Supper

It was a special supper because it was the Passover meal. It was even more special because it was the last supper they would share together. And it was even *more* special because of what Jesus did at this supper. **Get all the details in John 13:1-20!**

Dead...or Alive!

Jesus had died. His followers had placed his body in a tomb.

So why wasn't his body *still* in the tomb?

Read John's eyewitness account of the most amazing event in the history of the world! **It's in John 20:1-18.**

Go to Your Room

In heaven, going to your room will be a good thing! **Read all about it in John 14:1-3.**

Which room is Mine?!

Timeline

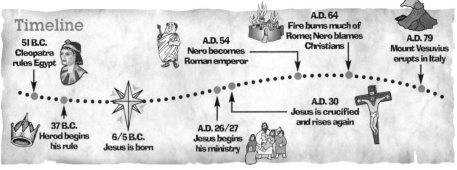

51 B.C. Cleopatra rules Egypt

37 B.C. Herod begins his rule

6/5 B.C. Jesus is born

A.D. 26/27 Jesus begins his ministry

A.D. 30 Jesus is crucified and rises again

A.D. 54 Nero becomes Roman emperor

A.D. 64 Fire burns much of Rome; Nero blames Christians

A.D. 79 Mount Vesuvius erupts in Italy

The JESUS CONNECTION

The book of John shows without question who Jesus really is—the Son of God, the living Savior! As you read this book, remember that the powerful Savior who once walked on earth and did many miracles is still with us today. He is powerful and loving enough to help you through tough times. And more than anything, he wants to have a relationship with you. **Ask God to help you get to know and love his Son more and more.**

CHAPTER **1**

Prologue: Christ, the Eternal Word

1 In the beginning the Word
already existed.
The Word was with God,
and the Word was God.
2 He existed in the beginning
with God.
3 God created everything through him,
and nothing was created except
through him.
4 The Word gave life to everything that
was created,
and his life brought light to everyone.
5 The light shines in the darkness,
and the darkness can never extinguish it.

6 God sent a man, John the Baptist, 7 to tell about the light so that everyone might believe because of his testimony. 8 John himself was not the light; he was simply a witness to tell about the light. 9 The one who is the true light, who gives light to everyone, was coming into the world.

10 He came into the very world he created, but the world didn't recognize him. 11 He came to his own people, and even they rejected him. 12 But to all who believed him and accepted him, he gave the right to become children of God. 13 They are reborn—not with a physical birth resulting from human passion or plan, but a birth that comes from God.

14 So the Word became human and made his home among us. He was full of unfailing love and faithfulness. And we have seen his glory, the glory of the Father's one and only Son.

15 John testified about him when he shouted to the crowds, "This is the one I was talking about when I said, 'Someone is coming after me who is far greater than I am, for he existed long before me.'"

16 From his abundance we have all received one gracious blessing after another. 17 For the law was given through Moses, but God's unfailing love and faithfulness came through Jesus Christ. 18 No one has ever seen God. But the unique One, who is himself God, is near to the Father's heart. He has revealed God to us.

The Testimony of John the Baptist

19 This was John's testimony when the Jewish leaders sent priests and Temple assistants from Jerusalem to ask John, "Who are you?" 20 He came right out and said, "I am not the Messiah."

21 "Well then, who are you?" they asked. "Are you Elijah?"

"No," he replied.

"Are you the Prophet we are expecting?"

"No."

22 "Then who are you? We need an answer for those who sent us. What do you have to say about yourself?"

23 John replied in the words of the prophet Isaiah:

"I am a voice shouting in the wilderness,
'Clear the way for the LORD's coming!'"

24 Then the Pharisees who had been sent 25 asked him, "If you aren't the Messiah or Elijah or the Prophet, what right do you have to baptize?"

26 John told them, "I baptize with water, but right here in the crowd is someone you do not recognize. 27 Though his ministry follows mine, I'm not even worthy to be his slave and untie the straps of his sandal."

28 This encounter took place in Bethany, an area east of the Jordan River, where John was baptizing.

Jesus, the Lamb of God

29 The next day John saw Jesus coming toward him and said, "Look! The Lamb of God who takes away the sin of the world! 30 He is the one I was talking about when I said, 'A man is coming after me who is far greater than I am, for he existed long before me.' 31 I did not recognize him as the Messiah, but I have been baptizing with water so that he might be revealed to Israel."

32 Then John testified, "I saw the Holy Spirit descending like a dove from heaven and resting upon him. 33 I didn't know he was the one, but when God sent me to baptize with water, he told me, 'The one on whom you see the Spirit descend and rest is the one who will baptize with the Holy Spirit.' 34 I saw this happen to Jesus, so I testify that he is the Chosen One of God."

The First Disciples

35 The following day John was again standing with two of his disciples. 36 As Jesus walked by, John looked at him and declared, "Look! There is the Lamb of God!" 37 When John's two disciples heard this, they followed Jesus.

38 Jesus looked around and saw them following. "What do you want?" he asked them.

Three in One 3

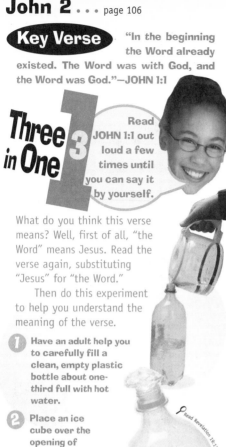

Read JOHN 1:1 out loud a few times until you can say it by yourself.

What do you think this verse means? Well, first of all, "the Word" means Jesus. Read the verse again, substituting "Jesus" for "the Word."

Then do this experiment to help you understand the meaning of the verse.

1. Have an adult help you to carefully fill a clean, empty plastic bottle about one-third full with hot water.

2. Place an ice cube over the opening of the bottle.

Read Revelation 19:13 for more on Jesus as the Word of God.

WHAT HAPPENS? Fog begins to develop. That's three different forms of water— fog, ice, and water— but they're all still water. It's sort of the same with God, Jesus, and the Holy Spirit. All three are God, but each is a distinct person. **Now read JOHN 1:1 again, and then read JOHN 1:14.** Below, write the verses in your own words.

_____
_____
_____

They replied, "Rabbi" (which means "Teacher"), "where are you staying?"

39"Come and see," he said. It was about four o'clock in the afternoon when they went with him to the place where he was staying, and they remained with him the rest of the day.

40Andrew, Simon Peter's brother, was one of these men who heard what John said and then followed Jesus. 41Andrew went to find his brother, Simon, and told him, "We have found the Messiah" (which means "Christ").

42Then Andrew brought Simon to meet Jesus. Looking intently at Simon, Jesus said, "Your name is Simon, son of John—but you will be called Cephas" (which means "Peter").

43The next day Jesus decided to go to Galilee. He found Philip and said to him, "Come, follow me." 44Philip was from Bethsaida, Andrew and Peter's hometown.

45Philip went to look for Nathanael and told him, "We have found the very person Moses and the prophets wrote about! His name is Jesus, the son of Joseph from Nazareth."

46"Nazareth!" exclaimed Nathanael. "Can anything good come from Nazareth?"

"Come and see for yourself," Philip replied.

47As they approached, Jesus said, "Now here is a genuine son of Israel—a man of complete integrity."

48"How do you know about me?" Nathanael asked.

Jesus replied, "I could see you under the fig tree before Philip found you."

49Then Nathanael exclaimed, "Rabbi, you are the Son of God—the King of Israel!"

50Jesus asked him, "Do you believe this just because I told you I had seen you under the fig tree? You will see greater things than this." 51Then he said, "I tell you the truth, you will all see heaven open and the angels of God going up and down on the Son of Man, the one who is the stairway between heaven and earth."

CHAPTER **2**
The Wedding at Cana

The next day there was a wedding celebration in the village of Cana in Galilee. Jesus' mother was there, 2and Jesus and his disciples were also invited to the celebration. 3The wine supply ran out during the festivities, so Jesus' mother told him, "They have no more wine."

4"Dear woman, that's not our problem," Jesus replied. "My time has not yet come."

5But his mother told the servants, "Do whatever he tells you."

⁶Standing nearby were six stone water jars, used for Jewish ceremonial washing. Each could hold twenty to thirty gallons. ⁷Jesus told the servants, "Fill the jars with water." When the jars had been filled, ⁸he said, "Now dip some out, and take it to the master of ceremonies." So the servants followed his instructions.

⁹When the master of ceremonies tasted the water that was now wine, not knowing where it had come from (though, of course, the servants knew), he called the bridegroom over. ¹⁰"A host always serves the best wine first," he said. "Then, when everyone has had a lot to drink, he brings out the less expensive wine. But you have kept the best until now!"

¹¹This miraculous sign at Cana in Galilee was the first time Jesus revealed his glory. And his disciples believed in him.

¹²After the wedding he went to Capernaum for a few days with his mother, his brothers, and his disciples.

Jesus Clears the Temple

¹³It was nearly time for the Jewish Passover celebration, so Jesus went to Jerusalem. ¹⁴In the Temple area he saw merchants selling cattle, sheep, and doves for sacrifices; he also saw dealers at tables exchanging foreign money. ¹⁵Jesus made a whip from some ropes and chased them all out of the Temple. He drove out the sheep and cattle, scattered the money changers' coins over the floor, and turned over their tables. ¹⁶Then, going over to the people who sold doves, he told them, "Get these things out of here. Stop turning my Father's house into a marketplace!"

¹⁷Then his disciples remembered this prophecy from the Scriptures: "Passion for God's house will consume me."

¹⁸But the Jewish leaders demanded, "What are you doing? If God gave you authority to do this, show us a miraculous sign to prove it."

¹⁹"All right," Jesus replied. "Destroy this temple, and in three days I will raise it up."

²⁰"What!" they exclaimed. "It has taken forty-six years to build this Temple, and you can rebuild it in three days?" ²¹But when Jesus said "this temple," he meant his own body. ²²After he was raised from the dead, his disciples remembered he had said this, and they believed both the Scriptures and what Jesus had said.

Jesus and Nicodemus

²³Because of the miraculous signs Jesus did in Jerusalem at the Passover celebration, many began to trust in him. ²⁴But Jesus didn't trust

A Wonderful Wedding

Find JOHN 2:1-12, and read about Jesus' very first miracle!

Jesus turned water into wine. You can't do that, but you *can* turn something red. Here's how!

Have an adult help gather these supplies:
- shallow pan
- small bowl
- ¹/₄ cup liquid dish soap
- ¹/₂ cup vinegar
- 1 tablespoon baking soda
- 1 cup water
- 1 packet of red powdered drink mix

Cover a table with newspaper.

1 Pour the dish soap and vinegar into the bowl, and set it inside the shallow pan.

2 In a separate container, add the baking soda to the water and stir. Sprinkle some of the powdered drink mix into the water and baking soda until it turns dark red like wine.

3 Slowly pour the water mixture into the soap and vinegar mixture, and watch as it erupts into a foaming red volcano!

SURPRISED?

The chemical reaction that made your cool red volcano was *nothing* compared to Jesus turning water into wine!

Use the red foam and a paintbrush to paint the words, **"Jesus can do anything!"** on a sheet of paper. Hang the paper in your room to remind you of Jesus' first miracle!

them, because he knew human nature. 25No one needed to tell him what mankind is really like.

CHAPTER 3

There was a man named Nicodemus, a Jewish religious leader who was a Pharisee. 2After dark one evening, he came to speak with Jesus. "Rabbi," he said, "we all know that God has sent you to teach us. Your miraculous signs are evidence that God is with you."

3Jesus replied, "I tell you the truth, unless you are born again, you cannot see the Kingdom of God."

4"What do you mean?" exclaimed Nicodemus. "How can an old man go back into his mother's womb and be born again?"

5Jesus replied, "I assure you, no one can enter the Kingdom of God without being born of water and the Spirit. 6Humans can reproduce only human life, but the Holy Spirit gives birth to spiritual life. 7So don't be surprised when I say, 'You must be born again.' 8The wind blows wherever it wants. Just as you can hear the wind but can't tell where it comes from or where it is going, so you can't explain how people are born of the Spirit."

9"How are these things possible?" Nicodemus asked.

10Jesus replied, "You are a respected Jewish teacher, and yet you don't understand these things? 11I assure you, we tell you what we know and have seen, and yet you won't believe our testimony. 12But if you don't believe me when I tell you about earthly things, how can you possibly believe if I tell you about heavenly things? 13No one has ever gone to heaven and returned. But the Son of Man has come down from heaven. 14And as Moses lifted up the bronze snake on a pole in the wilderness, so the Son of Man must be lifted up, 15so that everyone who believes in him will have eternal life.

16**"For God loved the world so much that he gave his one and only Son, so that everyone who believes in him will not perish but have eternal life.** 17God sent his Son into the world not to judge the world, but to save the world through him.

18"There is no judgment against anyone who believes in him. But anyone who does not believe in him has already been judged for not believing in God's one and only Son. 19And the judgment is based on this fact: God's light came into the world, but people loved the darkness more than the light, for their actions were evil. 20All who do evil hate the light and refuse to go near it for fear

Key Verse

"For God loved the world so much that he gave his one and only Son, so that everyone who believes in him will not perish but have eternal life."—JOHN 3:16

Read JOHN 3:16 a bunch of times. Practice saying it out loud too.

God loves us, he sent his Son to save us, and if we believe in Jesus we'll have eternal life with him.

Just so you *really* understand this verse, fill in your name in the blanks below.

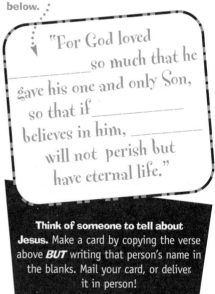

"For God loved _____ so much that he gave his one and only Son, so that if _____ believes in him, _____ will not perish but have eternal life."

Think of someone to tell about Jesus. Make a card by copying the verse above **BUT** writing that person's name in the blanks. Mail your card, or deliver it in person!

their sins will be exposed. 21But those who do what is right come to the light so others can see that they are doing what God wants."

John the Baptist Exalts Jesus

22Then Jesus and his disciples left Jerusalem and went into the Judean countryside. Jesus spent some time with them there, baptizing people.

23 At this time John the Baptist was baptizing at Aenon, near Salim, because there was plenty of water there; and people kept coming to him for baptism. 24(This was before John was thrown into prison.) 25 A debate broke out between John's disciples and a certain Jew over ceremonial cleansing. 26 So John's disciples came to him and said, "Rabbi, the man you met on the other side of the Jordan River, the one you identified as the Messiah, is also baptizing people. And everybody is going to him instead of coming to us."

27 John replied, "No one can receive anything unless God gives it from heaven. 28 You yourselves know how plainly I told you, 'I am not the Messiah. I am only here to prepare the way for him.' 29 It is the bridegroom who marries the bride, and the best man is simply glad to stand with him and hear his vows. Therefore, I am filled with joy at his success. 30 He must become greater and greater, and I must become less and less.

31 "He has come from above and is greater than anyone else. We are of the earth, and we speak of earthly things, but he has come from heaven and is greater than anyone else. 32 He testifies about what he has seen and heard, but how few believe what he tells them! 33 Anyone who accepts his testimony can affirm that God is true. 34 For he is sent by God. He speaks God's words, for God gives him the Spirit without limit. 35 The Father loves his Son and has put everything into his hands. 36 And anyone who believes in God's Son has eternal life. Anyone who doesn't obey the Son will never experience eternal life but remains under God's angry judgment."

CHAPTER **4**

Jesus and the Samaritan Woman

Jesus knew the Pharisees had heard that he was baptizing and making more disciples than John 2(though Jesus himself didn't baptize them—his disciples did). 3 So he left Judea and returned to Galilee.

4 He had to go through Samaria on the way. 5 Eventually he came to the Samaritan village of Sychar, near the field that Jacob gave to his son Joseph. 6 Jacob's well was there; and Jesus, tired from the long walk, sat wearily beside the well about noontime. 7 Soon a Samaritan woman came to draw water, and Jesus said to her, "Please give me a drink." 8 He was alone at the time because his disciples had gone into the village to buy some food.

9 The woman was surprised, for Jews refuse to have anything to do with Samaritans. She said to Jesus, "You are a Jew, and I am a Samaritan woman. Why are you asking me for a drink?"

10 Jesus replied, "If you only knew the gift God has for you and who you are speaking to, you would ask me, and I would give you living water."

11 "But sir, you don't have a rope or a bucket," she said, "and this well is very deep. Where would you get this living water? 12 And besides, do you think you're greater than our ancestor Jacob, who gave us this well? How can you offer better water than he and his sons and his animals enjoyed?"

13 Jesus replied, "Anyone who drinks this water will soon become thirsty again. 14 But those who drink the water I give will never be thirsty again. It becomes a fresh, bubbling spring within them, giving them eternal life."

15 "Please, sir," the woman said, "give me this water! Then I'll never be thirsty again, and I won't have to come here to get water."

16 "Go and get your husband," Jesus told her.

17 "I don't have a husband," the woman replied.

Jesus said, "You're right! You don't have a husband—18 for you have had five husbands, and you aren't even married to the man you're living with now. You certainly spoke the truth!"

19 "Sir," the woman said, "you must be a prophet. 20 So tell me, why is it that you Jews insist that Jerusalem is the only place of worship, while we Samaritans claim it is here at Mount Gerizim, where our ancestors worshiped?"

21 Jesus replied, "Believe me, dear woman, the time is coming when it will no longer matter whether you worship the Father on this mountain or in Jerusalem. 22 You Samaritans know very little about the one you worship, while we Jews know all about him, for salvation comes through the Jews. 23 But the time is coming—indeed it's here now—when true worshipers will worship the Father in spirit and in truth. The Father is looking for those who will worship him that way. 24 For God is Spirit, so those who worship him must worship in spirit and in truth."

25 The woman said, "I know the Messiah is coming—the one who is called Christ. When he comes, he will explain everything to us."

26 Then Jesus told her, "I AM the Messiah!"

27 Just then his disciples came back. They were shocked to find him talking to a woman, but none of them had the nerve to ask, "What do you want with her?" or "Why are you talking to

her?" 28The woman left her water jar beside the well and ran back to the village, telling everyone, 29"Come and see a man who told me everything I ever did! Could he possibly be the Messiah?" 30So the people came streaming from the village to see him.

31Meanwhile, the disciples were urging Jesus, "Rabbi, eat something."

32But Jesus replied, "I have a kind of food you know nothing about."

33"Did someone bring him food while we were gone?" the disciples asked each other.

34Then Jesus explained: "My nourishment comes from doing the will of God, who sent me, and from finishing his work. 35You know the saying, 'Four months between planting and harvest.' But I say, wake up and look around. The fields are already ripe for harvest. 36The harvesters are paid good wages, and the fruit they harvest is people brought to eternal life. What joy awaits both the planter and the harvester alike! 37You know the saying, 'One plants and another harvests.' And it's true. 38I sent you to harvest where you didn't plant; others had already done the work, and now you will get to gather the harvest."

Many Samaritans Believe

39Many Samaritans from the village believed in Jesus because the woman had said, "He told me everything I ever did!" 40When they came out to see him, they begged him to stay in their village. So he stayed for two days, 41long enough for many more to hear his message and believe. 42Then they said to the woman, "Now we believe, not just because of what you told us, but because we have heard him ourselves. Now we know that he is indeed the Savior of the world."

Jesus Heals an Official's Son

43At the end of the two days, Jesus went on to Galilee. 44He himself had said that a prophet is not honored in his own hometown. 45Yet the Galileans welcomed him, for they had been in Jerusalem at the Passover celebration and had seen everything he did there.

46As he traveled through Galilee, he came to Cana, where he had turned the water into wine. There was a government official in nearby Capernaum whose son was very sick. 47When he heard that Jesus had come from Judea to Galilee, he went and begged Jesus to come to Capernaum to heal his son, who was about to die.

48Jesus asked, "Will you never believe in me unless you see miraculous signs and wonders?"

49The official pleaded, "Lord, please come now before my little boy dies."

50Then Jesus told him, "Go back home. Your son will live!" And the man believed what Jesus said and started home.

51While the man was on his way, some of his servants met him with the news that his son was alive and well. 52He asked them when the boy had begun to get better, and they replied, "Yesterday afternoon at one o'clock his fever suddenly disappeared!" 53Then the father realized that that was the very time Jesus had told him, "Your son will live." And he and his entire household believed in Jesus. 54This was the second miraculous sign Jesus did in Galilee after coming from Judea.

CHAPTER **5**

Jesus Heals a Lame Man

Afterward Jesus returned to Jerusalem for one of the Jewish holy days. 2Inside the city, near the Sheep Gate, was the pool of Bethesda, with five covered porches. 3Crowds of sick people—blind, lame, or paralyzed—lay on the porches.* 5One of the men lying there had been sick for thirty-eight years. 6When Jesus saw him and knew he had been ill for a long time, he asked him, "Would you like to get well?"

7"I can't, sir," the sick man said, "for I have no one to put me into the pool when the water bubbles up. Someone else always gets there ahead of me."

8Jesus told him, "Stand up, pick up your mat, and walk!"

9Instantly, the man was healed! He rolled up his sleeping mat and began walking! But this miracle happened on the Sabbath, 10so the Jewish leaders objected. They said to the man who was cured, "You can't work on the Sabbath! The law doesn't allow you to carry that sleeping mat!"

11But he replied, "The man who healed me told me, 'Pick up your mat and walk.'"

12"Who said such a thing as that?" they demanded.

13The man didn't know, for Jesus had disappeared into the crowd. 14But afterward Jesus found him in the Temple and told him, "Now you are well; so stop sinning, or something even worse may happen to you." 15Then the man went and told the Jewish leaders that it was Jesus who had healed him.

5:3 Some manuscripts add an expanded conclusion to verse 3 and all of verse 4: *waiting for a certain movement of the water, 4for an angel of the Lord came from time to time and stirred up the water. And the first person to step in after the water was stirred was healed of whatever disease he had.*

Jesus Claims to Be the Son of God

16So the Jewish leaders began harassing Jesus for breaking the Sabbath rules. 17But Jesus replied, "My Father is always working, and so am I." 18So the Jewish leaders tried all the harder to find a way to kill him. For he not only broke the Sabbath, he called God his Father, thereby making himself equal with God.

19So Jesus explained, "I tell you the truth, the Son can do nothing by himself. He does only what he sees the Father doing. Whatever the Father does, the Son also does. 20For the Father loves the Son and shows him everything he is doing. In fact, the Father will show him how to do even greater works than healing this man. Then you will truly be astonished. 21For just as the Father gives life to those he raises from the dead, so the Son gives life to anyone he wants. 22In addition, the Father judges no one. Instead, he has given the Son absolute authority to judge, 23so that everyone will honor the Son, just as they honor the Father. Anyone who does not honor the Son is certainly not honoring the Father who sent him.

24"I tell you the truth, those who listen to my message and believe in God who sent me have eternal life. They will never be condemned for their sins, but they have already passed from death into life.

25"And I assure you that the time is coming, indeed it's here now, when the dead will hear my voice—the voice of the Son of God. And those who listen will live. 26The Father has life in himself, and he has granted that same life-giving power to his Son. 27And he has given him authority to judge everyone because he is the Son of Man. 28Don't be so surprised! Indeed, the time is coming when all the dead in their graves will hear the voice of God's Son, 29and they will rise again. Those who have done good will rise to experience eternal life, and those who have continued in evil will rise to experience judgment. 30I can do nothing on my own. I judge as God tells me. Therefore, my judgment is just, because I carry out the will of the one who sent me, not my own will.

Witnesses to Jesus

31"If I were to testify on my own behalf, my testimony would not be valid. 32But someone else is also testifying about me, and I assure you that everything he says about me is true. 33In fact, you sent investigators to listen to John the Baptist, and his testimony about me was true. 34Of

Living Water

What's the best thing to drink when you're really, really thirsty? Cool, fresh water. Read **JOHN 4:1-26** to see what Jesus said about special living water!

WOW! Jesus said he could offer people living water. That living water is Jesus himself! Because Jesus died on the cross for our sins, we can live forever in heaven. That's what living water is all about.

FIND A FRIEND, AND TOGETHER CREATE A COMMERCIAL FOR THE LIVING WATER OF JESUS.

You need THIS!

You could draw a poster, act out a skit, or record your oices.

1 Make your commercial as convincing as you can.

2 Show or perform your commercial for at least three people. Have your Bible handy so you can read **JOHN 4:13-14** and 26 to your audience!

3 Sit with your friend and enjoy a cold glass of water together. Discuss other ways you can tell people about Jesus. Write your favorite idea here:

NOW COMMIT WITH YOUR FRIEND TO FOLLOW THROUGH!

course, I have no need of human witnesses, but I say these things so you might be saved. 35John was like a burning and shining lamp, and you were excited for a while about his message. 36But I have a greater witness than John—my teachings and my miracles. The Father gave me these works to accomplish, and they prove that he sent me. 37And the Father who sent me has testified about me himself. You have never heard his voice or seen him face to face, 38and you do not have his message in your hearts, because you do not believe me—the one he sent to you.

39"You search the Scriptures because you think they give you eternal life. But the Scriptures point to me! 40Yet you refuse to come to me to receive this life.

41"Your approval means nothing to me, 42because I know you don't have God's love within you. 43For I have come to you in my Father's name, and you have rejected me. Yet if others come in their own name, you gladly welcome them. 44No wonder you can't believe! For you gladly honor each other, but you don't care about the honor that comes from the one who alone is God.

45"Yet it isn't I who will accuse you before the Father. Moses will accuse you! Yes, Moses, in whom you put your hopes. 46If you really believed Moses, you would believe me, because he wrote about me. 47But since you don't believe what he wrote, how will you believe what I say?"

CHAPTER **6**
Jesus Feeds Five Thousand
After this, Jesus crossed over to the far side of the Sea of Galilee, also known as the Sea of Tiberias. 2A huge crowd kept following him wherever he went, because they saw his miraculous signs as he healed the sick. 3Then Jesus climbed a hill and sat down with his disciples around him. 4(It was nearly time for the Jewish Passover celebration.) 5Jesus soon saw a huge crowd of people coming to look for him. Turning to Philip, he asked, "Where can we buy bread to feed all these people?" 6He was testing Philip, for he already knew what he was going to do.

7Philip replied, "Even if we worked for months, we wouldn't have enough money to feed them!"

8Then Andrew, Simon Peter's brother, spoke up. 9"There's a young boy here with five barley loaves and two fish. But what good is that with this huge crowd?"

10"Tell everyone to sit down," Jesus said. So they all sat down on the grassy slopes. (The men alone numbered about 5,000.) 11Then Jesus took the loaves, gave thanks to God, and distributed them to the people. Afterward he did the same with the fish. And they all ate as much as they wanted. 12After everyone was full, Jesus told his disciples, "Now gather the leftovers, so that nothing is wasted." 13So they picked up the pieces and filled twelve baskets with scraps left by the people who had eaten from the five barley loaves.

14When the people saw him do this miraculous sign, they exclaimed, "Surely, he is the Prophet we have been expecting!" 15When Jesus saw that they were ready to force him to be their king, he slipped away into the hills by himself.

Jesus Walks on Water
16That evening Jesus' disciples went down to the shore to wait for him. 17But as darkness fell and Jesus still hadn't come back, they got into the boat and headed across the lake toward Capernaum. 18Soon a gale swept down upon them, and the sea grew very rough. 19They had rowed three or four miles when suddenly they saw Jesus walking on the water toward the boat. They were terrified, 20but he called out to them, "Don't be afraid. I am here!" 21Then they were eager to let him in the boat, and immediately they arrived at their destination!

Jesus, the Bread of Life
22The next day the crowd that had stayed on the far shore saw that the disciples had taken the only boat, and they realized Jesus had not gone with them. 23Several boats from Tiberias landed near the place where the Lord had blessed the bread and the people had eaten. 24So when the crowd saw that neither Jesus nor his disciples were there, they got into the boats and went across to Capernaum to look for him. 25They found him on the other side of the lake and asked, "Rabbi, when did you get here?"

26Jesus replied, "I tell you the truth, you want to be with me because I fed you, not because you understood the miraculous signs. 27But don't be so concerned about perishable things like food. Spend your energy seeking the eternal life that the Son of Man can give you. For God the Father has given me the seal of his approval."

28They replied, "We want to perform God's works, too. What should we do?"

29Jesus told them, "This is the only work God wants from you: Believe in the one he has sent."

30They answered, "Show us a miraculous sign if you want us to believe in you. What can you do? 31After all, our ancestors ate manna while they journeyed through the wilderness! The

Scriptures say, 'Moses gave them bread from heaven to eat.'"

³²Jesus said, "I tell you the truth, Moses didn't give you bread from heaven. My Father did. And now he offers you the true bread from heaven. ³³The true bread of God is the one who comes down from heaven and gives life to the world."

³⁴"Sir," they said, "give us that bread every day."

³⁵Jesus replied, "I am the bread of life. Whoever comes to me will never be hungry again. Whoever believes in me will never be thirsty. ³⁶But you haven't believed in me even though you have seen me. ³⁷However, those the Father has given me will come to me, and I will never reject them. ³⁸For I have come down from heaven to do the will of God who sent me, not to do my own will. ³⁹And this is the will of God, that I should not lose even one of all those he has given me, but that I should raise them up at the last day. ⁴⁰For it is my Father's will that all who see his Son and believe in him should have eternal life. I will raise them up at the last day."

⁴¹Then the people began to murmur in disagreement because he had said, "I am the bread that came down from heaven." ⁴²They said, "Isn't this Jesus, the son of Joseph? We know his father and mother. How can he say, 'I came down from heaven'?"

⁴³But Jesus replied, "Stop complaining about what I said. ⁴⁴For no one can come to me unless the Father who sent me draws them to me, and at the last day I will raise them up. ⁴⁵As it is written in the Scriptures, 'They will all be taught by God.' Everyone who listens to the Father and learns from him comes to me. ⁴⁶(Not that anyone has ever seen the Father; only I, who was sent from God, have seen him.)

⁴⁷"I tell you the truth, anyone who believes has eternal life. ⁴⁸Yes, I am the bread of life! ⁴⁹Your ancestors ate manna in the wilderness, but they all died. ⁵⁰Anyone who eats the bread from heaven, however, will never die. ⁵¹I am the living bread that came down from heaven. Anyone who eats this bread will live forever; and this bread, which I will offer so the world may live, is my flesh."

⁵²Then the people began arguing with each other about what he meant. "How can this man give us his flesh to eat?" they asked.

⁵³So Jesus said again, "I tell you the truth, unless you eat the flesh of the Son of Man and drink his blood, you cannot have eternal life within you. ⁵⁴But anyone who eats my flesh and drinks my blood has eternal life, and I will raise that person at the last day. ⁵⁵For my flesh is true food, and my blood is true drink. ⁵⁶Anyone who eats my flesh and drinks my blood remains in me, and I in him. ⁵⁷I live because of the living Father who sent me; in the same way, anyone who feeds on me will live because of me. ⁵⁸I am the true bread that came down from heaven. Anyone who eats this bread will not die as your ancestors did (even though they ate the manna) but will live forever."

⁵⁹He said these things while he was teaching in the synagogue in Capernaum.

Many Disciples Desert Jesus

⁶⁰Many of his disciples said, "This is very hard to understand. How can anyone accept it?"

⁶¹Jesus was aware that his disciples were complaining, so he said to them, "Does this offend you? ⁶²Then what will you think if you see the Son of Man ascend to heaven again? ⁶³The Spirit alone gives eternal life. Human effort accomplishes nothing. And the very words I have spoken to you are spirit and life. ⁶⁴But some of you do not believe me." (For Jesus knew from the beginning which ones didn't believe, and he knew who would betray him.) ⁶⁵Then he said, "That is why I said that people can't come to me unless the Father gives them to me."

⁶⁶At this point many of his disciples turned away and deserted him. ⁶⁷Then Jesus turned to the Twelve and asked, "Are you also going to leave?"

⁶⁸Simon Peter replied, "Lord, to whom would we go? You have the words that give eternal life. ⁶⁹We believe, and we know you are the Holy One of God."

⁷⁰Then Jesus said, "I chose the twelve of you, but one is a devil." ⁷¹He was speaking of Judas, son of Simon Iscariot, one of the Twelve, who would later betray him.

CHAPTER **7**
Jesus and His Brothers

After this, Jesus traveled around Galilee. He wanted to stay out of Judea, where the Jewish leaders were plotting his death. ²But soon it was time for the Jewish Festival of Shelters, ³and Jesus' brothers said to him, "Leave here and go to Judea, where your followers can see your miracles! ⁴You can't become famous if you hide like this! If you can do such wonderful things, show yourself to the world!" ⁵For even his brothers didn't believe in him.

⁶Jesus replied, "Now is not the right time for me to go, but you can go anytime. ⁷The world can't hate you, but it does hate me because I accuse it of doing evil. ⁸You go on. I'm not going

What's up WITH THAT?

Several stories in the New Testament mention some bad feelings that Jews had toward Samaritans.

It goes way back! When Assyria and Babylon took the Jews captive, some Jews stayed in the land. They married people who weren't Jews. Their children from those marriages grew up and had their own children, and that whole race of people became known as Samaritans. The Jews looked down on them because they came from marriages outside the Jewish faith. But Jesus showed that God loves all people the same.

Think of one action you can take this week to work against discrimination or racism. Maybe you'll stand up for someone who's being made fun of because of his or her family background.

Write below what you plan to do.

THEN DO IT!
(Add the date that you did it!)

to this festival, because my time has not yet come." 9 After saying these things, Jesus remained in Galilee.

Jesus Teaches Openly at the Temple

10 But after his brothers left for the festival, Jesus also went, though secretly, staying out of public view. 11 The Jewish leaders tried to find him at the festival and kept asking if anyone had seen him. 12 There was a lot of grumbling about him among the crowds. Some argued, "He's a good man," but others said, "He's nothing but a fraud who deceives the people." 13 But no one had the courage to speak favorably about him in public, for they were afraid of getting in trouble with the Jewish leaders.

14 Then, midway through the festival, Jesus went up to the Temple and began to teach. 15 The people were surprised when they heard him. "How does he know so much when he hasn't been trained?" they asked.

16 So Jesus told them, "My message is not my own; it comes from God who sent me. 17 Anyone who wants to do the will of God will know whether my teaching is from God or is merely my own. 18 Those who speak for themselves want glory only for themselves, but a person who seeks to honor the one who sent him speaks truth, not lies. 19 Moses gave you the law, but none of you obeys it! In fact, you are trying to kill me."

20 The crowd replied, "You're demon possessed! Who's trying to kill you?"

21 Jesus replied, "I did one miracle on the Sabbath, and you were amazed. 22 But you work on the Sabbath, too, when you obey Moses' law of circumcision. (Actually, this tradition of circumcision began with the patriarchs, long before the law of Moses.) 23 For if the correct time for circumcising your son falls on the Sabbath, you go ahead and do it so as not to break the law of Moses. So why should you be angry with me for healing a man on the Sabbath? 24 Look beneath the surface so you can judge correctly."

Is Jesus the Messiah?

25 Some of the people who lived in Jerusalem started to ask each other, "Isn't this the man they are trying to kill? 26 But here he is, speaking in public, and they say nothing to him. Could our leaders possibly believe that he is the Messiah? 27 But how could he be? For we know where this man comes from. When the Messiah comes, he will simply appear; no one will know where he comes from."

28While Jesus was teaching in the Temple, he called out, "Yes, you know me, and you know where I come from. But I'm not here on my own. The one who sent me is true, and you don't know him. 29But I know him because I come from him, and he sent me to you." 30Then the leaders tried to arrest him; but no one laid a hand on him, because his time had not yet come.

31Many among the crowds at the Temple believed in him. "After all," they said, "would you expect the Messiah to do more miraculous signs than this man has done?"

32When the Pharisees heard that the crowds were whispering such things, they and the leading priests sent Temple guards to arrest Jesus. 33But Jesus told them, "I will be with you only a little longer. Then I will return to the one who sent me. 34You will search for me but not find me. And you cannot go where I am going."

35The Jewish leaders were puzzled by this statement. "Where is he planning to go?" they asked. "Is he thinking of leaving the country and going to the Jews in other lands? Maybe he will even teach the Greeks! 36What does he mean when he says, 'You will search for me but not find me,' and 'You cannot go where I am going'?"

Jesus Promises Living Water

37On the last day, the climax of the festival, Jesus stood and shouted to the crowds, "Anyone who is thirsty may come to me! 38Anyone who believes in me may come and drink! For the Scriptures declare, 'Rivers of living water will flow from his heart.'" 39(When he said "living water," he was speaking of the Spirit, who would be given to everyone believing in him. But the Spirit had not yet been given, because Jesus had not yet entered into his glory.)

Division and Unbelief

40When the crowds heard him say this, some of them declared, "Surely this man is the Prophet we've been expecting." 41Others said, "He is the Messiah." Still others said, "But he can't be! Will the Messiah come from Galilee? 42For the Scriptures clearly state that the Messiah will be born of the royal line of David, in Bethlehem, the village where King David was born." 43So the crowd was divided about him. 44Some even wanted him arrested, but no one laid a hand on him.

45When the Temple guards returned without having arrested Jesus, the leading priests and Pharisees demanded, "Why didn't you bring him in?"

46"We have never heard anyone speak like this!" the guards responded.

47"Have you been led astray, too?" the Pharisees mocked. 48"Is there a single one of us rulers or Pharisees who believes in him? 49This foolish crowd follows him, but they are ignorant of the law. God's curse is on them!"

50Then Nicodemus, the leader who had met with Jesus earlier, spoke up. 51"Is it legal to convict a man before he is given a hearing?" he asked.

52They replied, "Are you from Galilee, too? Search the Scriptures and see for yourself—no prophet ever comes from Galilee!"

[The most ancient Greek manuscripts do not include John 7:53–8:11.]

53Then the meeting broke up, and everybody went home.

CHAPTER **8**
A Woman Caught in Adultery

Jesus returned to the Mount of Olives, 2but early the next morning he was back again at the Temple. A crowd soon gathered, and he sat down and taught them. 3As he was speaking, the teachers of religious law and the Pharisees brought a woman who had been caught in the act of adultery. They put her in front of the crowd.

4"Teacher," they said to Jesus, "this woman was caught in the act of adultery. 5The law of Moses says to stone her. What do you say?"

6They were trying to trap him into saying something they could use against him, but Jesus stooped down and wrote in the dust with his finger. 7They kept demanding an answer, so he stood up again and said, "All right, but let the one who has never sinned throw the first stone!" 8Then he stooped down again and wrote in the dust.

9When the accusers heard this, they slipped away one by one, beginning with the oldest, until only Jesus was left in the middle of the crowd with the woman. 10Then Jesus stood up again and said to the woman, "Where are your accusers? Didn't even one of them condemn you?"

11"No, Lord," she said.

And Jesus said, "Neither do I. Go and sin no more."

Jesus, the Light of the World

12Jesus spoke to the people once more and said, "I am the light of the world. If you follow me, you won't have to walk in darkness, because you will have the light that leads to life."

13 The Pharisees replied, "You are making those claims about yourself! Such testimony is not valid."

14 Jesus told them, "These claims are valid even though I make them about myself. For I know where I came from and where I am going, but you don't know this about me. 15 You judge me by human standards, but I do not judge anyone. 16 And if I did, my judgment would be correct in every respect because I am not alone. The Father who sent me is with me. 17 Your own law says that if two people agree about something, their witness is accepted as fact. 18 I am one witness, and my Father who sent me is the other."

19 "Where is your father?" they asked.

Jesus answered, "Since you don't know who I am, you don't know who my Father is. If you knew me, you would also know my Father." 20 Jesus made these statements while he was teaching in the section of the Temple known as the Treasury. But he was not arrested, because his time had not yet come.

The Unbelieving People Warned

21 Later Jesus said to them again, "I am going away. You will search for me but will die in your sin. You cannot come where I am going."

22 The people asked, "Is he planning to commit suicide? What does he mean, 'You cannot come where I am going'?"

23 Jesus continued, "You are from below; I am from above. You belong to this world; I do not. 24 That is why I said that you will die in your sins; for unless you believe that I AM who I claim to be, you will die in your sins."

25 "Who are you?" they demanded.

Jesus replied, "The one I have always claimed to be. 26 I have much to say about you and much to condemn, but I won't. For I say only what I have heard from the one who sent me, and he is completely truthful." 27 But they still didn't understand that he was talking about his Father.

28 So Jesus said, "When you have lifted up the Son of Man on the cross, then you will understand that I AM he. I do nothing on my own but say only what the Father taught me. 29 And the one who sent me is with me—he has not deserted me. For I always do what pleases him." 30 Then many who heard him say these things believed in him.

Jesus and Abraham

31 Jesus said to the people who believed in him, "You are truly my disciples if you remain faithful to my teachings. 32 And you will know the truth, and the truth will set you free."

33 "But we are descendants of Abraham," they said. "We have never been slaves to anyone. What do you mean, 'You will be set free'?"

34 Jesus replied, "I tell you the truth, everyone who sins is a slave of sin. 35 A slave is not a permanent member of the family, but a son is part of the family forever. 36 **So if the Son sets you free, you are truly free.** 37 Yes, I realize that you are descendants of Abraham. And yet some of you are trying to kill me because there's no room in your hearts for my message. 38 I am telling you what I saw when I was with my Father. But you are following the advice of your father."

39 "Our father is Abraham!" they declared.

"No," Jesus replied, "for if you were really the children of Abraham, you would follow his example. 40 Instead, you are trying to kill me because I told you the truth, which I heard from God. Abraham never did such a thing. 41 No, you are imitating your real father."

They replied, "We aren't illegitimate children! God himself is our true Father."

42 Jesus told them, "If God were your Father, you would love me, because I have come to you from God. I am not here on my own, but he sent me. 43 Why can't you understand what I am saying? It's because you can't even hear me! 44 For you are the children of your father the devil, and you love to do the evil things he does. He was a murderer from the beginning. He has always hated the truth, because there is no truth in him. When he lies, it is consistent with his character; for he is a liar and the father of lies. 45 So when I tell the truth, you just naturally don't believe me! 46 Which of you can truthfully accuse me of sin? And since I am telling you the truth, why don't you believe me? 47 Anyone who belongs to God listens gladly to the words of God. But you don't listen because you don't belong to God."

48 The people retorted, "You Samaritan devil! Didn't we say all along that you were possessed by a demon?"

49 "No," Jesus said, "I have no demon in me. For I honor my Father—and you dishonor me. 50 And though I have no wish to glorify myself, God is going to glorify me. He is the true judge. 51 I tell you the truth, anyone who obeys my teaching will never die!"

52 The people said, "Now we know you are possessed by a demon. Even Abraham and the prophets died, but you say, 'Anyone who obeys

my teaching will never die!' 53 Are you greater than our father Abraham? He died, and so did the prophets. Who do you think you are?"

54 Jesus answered, "If I want glory for myself, it doesn't count. But it is my Father who will glorify me. You say, 'He is our God,' 55 but you don't even know him. I know him. If I said otherwise, I would be as great a liar as you! But I do know him and obey him. 56 Your father Abraham rejoiced as he looked forward to my coming. He saw it and was glad."

57 The people said, "You aren't even fifty years old. How can you say you have seen Abraham?"

58 Jesus answered, "I tell you the truth, before Abraham was even born, I Am!" 59 At that point they picked up stones to throw at him. But Jesus was hidden from them and left the Temple.

Jesus Heals a Man Born Blind

As Jesus was walking along, he saw a man who had been blind from birth. 2 "Rabbi," his disciples asked him, "why was this man born blind? Was it because of his own sins or his parents' sins?"

3 "It was not because of his sins or his parents' sins," Jesus answered. "This happened so the power of God could be seen in him. 4 We must quickly carry out the tasks assigned us by the one who sent us. The night is coming, and then no one can work. 5 But while I am here in the world, I am the light of the world."

6 Then he spit on the ground, made mud with the saliva, and spread the mud over the blind man's eyes. 7 He told him, "Go wash yourself in the pool of Siloam" (Siloam means "sent"). So the man went and washed and came back seeing!

8 His neighbors and others who knew him as a blind beggar asked each other, "Isn't this the man who used to sit and beg?" 9 Some said he was, and others said, "No, he just looks like him!"

But the beggar kept saying, "Yes, I am the same one!"

10 They asked, "Who healed you? What happened?"

11 He told them, "The man they call Jesus made mud and spread it over my eyes and told me, 'Go to the pool of Siloam and wash yourself.' So I went and washed, and now I can see!"

12 "Where is he now?" they asked.

"I don't know," he replied.

13 Then they took the man who had been blind to the Pharisees, 14 because it was on the Sabbath that Jesus had made the mud and healed him. 15 The Pharisees asked the man all about it. So he told them, "He put the mud over my eyes, and when I washed it away, I could see!"

16 Some of the Pharisees said, "This man Jesus is not from God, for he is working on the Sabbath." Others said, "But how could an ordinary sinner do such miraculous signs?" So there was a deep division of opinion among them.

17 Then the Pharisees again questioned the man who had been blind and demanded, "What's your opinion about this man who healed you?"

The man replied, "I think he must be a prophet."

18 The Jewish leaders still refused to believe the man had been blind and could now see, so they called in his parents. 19 They asked them, "Is this your son? Was he born blind? If so, how can he now see?"

20 His parents replied, "We know this is our son and that he was born blind, 21 but we don't know how he can see or who healed him. Ask him. He is old enough to speak for himself."

22 His parents said this because they were afraid of the Jewish leaders, who had announced that anyone saying Jesus was the Messiah would be expelled from the synagogue. 23 That's why they said, "He is old enough. Ask him."

24 So for the second time they called in the man who had been blind and told him, "God should get the glory for this, because we know this man Jesus is a sinner."

25 "I don't know whether he is a sinner," the man replied. "But I know this: I was blind, and now I can see!"

26 "But what did he do?" they asked. "How did he heal you?"

27 "Look!" the man exclaimed. "I told you once. Didn't you listen? Why do you want to hear it again? Do you want to become his disciples, too?"

28 Then they cursed him and said, "You are his disciple, but we are disciples of Moses! 29 We know God spoke to Moses, but we don't even know where this man comes from."

30 "Why, that's very strange!" the man replied. "He healed my eyes, and yet you don't know where he comes from? 31 We know that God doesn't listen to sinners, but he is ready to hear those who worship him and do his will. 32 Ever since the world began, no one has been able to open the eyes of someone born blind. 33 If this man were not from God, he couldn't have done it."

34 "You were born a total sinner!" they answered. "Are you trying to teach us?" And they threw him out of the synagogue.

Spiritual Blindness

35 When Jesus heard what had happened, he found the man and asked, "Do you believe in the Son of Man?"

36 The man answered, "Who is he, sir? I want to believe in him."

37 "You have seen him," Jesus said, "and he is speaking to you!"

38 "Yes, Lord, I believe!" the man said. And he worshiped Jesus.

39 Then Jesus told him, "I entered this world to render judgment—to give sight to the blind and to show those who think they see that they are blind."

40 Some Pharisees who were standing nearby heard him and asked, "Are you saying we're blind?"

41 "If you were blind, you wouldn't be guilty," Jesus replied. "But you remain guilty because you claim you can see.

CHAPTER **10**

The Good Shepherd and His Sheep

"I tell you the truth, anyone who sneaks over the wall of a sheepfold, rather than going through the gate, must surely be a thief and a robber! 2 But the one who enters through the gate is the shepherd of the sheep. 3 The gatekeeper opens the gate for him, and the sheep recognize his voice and come to him. He calls his own sheep by name and leads them out. 4 After he has gathered his own flock, he walks ahead of them, and they follow him because they know his voice. 5 They won't follow a stranger; they will run from him because they don't know his voice."

6 Those who heard Jesus use this illustration didn't understand what he meant, 7 so he explained it to them: "I tell you the truth, I am the gate for the sheep. 8 All who came before me were thieves and robbers. But the true sheep did not listen to them. 9 Yes, I am the gate. Those who come in through me will be saved. They will come and go freely and will find good pastures. 10 The thief's purpose is to steal and kill and destroy. My purpose is to give them a rich and satisfying life.

11 "I am the good shepherd. The good shepherd sacrifices his life for the sheep. 12 A hired hand will run when he sees a wolf coming. He will abandon the sheep because they don't belong to him and he isn't their shepherd. And so the wolf attacks them and scatters the flock. 13 The hired hand runs away because he's working only for the money and doesn't really care about the sheep.

14 "I am the good shepherd; I know my own sheep, and they know me, 15 just as my Father knows me and I know the Father. So I sacrifice my life for the sheep. 16 I have other sheep, too, that are not in this sheepfold. I must bring them also. They will listen to my voice, and there will be one flock with one shepherd.

17 "The Father loves me because I sacrifice my life so I may take it back again. 18 No one can take my life from me. I sacrifice it voluntarily. For I have the authority to lay it down when I want to and also to take it up again. For this is what my Father has commanded."

19 When he said these things, the people were again divided in their opinions about him. 20 Some said, "He's demon possessed and out of his mind. Why listen to a man like that?" 21 Others said, "This doesn't sound like a man possessed by a demon! Can a demon open the eyes of the blind?"

Jesus Claims to Be the Son of God

22 It was now winter, and Jesus was in Jerusalem at the time of Hanukkah, the Festival of Dedication. 23 He was in the Temple, walking through the section known as Solomon's Colonnade. 24 The people surrounded him and asked, "How long are you going to keep us in suspense? If you are the Messiah, tell us plainly."

25 Jesus replied, "I have already told you, and you don't believe me. The proof is the work I do in my Father's name. 26 But you don't believe me because you are not my sheep. 27 My sheep listen to my voice; I know them, and they follow me. 28 I give them eternal life, and they will never perish. No one can snatch them away from me, 29 for my Father has given them to me, and he is more powerful than anyone else. No one can snatch them from the Father's hand. 30 The Father and I are one."

31 Once again the people picked up stones to kill him. 32 Jesus said, "At my Father's direction I have done many good works. For which one are you going to stone me?"

33 They replied, "We're stoning you not for any good work, but for blasphemy! You, a mere man, claim to be God."

34 Jesus replied, "It is written in your own Scriptures that God said to certain leaders of the people, 'I say, you are gods!' 35 And you know that the Scriptures cannot be altered. So if those people who received God's message were called 'gods,' 36 why do you call it blasphemy when I say, 'I am the Son of God'? After all, the Father set me

Roll Away That Stone!

You probably already know that Jesus can do anything. **Read JOHN 11:1-44 to discover one of the most amazing things Jesus did!**

AWESOME! Jesus can even bring the dead back to life! Lazarus didn't need that tomb anymore!

MAKE THIS COOL CRAFT TO REMIND YOU OF THIS STORY.

1 Poke a small hole in the bottom of a paper cup.

Read Mark 5:35-43 to learn about another time Jesus raised the dead.

2 Thread a 12-inch length of string through the hole. Knot the string on the outside of the bottom of the cup.

3 Crumple a piece of paper into a ball that's just big enough to sit inside the rim of the cup. Tape the free end of the string to the paper ball.

Think of the cup as the empty tomb of Lazarus and the paper ball as the stone they rolled away. See how many times you can catch the paper ball "stone" in the paper cup "tomb."

Use your "tomb" and "stone" as you tell a friend the Bible story!

apart and sent me into the world. ³⁷Don't believe me unless I carry out my Father's work. ³⁸But if I do his work, believe in the evidence of the miraculous works I have done, even if you don't believe me. Then you will know and understand that the Father is in me, and I am in the Father."

³⁹Once again they tried to arrest him, but he got away and left them. ⁴⁰He went beyond the Jordan River near the place where John was first baptizing and stayed there awhile. ⁴¹And many followed him. "John didn't perform miraculous signs," they remarked to one another, "but everything he said about this man has come true." ⁴²And many who were there believed in Jesus.

CHAPTER **11**

The Raising of Lazarus

A man named Lazarus was sick. He lived in Bethany with his sisters, Mary and Martha. ²This is the Mary who later poured the expensive perfume on the Lord's feet and wiped them with her hair. Her brother, Lazarus, was sick. ³So the two sisters sent a message to Jesus telling him, "Lord, your dear friend is very sick."

⁴But when Jesus heard about it he said, "Lazarus's sickness will not end in death. No, it happened for the glory of God so that the Son of God will receive glory from this." ⁵So although Jesus loved Martha, Mary, and Lazarus, ⁶he stayed where he was for the next two days. ⁷Finally, he said to his disciples, "Let's go back to Judea."

⁸But his disciples objected. "Rabbi," they said, "only a few days ago the people in Judea were trying to stone you. Are you going there again?"

⁹Jesus replied, "There are twelve hours of daylight every day. During the day people can walk safely. They can see because they have the light of this world. ¹⁰But at night there is danger of stumbling because they have no light." ¹¹Then he said, "Our friend Lazarus has fallen asleep, but now I will go and wake him up."

¹²The disciples said, "Lord, if he is sleeping, he will soon get better!" ¹³They thought Jesus meant Lazarus was simply sleeping, but Jesus meant Lazarus had died.

¹⁴So he told them plainly, "Lazarus is dead. ¹⁵And for your sakes, I'm glad I wasn't there, for now you will really believe. Come, let's go see him."

¹⁶Thomas, nicknamed the Twin, said to his fellow disciples, "Let's go, too—and die with Jesus."

¹⁷When Jesus arrived at Bethany, he was told that Lazarus had already been in his grave for four days. ¹⁸Bethany was only a few miles down

the road from Jerusalem, [19]and many of the people had come to console Martha and Mary in their loss. [20]When Martha got word that Jesus was coming, she went to meet him. But Mary stayed in the house. [21]Martha said to Jesus, "Lord, if only you had been here, my brother would not have died. [22]But even now I know that God will give you whatever you ask."

[23]Jesus told her, "Your brother will rise again."

[24]"Yes," Martha said, "he will rise when everyone else rises, at the last day."

[25]**Jesus told her, "I am the resurrection and the life. Anyone who believes in me will live, even after dying.** [26]Everyone who lives in me and believes in me will never ever die. Do you believe this, Martha?"

[27]"Yes, Lord," she told him. "I have always believed you are the Messiah, the Son of God, the one who has come into the world from God." [28]Then she returned to Mary. She called Mary aside from the mourners and told her, "The Teacher is here and wants to see you." [29]So Mary immediately went to him.

[30]Jesus had stayed outside the village, at the place where Martha met him. [31]When the people who were at the house consoling Mary saw her leave so hastily, they assumed she was going to Lazarus's grave to weep. So they followed her there. [32]When Mary arrived and saw Jesus, she fell at his feet and said, "Lord, if only you had been here, my brother would not have died."

[33]When Jesus saw her weeping and saw the other people wailing with her, a deep anger welled up within him, and he was deeply troubled. [34]"Where have you put him?" he asked them.

They told him, "Lord, come and see." [35]Then Jesus wept. [36]The people who were standing nearby said, "See how much he loved him!" [37]But some said, "This man healed a blind man. Couldn't he have kept Lazarus from dying?"

[38]Jesus was still angry as he arrived at the tomb, a cave with a stone rolled across its entrance. [39]"Roll the stone aside," Jesus told them.

But Martha, the dead man's sister, protested, "Lord, he has been dead for four days. The smell will be terrible."

[40]Jesus responded, "Didn't I tell you that you would see God's glory if you believe?" [41]So they rolled the stone aside. Then Jesus looked up to heaven and said, "Father, thank you for hearing me. [42]You always hear me, but I said it out loud for the sake of all these people standing here, so that they will believe you sent me." [43]Then Jesus shouted, "Lazarus, come out!" [44]And the dead man came out, his hands and feet bound in graveclothes, his face wrapped in a headcloth. Jesus told them, "Unwrap him and let him go!"

The Plot to Kill Jesus

[45]Many of the people who were with Mary believed in Jesus when they saw this happen. [46]But some went to the Pharisees and told them what Jesus had done. [47]Then the leading priests and Pharisees called the high council together. "What are we going to do?" they asked each other. "This man certainly performs many miraculous signs. [48]If we allow him to go on like this, soon everyone will believe in him. Then the Roman army will come and destroy both our Temple and our nation."

[49]Caiaphas, who was high priest at that time, said, "You don't know what you're talking about! [50]You don't realize that it's better for you that one man should die for the people than for the whole nation to be destroyed."

[51]He did not say this on his own; as high priest at that time he was led to prophesy that Jesus would die for the entire nation. [52]And not only for that nation, but to bring together and unite all the children of God scattered around the world.

[53]So from that time on, the Jewish leaders began to plot Jesus' death. [54]As a result, Jesus stopped his public ministry among the people and left Jerusalem. He went to a place near the wilderness, to the village of Ephraim, and stayed there with his disciples.

[55]It was now almost time for the Jewish Passover celebration, and many people from all over the country arrived in Jerusalem several days early so they could go through the purification ceremony before Passover began. [56]They kept looking for Jesus, but as they stood around in the Temple, they said to each other, "What do you think? He won't come for Passover, will he?" [57]Meanwhile, the leading priests and Pharisees had publicly ordered that anyone seeing Jesus must report it immediately so they could arrest him.

CHAPTER **12**
Jesus Anointed at Bethany

Six days before the Passover celebration began, Jesus arrived in Bethany, the home of Lazarus—the man he had raised from the dead. [2]A dinner was prepared in Jesus' honor. Martha served, and Lazarus was among those who ate with him. [3]Then Mary took a twelve-ounce jar of expensive perfume made from essence of nard, and she anointed Jesus' feet with it, wiping his feet with her hair. The house was filled with the fragrance.

⁴But Judas Iscariot, the disciple who would soon betray him, said, ⁵"That perfume was worth a year's wages. It should have been sold and the money given to the poor." ⁶Not that he cared for the poor—he was a thief, and since he was in charge of the disciples' money, he often stole some for himself.

⁷Jesus replied, "Leave her alone. She did this in preparation for my burial. ⁸You will always have the poor among you, but you will not always have me."

⁹When all the people heard of Jesus' arrival, they flocked to see him and also to see Lazarus, the man Jesus had raised from the dead. ¹⁰Then the leading priests decided to kill Lazarus, too, ¹¹for it was because of him that many of the people had deserted them and believed in Jesus.

Jesus' Triumphant Entry

¹²The next day, the news that Jesus was on the way to Jerusalem swept through the city. A large crowd of Passover visitors ¹³took palm branches and went down the road to meet him. They shouted,

"Praise God!
Blessings on the one who comes
    in the name of the LORD!
Hail to the King of Israel!"

¹⁴Jesus found a young donkey and rode on it, fulfilling the prophecy that said:

¹⁵ "Don't be afraid, people of Jerusalem.
Look, your King is coming,
    riding on a donkey's colt."

¹⁶His disciples didn't understand at the time that this was a fulfillment of prophecy. But after Jesus entered into his glory, they remembered what had happened and realized that these things had been written about him.

¹⁷Many in the crowd had seen Jesus call Lazarus from the tomb, raising him from the dead, and they were telling others about it. ¹⁸That was the reason so many went out to meet him—because they had heard about this miraculous sign. ¹⁹Then the Pharisees said to each other, "There's nothing we can do. Look, everyone has gone after him!"

Jesus Predicts His Death

²⁰Some Greeks who had come to Jerusalem for the Passover celebration ²¹paid a visit to Philip, who was from Bethsaida in Galilee. They said, "Sir, we want to meet Jesus." ²²Philip told Andrew about it, and they went together to ask Jesus.

²³Jesus replied, "Now the time has come for the Son of Man to enter into his glory. ²⁴I tell you the truth, unless a kernel of wheat is planted in the soil and dies, it remains alone. But its death will produce many new kernels—a plentiful harvest of new lives. ²⁵Those who love their life in this world will lose it. Those who care nothing for their life in this world will keep it for eternity. ²⁶Anyone who wants to be my disciple must follow me, because my servants must be where I am. And the Father will honor anyone who serves me.

²⁷"Now my soul is deeply troubled. Should I pray, 'Father, save me from this hour'? But this is the very reason I came! ²⁸Father, bring glory to your name."

Then a voice spoke from heaven, saying, "I have already brought glory to my name, and I will do so again." ²⁹When the crowd heard the voice, some thought it was thunder, while others declared an angel had spoken to him.

³⁰Then Jesus told them, "The voice was for your benefit, not mine. ³¹The time for judging this world has come, when Satan, the ruler of this world, will be cast out. ³²And when I am lifted up from the earth, I will draw everyone to myself." ³³He said this to indicate how he was going to die.

³⁴The crowd responded, "We understood from Scripture that the Messiah would live forever. How can you say the Son of Man will die? Just who is this Son of Man, anyway?"

³⁵Jesus replied, "My light will shine for you just a little longer. Walk in the light while you can, so the darkness will not overtake you. Those who walk in the darkness cannot see where they are going. ³⁶Put your trust in the light while there is still time; then you will become children of the light."

After saying these things, Jesus went away and was hidden from them.

The Unbelief of the People

³⁷But despite all the miraculous signs Jesus had done, most of the people still did not believe in him. ³⁸This is exactly what Isaiah the prophet had predicted:

"LORD, who has believed our message?
    To whom has the LORD revealed his
        powerful arm?"

³⁹But the people couldn't believe, for as Isaiah also said,

40 "The Lord has blinded their eyes
  and hardened their hearts—
so that their eyes cannot see,
  and their hearts cannot understand,
and they cannot turn to me
  and have me heal them."

41 Isaiah was referring to Jesus when he said this, because he saw the future and spoke of the Messiah's glory. 42 Many people did believe in him, however, including some of the Jewish leaders. But they wouldn't admit it for fear that the Pharisees would expel them from the synagogue. 43 For they loved human praise more than the praise of God.

44 Jesus shouted to the crowds, "If you trust me, you are trusting not only me, but also God who sent me. 45 For when you see me, you are seeing the one who sent me. 46 I have come as a light to shine in this dark world, so that all who put their trust in me will no longer remain in the dark. 47 I will not judge those who hear me but don't obey me, for I have come to save the world and not to judge it. 48 But all who reject me and my message will be judged on the day of judgment by the truth I have spoken. 49 I don't speak on my own authority. The Father who sent me has commanded me what to say and how to say it. 50 And I know his commands lead to eternal life; so I say whatever the Father tells me to say."

CHAPTER **13**

Jesus Washes His Disciples' Feet

Before the Passover celebration, Jesus knew that his hour had come to leave this world and return to his Father. He had loved his disciples during his ministry on earth, and now he loved them to the very end. 2 It was time for supper, and the devil had already prompted Judas, son of Simon Iscariot, to betray Jesus. 3 Jesus knew that the Father had given him authority over everything and that he had come from God and would return to God. 4 So he got up from the table, took off his robe, wrapped a towel around his waist, 5 and poured water into a basin. Then he began to wash the disciples' feet, drying them with the towel he had around him.

6 When Jesus came to Simon Peter, Peter said to him, "Lord, are you going to wash my feet?"

7 Jesus replied, "You don't understand now what I am doing, but someday you will."

8 "No," Peter protested, "you will never ever wash my feet!"

Jesus replied, "Unless I wash you, you won't belong to me."

Jesus, the Son of God, served his disciples in an incredible way. **Read all about it in JOHN 13:1-17!** Imagine having no paved roads or sidewalks. And wearing sandals all the time. In Jesus' time, servants would wash the feet of guests. It was a lowly job. But Jesus washed the disciples' feet himself! He showed that we should serve others.

How can you serve others this week? Write your ideas below.

Date

_____ _____

_____ _____

_____ _____

When you accomplish each service idea, write the date you did it.

JESUS IS THE BEST EXAMPLE EVER!

9 Simon Peter exclaimed, "Then wash my hands and head as well, Lord, not just my feet!"

10 Jesus replied, "A person who has bathed all over does not need to wash, except for the feet, to be entirely clean. And you disciples are clean, but not all of you." 11 For Jesus knew who would betray him. That is what he meant when he said, "Not all of you are clean."

12 After washing their feet, he put on his robe again and sat down and asked, "Do you understand what I was doing? 13 You call me 'Teacher' and 'Lord,' and you are right, because that's what I

am. ¹⁴And since I, your Lord and Teacher, have washed your feet, you ought to wash each other's feet. ¹⁵I have given you an example to follow. Do as I have done to you. ¹⁶I tell you the truth, slaves are not greater than their master. Nor is the messenger more important than the one who sends the message. ¹⁷Now that you know these things, God will bless you for doing them.

Jesus Predicts His Betrayal

¹⁸"I am not saying these things to all of you; I know the ones I have chosen. But this fulfills the Scripture that says, 'The one who eats my food has turned against me.' ¹⁹I tell you this beforehand, so that when it happens you will believe that I AM the Messiah. ²⁰I tell you the truth, anyone who welcomes my messenger is welcoming me, and anyone who welcomes me is welcoming the Father who sent me."

²¹Now Jesus was deeply troubled, and he exclaimed, "I tell you the truth, one of you will betray me!"

²²The disciples looked at each other, wondering whom he could mean. ²³The disciple Jesus loved was sitting next to Jesus at the table. ²⁴Simon Peter motioned to him to ask, "Who's he talking about?" ²⁵So that disciple leaned over to Jesus and asked, "Lord, who is it?"

²⁶Jesus responded, "It is the one to whom I give the bread I dip in the bowl." And when he had dipped it, he gave it to Judas, son of Simon Iscariot. ²⁷When Judas had eaten the bread, Satan entered into him. Then Jesus told him, "Hurry and do what you're going to do." ²⁸None of the others at the table knew what Jesus meant. ²⁹Since Judas was their treasurer, some thought Jesus was telling him to go and pay for the food or to give some money to the poor. ³⁰So Judas left at once, going out into the night.

Jesus Predicts Peter's Denial

³¹As soon as Judas left the room, Jesus said, "The time has come for the Son of Man to enter into his glory, and God will be glorified because of him. ³²And since God receives glory because of the Son, he will soon give glory to the Son. ³³Dear children, I will be with you only a little longer. And as I told the Jewish leaders, you will search for me, but you can't come where I am going. **³⁴So now I am giving you a new commandment: Love each other. Just as I have loved you, you should love each other. ³⁵Your love for one another will prove to the world that you are my disciples."**

³⁶Simon Peter asked, "Lord, where are you going?"

And Jesus replied, "You can't go with me now, but you will follow me later."

³⁷"But why can't I come now, Lord?" he asked. "I'm ready to die for you."

³⁸Jesus answered, "Die for me? I tell you the truth, Peter—before the rooster crows tomorrow morning, you will deny three times that you even know me.

CHAPTER **14**
Jesus, the Way to the Father

"Don't let your hearts be troubled. Trust in God, and trust also in me. ²There is more than enough room in my Father's home. If this were not so, would I have told you that I am going to prepare a place for you? ³When everything is ready, I will come and get you, so that you will always be with me where I am. ⁴And you know the way to where I am going."

⁵"No, we don't know, Lord," Thomas said. "We have no idea where you are going, so how can we know the way?"

⁶Jesus told him, "I am the way, the truth, and the life. No one can come to the Father except through me. ⁷If you had really known me, you would know who my Father is. From now on, you do know him and have seen him!"

⁸Philip said, "Lord, show us the Father, and we will be satisfied."

⁹Jesus replied, "Have I been with you all this time, Philip, and yet you still don't know who I am? Anyone who has seen me has seen the Father! So why are you asking me to show him to you? ¹⁰Don't you believe that I am in the Father and the Father is in me? The words I speak are not my own, but my Father who lives in me does his work through me. ¹¹Just believe that I am in the Father and the Father is in me. Or at least believe because of the work you have seen me do.

¹²"I tell you the truth, anyone who believes in me will do the same works I have done, and even greater works, because I am going to be with the Father. ¹³You can ask for anything in my name, and I will do it, so that the Son can bring glory to the Father. ¹⁴Yes, ask me for anything in my name, and I will do it!

Jesus Promises the Holy Spirit

¹⁵"If you love me, obey my commandments. ¹⁶And I will ask the Father, and he will give you another Advocate, who will never leave you. ¹⁷He is the Holy Spirit, who leads into all truth. The

Key Verse

"I am the way, the truth, and the life. No one can come to the Father except through me."
—JOHN 14:6

The Only Way

Ever want to be an artist? Now's your chance. **But first, read JOHN 14:6 a couple of times.**

Jesus says he's the only way to the Father. Think of it this way: You and God are separated because of your sin. When you believe in Jesus, he acts as the bridge so you can get close to God and be forgiven:

DRAW A PICTURE OF YOUR OWN IDEA TO EXPLAIN THE VERSE.

Maybe you'll draw yourself in one city and God in another, and Jesus is the only bus that runs between the cities.

The ONLY Way

Now read JOHN 14:6 to someone else, and explain your picture.

Ask that person to draw a picture and explain the verse to someone. Who knows how many people will learn this verse because of you!

world cannot receive him, because it isn't looking for him and doesn't recognize him. But you know him, because he lives with you now and later will be in you. 18No, I will not abandon you as orphans—I will come to you. 19Soon the world will no longer see me, but you will see me. Since I live, you also will live. 20When I am raised to life again, you will know that I am in my Father, and you are in me, and I am in you. 21Those who accept my commandments and obey them are the ones who love me. And because they love me, my

Father will love them. And I will love them and reveal myself to each of them."

22Judas (not Judas Iscariot, but the other disciple with that name) said to him, "Lord, why are you going to reveal yourself only to us and not to the world at large?"

23Jesus replied, "All who love me will do what I say. My Father will love them, and we will come and make our home with each of them. 24Anyone who doesn't love me will not obey me. And remember, my words are not my own. What I am telling you is from the Father who sent me. 25I am telling you these things now while I am still with you. 26But when the Father sends the Advocate as my representative—that is, the Holy Spirit—he will teach you everything and will remind you of everything I have told you.

27"I am leaving you with a gift—peace of mind and heart. And the peace I give is a gift the world cannot give. So don't be troubled or afraid. 28Remember what I told you: I am going away, but I will come back to you again. If you really loved me, you would be happy that I am going to the Father, who is greater than I am. 29I have told you these things before they happen so that when they do happen, you will believe.

30"I don't have much more time to talk to you, because the ruler of this world approaches. He has no power over me, 31but I will do what the Father requires of me, so that the world will know that I love the Father. Come, let's be going.

CHAPTER 15

Jesus, the True Vine

"I am the true grapevine, and my Father is the gardener. 2He cuts off every branch of mine that doesn't produce fruit, and he prunes the branches that do bear fruit so they will produce even more. 3You have already been pruned and purified by the message I have given you. 4Remain in me, and I will remain in you. For a branch cannot produce fruit if it is severed from the vine, and you cannot be fruitful unless you remain in me.

5**"Yes, I am the vine; you are the branches. Those who remain in me, and I in them, will produce much fruit. For apart from me you can do nothing.** 6Anyone who does not remain in me is thrown away like a useless branch and withers. Such branches are gathered into a pile to be burned. 7But if you remain in me and my words remain in you, you may ask for anything you want, and it will be granted! 8When you produce much fruit, you are my true disciples. This brings great glory to my Father.

9"I have loved you even as the Father has loved me. Remain in my love. 10When you obey my commandments, you remain in my love, just as I obey my Father's commandments and remain in his love. 11I have told you these things so that you will be filled with my joy. Yes, your joy will overflow! 12This is my commandment: Love each other in the same way I have loved you. 13There is no greater love than to lay down one's life for one's friends. 14You are my friends if you do what I command. 15I no longer call you slaves, because a master doesn't confide in his slaves. Now you are my friends, since I have told you everything the Father told me. 16You didn't choose me. I chose you. I appointed you to go and produce lasting fruit, so that the Father will give you whatever you ask for, using my name. 17This is my command: Love each other.

The World's Hatred

18"If the world hates you, remember that it hated me first. 19The world would love you as one of its own if you belonged to it, but you are no longer part of the world. I chose you to come out of the world, so it hates you. 20Do you remember what I told you? 'A slave is not greater than the master.' Since they persecuted me, naturally they will persecute you. And if they had listened to me, they would listen to you. 21They will do all this to you because of me, for they have rejected the One who sent me. 22They would not be guilty if I had not come and spoken to them. But now they have no excuse for their sin. 23Anyone who hates me also hates my Father. 24If I hadn't done such miraculous signs among them that no one else could do, they would not be guilty. But as it is, they have seen everything I did, yet they still hate me and my Father. 25This fulfills what is written in their Scriptures: 'They hated me without cause.'

26"But I will send you the Advocate—the Spirit of truth. He will come to you from the Father and will testify all about me. 27And you must also testify about me because you have been with me from the beginning of my ministry.

CHAPTER **16**

"I have told you these things so that you won't abandon your faith. 2For you will be expelled from the synagogues, and the time is coming when those who kill you will think they are doing a holy service for God. 3This is because they have never known the Father or me. 4Yes, I'm telling you these things now, so that when they happen, you will remember my warning. I didn't tell you earlier because I was going to be with you for a while longer.

The Work of the Holy Spirit

5"But now I am going away to the One who sent me, and not one of you is asking where I am going. 6Instead, you grieve because of what I've told you. 7But in fact, it is best for you that I go away, because if I don't, the Advocate won't come. If I do go away, then I will send him to you. 8And when he comes, he will convict the world of its sin, and of God's righteousness, and of the coming judgment. 9The world's sin is that it refuses to believe in me. 10Righteousness is available because I go to the Father, and you will see me no more. 11Judgment will come because the ruler of this world has already been judged.

12"There is so much more I want to tell you, but you can't bear it now. 13When the Spirit of truth comes, he will guide you into all truth. He will not speak on his own but will tell you what he has heard. He will tell you about the future. 14He will bring me glory by telling you whatever he receives from me. 15All that belongs to the Father is mine; this is why I said, 'The Spirit will tell you whatever he receives from me.'

Sadness Will Be Turned to Joy

16"In a little while you won't see me anymore. But a little while after that, you will see me again."

17Some of the disciples asked each other, "What does he mean when he says, 'In a little while you won't see me, but then you will see me,' and 'I am going to the Father'? 18And what does he mean by 'a little while'? We don't understand."

19Jesus realized they wanted to ask him about it, so he said, "Are you asking yourselves what I meant? I said in a little while you won't see me, but a little while after that you will see me again. 20I tell you the truth, you will weep and mourn over what is going to happen to me, but the world will rejoice. You will grieve, but your grief will suddenly turn to wonderful joy. 21It will be like a woman suffering the pains of labor. When her child is born, her anguish gives way to joy because she has brought a new baby into the world. 22So you have sorrow now, but I will see you again; then you will rejoice, and no one can rob you of that joy. 23At that time you won't need to ask me for anything. I tell you the truth, you will ask the Father directly, and he will grant your request because you use my name. 24You haven't done this before. Ask, using my name, and you will receive, and you will have abundant joy.

25"I have spoken of these matters in figures of speech, but soon I will stop speaking figuratively and will tell you plainly all about the Father. 26Then you will ask in my name. I'm not saying I will ask the Father on your behalf, 27for the Father himself loves you dearly because you love me and believe that I came from God. 28Yes, I came from the Father into the world, and now I will leave the world and return to the Father."

29Then his disciples said, "At last you are speaking plainly and not figuratively. 30Now we understand that you know everything, and there's no need to question you. From this we believe that you came from God."

31Jesus asked, "Do you finally believe? 32But the time is coming—indeed it's here now—when you will be scattered, each one going his own way, leaving me alone. Yet I am not alone because the Father is with me. 33I have told you all this so that you may have peace in me. Here on earth you will have many trials and sorrows. But take heart, because I have overcome the world."

CHAPTER 17
The Prayer of Jesus

After saying all these things, Jesus looked up to heaven and said, "Father, the hour has come. Glorify your Son so he can give glory back to you. 2For you have given him authority over everyone. He gives eternal life to each one you have given him. 3And this is the way to have eternal life—to know you, the only true God, and Jesus Christ, the one you sent to earth. 4I brought glory to you here on earth by completing the work you gave me to do. 5Now, Father, bring me into the glory we shared before the world began.

6"I have revealed you to the ones you gave me from this world. They were always yours. You gave them to me, and they have kept your word. 7Now they know that everything I have is a gift from you, 8for I have passed on to them the message you gave me. They accepted it and know that I came from you, and they believe you sent me.

9"My prayer is not for the world, but for those you have given me, because they belong to you. 10All who are mine belong to you, and you have given them to me, so they bring me glory. 11Now I am departing from the world; they are staying in this world, but I am coming to you. Holy Father, you have given me your name; now protect them by the power of your name so that they will be

Key Verse

"Yes, I am the vine; you are the branches. Those who remain in me, and I in them, will produce much fruit. For apart from me you can do nothing."—JOHN 15:5

Chain Reaction

Find a friend, and read JOHN 15:5 a few times until you can say it to each other without reading it. Discuss these questions with your friend:

- Why can't a branch survive if it's not connected to the main vine?

- Why is it so important for us to be connected to Jesus?

- What are some ways to stay connected to Jesus?

Brainstorm with your friend ways to stay connected to Jesus. (You might say reading the Bible.) Then think of fruit you can produce by staying connected to Jesus. (You might say being loving.)

Make a green paper chain to remind you that Jesus is the vine. On each loop, write one of your ideas. Then hang the "vine" in your room to remind you to stay connected to Jesus!

united just as we are. 12During my time here, I protected them by the power of the name you gave me. I guarded them so that not one was lost, except the one headed for destruction, as the Scriptures foretold.

13"Now I am coming to you. I told them many things while I was with them in this world so they would be filled with my joy. 14I have given them your word. And the world hates them because they do not belong to the world, just as I do not belong to the world. 15I'm not asking you to take them out of the world, but to keep them safe from the evil one. 16They do not belong to this world any more than I do. 17Make them holy by your truth; teach them your word, which is truth. 18Just as you sent me into the world, I am sending them into the world. 19And I give myself as a holy sacrifice for them so they can be made holy by your truth.

20"I am praying not only for these disciples but also for all who will ever believe in me through their message. 21I pray that they will all be one, just as you and I are one—as you are in me, Father, and I am in you. And may they be in us so that the world will believe you sent me.

22"I have given them the glory you gave me, so they may be one as we are one. 23I am in them and you are in me. May they experience such perfect unity that the world will know that you sent me and that you love them as much as you love me. 24Father, I want these whom you have given me to be with me where I am. Then they can see all the glory you gave me because you loved me even before the world began!

25"O righteous Father, the world doesn't know you, but I do; and these disciples know you sent me. 26I have revealed you to them, and I will continue to do so. Then your love for me will be in them, and I will be in them."

CHAPTER **18**
Jesus Is Betrayed and Arrested

After saying these things, Jesus crossed the Kidron Valley with his disciples and entered a grove of olive trees. 2Judas, the betrayer, knew this place, because Jesus had often gone there with his disciples. 3The leading priests and Pharisees had given Judas a contingent of Roman soldiers and Temple guards to accompany him. Now with blazing torches, lanterns, and weapons, they arrived at the olive grove.

4Jesus fully realized all that was going to happen to him, so he stepped forward to meet them. "Who are you looking for?" he asked.

5"Jesus the Nazarene," they replied.

"I AM he," Jesus said. (Judas, who betrayed him, was standing with them.) 6As Jesus said "I AM he," they all drew back and fell to the ground! 7Once more he asked them, "Who are you looking for?"

And again they replied, "Jesus the Nazarene."

8"I told you that I AM he," Jesus said. "And since I am the one you want, let these others go." 9He did this to fulfill his own statement: "I did not lose a single one of those you have given me."

10Then Simon Peter drew a sword and slashed off the right ear of Malchus, the high priest's slave. 11But Jesus said to Peter, "Put your sword back into its sheath. Shall I not drink from the cup of suffering the Father has given me?"

Jesus at the High Priest's House

12So the soldiers, their commanding officer, and the Temple guards arrested Jesus and tied him up. 13First they took him to Annas, the father-in-law of Caiaphas, the high priest at that time. 14Caiaphas was the one who had told the other Jewish leaders, "It's better that one man should die for the people."

Peter's First Denial

15Simon Peter followed Jesus, as did another of the disciples. That other disciple was acquainted with the high priest, so he was allowed to enter the high priest's courtyard with Jesus. 16Peter had to stay outside the gate. Then the disciple who knew the high priest spoke to the woman watching at the gate, and she let Peter in. 17The woman asked Peter, "You're not one of that man's disciples, are you?"

"No," he said, "I am not."

18Because it was cold, the household servants and the guards had made a charcoal fire. They stood around it, warming themselves, and Peter stood with them, warming himself.

The High Priest Questions Jesus

19Inside, the high priest began asking Jesus about his followers and what he had been teaching them. 20Jesus replied, "Everyone knows what I teach. I have preached regularly in the synagogues and the Temple, where the people gather. I have not spoken in secret. 21Why are you asking me this question? Ask those who heard me. They know what I said."

22Then one of the Temple guards standing nearby slapped Jesus across the face. "Is that the way to answer the high priest?" he demanded.

23Jesus replied, "If I said anything wrong, you must prove it. But if I'm speaking the truth, why are you beating me?"

24Then Annas bound Jesus and sent him to Caiaphas, the high priest.

Peter's Second and Third Denials

25Meanwhile, as Simon Peter was standing by the fire warming himself, they asked him again, "You're not one of his disciples, are you?"

He denied it, saying, "No, I am not."

26 But one of the household slaves of the high priest, a relative of the man whose ear Peter had cut off, asked, "Didn't I see you out there in the olive grove with Jesus?" 27 Again Peter denied it. And immediately a rooster crowed.

Jesus' Trial before Pilate

28 Jesus' trial before Caiaphas ended in the early hours of the morning. Then he was taken to the headquarters of the Roman governor. His accusers didn't go inside because it would defile them, and they wouldn't be allowed to celebrate the Passover. 29 So Pilate, the governor, went out to them and asked, "What is your charge against this man?"

30 "We wouldn't have handed him over to you if he weren't a criminal!" they retorted.

31 "Then take him away and judge him by your own law," Pilate told them.

"Only the Romans are permitted to execute someone," the Jewish leaders replied. 32 (This fulfilled Jesus' prediction about the way he would die.)

33 Then Pilate went back into his headquarters and called for Jesus to be brought to him. "Are you the king of the Jews?" he asked him.

34 Jesus replied, "Is this your own question, or did others tell you about me?"

35 "Am I a Jew?" Pilate retorted. "Your own people and their leading priests brought you to me for trial. Why? What have you done?"

36 Jesus answered, "My Kingdom is not an earthly kingdom. If it were, my followers would fight to keep me from being handed over to the Jewish leaders. But my Kingdom is not of this world."

37 Pilate said, "So you are a king?"

Jesus responded, "You say I am a king. Actually, I was born and came into the world to testify to the truth. All who love the truth recognize that what I say is true."

38 "What is truth?" Pilate asked. Then he went out again to the people and told them, "He is not guilty of any crime. 39 But you have a custom of asking me to release one prisoner each year at Passover. Would you like me to release this 'King of the Jews'?"

40 But they shouted back, "No! Not this man. We want Barabbas!" (Barabbas was a revolutionary.)

CHAPTER **19**

Jesus Sentenced to Death

Then Pilate had Jesus flogged with a lead-tipped whip. 2 The soldiers wove a crown of thorns and put it on his head, and they put a purple robe on him. 3 "Hail! King of the Jews!" they mocked, as they slapped him across the face.

4 Pilate went outside again and said to the people, "I am going to bring him out to you now, but understand clearly that I find him not guilty."

5 Then Jesus came out wearing the crown of thorns and the purple robe. And Pilate said, "Look, here is the man!"

6 When they saw him, the leading priests and Temple guards began shouting, "Crucify him! Crucify him!"

"Take him yourselves and crucify him," Pilate said. "I find him not guilty."

7 The Jewish leaders replied, "By our law he ought to die because he called himself the Son of God."

8 When Pilate heard this, he was more frightened than ever. 9 He took Jesus back into the headquarters again and asked him, "Where are you from?" But Jesus gave no answer. 10 "Why don't you talk to me?" Pilate demanded. "Don't you realize that I have the power to release you or crucify you?"

11 Then Jesus said, "You would have no power over me at all unless it were given to you from above. So the one who handed me over to you has the greater sin."

12 Then Pilate tried to release him, but the Jewish leaders shouted, "If you release this man, you are no 'friend of Caesar.' Anyone who declares himself a king is a rebel against Caesar."

13 When they said this, Pilate brought Jesus out to them again. Then Pilate sat down on the judgment seat on the platform that is called the Stone Pavement (in Hebrew, *Gabbatha*). 14 It was now about noon on the day of preparation for the Passover. And Pilate said to the people, "Look, here is your king!"

15 "Away with him," they yelled. "Away with him! Crucify him!"

"What? Crucify your king?" Pilate asked.

"We have no king but Caesar," the leading priests shouted back.

16 Then Pilate turned Jesus over to them to be crucified.

The Crucifixion

So they took Jesus away. 17 Carrying the cross by himself, he went to the place called Place of the Skull (in Hebrew, *Golgotha*). 18 There they nailed him to the cross. Two others were crucified with him, one on either side, with Jesus between them. 19 And Pilate posted a sign over him that read, "Jesus of Nazareth, the King of the Jews." 20 The place where Jesus was crucified was near the city, and the sign was written in Hebrew, Latin, and Greek, so that many people could read it. ²¹Then the leading priests objected and said to Pilate, "Change it from 'The King of the Jews' to 'He said, I am King of the Jews.'"

²²Pilate replied, "No, what I have written, I have written."

²³When the soldiers had crucified Jesus, they divided his clothes among the four of them. They also took his robe, but it was seamless, woven in one piece from top to bottom. ²⁴So they said, "Rather than tearing it apart, let's throw dice for it." This fulfilled the Scripture that says, "They divided my garments among themselves and threw dice for my clothing." So that is what they did.

²⁵Standing near the cross were Jesus' mother, and his mother's sister, Mary (the wife of Clopas), and Mary Magdalene. ²⁶When Jesus saw his mother standing there beside the disciple he loved, he said to her, "Dear woman, here is your son." ²⁷And he said to this disciple, "Here is your mother." And from then on this disciple took her into his home.

The Death of Jesus

²⁸Jesus knew that his mission was now finished, and to fulfill Scripture he said, "I am thirsty." ²⁹A jar of sour wine was sitting there, so they soaked a sponge in it, put it on a hyssop branch, and held it up to his lips. ³⁰When Jesus had tasted it, he said, "It is finished!" Then he bowed his head and released his spirit.

³¹It was the day of preparation, and the Jewish leaders didn't want the bodies hanging there the next day, which was the Sabbath (and a very special Sabbath, because it was the Passover). So they asked Pilate to hasten their deaths by ordering that their legs be broken. Then their bodies could be taken down. ³²So the soldiers came and broke the legs of the two men crucified with Jesus. ³³But when they came to Jesus, they saw that he was already dead, so they didn't break his legs. ³⁴One of the soldiers, however, pierced his side with a spear, and immediately blood and water flowed out. ³⁵(This report is from an eyewitness giving an accurate account. He speaks the truth so that you also can believe.) ³⁶These things happened in fulfillment of the Scriptures that say, "Not one of his bones will be broken," ³⁷and "They will look on the one they pierced."

The Burial of Jesus

³⁸Afterward Joseph of Arimathea, who had been a secret disciple of Jesus (because he feared the Jewish leaders), asked Pilate for permission to take down Jesus' body. When Pilate gave permission, Joseph came and took the body away. ³⁹With him came Nicodemus, the man who had come to Jesus at night. He brought seventy-five pounds of perfumed ointment made from myrrh and aloes. ⁴⁰Following Jewish burial custom, they wrapped Jesus' body with the spices in long sheets of linen cloth. ⁴¹The place of crucifixion was near a garden, where there was a new tomb, never used before. ⁴²And so, because it was the day of preparation for the Jewish Passover and since the tomb was close at hand, they laid Jesus there.

FUN-fact

Pack It Up

If you were a Bible-times traveler, you might have carried a **hollowed-out gourd** weighted with a stone for drawing water from wells. You might also have carried a **stick** and a **money belt.** You may not have to travel to tell others about Jesus but you can still be prepared just the same!

What three items can you carry with you to tell others about Jesus?

Maybe you can keep a pocket Bible in your backpack. Or maybe you can write invitations to your church and keep them with you. Write your ideas below.

1. _____

2. _____

3. _____

Then start telling others about Jesus!

DON'T DOUBT

Have you ever doubted God? Guess what: You're not alone. **Read JOHN 20:24-31 to meet a doubting disciple.**

One good thing to do when you have doubts is to separate what you *know* from what you *feel*. **Here's an example:** You may doubt that God loves you because you didn't make the soccer team. You *feel* alone and unloved.

But the Bible says that God loves you, and that he'll take care of you. Because the Bible says it, you *know* it's true, even if it doesn't *feel* that way right now.

Fill in this chart with what you feel and what you know from the Bible.

What I Feel

Lonely

What I Know

God is with me.
—MATTHEW 28:20

Turn to John 13:34-35 to read more about love.

The index in this Bible can help you know where to look in the Bible!

CHAPTER 20
The Resurrection

Early on Sunday morning, while it was still dark, Mary Magdalene came to the tomb and found that the stone had been rolled away from the entrance. ²She ran and found Simon Peter and the other disciple, the one whom Jesus loved. She said, "They have taken the Lord's body out of the tomb, and we don't know where they have put him!"

³Peter and the other disciple started out for the tomb. ⁴They were both running, but the other disciple outran Peter and reached the tomb first. ⁵He stooped and looked in and saw the linen wrappings lying there, but he didn't go in. ⁶Then Simon Peter arrived and went inside. He also noticed the linen wrappings lying there, ⁷while the cloth that had covered Jesus' head was folded up and lying apart from the other wrappings. ⁸Then the disciple who had reached the tomb first also went in, and he saw and believed—⁹for until then they still hadn't understood the Scriptures that said Jesus must rise from the dead. ¹⁰Then they went home.

Jesus Appears to Mary Magdalene

¹¹Mary was standing outside the tomb crying, and as she wept, she stooped and looked in. ¹²She saw two white-robed angels, one sitting at the head and the other at the foot of the place where the body of Jesus had been lying. ¹³"Dear woman, why are you crying?" the angels asked her.

"Because they have taken away my Lord," she replied, "and I don't know where they have put him."

¹⁴She turned to leave and saw someone standing there. It was Jesus, but she didn't recognize him. ¹⁵"Dear woman, why are you crying?" Jesus asked her. "Who are you looking for?"

She thought he was the gardener. "Sir," she said, "if you have taken him away, tell me where you have put him, and I will go and get him."

¹⁶"Mary!" Jesus said.

She turned to him and cried out, "Rabboni!" (which is Hebrew for "Teacher").

¹⁷"Don't cling to me," Jesus said, "for I haven't yet ascended to the Father. But go find my brothers and tell them, 'I am ascending to my Father and your Father, to my God and your God.'"

¹⁸Mary Magdalene found the disciples and told them, "I have seen the Lord!" Then she gave them his message.

Jesus Appears to His Disciples

¹⁹That Sunday evening the disciples were meeting behind locked doors because they were afraid of the Jewish leaders. Suddenly, Jesus was standing there among them! "Peace be with you," he said. ²⁰As he spoke, he showed them the wounds in his hands and his side. They were filled with joy when they saw the Lord! ²¹Again he said, "Peace be with you. As the Father has sent me, so I am sending you." ²²Then he breathed on them and said, "Receive the Holy Spirit. ²³If you forgive anyone's sins, they are forgiven. If you do not forgive them, they are not forgiven."

Jesus Appears to Thomas

²⁴One of the twelve disciples, Thomas (nicknamed the Twin), was not with the others when Jesus came. ²⁵They told him, "We have seen the Lord!"

But he replied, "I won't believe it unless I see the nail wounds in his hands, put my fingers into them, and place my hand into the wound in his side."

²⁶Eight days later the disciples were together again, and this time Thomas was with them. The doors were locked; but suddenly, as before, Jesus was standing among them. "Peace be with you," he said. ²⁷Then he said to Thomas, "Put your finger here, and look at my hands. Put your hand into the wound in my side. Don't be faithless any longer. Believe!"

²⁸"My Lord and my God!" Thomas exclaimed.

²⁹Then Jesus told him, "You believe because you have seen me. Blessed are those who believe without seeing me."

Purpose of the Book

³⁰The disciples saw Jesus do many other miraculous signs in addition to the ones recorded in this book. ³¹But these are written so that you may continue to believe that Jesus is the Messiah, the Son of God, and that by believing in him you will have life by the power of his name.

CHAPTER **21**

Epilogue: Jesus Appears to Seven Disciples

Later, Jesus appeared again to the disciples beside the Sea of Galilee. This is how it happened. ²Several of the disciples were there—Simon Peter, Thomas (nicknamed the Twin), Nathanael from Cana in Galilee, the sons of Zebedee, and two other disciples.

³Simon Peter said, "I'm going fishing."

"We'll come, too," they all said. So they went out in the boat, but they caught nothing all night.

⁴At dawn Jesus was standing on the beach, but the disciples couldn't see who he was. ⁵He called out, "Fellows, have you caught any fish?"

"No," they replied.

⁶Then he said, "Throw out your net on the right-hand side of the boat, and you'll get some!" So they did, and they couldn't haul in the net because there were so many fish in it.

⁷Then the disciple Jesus loved said to Peter, "It's the Lord!" When Simon Peter heard that it was the Lord, he put on his tunic (for he had stripped for work), jumped into the water, and headed to shore. ⁸The others stayed with the boat and pulled the loaded net to the shore, for they were only about a hundred yards from shore. ⁹When they got there, they found breakfast waiting for them—fish cooking over a charcoal fire, and some bread.

¹⁰"Bring some of the fish you've just caught," Jesus said. ¹¹So Simon Peter went aboard and dragged the net to the shore. There were 153 large fish, and yet the net hadn't torn.

¹²"Now come and have some breakfast!" Jesus said. None of the disciples dared to ask him, "Who are you?" They knew it was the Lord. ¹³Then Jesus served them the bread and the fish. ¹⁴This was the third time Jesus had appeared to his disciples since he had been raised from the dead.

¹⁵After breakfast Jesus asked Simon Peter, "Simon son of John, do you love me more than these?"

"Yes, Lord," Peter replied, "you know I love you."

"Then feed my lambs," Jesus told him.

¹⁶Jesus repeated the question: "Simon son of John, do you love me?"

"Yes, Lord," Peter said, "you know I love you."

"Then take care of my sheep," Jesus said.

¹⁷A third time he asked him, "Simon son of John, do you love me?"

Peter was hurt that Jesus asked the question a third time. He said, "Lord, you know everything. You know that I love you."

Jesus said, "Then feed my sheep.

¹⁸"I tell you the truth, when you were young, you were able to do as you liked; you dressed yourself and went wherever you wanted to go. But when you are old, you will stretch out your hands, and others will dress you and take you where you don't want to go." ¹⁹Jesus said this to let him know by what kind of death he would glorify God. Then Jesus told him, "Follow me."

20 Peter turned around and saw behind them the disciple Jesus loved—the one who had leaned over to Jesus during supper and asked, "Lord, who will betray you?" 21 Peter asked Jesus, "What about him, Lord?"

22 Jesus replied, "If I want him to remain alive until I return, what is that to you? As for you, follow me." 23 So the rumor spread among the community of believers that this disciple wouldn't die. But that isn't what Jesus said at all. He only said, "If I want him to remain alive until I return, what is that to you?"

24 This disciple is the one who testifies to these events and has recorded them here. And we know that his account of these things is accurate.

25 Jesus also did many other things. If they were all written down, I suppose the whole world could not contain the books that would be written.

ACTS *A Book of Amazing Adventures!*

Look for **4** hidden messages in Acts!

Acts is about an exciting time that completely changed the world. It tells about
- **TONGUES ON FIRE**
- **MANY, MANY MIRACLES BY MANY DISCIPLES**
- **A BLINDING CHANGE OF HEART**
- **THOUSANDS TURNING TO JESUS**

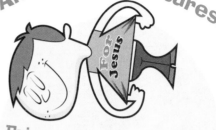

Friend or Foe?

Saul thought he was on the right side. One day, though, something happened that changed his mind, and he switched sides pretty quickly! **Find out what happened in Acts 9:1-31!**

Tongues of Fire and Tongues on Fire

Call the fire department! Burning to know more? **Read Acts 2.**

Up, Up, and Away

One day Jesus was standing on the ground talking to his disciples, and the next minute he was in the air. **Read the whole uplifting story for yourself in Acts 1:1-11!**

Workin' on a Chain Gang

The disciples couldn't seem to stay out of jail. But God always came to their rescue. **Read about their troubles with the authorities in the book of Acts. Here are just a few of the stories: Acts 4:1-31; Acts 5:12-42; Acts 12:1-19; and Acts 16:16-40.**

Smooth Sailin'

Gale force winds.
Smashing waves.
Driving rain. Why
wasn't Paul worried?
Find out in Acts 27:13-44.

Hit the Beach

Paul spent part of one winter on an island, but it was no vacation! **Read Acts 28:1-14 to find out what he was doing there!**

Keepin' On Keepin' On

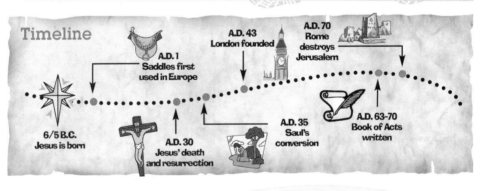

Paul walked lots of miles and started lots of churches, and he kept in touch with them by writing lots of letters. (Those letters make up a lot of the New Testament!)

See Acts 13:1-3 to read about a big missionary send-off.

Timeline

A.D. 1
Saddles first used in Europe

A.D. 43
London founded

A.D. 70
Rome destroys Jerusalem

6/5 B.C.
Jesus is born

A.D. 30
Jesus' death and resurrection

A.D. 35
Saul's conversion

A.D. 63-70
Book of Acts written

The JESUS CONNECTION

The whole Bible centers around Jesus. From the time Adam and Eve first sinned, God had been working on a plan to forgive people's sin. In Acts, the first part of God's plan had been completed. Jesus took the punishment for our sins when he died on the cross. After he rose from the dead, there was only one thing left to do—people had to find out about what Jesus did. That's why Jesus told his followers to go around the world with the good news about him. (Who can *you* tell about Jesus?)

The second part of God's plan will be completed when Jesus comes back to redeem his believers and establish a new heaven and earth.

What an amazing plan!

CHAPTER **1**

The Promise of the Holy Spirit

In my first book I told you, Theophilus, about everything Jesus began to do and teach 2until the day he was taken up to heaven after giving his chosen apostles further instructions through the Holy Spirit. 3During the forty days after his crucifixion, he appeared to the apostles from time to time, and he proved to them in many ways that he was actually alive. And he talked to them about the Kingdom of God.

4Once when he was eating with them, he commanded them, "Do not leave Jerusalem until the Father sends you the gift he promised, as I told you before. 5John baptized with water, but in just a few days you will be baptized with the Holy Spirit."

The Ascension of Jesus

6So when the apostles were with Jesus, they kept asking him, "Lord, has the time come for you to free Israel and restore our kingdom?"

7He replied, "The Father alone has the authority to set those dates and times, and they are not for you to know. 8But you will receive power when the Holy Spirit comes upon you. And you will be my witnesses, telling people about me everywhere—in Jerusalem, throughout Judea, in Samaria, and to the ends of the earth."

9After saying this, he was taken up into a cloud while they were watching, and they could no longer see him. 10As they strained to see him rising into heaven, two white-robed men suddenly stood among them. 11"Men of Galilee," they said, "why are you standing here staring into heaven? Jesus has been taken from you into heaven, but someday he will return from heaven in the same way you saw him go!"

Matthias Replaces Judas

12Then the apostles returned to Jerusalem from the Mount of Olives, a distance of half a mile. 13When they arrived, they went to the upstairs room of the house where they were staying.

Here are the names of those who were present: Peter, John, James, Andrew, Philip, Thomas, Bartholomew, Matthew, James (son of Alphaeus), Simon (the Zealot), and Judas (son of James). 14They all met together and were constantly united in prayer, along with Mary the mother of Jesus, several other women, and the brothers of Jesus.

15During this time, when about 120 believers were together in one place, Peter stood up and addressed them. 16"Brothers," he said, "the Scriptures had to be fulfilled concerning Judas, who guided those who arrested Jesus. This was predicted long ago by the Holy Spirit, speaking through King David. 17Judas was one of us and shared in the ministry with us."

18(Judas had bought a field with the money he received for his treachery. Falling headfirst there, his body split open, spilling out all his intestines. 19The news of his death spread to all the people of Jerusalem, and they gave the place the Aramaic name *Akeldama*, which means "Field of Blood.")

20Peter continued, "This was written in the book of Psalms, where it says, 'Let his home become desolate, with no one living in it.' It also says, 'Let someone else take his position.'

21"So now we must choose a replacement for Judas from among the men who were with us the entire time we were traveling with the Lord Jesus—22from the time he was baptized by John until the day he was taken from us. Whoever is chosen will join us as a witness of Jesus' resurrection."

23So they nominated two men: Joseph called Barsabbas (also known as Justus) and Matthias. 24Then they all prayed, "O Lord, you know every heart. Show us which of these men you have chosen 25as an apostle to replace Judas in this ministry, for he has deserted us and gone where he belongs." 26Then they cast lots, and Matthias was selected to become an apostle with the other eleven.

CHAPTER **2**

The Holy Spirit Comes

On the day of Pentecost all the believers were meeting together in one place. 2Suddenly, there was a sound from heaven like the roaring of a mighty windstorm, and it filled the house where they were sitting. 3Then, what looked like flames or tongues of fire appeared and settled on each of them. 4And everyone present was filled with the Holy Spirit and began speaking in other languages, as the Holy Spirit gave them this ability.

5At that time there were devout Jews from every nation living in Jerusalem. 6When they heard the loud noise, everyone came running, and they were bewildered to hear their own languages being spoken by the believers.

7They were completely amazed. "How can this be?" they exclaimed. "These people are all from Galilee, 8and yet we hear them speaking in our own native languages! 9Here we are—Parthians, Medes, Elamites, people from Mesopotamia, Judea, Cappadocia, Pontus, the province of Asia, 10Phrygia, Pamphylia, Egypt, and

SAY AGAIN? GUTEN TAG CIAO BONJOUR

HUH?

All those words mean "hello" in a different language. There's a cool story in the Bible about people speaking different languages. But they were speaking in languages they didn't even know! **Read the whole amazing story in ACTS 2:1-42.**

GRAB A FRIEND AND TRY THIS.

Together, make up your own foreign language. In your new language, what words represent these pictures?

Now, with your friend, go talk to three people using only your new language. They didn't understand you, did they? So how come on the day of Pentecost the people were able to speak in new languages and others were able to understand them? Because of God! God poured out his Holy Spirit on the people!

Think of three things you can tell about Jesus, and tell them to three people this week.

SPREAD THE NEWS, JUST LIKE THE DISCIPLES DID!

the areas of Libya around Cyrene, visitors from Rome 11(both Jews and converts to Judaism), Cretans, and Arabs. And we all hear these people speaking in our own languages about the wonderful things God has done!" 12They stood there amazed and perplexed. "What can this mean?" they asked each other.

13But others in the crowd ridiculed them, saying, "They're just drunk, that's all!"

Peter Preaches to the Crowd

14Then Peter stepped forward with the eleven other apostles and shouted to the crowd, "Listen carefully, all of you, fellow Jews and residents of Jerusalem! Make no mistake about this. 15These people are not drunk, as some of you are assuming. Nine o'clock in the morning is much too early for that. 16No, what you see was predicted long ago by the prophet Joel:

17 'In the last days,' God says,
    'I will pour out my Spirit upon all people.
  Your sons and daughters will prophesy.
    Your young men will see visions,
    and your old men will dream dreams.
18 In those days I will pour out my Spirit
        even on my servants—men and women
        alike—
    and they will prophesy.
19 And I will cause wonders in the heavens
        above
    and signs on the earth below—
    blood and fire and clouds of smoke.
20 The sun will become dark,
    and the moon will turn blood red
        before that great and glorious day
        of the LORD arrives.
21 But everyone who calls on the name
        of the LORD
    will be saved.'

22"People of Israel, listen! God publicly endorsed Jesus the Nazarene by doing powerful miracles, wonders, and signs through him, as you well know. 23But God knew what would happen, and his prearranged plan was carried out when Jesus was betrayed. With the help of lawless Gentiles, you nailed him to a cross and killed him. 24But God released him from the horrors of death and raised him back to life, for death could not keep him in its grip. 25King David said this about him:

  'I see that the LORD is always with me.
    I will not be shaken, for he is right
        beside me.

26 No wonder my heart is glad,
and my tongue shouts his praises!
My body rests in hope.
27 For you will not leave my soul among
the dead
or allow your Holy One to rot
in the grave.
28 You have shown me the way of life,
and you will fill me with the joy
of your presence.'

29 "Dear brothers, think about this! You can be sure that the patriarch David wasn't referring to himself, for he died and was buried, and his tomb is still here among us. 30 But he was a prophet, and he knew God had promised with an oath that one of David's own descendants would sit on his throne. 31 David was looking into the future and speaking of the Messiah's resurrection. He was saying that God would not leave him among the dead or allow his body to rot in the grave.

32 "God raised Jesus from the dead, and we are all witnesses of this. 33 Now he is exalted to the place of highest honor in heaven, at God's right hand. And the Father, as he had promised, gave him the Holy Spirit to pour out upon us, just as you see and hear today. 34 For David himself never ascended into heaven, yet he said,

'The LORD said to my Lord,
"Sit in the place of honor at my
right hand
35 until I humble your enemies,
making them a footstool under
your feet."'

36 "So let everyone in Israel know for certain that God has made this Jesus, whom you crucified, to be both Lord and Messiah!"

37 Peter's words pierced their hearts, and they said to him and to the other apostles, "Brothers, what should we do?"

38 Peter replied, "Each of you must repent of your sins and turn to God, and be baptized in the name of Jesus Christ for the forgiveness of your sins. Then you will receive the gift of the Holy Spirit. 39 This promise is to you, and to your children, and even to the Gentiles—all who have been called by the Lord our God." 40 Then Peter continued preaching for a long time, strongly urging all his listeners, "Save yourselves from this crooked generation!"

41 Those who believed what Peter said were baptized and added to the church that day—about 3,000 in all.

The Believers Form a Community

42 All the believers devoted themselves to the apostles' teaching, and to fellowship, and to sharing in meals (including the Lord's Supper), and to prayer.

43 A deep sense of awe came over them all, and the apostles performed many miraculous signs and wonders. 44 And all the believers met together in one place and shared everything they had. 45 They sold their property and possessions and shared the money with those in need. 46 They worshiped together at the Temple each day, met in homes for the Lord's Supper, and shared their meals with great joy and generosity—47 all the while praising God and enjoying the goodwill of all the people. And each day the Lord added to their fellowship those who were being saved.

CHAPTER **3**

Peter Heals a Crippled Beggar

Peter and John went to the Temple one afternoon to take part in the three o'clock prayer service. 2 As they approached the Temple, a man lame from birth was being carried in. Each day he was put beside the Temple gate, the one called the Beautiful Gate, so he could beg from the people going into the Temple. 3 When he saw Peter and John about to enter, he asked them for some money.

4 Peter and John looked at him intently, and Peter said, "Look at us!" 5 The lame man looked at them eagerly, expecting some money. 6 But Peter said, "I don't have any silver or gold for you. But I'll give you what I have. In the name of Jesus Christ the Nazarene, get up and walk!"

7 Then Peter took the lame man by the right hand and helped him up. And as he did, the man's feet and ankles were instantly healed and strengthened. 8 He jumped up, stood on his feet, and began to walk! Then, walking, leaping, and praising God, he went into the Temple with them.

9 All the people saw him walking and heard him praising God. 10 When they realized he was the lame beggar they had seen so often at the Beautiful Gate, they were absolutely astounded! 11 They all rushed out in amazement to Solomon's Colonnade, where the man was holding tightly to Peter and John.

Peter Preaches in the Temple

12 Peter saw his opportunity and addressed the crowd. "People of Israel," he said, "what is so surprising about this? And why stare at us as though

we had made this man walk by our own power or godliness? 13 For it is the God of Abraham, Isaac, and Jacob—the God of all our ancestors—who has brought glory to his servant Jesus by doing this. This is the same Jesus whom you handed over and rejected before Pilate, despite Pilate's decision to release him. 14 You rejected this holy, righteous one and instead demanded the release of a murderer. 15 You killed the author of life, but God raised him from the dead. And we are witnesses of this fact!

16 "Through faith in the name of Jesus, this man was healed—and you know how crippled he was before. Faith in Jesus' name has healed him before your very eyes.

17 "Friends, I realize that what you and your leaders did to Jesus was done in ignorance. 18 But God was fulfilling what all the prophets had foretold about the Messiah—that he must suffer these things. 19 Now repent of your sins and turn to God, so that your sins may be wiped away. 20 Then times of refreshment will come from the presence of the Lord, and he will again send you Jesus, your appointed Messiah. 21 For he must remain in heaven until the time for the final restoration of all things, as God promised long ago through his holy prophets. 22 Moses said, 'The LORD your God will raise up for you a Prophet like me from among your own people. Listen carefully to everything he tells you.' 23 Then Moses said, 'Anyone who will not listen to that Prophet will be completely cut off from God's people.'

24 "Starting with Samuel, every prophet spoke about what is happening today. 25 You are the children of those prophets, and you are included in the covenant God promised to your ancestors. For God said to Abraham, 'Through your descendants all the families on earth will be blessed.' 26 When God raised up his servant, Jesus, he sent him first to you people of Israel, to bless you by turning each of you back from your sinful ways."

CHAPTER 4

Peter and John before the Council

While Peter and John were speaking to the people, they were confronted by the priests, the captain of the Temple guard, and some of the Sadducees. 2 These leaders were very disturbed that Peter and John were teaching the people that through Jesus there is a resurrection of the dead. 3 They arrested them and, since it was already evening, put them in jail until morning.

4 But many of the people who heard their message believed it, so the number of believers now totaled about 5,000 men, not counting women and children.

5 The next day the council of all the rulers and elders and teachers of religious law met in Jerusalem. 6 Annas the high priest was there, along with Caiaphas, John, Alexander, and other relatives of the high priest. 7 They brought in the two disciples and demanded, "By what power, or in whose name, have you done this?"

8 Then Peter, filled with the Holy Spirit, said to them, "Rulers and elders of our people, 9 are we being questioned today because we've done a good deed for a crippled man? Do you want to know how he was healed? 10 Let me clearly state to all of you and to all the people of Israel that he was healed by the powerful name of Jesus Christ the Nazarene, the man you crucified but whom God raised from the dead. 11 For Jesus is the one referred to in the Scriptures, where it says,

'The stone that you builders rejected
has now become the cornerstone.'

12 There is salvation in no one else! God has given no other name under heaven by which we must be saved."

13 The members of the council were amazed when they saw the boldness of Peter and John, for they could see that they were ordinary men with no special training in the Scriptures. They also recognized them as men who had been with Jesus. 14 But since they could see the man who had been healed standing right there among them, there was nothing the council could say. 15 So they ordered Peter and John out of the council chamber and conferred among themselves.

16 "What should we do with these men?" they asked each other. "We can't deny that they have performed a miraculous sign, and everybody in Jerusalem knows about it. 17 But to keep them from spreading their propaganda any further, we must warn them not to speak to anyone in Jesus' name again." 18 So they called the apostles back in and commanded them never again to speak or teach in the name of Jesus.

19 But Peter and John replied, "Do you think God wants us to obey you rather than him? 20 We cannot stop telling about everything we have seen and heard."

21 The council then threatened them further, but they finally let them go because they didn't know how to punish them without starting a riot. For everyone was praising God 22 for this mirac-

ulous sign—the healing of a man who had been lame for more than forty years.

The Believers Pray for Courage

23 As soon as they were freed, Peter and John returned to the other believers and told them what the leading priests and elders had said. 24 When they heard the report, all the believers lifted their voices together in prayer to God: "O Sovereign Lord, Creator of heaven and earth, the sea, and everything in them—25 you spoke long ago by the Holy Spirit through our ancestor David, your servant, saying,

'Why were the nations so angry?
  Why did they waste their time
    with futile plans?
26 The kings of the earth prepared for battle;
  the rulers gathered together
against the LORD
  and against his Messiah.'

27 "In fact, this has happened here in this very city! For Herod Antipas, Pontius Pilate the governor, the Gentiles, and the people of Israel were all united against Jesus, your holy servant, whom you anointed. 28 But everything they did was determined beforehand according to your will. 29 And now, O Lord, hear their threats, and give us, your servants, great boldness in preaching your word. 30 Stretch out your hand with healing power; may miraculous signs and wonders be done through the name of your holy servant Jesus."

31 After this prayer, the meeting place shook, and they were all filled with the Holy Spirit. Then they preached the word of God with boldness.

The Believers Share Their Possessions

32 All the believers were united in heart and mind. And they felt that what they owned was not their own, so they shared everything they had. 33 The apostles testified powerfully to the resurrection of the Lord Jesus, and God's great blessing was upon them all. 34 There were no needy people among them, because those who owned land or houses would sell them 35 and bring the money to the apostles to give to those in need.

36 For instance, there was Joseph, the one the apostles nicknamed Barnabas (which means "Son of Encouragement"). He was from the tribe of Levi and came from the island of Cyprus. 37 He sold a field he owned and brought the money to the apostles.

Ananias and Sapphira

But there was a certain man named Ananias who, with his wife, Sapphira, sold some property. 2 He brought part of the money to the apostles, claiming it was the full amount. With his wife's consent, he kept the rest.

3 Then Peter said, "Ananias, why have you let Satan fill your heart? You lied to the Holy Spirit, and you kept some of the money for yourself. 4 The property was yours to sell or not sell, as you wished. And after selling it, the money was also yours to give away. How could you do a thing like this? You weren't lying to us but to God!"

5 As soon as Ananias heard these words, he fell to the floor and died. Everyone who heard about it was terrified. 6 Then some young men got up, wrapped him in a sheet, and took him out and buried him.

7 About three hours later his wife came in, not knowing what had happened. 8 Peter asked her, "Was this the price you and your husband received for your land?"

"Yes," she replied, "that was the price."

9 And Peter said, "How could the two of you even think of conspiring to test the Spirit of the Lord like this? The young men who buried your husband are just outside the door, and they will carry you out, too."

10 Instantly, she fell to the floor and died. When the young men came in and saw that she was dead, they carried her out and buried her beside her husband. 11 Great fear gripped the entire church and everyone else who heard what had happened.

The Apostles Heal Many

12 The apostles were performing many miraculous signs and wonders among the people. And all the believers were meeting regularly at the Temple in the area known as Solomon's Colonnade. 13 But no one else dared to join them, even though all the people had high regard for them. 14 Yet more and more people believed and were brought to the Lord—crowds of both men and women. 15 As a result of the apostles' work, sick people were brought out into the streets on beds and mats so that Peter's shadow might fall across some of them as he went by. 16 Crowds came from the villages around Jerusalem, bringing their sick and those possessed by evil spirits, and they were all healed.

The Apostles Meet Opposition

17 The high priest and his officials, who were Sadducees, were filled with jealousy. 18 They arrested

the apostles and put them in the public jail. ¹⁹But an angel of the Lord came at night, opened the gates of the jail, and brought them out. Then he told them, ²⁰"Go to the Temple and give the people this message of life!"

²¹So at daybreak the apostles entered the Temple, as they were told, and immediately began teaching.

When the high priest and his officials arrived, they convened the high council—the full assembly of the elders of Israel. Then they sent for the apostles to be brought from the jail for trial. ²²But when the Temple guards went to the jail, the men were gone. So they returned to the council and reported, ²³"The jail was securely locked, with the guards standing outside, but when we opened the gates, no one was there!"

²⁴When the captain of the Temple guard and the leading priests heard this, they were perplexed, wondering where it would all end. ²⁵Then someone arrived with startling news: "The men you put in jail are standing in the Temple, teaching the people!"

²⁶The captain went with his Temple guards and arrested the apostles, but without violence, for they were afraid the people would stone them. ²⁷Then they brought the apostles before the high council, where the high priest confronted them. ²⁸"Didn't we tell you never again to teach in this man's name?" he demanded. "Instead, you have filled all Jerusalem with your teaching about him, and you want to make us responsible for his death!"

²⁹**But Peter and the apostles replied, "We must obey God rather than any human authority.** ³⁰The God of our ancestors raised Jesus from the dead after you killed him by hanging him on a cross. ³¹Then God put him in the place of honor at his right hand as Prince and Savior. He did this so the people of Israel would repent of their sins and be forgiven. ³²We are witnesses of these things and so is the Holy Spirit, who is given by God to those who obey him."

³³When they heard this, the high council was furious and decided to kill them. ³⁴But one member, a Pharisee named Gamaliel, who was an expert in religious law and respected by all the people, stood up and ordered that the men be sent outside the council chamber for a while. ³⁵Then he said to his colleagues, "Men of Israel, take care what you are planning to do to these men! ³⁶Some time ago there was that fellow Theudas, who pretended to be someone great. About 400 others joined him, but he was killed,

and all his followers went their various ways. The whole movement came to nothing. ³⁷After him, at the time of the census, there was Judas of Galilee. He got people to follow him, but he was killed, too, and all his followers were scattered.

³⁸"So my advice is, leave these men alone. Let them go. If they are planning and doing these things merely on their own, it will soon be overthrown. ³⁹But if it is from God, you will not be able to overthrow them. You may even find yourselves fighting against God!"

⁴⁰The others accepted his advice. They called in the apostles and had them flogged. Then they ordered them never again to speak in the name of Jesus, and they let them go.

⁴¹The apostles left the high council rejoicing that God had counted them worthy to suffer disgrace for the name of Jesus. ⁴²And every day, in the Temple and from house to house, they continued to teach and preach this message: "Jesus is the Messiah."

CHAPTER **6**

Seven Men Chosen to Serve

But as the believers rapidly multiplied, there were rumblings of discontent. The Greek-speaking believers complained about the Hebrew-speaking believers, saying that their widows were being discriminated against in the daily distribution of food.

²So the Twelve called a meeting of all the believers. They said, "We apostles should spend our time teaching the word of God, not running a food program. ³And so, brothers, select seven men who are well respected and are full of the Spirit and wisdom. We will give them this responsibility. ⁴Then we apostles can spend our time in prayer and teaching the word."

⁵Everyone liked this idea, and they chose the following: Stephen (a man full of faith and the Holy Spirit), Philip, Procorus, Nicanor, Timon, Parmenas, and Nicolas of Antioch (an earlier convert to the Jewish faith). ⁶These seven were presented to the apostles, who prayed for them as they laid their hands on them.

⁷So God's message continued to spread. The number of believers greatly increased in Jerusalem, and many of the Jewish priests were converted, too.

Stephen Is Arrested

⁸Stephen, a man full of God's grace and power, performed amazing miracles and signs among the people. ⁹But one day some men from the Synagogue of Freed Slaves, as it was called, started to

debate with him. They were Jews from Cyrene, Alexandria, Cilicia, and the province of Asia. ¹⁰None of them could stand against the wisdom and the Spirit with which Stephen spoke.

¹¹So they persuaded some men to lie about Stephen, saying, "We heard him blaspheme Moses, and even God." ¹²This roused the people, the elders, and the teachers of religious law. So they arrested Stephen and brought him before the high council.

¹³The lying witnesses said, "This man is always speaking against the holy Temple and against the law of Moses. ¹⁴We have heard him say that this Jesus of Nazareth will destroy the Temple and change the customs Moses handed down to us."

¹⁵At this point everyone in the high council stared at Stephen, because his face became as bright as an angel's.

CHAPTER 7

Stephen Addresses the Council
Then the high priest asked Stephen, "Are these accusations true?"

Heroes
of the Faith

You've heard of superheroes, right?

Want to learn about a *real* superhero? **Read ACTS 6:8-15 and ACTS 7:54-60.**

Stephen died for his faith. But all around us are heroes who live their lives for Jesus. Think about someone you know who's a hero of the faith.

Write your hero's name below.

• •

Now write that person a note, to thank him or her for being an example of faith for you.

WRITE NOTES TO EVERY HERO OF THE FAITH YOU KNOW!

²This was Stephen's reply: "Brothers and fathers, listen to me. Our glorious God appeared to our ancestor Abraham in Mesopotamia before he settled in Haran. ³God told him, 'Leave your native land and your relatives, and come into the land that I will show you.' ⁴So Abraham left the land of the Chaldeans and lived in Haran until his father died. Then God brought him here to the land where you now live.

⁵"But God gave him no inheritance here, not even one square foot of land. God did promise, however, that eventually the whole land would belong to Abraham and his descendants—even though he had no children yet. ⁶God also told him that his descendants would live in a foreign land, where they would be oppressed as slaves for 400 years. ⁷'But I will punish the nation that enslaves them,' God said, 'and in the end they will come out and worship me here in this place.'

⁸"God also gave Abraham the covenant of circumcision at that time. So when Abraham became the father of Isaac, he circumcised him on the eighth day. And the practice was continued when Isaac became the father of Jacob, and when Jacob became the father of the twelve patriarchs of the Israelite nation.

⁹"These patriarchs were jealous of their brother Joseph, and they sold him to be a slave in Egypt. But God was with him ¹⁰and rescued him from all his troubles. And God gave him favor before Pharaoh, king of Egypt. God also gave Joseph unusual wisdom, so that Pharaoh appointed him governor over all of Egypt and put him in charge of the palace.

¹¹"But a famine came upon Egypt and Canaan. There was great misery, and our ancestors ran out of food. ¹²Jacob heard that there was still grain in Egypt, so he sent his sons—our ancestors—to buy some. ¹³The second time they went, Joseph revealed his identity to his brothers, and they were introduced to Pharaoh. ¹⁴Then Joseph sent for his father, Jacob, and all his relatives to come to Egypt, seventy-five persons in all. ¹⁵So Jacob went to Egypt. He died there, as did our ancestors. ¹⁶Their bodies were taken to Shechem and buried in the tomb Abraham had bought for a certain price from Hamor's sons in Shechem.

¹⁷"As the time drew near when God would fulfill his promise to Abraham, the number of our people in Egypt greatly increased. ¹⁸But then a new king came to the throne of Egypt who knew nothing about Joseph. ¹⁹This king exploited our people and oppressed them, forcing parents to abandon their newborn babies so they would die.

20"At that time Moses was born—a beautiful child in God's eyes. His parents cared for him at home for three months. 21When they had to abandon him, Pharaoh's daughter adopted him and raised him as her own son. 22Moses was taught all the wisdom of the Egyptians, and he was powerful in both speech and action.

23"One day when Moses was forty years old, he decided to visit his relatives, the people of Israel. 24He saw an Egyptian mistreating an Israelite. So Moses came to the man's defense and avenged him, killing the Egyptian. 25Moses assumed his fellow Israelites would realize that God had sent him to rescue them, but they didn't.

26"The next day he visited them again and saw two men of Israel fighting. He tried to be a peacemaker. 'Men,' he said, 'you are brothers. Why are you fighting each other?'

27"But the man in the wrong pushed Moses aside. 'Who made you a ruler and judge over us?' he asked. 28'Are you going to kill me as you killed that Egyptian yesterday?' 29When Moses heard that, he fled the country and lived as a foreigner in the land of Midian. There his two sons were born.

30"Forty years later, in the desert near Mount Sinai, an angel appeared to Moses in the flame of a burning bush. 31When Moses saw it, he was amazed at the sight. As he went to take a closer look, the voice of the LORD called out to him, 32'I am the God of your ancestors—the God of Abraham, Isaac, and Jacob.' Moses shook with terror and did not dare to look.

33"Then the LORD said to him, 'Take off your sandals, for you are standing on holy ground. 34I have certainly seen the oppression of my people in Egypt. I have heard their groans and have come down to rescue them. Now go, for I am sending you back to Egypt.'

35"So God sent back the same man his people had previously rejected when they demanded, 'Who made you a ruler and judge over us?' Through the angel who appeared to him in the burning bush, God sent Moses to be their ruler and savior. 36And by means of many wonders and miraculous signs, he led them out of Egypt, through the Red Sea, and through the wilderness for forty years.

37"Moses himself told the people of Israel, 'God will raise up for you a Prophet like me from among your own people.' 38Moses was with our ancestors, the assembly of God's people in the wilderness, when the angel spoke to him at Mount Sinai. And there Moses received life-giving words to pass on to us.

39"But our ancestors refused to listen to Moses. They rejected him and wanted to return to Egypt. 40They told Aaron, 'Make us some gods who can lead us, for we don't know what has become of this Moses, who brought us out of Egypt.' 41So they made an idol shaped like a calf, and they sacrificed to it and celebrated over this thing they had made. 42Then God turned away from them and abandoned them to serve the stars of heaven as their gods! In the book of the prophets it is written,

'Was it to me you were bringing sacrifices
     and offerings
  during those forty years in the
     wilderness, Israel?
43 No, you carried your pagan gods—
     the shrine of Molech,
  the star of your god Rephan,
  and the images you made to
     worship them.
So I will send you into exile
  as far away as Babylon.'

44"Our ancestors carried the Tabernacle with them through the wilderness. It was constructed according to the plan God had shown to Moses. 45Years later, when Joshua led our ancestors in battle against the nations that God drove out of this land, the Tabernacle was taken with them into their new territory. And it stayed there until the time of King David.

46"David found favor with God and asked for the privilege of building a permanent Temple for the God of Jacob. 47But it was Solomon who actually built it. 48However, the Most High doesn't live in temples made by human hands. As the prophet says,

49 'Heaven is my throne,
     and the earth is my footstool.
  Could you build me a temple as good as that?'
     asks the LORD.
  'Could you build me such a resting place?
50   Didn't my hands make both heaven
     and earth?'

51"You stubborn people! You are heathen at heart and deaf to the truth. Must you forever resist the Holy Spirit? That's what your ancestors did, and so do you! 52Name one prophet your ancestors didn't persecute! They even killed the ones who predicted the coming of the Righteous One—the Messiah whom you betrayed and murdered. 53You deliberately disobeyed God's law, even though you received it from the hands of angels."

54The Jewish leaders were infuriated by Stephen's accusation, and they shook their fists at him in rage. 55But Stephen, full of the Holy Spirit, gazed steadily into heaven and saw the glory of God, and he saw Jesus standing in the place of honor at God's right hand. 56And he told them, "Look, I see the heavens opened and the Son of Man standing in the place of honor at God's right hand!"

57Then they put their hands over their ears and began shouting. They rushed at him 58and dragged him out of the city and began to stone him. His accusers took off their coats and laid them at the feet of a young man named Saul.

59As they stoned him, Stephen prayed, "Lord Jesus, receive my spirit." 60He fell to his knees, shouting, "Lord, don't charge them with this sin!" And with that, he died.

CHAPTER **8**

Saul was one of the witnesses, and he agreed completely with the killing of Stephen.

Persecution Scatters the Believers

A great wave of persecution began that day, sweeping over the church in Jerusalem; and all the believers except the apostles were scattered through the regions of Judea and Samaria. 2(Some devout men came and buried Stephen with great mourning.) 3But Saul was going everywhere to destroy the church. He went from house to house, dragging out both men and women to throw them into prison.

Philip Preaches in Samaria

4But the believers who were scattered preached the Good News about Jesus wherever they went. 5Philip, for example, went to the city of Samaria and told the people there about the Messiah. 6Crowds listened intently to Philip because they were eager to hear his message and see the miraculous signs he did. 7Many evil spirits were cast out, screaming as they left their victims. And many who had been paralyzed or lame were healed. 8So there was great joy in that city.

9A man named Simon had been a sorcerer there for many years, amazing the people of Samaria and claiming to be someone great. 10Everyone, from the least to the greatest, often spoke of him as "the Great One—the Power of God." 11They listened closely to him because for a long time he had astounded them with his magic.

12But now the people believed Philip's

Reflection of Love

Look in the mirror and what do you see? Yup—you see a reflection. **Read ACTS 8:26-40 to meet a man who reflected the love of Jesus!**

THEN TRY THIS!

Gather two empty paper towel tubes, a mirror, a flashlight — and a friend!

Read what Jesus had to say about sharing your faith in him. Check out Matthew 28:19-20.

1 Set the paper towel tubes on a table in front of a mirror. Place them in a V-shape pointing toward the mirror.

2 Use a flashlight to shine light through one tube toward the mirror. Angle the second tube until you see the light reflected back through the second tube.

THAT'S ENLIGHTENING!

When we treat others the way Jesus says to, we reflect the love Jesus shows us. Philip reflected Jesus' love when he helped the Ethiopian understand the Scripture.

WHO CAN YOU REFLECT THE LOVE OF JESUS TO THIS WEEK?

Write that person's name below.

message of Good News concerning the King-dom of God and the name of Jesus Christ. As a result, many men and women were baptized. [13]Then Simon himself believed and was baptized. He began following Philip wherever he went, and he was amazed by the signs and great miracles Philip performed.

[14]When the apostles in Jerusalem heard that the people of Samaria had accepted God's message, they sent Peter and John there. [15]As soon as they arrived, they prayed for these new believers to receive the Holy Spirit. [16]The Holy Spirit had not yet come upon any of them, for they had only been baptized in the name of the Lord Jesus. [17]Then Peter and John laid their hands upon these believers, and they received the Holy Spirit.

[18]When Simon saw that the Spirit was given when the apostles laid their hands on people, he offered them money to buy this power. [19]"Let me have this power, too," he exclaimed, "so that when I lay my hands on people, they will receive the Holy Spirit!"

[20]But Peter replied, "May your money be destroyed with you for thinking God's gift can be bought! [21]You can have no part in this, for your heart is not right with God. [22]Repent of your wickedness and pray to the Lord. Perhaps he will forgive your evil thoughts, [23]for I can see that you are full of bitter jealousy and are held captive by sin."

[24]"Pray to the Lord for me," Simon exclaimed, "that these terrible things you've said won't happen to me!"

[25]After testifying and preaching the word of the Lord in Samaria, Peter and John returned to Jerusalem. And they stopped in many Samaritan villages along the way to preach the Good News.

Philip and the Ethiopian Eunuch

[26]As for Philip, an angel of the Lord said to him, "Go south down the desert road that runs from Jerusalem to Gaza." [27]So he started out, and he met the treasurer of Ethiopia, a eunuch of great authority under the Kandake, the queen of Ethiopia. The eunuch had gone to Jerusalem to worship, [28]and he was now returning. Seated in his carriage, he was reading aloud from the book of the prophet Isaiah.

[29]The Holy Spirit said to Philip, "Go over and walk along beside the carriage."

[30]Philip ran over and heard the man reading from the prophet Isaiah. Philip asked, "Do you understand what you are reading?"

Inside Out

You can't tell what a person's like on the inside by looking at the outside. That was sure true for Saul in Acts! **Read about his amazing change in ACTS 9:1-20!**

NOW FIND A FRIEND AND TRY THIS!

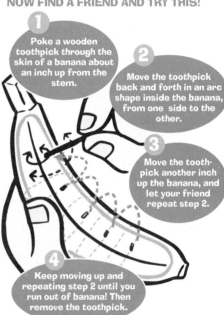

1 Poke a wooden toothpick through the skin of a banana about an inch up from the stem.

2 Move the toothpick back and forth in an arc shape inside the banana, from one side to the other.

3 Move the toothpick another inch up the banana, and let your friend repeat step 2.

4 Keep moving up and repeating step 2 until you run out of banana! Then remove the toothpick.

The banana doesn't look different on the outside, does it? But inside it's already cut into bite-size pieces!

Dip the banana pieces in chocolate. Before you eat, think of something that needs to change in your heart.

PRAY WITH YOUR FRIEND AND ASK GOD TO CHANGE EACH OF YOU ON THE INSIDE!

31The man replied, "How can I, unless someone instructs me?" And he urged Philip to come up into the carriage and sit with him.

32The passage of Scripture he had been reading was this:

"He was led like a sheep to the slaughter.
　And as a lamb is silent before the shearers,
　he did not open his mouth.
33 He was humiliated and received no justice.
　Who can speak of his descendants?
　For his life was taken from the earth."

34The eunuch asked Philip, "Tell me, was the prophet talking about himself or someone else?" 35So beginning with this same Scripture, Philip told him the Good News about Jesus.

36As they rode along, they came to some water, and the eunuch said, "Look! There's some water! Why can't I be baptized?"* 38He ordered the carriage to stop, and they went down into the water, and Philip baptized him.

39When they came up out of the water, the Spirit of the Lord snatched Philip away. The eunuch never saw him again but went on his way rejoicing. 40Meanwhile, Philip found himself farther north at the town of Azotus. He preached the Good News there and in every town along the way until he came to Caesarea.

CHAPTER **9**
Saul's Conversion

Meanwhile, Saul was uttering threats with every breath and was eager to kill the Lord's followers. So he went to the high priest. 2He requested letters addressed to the synagogues in Damascus, asking for their cooperation in the arrest of any followers of the Way he found there. He wanted to bring them—both men and women—back to Jerusalem in chains.

3As he was approaching Damascus on this mission, a light from heaven suddenly shone down around him. 4He fell to the ground and heard a voice saying to him, "Saul! Saul! Why are you persecuting me?"

5"Who are you, lord?" Saul asked.

And the voice replied, "I am Jesus, the one you are persecuting! 6Now get up and go into the city, and you will be told what you must do."

7The men with Saul stood speechless, for they heard the sound of someone's voice but saw no one! 8Saul picked himself up off the ground, but when he opened his eyes he was blind. So his companions led him by the hand to Damascus.

9He remained there blind for three days and did not eat or drink.

10Now there was a believer in Damascus named Ananias. The Lord spoke to him in a vision, calling, "Ananias!"

"Yes, Lord!" he replied.

11The Lord said, "Go over to Straight Street, to the house of Judas. When you get there, ask for a man from Tarsus named Saul. He is praying to me right now. 12I have shown him a vision of a man named Ananias coming in and laying hands on him so he can see again."

13"But Lord," exclaimed Ananias, "I've heard many people talk about the terrible things this man has done to the believers in Jerusalem! 14And he is authorized by the leading priests to arrest everyone who calls upon your name."

15But the Lord said, "Go, for Saul is my chosen instrument to take my message to the Gentiles and to kings, as well as to the people of Israel. 16And I will show him how much he must suffer for my name's sake."

17So Ananias went and found Saul. He laid his hands on him and said, "Brother Saul, the Lord Jesus, who appeared to you on the road, has sent me so that you might regain your sight and be filled with the Holy Spirit." 18Instantly something like scales fell from Saul's eyes, and he regained his sight. Then he got up and was baptized. 19Afterward he ate some food and regained his strength.

Saul in Damascus and Jerusalem

Saul stayed with the believers in Damascus for a few days. 20And immediately he began preaching about Jesus in the synagogues, saying, "He is indeed the Son of God!"

21All who heard him were amazed. "Isn't this the same man who caused such devastation among Jesus' followers in Jerusalem?" they asked. "And didn't he come here to arrest them and take them in chains to the leading priests?"

22Saul's preaching became more and more powerful, and the Jews in Damascus couldn't refute his proofs that Jesus was indeed the Messiah. 23After a while some of the Jews plotted together to kill him. 24They were watching for him day and night at the city gate so they could murder him, but Saul was told about their plot. 25So during the night, some of the other believers lowered him in a large basket through an opening in the city wall.

8:36 Some manuscripts add verse 37, "You can," Philip answered, "if you believe with all your heart." And the eunuch replied, "I believe that Jesus Christ is the Son of God."

26When Saul arrived in Jerusalem, he tried to meet with the believers, but they were all afraid of him. They did not believe he had truly become a believer! 27Then Barnabas brought him to the apostles and told them how Saul had seen the Lord on the way to Damascus and how the Lord had spoken to Saul. He also told them that Saul had preached boldly in the name of Jesus in Damascus.

28So Saul stayed with the apostles and went all around Jerusalem with them, preaching boldly in the name of the Lord. 29He debated with some Greek-speaking Jews, but they tried to murder him. 30When the believers heard about this, they took him down to Caesarea and sent him away to Tarsus, his hometown.

31The church then had peace throughout Judea, Galilee, and Samaria, and it became stronger as the believers lived in the fear of the Lord. And with the encouragement of the Holy Spirit, it also grew in numbers.

Peter Heals Aeneas and Raises Dorcas

32Meanwhile, Peter traveled from place to place, and he came down to visit the believers in the town of Lydda. 33There he met a man named Aeneas, who had been paralyzed and bedridden for eight years. 34Peter said to him, "Aeneas, Jesus Christ heals you! Get up, and roll up your sleeping mat!" And he was healed instantly. 35Then the whole population of Lydda and Sharon saw Aeneas walking around, and they turned to the Lord.

36There was a believer in Joppa named Tabitha (which in Greek is Dorcas). She was always doing kind things for others and helping the poor. 37About this time she became ill and died. Her body was washed for burial and laid in an upstairs room. 38But the believers had heard that Peter was nearby at Lydda, so they sent two men to beg him, "Please come as soon as possible!"

39So Peter returned with them; and as soon as he arrived, they took him to the upstairs room. The room was filled with widows who were weeping and showing him the coats and other clothes Dorcas had made for them. 40But Peter asked them all to leave the room; then he knelt and prayed. Turning to the body he said, "Get up, Tabitha." And she opened her eyes! When she saw Peter, she sat up! 41He gave her his hand and helped her up. Then he called in the widows and all the believers, and he presented her to them alive.

42The news spread through the whole town, and many believed in the Lord. 43And Peter stayed a long time in Joppa, living with Simon, a tanner of hides.

CHAPTER 10
Cornelius Calls for Peter

In Caesarea there lived a Roman army officer named Cornelius, who was a captain of the Italian Regiment. 2He was a devout, God-fearing man, as was everyone in his household. He gave generously to the poor and prayed regularly to God. 3One afternoon about three o'clock, he had a vision in which he saw an angel of God coming toward him. "Cornelius!" the angel said.

4Cornelius stared at him in terror. "What is it, sir?" he asked the angel.

And the angel replied, "Your prayers and gifts to the poor have been received by God as an offering! 5Now send some men to Joppa, and summon a man named Simon Peter. 6He is staying with Simon, a tanner who lives near the seashore.

7As soon as the angel was gone, Cornelius called two of his household servants and a devout soldier, one of his personal attendants. 8He told them what had happened and sent them off to Joppa.

Peter Visits Cornelius

9The next day as Cornelius's messengers were nearing the town, Peter went up on the flat roof to pray. It was about noon, 10and he was hungry. But while a meal was being prepared, he fell into a trance. 11He saw the sky open, and something like a large sheet was let down by its four corners. 12In the sheet were all sorts of animals, reptiles, and birds. 13Then a voice said to him, "Get up, Peter; kill and eat them."

14"No, Lord," Peter declared. "I have never eaten anything that our Jewish laws have declared impure and unclean."

15But the voice spoke again: "Do not call something unclean if God has made it clean." 16The same vision was repeated three times. Then the sheet was suddenly pulled up to heaven.

17Peter was very perplexed. What could the vision mean? Just then the men sent by Cornelius found Simon's house. Standing outside the gate, 18they asked if a man named Simon Peter was staying there.

19Meanwhile, as Peter was puzzling over the vision, the Holy Spirit said to him, "Three men have come looking for you. 20Get up, go downstairs, and go with them without hesitation. Don't worry, for I have sent them."

²¹So Peter went down and said, "I'm the man you are looking for. Why have you come?" ²²They said, "We were sent by Cornelius, a Roman officer. He is a devout and God-fearing man, well respected by all the Jews. A holy angel instructed him to summon you to his house so that he can hear your message." ²³So Peter invited the men to stay for the night. The next day he went with them, accompanied by some of the brothers from Joppa.

²⁴They arrived in Caesarea the following day. Cornelius was waiting for them and had called together his relatives and close friends. ²⁵As Peter entered his home, Cornelius fell at his feet and worshiped him. ²⁶But Peter pulled him up and said, "Stand up! I'm a human being just like you!" ²⁷So they talked together and went inside, where many others were assembled.

²⁸Peter told them, "You know it is against our laws for a Jewish man to enter a Gentile home like this or to associate with you. But God has shown me that I should no longer think of anyone as impure or unclean. ²⁹So I came without objection as soon as I was sent for. Now tell me why you sent for me."

³⁰Cornelius replied, "Four days ago I was praying in my house about this same time, three o'clock in the afternoon. Suddenly, a man in dazzling clothes was standing in front of me. ³¹He told me, 'Cornelius, your prayer has been heard, and your gifts to the poor have been noticed by God! ³²Now send messengers to Joppa, and summon a man named Simon Peter. He is staying in the home of Simon, a tanner who lives near the seashore.' ³³So I sent for you at once, and it was good of you to come. Now we are all here, waiting before God to hear the message the Lord has given you."

The Gentiles Hear the Good News

³⁴Then Peter replied, "I see very clearly that God shows no favoritism. ³⁵In every nation he accepts those who fear him and do what is right. ³⁶This is the message of Good News for the people of Israel—that there is peace with God through Jesus Christ, who is Lord of all. ³⁷You know what happened throughout Judea, beginning in Galilee, after John began preaching his message of baptism. ³⁸And you know that God anointed Jesus of Nazareth with the Holy Spirit and with power. Then Jesus went around doing good and healing all who were oppressed by the devil, for God was with him.

³⁹"And we apostles are witnesses of all he did throughout Judea and in Jerusalem. They put him to death by hanging him on a cross, ⁴⁰but God raised him to life on the third day. Then God allowed him to appear, ⁴¹not to the general public, but to us whom God had chosen in advance to be his witnesses. We were those who ate and drank with him after he rose from the dead. ⁴²And he ordered us to preach everywhere and to testify that Jesus is the one appointed by God to be the judge of all—the living and the dead. ⁴³He is the one all the prophets testified about, saying that everyone who believes in him will have their sins forgiven through his name."

The Gentiles Receive the Holy Spirit

⁴⁴Even as Peter was saying these things, the Holy Spirit fell upon all who were listening to the message. ⁴⁵The Jewish believers who came with Peter were amazed that the gift of the Holy Spirit had been poured out on the Gentiles, too. ⁴⁶For they heard them speaking in tongues and praising God.

Then Peter asked, ⁴⁷"Can anyone object to their being baptized, now that they have received the Holy Spirit just as we did?" ⁴⁸So he gave orders for them to be baptized in the name of Jesus Christ. Afterward Cornelius asked him to stay with them for several days.

CHAPTER **11**

Peter Explains His Actions

Soon the news reached the apostles and other believers in Judea that the Gentiles had received the word of God. ²But when Peter arrived back in Jerusalem, the Jewish believers criticized him. ³"You entered the home of Gentiles and even ate with them!" they said.

⁴Then Peter told them exactly what had happened. ⁵"I was in the town of Joppa," he said, "and while I was praying, I went into a trance and saw a vision. Something like a large sheet was let down by its four corners from the sky. And it came right down to me. ⁶When I looked inside the sheet, I saw all sorts of small animals, wild animals, reptiles, and birds. ⁷And I heard a voice say, 'Get up, Peter; kill and eat them.'

⁸"'No, Lord,' I replied. 'I have never eaten anything that our Jewish laws have declared impure or unclean.'

⁹"But the voice from heaven spoke again: 'Do not call something unclean if God has made it clean.' ¹⁰This happened three times before the sheet and all it contained was pulled back up to heaven.

11"Just then three men who had been sent from Caesarea arrived at the house where we were staying. 12The Holy Spirit told me to go with them and not to worry that they were Gentiles. These six brothers here accompanied me, and we soon entered the home of the man who had sent for us. 13He told us how an angel had appeared to him in his home and had told him, 'Send messengers to Joppa, and summon a man named Simon Peter. 14He will tell you how you and everyone in your household can be saved!'

15"As I began to speak," Peter continued, "the Holy Spirit fell on them, just as he fell on us at the beginning. 16Then I thought of the Lord's words when he said, 'John baptized with water, but you will be baptized with the Holy Spirit.' 17And since God gave these Gentiles the same gift he gave us when we believed in the Lord Jesus Christ, who was I to stand in God's way?"

18When the others heard this, they stopped objecting and began praising God. They said, "We can see that God has also given the Gentiles the privilege of repenting of their sins and receiving eternal life."

The Church in Antioch of Syria

19Meanwhile, the believers who had been scattered during the persecution after Stephen's death traveled as far as Phoenicia, Cyprus, and Antioch of Syria. They preached the word of God, but only to Jews. 20However, some of the believers who went to Antioch from Cyprus and Cyrene began preaching to the Gentiles about the Lord Jesus. 21The power of the Lord was with them, and a large number of these Gentiles believed and turned to the Lord.

22When the church at Jerusalem heard what had happened, they sent Barnabas to Antioch. 23When he arrived and saw this evidence of God's blessing, he was filled with joy, and he encouraged the believers to stay true to the Lord. 24Barnabas was a good man, full of the Holy Spirit and strong in faith. And many people were brought to the Lord.

25Then Barnabas went on to Tarsus to look for Saul. 26When he found him, he brought him back to Antioch. Both of them stayed there with the church for a full year, teaching large crowds of people. (It was at Antioch that the believers were first called Christians.)

27During this time some prophets traveled from Jerusalem to Antioch. 28One of them named Agabus stood up in one of the meetings and predicted by the Spirit that a great famine was coming upon the entire Roman world. (This was fulfilled during the reign of Claudius.) 29So the believers in Antioch decided to send relief to the brothers and sisters in Judea, everyone giving as much as they could. 30This they did, entrusting their gifts to Barnabas and Saul to take to the elders of the church in Jerusalem.

CHAPTER **12**
James Is Killed and Peter Is Imprisoned

About that time King Herod Agrippa began to persecute some believers in the church. 2He had the apostle James (John's brother) killed with a sword. 3When Herod saw how much this pleased the Jewish people, he also arrested Peter. (This took place during the Passover celebration.) 4Then he imprisoned him, placing him under the guard of four squads of four soldiers each. Herod intended to bring Peter out for public trial after the Passover. 5But while Peter was in prison, the church prayed very earnestly for him.

Peter's Miraculous Escape from Prison

6The night before Peter was to be placed on trial, he was asleep, fastened with two chains between two soldiers. Others stood guard at the prison gate. 7Suddenly, there was a bright light in the cell, and an angel of the Lord stood before Peter. The angel struck him on the side to awaken him and said, "Quick! Get up!" And the chains fell off his wrists. 8Then the angel told him, "Get dressed and put on your sandals." And he did. "Now put on your coat and follow me," the angel ordered.

9So Peter left the cell, following the angel. But all the time he thought it was a vision. He didn't realize it was actually happening. 10They passed the first and second guard posts and came to the iron gate leading to the city, and this opened for them all by itself. So they passed through and started walking down the street, and then the angel suddenly left him.

11Peter finally came to his senses. "It's really true!" he said. "The Lord has sent his angel and saved me from Herod and from what the Jewish leaders had planned to do to me!"

12When he realized this, he went to the home of Mary, the mother of John Mark, where many were gathered for prayer. 13He knocked at the door in the gate, and a servant girl named Rhoda came to open it. 14When she recognized Peter's voice, she was so overjoyed that, instead of open-

Knock, Knock

WHO'S THERE?

NO WAY, PETER'S IN PRISON!

PETER.

Hey, it was an honest mistake.

Peter *was* in jail. But not for long. **Read ACTS 12:6-19 for an account of a most amazing jailbreak!**

NOW TRY THIS!

1 Hold a large book in one hand and a sheet of paper in the other.

2 Drop them both at the same time.

Read about another prison adventure in Acts 16:16-34.

WHICH HITS THE FLOOR FIRST? YOU'RE RIGHT! THE BOOK.

NOW TRY IT AGAIN, WITH THIS CHANGE.

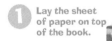

1 Lay the sheet of paper on top of the book.

2 Drop them together.

SEE?

The paper followed the book right down to the floor, just like Peter followed the angel out of jail!

On your paper, draw a picture of this Bible story. Then use your picture to tell the Bible story to two people this week. Write on your paper the names of the people you tell and the dates you talked to them.

ing the door, she ran back inside and told everyone, "Peter is standing at the door!"

15 "You're out of your mind!" they said. When she insisted, they decided, "It must be his angel."

16 Meanwhile, Peter continued knocking. When they finally opened the door and saw him, they were amazed. 17 He motioned for them to quiet down and told them how the Lord had led him out of prison. "Tell James and the other brothers what happened," he said. And then he went to another place.

18 At dawn there was a great commotion among the soldiers about what had happened to Peter. 19 Herod Agrippa ordered a thorough search for him. When he couldn't be found, Herod interrogated the guards and sentenced them to death. Afterward Herod left Judea to stay in Caesarea for a while.

The Death of Herod Agrippa

20 Now Herod was very angry with the people of Tyre and Sidon. So they sent a delegation to make peace with him because their cities were dependent upon Herod's country for food. The delegates won the support of Blastus, Herod's personal assistant, 21 and an appointment with Herod was granted. When the day arrived, Herod put on his royal robes, sat on his throne, and made a speech to them. 22 The people gave him a great ovation, shouting, "It's the voice of a god, not of a man!"

23 Instantly, an angel of the Lord struck Herod with a sickness, because he accepted the people's worship instead of giving the glory to God. So he was consumed with worms and died.

24 Meanwhile, the word of God continued to spread, and there were many new believers.

25 When Barnabas and Saul had finished their mission to Jerusalem, they returned, taking John Mark with them.

CHAPTER 13

Barnabas and Saul Are Commissioned

Among the prophets and teachers of the church at Antioch of Syria were Barnabas, Simeon (called "the black man"), Lucius (from Cyrene), Manaen (the childhood companion of King Herod Antipas), and Saul. 2 One day as these men were worshiping the Lord and fasting, the Holy Spirit said, "Dedicate Barnabas and Saul for the special work to which I have called them." 3 So after more fasting and prayer, the men laid their hands on them and sent them on their way.

Paul's First Missionary Journey

4 So Barnabas and Saul were sent out by the Holy Spirit. They went down to the seaport of Seleucia and then sailed for the island of Cyprus. 5 There, in the town of Salamis, they went to the Jewish synagogues and preached the word of God. John Mark went with them as their assistant.

6 Afterward they traveled from town to town across the entire island until finally they reached Paphos, where they met a Jewish sorcerer, a false prophet named Bar-Jesus. 7 He had attached himself to the governor, Sergius Paulus, who was an intelligent man. The governor invited Barnabas and Saul to visit him, for he wanted to hear the word of God. 8 But Elymas, the sorcerer (as his name means in Greek), interfered and urged the governor to pay no attention to what Barnabas and Saul said. He was trying to keep the governor from believing.

9 Saul, also known as Paul, was filled with the Holy Spirit, and he looked the sorcerer in the eye. 10 Then he said, "You son of the devil, full of every sort of deceit and fraud, and enemy of all that is good! Will you never stop perverting the true ways of the Lord? 11 Watch now, for the Lord has laid his hand of punishment upon you, and you will be struck blind. You will not see the sunlight for some time." Instantly mist and darkness came over the man's eyes, and he began groping around begging for someone to take his hand and lead him.

12 When the governor saw what had happened, he became a believer, for he was astonished at the teaching about the Lord.

Paul Preaches in Antioch of Pisidia

13 Paul and his companions then left Paphos by ship for Pamphylia, landing at the port town of Perga. There John Mark left them and returned to Jerusalem. 14 But Paul and Barnabas traveled inland to Antioch of Pisidia.

On the Sabbath they went to the synagogue for the services. 15 After the usual readings from the books of Moses and the prophets, those in charge of the service sent them this message: "Brothers, if you have any word of encouragement for the people, come and give it."

16 So Paul stood, lifted his hand to quiet them, and started speaking. "Men of Israel," he said, "and you God-fearing Gentiles, listen to me. 17 The God of this nation of Israel chose our ancestors and made them multiply and grow strong during their stay in Egypt. Then with a powerful arm he led them out of their slavery. 18 He put up with them through forty years of wandering in the wilderness. 19 Then he destroyed seven nations in Canaan and gave their land to Israel as an inheritance. 20 All this took about 450 years.

"After that, God gave them judges to rule until the time of Samuel the prophet. 21 Then the people begged for a king, and God gave them Saul son of Kish, a man of the tribe of Benjamin, who reigned for forty years. 22 But God removed Saul and replaced him with David, a man about whom God said, 'I have found David son of Jesse, a man after my own heart. He will do everything I want him to do.'

23 "And it is one of King David's descendants, Jesus, who is God's promised Savior of Israel! 24 Before he came, John the Baptist preached that all the people of Israel needed to repent of their sins and turn to God and be baptized. 25 As John was finishing his ministry he asked, 'Do you think I am the Messiah? No, I am not! But he is coming soon—and I'm not even worthy to be his slave and untie the sandals on his feet.'

26 "Brothers—you sons of Abraham, and also you God-fearing Gentiles—this message of salvation has been sent to us! 27 The people in Jerusalem and their leaders did not recognize Jesus as the one the prophets had spoken about. Instead, they condemned him, and in doing this they fulfilled the prophets' words that are read every Sabbath. 28 They found no legal reason to execute him, but they asked Pilate to have him killed anyway.

29 "When they had done all that the prophecies said about him, they took him down from the cross and placed him in a tomb. 30 But God raised him from the dead! 31 And over a period of many days he appeared to those who had gone with him from Galilee to Jerusalem. They are now his witnesses to the people of Israel.

32 "And now we are here to bring you this Good News. The promise was made to our ancestors, 33 and God has now fulfilled it for us, their descendants, by raising Jesus. This is what the second psalm says about Jesus:

'You are my Son.
Today I have become your Father.'

34 For God had promised to raise him from the dead, not leaving him to rot in the grave. He said, 'I will give you the sacred blessings I promised to David.' 35 Another psalm explains it more fully: 'You will not allow your Holy One to rot in the grave.' 36 This is not a reference to David, for af-

ter David had done the will of God in his own generation, he died and was buried with his ancestors, and his body decayed. 37No, it was a reference to someone else—someone whom God raised and whose body did not decay.

38"Brothers, listen! We are here to proclaim that through this man Jesus there is forgiveness for your sins. 39Everyone who believes in him is declared right with God—something the law of Moses could never do. 40Be careful! Don't let the prophets' words apply to you. For they said,

41 'Look, you mockers,
      be amazed and die!
   For I am doing something in your
      own day,
      something you wouldn't believe
      even if someone told you about it.'"

42As Paul and Barnabas left the synagogue that day, the people begged them to speak about these things again the next week. 43Many Jews and devout converts to Judaism followed Paul and Barnabas, and the two men urged them to continue to rely on the grace of God.

Paul Turns to the Gentiles

44The following week almost the entire city turned out to hear them preach the word of the Lord. 45But when some of the Jews saw the crowds, they were jealous; so they slandered Paul and argued against whatever he said.

46Then Paul and Barnabas spoke out boldly and declared, "It was necessary that we first preach the word of God to you Jews. But since you have rejected it and judged yourselves unworthy of eternal life, we will offer it to the Gentiles. 47For the Lord gave us this command when he said,

   'I have made you a light to the Gentiles,
      to bring salvation to the farthest corners
      of the earth.'"

48When the Gentiles heard this, they were very glad and thanked the Lord for his message; and all who were chosen for eternal life became believers. 49So the Lord's message spread throughout that region. 50Then the Jews stirred up the influential religious women and the leaders of the city, and they incited a mob against Paul and Barnabas and ran them out of town. 51So they shook the dust from their feet as a sign of rejection and went to the town of Iconium. 52And the believers were filled with joy and with the Holy Spirit.

CHAPTER **14**

Paul and Barnabas in Iconium

The same thing happened in Iconium. Paul and Barnabas went to the Jewish synagogue and preached with such power that a great number of both Jews and Greeks became believers. 2Some of the Jews, however, spurned God's message and poisoned the minds of the Gentiles against Paul and Barnabas. 3But the apostles stayed there a long time, preaching boldly about the grace of the Lord. And the Lord proved their message was true by giving them power to do miraculous signs and wonders. 4But the people of the town were divided in their opinion about them. Some sided with the Jews, and some with the apostles.

5Then a mob of Gentiles and Jews, along with their leaders, decided to attack and stone them. 6When the apostles learned of it, they fled to the region of Lycaonia—to the towns of Lystra and Derbe and the surrounding area. 7And there they preached the Good News.

Paul and Barnabas in Lystra and Derbe

8While they were at Lystra, Paul and Barnabas came upon a man with crippled feet. He had been that way from birth, so he had never walked. He was sitting 9and listening as Paul preached. Looking straight at him, Paul realized he had faith to be healed. 10So Paul called to him in a loud voice, "Stand up!" And the man jumped to his feet and started walking.

11When the crowd saw what Paul had done, they shouted in their local dialect, "These men are gods in human form!" 12They decided that Barnabas was the Greek god Zeus and that Paul was Hermes, since he was the chief speaker. 13Now the temple of Zeus was located just outside the town. So the priest of the temple and the crowd brought bulls and wreaths of flowers to the town gates, and they prepared to offer sacrifices to the apostles.

14But when the apostles Barnabas and Paul heard what was happening, they tore their clothing in dismay and ran out among the people, shouting, 15"Friends, why are you doing this? We are merely human beings—just like you! We have come to bring you the Good News that you should turn from these worthless things and turn to the living God, who made heaven and earth, the sea, and everything in them. 16In the past he permitted all the nations to go their own ways, 17but he never left them without evidence of himself and his goodness. For instance, he sends you rain and good crops and gives you food and joyful hearts." ¹⁸But even with these words, Paul and Barnabas could scarcely restrain the people from sacrificing to them.

¹⁹Then some Jews arrived from Antioch and Iconium and won the crowds to their side. They stoned Paul and dragged him out of town, thinking he was dead. ²⁰But as the believers gathered around him, he got up and went back into the town. The next day he left with Barnabas for Derbe.

Paul and Barnabas Return to Antioch of Syria

²¹After preaching the Good News in Derbe and making many disciples, Paul and Barnabas returned to Lystra, Iconium, and Antioch of Pisidia, ²²where they strengthened the believers. They encouraged them to continue in the faith, reminding them that we must suffer many hardships to enter the Kingdom of God. ²³Paul and Barnabas also appointed elders in every church. With prayer and fasting, they turned the elders over to the care of the Lord, in whom they had put their trust. ²⁴Then they traveled back through Pisidia to Pamphylia. ²⁵They preached the word in Perga, then went down to Attalia.

²⁶Finally, they returned by ship to Antioch of Syria, where their journey had begun. The believers there had entrusted them to the grace of God to do the work they had now completed. ²⁷Upon arriving in Antioch, they called the church together and reported everything God had done through them and how he had opened the door of faith to the Gentiles, too. ²⁸And they stayed there with the believers for a long time.

CHAPTER **15**
The Council at Jerusalem

While Paul and Barnabas were at Antioch of Syria, some men from Judea arrived and began to teach the believers: "Unless you are circumcised as required by the law of Moses, you cannot be saved." ²Paul and Barnabas disagreed with them, arguing vehemently. Finally, the church decided to send Paul and Barnabas to Jerusalem, accompanied by some local believers, to talk to the apostles and elders about this question. ³The church sent the delegates to Jerusalem, and they stopped along the way in Phoenicia and Samaria to visit the believers. They told them—much to everyone's joy—that the Gentiles, too, were being converted.

⁴When they arrived in Jerusalem, Barnabas and Paul were welcomed by the whole church, including the apostles and elders. They reported everything God had done through them. ⁵But then some of the believers who belonged to the sect of the Pharisees stood up and insisted, "The Gentile converts must be circumcised and required to follow the law of Moses."

⁶So the apostles and elders met together to resolve this issue. ⁷At the meeting, after a long discussion, Peter stood and addressed them as follows: "Brothers, you all know that God chose me from among you some time ago to preach to the Gentiles so that they could hear the Good News and believe. ⁸God knows people's hearts, and he confirmed that he accepts Gentiles by giving them the Holy Spirit, just as he did to us. ⁹He made no distinction between us and them, for he cleansed their hearts through faith. ¹⁰So why are you now challenging God by burdening the Gentile believers with a yoke that neither we nor our ancestors were able to bear? ¹¹We believe that we are all saved the same way, by the undeserved grace of the Lord Jesus."

¹²Everyone listened quietly as Barnabas and Paul told about the miraculous signs and wonders God had done through them among the Gentiles.

¹³When they had finished, James stood and said, "Brothers, listen to me. ¹⁴Peter has told you about the time God first visited the Gentiles to take from them a people for himself. ¹⁵And this conversion of Gentiles is exactly what the prophets predicted. As it is written:

¹⁶ 'Afterward I will return
    and restore the fallen house of David.
  I will rebuild its ruins
    and restore it,
¹⁷ so that the rest of humanity might seek
      the Lord,
    including the Gentiles—
    all those I have called to be mine.
  The Lord has spoken—
¹⁸   he who made these things known
      so long ago.'

¹⁹"And so my judgment is that we should not make it difficult for the Gentiles who are turning to God. ²⁰Instead, we should write and tell them to abstain from eating food offered to idols, from sexual immorality, from eating the meat of strangled animals, and from consuming blood. ²¹For these laws of Moses have been preached in Jewish synagogues in every city on every Sabbath for many generations."

The Letter for Gentile Believers

22 Then the apostles and elders together with the whole church in Jerusalem chose delegates, and they sent them to Antioch of Syria with Paul and Barnabas to report on this decision. The men chosen were two of the church leaders—Judas (also called Barsabbas) and Silas. 23 This is the letter they took with them:

"This letter is from the apostles and elders, your brothers in Jerusalem. It is written to the Gentile believers in Antioch, Syria, and Cilicia. Greetings!

24 "We understand that some men from here have troubled you and upset you with their teaching, but we did not send them! 25 So we decided, having come to complete agreement, to send you official representatives, along with our beloved Barnabas and Paul, 26 who have risked their lives for the name of our Lord Jesus Christ. 27 We are sending Judas and Silas to confirm what we have decided concerning your question.

28 "For it seemed good to the Holy Spirit and to us to lay no greater burden on you than these few requirements: 29 You must abstain from eating food offered to idols, from consuming blood or the meat of strangled animals, and from sexual immorality. If you do this, you will do well. Farewell."

30 The messengers went at once to Antioch, where they called a general meeting of the believers and delivered the letter. 31 And there was great joy throughout the church that day as they read this encouraging message.

32 Then Judas and Silas, both being prophets, spoke at length to the believers, encouraging and strengthening their faith. 33 They stayed for a while, and then the believers sent them back to the church in Jerusalem with a blessing of peace.* 35 Paul and Barnabas stayed in Antioch. They and many others taught and preached the word of the Lord there.

Paul and Barnabas Separate

36 After some time Paul said to Barnabas, "Let's go back and visit each city where we previously preached the word of the Lord, to see how the new believers are doing." 37 Barnabas agreed and wanted to take along John Mark. 38 But Paul disagreed strongly, since John Mark had

15:33 Some manuscripts add verse 34, *But Silas decided to stay there.*

deserted them in Pamphylia and had not continued with them in their work. 39 Their disagreement was so sharp that they separated. Barnabas took John Mark with him and sailed for Cyprus. 40 Paul chose Silas, and as he left, the believers entrusted him to the Lord's gracious care. 41 Then he traveled throughout Syria and Cilicia, strengthening the churches there.

Stayin' Put

IF YOU WERE IN A TIGHT SPOT AND HAD THE CHANCE TO GET OUT OF IT, WOULD YOU?

Read ACTS 16:16-40 to see what two guys in the Bible did! Would you have stayed put like Paul and Silas did? Here's an experiment all about staying put!

1 Lay a playing card on top of a foam or paper cup, covering the opening.

2 Place a penny on top of the card.

3 Quickly pull the playing card from under the penny.

What happened? The penny didn't follow the card—it stayed put and dropped in the cup!

DO YOUR TRICK FOR A FRIEND.

Then tell your friend how Paul and Silas stayed put. Who knows—maybe the friend you tell will believe in Jesus too!

CHAPTER **16**
Paul's Second Missionary Journey

Paul went first to Derbe and then to Lystra, where there was a young disciple named Timothy. His mother was a Jewish believer, but his father was a Greek. [2]Timothy was well thought of by the believers in Lystra and Iconium, [3]so Paul wanted him to join them on their journey. In deference to the Jews of the area, he arranged for Timothy to be circumcised before they left, for everyone knew that his father was a Greek. [4]Then they went from town to town, instructing the believers to follow the decisions made by the apostles and elders in Jerusalem. [5]So the churches were strengthened in their faith and grew larger everyday.

A Call from Macedonia

[6]Next Paul and Silas traveled through the area of Phrygia and Galatia, because the Holy Spirit had prevented them from preaching the word in the province of Asia at that time. [7]Then coming to the borders of Mysia, they headed north for the province of Bithynia, but again the Spirit of Jesus did not allow them to go there. [8]So instead, they went on through Mysia to the seaport of Troas.

[9]That night Paul had a vision: A man from Macedonia in northern Greece was standing there, pleading with him, "Come over to Macedonia and help us!" [10]So we decided to leave for Macedonia at once, having concluded that God was calling us to preach the Good News there.

Lydia of Philippi Believes in Jesus

[11]We boarded a boat at Troas and sailed straight across to the island of Samothrace, and the next day we landed at Neapolis. [12]From there we reached Philippi, a major city of that district of Macedonia and a Roman colony. And we stayed there several days.

[13]On the Sabbath we went a little way outside the city to a riverbank, where we thought people would be meeting for prayer, and we sat down to speak with some women who had gathered there. [14]One of them was Lydia from Thyatira, a merchant of expensive purple cloth, who worshiped God. As she listened to us, the Lord opened her heart, and she accepted what Paul was saying. [15]She was baptized along with other members of her household, and she asked us to be her guests. "If you agree that I

am a true believer in the Lord," she said, "come and stay at my home." And she urged us until we agreed.

Paul and Silas in Prison

[16]One day as we were going down to the place of prayer, we met a demon-possessed slave girl. She was a fortune-teller who earned a lot of money for her masters. [17]She followed Paul and the rest of us, shouting, "These men are servants of the Most High God, and they have come to tell you how to be saved."

[18]This went on day after day until Paul got so exasperated that he turned and said to the demon within her, "I command you in the name of Jesus Christ to come out of her." And instantly it left her.

[19]Her masters' hopes of wealth were now shattered, so they grabbed Paul and Silas and dragged them before the authorities at the marketplace. [20]"The whole city is in an uproar because of these Jews!" they shouted to the city officials. [21]"They are teaching customs that are illegal for us Romans to practice."

[22]A mob quickly formed against Paul and Silas, and the city officials ordered them stripped and beaten with wooden rods. [23]They were severely beaten, and then they were thrown into prison. The jailer was ordered to make sure they didn't escape. [24]So the jailer put them into the inner dungeon and clamped their feet in the stocks.

[25]Around midnight Paul and Silas were praying and singing hymns to God, and the other prisoners were listening. [26]Suddenly, there was a massive earthquake, and the prison was shaken to its foundations. All the doors immediately flew open, and the chains of every prisoner fell off! [27]The jailer woke up to see the prison doors wide open. He assumed the prisoners had escaped, so he drew his sword to kill himself. [28]But Paul shouted to him, "Stop! Don't kill yourself! We are all here!"

[29]The jailer called for lights and ran to the dungeon and fell down trembling before Paul and Silas. **[30]Then he brought them out and asked, "Sirs, what must I do to be saved?"**

[31]They replied, "Believe in the Lord Jesus and you will be saved, along with everyone in your household." [32]And they shared the word of the Lord with him and with all who lived in his household. [33]Even at that hour of the night, the jailer cared for them and washed their wounds. Then he and everyone in his household were immediately baptized. ³⁴He brought them into his house and set a meal before them, and he and his entire household rejoiced because they all believed in God.

³⁵The next morning the city officials sent the police to tell the jailer, "Let those men go!" ³⁶So the jailer told Paul, "The city officials have said you and Silas are free to leave. Go in peace."

³⁷But Paul replied, "They have publicly beaten us without a trial and put us in prison—and we are Roman citizens. So now they want us to leave secretly? Certainly not! Let them come themselves to release us!"

³⁸When the police reported this, the city officials were alarmed to learn that Paul and Silas were Roman citizens. ³⁹So they came to the jail and apologized to them. Then they brought them out and begged them to leave the city. ⁴⁰When Paul and Silas left the prison, they returned to the home of Lydia. There they met with the believers and encouraged them once more. Then they left town.

CHAPTER **17**

Paul Preaches in Thessalonica

Paul and Silas then traveled through the towns of Amphipolis and Apollonia and came to Thessalonica, where there was a Jewish synagogue. ²As was Paul's custom, he went to the synagogue service, and for three Sabbaths in a row he used the Scriptures to reason with the people. ³He explained the prophecies and proved that the Messiah must suffer and rise from the dead. He said, "This Jesus I'm telling you about is the Messiah." ⁴Some of the Jews who listened were persuaded and joined Paul and Silas, along with many God-fearing Greek men and quite a few prominent women.

⁵But some of the Jews were jealous, so they gathered some troublemakers from the marketplace to form a mob and start a riot. They attacked the home of Jason, searching for Paul and Silas so they could drag them out to the crowd. ⁶Not finding them there, they dragged out Jason and some of the other believers instead and took them before the city council. "Paul and Silas have caused trouble all over the world," they shouted, "and now they are here disturbing our city, too. ⁷And Jason has welcomed them into his home. They are all guilty of treason against Caesar, for they profess allegiance to another king, named Jesus."

⁸The people of the city, as well as the city council, were thrown into turmoil by these reports. ⁹So the officials forced Jason and the other believers to post bond, and then they released them.

Paul and Silas in Berea

¹⁰That very night the believers sent Paul and Silas to Berea. When they arrived there, they went to the Jewish synagogue. ¹¹And the people of Berea were more open-minded than those in Thessalonica, and they listened eagerly to Paul's message. They searched the Scriptures day after day to see if Paul and Silas were teaching the truth. ¹²As a result, many Jews believed, as did many of the prominent Greek women and men.

¹³But when some Jews in Thessalonica learned that Paul was preaching the word of God in Berea, they went there and stirred up trouble. ¹⁴The believers acted at once, sending Paul on to the coast, while Silas and Timothy remained behind. ¹⁵Those escorting Paul went with him all the way to Athens; then they returned to Berea with instructions for Silas and Timothy to hurry and join him.

Paul Preaches in Athens

¹⁶While Paul was waiting for them in Athens, he was deeply troubled by all the idols he saw everywhere in the city. ¹⁷He went to the synagogue to reason with the Jews and the God-fearing Gentiles, and he spoke daily in the public square to all who happened to be there.

¹⁸He also had a debate with some of the Epicurean and Stoic philosophers. When he told them about Jesus and his resurrection, they said, "What's this babbler trying to say with these strange ideas he's picked up?" Others said, "He seems to be preaching about some foreign gods."

¹⁹Then they took him to the high council of the city. "Come and tell us about this new teaching," they said. ²⁰"You are saying some rather strange things, and we want to know what it's all about." ²¹(It should be explained that all the Athenians as well as the foreigners in Athens seemed to spend all their time discussing the latest ideas.)

²²So Paul, standing before the council, addressed them as follows: "Men of Athens, I notice that you are very religious in every way, ²³for as I was walking along I saw your many shrines. And one of your altars had this inscription on it: 'To an Unknown God.' This God, whom you worship without knowing, is the one I'm telling you about.

²⁴"He is the God who made the world and

everything in it. Since he is Lord of heaven and earth, he doesn't live in man-made temples, 25 and human hands can't serve his needs—for he has no needs. He himself gives life and breath to everything, and he satisfies every need. 26 From one man he created all the nations throughout the whole earth. He decided beforehand when they should rise and fall, and he determined their boundaries.

27 "His purpose was for the nations to seek after God and perhaps feel their way toward him and find him—though he is not far from any one of us. 28 For in him we live and move and exist. As some of your own poets have said, 'We are his offspring.' 29 And since this is true, we shouldn't think of God as an idol designed by craftsmen from gold or silver or stone.

30 "God overlooked people's ignorance about these things in earlier times, but now he commands everyone everywhere to repent of their sins and turn to him. 31 For he has set a day for judging the world with justice by the man he has appointed, and he proved to everyone who this is by raising him from the dead."

32 When they heard Paul speak about the resurrection of the dead, some laughed in contempt, but others said, "We want to hear more about this later." 33 That ended Paul's discussion with them, 34 but some joined him and became believers. Among them were Dionysius, a member of the council, a woman named Damaris, and others with them.

CHAPTER 18
Paul Meets Priscilla and Aquila in Corinth

Then Paul left Athens and went to Corinth. 2 There he became acquainted with a Jew named Aquila, born in Pontus, who had recently arrived from Italy with his wife, Priscilla. They had left Italy when Claudius Caesar deported all Jews from Rome. 3 Paul lived and worked with them, for they were tentmakers just as he was.

4 Each Sabbath found Paul at the synagogue, trying to convince the Jews and Greeks alike. 5 And after Silas and Timothy came down from Macedonia, Paul spent all his time preaching the word. He testified to the Jews that Jesus was the Messiah. 6 But when they opposed and insulted him, Paul shook the dust from his clothes and said, "Your blood is upon your own heads—I am innocent. From now on I will go preach to the Gentiles."

7 Then he left and went to the home of Titius Justus, a Gentile who worshiped God and lived next door to the synagogue. 8 Crispus, the leader of the synagogue, and everyone in his household believed in the Lord. Many others in Corinth also heard Paul, became believers, and were baptized.

9 One night the Lord spoke to Paul in a vision and told him, "Don't be afraid! Speak out! Don't be silent! 10 For I am with you, and no one will attack and harm you, for many people in this city belong to me." 11 So Paul stayed there for the next year and a half, teaching the word of God.

12 But when Gallio became governor of Achaia, some Jews rose up together against Paul and brought him before the governor for judgment. 13 They accused Paul of "persuading people to worship God in ways that are contrary to our law."

14 But just as Paul started to make his defense, Gallio turned to Paul's accusers and said, "Listen, you Jews, if this were a case involving some wrongdoing or a serious crime, I would have a reason to accept your case. 15 But since it is merely a question of words and names and your Jewish law, take care of it yourselves. I refuse to judge such matters." 16 And he threw them out of the courtroom.

17 The crowd then grabbed Sosthenes, the leader of the synagogue, and beat him right there in the courtroom. But Gallio paid no attention.

Paul Returns to Antioch of Syria

18 Paul stayed in Corinth for some time after that, then said good-bye to the brothers and sisters and went to nearby Cenchrea. There he shaved his head according to Jewish custom, marking the end of a vow. Then he set sail for Syria, taking Priscilla and Aquila with him.

19 They stopped first at the port of Ephesus, where Paul left the others behind. While he was there, he went to the synagogue to reason with the Jews. 20 They asked him to stay longer, but he declined. 21 As he left, however, he said, "I will come back later, God willing." Then he set sail from Ephesus. 22 The next stop was at the port of Caesarea. From there he went up and visited the church at Jerusalem and then went back to Antioch.

23 After spending some time in Antioch, Paul went back through Galatia and Phrygia, visiting and strengthening all the believers.

Apollos Instructed at Ephesus

24 Meanwhile, a Jew named Apollos, an eloquent speaker who knew the Scriptures well, had arrived in Ephesus from Alexandria in Egypt. 25 He

had been taught the way of the Lord, and he taught others about Jesus with an enthusiastic spirit and with accuracy. However, he knew only about John's baptism. 26When Priscilla and Aquila heard him preaching boldly in the synagogue, they took him aside and explained the way of God even more accurately.

27Apollos had been thinking about going to Achaia, and the brothers and sisters in Ephesus encouraged him to go. They wrote to the believers in Achaia, asking them to welcome him. When he arrived there, he proved to be of great benefit to those who, by God's grace, had believed. 28He refuted the Jews with powerful arguments in public debate. Using the Scriptures, he explained to them that Jesus was the Messiah.

CHAPTER **19**

Paul's Third Missionary Journey

While Apollos was in Corinth, Paul traveled through the interior regions until he reached Ephesus, on the coast, where he found several believers. 2"Did you receive the Holy Spirit when you believed?" he asked them.

"No," they replied, "we haven't even heard that there is a Holy Spirit."

3"Then what baptism did you experience?" he asked.

And they replied, "The baptism of John."

4Paul said, "John's baptism called for repentance from sin. But John himself told the people to believe in the one who would come later, meaning Jesus."

5As soon as they heard this, they were baptized in the name of the Lord Jesus. 6Then when Paul laid his hands on them, the Holy Spirit came on them, and they spoke in other tongues and prophesied. 7There were about twelve men in all.

Paul Ministers in Ephesus

8Then Paul went to the synagogue and preached boldly for the next three months, arguing persuasively about the Kingdom of God. 9But some became stubborn, rejecting his message and publicly speaking against the Way. So Paul left the synagogue and took the believers with him. Then he held daily discussions at the lecture hall of Tyrannus. 10This went on for the next two years, so that people throughout the province of Asia—both Jews and Greeks—heard the word of the Lord.

11God gave Paul the power to perform unusual miracles. 12When handkerchiefs or aprons that had merely touched his skin were placed on sick people, they were healed of their diseases, and evil spirits were expelled.

13A group of Jews was traveling from town to town casting out evil spirits. They tried to use the name of the Lord Jesus in their incantation, saying, "I command you in the name of Jesus, whom Paul preaches, to come out!" 14Seven sons of Sceva, a leading priest, were doing this. 15But one time when they tried it, the evil spirit replied, "I know Jesus, and I know Paul, but who are you?" 16Then the man with the evil spirit leaped on them, overpowered them, and attacked them with such violence that they fled from the house, naked and battered.

17The story of what happened spread quickly all through Ephesus, to Jews and Greeks alike. A solemn fear descended on the city, and the name of the Lord Jesus was greatly honored. 18Many who became believers confessed their sinful practices. 19A number of them who had been practicing sorcery brought their incantation books and burned them at a public bonfire. The value of the books was several million dollars. 20So the message about the Lord spread widely and had a powerful effect.

21Afterward Paul felt compelled by the Spirit to go over to Macedonia and Achaia before going to Jerusalem. "And after that," he said, "I must go on to Rome!" 22He sent his two assistants, Timothy and Erastus, ahead to Macedonia while he stayed awhile longer in the province of Asia.

The Riot in Ephesus

23About that time, serious trouble developed in Ephesus concerning the Way. 24It began with Demetrius, a silversmith who had a large business manufacturing silver shrines of the Greek goddess Artemis. He kept many craftsmen busy. 25He called them together, along with others employed in similar trades, and addressed them as follows:

"Gentlemen, you know that our wealth comes from this business. 26But as you have seen and heard, this man Paul has persuaded many people that handmade gods aren't really gods at all. And he's done this not only here in Ephesus but throughout the entire province! 27Of course, I'm not just talking about the loss of public respect for our business. I'm also concerned that the temple of the great goddess Artemis will lose its influence and that Artemis—this magnificent goddess worshiped throughout the province of Asia and all around the world—will be robbed of her great prestige!"

28At this their anger boiled, and they began

shouting, "Great is Artemis of the Ephesians!" 29Soon the whole city was filled with confusion. Everyone rushed to the amphitheater, dragging along Gaius and Aristarchus, who were Paul's traveling companions from Macedonia. 30Paul wanted to go in, too, but the believers wouldn't let him. 31Some of the officials of the province, friends of Paul, also sent a message to him, begging him not to risk his life by entering the amphitheater.

32Inside, the people were all shouting, some one thing and some another. Everything was in confusion. In fact, most of them didn't even know why they were there. 33The Jews in the crowd pushed Alexander forward and told him to explain the situation. He motioned for silence and tried to speak. 34But when the crowd realized he was a Jew, they started shouting again and kept it up for two hours: "Great is Artemis of the Ephesians! Great is Artemis of the Ephesians!"

35At last the mayor was able to quiet them down enough to speak. "Citizens of Ephesus," he said. "Everyone knows that Ephesus is the official guardian of the temple of the great Artemis, whose image fell down to us from heaven. 36Since this is an undeniable fact, you should stay calm and not do anything rash. 37You have brought these men here, but they have stolen nothing from the temple and have not spoken against our goddess.

38"If Demetrius and the craftsmen have a case against them, the courts are in session and the officials can hear the case at once. Let them make formal charges. 39And if there are complaints about other matters, they can be settled in a legal assembly. 40I am afraid we are in danger of being charged with rioting by the Roman government, since there is no cause for all this commotion. And if Rome demands an explanation, we won't know what to say." 41Then he dismissed them, and they dispersed.

CHAPTER 20
Paul Goes to Macedonia and Greece

When the uproar was over, Paul sent for the believers and encouraged them. Then he said good-bye and left for Macedonia. 2While there, he encouraged the believers in all the towns he passed through. Then he traveled down to Greece, 3where he stayed for three months. He was preparing to sail back to Syria when he discovered a plot by some Jews against his life, so he decided to return through Macedonia.

4Several men were traveling with him. They were Sopater son of Pyrrhus from Berea; Aristarchus and Secundus from Thessalonica; Gaius from Derbe; Timothy; and Tychicus and Trophimus from the province of Asia. 5They went on ahead and waited for us at Troas. 6After the Passover ended, we boarded a ship at Philippi in Macedonia and five days later joined them in Troas, where we stayed a week.

Paul's Final Visit to Troas

7On the first day of the week, we gathered with the local believers to share in the Lord's Supper. Paul was preaching to them, and since he was leaving the next day, he kept talking until midnight. 8The upstairs room where we met was lighted with many flickering lamps. 9As Paul spoke on and on, a young man named Eutychus, sitting on the windowsill, became very drowsy. Finally, he fell sound asleep and dropped three stories to his death below. 10Paul went down, bent over him, and took him into his arms. "Don't worry," he said, "he's alive!" 11Then they all went back upstairs, shared in the Lord's Supper, and ate together. Paul continued talking to them until dawn, and then he left. 12Meanwhile, the young man was taken home unhurt, and everyone was greatly relieved.

Paul Meets the Ephesian Elders

13Paul went by land to Assos, where he had arranged for us to join him, while we traveled by ship. 14He joined us there, and we sailed together to Mitylene. 15The next day we sailed past the island of Kios. The following day we crossed to the island of Samos, and a day later we arrived at Miletus.

16Paul had decided to sail on past Ephesus, for he didn't want to spend any more time in the province of Asia. He was hurrying to get to Jerusalem, if possible, in time for the Festival of Pentecost. 17But when we landed at Miletus, he sent a message to the elders of the church at Ephesus, asking them to come and meet him.

18When they arrived he declared, "You know that from the day I set foot in the province of Asia until now 19I have done the Lord's work humbly and with many tears. I have endured the trials that came to me from the plots of the Jews. 20I never shrank back from telling you what you needed to hear, either publicly or in your homes. 21I have had one message for Jews and Greeks alike—the necessity of repenting from sin and turning to God, and of having faith in our Lord Jesus.

22"And now I am bound by the Spirit to go to

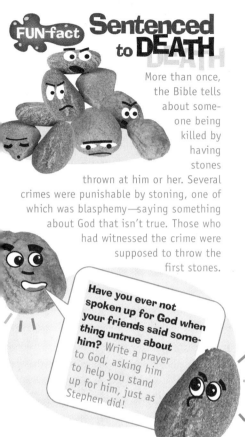

Sentenced to **DEATH**

More than once, the Bible tells about someone being killed by having stones thrown at him or her. Several crimes were punishable by stoning, one of which was blasphemy—saying something about God that isn't true. Those who had witnessed the crime were supposed to throw the first stones.

Have you ever not spoken up for God when your friends said something untrue about him? Write a prayer to God, asking him to help you stand up for him, just as Stephen did!

lowing. 31 Watch out! Remember the three years I was with you—my constant watch and care over you night and day, and my many tears for you.

32 "And now I entrust you to God and the message of his grace that is able to build you up and give you an inheritance with all those he has set apart for himself.

33 "I have never coveted anyone's silver or gold or fine clothes. 34 You know that these hands of mine have worked to supply my own needs and even the needs of those who were with me. 35 And I have been a constant example of how you can help those in need by working hard. You should remember the words of the Lord Jesus: 'It is more blessed to give than to receive.'"

36 When he had finished speaking, he knelt and prayed with them. 37 They all cried as they embraced and kissed him good-bye. 38 They were sad most of all because he had said that they would never see him again. Then they escorted him down to the ship.

CHAPTER **21**
Paul's Journey to Jerusalem

After saying farewell to the Ephesian elders, we sailed straight to the island of Cos. The next day we reached Rhodes and then went to Patara. 2 There we boarded a ship sailing for Phoenicia. 3 We sighted the island of Cyprus, passed it on our left, and landed at the harbor of Tyre, in Syria, where the ship was to unload its cargo.

4 We went ashore, found the local believers, and stayed with them a week. These believers prophesied through the Holy Spirit that Paul should not go on to Jerusalem. 5 When we returned to the ship at the end of the week, the entire congregation, including women and children, left the city and came down to the shore with us. There we knelt, prayed, 6 and said our farewells. Then we went aboard, and they returned home.

7 The next stop after leaving Tyre was Ptolemais, where we greeted the brothers and sisters and stayed for one day. 8 The next day we went on to Caesarea and stayed at the home of Philip the Evangelist, one of the seven men who had been chosen to distribute food. 9 He had four unmarried daughters who had the gift of prophecy.

10 Several days later a man named Agabus, who also had the gift of prophecy, arrived from Judea. 11 He came over, took Paul's belt, and bound his own feet and hands with it. Then he said, "The Holy Spirit declares, 'So shall the owner of this belt be bound by the Jewish leaders

Jerusalem. I don't know what awaits me, 23 except that the Holy Spirit tells me in city after city that jail and suffering lie ahead. 24 But my life is worth nothing to me unless I use it for finishing the work assigned me by the Lord Jesus—the work of telling others the Good News about the wonderful grace of God.

25 "And now I know that none of you to whom I have preached the Kingdom will ever see me again. 26 I declare today that I have been faithful. If anyone suffers eternal death, it's not my fault, 27 for I didn't shrink from declaring all that God wants you to know.

28 "So guard yourselves and God's people. Feed and shepherd God's flock—his church, purchased with his own blood—over which the Holy Spirit has appointed you as elders. 29 I know that false teachers, like vicious wolves, will come in among you after I leave, not sparing the flock. 30 Even some men from your own group will rise up and distort the truth in order to draw a fol-

in Jerusalem and turned over to the Gentiles.'" [12]When we heard this, we and the local believers all begged Paul not to go on to Jerusalem.

[13]But he said, "Why all this weeping? You are breaking my heart! I am ready not only to be jailed at Jerusalem but even to die for the sake of the Lord Jesus." [14]When it was clear that we couldn't persuade him, we gave up and said, "The Lord's will be done."

Paul Arrives at Jerusalem

[15]After this we packed our things and left for Jerusalem. [16]Some believers from Caesarea accompanied us, and they took us to the home of Mnason, a man originally from Cyprus and one of the early believers. [17]When we arrived, the brothers and sisters in Jerusalem welcomed us warmly.

[18]The next day Paul went with us to meet with James, and all the elders of the Jerusalem church were present. [19]After greeting them, Paul gave a detailed account of the things God had accomplished among the Gentiles through his ministry.

[20]After hearing this, they praised God. And then they said, "You know, dear brother, how many thousands of Jews have also believed, and they all follow the law of Moses very seriously. [21]But the Jewish believers here in Jerusalem have been told that you are teaching all the Jews who live among the Gentiles to turn their backs on the laws of Moses. They've heard that you teach them not to circumcise their children or follow other Jewish customs. [22]What should we do? They will certainly hear that you have come.

[23]"Here's what we want you to do. We have four men here who have completed their vow. [24]Go with them to the Temple and join them in the purification ceremony, paying for them to have their heads ritually shaved. Then everyone will know that the rumors are all false and that you yourself observe the Jewish laws.

[25]"As for the Gentile believers, they should do what we already told them in a letter: They should abstain from eating food offered to idols, from consuming blood or the meat of strangled animals, and from sexual immorality."

Paul Is Arrested

[26]So Paul went to the Temple the next day with the other men. They had already started the purification ritual, so he publicly announced the date when their vows would end and sacrifices would be offered for each of them.

[27]The seven days were almost ended when some Jews from the province of Asia saw Paul in the Temple and roused a mob against him. They grabbed him, [28]yelling, "Men of Israel, help us! This is the man who preaches against our people everywhere and tells everybody to disobey the Jewish laws. He speaks against the Temple—and even defiles this holy place by bringing in Gentiles." [29](For earlier that day they had seen him in the city with Trophimus, a Gentile from Ephesus, and they assumed Paul had taken him into the Temple.)

[30]The whole city was rocked by these accusations, and a great riot followed. Paul was grabbed and dragged out of the Temple, and immediately the gates were closed behind him. [31]As they were trying to kill him, word reached the commander of the Roman regiment that all Jerusalem was in an uproar. [32]He immediately called out his soldiers and officers and ran down among the crowd. When the mob saw the commander and the troops coming, they stopped beating Paul.

[33]Then the commander arrested him and ordered him bound with two chains. He asked the crowd who he was and what he had done. [34]Some shouted one thing and some another. Since he couldn't find out the truth in all the uproar and confusion, he ordered that Paul be taken to the fortress. [35]As Paul reached the stairs, the mob grew so violent the soldiers had to lift him to their shoulders to protect him. [36]And the crowd followed behind, shouting, "Kill him, kill him!"

Paul Speaks to the Crowd

[37]As Paul was about to be taken inside, he said to the commander, "May I have a word with you?"

"Do you know Greek?" the commander asked, surprised. [38]"Aren't you the Egyptian who led a rebellion some time ago and took 4,000 members of the Assassins out into the desert?"

[39]"No," Paul replied, "I am a Jew and a citizen of Tarsus in Cilicia, which is an important city. Please, let me talk to these people." [40]The commander agreed, so Paul stood on the stairs and motioned to the people to be quiet. Soon a deep silence enveloped the crowd, and he addressed them in their own language, Aramaic.

CHAPTER **22**

"Brothers and esteemed fathers," Paul said, "listen to me as I offer my defense." [2]When they heard him speaking in their own language, the silence was even greater.

[3]Then Paul said, "I am a Jew, born in Tarsus, a

city in Cilicia, and I was brought up and educated here in Jerusalem under Gamaliel. As his student, I was carefully trained in our Jewish laws and customs. I became very zealous to honor God in everything I did, just like all of you today. ⁴And I persecuted the followers of the Way, hounding some to death, arresting both men and women and throwing them in prison. ⁵The high priest and the whole council of elders can testify that this is so. For I received letters from them to our Jewish brothers in Damascus, authorizing me to bring the Christians from there to Jerusalem, in chains, to be punished.

⁶"As I was on the road, approaching Damascus about noon, a very bright light from heaven suddenly shone down around me. ⁷I fell to the ground and heard a voice saying to me, 'Saul, Saul, why are you persecuting me?'

⁸"'Who are you, lord?' I asked.

"And the voice replied, 'I am Jesus the Nazarene, the one you are persecuting.' ⁹The people with me saw the light but didn't understand the voice speaking to me.

¹⁰"I asked, 'What should I do, Lord?'

"And the Lord told me, 'Get up and go into Damascus, and there you will be told everything you are to do.'

¹¹"I was blinded by the intense light and had to be led by the hand to Damascus by my companions. ¹²A man named Ananias lived there. He was a godly man, deeply devoted to the law, and well regarded by all the Jews of Damascus. ¹³He came and stood beside me and said, 'Brother Saul, regain your sight.' And that very moment I could see him!

¹⁴"Then he told me, 'The God of our ancestors has chosen you to know his will and to see the Righteous One and hear him speak. ¹⁵For you are to be his witness, telling everyone what you have seen and heard. ¹⁶What are you waiting for? Get up and be baptized. Have your sins washed away by calling on the name of the Lord.'

¹⁷"After I returned to Jerusalem, I was praying in the Temple and fell into a trance. ¹⁸I saw a vision of Jesus saying to me, 'Hurry! Leave Jerusalem, for the people here won't accept your testimony about me.'

¹⁹"'But Lord,' I argued, 'they certainly know that in every synagogue I imprisoned and beat those who believed in you. ²⁰And I was in complete agreement when your witness Stephen was killed. I stood by and kept the coats they took off when they stoned him.'

²¹"But the Lord said to me, 'Go, for I will send you far away to the Gentiles!'"

²²The crowd listened until Paul said that word. Then they all began to shout, "Away with such a fellow! He isn't fit to live!" ²³They yelled, threw off their coats, and tossed handfuls of dust into the air.

Paul Reveals His Roman Citizenship

²⁴The commander brought Paul inside and ordered him lashed with whips to make him confess his crime. He wanted to find out why the crowd had become so furious. ²⁵When they tied Paul down to lash him, Paul said to the officer standing there, "Is it legal for you to whip a Roman citizen who hasn't even been tried?"

²⁶When the officer heard this, he went to the commander and asked, "What are you doing? This man is a Roman citizen!"

²⁷So the commander went over and asked Paul, "Tell me, are you a Roman citizen?"

"Yes, I certainly am," Paul replied.

²⁸"I am, too," the commander muttered, "and it cost me plenty!"

Paul answered, "But I am a citizen by birth!"

²⁹The soldiers who were about to interrogate Paul quickly withdrew when they heard he was a Roman citizen, and the commander was frightened because he had ordered him bound and whipped.

Paul before the High Council

³⁰The next day the commander ordered the leading priests into session with the Jewish high council. He wanted to find out what the trouble was all about, so he released Paul to have him stand before them.

CHAPTER **23**

Gazing intently at the high council, Paul began: "Brothers, I have always lived before God with a clear conscience!"

²Instantly Ananias the high priest commanded those close to Paul to slap him on the mouth. ³But Paul said to him, "God will slap you, you corrupt hypocrite! What kind of judge are you to break the law yourself by ordering me struck like that?"

⁴Those standing near Paul said to him, "Do you dare to insult God's high priest?"

⁵"I'm sorry, brothers. I didn't realize he was the high priest," Paul replied, "for the Scriptures say, 'You must not speak evil of any of your rulers.'"

⁶Paul realized that some members of the high council were Sadducees and some were

Pharisees, so he shouted, "Brothers, I am a Pharisee, as were my ancestors! And I am on trial because my hope is in the resurrection of the dead!"

7This divided the council—the Pharisees against the Sadducees—8for the Sadducees say there is no resurrection or angels or spirits, but the Pharisees believe in all of these. 9So there was a great uproar. Some of the teachers of religious law who were Pharisees jumped up and began to argue forcefully. "We see nothing wrong with him," they shouted. "Perhaps a spirit or an angel spoke to him." 10As the conflict grew more violent, the commander was afraid they would tear Paul apart. So he ordered his soldiers to go and rescue him by force and take him back to the fortress.

11That night the Lord appeared to Paul and said, "Be encouraged, Paul. Just as you have been a witness to me here in Jerusalem, you must preach the Good News in Rome as well."

FUN-fact

A Tough JOB

In Bible times, Jewish people would often shake the dust off their feet when leaving a Gentile town. This was a symbolic way of cleansing themselves. But the tables turned!

Sometimes the Jewish people and leaders didn't want to hear about Jesus. One time, Paul and Barnabas were run out of town for talking about Jesus. But as they left, they shook the dust off their feet!

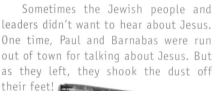

Even today, missionaries face opposition. SO WRITE A LETTER TO ENCOURAGE THE MISSIONARIES YOUR CHURCH SUPPORTS!

The Plan to Kill Paul

12The next morning a group of Jews got together and bound themselves with an oath not to eat or drink until they had killed Paul. 13There were more than forty of them in the conspiracy. 14They went to the leading priests and elders and told them, "We have bound ourselves with an oath to eat nothing until we have killed Paul. 15So you and the high council should ask the commander to bring Paul back to the council again. Pretend you want to examine his case more fully. We will kill him on the way."

16But Paul's nephew—his sister's son—heard of their plan and went to the fortress and told Paul. 17Paul called for one of the Roman officers and said, "Take this young man to the commander. He has something important to tell him."

18So the officer did, explaining, "Paul, the prisoner, called me over and asked me to bring this young man to you because he has something to tell you."

19The commander took his hand, led him aside, and asked, "What is it you want to tell me?"

20Paul's nephew told him, "Some Jews are going to ask you to bring Paul before the high council tomorrow, pretending they want to get some more information. 21But don't do it! There are more than forty men hiding along the way ready to ambush him. They have vowed not to eat or drink anything until they have killed him. They are ready now, just waiting for your consent."

22"Don't let anyone know you told me this," the commander warned the young man.

Paul Is Sent to Caesarea

23Then the commander called two of his officers and ordered, "Get 200 soldiers ready to leave for Caesarea at nine o'clock tonight. Also take 200 spearmen and 70 mounted troops. 24Provide horses for Paul to ride, and get him safely to Governor Felix." 25Then he wrote this letter to the governor:

26"From Claudius Lysias, to his Excellency, Governor Felix: Greetings!

27"This man was seized by some Jews, and they were about to kill him when I arrived with the troops. When I learned that he was a Roman citizen, I removed him to safety. 28Then I took him to their high council to try to learn the basis of the accusations against him. 29I soon discovered the charge was something regarding their religious law—certainly nothing worthy of imprisonment or death. ³⁰But when I was informed of a plot to kill him, I immediately sent him on to you. I have told his accusers to bring their charges before you."

³¹So that night, as ordered, the soldiers took Paul as far as Antipatris. ³²They returned to the fortress the next morning, while the mounted troops took him on to Caesarea. ³³When they arrived in Caesarea, they presented Paul and the letter to Governor Felix. ³⁴He read it and then asked Paul what province he was from. "Cilicia," Paul answered.

³⁵"I will hear your case myself when your accusers arrive," the governor told him. Then the governor ordered him kept in the prison at Herod's headquarters.

CHAPTER **24**
Paul Appears before Felix
Five days later Ananias, the high priest, arrived with some of the Jewish elders and the lawyer Tertullus, to present their case against Paul to the governor. ²When Paul was called in, Tertullus presented the charges against Paul in the following address to the governor:

"Your Excellency, you have provided a long period of peace for us Jews and with foresight have enacted reforms for us. ³For all of this we are very grateful to you. ⁴But I don't want to bore you, so please give me your attention for only a moment. ⁵We have found this man to be a troublemaker who is constantly stirring up riots among the Jews all over the world. He is a ringleader of the cult known as the Nazarenes. ⁶Furthermore, he was trying to desecrate the Temple when we arrested him.* ⁸You can find out the truth of our accusations by examining him yourself." ⁹Then the other Jews chimed in, declaring that everything Tertullus said was true.

¹⁰The governor then motioned for Paul to speak. Paul said, "I know, sir, that you have been a judge of Jewish affairs for many years, so I gladly present my defense before you. ¹¹You can quickly discover that I arrived in Jerusalem no more than twelve days ago to worship at the Temple. ¹²My accusers never found me arguing with anyone in the Temple, nor stirring up a riot in any synagogue or on the streets of the city. ¹³These men cannot prove the things they accuse me of doing.

¹⁴"But I admit that I follow the Way, which they call a cult. I worship the God of our ancestors, and I firmly believe the Jewish law and

everything written in the prophets. ¹⁵I have the same hope in God that these men have, that he will raise both the righteous and the unrighteous. ¹⁶Because of this, I always try to maintain a clear conscience before God and all people.

¹⁷"After several years away, I returned to Jerusalem with money to aid my people and to offer sacrifices to God. ¹⁸My accusers saw me in the Temple as I was completing a purification ceremony. There was no crowd around me and no rioting. ¹⁹But some Jews from the province of Asia were there—and they ought to be here to bring charges if they have anything against me! ²⁰Ask these men here what crime the Jewish high council found me guilty of, ²¹except for the one time I shouted out, 'I am on trial before you today because I believe in the resurrection of the dead!'"

²²At that point Felix, who was quite familiar with the Way, adjourned the hearing and said, "Wait until Lysias, the garrison commander, arrives. Then I will decide the case." ²³He ordered an officer to keep Paul in custody but to give him some freedom and allow his friends to visit him and take care of his needs.

²⁴A few days later Felix came back with his wife, Drusilla, who was Jewish. Sending for Paul, they listened as he told them about faith in Christ Jesus. ²⁵As he reasoned with them about righteousness and self-control and the coming day of judgment, Felix became frightened. "Go away for now," he replied. "When it is more convenient, I'll call for you again." ²⁶He also hoped that Paul would bribe him, so he sent for him quite often and talked with him.

²⁷After two years went by in this way, Felix was succeeded by Porcius Festus. And because Felix wanted to gain favor with the Jewish people, he left Paul in prison.

CHAPTER **25**
Paul Appears before Festus
Three days after Festus arrived in Caesarea to take over his new responsibilities, he left for Jerusalem, ²where the leading priests and other Jewish leaders met with him and made their accusations against Paul. ³They asked Festus as a favor to transfer Paul to Jerusalem (planning to ambush and kill him on the way). ⁴But Festus replied that Paul was at Caesarea and he himself would be returning there soon. ⁵So he said, "Those of you in authority can return with me. If Paul has done anything wrong, you can make your accusations."

24:6 Some manuscripts add an expanded conclusion to verse 6, all of verse 7, and an additional phrase in verse 8: *We would have judged him by our law,* ⁷*but Lysias, the commander of the garrison, came and violently took him away from us,* ⁸*commanding his accusers to come before you.*

6 About eight or ten days later Festus returned to Caesarea, and on the following day he took his seat in court and ordered that Paul be brought in. 7 When Paul arrived, the Jewish leaders from Jerusalem gathered around and made many serious accusations they couldn't prove.

8 Paul denied the charges. "I am not guilty of any crime against the Jewish laws or the Temple or the Roman government," he said.

9 Then Festus, wanting to please the Jews, asked him, "Are you willing to go to Jerusalem and stand trial before me there?"

10 But Paul replied, "No! This is the official Roman court, so I ought to be tried right here. You know very well I am not guilty of harming the Jews. 11 If I have done something worthy of death, I don't refuse to die. But if I am innocent, no one has a right to turn me over to these men to kill me. I appeal to Caesar!"

12 Festus conferred with his advisers and then replied, "Very well! You have appealed to Caesar, and to Caesar you will go!"

13 A few days later King Agrippa arrived with his sister, Bernice, to pay their respects to Festus. 14 During their stay of several days, Festus discussed Paul's case with the king. "There is a prisoner here," he told him, "whose case was left for me by Felix. 15 When I was in Jerusalem, the leading priests and Jewish elders pressed charges against him and asked me to condemn him. 16 I pointed out to them that Roman law does not convict people without a trial. They must be given an opportunity to confront their accusers and defend themselves.

17 "When his accusers came here for the trial, I didn't delay. I called the case the very next day and ordered Paul brought in. 18 But the accusations made against him weren't any of the crimes I expected. 19 Instead, it was something about their religion and a dead man named Jesus, who Paul insists is alive. 20 I was at a loss to know how to investigate these things, so I asked him whether he would be willing to stand trial on these charges in Jerusalem. 21 But Paul appealed to have his case decided by the emperor. So I ordered that he be held in custody until I could arrange to send him to Caesar."

22 "I'd like to hear the man myself," Agrippa said.

And Festus replied, "You will—tomorrow!"

Paul Speaks to Agrippa

23 So the next day Agrippa and Bernice arrived at the auditorium with great pomp, accompanied by military officers and prominent men of the city. Festus ordered that Paul be brought in. 24 Then Festus said, "King Agrippa and all who are here, this is the man whose death is demanded by all the Jews, both here and in Jerusalem. 25 But in my opinion he has done nothing deserving death. However, since he appealed his case to the emperor, I have decided to send him to Rome. 26 "But what shall I write the emperor? For there is no clear charge against him. So I have brought him before all of you, and especially you, King Agrippa, so that after we examine him, I might have something to write. 27 For it makes no sense to send a prisoner to the emperor without specifying the charges against him!"

CHAPTER 26

Then Agrippa said to Paul, "You may speak in your defense."

So Paul, gesturing with his hand, started his defense: 2 "I am fortunate, King Agrippa, that you are the one hearing my defense today against all these accusations made by the Jewish leaders, 3 for I know you are an expert on all Jewish customs and controversies. Now please listen to me patiently!

4 "As the Jewish leaders are well aware, I was given a thorough Jewish training from my earliest childhood among my own people and in Jerusalem. 5 If they would admit it, they know that I have been a member of the Pharisees, the strictest sect of our religion. 6 Now I am on trial because of my hope in the fulfillment of God's promise made to our ancestors. 7 In fact, that is why the twelve tribes of Israel zealously worship God night and day, and they share the same hope I have. Yet, Your Majesty, they accuse me for having this hope! 8 Why does it seem incredible to any of you that God can raise the dead?

9 "I used to believe that I ought to do everything I could to oppose the very name of Jesus the Nazarene. 10 Indeed, I did just that in Jerusalem. Authorized by the leading priests, I caused many believers there to be sent to prison. And I cast my vote against them when they were condemned to death. 11 Many times I had them punished in the synagogues to get them to curse Jesus. I was so violently opposed to them that I even chased them down in foreign cities.

12 "One day I was on such a mission to Damascus, armed with the authority and commission of the leading priests. 13 About noon, Your Majesty, as I was on the road, a light from heaven brighter than the sun shone down on me and my companions. 14 We all fell down, and I heard a

voice saying to me in Aramaic, 'Saul, Saul, why are you persecuting me? It is useless for you to fight against my will.'

15"'Who are you, lord?' I asked.

"And the Lord replied, 'I am Jesus, the one you are persecuting. 16Now get to your feet! For I have appeared to you to appoint you as my servant and witness. You are to tell the world what you have seen and what I will show you in the future. 17And I will rescue you from both your own people and the Gentiles. Yes, I am sending you to the Gentiles 18to open their eyes, so they may turn from darkness to light and from the power of Satan to God. Then they will receive forgiveness for their sins and be given a place among God's people, who are set apart by faith in me.'

19"And so, King Agrippa, I obeyed that vision from heaven. 20I preached first to those in Damascus, then in Jerusalem and throughout all Judea, and also to the Gentiles, that all must repent of their sins and turn to God—and prove they have changed by the good things they do. 21Some Jews arrested me in the Temple for preaching this, and they tried to kill me. 22But God has protected me right up to this present time so I can testify to everyone, from the least to the greatest. I teach nothing except what the prophets and Moses said would happen—23that the Messiah would suffer and be the first to rise from the dead, and in this way announce God's light to Jews and Gentiles alike."

24Suddenly, Festus shouted, "Paul, you are insane. Too much study has made you crazy!"

25But Paul replied, "I am not insane, Most Excellent Festus. What I am saying is the sober truth. 26And King Agrippa knows about these things. I speak boldly, for I am sure these events are all familiar to him, for they were not done in a corner! 27King Agrippa, do you believe the prophets? I know you do—"

28Agrippa interrupted him. "Do you think you can persuade me to become a Christian so quickly?"

29Paul replied, "Whether quickly or not, I pray to God that both you and everyone here in this audience might become the same as I am, except for these chains."

30Then the king, the governor, Bernice, and all the others stood and left. 31As they went out, they talked it over and agreed, "This man hasn't done anything to deserve death or imprisonment."

32And Agrippa said to Festus, "He could have been set free if he hadn't appealed to Caesar."

CHAPTER **27**
Paul Sails for Rome

When the time came, we set sail for Italy. Paul and several other prisoners were placed in the custody of a Roman officer named Julius, a captain of the Imperial Regiment. 2Aristarchus, a Macedonian from Thessalonica, was also with us. We left on a ship whose home port was Adramyttium on the northwest coast of the province of Asia; it was scheduled to make several stops at ports along the coast of the province.

3The next day when we docked at Sidon, Julius was very kind to Paul and let him go ashore to visit with friends so they could provide for his needs. 4Putting out to sea from there, we encountered strong headwinds that made it difficult to keep the ship on course, so we sailed north of Cyprus between the island and the mainland. 5Keeping to the open sea, we passed along the coast of Cilicia and Pamphylia, landing at Myra, in the province of Lycia. 6There the commanding officer found an Egyptian ship from Alexandria that was bound for Italy, and he put us on board.

7We had several days of slow sailing, and after great difficulty we finally neared Cnidus. But the wind was against us, so we sailed across to Crete and along the sheltered coast of the island, past the cape of Salmone. 8We struggled along the coast with great difficulty and finally arrived at Fair Havens, near the town of Lasea. 9We had lost a lot of time. The weather was becoming dangerous for sea travel because it was so late in the fall, and Paul spoke to the ship's officers about it.

10"Men," he said, "I believe there is trouble ahead if we go on—shipwreck, loss of cargo, and danger to our lives as well." 11But the officer in charge of the prisoners listened more to the ship's captain and the owner than to Paul. 12And since Fair Havens was an exposed harbor—a poor place to spend the winter—most of the crew wanted to go on to Phoenix, farther up the coast of Crete, and spend the winter there. Phoenix was a good harbor with only a southwest and northwest exposure.

The Storm at Sea

13When a light wind began blowing from the south, the sailors thought they could make it. So they pulled up anchor and sailed close to the shore of Crete. 14But the weather changed abruptly, and a wind of typhoon strength (called a "northeaster") burst across the island and blew us out to sea. 15The sailors couldn't turn the ship into the wind, so they gave up and let it run before the gale.

Ship wrecked!

A TERRIBLE STORM...

A HORRIBLE SHIPWRECK...

STRANDED FOR MONTHS ON

A REMOTE ISLAND...

An adventure movie? Wrong. It's what happened to Paul and a couple of Jesus' other followers. Read it for yourself in **ACTS 27!**

This story reads kind of like a journal entry. Write a journal story of your own about a time God brought *you* through a scary or hard time.

1 Have an adult steep a tea bag or two in a pot of very warm water.

2 Let the tea cool. Dip a sheet of paper in the tea, then set the paper on newspaper to dry.

When your paper dries, it'll look antique—kind of like paper from a long time ago!

Read Acts 28:1-10 for more of Paul's island adventures!

Now write your journal story. Roll up your paper, and put it in a bottle like stranded sailors used to do. The bottle can remind you that **God will help you during hard times!**

16 We sailed along the sheltered side of a small island named Cauda, where with great difficulty we hoisted aboard the lifeboat being towed behind us. 17 Then the sailors bound ropes around the hull of the ship to strengthen it. They were afraid of being driven across to the sandbars of Syrtis off the African coast, so they lowered the sea anchor to slow the ship and were driven before the wind.

18 The next day, as gale-force winds continued to batter the ship, the crew began throwing the cargo overboard. 19 The following day they even took some of the ship's gear and threw it overboard. 20 The terrible storm raged for many days, blotting out the sun and the stars, until at last all hope was gone.

21 No one had eaten for a long time. Finally, Paul called the crew together and said, "Men, you should have listened to me in the first place and not left Crete. You would have avoided all this damage and loss. 22 But take courage! None of you will lose your lives, even though the ship will go down. 23 For last night an angel of the God to whom I belong and whom I serve stood beside me, 24 and he said, 'Don't be afraid, Paul, for you will surely stand trial before Caesar! What's more, God in his goodness has granted safety to everyone sailing with you.' 25 So take courage! For I believe God. It will be just as he said. 26 But we will be shipwrecked on an island."

The Shipwreck

27 About midnight on the fourteenth night of the storm, as we were being driven across the Sea of Adria, the sailors sensed land was near. 28 They dropped a weighted line and found that the water was 120 feet deep. But a little later they measured again and found it was only 90 feet deep. 29 At this rate they were afraid we would soon be driven against the rocks along the shore, so they threw out four anchors from the back of the ship and prayed for daylight.

30 Then the sailors tried to abandon the ship; they lowered the lifeboat as though they were going to put out anchors from the front of the ship. 31 But Paul said to the commanding officer and the soldiers, "You will all die unless the sailors stay aboard." 32 So the soldiers cut the ropes to the lifeboat and let it drift away.

33 Just as day was dawning, Paul urged everyone to eat. "You have been so worried that you haven't touched food for two weeks," he said. 34 "Please eat something now for your own good. For not a hair of your heads will perish."

35 Then he took some bread, gave thanks to God before them all, and broke off a piece and ate it. 36 Then everyone was encouraged and began to eat—37 all 276 of us who were on board. 38 After eating, the crew lightened the ship further by throwing the cargo of wheat overboard.

39 When morning dawned, they didn't recognize the coastline, but they saw a bay with a beach and wondered if they could get to shore by running the ship aground. 40 So they cut off the anchors and left them in the sea. Then they lowered the rudders, raised the foresail, and headed toward shore. 41 But they hit a shoal and ran the ship aground too soon. The bow of the ship stuck fast, while the stern was repeatedly smashed by the force of the waves and began to break apart.

42 The soldiers wanted to kill the prisoners to make sure they didn't swim ashore and escape. 43 But the commanding officer wanted to spare Paul, so he didn't let them carry out their plan. Then he ordered all who could swim to jump overboard first and make for land. 44 The others held onto planks or debris from the broken ship. So everyone escaped safely to shore.

CHAPTER **28**
Paul on the Island of Malta
Once we were safe on shore, we learned that we were on the island of Malta. 2 The people of the island were very kind to us. It was cold and rainy, so they built a fire on the shore to welcome us.

3 As Paul gathered an armful of sticks and was laying them on the fire, a poisonous snake, driven out by the heat, bit him on the hand. 4 The people of the island saw it hanging from his hand and said to each other, "A murderer, no doubt! Though he escaped the sea, justice will not permit him to live." 5 But Paul shook off the snake into the fire and was unharmed. 6 The people waited for him to swell up or suddenly drop dead. But when they had waited a long time and saw that he wasn't harmed, they changed their minds and decided he was a god.

7 Near the shore where we landed was an estate belonging to Publius, the chief official of the island. He welcomed us and treated us kindly for three days. 8 As it happened, Publius's father was ill with fever and dysentery. Paul went in and prayed for him, and laying his hands on him, he healed him. 9 Then all the other sick people on the island came and were healed. 10 As a result we were showered with honors, and when the time came to sail, people supplied us with everything we would need for the trip.

Paul Arrives at Rome
11 It was three months after the shipwreck that we set sail on another ship that had wintered at the island—an Alexandrian ship with the twin gods as its figurehead. 12 Our first stop was Syracuse, where we stayed three days. 13 From there we sailed across to Rhegium. A day later a south wind began blowing, so the following day we sailed up the coast to Puteoli. 14 There we found some believers, who invited us to spend a week with them. And so we came to Rome.

15 The brothers and sisters in Rome had heard we were coming, and they came to meet us at the Forum on the Appian Way. Others joined us at The Three Taverns. When Paul saw them, he was encouraged and thanked God.

16 When we arrived in Rome, Paul was permitted to have his own private lodging, though he was guarded by a soldier.

Paul Preaches at Rome under Guard
17 Three days after Paul's arrival, he called together the local Jewish leaders. He said to them, "Brothers, I was arrested in Jerusalem and handed over to the Roman government, even though I had done nothing against our people or the customs of our ancestors. 18 The Romans tried me and wanted to release me, because they found no cause for the death sentence. 19 But when the Jewish leaders protested the decision, I felt it necessary to appeal to Caesar, even though I had no desire to press charges against my own people. 20 I asked you to come here today so we could get acquainted and so I could explain to you that I am bound with this chain because I believe that the hope of Israel—the Messiah—has already come."

21 They replied, "We have had no letters from Judea or reports against you from anyone who has come here. 22 But we want to hear what you believe, for the only thing we know about this movement is that it is denounced everywhere."

23 So a time was set, and on that day a large number of people came to Paul's lodging. He explained and testified about the Kingdom of God and tried to persuade them about Jesus from the Scriptures. Using the law of Moses and the books of the prophets, he spoke to them from morning until evening. 24 Some were persuaded by the things he said, but others did not believe. 25 And after they had argued back and forth among themselves, they left with this final word from Paul: "The Holy Spirit was right

when he said to your ancestors through Isaiah the prophet,

26 'Go and say to this people:
When you hear what I say,
    you will not understand.
When you see what I do,
    you will not comprehend.
27 For the hearts of these people are
        hardened,
    and their ears cannot hear,
    and they have closed their eyes—
so their eyes cannot see,
    and their ears cannot hear,
    and their hearts cannot understand,
and they cannot turn to me
    and let me heal them.'

28 So I want you to know that this salvation from God has also been offered to the Gentiles, and they will accept it."*

30 For the next two years, Paul lived in Rome at his own expense. He welcomed all who visited him, 31 boldly proclaiming the Kingdom of God and teaching about the Lord Jesus Christ. And no one tried to stop him.

28:28 Some manuscripts add verse 29, *And when he had said these words, the Jews departed, greatly disagreeing with each other.*

RoMANS
A State of Grace

Look for **2** hidden messages in Romans!

Paul wrote to the believers living in Rome to explain the basics of the Christian faith. He talked about

- **LAW VS. GRACE**
- **FAITH VS. DEEDS**
- **DEAD VS. ALIVE**
- **WEAK VS. STRONG**

Why, I remember...

Feeling Bad!

Having a hard time? Feeling a little down? Things aren't going all that well? **Take heart! Find out why in Romans 5:3-5.**

A Good Example

In his letter to the Romans, Paul talked about a hero from the past. **Find out who, and why he remembered him. Read Romans 4:1-25.**

Perfect Timing

God doesn't wear a watch, but his timing is perfect. **Read Romans 5:6-8 to see what God timed so perfectly!**

We're All the Same

Think you're different from other people? Think again! **Read Romans 3:22-23 to find out how and why we're all the same.**

We're All the Same —Again!

I'm OK. You're OK. *Not!*

Think you're the only one who struggles to do right? Well, Paul had exactly the same problems. **Read Romans 7:21-25 to see how Paul struggled with sin, just like we do!**

Not to Worry

Ever worry about why things happen the way they do? Well, stop worrying! God has a perfect plan for those who believe in him. **Read Romans 8:28 for proof of that perfect plan!**

And the Winner Is...

I'm the greatest! No, I'm the greatest! No, no, no —*I'm* the greatest! Which of God's commandments is the greatest? **Read Romans 13:8-10 to find the winner!**

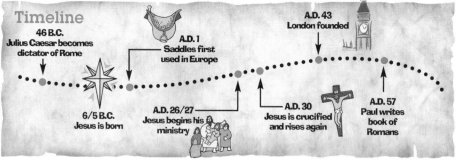

Timeline

46 B.C.
Julius Caesar becomes dictator of Rome

6/5 B.C.
Jesus is born

A.D. 1
Saddles first used in Europe

A.D. 26/27
Jesus begins his ministry

A.D. 30
Jesus is crucified and rises again

A.D. 43
London founded

A.D. 57
Paul writes book of Romans

The book of Romans is a great guideline for what it means to be a follower of Jesus. In his letter to the Roman believers, Paul laid it all out—ask God to forgive your sins and believe in Jesus to be saved. He made it clear that you can't be saved by doing good deeds. You can be saved only by believing that Jesus died to save you. Paul's words were true back then, and they're true today. **Just believe—it's that simple.**

CHAPTER **1**
Greetings from Paul

This letter is from Paul, a slave of Christ Jesus, chosen by God to be an apostle and sent out to preach his Good News. ²God promised this Good News long ago through his prophets in the holy Scriptures. ³The Good News is about his Son. In his earthly life he was born into King David's family line, ⁴and he was shown to be the Son of God when he was raised from the dead by the power of the Holy Spirit. He is Jesus Christ our Lord. ⁵Through Christ, God has given us the privilege and authority as apostles to tell Gentiles everywhere what God has done for them, so that they will believe and obey him, bringing glory to his name.

⁶And you are included among those Gentiles who have been called to belong to Jesus Christ. ⁷I am writing to all of you in Rome who are loved by God and are called to be his own holy people.

May God our Father and the Lord Jesus Christ give you grace and peace.

God's Good News

⁸Let me say first that I thank my God through Jesus Christ for all of you, because your faith in him is being talked about all over the world. ⁹God knows how often I pray for you. Day and night I bring you and your needs in prayer to God, whom I serve with all my heart by spreading the Good News about his Son.

¹⁰One of the things I always pray for is the opportunity, God willing, to come at last to see you. ¹¹For I long to visit you so I can bring you some spiritual gift that will help you grow strong in the Lord. ¹²When we get together, I want to encourage you in your faith, but I also want to be encouraged by yours.

¹³I want you to know, dear brothers and sisters, that I planned many times to visit you, but I was prevented until now. I want to work among you and see spiritual fruit, just as I have seen among other Gentiles. ¹⁴For I have a great sense of obligation to people in both the civilized world and the rest of the world, to the educated and uneducated alike. ¹⁵So I am eager to come to you in Rome, too, to preach the Good News.

¹⁶**For I am not ashamed of this Good News about Christ. It is the power of God at work, saving everyone who believes—the Jew first and also the Gentile.** ¹⁷This Good News tells us how God makes us right in his sight. This is accomplished from start to finish by faith. As the Scriptures say, "It is through faith that a righteous person has life."

God's Anger at Sin

¹⁸But God shows his anger from heaven against all sinful, wicked people who suppress the truth by their wickedness. ¹⁹They know the truth about God because he has made it obvious to them. ²⁰For ever since the world was created, people have seen the earth and sky. Through everything God made, they can clearly see his invisible qualities—his eternal power and divine nature. So they have no excuse for not knowing God.

²¹Yes, they knew God, but they wouldn't worship him as God or even give him thanks. And they began to think up foolish ideas of what God was like. As a result, their minds became dark and confused. ²²Claiming to be wise, they instead became utter fools. ²³And instead of worshiping the glorious, ever-living God, they worshiped idols made to look like mere people and birds and animals and reptiles.

²⁴So God abandoned them to do whatever shameful things their hearts desired. As a result, they did vile and degrading things with each other's bodies. ²⁵They traded the truth about God for a lie. So they worshiped and served the things God created instead of the Creator himself, who is worthy of eternal praise! Amen. ²⁶That is why God abandoned them to their shameful desires. Even the women turned against the natural way to have sex and instead indulged in sex with each other. ²⁷And the men, instead of having normal sexual relations with women, burned with lust for each other. Men did shameful things with other men, and as a result of this sin, they suffered within themselves the penalty they deserved.

²⁸Since they thought it foolish to acknowledge God, he abandoned them to their foolish thinking and let them do things that should never be done. ²⁹Their lives became full of every kind of wickedness, sin, greed, hate, envy, murder, quarreling, deception, malicious behavior, and gossip. ³⁰They are backstabbers, haters of God, insolent, proud, and boastful. They invent new ways of sinning, and they disobey their parents. ³¹They refuse to understand, break their promises, are heartless, and have no mercy. ³²They know God's justice requires that those who do these things deserve to die, yet they do them anyway. Worse yet, they encourage others to do them, too.

"For I am not ashamed of this Good News about Christ. It is the power of God at work, saving everyone who believes—the Jew first and also the Gentile."—**ROMANS 1:16**

Read ROMANS 1:16 out loud a few times until you know it by heart.

Whoever believes in Jesus will be saved and live with him forever in heaven. Now *that's* power!

> Believing in Jesus has the awesome power to save you, change your life, and let you live in heaven forever.

Here's an experiment about SIMPLE POWER!

1 Zip a resealable gallon-size plastic bag closed.

2 Poke a hole in the side of the bag with a drinking straw. Tape around the straw where it's poked inside the bag.

3 Place a heavy book on the bag. Now blow through the straw, and watch what happens.

AMAZING! You may not have thought the bag was powerful at first, but it turned out to be very powerful!

You may not think at first that believing in Jesus is powerful, but it is. It's the only thing that can get you into heaven!

> Show this experiment to a friend, then explain the power of believing in Jesus!

CHAPTER **2**
God's Judgment of Sin

You may think you can condemn such people, but you are just as bad, and you have no excuse! When you say they are wicked and should be punished, you are condemning yourself, for you who judge others do these very same things. 2And we know that God, in his justice, will punish anyone who does such things. 3Since you judge others for doing these things, why do you think you can avoid God's judgment when you do the same things? 4Don't you see how wonderfully kind, tolerant, and patient God is with you? Does this mean nothing to you? Can't you see that his kindness is intended to turn you from your sin?

5But because you are stubborn and refuse to turn from your sin, you are storing up terrible punishment for yourself. For a day of anger is coming, when God's righteous judgment will be revealed. 6He will judge everyone according to what they have done. 7He will give eternal life to those who keep on doing good, seeking after the glory and honor and immortality that God offers. 8But he will pour out his anger and wrath on those who live for themselves, who refuse to obey the truth and instead live lives of wickedness. 9There will be trouble and calamity for everyone who keeps on doing what is evil—for the Jew first and also for the Gentile. 10But there will be glory and honor and peace from God for all who do good—for the Jew first and also for the Gentile. 11For God does not show favoritism.

12When the Gentiles sin, they will be destroyed, even though they never had God's written law. And the Jews, who do have God's law, will be judged by that law when they fail to obey it. 13For merely listening to the law doesn't make us right with God. It is obeying the law that makes us right in his sight. 14Even Gentiles, who do not have God's written law, show that they know his law when they instinctively obey it, even without having heard it. 15They demonstrate that God's law is written in their hearts, for their own conscience and thoughts either accuse them or tell them they are doing right. 16And this is the message I proclaim—that the day is coming when God, through Christ Jesus, will judge everyone's secret life.

The Jews and the Law

17You who call yourselves Jews are relying on God's law, and you boast about your special relationship with him. 18You know what he wants; you know what is right because you have been taught his law. 19You are convinced that you are a guide for the blind and a light for people who are lost in darkness. 20 You think you can instruct the ignorant and teach children the ways of God. For you are certain that God's law gives you complete knowledge and truth.

21 Well then, if you teach others, why don't you teach yourself? You tell others not to steal, but do you steal? 22 You say it is wrong to commit adultery, but do you commit adultery? You condemn idolatry, but do you use items stolen from pagan temples? 23 You are so proud of knowing the law, but you dishonor God by breaking it. 24 No wonder the Scriptures say, "The Gentiles blaspheme the name of God because of you."

25 The Jewish ceremony of circumcision has value only if you obey God's law. But if you don't obey God's law, you are no better off than an uncircumcised Gentile. 26 And if the Gentiles obey God's law, won't God declare them to be his own people? 27 In fact, uncircumcised Gentiles who keep God's law will condemn you Jews who are circumcised and possess God's law but don't obey it.

28 For you are not a true Jew just because you were born of Jewish parents or because you have gone through the ceremony of circumcision. 29 No, a true Jew is one whose heart is right with God. And true circumcision is not merely obeying the letter of the law; rather, it is a change of heart produced by God's Spirit. And a person with a changed heart seeks praise from God, not from people.

CHAPTER **3**
God Remains Faithful

Then what's the advantage of being a Jew? Is there any value in the ceremony of circumcision? 2 Yes, there are great benefits! First of all, the Jews were entrusted with the whole revelation of God.

3 True, some of them were unfaithful; but just because they were unfaithful, does that mean God will be unfaithful? 4 Of course not! Even if everyone else is a liar, God is true. As the Scriptures say about him,

"You will be proved right in what you say,
and you will win your case in court."

5 "But," some might say, "our sinfulness serves a good purpose, for it helps people see how righteous God is. Isn't it unfair, then, for him to punish us?" (This is merely a human point of view.) 6 Of course not! If God were not entirely fair, how would he be qualified to judge the world? 7 "But," someone might still argue, "how can God

condemn me as a sinner if my dishonesty highlights his truthfulness and brings him more glory?" 8 And some people even slander us by claiming that we say, "The more we sin, the better it is!" Those who say such things deserve to be condemned.

All People Are Sinners

9 Well then, should we conclude that we Jews are better than others? No, not at all, for we have already shown that all people, whether Jews or Gentiles, are under the power of sin. 10 As the Scriptures say,

"No one is righteous—
    not even one.
11 No one is truly wise;
    no one is seeking God.
12 All have turned away;
    all have become useless.
No one does good,
    not a single one."
13 "Their talk is foul, like the stench from
    an open grave.
Their tongues are filled with lies."
"Snake venom drips from their lips."
14   "Their mouths are full of cursing
    and bitterness."
15 "They rush to commit murder.
16   Destruction and misery always
    follow them.
17 They don't know where to find peace."
18   "They have no fear of God at all."

19 Obviously, the law applies to those to whom it was given, for its purpose is to keep people from having excuses, and to show that the entire world is guilty before God. 20 For no one can ever be made right with God by doing what the law commands. The law simply shows us how sinful we are.

Christ Took Our Punishment

21 But now God has shown us a way to be made right with him without keeping the requirements of the law, as was promised in the writings of Moses and the prophets long ago. 22 We are made right with God by placing our faith in Jesus Christ. And this is true for everyone who believes, no matter who we are.

23 **For everyone has sinned; we all fall short of God's glorious standard.** 24 Yet God, with undeserved kindness, declares that we are righteous. He did this through Christ Jesus when he freed us from the penalty for our sins. 25 For God presented Jesus as the sacrifice

for sin. People are made right with God when they believe that Jesus sacrificed his life, shedding his blood. This sacrifice shows that God was being fair when he held back and did not punish those who sinned in times past, 26for he was looking ahead and including them in what he would do in this present time. God did this to demonstrate his righteousness, for he himself is fair and just, and he declares sinners to be right in his sight when they believe in Jesus.

27Can we boast, then, that we have done anything to be accepted by God? No, because our acquittal is not based on obeying the law. It is based on faith. 28So we are made right with God through faith and not by obeying the law.

29After all, is God the God of the Jews only? Isn't he also the God of the Gentiles? Of course he is. 30There is only one God, and he makes people right with himself only by faith, whether they are Jews or Gentiles. 31Well then, if we emphasize faith, does this mean that we can forget about the law? Of course not! In fact, only when we have faith do we truly fulfill the law.

CHAPTER **4**
The Faith of Abraham

Abraham was, humanly speaking, the founder of our Jewish nation. What did he discover about being made right with God? 2If his good deeds had made him acceptable to God, he would have had something to boast about. But that was not God's way. 3For the Scriptures tell us, "Abraham believed God, and God counted him as righteous because of his faith."

4When people work, their wages are not a gift, but something they have earned. 5But people are counted as righteous, not because of their work, but because of their faith in God who forgives sinners. 6David also spoke of this when he described the happiness of those who are declared righteous without working for it:

7 "Oh, what joy for those
whose disobedience is forgiven,
whose sins are put out of sight.
8 Yes, what joy for those
whose record the LORD has cleared of sin."

9Now, is this blessing only for the Jews, or is it also for uncircumcised Gentiles? Well, we have been saying that Abraham was counted as righteous by God because of his faith. 10But how did this happen? Was he counted as righteous only after he was circumcised, or was it before he was circumcised? Clearly, God accepted Abraham before he was circumcised!

EVERYONE Has Sinned

Read ROMANS 3:23 out loud a few times until you have it stuck in your brain.

No matter how much we try, we just can't be as good as God.

IT'S KIND OF LIKE THIS!

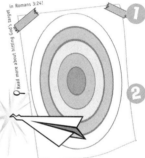

Read more about hitting God's target in Romans 3:24!

1 Draw a bull's-eye target on a sheet of paper. Tape the paper to a wall.

2 Use more paper to make paper wads or paper airplanes.

3 Step as far away from the target as the room allows, and try to hit the center of the target with your paper wads or airplanes. Play several rounds.

If you think of God as the center of the target, we just can't hit the target every time. **But that's OK. Do you know why? BECAUSE OF JESUS!**

Jesus took the punishment for our sins when he died on the cross. After we believe in Jesus, God helps us choose to follow Jesus so we can be on target.

THAT'S THE ONLY WAY TO HIT GOD'S TARGET—TO BELIEVE IN JESUS!

¹¹Circumcision was a sign that Abraham already had faith and that God had already accepted him and declared him to be righteous—even before he was circumcised. So Abraham is the spiritual father of those who have faith but have not been circumcised. They are counted as righteous because of their faith. ¹²And Abraham is also the spiritual father of those who have been circumcised, but only if they have the same kind of faith Abraham had before he was circumcised.

¹³Clearly, God's promise to give the whole earth to Abraham and his descendants was based not on his obedience to God's law, but on a right relationship with God that comes by faith. ¹⁴If God's promise is only for those who obey the law, then faith is not necessary and the promise is pointless. ¹⁵For the law always brings punishment on those who try to obey it. (The only way to avoid breaking the law is to have no law to break!)

¹⁶So the promise is received by faith. It is given as a free gift. And we are all certain to receive it, whether or not we live according to the law of Moses, if we have faith like Abraham's. For Abraham is the father of all who believe. ¹⁷That is what the Scriptures mean when God told him, "I have made you the father of many nations." This happened because Abraham believed in the God who brings the dead back to life and who creates new things out of nothing.

¹⁸Even when there was no reason for hope, Abraham kept hoping—believing that he would become the father of many nations. For God had said to him, "That's how many descendants you will have!" ¹⁹And Abraham's faith did not weaken, even though, at about 100 years of age, he figured his body was as good as dead—and so was Sarah's womb.

²⁰Abraham never wavered in believing God's promise. In fact, his faith grew stronger, and in this he brought glory to God. ²¹He was fully convinced that God is able to do whatever he promises. ²²And because of Abraham's faith, God counted him as righteous. ²³And when God counted him as righteous, it wasn't just for Abraham's benefit. It was recorded ²⁴for our benefit, too, assuring us that God will also count us as righteous if we believe in him, the one who raised Jesus our Lord from the dead. ²⁵He was handed over to die because of our sins, and he was raised to life to make us right with God.

CHAPTER **5**
Faith Brings Joy
Therefore, since we have been made right in God's sight by faith, we have peace with God be- cause of what Jesus Christ our Lord has done for us. ²Because of our faith, Christ has brought us into this place of undeserved privilege where we now stand, and we confidently and joyfully look forward to sharing God's glory.

³We can rejoice, too, when we run into problems and trials, for we know that they help us develop endurance. ⁴And endurance develops strength of character, and character strengthens our confident hope of salvation. ⁵And this hope will not lead to disappointment. For we know how dearly God loves us, because he has given us the Holy Spirit to fill our hearts with his love.

⁶When we were utterly helpless, Christ came at just the right time and died for us sinners. ⁷Now, most people would not be willing to die for an upright person, though someone might perhaps be willing to die for a person who is especially good. **⁸But God showed his great love for us by sending Christ to die for us while we were still sinners.** ⁹And since we have been made right in God's sight by the blood of Christ, he will certainly save us from God's condemnation. ¹⁰For since our friendship with God was restored by the death of his Son while we were still his enemies, we will certainly be saved through the life of his Son. ¹¹So now we can rejoice in our wonderful new relationship with God because our Lord Jesus Christ has made us friends of God.

Adam and Christ Contrasted
¹²When Adam sinned, sin entered the world. Adam's sin brought death, so death spread to everyone, for everyone sinned. ¹³Yes, people sinned even before the law was given. But it was not counted as sin because there was not yet any law to break. ¹⁴Still, everyone died—from the time of Adam to the time of Moses—even those who did not disobey an explicit commandment of God, as Adam did. Now Adam is a symbol, a representation of Christ, who was yet to come. ¹⁵But there is a great difference between Adam's sin and God's gracious gift. For the sin of this one man, Adam, brought death to many. But even greater is God's wonderful grace and his gift of forgiveness to many through this other man, Jesus Christ. ¹⁶And the result of God's gracious gift is very different from the result of that one man's sin. For Adam's sin led to condemnation, but God's free gift leads to our being made right with God, even though we are guilty of many sins. ¹⁷For

the sin of this one man, Adam, caused death to rule over many. But even greater is God's wonderful grace and his gift of righteousness, for all who receive it will live in triumph over sin and death through this one man, Jesus Christ.

18 Yes, Adam's one sin brings condemnation for everyone, but Christ's one act of righteousness brings a right relationship with God and new life for everyone. 19 Because one person disobeyed God, many became sinners. But because one other person obeyed God, many will be made righteous.

20 God's law was given so that all people could see how sinful they were. But as people sinned more and more, God's wonderful grace became more abundant. 21 So just as sin ruled over all people and brought them to death, now God's wonderful grace rules instead, giving us right standing with God and resulting in eternal life through Jesus Christ our Lord.

CHAPTER 6
Sin's Power Is Broken

Well then, should we keep on sinning so that God can show us more and more of his wonderful grace? 2 Of course not! Since we have died to sin, how can we continue to live in it? 3 Or have you forgotten that when we were joined with Christ Jesus in baptism, we joined him in his death? 4 For we died and were buried with Christ by baptism. And just as Christ was raised from the dead by the glorious power of the Father, now we also may live new lives.

5 Since we have been united with him in his death, we will also be raised to life as he was. 6 We know that our old sinful selves were crucified with Christ so that sin might lose its power in our lives. We are no longer slaves to sin. 7 For when we died with Christ we were set free from the power of sin. 8 And since we died with Christ, we know we will also live with him. 9 We are sure of this because Christ was raised from the dead, and he will never die again. Death no longer has any power over him. 10 When he died, he died once to break the power of sin. But now that he lives, he lives for the glory of God. 11 So you also should consider yourselves to be dead to the power of sin and alive to God through Christ Jesus.

12 Do not let sin control the way you live; do not give in to sinful desires. 13 Do not let any part of your body become an instrument of evil to serve sin. Instead, give yourselves completely to God, for you were dead, but now you have new life. So use your whole body as an instrument to do what is right for the glory of God. 14 Sin is no longer your master, for you no longer live under the requirements of the law. Instead, you live under the freedom of God's grace.

15 Well then, since God's grace has set us free from the law, does that mean we can go on sinning? Of course not! 16 Don't you realize that you become the slave of whatever you choose to obey? You can be a slave to sin, which leads to death, or you can choose to obey God, which leads to righteous living. 17 Thank God! Once you were slaves of sin, but now you wholeheartedly obey this teaching we have given you. 18 Now you are free from your slavery to sin, and you have become slaves to righteous living.

19 Because of the weakness of your human nature, I am using the illustration of slavery to help you understand all this. Previously, you let yourselves be slaves to impurity and lawlessness, which led ever deeper into sin. Now you must give yourselves to be slaves to righteous living so that you will become holy.

20 When you were slaves to sin, you were free from the obligation to do right. 21 And what was the result? You are now ashamed of the things you used to do, things that end in eternal doom. 22 But now you are free from the power of sin and have become slaves of God. Now you do those things that lead to holiness and result in eternal life. **23 For the wages of sin is death, but the free gift of God is eternal life through Christ Jesus our Lord.**

CHAPTER 7
No Longer Bound to the Law

Now, dear brothers and sisters—you who are familiar with the law—don't you know that the law applies only while a person is living? 2 For example, when a woman marries, the law binds her to her husband as long as he is alive. But if he dies, the laws of marriage no longer apply to her. 3 So while her husband is alive, she would be committing adultery if she married another man. But if her husband dies, she is free from that law and does not commit adultery when she remarries.

4 So, my dear brothers and sisters, this is the point: You died to the power of the law when you died with Christ. And now you are united with the one who was raised from the dead. As a result, we can produce a harvest of good deeds for God. 5 When we were controlled by our old nature, sinful desires were at work within us, and the law aroused these evil desires that produced a har-

vest of sinful deeds, resulting in death. 6But now we have been released from the law, for we died to it and are no longer captive to its power. Now we can serve God, not in the old way of obeying the letter of the law, but in the new way of living in the Spirit.

God's Law Reveals Our Sin

7Well then, am I suggesting that the law of God is sinful? Of course not! In fact, it was the law that showed me my sin. I would never have known that coveting is wrong if the law had not said, "You must not covet." 8But sin used this command to arouse all kinds of covetous desires within me! If there were no law, sin would not have that power. 9At one time I lived without understanding the law. But when I learned the command not to covet, for instance, the power of sin came to life, 10and I died. So I discovered that the law's commands, which were supposed to bring life, brought spiritual death instead. 11Sin took advantage of those commands and deceived me; it used the commands to kill me. 12But still, the law itself is holy, and its commands are holy and right and good.

13But how can that be? Did the law, which is good, cause my death? Of course not! Sin used what was good to bring about my condemnation to death. So we can see how terrible sin really is. It uses God's good commands for its own evil purposes.

Struggling with Sin

14So the trouble is not with the law, for it is spiritual and good. The trouble is with me, for I am all too human, a slave to sin. 15I don't really understand myself, for I want to do what is right, but I don't do it. Instead, I do what I hate. 16But if I know that what I am doing is wrong, this shows that I agree that the law is good. 17So I am not the one doing wrong; it is sin living in me that does it.

18And I know that nothing good lives in me, that is, in my sinful nature. I want to do what is right, but I can't. 19I want to do what is good, but I don't. I don't want to do what is wrong, but I do it anyway. 20But if I do what I don't want to do, I am not really the one doing wrong; it is sin living in me that does it.

21I have discovered this principle of life—that when I want to do what is right, I inevitably do what is wrong. 22I love God's law with all my heart. 23But there is another power within me that is at war with my mind. This power makes me a slave to the sin that is still within me. 24Oh,

Key Verse "But God showed his great love for us by sending Christ to die for us while we were still sinners."—ROMANS 5:8

GOD LOVES YOU!

Read ROMANS 5:8 out loud. Then read it again. And again.

God loves you so much that he sent his Son to die for you, just as you are. He didn't wait until you cleaned up your act. *That's* how much he loves you!

THINK OF SOMEONE IN YOUR LIFE WHO LOVES YOU.

1. Write that person's name in the sentence on the left of the chart below. Then write a few ways that person shows love for you.

2. On the right, write ways that God shows love for you. (The most important way is already written there!)

THIS IS HOW _____ SHOWS LOVE FOR ME:	THIS IS HOW GOD SHOWS LOVE FOR ME:
	He sent Jesus to die for me.

Read more about love in 1 Corinthians 13:4-7.

Whenever you feel alone, open your Bible to this verse and remind yourself that God sent his Son to die for you!

what a miserable person I am! Who will free me from this life that is dominated by sin and death? 25 Thank God! The answer is in Jesus Christ our Lord. So you see how it is: In my mind I really want to obey God's law, but because of my sinful nature I am a slave to sin.

CHAPTER **8**
Life in the Spirit

So now there is no condemnation for those who belong to Christ Jesus. 2 And because you belong to him, the power of the life-giving Spirit has freed you from the power of sin that leads to death. 3 The law of Moses was unable to save us because of the weakness of our sinful nature. So God did what the law could not do. He sent his own Son in a body like the bodies we sinners have. And in that body God declared an end to sin's control over us by giving his Son as a sacrifice for our sins. 4 He did this so that the just requirement of the law would be fully satisfied for us, who no longer follow our sinful nature but instead follow the Spirit.

5 Those who are dominated by the sinful nature think about sinful things, but those who are controlled by the Holy Spirit think about things that please the Spirit. 6 So letting your sinful nature control your mind leads to death. But letting the Spirit control your mind leads to life and peace. 7 For the sinful nature is always hostile to God. It never did obey God's laws, and it never will. 8 That's why those who are still under the control of their sinful nature can never please God.

9 But you are not controlled by your sinful nature. You are controlled by the Spirit if you have the Spirit of God living in you. (And remember that those who do not have the Spirit of Christ living in them do not belong to him at all.) 10 And Christ lives within you, so even though your body will die because of sin, the Spirit gives you life because you have been made right with God. 11 The Spirit of God, who raised Jesus from the dead, lives in you. And just as God raised Christ Jesus from the dead, he will give life to your mortal bodies by this same Spirit living within you.

12 Therefore, dear brothers and sisters, you have no obligation to do what your sinful nature urges you to do. 13 For if you live by its dictates, you will die. But if through the power of the Spirit you put to death the deeds of your sinful nature, you will live. 14 For all who are led by the Spirit of God are children of God.

15 So you have not received a spirit that makes you fearful slaves. Instead, you received God's Spirit when he adopted you as his own children. Now we call him, "Abba, Father." 16 For his Spirit joins with our spirit to affirm that we are God's children. 17 And since we are his children, we are his heirs. In fact, together with Christ we are heirs of God's glory. But if we are to share his glory, we must also share his suffering.

Key Verse

"For the wages of sin is death, but the free gift of God is eternal life through Christ Jesus our Lord."
—ROMANS 6:23

Gift Giving

Read ROMANS 6:23 out loud to a friend or family member.

HEY, WHO DOESN'T LIKE A FREE GIFT? God gives us the free gift of eternal life through Jesus. That's a gift worth sharing, don't you think?

HERE'S HOW!

1. Write the words of the verse on a sheet of paper. Decorate the paper any way you choose.

2. Put the paper in a box and gift-wrap the box.

3. Make a gift tag that says, "Here's the greatest gift of all!"

GIVE THE GIFT TO SOMEONE WHO NEEDS TO KNOW ABOUT JESUS. Then make another gift box, and another. *Everyone* needs to know about Jesus!

The Future Glory

18 Yet what we suffer now is nothing compared to the glory he will reveal to us later. 19 For all creation is waiting eagerly for that future day when God will reveal who his children really are. 20 Against its will, all creation was subjected to God's curse. But with eager hope, 21 the creation looks forward to the day when it will join God's children in glorious freedom from death and decay. 22 For we know that all creation has been groaning as in the pains of childbirth right up to the present time. 23 And we believers also groan, even though we have the Holy Spirit within us as a foretaste of future glory, for we long for our bodies to be released from sin and suffering. We, too, wait with eager hope for the day when God will give us our full rights as his adopted children, including the new bodies he has promised us. 24 We were given this hope when we were saved. (If we already have something, we don't need to hope for it. 25 But if we look forward to something we don't yet have, we must wait patiently and confidently.)

26 And the Holy Spirit helps us in our weakness. For example, we don't know what God wants us to pray for. But the Holy Spirit prays for us with groanings that cannot be expressed in words. 27 And the Father who knows all hearts knows what the Spirit is saying, for the Spirit pleads for us believers in harmony with God's own will. **28 And we know that God causes everything to work together for the good of those who love God and are called according to his purpose for them.** 29 For God knew his people in advance, and he chose them to become like his Son, so that his Son would be the firstborn among many brothers and sisters. 30 And having chosen them, he called them to come to him. And having called them, he gave them right standing with himself. And having given them right standing, he gave them his glory.

Nothing Can Separate Us from God's Love

31 What shall we say about such wonderful things as these? If God is for us, who can ever be against us? 32 Since he did not spare even his own Son but gave him up for us all, won't he also give us everything else? 33 Who dares accuse us whom God has chosen for his own? No one—for God himself has given us right standing with himself. 34 Who then will condemn us? No one—for Christ Jesus died for us and was raised to life for us, and he is sitting in the place of honor at God's right hand, pleading for us.

35 Can anything ever separate us from Christ's love? Does it mean he no longer loves us if we have trouble or calamity, or are persecuted, or hungry, or destitute, or in danger, or threatened with death? 36 (As the Scriptures say, "For your sake we are killed every day; we are being slaughtered like sheep.") 37 No, despite all these things, overwhelming victory is ours through Christ, who loved us.

38 And I am convinced that nothing can ever separate us from God's love. Neither death nor life, neither angels nor demons, neither our fears for today nor our worries about tomorrow—not even the powers of hell can separate us from God's love. 39 No power in the sky above or in the earth below—indeed, nothing in all creation will ever be able to separate us from the love of God that is revealed in Christ Jesus our Lord.

CHAPTER **9**

God's Selection of Israel

With Christ as my witness, I speak with utter truthfulness. My conscience and the Holy Spirit confirm it. 2 My heart is filled with bitter sorrow and unending grief 3 for my people, my Jewish brothers and sisters. I would be willing to be forever cursed—cut off from Christ!—if that would save them. 4 They are the people of Israel, chosen to be God's adopted children. God revealed his glory to them. He made covenants with them and gave them his law. He gave them the privilege of worshiping him and receiving his wonderful promises. 5 Abraham, Isaac, and Jacob are their ancestors, and Christ himself was an Israelite as far as his human nature is concerned. And he is God, the one who rules over everything and is worthy of eternal praise! Amen.

6 Well then, has God failed to fulfill his promise to Israel? No, for not all who are born into the nation of Israel are truly members of God's people! 7 Being descendants of Abraham doesn't make them truly Abraham's children. For the Scriptures say, "Isaac is the son through whom your descendants will be counted," though Abraham had other children, too. 8 This means that Abraham's physical descendants are not necessarily children of God. Only the children of the promise are considered to be Abraham's children. 9 For God had promised, "I will return about this time next year, and Sarah will have a son."

10 This son was our ancestor Isaac. When he married Rebekah, she gave birth to twins. 11 But before they were born, before they had done

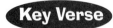

Key Verse — "And we know that God causes everything to work together for the good of those who love God and are called according to his purpose for them." —ROMANS 8:28

Read ROMANS 8:28 out loud to a friend.

The Pieces Fit!

THEN DO THIS.

1 Find an old puzzle, and spread the pieces out on a table, leaving a clear space in the center.

2 Take turns with your friend picking up a puzzle piece and laying it in the clear space. For each piece you pick up, tell your friend about a time you were confused or troubled.

The picture on the puzzle box is a complete picture, made up of little pieces that all fit together like the pieces of your life. Glue some puzzle pieces to a square of colored poster board. Write the words of **ROMANS 8:28** around the border.

DO THIS! Keep your puzzle in your room to remind you that God sees the big picture of your life!

anything good or bad, she received a message from God. (This message shows that God chooses people according to his own purposes; 12he calls people, but not according to their good or bad works.) She was told, "Your older son will serve your younger son." 13In the words of the Scriptures, "I loved Jacob, but I rejected Esau."

14Are we saying, then, that God was unfair? Of course not! 15For God said to Moses,

"I will show mercy to anyone I choose,
and I will show compassion to anyone
I choose."

16So it is God who decides to show mercy. We can neither choose it nor work for it.

17For the Scriptures say that God told Pharaoh, "I have appointed you for the very purpose of displaying my power in you and to spread my fame throughout the earth." 18So you see, God chooses to show mercy to some, and he chooses to harden the hearts of others so they refuse to listen.

19Well then, you might say, "Why does God blame people for not responding? Haven't they simply done what he makes them do?"

20No, don't say that. Who are you, a mere human being, to argue with God? Should the thing that was created say to the one who created it, "Why have you made me like this?" 21When a potter makes jars out of clay, doesn't he have a right to use the same lump of clay to make one jar for decoration and another to throw garbage into? 22In the same way, even though God has the right to show his anger and his power, he is very patient with those on whom his anger falls, who are destined for destruction. 23He does this to make the riches of his glory shine even brighter on those to whom he shows mercy, who were prepared in advance for glory. 24And we are among those whom he selected, both from the Jews and from the Gentiles.

25Concerning the Gentiles, God says in the prophecy of Hosea,

"Those who were not my people,
I will now call my people.
And I will love those
whom I did not love before."

26And,

"Then, at the place where they were told,
'You are not my people,'
there they will be called
'children of the living God.'"

27And concerning Israel, Isaiah the prophet cried out,

"Though the people of Israel are as
numerous as the sand of the seashore,
only a remnant will be saved.
28 For the LORD will carry out his sentence
upon the earth
quickly and with finality."

29 And Isaiah said the same thing in another place:

"If the LORD of Heaven's Armies
had not spared a few of our children,
we would have been wiped out like Sodom,
destroyed like Gomorrah."

Israel's Unbelief

30 What does all this mean? Even though the Gentiles were not trying to follow God's standards, they were made right with God. And it was by faith that this took place. 31 But the people of Israel, who tried so hard to get right with God by keeping the law, never succeeded. 32 Why not? Because they were trying to get right with God by keeping the law instead of by trusting in him. They stumbled over the great rock in their path. 33 God warned them of this in the Scriptures when he said,

"I am placing a stone in Jerusalem
that makes people stumble,
a rock that makes them fall.
But anyone who trusts in him
will never be disgraced."

CHAPTER **10**

Dear brothers and sisters, the longing of my heart and my prayer to God is for the people of Israel to be saved. 2 I know what enthusiasm they have for God, but it is misdirected zeal. 3 For they don't understand God's way of making people right with himself. Refusing to accept God's way, they cling to their own way of getting right with God by trying to keep the law. 4 For Christ has already accomplished the purpose for which the law was given. As a result, all who believe in him are made right with God.

Salvation Is for Everyone

5 For Moses writes that the law's way of making a person right with God requires obedience to all of its commands. 6 But faith's way of getting right with God says, "Don't say in your heart, 'Who will go up to heaven' (to bring Christ down to earth). 7 And don't say, 'Who will go down to the place of the dead' (to bring Christ back to life again)." 8 In fact, it says,

"The message is very close at hand;
it is on your lips and in your heart."

And that message is the very message about faith that we preach: 9 **If you confess with your mouth that Jesus is Lord and believe in your heart that God raised him from the dead, you will be saved.** 10 For it is by believing in your heart that you are made right with God, and it is by confessing with your mouth that you are saved. 11 As the Scriptures tell us, "Anyone who trusts in him will never be disgraced." 12 Jew and Gentile are the same in this respect. They have the same Lord, who gives generously to all who call on him. 13 For "Everyone who calls on the name of the LORD will be saved."

14 But how can they call on him to save them unless they believe in him? And how can they believe in him if they have never heard about him? And how can they hear about him unless someone tells them? 15 And how will anyone go and tell them without being sent? That is why the Scriptures say, "How beautiful are the feet of messengers who bring good news!"

16 But not everyone welcomes the Good News, for Isaiah the prophet said, "LORD, who has believed our message?" 17 So faith comes from hearing, that is, hearing the Good News about Christ. 18 But I ask, have the people of Israel actually heard the message? Yes, they have:

"The message has gone throughout the earth,
and the words to all the world."

19 But I ask, did the people of Israel really understand? Yes, they did, for even in the time of Moses, God said,

"I will rouse your jealousy through people
who are not even a nation.
I will provoke your anger through the
foolish Gentiles."

20 And later Isaiah spoke boldly for God, saying,

"I was found by people who were not
looking for me.
I showed myself to those who were
not asking for me."

21 But regarding Israel, God said,

"All day long I opened my arms to them,
but they were disobedient and rebellious."

CHAPTER **11**

God's Mercy on Israel

I ask, then, has God rejected his own people, the nation of Israel? Of course not! I myself am an

Israelite, a descendant of Abraham and a member of the tribe of Benjamin.

2No, God has not rejected his own people, whom he chose from the very beginning. Do you realize what the Scriptures say about this? Elijah the prophet complained to God about the people of Israel and said, 3"LORD, they have killed your prophets and torn down your altars. I am the only one left, and now they are trying to kill me, too."

4And do you remember God's reply? He said, "No, I have 7,000 others who have never bowed down to Baal!"

5It is the same today, for a few of the people of Israel have remained faithful because of God's grace—his undeserved kindness in choosing them. 6And since it is through God's kindness, then it is not by their good works. For in that case, God's grace would not be what it really is— free and undeserved.

7So this is the situation: Most of the people of Israel have not found the favor of God they are looking for so earnestly. A few have—the ones God has chosen—but the hearts of the rest were hardened. 8As the Scriptures say,

"God has put them into a deep sleep.
To this day he has shut their eyes so they
do not see,
and closed their ears so they do not hear."

9Likewise, David said,

"Let their bountiful table become a snare,
a trap that makes them think all is well.
Let their blessings cause them to stumble,
and let them get what they deserve.
10 Let their eyes go blind so they cannot see,
and let their backs be bent forever."

11Did God's people stumble and fall beyond recovery? Of course not! They were disobedient, so God made salvation available to the Gentiles. But he wanted his own people to become jealous and claim it for themselves. 12Now if the Gentiles were enriched because the people of Israel turned down God's offer of salvation, think how much greater a blessing the world will share when they finally accept it.

13I am saying all this especially for you Gentiles. God has appointed me as the apostle to the Gentiles. I stress this, 14for I want somehow to make the people of Israel jealous of what you Gentiles have, so I might save some of them. 15For since their rejection meant that God offered salvation to the rest of the world, their acceptance will be even more wonderful. It will be life for those who were dead! 16And since Abraham and the other patriarchs were holy, their descendants will also be holy—just as the entire batch of dough is holy because the portion given as an offering is holy. For if the roots of the tree are holy, the branches will be, too.

17But some of these branches from Abraham's tree—some of the people of Israel—have been broken off. And you Gentiles, who were branches from a wild olive tree, have been grafted in. So now you also receive the blessing God has promised Abraham and his children, sharing in the rich nourishment from the root of God's special olive tree. 18But you must not brag about being grafted in to replace the branches that were broken off. You are just a branch, not the root.

19"Well," you may say, "those branches were broken off to make room for me." 20Yes, but remember—those branches were broken off because they didn't believe in Christ, and you are there because you do believe. So don't think highly of yourself, but fear what could happen. 21For if God did not spare the original branches, he won't spare you either.

22Notice how God is both kind and severe. He is severe toward those who disobeyed, but kind to you if you continue to trust in his kindness. But if you stop trusting, you also will be cut off. 23And if the people of Israel turn from their unbelief, they will be grafted in again, for God has the power to graft them back into the tree. 24You, by nature, were a branch cut from a wild olive tree. So if God was willing to do something contrary to nature by grafting you into his cultivated tree, he will be far more eager to graft the original branches back into the tree where they belong.

God's Mercy Is for Everyone

25I want you to understand this mystery, dear brothers and sisters, so that you will not feel proud about yourselves. Some of the people of Israel have hard hearts, but this will last only until the full number of Gentiles comes to Christ. 26And so all Israel will be saved. As the Scriptures say,

"The one who rescues will come from
Jerusalem,
and he will turn Israel away from
ungodliness.
27 And this is my covenant with them,
that I will take away their sins."

28Many of the people of Israel are now enemies of the Good News, and this benefits you

Gentiles. Yet they are still the people he loves because he chose their ancestors Abraham, Isaac, and Jacob. 29For God's gifts and his call can never be withdrawn. 30Once, you Gentiles were rebels against God, but when the people of Israel rebelled against him, God was merciful to you instead. 31Now they are the rebels, and God's mercy has come to you so that they, too, will share in God's mercy. 32For God has imprisoned everyone in disobedience so he could have mercy on everyone.

33Oh, how great are God's riches and wisdom and knowledge! How impossible it is for us to understand his decisions and his ways!

34 For who can know the LORD's thoughts?
    Who knows enough to give him advice?
35 And who has given him so much
    that he needs to pay it back?

36For everything comes from him and exists by his power and is intended for his glory. All glory to him forever! Amen.

CHAPTER **12**
A Living Sacrifice to God
And so, dear brothers and sisters, I plead with you to give your bodies to God because of all he has done for you. Let them be a living and holy sacrifice—the kind he will find acceptable. This is truly the way to worship him. 2Don't copy the behavior and customs of this world, but let God transform you into a new person by changing the way you think. Then you will learn to know God's will for you, which is good and pleasing and perfect.

3Because of the privilege and authority God has given me, I give each of you this warning: Don't think you are better than you really are. Be honest in your evaluation of yourselves, measuring yourselves by the faith God has given us. 4Just as our bodies have many parts and each part has a special function, 5so it is with Christ's body. We are many parts of one body, and we all belong to each other.

6In his grace, God has given us different gifts for doing certain things well. So if God has given you the ability to prophesy, speak out with as much faith as God has given you. 7If your gift is serving others, serve them well. If you are a teacher, teach well. 8If your gift is to encourage others, be encouraging. If it is giving, give generously. If God has given you leadership ability, take the responsibility seriously. And if you have a gift for showing kindness to others, do it gladly.

9Don't just pretend to love others. Really love them. Hate what is wrong. Hold tightly to what is good. 10**Love each other with genuine affection, and take delight in honoring each other.** 11Never be lazy, but work hard and serve the Lord enthusiastically. 12Rejoice in our confident hope. Be patient in trouble, and keep on praying. 13When God's people are in need, be ready to help them. Always be eager to practice hospitality.

14Bless those who persecute you. Don't curse them; pray that God will bless them. 15Be happy with those who are happy, and weep with those who weep. 16Live in harmony with each other. Don't be too proud to enjoy the company of ordinary people. And don't think you know it all!

17Never pay back evil with more evil. Do things in such a way that everyone can see you are honorable. 18Do all that you can to live in peace with everyone.

19Dear friends, never take revenge. Leave that to the righteous anger of God. For the Scriptures say,

"I will take revenge;
    I will pay them back,"
    says the LORD.

20Instead,

"If your enemies are hungry, feed them.
    If they are thirsty, give them something
        to drink.
In doing this, you will heap
    burning coals of shame on their heads."

21Don't let evil conquer you, but conquer evil by doing good.

CHAPTER **13**
Respect for Authority
Everyone must submit to governing authorities. For all authority comes from God, and those in positions of authority have been placed there by God. 2So anyone who rebels against authority is rebelling against what God has instituted, and they will be punished. 3For the authorities do not strike fear in people who are doing right, but in those who are doing wrong. Would you like to live without fear of the authorities? Do what is right, and they will honor you. 4The authorities are God's servants, sent for your good. But if you are doing wrong, of course you should be afraid, for they have the power to punish you. They are God's servants, sent for the very purpose of punishing those who do what is wrong. 5So you must submit to them,

not only to avoid punishment, but also to keep a clear conscience.

⁶Pay your taxes, too, for these same reasons. For government workers need to be paid. They are serving God in what they do. ⁷Give to everyone what you owe them: Pay your taxes and government fees to those who collect them, and give respect and honor to those who are in authority.

Love Fulfills God's Requirements

⁸Owe nothing to anyone—except for your obligation to love one another. If you love your neighbor, you will fulfill the requirements of God's law. ⁹For the commandments say, "You must not commit adultery. You must not murder. You must not steal. You must not covet." These—and other such commandments—are summed up in this one commandment: "Love your neighbor as yourself." ¹⁰Love does no wrong to others, so love fulfills the requirements of God's law.

¹¹This is all the more urgent, for you know how late it is; time is running out. Wake up, for our salvation is nearer now than when we first believed. ¹²The night is almost gone; the day of salvation will soon be here. So remove your dark deeds like dirty clothes, and put on the shining armor of right living. ¹³Because we belong to the day, we must live decent lives for all to see. Don't participate in the darkness of wild parties and drunkenness, or in sexual promiscuity and immoral living, or in quarreling and jealousy. ¹⁴Instead, clothe yourself with the presence of the Lord Jesus Christ. And don't let yourself think about ways to indulge your evil desires.

CHAPTER 14
The Danger of Criticism

Accept other believers who are weak in faith, and don't argue with them about what they think is right or wrong. ²For instance, one person believes it's all right to eat anything. But another believer with a sensitive conscience will eat only vegetables. ³Those who feel free to eat anything must not look down on those who don't. And those who don't eat certain foods must not condemn those who do, for God has accepted them. ⁴Who are you to condemn someone else's servants? They are responsible to the Lord, so let him judge whether they are right or wrong. And with the Lord's help, they will do what is right and will receive his approval.

⁵In the same way, some think one day is more holy than another day, while others think every

You've Got Mail!

The Apostle Paul wrote letters to tell others about Jesus. Some of those letters became books of the Bible! **For instance, Paul wrote a letter to the Christians in Rome, and that letter became the book of ROMANS!** Paul wanted to go to Rome to teach the people there about Jesus, but he also had to return to Jerusalem (which was in the opposite direction). So Paul wrote a letter instead!

GRAB A PENCIL!

Write a letter to someone who doesn't know Jesus. Maybe you'll write to a stranger in another country like Paul wrote to the Romans. In your letter, tell what you know about Jesus and what he means to you just like Paul did!

day is alike. You should each be fully convinced that whichever day you choose is acceptable. ⁶Those who worship the Lord on a special day do it to honor him. Those who eat any kind of food do so to honor the Lord, since they give thanks to God before eating. And those who refuse to eat certain foods also want to please the Lord and give thanks to God. ⁷For we don't live for ourselves or die for ourselves. ⁸If we live, it's to honor the Lord. And if we die, it's to honor the Lord. So whether we live or die, we belong to the Lord. ⁹Christ died and rose again for this very purpose—to be Lord both of the living and of the dead.

¹⁰So why do you condemn another believer? Why do you look down on another believer? Remember, we will all stand before the judgment seat of God. ¹¹For the Scriptures say,

"'As surely as I live,' says the LORD,
'every knee will bend to me,
and every tongue will confess and give
praise to God.'"

¹²Yes, each of us will give a personal account to God. ¹³So let's stop condemning each other. Decide instead to live in such a way that you will not cause another believer to stumble and fall.

¹⁴I know and am convinced on the authority of the Lord Jesus that no food, in and of itself, is wrong to eat. But if someone believes it is wrong, then for that person it is wrong. ¹⁵And if another believer is distressed by what you eat, you are not acting in love if you eat it. Don't let your eating ruin someone for whom Christ died. ¹⁶Then you will not be criticized for doing something you believe is good. ¹⁷For the Kingdom of God is not a matter of what we eat or drink, but of living a life of goodness and peace and joy in the Holy Spirit. ¹⁸If you serve Christ with this attitude, you will please God, and others will approve of you, too. ¹⁹So then, let us aim for harmony in the church and try to build each other up.

²⁰Don't tear apart the work of God over what you eat. Remember, all foods are acceptable, but it is wrong to eat something if it makes another person stumble. ²¹It is better not to eat meat or drink wine or do anything else if it might cause another believer to stumble. ²²You may believe there's nothing wrong with what you are doing, but keep it between yourself and God. Blessed are those who don't feel guilty for doing something they have decided is right. ²³But if you have doubts about whether or not you should eat something, you are sinning if you go ahead and do it. For you are not following your convictions. If you do anything you believe is not right, you are sinning.

CHAPTER **15**
Living to Please Others

We who are strong must be considerate of those who are sensitive about things like this. We must not just please ourselves. ²We should help others do what is right and build them up in the Lord. ³For even Christ didn't live to please himself. As the Scriptures say, "The insults of those who insult you, O God, have fallen on me." ⁴Such things were written in the Scriptures long ago to teach us. And the Scriptures give us hope and encouragement as we wait patiently for God's promises to be fulfilled.

⁵May God, who gives this patience and encouragement, help you live in complete harmony with each other, as is fitting for followers of Christ Jesus. ⁶Then all of you can join together with one voice, giving praise and glory to God, the Father of our Lord Jesus Christ.

⁷Therefore, accept each other just as Christ has accepted you so that God will be given glory. ⁸Remember that Christ came as a servant to the Jews to show that God is true to the promises he made to their ancestors. ⁹He also came so that the Gentiles might give glory to God for his mercies to them. That is what the psalmist meant when he wrote:

"For this, I will praise you among
the Gentiles;
I will sing praises to your name."

¹⁰And in another place it is written,

"Rejoice with his people,
you Gentiles."

¹¹And yet again,

"Praise the LORD, all you Gentiles.
Praise him, all you people of the earth."

¹²And in another place Isaiah said,

"The heir to David's throne will come,
and he will rule over the Gentiles.
They will place their hope on him."

¹³I pray that God, the source of hope, will fill you completely with joy and peace because you trust in him. Then you will overflow with confident hope through the power of the Holy Spirit.

Paul's Reason for Writing

¹⁴I am fully convinced, my dear brothers and sisters, that you are full of goodness. You know these things so well you can teach each other all about them. ¹⁵Even so, I have been bold enough to write about some of these points, knowing that all you need is this reminder. For by God's grace, ¹⁶I am a special messenger from Christ Jesus to you Gentiles. I bring you the Good News so that I might present you as an acceptable offering to God, made holy by the Holy Spirit. ¹⁷So I have reason to be enthusiastic about all Christ Jesus has done through me in my service to God. ¹⁸Yet I dare not boast about anything except

what Christ has done through me, bringing the Gentiles to God by my message and by the way I worked among them. [19]They were convinced by the power of miraculous signs and wonders and by the power of God's Spirit. In this way, I have fully presented the Good News of Christ from Jerusalem all the way to Illyricum.

[20]My ambition has always been to preach the Good News where the name of Christ has never been heard, rather than where a church has already been started by someone else. [21]I have been following the plan spoken of in the Scriptures, where it says,

"Those who have never been told about
   him will see,
and those who have never heard of him
   will understand."

[22]In fact, my visit to you has been delayed so long because I have been preaching in these places.

Paul's Travel Plans

[23]But now I have finished my work in these regions, and after all these long years of waiting, I am eager to visit you. [24]I am planning to go to Spain, and when I do, I will stop off in Rome. And after I have enjoyed your fellowship for a little while, you can provide for my journey.

[25]But before I come, I must go to Jerusalem to take a gift to the believers there. [26]For you see, the believers in Macedonia and Achaia have eagerly taken up an offering for the poor among the believers in Jerusalem. [27]They were glad to do this because they feel they owe a real debt to them. Since the Gentiles received the spiritual blessings of the Good News from the believers in Jerusalem, they feel the least they can do in return is to help them financially. [28]As soon as I have delivered this money and completed this good deed of theirs, I will come to see you on my way to Spain. [29]And I am sure that when I come, Christ will richly bless our time together.

[30]Dear brothers and sisters, I urge you in the name of our Lord Jesus Christ to join in my struggle by praying to God for me. Do this because of your love for me, given to you by the Holy Spirit. [31]Pray that I will be rescued from those in Judea who refuse to obey God. Pray also that the believers there will be willing to accept the donation I am taking to Jerusalem. [32]Then, by the will of God, I will be able to come to you with a joyful heart, and we will be an encouragement to each other.

[33]And now may God, who gives us his peace, be with you all. Amen.

CHAPTER **16**

Paul Greets His Friends

I commend to you our sister Phoebe, who is a deacon in the church in Cenchrea. [2]Welcome her in the Lord as one who is worthy of honor among God's people. Help her in whatever she needs, for she has been helpful to many, and especially to me.

[3]Give my greetings to Priscilla and Aquila, my co-workers in the ministry of Christ Jesus. [4]In fact, they once risked their lives for me. I am thankful to them, and so are all the Gentile churches. [5]Also give my greetings to the church that meets in their home.

Greet my dear friend Epenetus. He was the first person from the province of Asia to become a follower of Christ. [6]Give my greetings to Mary, who has worked so hard for your benefit. [7]Greet Andronicus and Junia, my fellow Jews, who were in prison with me. They are highly respected among the apostles and became followers of Christ before I did. [8]Greet Ampliatus, my dear friend in the Lord. [9]Greet Urbanus, our co-worker in Christ, and my dear friend Stachys.

[10]Greet Apelles, a good man whom Christ approves. And give my greetings to the believers from the household of Aristobulus. [11]Greet Herodion, my fellow Jew. Greet the Lord's people from the household of Narcissus. [12]Give my greetings to Tryphena and Tryphosa, the Lord's workers, and to dear Persis, who has worked so hard for the Lord. [13]Greet Rufus, whom the Lord picked out to be his very own; and also his dear mother, who has been a mother to me.

[14]Give my greetings to Asyncritus, Phlegon, Hermes, Patrobas, Hermas, and the brothers and sisters who meet with them. [15]Give my greetings to Philologus, Julia, Nereus and his sister, and to Olympas and all the believers who meet with them. [16]Greet each other in Christian love. All the churches of Christ send you their greetings.

Paul's Final Instructions

[17]And now I make one more appeal, my dear brothers and sisters. Watch out for people who cause divisions and upset people's faith by teaching things contrary to what you have been taught. Stay away from them. [18]Such people are not serving Christ our Lord; they are serving their own personal interests. By smooth talk and glowing words they deceive innocent people. [19]But everyone knows that you are obedient to the Lord. This makes me very happy. I want

you to be wise in doing right and to stay innocent of any wrong. 20The God of peace will soon crush Satan under your feet. May the grace of our Lord Jesus be with you.

21Timothy, my fellow worker, sends you his greetings, as do Lucius, Jason, and Sosipater, my fellow Jews.

22I, Tertius, the one writing this letter for Paul, send my greetings, too, as one of the Lord's followers.

23Gaius says hello to you. He is my host and also serves as host to the whole church. Erastus, the city treasurer, sends you his greetings, and so does our brother Quartus.*

25Now all glory to God, who is able to make you strong, just as my Good News says. This message about Jesus Christ has revealed his plan for you Gentiles, a plan kept secret from the beginning of time. 26But now as the prophets foretold and as the eternal God has commanded, this message is made known to all Gentiles everywhere, so that they too might believe and obey him. 27All glory to the only wise God, through Jesus Christ, forever. Amen.

16:23 Some manuscripts add verse 24, *May the grace of our Lord Jesus Christ be with you all. Amen.* Still others add this sentence after verse 27.

1 CORINTHIANS Hot Topics

Look for **1** hidden message in 1 Corinthians!

Paul heard disturbing rumors that the Christians in the city of Corinth were having disagreements that could hurt the church. Look for

- **WISDOM AND WARNINGS**
- **MATTERS OF MARRIAGE**
- **SOME SPECIAL GIFTS**
- **LOTS AND LOTS ABOUT LOVE**

Straight From the Spirit

How can we begin to understand God's plan? Simple—through the Spirit. **Find out more in 1 Corinthians 2:9-12.**

Body Basics

Are you a foot? a hand? an eye? No matter—the body needs you! See what Paul said about body parts. **Check out 1 Corinthians 12:12-27.**

Love Rules!

Love never fails. That's what Paul wrote in his letter to the Corinthians. OK, he wrote more than that! **Read 1 Corinthians 13:4-8a for the perfect definition of love.**

Remember When

Paul retold the most important story of all time for the people in Corinth. **Find out what that important story is in 1 Corinthians 15:3-5.**

Timeline

46 B.C. Julius Caesar becomes dictator of Rome

A.D. 1 Saddles first used in Europe

A.D. 64 Fire burns much of Rome

6/5 B.C. Jesus is born

A.D. 26/27 Jesus begins his ministry

A.D. 30 Jesus is crucified and rises again

Around A.D. 55 Paul writes first letter to Corinthians

The JESUS CONNECTION

In his first letter to the Christians in Corinth, Paul addressed the tough problems the early church had. And he offered solutions. Those solutions still work today when we have problems. Trust God, believe in Jesus, recognize that Jesus died for *you*. **The answers that worked back then still work today.**

Greetings from Paul

This letter is from Paul, chosen by the will of God to be an apostle of Christ Jesus, and from our brother Sosthenes.

2 I am writing to God's church in Corinth, to you who have been called by God to be his own holy people. He made you holy by means of Christ Jesus, just as he did for all people everywhere who call on the name of our Lord Jesus Christ, their Lord and ours.

3 May God our Father and the Lord Jesus Christ give you grace and peace.

Paul Gives Thanks to God

4 I always thank my God for you and for the gracious gifts he has given you, now that you belong to Christ Jesus. 5 Through him, God has enriched your church in every way—with all of your eloquent words and all of your knowledge. 6 This confirms that what I told you about Christ is true. 7 Now you have every spiritual gift you need as you eagerly wait for the return of our Lord Jesus Christ. 8 He will keep you strong to the end so that you will be free from all blame on the day when our Lord Jesus Christ returns. 9 God will do this, for he is faithful to do what he says, and he has invited you into partnership with his Son, Jesus Christ our Lord.

Divisions in the Church

10 I appeal to you, dear brothers and sisters, by the authority of our Lord Jesus Christ, to live in harmony with each other. Let there be no divisions in the church. Rather, be of one mind, united in thought and purpose. 11 For some members of Chloe's household have told me about your quarrels, my dear brothers and sisters. 12 Some of you are saying, "I am a follower of Paul." Others are saying, "I follow Apollos," or "I follow Peter," or "I follow only Christ."

13 Has Christ been divided into factions? Was I, Paul, crucified for you? Were any of you baptized in the name of Paul? Of course not! 14 I thank God that I did not baptize any of you except Crispus and Gaius, 15 for now no one can say they were baptized in my name. 16 (Oh yes, I also baptized the household of Stephanas, but I don't remember baptizing anyone else.) 17 For Christ didn't send me to baptize, but to preach the Good News—and not with clever speech, for fear that the cross of Christ would lose its power.

The Wisdom of God

18 The message of the cross is foolish to those who are headed for destruction! But we who are being saved know it is the very power of God. 19 As the Scriptures say,

"I will destroy the wisdom of the wise
and discard the intelligence of the
intelligent."

20 So where does this leave the philosophers, the scholars, and the world's brilliant debaters? God has made the wisdom of this world look foolish. 21 Since God in his wisdom saw to it that the world would never know him through human wisdom, he has used our foolish preaching to save those who believe. 22 It is foolish to the Jews, who ask for signs from heaven. And it is foolish to the Greeks, who seek human wisdom. 23 So when we preach that Christ was crucified, the Jews are offended and the Gentiles say it's all nonsense.

24 But to those called by God to salvation, both Jews and Gentiles, Christ is the power of God and the wisdom of God. 25 This foolish plan of God is wiser than the wisest of human plans, and God's weakness is stronger than the greatest of human strength.

26 Remember, dear brothers and sisters, that few of you were wise in the world's eyes or powerful or wealthy when God called you. 27 Instead, God chose things the world considers foolish in order to shame those who think they are wise. And he chose things that are powerless to shame those who are powerful. 28 God chose things despised by the world, things counted as nothing at all, and used them to bring to nothing what the world considers important. 29 As a result, no one can ever boast in the presence of God.

30 God has united you with Christ Jesus. For our benefit God made him to be wisdom itself. Christ made us right with God; he made us pure and holy, and he freed us from sin. 31 Therefore, as the Scriptures say, "If you want to boast, boast only about the LORD."

Paul's Message of Wisdom

When I first came to you, dear brothers and sisters, I didn't use lofty words and impressive wisdom to tell you God's secret plan. 2 For I decided that while I was with you I would forget everything except Jesus Christ, the one who was crucified. 3 I came to you in weakness—timid and trembling. 4 And my message and my preaching were very plain. Rather than using clever and persuasive speeches, I relied only on the power of the Holy Spirit. 5 I did this so you would trust not in human wisdom but in the power of God.

Conflict Resolution

The Apostle Paul wrote lots of letters during his ministry. Sometimes he tried to help people solve problems and resolve conflicts. For example, in the city of Corinth, people worshiped a lot of different gods.

So Paul wrote to the church to guide the church toward what a church *should* be.

THINK OF A CONFLICT YOU HAVE WITH SOMEONE. Pray about how God might want you to resolve that conflict. Then go do what God says!

⁶Yet when I am among mature believers, I do speak with words of wisdom, but not the kind of wisdom that belongs to this world or to the rulers of this world, who are soon forgotten. ⁷No, the wisdom we speak of is the mystery of God—his plan that was previously hidden, even though he made it for our ultimate glory before the world began. ⁸But the rulers of this world have not understood it; if they had, they would not have crucified our glorious Lord. ⁹That is what the Scriptures mean when they say,

"No eye has seen, no ear has heard,
    and no mind has imagined
what God has prepared
    for those who love him."

¹⁰But it was to us that God revealed these things by his Spirit. For his Spirit searches out everything and shows us God's deep secrets. ¹¹No one can know a person's thoughts except that person's own spirit, and no one can know God's thoughts except God's own Spirit. ¹²And we have received God's Spirit (not the world's

spirit), so we can know the wonderful things God has freely given us.

¹³When we tell you these things, we do not use words that come from human wisdom. Instead, we speak words given to us by the Spirit, using the Spirit's words to explain spiritual truths. ¹⁴But people who aren't spiritual can't receive these truths from God's Spirit. It all sounds foolish to them and they can't understand it, for only those who are spiritual can understand what the Spirit means. ¹⁵Those who are spiritual can evaluate all things, but they themselves cannot be evaluated by others. ¹⁶For,

"Who can know the LORD's thoughts?
    Who knows enough to teach him?"

But we understand these things, for we have the mind of Christ.

CHAPTER **3**
Paul and Apollos, Servants of Christ

Dear brothers and sisters, when I was with you I couldn't talk to you as I would to spiritual people. I had to talk as though you belonged to this world or as though you were infants in the Christian life. ²I had to feed you with milk, not with solid food, because you weren't ready for anything stronger. And you still aren't ready, ³for you are still controlled by your sinful nature. You are jealous of one another and quarrel with each other. Doesn't that prove you are controlled by your sinful nature? Aren't you living like people of the world? ⁴When one of you says, "I am a follower of Paul," and another says, "I follow Apollos," aren't you acting just like people of the world?

⁵After all, who is Apollos? Who is Paul? We are only God's servants through whom you believed the Good News. Each of us did the work the Lord gave us. ⁶I planted the seed in your hearts, and Apollos watered it, but it was God who made it grow. ⁷It's not important who does the planting, or who does the watering. What's important is that God makes the seed grow. ⁸The one who plants and the one who waters work together with the same purpose. And both will be rewarded for their own hard work. ⁹For we are both God's workers. And you are God's field. You are God's building.

¹⁰Because of God's grace to me, I have laid the foundation like an expert builder. Now others are building on it. But whoever is building on this foundation must be very careful. ¹¹For no one can lay any foundation other than the one we already have—Jesus Christ.

¹²Anyone who builds on that foundation may use a variety of materials—gold, silver, jewels, wood, hay, or straw. ¹³But on the judgment day, fire will reveal what kind of work each builder has done. The fire will show if a person's work has any value. ¹⁴If the work survives, that builder will receive a reward. ¹⁵But if the work is burned up, the builder will suffer great loss. The builder will be saved, but like someone barely escaping through a wall of flames.

¹⁶Don't you realize that all of you together are the temple of God and that the Spirit of God lives in you? ¹⁷God will destroy anyone who destroys this temple. For God's temple is holy, and you are that temple.

¹⁸Stop deceiving yourselves. If you think you are wise by this world's standards, you need to become a fool to be truly wise. ¹⁹For the wisdom of this world is foolishness to God. As the Scriptures say,

"He traps the wise
    in the snare of their own cleverness."

²⁰And again,

"The LORD knows the thoughts of the wise;
    he knows they are worthless."

²¹So don't boast about following a particular human leader. For everything belongs to you: ²²whether Paul or Apollos or Peter, or the world, or life and death, or the present and the future. Everything belongs to you, ²³and you belong to Christ, and Christ belongs to God.

CHAPTER **4**
Paul's Relationship with the Corinthians

So look at Apollos and me as mere servants of Christ who have been put in charge of explaining God's mysteries. ²Now, a person who is put in charge as a manager must be faithful. ³As for me, it matters very little how I might be evaluated by you or by any human authority. I don't even trust my own judgment on this point. ⁴My conscience is clear, but that doesn't prove I'm right. It is the Lord himself who will examine me and decide.

⁵So don't make judgments about anyone ahead of time—before the Lord returns. For he will bring our darkest secrets to light and will reveal our private motives. Then God will give to each one whatever praise is due.

⁶Dear brothers and sisters, I have used Apollos and myself to illustrate what I've been saying. If you pay attention to what I have quoted from the Scriptures, you won't be proud of one of your leaders at the expense of another. ⁷For what gives you the right to make such a judgment? What do you have that God hasn't given you? And if everything you have is from God, why boast as though it were not a gift?

⁸You think you already have everything you need. You think you are already rich. You have begun to reign in God's kingdom without us! I wish you really were reigning already, for then we would be reigning with you. ⁹Instead, I sometimes think God has put us apostles on display, like prisoners of war at the end of a victor's parade, condemned to die. We have become a spectacle to the entire world—to people and angels alike.

¹⁰Our dedication to Christ makes us look like fools, but you claim to be so wise in Christ! We are weak, but you are so powerful! You are honored, but we are ridiculed. ¹¹Even now we go hungry and thirsty, and we don't have enough clothes to keep warm. We are often beaten and have no home. ¹²We work wearily with our own hands to earn our living. We bless those who curse us. We are patient with those who abuse us. ¹³We appeal gently when evil things are said about us. Yet we are treated like the world's garbage, like everybody's trash—right up to the present moment.

¹⁴I am not writing these things to shame you, but to warn you as my beloved children. ¹⁵For even if you had ten thousand others to teach you about Christ, you have only one spiritual father. For I became your father in Christ Jesus when I preached the Good News to you. ¹⁶So I urge you to imitate me.

¹⁷That's why I have sent Timothy, my beloved and faithful child in the Lord. He will remind you of how I follow Christ Jesus, just as I teach in all the churches wherever I go.

¹⁸Some of you have become arrogant, thinking I will not visit you again. ¹⁹But I will come—and soon—if the Lord lets me, and then I'll find out whether these arrogant people just give pretentious speeches or whether they really have God's power. ²⁰For the Kingdom of God is not just a lot of talk; it is living by God's power. ²¹Which do you choose? Should I come with a rod to punish you, or should I come with love and a gentle spirit?

CHAPTER **5**
Paul Condemns Spiritual Pride

I can hardly believe the report about the sexual immorality going on among you—something that even pagans don't do. I am told that a man in

Hi, my name is

JOHN the BAPTIST *(prophet, baptizer, advance man for Jesus)*

My greatest claim to fame is being the one who prepared the way for Jesus' coming. That doesn't mean that I rolled out a red carpet or anything like that, but I did try to prepare peoples' hearts for Jesus by encouraging them to repent of their sins.

I lived out in the country, away from the distractions of the city. I preached repentance, and people came to me to be baptized. That's where I got my nickname, the Baptist. I baptized people in water, which symbolized washing away the sins. You might think my lifestyle was strange because I just lived out in the desert, eating whatever I could find —mostly locusts and wild honey. And I wore clothing made out of camel skins. But hey, it worked for me!

> **Want to know more about John's attitude toward Jesus? Read JOHN 3:27-30.**

My strange dress and eating habits didn't keep people from coming out to hear me preach though. In fact, I became so popular that some people actually thought that I might be the Messiah. But I was careful to set them straight! I was not even worthy to untie the sandals of the real Messiah, Jesus.

> **Read all about John's baptism of Jesus in MATTHEW 3:13-17.**

One of the finest moments of my life was when Jesus came to me to be baptized. There was no way I felt worthy—I would rather he baptized me! But Jesus insisted, so I baptized him. And God spoke from heaven when I did! Wow, what an experience!

I guess I'd have to say that the thing I look back on most fondly is what Jesus said about me. He once told a crowd of people that "of all who have ever lived, none is greater than John the Baptist." I've never thought of myself as being better than any other prophet, but it sure felt good to know that the Savior of the world thought that about me!

How can you follow Jesus?

Jot down on a note card one way you could serve Jesus more faithfully. Keep that note card with you so you can see it every day as a reminder. Really work on the action you wrote down. Then next month, read the Bible and make a new note card with another way you could follow Jesus more faithfully. Keep your note cards in a special "Follow Jesus" box. Pretty soon you'll be a much better follower of Jesus than you are right now!

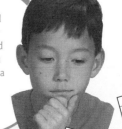

trust god

help others

be kind!

be thankful

pray more

FORGIVE!

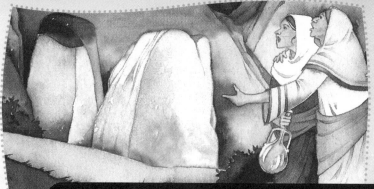

THE MARYS *(mother of Jesus; friend of Jesus)*

"Hi! I'm Mary, the mother of Jesus!"

"Hi from me, too! I'm Mary Magdalene. Jesus' mother and I have the same name, so sometimes people get us confused. But we're two very different women. I'll let the other Mary, Jesus' mother, tell her story first."

"Thanks, Mary. My story begins when I was a young woman. I was engaged to marry Joseph. An angel appeared to me, and wow, was I shocked. God had chosen *me* to be the mother of his own Son, Jesus! Then an angel appeared to Joseph, too, and told him the same thing.

I got to watch Jesus grow up. He went out on his own, preaching and healing. About three years later I had to watch him die. That was the darkest day of my life. But then came Sunday! I'll let Mary Magdalene tell the rest of that story!"

> **Want to know more about Mary and the birth of Jesus? Read LUKE 2:1-21.**

"Thanks, Mary. What an incredible morning that was! On that Sunday morning after Jesus died, Mary and I and a couple other women went to Jesus' tomb, where we were met by angels. Jesus wasn't there! The angels said that Jesus had risen. After we ran and told the disciples, I went back and hung around the tomb, confused about what was really happening. When I realized someone was standing near me, I thought it was the gardener, and I asked him if he knew where Jesus was. But then he said my name, and it had never sounded so good! I knew it was Jesus. He really *was* alive!

> **For the whole story of Mary's encounter with Jesus at the tomb, read LUKE 24:1-10.**

Chronicle of Change

How has Jesus changed your life or the lives of people you know? Create a booklet that tells all about it. Interview as many Christians as you can, asking them to tell you how Jesus has changed their lives. Decorate the cover of your booklet with pictures that remind you of Jesus. Show your booklet to at least two other people, so they can get to know Jesus too!

> **"I always have a friend in Jesus."**
> **Aunt Pat**

> **"Because of Jesus, I know I'm going to heaven."**
> **Dad**

your church is living in sin with his stepmother. ²You are so proud of yourselves, but you should be mourning in sorrow and shame. And you should remove this man from your fellowship.

³Even though I am not with you in person, I am with you in the Spirit. And as though I were there, I have already passed judgment on this man ⁴in the name of the Lord Jesus. You must call a meeting of the church. I will be present with you in spirit, and so will the power of our Lord Jesus. ⁵Then you must throw this man out and hand him over to Satan so that his sinful nature will be destroyed and he himself will be saved on the day the Lord returns.

⁶Your boasting about this is terrible. Don't you realize that this sin is like a little yeast that spreads through the whole batch of dough? ⁷Get rid of the old "yeast" by removing this wicked person from among you. Then you will be like a fresh batch of dough made without yeast, which is what you really are. Christ, our Passover Lamb, has been sacrificed for us. ⁸So let us celebrate the festival, not with the old bread of wickedness and evil, but with the new bread of sincerity and truth.

⁹When I wrote to you before, I told you not to associate with people who indulge in sexual sin. ¹⁰But I wasn't talking about unbelievers who indulge in sexual sin, or are greedy, or cheat people, or worship idols. You would have to leave this world to avoid people like that. ¹¹I meant that you are not to associate with anyone who claims to be a believer yet indulges in sexual sin, or is greedy, or worships idols, or is abusive, or is a drunkard, or cheats people. Don't even eat with such people.

¹²It isn't my responsibility to judge outsiders, but it certainly is your responsibility to judge those inside the church who are sinning. ¹³God will judge those on the outside; but as the Scriptures say, "You must remove the evil person from among you."

CHAPTER **6**
Avoiding Lawsuits with Christians

When one of you has a dispute with another believer, how dare you file a lawsuit and ask a secular court to decide the matter instead of taking it to other believers! ²Don't you realize that someday we believers will judge the world? And since you are going to judge the world, can't you decide even these little things among yourselves? ³Don't you realize that we will judge angels? So you should surely be able to resolve ordinary disputes in this life. ⁴If you have legal disputes about such matters, why go to outside judges who are not respected by the church? ⁵I am saying this to shame you. Isn't there anyone in all the church who is wise enough to decide these issues? ⁶But instead, one believer sues another—right in front of unbelievers!

⁷Even to have such lawsuits with one another is a defeat for you. Why not just accept the injustice and leave it at that? Why not let yourselves be cheated? ⁸Instead, you yourselves are the ones who do wrong and cheat even your fellow believers.

⁹Don't you realize that those who do wrong will not inherit the Kingdom of God? Don't fool yourselves. Those who indulge in sexual sin, or who worship idols, or commit adultery, or are male prostitutes, or practice homosexuality, ¹⁰or are thieves, or greedy people, or drunkards, or are abusive, or cheat people—none of these will inherit the Kingdom of God. ¹¹Some of you were once like that. But you were cleansed; you were made holy; you were made right with God by calling on the name of the Lord Jesus Christ and by the Spirit of our God.

Avoiding Sexual Sin

¹²You say, "I am allowed to do anything"—but not everything is good for you. And even though "I am allowed to do anything," I must not become a slave to anything. ¹³You say, "Food was made for the stomach, and the stomach for food." (This is true, though someday God will do away with both of them.) But you can't say that our bodies were made for sexual immorality. They were made for the Lord, and the Lord cares about our bodies. ¹⁴And God will raise us from the dead by his power, just as he raised our Lord from the dead.

¹⁵Don't you realize that your bodies are actually parts of Christ? Should a man take his body, which is part of Christ, and join it to a prostitute? Never! ¹⁶And don't you realize that if a man joins himself to a prostitute, he becomes one body with her? For the Scriptures say, "The two are united into one." ¹⁷But the person who is joined to the Lord is one spirit with him.

¹⁸Run from sexual sin! No other sin so clearly affects the body as this one does. For sexual immorality is a sin against your own body. ¹⁹Don't you realize that your body is the temple of the Holy Spirit, who lives in you and was given to you by God? You do not belong to yourself, ²⁰for God bought you with a high price. So you must honor God with your body.

CHAPTER **7**

Instruction on Marriage

Now regarding the questions you asked in your letter. Yes, it is good to live a celibate life. ²But because there is so much sexual immorality, each man should have his own wife, and each woman should have her own husband.

³The husband should fulfill his wife's sexual needs, and the wife should fulfill her husband's needs. ⁴The wife gives authority over her body to her husband, and the husband gives authority over his body to his wife.

⁵Do not deprive each other of sexual relations, unless you both agree to refrain from sexual intimacy for a limited time so you can give yourselves more completely to prayer. Afterward, you should come together again so that Satan won't be able to tempt you because of your lack of self-control. ⁶I say this as a concession, not as a command. ⁷But I wish everyone were single, just as I am. But God gives to some the gift of marriage, and to others the gift of singleness.

⁸So I say to those who aren't married and to widows—it's better to stay unmarried, just as I am. ⁹But if they can't control themselves, they should go ahead and marry. It's better to marry than to burn with lust.

¹⁰But for those who are married, I have a command that comes not from me, but from the Lord. A wife must not leave her husband. ¹¹But if she does leave him, let her remain single or else be reconciled to him. And the husband must not leave his wife.

¹²Now, I will speak to the rest of you, though I do not have a direct command from the Lord. If a Christian man has a wife who is not a believer and she is willing to continue living with him, he must not leave her. ¹³And if a Christian woman has a husband who is not a believer and he is willing to continue living with her, she must not leave him. ¹⁴For the Christian wife brings holiness to her marriage, and the Christian husband brings holiness to his marriage. Otherwise, your children would not be holy, but now they are holy. ¹⁵(But if the husband or wife who isn't a believer insists on leaving, let them go. In such cases the Christian husband or wife is no longer bound to the other, for God has called you to live in peace.) ¹⁶Don't you wives realize that your husbands might be saved because of you? And don't you husbands realize that your wives might be saved because of you?

¹⁷Each of you should continue to live in whatever situation the Lord has placed you, and remain as you were when God first called you. This is my rule for all the churches. ¹⁸For instance, a man who was circumcised before he became a believer should not try to reverse it. And the man who was uncircumcised when he became a believer should not be circumcised now. ¹⁹For it makes no difference whether or not a man has been circumcised. The important thing is to keep God's commandments.

²⁰Yes, each of you should remain as you were when God called you. ²¹Are you a slave? Don't let that worry you—but if you get a chance to be free, take it. ²²And remember, if you were a slave when the Lord called you, you are now free in the Lord. And if you were free when the Lord called you, you are now a slave of Christ. ²³God paid a high price for you, so don't be enslaved by the world. ²⁴Each of you, dear brothers and sisters, should remain as you were when God first called you.

²⁵Now regarding your question about the young women who are not yet married. I do not have a command from the Lord for them. But the Lord in his mercy has given me wisdom that can be trusted, and I will share it with you. ²⁶Because of the present crisis, I think it is best to remain as you are. ²⁷If you have a wife, do not seek to end the marriage. If you do not have a wife, do not seek to get married. ²⁸But if you do get married, it is not a sin. And if a young woman gets married, it is not a sin. However, those who get married at this time will have troubles, and I am trying to spare you those problems.

²⁹But let me say this, dear brothers and sisters: The time that remains is very short. So from now on, those with wives should not focus only on their marriage. ³⁰Those who weep or who rejoice or who buy things should not be absorbed by their weeping or their joy or their possessions. ³¹Those who use the things of the world should not become attached to them. For this world as we know it will soon pass away.

³²I want you to be free from the concerns of this life. An unmarried man can spend his time doing the Lord's work and thinking how to please him. ³³But a married man has to think about his earthly responsibilities and how to please his wife. ³⁴His interests are divided. In the same way, a woman who is no longer married or has never been married can be devoted to the Lord and holy in body and in spirit. But a married woman has to think about her earthly responsibilities and how to please her husband. ³⁵I am saying this for your benefit, not to place restrictions on you. I want you to do whatever will help you serve the Lord best, with as few distractions as possible.

36But if a man thinks that he's treating his fiancée improperly and will inevitably give in to his passion, let him marry her as he wishes. It is not a sin. **37**But if he has decided firmly not to marry and there is no urgency and he can control his passion, he does well not to marry. **38**So the person who marries his fiancée does well, and the person who doesn't marry does even better.

39A wife is bound to her husband as long as he lives. If her husband dies, she is free to marry anyone she wishes, but only if he loves the Lord. **40**But in my opinion it would be better for her to stay single, and I think I am giving you counsel from God's Spirit when I say this.

CHAPTER **8**
Food Sacrificed to Idols

Now regarding your question about food that has been offered to idols. Yes, we know that "we all have knowledge" about this issue. But while knowledge makes us feel important, it is love that strengthens the church. **2**Anyone who claims to know all the answers doesn't really know very much. **3**But the person who loves God is the one whom God recognizes.

4So, what about eating meat that has been offered to idols? Well, we all know that an idol is not really a god and that there is only one God. **5**There may be so-called gods both in heaven and on earth, and some people actually worship many gods and many lords. **6**But we know that there is only one God, the Father, who created everything, and we live for him. And there is only one Lord, Jesus Christ, through whom God made everything and through whom we have been given life.

7However, not all believers know this. Some are accustomed to thinking of idols as being real, so when they eat food that has been offered to idols, they think of it as the worship of real gods, and their weak consciences are violated. **8**It's true that we can't win God's approval by what we eat. We don't lose anything if we don't eat it, and we don't gain anything if we do.

9But you must be careful so that your freedom does not cause others with a weaker conscience to stumble. **10**For if others see you—with your "superior knowledge"—eating in the temple of an idol, won't they be encouraged to violate their conscience by eating food that has been offered to an idol? **11**So because of your superior knowledge, a weak believer for whom Christ died will be destroyed. **12**And when you sin against other believers by encouraging them to do something they believe is wrong, you are sinning against Christ. **13**So if what I eat causes another believer to sin, I will never eat meat again as long as I live—for I don't want to cause another believer to stumble.

CHAPTER **9**
Paul Gives Up His Rights

Am I not as free as anyone else? Am I not an apostle? Haven't I seen Jesus our Lord with my own eyes? Isn't it because of my work that you belong to the Lord? **2**Even if others think I am not an apostle, I certainly am to you. You yourselves are proof that I am the Lord's apostle.

3This is my answer to those who question my authority. **4**Don't we have the right to live in your homes and share your meals? **5**Don't we have the right to bring a Christian wife with us as the other apostles and the Lord's brothers do, and as Peter does? **6**Or is it only Barnabas and I who have to work to support ourselves?

7What soldier has to pay his own expenses? What farmer plants a vineyard and doesn't have the right to eat some of its fruit? What shepherd cares for a flock of sheep and isn't allowed to drink some of the milk? **8**Am I expressing merely a human opinion, or does the law say the same thing? **9**For the law of Moses says, "You must not muzzle an ox to keep it from eating as it treads out the grain." Was God thinking only about oxen when he said this? **10**Wasn't he actually speaking to us? Yes, it was written for us, so that the one who plows and the one who threshes the grain might both expect a share of the harvest.

11Since we have planted spiritual seed among you, aren't we entitled to a harvest of physical food and drink? **12**If you support others who preach to you, shouldn't we have an even greater right to be supported? But we have never used this right. We would rather put up with anything than be an obstacle to the Good News about Christ.

13Don't you realize that those who work in the temple get their meals from the offerings brought to the temple? And those who serve at the altar get a share of the sacrificial offerings. **14**In the same way, the Lord ordered that those who preach the Good News should be supported by those who benefit from it. **15**Yet I have never used any of these rights. And I am not writing this to suggest that I want to start now. In fact, I would rather die than lose my right to boast about preaching without charge. **16**Yet preaching the Good News is not something I can boast about. I am compelled by God to do it. How terrible for me if I didn't preach the Good News!

17If I were doing this on my own initiative, I would deserve payment. But I have no choice, for God has given me this sacred trust. 18What then is my pay? It is the opportunity to preach the Good News without charging anyone. That's why I never demand my rights when I preach the Good News.

19Even though I am a free man with no master, I have become a slave to all people to bring many to Christ. 20When I was with the Jews, I lived like a Jew to bring the Jews to Christ. When I was with those who follow the Jewish law, I too lived under that law. Even though I am not subject to the law, I did this so I could bring to Christ those who are under the law. 21When I am with the Gentiles who do not follow the Jewish law, I too live apart from that law so I can bring them to Christ. But I do not ignore the law of God; I obey the law of Christ.

22When I am with those who are weak, I share their weakness, for I want to bring the weak to Christ. Yes, I try to find common ground with everyone, doing everything I can to save some. 23I do everything to spread the Good News and share in its blessings.

24Don't you realize that in a race everyone runs, but only one person gets the prize? So run to win! 25All athletes are disciplined in their training. They do it to win a prize that will fade away, but we do it for an eternal prize. 26So I run with purpose in every step. I am not just shadowboxing. 27I discipline my body like an athlete, training it to do what it should. Otherwise, I fear that after preaching to others I myself might be disqualified.

CHAPTER **10**
Lessons from Israel's Idolatry

I don't want you to forget, dear brothers and sisters, about our ancestors in the wilderness long ago. All of them were guided by a cloud that moved ahead of them, and all of them walked through the sea on dry ground. 2In the cloud and in the sea, all of them were baptized as followers of Moses. 3All of them ate the same spiritual food, 4and all of them drank the same spiritual water. For they drank from the spiritual rock that traveled with them, and that rock was Christ. 5Yet God was not pleased with most of them, and their bodies were scattered in the wilderness.

6These things happened as a warning to us, so that we would not crave evil things as they did, 7or worship idols as some of them did. As the Scriptures say, "The people celebrated with feasting and drinking, and they indulged in pagan revelry." 8And we must not engage in sexual immorality as some of them did, causing 23,000 of them to die in one day.

9Nor should we put Christ to the test, as some of them did and then died from snakebites. 10And don't grumble as some of them did, and then were destroyed by the angel of death. 11These things happened to them as examples for us. They were written down to warn us who live at the end of the age.

12If you think you are standing strong, be careful not to fall. 13The temptations in your life are no different from what others experience. And God is faithful. He will not allow the temptation to be more than you can stand. When you are tempted, he will show you a way out so that you can endure.

14So, my dear friends, flee from the worship of idols. 15You are reasonable people. Decide for yourselves if what I am saying is true. 16When we bless the cup at the Lord's Table, aren't we sharing in the blood of Christ? And when we break the bread, aren't we sharing in the body of Christ? 17And though we are many, we all eat from one loaf of bread, showing that we are one body. 18Think about the people of Israel. Weren't they united by eating the sacrifices at the altar?

19What am I trying to say? Am I saying that food offered to idols has some significance, or that idols are real gods? 20No, not at all. I am saying that these sacrifices are offered to demons, not to God. And I don't want you to participate with demons. 21You cannot drink from the cup of the Lord and from the cup of demons, too. You cannot eat at the Lord's Table and at the table of demons, too. 22What? Do we dare to rouse the Lord's jealousy? Do you think we are stronger than he is?

23You say, "I am allowed to do anything"—but not everything is good for you. You say, "I am allowed to do anything"—but not everything is beneficial. 24Don't be concerned for your own good but for the good of others.

25So you may eat any meat that is sold in the marketplace without raising questions of conscience. 26For "the earth is the LORD's, and everything in it."

27If someone who isn't a believer asks you home for dinner, accept the invitation if you want to. Eat whatever is offered to you without raising questions of conscience. 28(But suppose someone tells you, "This meat was offered to an idol." Don't eat it, out of consideration for the conscience of the one who told you. 29It might not be a matter of conscience for you, but it is for the other person.) For why should my freedom be limited by what someone else thinks? 30If I can thank God for the food and enjoy it, why should I be condemned for eating it?

31**So whether you eat or drink, or whatever you do, do it all for the glory of God.** 32Don't give offense to Jews or Gentiles or the church of God. 33I, too, try to please everyone in everything I do. I don't just do what is best for me; I do what is best for others so that many may be saved. 11:1And you should imitate me, just as I imitate Christ.

CHAPTER **11**
Instructions for Public Worship

2I am so glad that you always keep me in your thoughts, and that you are following the teachings I passed on to you. 3But there is one thing I want you to know: The head of every man is Christ, the head of woman is man, and the head of Christ is God. 4A man dishonors his head if he covers his head while praying or prophesying. 5But a woman dishonors her head if she prays or prophesies without a covering on her head, for this is the same as shaving her head. 6Yes, if she refuses to wear a head covering, she should cut off all her hair! But since it is shameful for a woman to have her hair cut or her head shaved, she should wear a covering.

7A man should not wear anything on his head when worshiping, for man is made in God's image and reflects God's glory. And woman reflects man's glory. 8For the first man didn't come from woman, but the first woman came from man. 9And man was not made for woman, but woman was made for man. 10For this reason, and because the angels are watching, a woman should wear a covering on her head to show she is under authority.

11But among the Lord's people, women are not independent of men, and men are not independent of women. 12For although the first woman came from man, every other man was born from a woman, and everything comes from God.

13Judge for yourselves. Is it right for a woman to pray to God in public without covering her head? 14Isn't it obvious that it's disgraceful for a man to have long hair? 15And isn't long hair a woman's pride and joy? For it has been given to her as a covering. 16But if anyone wants to argue about this, I simply say that we have no other custom than this, and neither do God's other churches.

Order at the Lord's Supper

17But in the following instructions, I cannot praise you. For it sounds as if more harm than good is done when you meet together. 18First, I hear that there are divisions among you when you meet as a church, and to some extent I believe it. 19But, of course, there must be divisions among you so that you who have God's approval will be recognized!

20When you meet together, you are not really interested in the Lord's Supper. 21For some of you hurry to eat your own meal without sharing with others. As a result, some go hungry while others get drunk. 22What? Don't you have your own homes for eating and drinking? Or do you really want to disgrace God's church and shame the poor? What am I supposed to say? Do you

Key Verse

"So whether you eat or drink, or whatever you do, do it all for the glory of God."
—1 CORINTHIANS 10:31

Give God Your Best

Read 1 CORINTHIANS 10:31 out loud to your family. Ask each person to say what he or she thinks this verse means. Whatever we do, we should do it so we honor and glorify God—even if all we're doing is eating and drinking.

Have a "GIVE GOD YOUR BEST" dinner with your family.

Use your **best tablecloth**, wear your **best clothes**, make your **favorite food**, and serve your **best dessert.**

Ask each person to name one way to honor God this week with words or actions.

want me to praise you? Well, I certainly will not praise you for this!

²³For I pass on to you what I received from the Lord himself. On the night when he was betrayed, the Lord Jesus took some bread ²⁴and gave thanks to God for it. Then he broke it in pieces and said, "This is my body, which is given for you. Do this to remember me." ²⁵In the same way, he took the cup of wine after supper, saying, "This cup is the new covenant between God and his people—an agreement confirmed with my blood. Do this to remember me as often as you drink it." ²⁶For every time you eat this bread and drink this cup, you are announcing the Lord's death until he comes again.

²⁷So anyone who eats this bread or drinks this cup of the Lord unworthily is guilty of sinning against the body and blood of the Lord. ²⁸That is why you should examine yourself before eating the bread and drinking the cup. ²⁹For if you eat the bread or drink the cup without honoring the body of Christ, you are eating and drinking God's judgment upon yourself. ³⁰That is why many of you are weak and sick and some have even died.

³¹But if we would examine ourselves, we would not be judged by God in this way. ³²Yet when we are judged by the Lord, we are being disciplined so that we will not be condemned along with the world.

³³So, my dear brothers and sisters, when you gather for the Lord's Supper, wait for each other. ³⁴If you are really hungry, eat at home so you won't bring judgment upon yourselves when you meet together. I'll give you instructions about the other matters after I arrive.

CHAPTER **12**
Spiritual Gifts

Now, dear brothers and sisters, regarding your question about the special abilities the Spirit gives us. I don't want you to misunderstand this. ²You know that when you were still pagans, you were led astray and swept along in worshiping speechless idols. ³So I want you to know that no one speaking by the Spirit of God will curse Jesus, and no one can say Jesus is Lord, except by the Holy Spirit.

⁴There are different kinds of spiritual gifts, but the same Spirit is the source of them all. ⁵There are different kinds of service, but we serve the same Lord. ⁶God works in different ways, but it is the same God who does the work in all of us.

⁷A spiritual gift is given to each of us so we

L♥ve All Ar♥und

YOU KNOW WHAT A DICTIONARY'S FOR, RIGHT?

IT GIVES YOU DEFINITIONS OF WORDS.

Well, there's a cool definition in the Bible, too! **Read 1 CORINTHIANS 13:4-7.**

To help you remember everything that love is, make this rolling reminder.

FIRST GATHER

- glue
- cup
- water
- paintbrush
- magazines
- permanent markers
- inexpensive ball (the bigger the better, like a soccer ball).

1 In a cup, add a little water to some white glue.

2 Look through old magazines, and tear out words that remind you of what the Bible says love is. Use the paintbrush and glue mixture to attach the words to the ball, and paint a little of the mixture over the words so they're smooth.

3 Set the ball on an empty aluminum can to dry.

patient
kind
not proud
hopeful
Read more about love in 1 John 4:8.

Find a friend, and bounce the ball to each other. Whatever words your hands land on when you catch the ball, ask yourselves, **"Is this how I treat others?"**

NOW TRY THIS!

can help each other. ⁸To one person the Spirit gives the ability to give wise advice; to another the same Spirit gives a message of special knowledge. ⁹The same Spirit gives great faith to another, and to someone else the one Spirit gives the gift of healing. ¹⁰He gives one person the power to perform miracles, and another the ability to prophesy. He gives someone else the ability to discern whether a message is from the Spirit of God or from another spirit. Still another person is given the ability to speak in unknown languages, while another is given the ability to interpret what is being said. ¹¹It is the one and only Spirit who distributes all these gifts. He alone decides which gift each person should have.

One Body with Many Parts

¹²The human body has many parts, but the many parts make up one whole body. So it is with the body of Christ. ¹³Some of us are Jews, some are Gentiles, some are slaves, and some are free. But we have all been baptized into one body by one Spirit, and we all share the same Spirit.

¹⁴Yes, the body has many different parts, not just one part. ¹⁵If the foot says, "I am not a part of the body because I am not a hand," that does not make it any less a part of the body. ¹⁶And if the ear says, "I am not part of the body because I am not an eye," would that make it any less a part of the body? ¹⁷If the whole body were an eye, how would you hear? Or if your whole body were an ear, how would you smell anything?

¹⁸But our bodies have many parts, and God has put each part just where he wants it. ¹⁹How strange a body would be if it had only one part! ²⁰Yes, there are many parts, but only one body. ²¹The eye can never say to the hand, "I don't need you." The head can't say to the feet, "I don't need you."

²²In fact, some parts of the body that seem weakest and least important are actually the most necessary. ²³And the parts we regard as less honorable are those we clothe with the greatest care. So we carefully protect those parts that should not be seen, ²⁴while the more honorable parts do not require this special care. So God has put the body together such that extra honor and care are given to those parts that have less dignity. ²⁵This makes for harmony among the members, so that all the members care for each other. ²⁶If one part suffers, all the parts suffer with it, and if one part is honored, all the parts are glad.

²⁷All of you together are Christ's body, and each of you is a part of it. ²⁸Here are some of the parts God has appointed for the church:

first are apostles,
second are prophets,
third are teachers,
then those who do miracles,
those who have the gift of healing,
those who can help others,
those who have the gift of leadership,
those who speak in unknown languages.

²⁹Are we all apostles? Are we all prophets? Are we all teachers? Do we all have the power to do miracles? ³⁰Do we all have the gift of healing? Do we all have the ability to speak in unknown languages? Do we all have the ability to interpret unknown languages? Of course not! ³¹So you should earnestly desire the most helpful gifts.

But now let me show you a way of life that is best of all.

CHAPTER **13**
Love Is the Greatest

If I could speak all the languages of earth and of angels, but didn't love others, I would only be a noisy gong or a clanging cymbal. ²If I had the gift of prophecy, and if I understood all of God's secret plans and possessed all knowledge, and if I had such faith that I could move mountains, but didn't love others, I would be nothing. ³If I gave everything I have to the poor and even sacrificed my body, I could boast about it; but if I didn't love others, I would have gained nothing.

⁴Love is patient and kind. Love is not jealous or boastful or proud ⁵or rude. It does not demand its own way. It is not irritable, and it keeps no record of being wronged. ⁶It does not rejoice about injustice but rejoices whenever the truth wins out. ⁷Love never gives up, never loses faith, is always hopeful, and endures through every circumstance.

⁸Prophecy and speaking in unknown languages and special knowledge will become useless. But love will last forever! ⁹Now our knowledge is partial and incomplete, and even the gift of prophecy reveals only part of the whole picture! ¹⁰But when full understanding comes, these partial things will become useless.

¹¹When I was a child, I spoke and thought and reasoned as a child. But when I grew up, I put away childish things. ¹²Now we see things imperfectly as in a cloudy mirror, but then we will see everything with perfect clarity. All that I

know now is partial and incomplete, but then I will know everything completely, just as God now knows me completely.

13 Three things will last forever—faith, hope, and love—and the greatest of these is love.

Tongues and Prophecy

Let love be your highest goal! But you should also desire the special abilities the Spirit gives—especially the ability to prophesy. 2 For if you have the ability to speak in tongues, you will be talking only to God, since people won't be able to understand you. You will be speaking by the power of the Spirit, but it will all be mysterious. 3 But one who prophesies strengthens others, encourages them, and comforts them. 4 A person who speaks in tongues is strengthened personally, but one who speaks a word of prophecy strengthens the entire church.

5 I wish you could all speak in tongues, but even more I wish you could all prophesy. For prophecy is greater than speaking in tongues, unless someone interprets what you are saying so that the whole church will be strengthened.

6 Dear brothers and sisters, if I should come to you speaking in an unknown language, how would that help you? But if I bring you a revelation or some special knowledge or prophecy or teaching, that will be helpful. 7 Even lifeless instruments like the flute or the harp must play the notes clearly, or no one will recognize the melody. 8 And if the bugler doesn't sound a clear call, how will the soldiers know they are being called to battle?

9 It's the same for you. If you speak to people in words they don't understand, how will they know what you are saying? You might as well be talking into empty space.

10 There are many different languages in the world, and every language has meaning. 11 But if I don't understand a language, I will be a foreigner to someone who speaks it, and the one who speaks it will be a foreigner to me. 12 And the same is true for you. Since you are so eager to have the special abilities the Spirit gives, seek those that will strengthen the whole church.

13 So anyone who speaks in tongues should pray also for the ability to interpret what has been said. 14 For if I pray in tongues, my spirit is praying, but I don't understand what I am saying.

15 Well then, what shall I do? I will pray in the spirit, and I will also pray in words I understand. I will sing in the spirit, and I will also sing in words I understand. 16 For if you praise God only in the spirit, how can those who don't understand you praise God along with you? How can they join you in giving thanks when they don't understand what you are saying? 17 You will be giving thanks very well, but it won't strengthen the people who hear you.

18 I thank God that I speak in tongues more than any of you. 19 But in a church meeting I would rather speak five understandable words to help others than ten thousand words in an unknown language.

20 Dear brothers and sisters, don't be childish in your understanding of these things. Be innocent as babies when it comes to evil, but be mature in understanding matters of this kind. 21 It is written in the Scriptures:

"I will speak to my own people
through strange languages
and through the lips of foreigners.
But even then, they will not listen to me,"
says the Lord.

22 So you see that speaking in tongues is a sign, not for believers, but for unbelievers. Prophecy, however, is for the benefit of believers, not unbelievers. 23 Even so, if unbelievers or people who don't understand these things come into your church meeting and hear everyone speaking in an unknown language, they will think you are crazy. 24 But if all of you are prophesying, and unbelievers or people who don't understand these things come into your meeting, they will be convicted of sin and judged by what you say. 25 As they listen, their secret thoughts will be exposed, and they will fall to their knees and worship God, declaring, "God is truly here among you."

A Call to Orderly Worship

26 Well, my brothers and sisters, let's summarize. When you meet together, one will sing, another will teach, another will tell some special revelation God has given, one will speak in tongues, and another will interpret what is said. But everything that is done must strengthen all of you.

27 No more than two or three should speak in tongues. They must speak one at a time, and someone must interpret what they say. 28 But if no one is present who can interpret, they must be silent in your church meeting and speak in tongues to God privately.

29 Let two or three people prophesy, and let the others evaluate what is said. 30 But if someone is prophesying and another person receives

a revelation from the Lord, the one who is speaking must stop. 31In this way, all who prophesy will have a turn to speak, one after the other, so that everyone will learn and be encouraged. 32Remember that people who prophesy are in control of their spirit and can take turns. 33For God is not a God of disorder but of peace, as in all the meetings of God's holy people.

34Women should be silent during the church meetings. It is not proper for them to speak. They should be submissive, just as the law says. 35If they have any questions, they should ask their husbands at home, for it is improper for women to speak in church meetings.

36Or do you think God's word originated with you Corinthians? Are you the only ones to whom it was given? 37If you claim to be a prophet or think you are spiritual, you should recognize that what I am saying is a command from the Lord himself. 38But if you do not recognize this, you yourself will not be recognized.

39So, my dear brothers and sisters, be eager to prophesy, and don't forbid speaking in tongues. 40But be sure that everything is done properly and in order.

CHAPTER **15**
The Resurrection of Christ
Let me now remind you, dear brothers and sisters, of the Good News I preached to you before. You welcomed it then, and you still stand firm in it. 2It is this Good News that saves you if you continue to believe the message I told you—unless, of course, you believed something that was never true in the first place.

3I passed on to you what was most important and what had also been passed on to me. Christ died for our sins, just as the Scriptures said. 4He was buried, and he was raised from the dead on the third day, just as the Scriptures said. 5He was seen by Peter and then by the Twelve. 6After that, he was seen by more than 500 of his followers at one time, most of whom are still alive, though some have died. 7Then he was seen by James and later by all the apostles. 8Last of all, as though I had been born at the wrong time, I also saw him. 9For I am the least of all the apostles. In fact, I'm not even worthy to be called an apostle after the way I persecuted God's church.

10But whatever I am now, it is all because God poured out his special favor on me—and not without results. For I have worked harder than any of the other apostles; yet it was not I but God who was working through me by his grace. 11So it makes no difference whether I preach or they preach, for we all preach the same message you have already believed.

The Resurrection of the Dead
12But tell me this—since we preach that Christ rose from the dead, why are some of you saying there will be no resurrection of the dead? 13For if there is no resurrection of the dead, then Christ has not been raised either. 14And if Christ has not been raised, then all our preaching is useless, and your faith is useless. 15And we apostles would all be lying about God—for we have said that God raised Christ from the grave. But that can't be true if there is no resurrection of the dead. 16And if there is no resurrection of the dead, then Christ has not been raised. 17And if Christ has not been raised, then your faith is useless and you are still guilty of your sins. 18In that case, all who have died believing in Christ are lost! 19And if our hope in Christ is only for this life, we are more to be pitied than anyone in the world.

20But in fact, Christ has been raised from the dead. He is the first of a great harvest of all who have died.

21So you see, just as death came into the world through a man, now the resurrection from the dead has begun through another man. 22Just as everyone dies because we all belong to Adam, everyone who belongs to Christ will be given new life. 23But there is an order to this resurrection: Christ was raised as the first of the harvest; then all who belong to Christ will be raised when he comes back.

24After that the end will come, when he will turn the Kingdom over to God the Father, having destroyed every ruler and authority and power. 25For Christ must reign until he humbles all his enemies beneath his feet. 26And the last enemy to be destroyed is death. 27For the Scriptures say, "God has put all things under his authority." (Of course, when it says "all things are under his authority," that does not include God himself, who gave Christ his authority.) 28Then, when all things are under his authority, the Son will put himself under God's authority, so that God, who gave his Son authority over all things, will be utterly supreme over everything everywhere.

29If the dead will not be raised, what point is there in people being baptized for those who are dead? Why do it unless the dead will someday rise again?

30And why should we ourselves risk our lives hour by hour? 31For I swear, dear brothers and sisters, that I face death daily. This is as certain as my pride in what Christ Jesus our Lord has done in you. 32 And what value was there in fighting wild beasts—those people of Ephesus—if there will be no resurrection from the dead? And if there is no resurrection, "Let's feast and drink, for tomorrow we die!" 33 Don't be fooled by those who say such things, for "bad company corrupts good character." 34 Think carefully about what is right, and stop sinning. For to your shame I say that some of you don't know God at all.

The Resurrection Body

35 But someone may ask, "How will the dead be raised? What kind of bodies will they have?" 36 What a foolish question! When you put a seed into the ground, it doesn't grow into a plant unless it dies first. 37 And what you put in the ground is not the plant that will grow, but only a bare seed of wheat or whatever you are planting. 38 Then God gives it the new body he wants it to have. A different plant grows from each kind of seed. 39 Similarly there are different kinds of flesh—one kind for humans, another for animals, another for birds, and another for fish.

40 There are also bodies in the heavens and bodies on the earth. The glory of the heavenly bodies is different from the glory of the earthly bodies. 41 The sun has one kind of glory, while the moon and stars each have another kind. And even the stars differ from each other in their glory.

42 It is the same way with the resurrection of the dead. Our earthly bodies are planted in the ground when we die, but they will be raised to live forever. 43 Our bodies are buried in brokenness, but they will be raised in glory. They are buried in weakness, but they will be raised in strength. 44 They are buried as natural human bodies, but they will be raised as spiritual bodies. For just as there are natural bodies, there are also spiritual bodies.

45 The Scriptures tell us, "The first man, Adam, became a living person." But the last Adam—that is, Christ—is a life-giving Spirit. 46 What comes first is the natural body, then the spiritual body comes later. 47 Adam, the first man, was made from the dust of the earth, while Christ, the second man, came from heaven. 48 Earthly people are like the earthly man, and heavenly people are like the heavenly man. 49 Just as we are now like the earthly man, we will someday be like the heavenly man.

50 What I am saying, dear brothers and sisters, is that our physical bodies cannot inherit the Kingdom of God. These dying bodies cannot inherit what will last forever.

51 But let me reveal to you a wonderful secret. We will not all die, but we will all be transformed! 52 It will happen in a moment, in the blink of an eye, when the last trumpet is blown. For when the trumpet sounds, those who have died will be raised to live forever. And we who are living will also be transformed. 53 For our dying bodies must be transformed into bodies that will never die; our mortal bodies must be transformed into immortal bodies.

54 Then, when our dying bodies have been transformed into bodies that will never die, this Scripture will be fulfilled:

"Death is swallowed up in victory.
55 O death, where is your victory?
O death, where is your sting?"

56 For sin is the sting that results in death, and the law gives sin its power. 57 But thank God! He gives us victory over sin and death through our Lord Jesus Christ.

58 **So, my dear brothers and sisters, be strong and immovable. Always work enthusiastically for the Lord, for you know that nothing you do for the Lord is ever useless.**

CHAPTER **16**

The Collection for Jerusalem

Now regarding your question about the money being collected for God's people in Jerusalem. You should follow the same procedure I gave to the churches in Galatia. 2 On the first day of each week, you should each put aside a portion of the money you have earned. Don't wait until I get there and then try to collect it all at once. 3 When I come, I will write letters of recommendation for the messengers you choose to deliver your gift to Jerusalem. 4 And if it seems appropriate for me to go along, they can travel with me.

Paul's Final Instructions

5 I am coming to visit you after I have been to Macedonia, for I am planning to travel through Macedonia. 6 Perhaps I will stay awhile with you, possibly all winter, and then you can send me on my way to my next destination. 7 This time I don't want to make just a short visit and then go right on. I want to come and stay awhile, if the Lord will let me. 8 In the meantime, I will be staying here at Ephesus until the Festival of Pentecost. 9 There is a wide-open door for a great work here, although many oppose me.

¹⁰When Timothy comes, don't intimidate him. He is doing the Lord's work, just as I am. ¹¹Don't let anyone treat him with contempt. Send him on his way with your blessing when he returns to me. I expect him to come with the other believers.

¹²Now about our brother Apollos—I urged him to visit you with the other believers, but he was not willing to go right now. He will see you later when he has the opportunity.

¹³Be on guard. Stand firm in the faith. Be courageous. Be strong. ¹⁴And do everything with love.

¹⁵You know that Stephanas and his household were the first of the harvest of believers in Greece, and they are spending their lives in service to God's people. I urge you, dear brothers and sisters, ¹⁶to submit to them and others like them who serve with such devotion. ¹⁷I am very glad that Stephanas, Fortunatus, and Achaicus have come here. They have been providing the help you weren't here to give me. ¹⁸They have been a wonderful encouragement to me, as they have been to you. You must show your appreciation to all who serve so well.

Paul's Final Greetings

¹⁹The churches here in the province of Asia send greetings in the Lord, as do Aquila and Priscilla and all the others who gather in their home for church meetings. ²⁰All the brothers and sisters here send greetings to you. Greet each other with Christian love.

²¹HERE IS MY GREETING IN MY OWN HANDWRITING—PAUL.

²²If anyone does not love the Lord, that person is cursed. Our Lord, come!

²³May the grace of the Lord Jesus be with you. ²⁴My love to all of you in Christ Jesus.

2 CORINTHIANS A Calm Voice

Look for ① hidden message in 2 Corinthians!

Paul wrote another letter to the troubled church in Corinth, trying to help the people there resolve their problems. Look for
- **COMFORTING WORDS**
- **JARS OF CLAY**
- **NEW CREATIONS**
- **CARE AND CONCERN**

Comfort and Care

You know, there just may be a reason you're going through something hard right now. Find out what that reason could be in 2 Corinthians 1:3-4!

Jars of Clay

If you had a special treasure, where would you put it?

Where God put his special treasure—the Good News about Jesus—might just surprise you. Read 2 Corinthians 4:6-7 for the answer.

Cheerful Giving

God wants our gifts, but not if we don't really want to give them. Get it? You can, by reading 2 Corinthians 9:7-12!

Brand-New

Ready for a make-over? Well, God can do one for you! Find out how in 2 Corinthians 5:17.

It's Enough!

Sometimes we ask God to take away our problems, but he doesn't. The same thing happened to Paul. But Paul was happy about it! Read 2 Corinthians 12:6-10 to find out why.

Timeline

46 B.C.
Julius Caesar becomes dictator of Rome

A.D. 14
Tiberius becomes emperor of Rome

A.D. 54
Nero becomes emperor of Rome

6/5 B.C.
Jesus is born

A.D. 26/27
Jesus begins his ministry

A.D. 30
Jesus is crucified and rises again

Around A.D. 55-57
Paul writes second letter to Corinthians

The JESUS CONNECTION

In 2 Corinthians, Paul's emotions come through loud and clear—his joy in spreading the gospel, his pain in suffering for his faith, and his love and concern for the believers in Corinth. Paul put everything on the line to share the Good News about Jesus. He didn't care what he had to do to get the word out about Jesus. He knew that Jesus is the most important thing in the world!

CHAPTER 1

Greetings from Paul

This letter is from Paul, chosen by the will of God to be an apostle of Christ Jesus, and from our brother Timothy.

I am writing to God's church in Corinth and to all of his holy people throughout Greece.

2 May God our Father and the Lord Jesus Christ give you grace and peace.

God Offers Comfort to All

3 All praise to God, the Father of our Lord Jesus Christ. God is our merciful Father and the source of all comfort. 4 He comforts us in all our troubles so that we can comfort others. When they are troubled, we will be able to give them the same comfort God has given us. 5 For the more we suffer for Christ, the more God will shower us with his comfort through Christ. 6 Even when we are weighed down with troubles, it is for your comfort and salvation! For when we ourselves are comforted, we will certainly comfort you. Then you can patiently endure the same things we suffer. 7 We are confident that as you share in our sufferings, you will also share in the comfort God gives us.

8 We think you ought to know, dear brothers and sisters, about the trouble we went through in the province of Asia. We were crushed and overwhelmed beyond our ability to endure, and we thought we would never live through it. 9 In fact, we expected to die. But as a result, we stopped relying on ourselves and learned to rely only on God, who raises the dead. 10 And he did rescue us from mortal danger, and he will rescue us again. We have placed our confidence in him, and he will continue to rescue us. 11 And you are helping us by praying for us. Then many people will give thanks because God has graciously answered so many prayers for our safety.

Paul's Change of Plans

12 We can say with confidence and a clear conscience that we have lived with a God-given holiness and sincerity in all our dealings. We have depended on God's grace, not on our own human wisdom. That is how we have conducted ourselves before the world, and especially toward you. 13 Our letters have been straightforward, and there is nothing written between the lines and nothing you can't understand. I hope someday you will fully understand us, 14 even if you don't understand us now. Then on the day when the Lord Jesus returns, you will be proud of us in the same way we are proud of you.

15 Since I was so sure of your understanding and trust, I wanted to give you a double blessing by visiting you twice— 16 first on my way to Macedonia and again when I returned from Macedonia. Then you could send me on my way to Judea. 17 You may be asking why I changed my plan. Do you think I make my plans carelessly? Do you think I am like people of the world who say "Yes" when they really mean "No"? 18 As surely as God is faithful, my word to you does not waver between "Yes" and "No." 19 For Jesus Christ, the Son of God, does not waver between "Yes" and "No." He is the one whom Silas, Timothy, and I preached to you, and as God's ultimate "Yes," he always does what he says. 20 For all of God's promises have been fulfilled in Christ with a resounding "Yes!" And through Christ, our "Amen" (which means "Yes") ascends to God for his glory.

21 It is God who enables us, along with you, to stand firm for Christ. He has commissioned us, 22 and he has identified us as his own by placing the Holy Spirit in our hearts as the first installment that guarantees everything he has promised us.

23 Now I call upon God as my witness that I am telling the truth. The reason I didn't return to Corinth was to spare you from a severe rebuke. 24 But that does not mean we want to dominate you by telling you how to put your faith into practice. We want to work together with you so you will be full of joy, for it is by your own faith that you stand firm.

CHAPTER 2

So I decided that I would not bring you grief with another painful visit. 2 For if I cause you grief, who will make me glad? Certainly not someone I have grieved. 3 That is why I wrote to you as I did, so that when I do come, I won't be grieved by the very ones who ought to give me the greatest joy. Surely you all know that my joy comes from your being joyful. 4 I wrote that letter in great anguish, with a troubled heart and many tears. I didn't want to grieve you, but I wanted to let you know how much love I have for you.

Forgiveness for the Sinner

5 I am not overstating it when I say that the man who caused all the trouble hurt all of you more than he hurt me. 6 Most of you opposed him, and that was punishment enough. 7 Now, however, it is time to forgive and comfort him. Otherwise he may be overcome by discouragement. 8 So I urge you now to reaffirm your love for him.

⁹I wrote to you as I did to test you and see if you would fully comply with my instructions. ¹⁰When you forgive this man, I forgive him, too. And when I forgive whatever needs to be forgiven, I do so with Christ's authority for your benefit, ¹¹so that Satan will not outsmart us. For we are familiar with his evil schemes.

¹²When I came to the city of Troas to preach the Good News of Christ, the Lord opened a door of opportunity for me. ¹³But I had no peace of mind because my dear brother Titus hadn't yet arrived with a report from you. So I said good-bye and went on to Macedonia to find him.

Ministers of the New Covenant

¹⁴But thank God! He has made us his captives and continues to lead us along in Christ's triumphal procession. Now he uses us to spread the knowledge of Christ everywhere, like a sweet perfume. ¹⁵Our lives are a Christ-like fragrance rising up to God. But this fragrance is perceived differently by those who are being saved and by those who are perishing. ¹⁶To those who are perishing, we are a dreadful smell of death and doom. But to those who are being saved, we are a life-giving perfume. And who is adequate for such a task as this?

¹⁷You see, we are not like the many hucksters who preach for personal profit. We preach the word of God with sincerity and with Christ's authority, knowing that God is watching us.

CHAPTER **3**

Are we beginning to praise ourselves again? Are we like others, who need to bring you letters of recommendation, or who ask you to write such letters on their behalf? Surely not! ²The only letter of recommendation we need is you yourselves. Your lives are a letter written in our hearts; everyone can read it and recognize our good work among you. ³Clearly, you are a letter from Christ showing the result of our ministry among you. This "letter" is written not with pen and ink, but with the Spirit of the living God. It is carved not on tablets of stone, but on human hearts.

⁴We are confident of all this because of our great trust in God through Christ. ⁵It is not that we think we are qualified to do anything on our own. Our qualification comes from God. ⁶He has enabled us to be ministers of his new covenant. This is a covenant not of written laws, but of the Spirit. The old written covenant ends in death; but under the new covenant, the Spirit gives life.

The Glory of the New Covenant

⁷The old way, with laws etched in stone, led to death, though it began with such glory that the people of Israel could not bear to look at Moses' face. For his face shone with the glory of God, even though the brightness was already fading away. ⁸Shouldn't we expect far greater glory under the new way, now that the Holy Spirit is giving life? ⁹If the old way, which brings condemnation, was glorious, how much more glorious is the new way, which makes us right with God! ¹⁰In fact, that first glory was not glorious at all compared with the overwhelming glory of the new way. ¹¹So if the old way, which has been replaced, was glorious, how much more glorious is the new, which remains forever!

¹²Since this new way gives us such confidence, we can be very bold. ¹³We are not like Moses, who put a veil over his face so the people of Israel would not see the glory, even though it was destined to fade away. ¹⁴But the people's minds were hardened, and to this day whenever the old covenant is being read, the same veil covers their minds so they cannot understand the truth. And this veil can be removed only by believing in Christ. ¹⁵Yes, even today when they read Moses' writings, their hearts are covered with that veil, and they do not understand.

¹⁶But whenever someone turns to the Lord, the veil is taken away. ¹⁷For the Lord is the Spirit, and wherever the Spirit of the Lord is, there is freedom. ¹⁸So all of us who have had that veil removed can see and reflect the glory of the Lord. And the Lord—who is the Spirit—makes us more and more like him as we are changed into his glorious image.

CHAPTER **4**
Treasure in Fragile Clay Jars

Therefore, since God in his mercy has given us this new way, we never give up. ²We reject all shameful deeds and underhanded methods. We don't try to trick anyone or distort the word of God. We tell the truth before God, and all who are honest know this.

³If the Good News we preach is hidden behind a veil, it is hidden only from people who are perishing. ⁴Satan, who is the god of this world, has blinded the minds of those who don't believe. They are unable to see the glorious light of the Good News. They don't understand this message about the glory of Christ, who is the exact likeness of God.

⁵You see, we don't go around preaching about ourselves. We preach that Jesus Christ is Lord,

and we ourselves are your servants for Jesus' sake. ⁶For God, who said, "Let there be light in the darkness," has made this light shine in our hearts so we could know the glory of God that is seen in the face of Jesus Christ.

⁷We now have this light shining in our hearts, but we ourselves are like fragile clay jars containing this great treasure. This makes it clear that our great power is from God, not from ourselves.

⁸We are pressed on every side by troubles, but we are not crushed. We are perplexed, but not driven to despair. ⁹We are hunted down, but never abandoned by God. We get knocked down, but we are not destroyed. ¹⁰Through suffering, our bodies continue to share in the death of Jesus so that the life of Jesus may also be seen in our bodies.

¹¹Yes, we live under constant danger of death because we serve Jesus, so that the life of Jesus will be evident in our dying bodies. ¹²So we live in the face of death, but this has resulted in eternal life for you.

¹³But we continue to preach because we have the same kind of faith the psalmist had when he said, "I believed in God, so I spoke." ¹⁴We know that God, who raised the Lord Jesus, will also raise us with Jesus and present us to himself together with you. ¹⁵All of this is for your benefit. And as God's grace reaches more and more people, there will be great thanksgiving, and God will receive more and more glory.

¹⁶That is why we never give up. Though our bodies are dying, our spirits are being renewed every day. ¹⁷For our present troubles are small and won't last very long. Yet they produce for us a glory that vastly outweighs them and will last forever! ¹⁸So we don't look at the troubles we can see now; rather, we fix our gaze on things that cannot be seen. For the things we see now will soon be gone, but the things we cannot see will last forever.

CHAPTER **5**
New Bodies

For we know that when this earthly tent we live in is taken down (that is, when we die and leave this earthly body), we will have a house in heaven, an eternal body made for us by God himself and not by human hands. ²We grow weary in our present bodies, and we long to put on our heavenly bodies like new clothing. ³For we will put on heavenly bodies; we will not be spirits without bodies. ⁴While we live in these earthly bodies, we groan and sigh, but it's not that we want to die and get rid of these bodies that clothe us. Rather,

Key Verse

"This means that anyone who belongs to Christ has become a new person. The old life is gone; a new life has begun!"—2 CORINTHIANS 5:17

Presto Chango!

Read 2 CORINTHIANS 5:17 out loud a few times.

When we believe in Jesus, the Holy Spirit lives in us and begins teaching and guiding us.

THE CHANGE IS KIND OF LIKE THIS!

GATHER:

- old colored comic section from a newspaper
- container
- white glue
- liquid starch
- spoon

1. Mix two parts glue with one part liquid starch. Stir well.

2. Continue adding starch one spoonful at a time, using your fingers to work the mixture into a smooth putty.

3. Press the putty onto a colored comic picture, then pull it off.

The putty was plain. But after you pressed it onto the colored picture, it became colorful itself! That's kind of how it is when you believe in Jesus. Just like the putty changed when it came in contact with the picture, you change when you believe in Jesus. Then the Holy Spirit helps you become more and more like Jesus each day.

Do this experiment with a friend. Read this verse to your friend, and explain how your friend can become new by believing in Jesus!

Ever feel tired of doing the right thing? Check out Galatians 6:9.

we want to put on our new bodies so that these dying bodies will be swallowed up by life. ⁵God himself has prepared us for this, and as a guarantee he has given us his Holy Spirit.

⁶So we are always confident, even though we know that as long as we live in these bodies we are not at home with the Lord. ⁷For we live by believing and not by seeing. ⁸Yes, we are fully confident, and we would rather be away from these earthly bodies, for then we will be at home with the Lord. ⁹So whether we are here in this body or away from this body, our goal is to please him. ¹⁰For we must all stand before Christ to be judged. We will each receive whatever we deserve for the good or evil we have done in this earthly body.

We Are God's Ambassadors

¹¹Because we understand our fearful responsibility to the Lord, we work hard to persuade others. God knows we are sincere, and I hope you know this, too. ¹²Are we commending ourselves to you again? No, we are giving you a reason to be proud of us, so you can answer those who brag about having a spectacular ministry rather than having a sincere heart. ¹³If it seems we are crazy, it is to bring glory to God. And if we are in our right minds, it is for your benefit. ¹⁴Either way, Christ's love controls us. Since we believe that Christ died for all, we also believe that we have all died to our old life. ¹⁵He died for everyone so that those who receive his new life will no longer live for themselves. Instead, they will live for Christ, who died and was raised for them.

¹⁶So we have stopped evaluating others from a human point of view. At one time we thought of Christ merely from a human point of view. How differently we know him now! **¹⁷This means that anyone who belongs to Christ has become a new person. The old life is gone; a new life has begun!**
¹⁸And all of this is a gift from God, who brought us back to himself through Christ. And God has given us this task of reconciling people to him. ¹⁹For God was in Christ, reconciling the world to himself, no longer counting people's sins against them. And he gave us this wonderful message of reconciliation. ²⁰So we are Christ's ambassadors; God is making his appeal through us. We speak for Christ when we plead, "Come back to God!" ²¹For God made Christ, who never sinned, to be the offering for our sin, so that we could be made right with God through Christ.

CHAPTER **6**

As God's partners, we beg you not to accept this marvelous gift of God's kindness and then ignore it. ²For God says,

"At just the right time, I heard you.
  On the day of salvation, I helped you."

Indeed, the "right time" is now. Today is the day of salvation.

Paul's Hardships

³We live in such a way that no one will stumble because of us, and no one will find fault with our ministry. ⁴In everything we do, we show that we are true ministers of God. We patiently endure troubles and hardships and calamities of every kind. ⁵We have been beaten, been put in prison, faced angry mobs, worked to exhaustion, endured sleepless nights, and gone without food. ⁶We prove ourselves by our purity, our understanding, our patience, our kindness, by the Holy Spirit within us, and by our sincere love. ⁷We faithfully preach the truth. God's power is working in us. We use the weapons of righteousness in the right hand for attack and the left hand for defense. ⁸We serve God whether people honor us or despise us, whether they slander us or praise us. We are honest, but they call us impostors. ⁹We are ignored, even though we are well known. We live close to death, but we are still alive. We have been beaten, but we have not been killed. ¹⁰Our hearts ache, but we always have joy. We are poor, but we give spiritual riches to others. We own nothing, and yet we have everything.

¹¹Oh, dear Corinthian friends! We have spoken honestly with you, and our hearts are open to you. ¹²There is no lack of love on our part, but you have withheld your love from us. ¹³I am asking you to respond as if you were my own children. Open your hearts to us!

The Temple of the Living God

¹⁴Don't team up with those who are unbelievers. How can righteousness be a partner with wickedness? How can light live with darkness? ¹⁵What harmony can there be between Christ and the devil? How can a believer be a partner with an unbeliever? ¹⁶And what union can there be between God's temple and idols? For we are the temple of the living God. As God said:

"I will live in them
  and walk among them.
I will be their God,
  and they will be my people.

¹⁷ Therefore, come out from among
   unbelievers,
   and separate yourselves from them,
      says the LORD.
   Don't touch their filthy things,
      and I will welcome you.
¹⁸ And I will be your Father,
   and you will be my sons and daughters,
      says the LORD Almighty."

CHAPTER **7**

Because we have these promises, dear friends, let us cleanse ourselves from everything that can defile our body or spirit. And let us work toward complete holiness because we fear God.

²Please open your hearts to us. We have not done wrong to anyone, nor led anyone astray, nor taken advantage of anyone. ³I'm not saying this to condemn you. I said before that you are in our hearts, and we live or die together with you. ⁴I have the highest confidence in you, and I take great pride in you. You have greatly encouraged me and made me happy despite all our troubles.

Paul's Joy at the Church's Repentance

⁵When we arrived in Macedonia, there was no rest for us. We faced conflict from every direction, with battles on the outside and fear on the inside. ⁶But God, who encourages those who are discouraged, encouraged us by the arrival of Titus. ⁷His presence was a joy, but so was the news he brought of the encouragement he received from you. When he told us how much you long to see me, and how sorry you are for what happened, and how loyal you are to me, I was filled with joy!

⁸I am not sorry that I sent that severe letter to you, though I was sorry at first, for I know it was painful to you for a little while. ⁹Now I am glad I sent it, not because it hurt you, but because the pain caused you to repent and change your ways. It was the kind of sorrow God wants his people to have, so you were not harmed by us in any way. ¹⁰For the kind of sorrow God wants us to experience leads us away from sin and results in salvation. There's no regret for that kind of sorrow. But worldly sorrow, which lacks repentance, results in spiritual death.

¹¹Just see what this godly sorrow produced in you! Such earnestness, such concern to clear yourselves, such indignation, such alarm, such longing to see me, such zeal, and such a readiness to punish wrong. You showed that you have done everything necessary to make things right. ¹²My purpose, then, was not to write about who did the wrong or who was wronged. I wrote to you so that in the sight of God you could see for yourselves how loyal you are to us. ¹³We have been greatly encouraged by this.

In addition to our own encouragement, we were especially delighted to see how happy Titus was about the way all of you welcomed him and set his mind at ease. ¹⁴I had told him how proud I was of you—and you didn't disappoint me. I have always told you the truth, and now my boasting to Titus has also proved true! ¹⁵Now he cares for you more than ever when he remembers the way all of you obeyed him and welcomed him with such fear and deep respect. ¹⁶I am very happy now because I have complete confidence in you.

CHAPTER **8**
A Call to Generous Giving

Now I want you to know, dear brothers and sisters, what God in his kindness has done through the churches in Macedonia. ²They are being tested by many troubles, and they are very poor. But they are also filled with abundant joy, which has overflowed in rich generosity.

³For I can testify that they gave not only what they could afford, but far more. And they did it of their own free will. ⁴They begged us again and again for the privilege of sharing in the gift for the believers in Jerusalem. ⁵They even did more than we had hoped, for their first action was to give themselves to the Lord and to us, just as God wanted them to do.

⁶So we have urged Titus, who encouraged your giving in the first place, to return to you and encourage you to finish this ministry of giving. ⁷Since you excel in so many ways—in your faith, your gifted speakers, your knowledge, your enthusiasm, and your love from us—I want you to excel also in this gracious act of giving.

⁸I am not commanding you to do this. But I am testing how genuine your love is by comparing it with the eagerness of the other churches.

⁹You know the generous grace of our Lord Jesus Christ. Though he was rich, yet for your sakes he became poor, so that by his poverty he could make you rich.

¹⁰Here is my advice: It would be good for you to finish what you started a year ago. Last year you were the first who wanted to give, and you were the first to begin doing it. ¹¹Now you should finish what you started. Let the eagerness you showed in the beginning be matched now by your giving. Give in proportion to what you have. ¹²Whatever you give is acceptable if you give it eagerly. And give according to what you have,

not what you don't have. ¹³Of course, I don't mean your giving should make life easy for others and hard for yourselves. I only mean that there should be some equality. ¹⁴Right now you have plenty and can help those who are in need. Later, they will have plenty and can share with you when you need it. In this way, things will be equal. ¹⁵As the Scriptures say,

"Those who gathered a lot had nothing
    left over,
and those who gathered only a little
    had enough."

Titus and His Companions

¹⁶But thank God! He has given Titus the same enthusiasm for you that I have. ¹⁷Titus welcomed our request that he visit you again. In fact, he himself was very eager to go and see you. ¹⁸We are also sending another brother with Titus. All the churches praise him as a preacher of the Good News. ¹⁹He was appointed by the churches to accompany us as we take the offering to Jerusalem—a service that glorifies the Lord and shows our eagerness to help.

²⁰We are traveling together to guard against any criticism for the way we are handling this generous gift. ²¹We are careful to be honorable before the Lord, but we also want everyone else to see that we are honorable.

²²We are also sending with them another of our brothers who has proven himself many times and has shown on many occasions how eager he is. He is now even more enthusiastic because of his great confidence in you. ²³If anyone asks about Titus, say that he is my partner who works with me to help you. And the brothers with him have been sent by the churches, and they bring honor to Christ. ²⁴So show them your love, and prove to all the churches that our boasting about you is justified.

CHAPTER **9**
The Collection for Christians in Jerusalem

I really don't need to write to you about this ministry of giving for the believers in Jerusalem. ²For I know how eager you are to help, and I have been boasting to the churches in Macedonia that you in Greece were ready to send an offering a year ago. In fact, it was your enthusiasm that stirred up many of the Macedonian believers to begin giving.

³But I am sending these brothers to be sure you really are ready, as I have been telling them,

and that your money is all collected. I don't want to be wrong in my boasting about you. ⁴We would be embarrassed—not to mention your own embarrassment—if some Macedonian believers came with me and found that you weren't ready after all I had told them! ⁵So I thought I should send these brothers ahead of me to make sure the gift you promised is ready. But I want it to be a willing gift, not one given grudgingly.

⁶Remember this—a farmer who plants only a few seeds will get a small crop. But the one who plants generously will get a generous crop. **⁷You must each decide in your heart how much to give. And don't give reluctantly or in response to pressure. "For God loves a person who gives cheerfully."** ⁸And God will generously provide all you need. Then you will always have everything you need and plenty left over to share with others. ⁹As the Scriptures say,

"They share freely and give generously
    to the poor.
Their good deeds will be remembered
    forever."

¹⁰For God is the one who provides seed for the farmer and then bread to eat. In the same way, he will provide and increase your resources and then produce a great harvest of generosity in you. ¹¹Yes, you will be enriched in every way so that you can always be generous. And when we take your gifts to those who need them, they will thank God. ¹²So two good things will result from this ministry of giving—the needs of the believers in Jerusalem will be met, and they will joyfully express their thanks to God.

¹³As a result of your ministry, they will give glory to God. For your generosity to them and to all believers will prove that you are obedient to the Good News of Christ. ¹⁴And they will pray for you with deep affection because of the overflowing grace God has given to you. ¹⁵Thank God for this gift too wonderful for words!

CHAPTER **10**
Paul Defends His Authority

Now I, Paul, appeal to you with the gentleness and kindness of Christ—though I realize you think I am timid in person and bold only when I write from far away. ²Well, I am begging you now so that when I come I won't have to be bold with those who think we act from human motives.

³We are human, but we don't wage war as humans do. ⁴We use God's mighty weapons, not worldly weapons, to knock down the strongholds

of human reasoning and to destroy false arguments. 5We destroy every proud obstacle that keeps people from knowing God. We capture their rebellious thoughts and teach them to obey Christ. 6And after you have become fully obedient, we will punish everyone who remains disobedient.

7Look at the obvious facts. Those who say they belong to Christ must recognize that we belong to Christ as much as they do. 8I may seem to be boasting too much about the authority given to us by the Lord. But our authority builds you up; it doesn't tear you down. So I will not be ashamed of using my authority.

9I'm not trying to frighten you by my letters. 10For some say, "Paul's letters are demanding and forceful, but in person he is weak, and his speeches are worthless!" 11Those people should realize that our actions when we arrive in person will be as forceful as what we say in our letters from far away.

12Oh, don't worry; we wouldn't dare say that we are as wonderful as these other men who tell you how important they are! But they are only comparing themselves with each other, using themselves as the standard of measurement. How ignorant!

13We will not boast about things done outside our area of authority. We will boast only about what has happened within the boundaries of the work God has given us, which includes our working with you. 14We are not reaching beyond these boundaries when we claim authority over you, as if we had never visited you. For we were the first to travel all the way to Corinth with the Good News of Christ.

15Nor do we boast and claim credit for the work someone else has done. Instead, we hope that your faith will grow so that the boundaries of our work among you will be extended. 16Then we will be able to go and preach the Good News in other places far beyond you, where no one else is working. Then there will be no question of our boasting about work done in someone else's territory. 17As the Scriptures say, "If you want to boast, boast only about the LORD."

18When people commend themselves, it doesn't count for much. The important thing is for the Lord to commend them.

CHAPTER 11
Paul and the False Apostles

I hope you will put up with a little more of my foolishness. Please bear with me. 2For I am jealous for you with the jealousy of God himself. I promised you as a pure bride to one husband—Christ. 3But I fear that somehow your pure and undivided devotion to Christ will be corrupted, just as Eve was deceived by the cunning ways of the serpent. 4You happily put up with whatever anyone tells you, even if they preach a different Jesus than the one we preach, or a different kind of Spirit than the one you received, or a different kind of gospel than the one you believed.

5But I don't consider myself inferior in any way to these "super apostles" who teach such things. 6I may be unskilled as a speaker, but I'm not lacking in knowledge. We have made this clear to you in every possible way.

7Was I wrong when I humbled myself and honored you by preaching God's Good News to you without expecting anything in return? 8I "robbed" other churches by accepting their contributions so I could serve you at no cost. 9And when I was with you and didn't have enough to live on, I did not become a financial burden to anyone. For the brothers who came from Macedonia brought me all that I needed. I have never been a burden to you, and I never will be. 10As surely as the truth of Christ is in me, no one in all of Greece will ever stop me from boasting about this. 11Why? Because I don't love you? God knows that I do.

12But I will continue doing what I have always done. This will undercut those who are looking for an opportunity to boast that their work is just like ours. 13These people are false apostles. They are deceitful workers who disguise themselves as apostles of Christ. 14But I am not surprised! Even Satan disguises himself as an angel of light. 15So it is no wonder that his servants also disguise themselves as servants of righteousness. In the end they will get the punishment their wicked deeds deserve.

Paul's Many Trials

16Again I say, don't think that I am a fool to talk like this. But even if you do, listen to me, as you would to a foolish person, while I also boast a little. 17Such boasting is not from the Lord, but I am acting like a fool. 18And since others boast about their human achievements, I will, too. 19After all, you think you are so wise, but you enjoy putting up with fools! 20You put up with it when someone enslaves you, takes everything you have, takes advantage of you, takes control of everything, and slaps you in the face. 21I'm ashamed to say that we've been too "weak" to do that!

But whatever they dare to boast about—I'm talking like a fool again—I dare to boast about it, too. ²²Are they Hebrews? So am I. Are they Israelites? So am I. Are they descendants of Abraham? So am I. ²³Are they servants of Christ? I know I sound like a madman, but I have served him far more! I have worked harder, been put in prison more often, been whipped times without number, and faced death again and again. ²⁴Five different times the Jewish leaders gave me thirty-nine lashes. ²⁵Three times I was beaten with rods. Once I was stoned. Three times I was shipwrecked. Once I spent a whole night and a day adrift at sea. ²⁶I have traveled on many long journeys. I have faced danger from rivers and from robbers. I have faced danger from my own people, the Jews, as well as from the Gentiles. I have faced danger in the cities, in the deserts, and on the seas. And I have faced danger from men who claim to be believers but are not. ²⁷I have worked hard and long, enduring many sleepless nights. I have been hungry and thirsty and have often gone without food. I have shivered in the cold, without enough clothing to keep me warm.

²⁸Then, besides all this, I have the daily burden of my concern for all the churches. ²⁹Who is weak without my feeling that weakness? Who is led astray, and I do not burn with anger?

³⁰If I must boast, I would rather boast about the things that show how weak I am. ³¹God, the Father of our Lord Jesus, who is worthy of eternal praise, knows I am not lying. ³²When I was in Damascus, the governor under King Aretas kept guards at the city gates to catch me. ³³I had to be lowered in a basket through a window in the city wall to escape from him.

CHAPTER **12**
Paul's Vision and His Thorn in the Flesh

This boasting will do no good, but I must go on. I will reluctantly tell about visions and revelations from the Lord. ²I was caught up to the third heaven fourteen years ago. Whether I was in my body or out of my body, I don't know—only God knows. ³Yes, only God knows whether I was in my body or outside my body. But I do know ⁴that I was caught up to paradise and heard things so astounding that they cannot be expressed in words, things no human is allowed to tell.

⁵That experience is worth boasting about, but I'm not going to do it. I will boast only about my weaknesses. ⁶If I wanted to boast, I would be no fool in doing so, because I would be telling the truth. But I won't do it, because I don't want anyone to give me credit beyond what they can see in my life or hear in my message, ⁷even though I

have received such wonderful revelations from God. So to keep me from becoming proud, I was given a thorn in my flesh, a messenger from Satan to torment me and keep me from becoming proud.

⁸Three different times I begged the Lord to take it away. ⁹Each time he said, "My grace is all you need. My power works best in weakness." So now I am glad to boast about my weaknesses, so that the power of Christ can work through me. ¹⁰That's why I take pleasure in my weaknesses, and in the insults, hardships, persecutions, and troubles that I suffer for Christ. For when I am weak, then I am strong.

Paul's Concern for the Corinthians

¹¹You have made me act like a fool—boasting like this. You ought to be writing commendations for me, for I am not at all inferior to these "super apostles," even though I am nothing at all. ¹²When I was with you, I certainly gave you proof that I am an apostle. For I patiently did many signs and wonders and miracles among you. ¹³The only thing I failed to do, which I do in the other churches, was to become a financial burden to you. Please forgive me for this wrong!

¹⁴Now I am coming to you for the third time, and I will not be a burden to you. I don't want what you have—I want you. After all, children don't provide for their parents. Rather, parents provide for their children. ¹⁵I will gladly spend myself and all I have for you, even though it seems that the more I love you, the less you love me.

¹⁶Some of you admit I was not a burden to you. But others still think I was sneaky and took advantage of you by trickery. ¹⁷But how? Did any of the men I sent to you take advantage of you? ¹⁸When I urged Titus to visit you and sent our other brother with him, did Titus take advantage of you? No! For we have the same spirit and walk in each other's steps, doing things the same way.

¹⁹Perhaps you think we're saying these things just to defend ourselves. No, we tell you this as Christ's servants, and with God as our witness. Everything we do, dear friends, is to strengthen you. ²⁰For I am afraid that when I come I won't like what I find, and you won't like my response. I am afraid that I will find quarreling, jealousy, anger, selfishness, slander, gossip, arrogance, and disorderly behavior. ²¹Yes, I am afraid that when I come again, God will humble me in your presence. And I will be grieved because many of you have not given up your old sins. You have not

repented of your impurity, sexual immorality, and eagerness for lustful pleasure.

Paul's Final Advice

This is the third time I am coming to visit you (and as the Scriptures say, "The facts of every case must be established by the testimony of two or three witnesses"). ²I have already warned those who had been sinning when I was there on my second visit. Now I again warn them and all others, just as I did before, that next time I will not spare them.

³I will give you all the proof you want that Christ speaks through me. Christ is not weak when he deals with you; he is powerful among you. ⁴Although he was crucified in weakness, he now lives by the power of God. We, too, are weak, just as Christ was, but when we deal with you we will be alive with him and will have God's power.

⁵Examine yourselves to see if your faith is genuine. Test yourselves. Surely you know that Jesus Christ is among you; if not, you have failed the test of genuine faith. ⁶As you test yourselves, I hope you will recognize that we have not failed the test of apostolic authority.

⁷We pray to God that you will not do what is wrong by refusing our correction. I hope we won't need to demonstrate our authority when we arrive. Do the right thing before we come— even if that makes it look like we have failed to demonstrate our authority. ⁸For we cannot oppose the truth, but must always stand for the truth. ⁹We are glad to seem weak if it helps show that you are actually strong. We pray that you will become mature.

¹⁰I am writing this to you before I come, hoping that I won't need to deal severely with you when I do come. For I want to use the authority the Lord has given me to strengthen you, not to tear you down.

Paul's Final Greetings

¹¹Dear brothers and sisters, I close my letter with these last words: Be joyful. Grow to maturity. Encourage each other. Live in harmony and peace. Then the God of love and peace will be with you.

¹²Greet each other with Christian love. ¹³All of God's people here send you their greetings.

¹⁴May the grace of the Lord Jesus Christ, the love of God, and the fellowship of the Holy Spirit be with you all.

GALATiANS Back to Basics

Look for **1** hidden message in Galatians!

Paul wrote to the Christians in Galatia to help them get rid of false teachings. Look for
- **THE ONE AND ONLY GOSPEL**
- **THE LETTER OF THE LAW**
- **FREEDOM FROM SIN**
- **SALVATION AND THE SPIRIT**

Obituaries

Paul of Tarsus is dead. At least that's what he says. Hey, wait a minute! How can he say it if he's dead? **Read Galatians 2:20 to find the answer to this mystery.**

Farmer's Market

Fruit with personality. Huh? A patient pineapple? A kind kiwi? A faithful fig? **To find out more about this attitude-changing produce, read Galatians 5:22.**

Reality Show

The Bible is the ultimate reality show! Paul didn't pull any punches when he talked about his past life. **Read Galatians 1:11-24 to find out all the details of Paul's call.**

Healthy Harvest

If you plant a good seed, what do you think you'll harvest? **Dig up the whole story in Galatians 6:7-10.**

Timeline

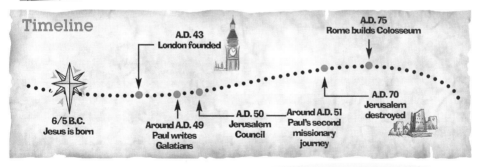

A.D. 75
Rome builds Colosseum

A.D. 43
London founded

6/5 B.C.
Jesus is born

Around A.D. 49
Paul writes
Galatians

A.D. 50
Jerusalem
Council

Around A.D. 51
Paul's second
missionary
journey

A.D. 70
Jerusalem
destroyed

The Jesus Connection

The book of Galatians shows us that our relationship with Jesus isn't about trying to be good—it's about the freedom from sin he gives us just because he loves us. When we put our faith in Jesus, he frees us from sin's enslaving power. The Holy Spirit helps us turn from temptation and do what is right. And even when we mess up, we're forgiven and free— because Jesus paid the price for our sins by dying on the cross. **Jesus really has set us free!**

CHAPTER 1
Greetings from Paul

This letter is from Paul, an apostle. I was not appointed by any group of people or any human authority, but by Jesus Christ himself and by God the Father, who raised Jesus from the dead.

²All the brothers and sisters here join me in sending this letter to the churches of Galatia.

³May God our Father and the Lord Jesus Christ give you grace and peace. ⁴Jesus gave his life for our sins, just as God our Father planned, in order to rescue us from this evil world in which we live. ⁵All glory to God forever and ever! Amen.

There Is Only One Good News

⁶I am shocked that you are turning away so soon from God, who called you to himself through the loving mercy of Christ. You are following a different way that pretends to be the Good News ⁷but is not the Good News at all. You are being fooled by those who deliberately twist the truth concerning Christ.

⁸Let God's curse fall on anyone, including us or even an angel from heaven, who preaches a different kind of Good News than the one we preached to you. ⁹I say again what we have said before: If anyone preaches any other Good News than the one you welcomed, let that person be cursed.

¹⁰Obviously, I'm not trying to win the approval of people, but of God. If pleasing people were my goal, I would not be Christ's servant.

Paul's Message Comes from Christ

¹¹Dear brothers and sisters, I want you to understand that the gospel message I preach is not based on mere human reasoning. ¹²I received my message from no human source, and no one taught me. Instead, I received it by direct revelation from Jesus Christ.

¹³You know what I was like when I followed the Jewish religion—how I violently persecuted God's church. I did my best to destroy it. ¹⁴I was far ahead of my fellow Jews in my zeal for the traditions of my ancestors.

¹⁵But even before I was born, God chose me and called me by his marvelous grace. Then it pleased him ¹⁶ to reveal his Son to me so that I would proclaim the Good News about Jesus to the Gentiles.

When this happened, I did not rush out to consult with any human being. ¹⁷Nor did I go up to Jerusalem to consult with those who were apostles

Key Verse

"It is no longer I who live, but Christ lives in me. So I live in this earthly body by trusting in the Son of God, who loved me and gave himself for me."—GALATIANS 2:20

Christ in Me

Read GALATIANS 2:20 out loud.

Then try this!

HAVE AN ADULT HELP YOU!

You'll need:
- water
- salt
- bowl
- saucepan with a lid
- way to heat the water

Read Romans 12:2 for more about how to live for Jesus.

1 Add salt to the water. Take a taste. Pretty salty, huh?

2 Heat the water in a microwave or on the stove until the water boils.

3 HAVE THE ADULT remove the bowl or pan from the heat source, and put the lid on.

4 After 30 seconds, remove the lid. Wait until the water on the lid cools and then take a taste.

THE SALTINESS IS GONE!

When we believe in Jesus, our sinful selves start to disappear, just like the salt disappeared.

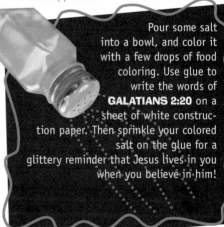

Pour some salt into a bowl, and color it with a few drops of food coloring. Use glue to write the words of **GALATIANS 2:20** on a sheet of white construction paper. Then sprinkle your colored salt on the glue for a glittery reminder that Jesus lives in you when you believe in him!

before I was. Instead, I went away into Arabia, and later I returned to the city of Damascus.

¹⁸Then three years later I went to Jerusalem to get to know Peter, and I stayed with him for fifteen days. ¹⁹The only other apostle I met at that time was James, the Lord's brother. ²⁰I declare before God that what I am writing to you is not a lie.

²¹After that visit I went north into the provinces of Syria and Cilicia. ²²And still the Christians in the churches in Judea didn't know me personally. ²³All they knew was that people were saying, "The one who used to persecute us is now preaching the very faith he tried to destroy!" ²⁴And they praised God because of me.

CHAPTER **2**
The Apostles Accept Paul

Then fourteen years later I went back to Jerusalem again, this time with Barnabas; and Titus came along, too. ²I went there because God revealed to me that I should go. While I was there I met privately with those considered to be leaders of the church and shared with them the message I had been preaching to the Gentiles. I wanted to make sure that we were in agreement, for fear that all my efforts had been wasted and I was running the race for nothing. ³And they supported me and did not even demand that my companion Titus be circumcised, though he was a Gentile.

⁴Even that question came up only because of some so-called Christians there—false ones, really—who were secretly brought in. They sneaked in to spy on us and take away the freedom we have in Christ Jesus. They wanted to enslave us and force us to follow their Jewish regulations. ⁵But we refused to give in to them for a single moment. We wanted to preserve the truth of the gospel message for you.

⁶And the leaders of the church had nothing to add to what I was preaching. (By the way, their reputation as great leaders made no difference to me, for God has no favorites.) ⁷Instead, they saw that God had given me the responsibility of preaching the gospel to the Gentiles, just as he had given Peter the responsibility of preaching to the Jews. ⁸For the same God who worked through Peter as the apostle to the Jews also worked through me as the apostle to the Gentiles.

⁹In fact, James, Peter, and John, who were known as pillars of the church, recognized the gift God had given me, and they accepted Barnabas and me as their co-workers. They encouraged us to keep preaching to the Gentiles, while they continued their work with the Jews. ¹⁰Their only suggestion was that we keep on helping the poor, which I have always been eager to do.

Paul Confronts Peter

¹¹But when Peter came to Antioch, I had to oppose him to his face, for what he did was very wrong. ¹²When he first arrived, he ate with the Gentile Christians, who were not circumcised. But afterward, when some friends of James came, Peter wouldn't eat with the Gentiles anymore. He was afraid of criticism from these people who insisted on the necessity of circumcision. ¹³As a result, other Jewish Christians followed Peter's hypocrisy, and even Barnabas was led astray by their hypocrisy.

¹⁴When I saw that they were not following the truth of the gospel message, I said to Peter in front of all the others, "Since you, a Jew by birth, have discarded the Jewish laws and are living like a Gentile, why are you now trying to make these Gentiles follow the Jewish traditions?

¹⁵"You and I are Jews by birth, not 'sinners' like the Gentiles. ¹⁶Yet we know that a person is made right with God by faith in Jesus Christ, not by obeying the law. And we have believed in Christ Jesus, so that we might be made right with God because of our faith in Christ, not because we have obeyed the law. For no one will ever be made right with God by obeying the law."

¹⁷But suppose we seek to be made right with God through faith in Christ and then we are found guilty because we have abandoned the law. Would that mean Christ has led us into sin? Absolutely not! ¹⁸Rather, I am a sinner if I rebuild the old system of law I already tore down. ¹⁹For when I tried to keep the law, it condemned me. So I died to the law—I stopped trying to meet all its requirements—so that I might live for God. **²⁰My old self has been crucified with Christ. It is no longer I who live, but Christ lives in me. So I live in this earthly body by trusting in the Son of God, who loved me and gave himself for me.** ²¹I do not treat the grace of God as meaningless. For if keeping the law could make us right with God, then there was no need for Christ to die.

CHAPTER **3**
The Law and Faith in Christ

Oh, foolish Galatians! Who has cast an evil spell on you? For the meaning of Jesus Christ's death was made as clear to you as if you had seen a picture of his death on the cross. ²Let me ask you this one question: Did you receive the Holy Spirit by obeying the law of Moses? Of course not! You received the Spirit because you believed the message you heard about Christ. 3 How foolish can you be? After starting your Christian lives in the Spirit, why are you now trying to become perfect by your own human effort? 4 Have you experienced so much for nothing? Surely it was not in vain, was it?

5 I ask you again, does God give you the Holy Spirit and work miracles among you because you obey the law? Of course not! It is because you believe the message you heard about Christ.

6 In the same way, "Abraham believed God, and God counted him as righteous because of his faith." 7 The real children of Abraham, then, are those who put their faith in God.

8 What's more, the Scriptures looked forward to this time when God would declare the Gentiles to be righteous because of their faith. God proclaimed this good news to Abraham long ago when he said, "All nations will be blessed through you." 9 So all who put their faith in Christ share the same blessing Abraham received because of his faith.

10 But those who depend on the law to make them right with God are under his curse, for the Scriptures say, "Cursed is everyone who does not observe and obey all the commands that are written in God's Book of the Law." 11 So it is clear that no one can be made right with God by trying to keep the law. For the Scriptures say, "It is through faith that a righteous person has life." 12 This way of faith is very different from the way of law, which says, "It is through obeying the law that a person has life."

13 But Christ has rescued us from the curse pronounced by the law. When he was hung on the cross, he took upon himself the curse for our wrongdoing. For it is written in the Scriptures, "Cursed is everyone who is hung on a tree." 14 Through Christ Jesus, God has blessed the Gentiles with the same blessing he promised to Abraham, so that we who are believers might receive the promised Holy Spirit through faith.

The Law and God's Promise

15 Dear brothers and sisters, here's an example from everyday life. Just as no one can set aside or amend an irrevocable agreement, so it is in this case. 16 God gave the promises to Abraham and his child. And notice that the Scripture doesn't say "to his children," as if it meant many descendants. Rather, it says "to his child"—and that, of course, means Christ. 17 This is what I am trying to say: The agreement God made with Abraham could not be canceled 430 years later when God gave the law to Moses. God would be breaking his promise. 18 For if the inheritance could be received by keeping the law, then it would not be the result of accepting God's promise. But God graciously gave it to Abraham as a promise.

19 Why, then, was the law given? It was given alongside the promise to show people their sins. But the law was designed to last only until the coming of the child who was promised. God gave his law through angels to Moses, who was the mediator between God and the people. 20 Now a mediator is helpful if more than one party must reach an agreement. But God, who is one, did not use a mediator when he gave his promise to Abraham.

21 Is there a conflict, then, between God's law and God's promises? Absolutely not! If the law could give us new life, we could be made right with God by obeying it. 22 But the Scriptures declare that we are all prisoners of sin, so we receive God's promise of freedom only by believing in Jesus Christ.

God's Children through Faith

23 Before the way of faith in Christ was available to us, we were placed under guard by the law. We were kept in protective custody, so to speak, until the way of faith was revealed.

24 Let me put it another way. The law was our guardian until Christ came; it protected us until we could be made right with God through faith. 25 And now that the way of faith has come, we no longer need the law as our guardian.

26 For you are all children of God through faith in Christ Jesus. 27 And all who have been united with Christ in baptism have put on Christ, like putting on new clothes. 28 There is no longer Jew or Gentile, slave or free, male and female. For you are all one in Christ Jesus. 29 And now that you belong to Christ, you are the true children of Abraham. You are his heirs, and God's promise to Abraham belongs to you.

CHAPTER **4**

Think of it this way. If a father dies and leaves an inheritance for his young children, those children are not much better off than slaves until they grow up, even though they actually own everything their father had. 2 They have to obey their guardians until they reach whatever age their father set. 3 And that's the way it was with us before Christ came. We were like children; we were slaves to the basic spiritual principles of this world.

all MiXeD-UP

In the early church, some Jewish Christians were mixing their Jewish faith with their new Christian faith. Not only that, some of them required new Christians who weren't Jewish to follow some of the Jewish laws.

But Paul clearly pointed out (in his letter to Galatia and through other writings) **that faith in Jesus is all that is required to be a Christian**—not any rituals we can perform or traditions we can follow.

Do you ever fall into the trap of thinking that you can earn your way to heaven? **If so, read what Paul says in GALATIANS 2:16.** Then make a reminder that faith in Jesus is what really matters. You could make up a song, draw a poster, or write a poem.

⁴But when the right time came, God sent his Son, born of a woman, subject to the law. ⁵God sent him to buy freedom for us who were slaves to the law, so that he could adopt us as his very own children. ⁶And because we are his children, God has sent the Spirit of his Son into our hearts, prompting us to call out, "Abba, Father." ⁷Now you are no longer a slave but God's own child. And since you are his child, God has made you his heir.

Paul's Concern for the Galatians

⁸Before you Gentiles knew God, you were slaves to so-called gods that do not even exist. ⁹So now that you know God (or should I say, now that God knows you), why do you want to go back again and become slaves once more to the weak and useless spiritual principles of this world? ¹⁰You are trying to earn favor with God by observing certain days or months or seasons or years. ¹¹I

fear for you. Perhaps all my hard work with you was for nothing. ¹²Dear brothers and sisters, I plead with you to live as I do in freedom from these things, for I have become like you Gentiles—free from those laws.

You did not mistreat me when I first preached to you. ¹³Surely you remember that I was sick when I first brought you the Good News. ¹⁴But even though my condition tempted you to reject me, you did not despise me or turn me away. No, you took me in and cared for me as though I were an angel from God or even Christ Jesus himself. ¹⁵Where is that joyful and grateful spirit you felt then? I am sure you would have taken out your own eyes and given them to me if it had been possible. ¹⁶Have I now become your enemy because I am telling you the truth?

¹⁷Those false teachers are so eager to win your favor, but their intentions are not good. They are trying to shut you off from me so that you will pay attention only to them. ¹⁸If someone is eager to do good things for you, that's all right; but let them do it all the time, not just when I'm with you.

¹⁹Oh, my dear children! I feel as if I'm going through labor pains for you again, and they will continue until Christ is fully developed in your lives. ²⁰I wish I were with you right now so I could change my tone. But at this distance I don't know how else to help you.

Abraham's Two Children

²¹Tell me, you who want to live under the law, do you know what the law actually says? ²²The Scriptures say that Abraham had two sons, one from his slave wife and one from his freeborn wife. ²³The son of the slave wife was born in a human attempt to bring about the fulfillment of God's promise. But the son of the freeborn wife was born as God's own fulfillment of his promise.

²⁴These two women serve as an illustration of God's two covenants. The first woman, Hagar, represents Mount Sinai where people received the law that enslaved them. ²⁵And now Jerusalem is just like Mount Sinai in Arabia, because she and her children live in slavery to the law. ²⁶But the other woman, Sarah, represents the heavenly Jerusalem. She is the free woman, and she is our mother. ²⁷As Isaiah said,

"Rejoice, O childless woman,
  you who have never given birth!
Break into a joyful shout,
  you who have never been in labor!

For the desolate woman now has more
children
than the woman who lives with her
husband!"

28 And you, dear brothers and sisters, are children of the promise, just like Isaac. 29 But you are now being persecuted by those who want you to keep the law, just as Ishmael, the child born by human effort, persecuted Isaac, the child born by the power of the Spirit.

30 But what do the Scriptures say about that?

Key Verse

"But the Holy Spirit produces this kind of fruit in our lives: love, joy, peace, patience, kindness, goodness, faithfulness, gentleness, and self-control." —GALATIANS 5:22-23a

Fruit of the Spirit

. Read GALATIANS 5:22-23. Keep reading it until you can say all nine fruits of the Spirit without looking at the verse.

Find an adult, and make this Fruit of the Spirit reminder.

1 Gather nine kinds of fruit. You could use red apples, green apples, bananas, strawberries, cantaloupe, red grapes, green grapes, pears, and pineapple.

2 Have an adult cut the fruit into bite-sized pieces.

3 Put nine different pieces of fruit on a wooden skewer to represent the fruit of the Spirit.

Invite friends and family to a **Fruit of the Spirit Festival.** Ask God to help each of you grow more and more good fruit in your life!

"Get rid of the slave and her son, for the son of the slave woman will not share the inheritance with the free woman's son." 31 So, dear brothers and sisters, we are not children of the slave woman; we are children of the free woman.

CHAPTER **5**
Freedom in Christ

So Christ has truly set us free. Now make sure that you stay free, and don't get tied up again in slavery to the law.

2 Listen! I, Paul, tell you this: If you are counting on circumcision to make you right with God, then Christ will be of no benefit to you. 3 I'll say it again. If you are trying to find favor with God by being circumcised, you must obey every regulation in the whole law of Moses. 4 For if you are trying to make yourselves right with God by keeping the law, you have been cut off from Christ! You have fallen away from God's grace.

5 But we who live by the Spirit eagerly wait to receive by faith the righteousness God has promised to us. 6 For when we place our faith in Christ Jesus, there is no benefit in being circumcised or being uncircumcised. What is important is faith expressing itself in love.

7 You were running the race so well. Who has held you back from following the truth? 8 It certainly isn't God, for he is the one who called you to freedom. 9 This false teaching is like a little yeast that spreads through the whole batch of dough! 10 I am trusting the Lord to keep you from believing false teachings. God will judge that person, whoever he is, who has been confusing you.

11 Dear brothers and sisters, if I were still preaching that you must be circumcised—as some say I do—why am I still being persecuted? If I were no longer preaching salvation through the cross of Christ, no one would be offended. 12 I just wish that those troublemakers who want to mutilate you by circumcision would mutilate themselves.

13 For you have been called to live in freedom, my brothers and sisters. But don't use your freedom to satisfy your sinful nature. Instead, use your freedom to serve one another in love. 14 For the whole law can be summed up in this one command: "Love your neighbor as yourself." 15 But if you are always biting and devouring one another, watch out! Beware of destroying one another.

Living by the Spirit's Power

16 So I say, let the Holy Spirit guide your lives. Then you won't be doing what your sinful nature

craves. 17The sinful nature wants to do evil, which is just the opposite of what the Spirit wants. And the Spirit gives us desires that are the opposite of what the sinful nature desires. These two forces are constantly fighting each other, so you are not free to carry out your good intentions. 18But when you are directed by the Spirit, you are not under obligation to the law of Moses.

19When you follow the desires of your sinful nature, the results are very clear: sexual immorality, impurity, lustful pleasures, 20idolatry, sorcery, hostility, quarreling, jealousy, outbursts of anger, selfish ambition, dissension, division, 21envy, drunkenness, wild parties, and other sins like these. Let me tell you again, as I have before, that anyone living that sort of life will not inherit the Kingdom of God.

22But the Holy Spirit produces this kind of fruit in our lives: love, joy, peace, patience, kindness, goodness, faithfulness, 23gentleness, and self-control. There is no law against these things!

24Those who belong to Christ Jesus have nailed the passions and desires of their sinful nature to his cross and crucified them there. 25Since we are living by the Spirit, let us follow the Spirit's leading in every part of our lives. 26Let us not become conceited, or provoke one another, or be jealous of one another.

CHAPTER **6**
We Harvest What We Plant

Dear brothers and sisters, if another believer is overcome by some sin, you who are godly should gently and humbly help that person back onto the right path. And be careful not to fall into the same temptation yourself. 2Share each other's burdens, and in this way obey the law of Christ. 3If you think you are too important to help someone, you are only fooling yourself. You are not that important.

4Pay careful attention to your own work, for then you will get the satisfaction of a job well done, and you won't need to compare yourself to anyone else. 5For we are each responsible for our own conduct.

6Those who are taught the word of God should provide for their teachers, sharing all good things with them.

7Don't be misled—you cannot mock the justice of God. You will always harvest what you plant. 8Those who live only to satisfy their own sinful nature will harvest decay and death from that sinful nature. But those who live to please the Spirit will harvest everlasting life from the Spirit. 9So let's not get tired of doing what is good. At just the right time we will reap a harvest of blessing if we don't give up. 10Therefore, whenever we have the opportunity, we should do good to everyone—especially to those in the family of faith.

Paul's Final Advice

11NOTICE WHAT LARGE LETTERS I USE AS I WRITE THESE CLOSING WORDS IN MY OWN HANDWRITING.

12Those who are trying to force you to be circumcised want to look good to others. They don't want to be persecuted for teaching that the cross of Christ alone can save. 13And even those who advocate circumcision don't keep the whole law themselves. They only want you to be circumcised so they can boast about it and claim you as their disciples.

14As for me, may I never boast about anything except the cross of our Lord Jesus Christ. Because of that cross, my interest in this world has been crucified, and the world's interest in me has also died. 15It doesn't matter whether we have been circumcised or not. What counts is whether we have been transformed into a new creation. 16May God's peace and mercy be upon all who live by this principle; they are the new people of God.

17From now on, don't let anyone trouble me with these things. For I bear on my body the scars that show I belong to Jesus.

18Dear brothers and sisters, may the grace of our Lord Jesus Christ be with your spirit. Amen.

EPHESIANS The Church Family

Look for **1** hidden message in Ephesians!

Ephesians is all about what it means to be part of the Christian church. It tells about

- **A NEW FAMILY**
- **NEW GIFTS**
- **NEW LIFE**
- **NEW RESPONSIBILITIES**

Gear Up, Dude!

Before you go boardin' you get geared up, right? I mean, you wouldn't ride fakie without protection! Well, God wants you to gear up too. **Go to Ephesians 6:10-17 to read about God's gear.**

Enjoy Life—Here's How!

No, it's not a new super-vitamin. It's not a new sports drink or diet. But it *is* a proven formula to help you enjoy life. **Read Ephesians 6:1-3 to learn the secret!**

WOW! That's Deep!

Did you know that the deepest part of the ocean is 36,201 feet deep? Did you know that the highest mountain is 29,035 feet high?

And did you know that God's love for you is deeper and higher than anything? **Check out the depths of God's love in Ephesians 3:17-19!**

Best Seat in the House

Have you ever gone to a game and gotten really horrible seats? Well, good seats aren't a problem for God! He has the best seats in the house reserved for you.

Check out Ephesians 2:4-10 to find out about the seats in heaven!

Timeline

A.D. 66 Painting on canvas

A.D. 74 China opens silk trade with the West

6/5 B.C. Jesus is born

A.D. 50-52 Paul's second missionary trip

About A.D. 60 Paul writes Ephesians

A.D. 70 Jerusalem destroyed

The JESUS CONNECTION

Becoming a Christian is the most important decision in your life, but it's only the first step in your relationship with God. Being a Christian means growing in Christ, following God in *everything* you do, and living for Jesus here on earth. If you've just begun your adventure with God, way to go! **But get ready, because God has so much more for you on your way to eternal life with him!**

CHAPTER **1**
Greetings from Paul
This letter is from Paul, chosen by the will of God to be an apostle of Christ Jesus.

I am writing to God's holy people in Ephesus, who are faithful followers of Christ Jesus.

2May God our Father and the Lord Jesus Christ give you grace and peace.

Spiritual Blessings
3All praise to God, the Father of our Lord Jesus Christ, who has blessed us with every spiritual blessing in the heavenly realms because we are united with Christ. 4Even before he made the world, God loved us and chose us in Christ to be holy and without fault in his eyes. 5God decided in advance to adopt us into his own family by bringing us to himself through Jesus Christ. This is what he wanted to do, and it gave him great pleasure. 6So we praise God for the glorious grace he has poured out on us who belong to his dear Son. 7He is so rich in kindness and grace that he purchased our freedom with the blood of his Son and forgave our sins. 8He has showered his kindness on us, along with all wisdom and understanding.

9God has now revealed to us his mysterious plan regarding Christ, a plan to fulfill his own good pleasure. 10And this is the plan: At the right time he will bring everything together under the authority of Christ—everything in heaven and on earth. 11Furthermore, because we are united with Christ, we have received an inheritance from God, for he chose us in advance, and he makes everything work out according to his plan.

12God's purpose was that we Jews who were the first to trust in Christ would bring praise and glory to God. 13And now you Gentiles have also heard the truth, the Good News that God saves you. And when you believed in Christ, he identified you as his own by giving you the Holy Spirit, whom he promised long ago. 14The Spirit is God's guarantee that he will give us the inheritance he promised and that he has purchased us to be his own people. He did this so we would praise and glorify him.

Paul's Prayer for Spiritual Wisdom
15Ever since I first heard of your strong faith in the Lord Jesus and your love for God's people everywhere, 16I have not stopped thanking God for you. I pray for you constantly, 17asking God, the glorious Father of our Lord Jesus Christ, to give you spiritual wisdom and insight so that you might grow in your knowledge of God. 18I pray that your hearts will be flooded with light so that you can understand the confident hope he has given to those he called—his holy people who are his rich and glorious inheritance.

19I also pray that you will understand the incredible greatness of God's power for us who believe him. This is the same mighty power 20that raised Christ from the dead and seated him in the place of honor at God's right hand in the heavenly realms. 21Now he is far above any ruler or authority or power or leader or anything else—not only in this world but also in the world to come. 22God has put all things under the authority of Christ and has made him head over all things for the benefit of the church. 23And the church is his body; it is made full and complete by Christ, who fills all things everywhere with himself.

CHAPTER **2**
Made Alive with Christ
Once you were dead because of your disobedience and your many sins. 2You used to live in sin, just like the rest of the world, obeying the devil—the commander of the powers in the unseen world. He is the spirit at work in the hearts of those who refuse to obey God. 3All of us used to live that way, following the passionate desires and inclinations of our sinful nature. By our very nature we were subject to God's anger, just like everyone else.

4But God is so rich in mercy, and he loved us so much, 5that even though we were dead because of our sins, he gave us life when he raised Christ from the dead. (It is only by God's grace that you have been saved!) 6For he raised us from the dead along with Christ and seated us with him in the heavenly realms because we are united with Christ Jesus. 7So God can point to us in all future ages as examples of the incredible wealth of his grace and kindness toward us, as shown in all he has done for us who are united with Christ Jesus.

8God saved you by his grace when you believed. And you can't take credit for this; it is a gift from God. 9Salvation is not a reward for the good things we have done, so none of us can boast about it. 10For we are God's masterpiece. He has created us anew in Christ Jesus, so we can do the good things he planned for us long ago.

Oneness and Peace in Christ
11Don't forget that you Gentiles used to be outsiders. You were called "uncircumcised heathens"

by the Jews, who were proud of their circumcision, even though it affected only their bodies and not their hearts. ¹²In those days you were living apart from Christ. You were excluded from citizenship among the people of Israel, and you did not know the covenant promises God had made to them. You lived in this world without God and without hope. ¹³But now you have been united with Christ Jesus. Once you were far away from God, but now you have been brought near to him through the blood of Christ.

¹⁴For Christ himself has brought peace to us. He united Jews and Gentiles into one people when, in his own body on the cross, he broke down the wall of hostility that separated us. ¹⁵He did this by ending the system of law with its commandments and regulations. He made peace between Jews and Gentiles by creating in himself one new people from the two groups. ¹⁶Together as one body, Christ reconciled both groups to God by means of his death on the cross, and our hostility toward each other was put to death.

¹⁷He brought this Good News of peace to you Gentiles who were far away from him, and peace to the Jews who were near. ¹⁸Now all of us can come to the Father through the same Holy Spirit because of what Christ has done for us.

A Temple for the Lord

¹⁹So now you Gentiles are no longer strangers and foreigners. You are citizens along with all of God's holy people. You are members of God's family. ²⁰Together, we are his house, built on the foundation of the apostles and the prophets. And the cornerstone is Christ Jesus himself. ²¹We are carefully joined together in him, becoming a holy temple for the Lord. ²²Through him you Gentiles are also being made part of this dwelling where God lives by his Spirit.

CHAPTER **3**
God's Mysterious Plan Revealed

When I think of all this, I, Paul, a prisoner of Christ Jesus for the benefit of you Gentiles . . . ²assuming, by the way, that you know God gave me the special responsibility of extending his grace to you Gentiles. ³As I briefly wrote earlier, God himself revealed his mysterious plan to me. ⁴As you read what I have written, you will understand my insight into this plan regarding Christ. ⁵God did not reveal it to previous generations, but now by his Spirit he has revealed it to his holy apostles and prophets.

⁶And this is God's plan: Both Gentiles and Jews

Key Verse "God saved you by his grace when you believed. And you can't take credit for this; it is a gift from God."
—EPHESIANS 2:8

It's FREE!

Read EPHESIANS 2:8 a few times until you really know it. Then write the verse in your own words below.

WOW! Being saved is a free gift that God gives us when we believe in Jesus. We can't earn it. We can't take credit for it. But we can *give* credit for it—to God, of course!

Write a thank you note to God, explaining how you feel about his free gift.

Now fill in your name in the verse below, so you remember that God has given this free gift to you!

"God saved _____ by his grace when _____ believed. And _____ can't take credit for this; it is a gift from God."

—EPHESIANS 2:8

who believe the Good News share equally in the riches inherited by God's children. Both are part of the same body, and both enjoy the promise of blessings because they belong to Christ Jesus. 7By God's grace and mighty power, I have been given the privilege of serving him by spreading this Good News.

8Though I am the least deserving of all God's people, he graciously gave me the privilege of telling the Gentiles about the endless treasures available to them in Christ. 9I was chosen to explain to everyone this mysterious plan that God, the Creator of all things, had kept secret from the beginning.

10God's purpose in all this was to use the church to display his wisdom in its rich variety to all the unseen rulers and authorities in the heavenly places. 11This was his eternal plan, which he carried out through Christ Jesus our Lord.

12Because of Christ and our faith in him, we can now come boldly and confidently into God's presence. 13So please don't lose heart because of my trials here. I am suffering for you, so you should feel honored.

Paul's Prayer for Spiritual Growth

14When I think of all this, I fall to my knees and pray to the Father, 15the Creator of everything in heaven and on earth. 16I pray that from his glorious, unlimited resources he will empower you with inner strength through his Spirit. 17Then Christ will make his home in your hearts as you trust in him. Your roots will grow down into God's love and keep you strong. 18And may you have the power to understand, as all God's people should, how wide, how long, how high, and how deep his love is. 19May you experience the love of Christ, though it is too great to understand fully. Then you will be made complete with all the fullness of life and power that comes from God.

20Now all glory to God, who is able, through his mighty power at work within us, to accomplish infinitely more than we might ask or think. 21Glory to him in the church and in Christ Jesus through all generations forever and ever! Amen.

CHAPTER **4**
Unity in the Body

Therefore I, a prisoner for serving the Lord, beg you to lead a life worthy of your calling, for you have been called by God. 2Always be humble and gentle. Be patient with each other, making allowance for each other's faults because of your love. 3Make every effort to keep yourselves united in the Spirit, binding yourselves together with peace. 4For there is one body and one Spirit, just as you have been called to one glorious hope for the future. 5There is one Lord, one faith, one baptism, 6and one God and Father, who is over all and in all and living through all.

7However, he has given each one of us a special gift through the generosity of Christ. 8That is why the Scriptures say,

"When he ascended to the heights,
he led a crowd of captives
and gave gifts to his people."

9Notice that it says "he ascended." This clearly means that Christ also descended to our lowly world. 10And the same one who descended is the one who ascended higher than all the heavens, so that he might fill the entire universe with himself.

11Now these are the gifts Christ gave to the church: the apostles, the prophets, the evangelists, and the pastors and teachers. 12Their responsibility is to equip God's people to do his work and build up the church, the body of Christ. 13This will continue until we all come to such unity in our faith and knowledge of God's Son that we will be mature in the Lord, measuring up to the full and complete standard of Christ.

14Then we will no longer be immature like children. We won't be tossed and blown about by every wind of new teaching. We will not be influenced when people try to trick us with lies so clever they sound like the truth. 15Instead, we will speak the truth in love, growing in every way more and more like Christ, who is the head of his body, the church. 16He makes the whole body fit together perfectly. As each part does its own special work, it helps the other parts grow, so that the whole body is healthy and growing and full of love.

Living as Children of Light

17With the Lord's authority I say this: Live no longer as the Gentiles do, for they are hopelessly confused. 18Their minds are full of darkness; they wander far from the life God gives because they have closed their minds and hardened their hearts against him. 19They have no sense of shame. They live for lustful pleasure and eagerly practice every kind of impurity.

20But that isn't what you learned about Christ. 21Since you have heard about Jesus and have learned the truth that comes from him, 22throw off your old sinful nature and your former way of life, which is corrupted by lust and deception.

23 Instead, let the Spirit renew your thoughts and attitudes. 24 Put on your new nature, created to be like God—truly righteous and holy.

25 So stop telling lies. Let us tell our neighbors the truth, for we are all parts of the same body. 26 And "don't sin by letting anger control you." Don't let the sun go down while you are still angry, 27 for anger gives a foothold to the devil.

28 If you are a thief, quit stealing. Instead, use your hands for good hard work, and then give generously to others in need. 29 Don't use foul or abusive language. Let everything you say be good and helpful, so that your words will be an encouragement to those who hear them.

30 And do not bring sorrow to God's Holy Spirit by the way you live. Remember, he has identified you as his own, guaranteeing that you will be saved on the day of redemption.

31 **Get rid of all bitterness, rage, anger, harsh words, and slander, as well as all types of evil behavior. 32 Instead, be kind to each other, tenderhearted, forgiving one another, just as God through Christ has forgiven you.**

CHAPTER **5**
Living in the Light
Imitate God, therefore, in everything you do, because you are his dear children. 2 Live a life filled with love, following the example of Christ. He loved us and offered himself as a sacrifice for us, a pleasing aroma to God.

3 Let there be no sexual immorality, impurity, or greed among you. Such sins have no place among God's people. 4 Obscene stories, foolish talk, and coarse jokes—these are not for you. Instead, let there be thankfulness to God. 5 You can be sure that no immoral, impure, or greedy person will inherit the Kingdom of Christ and God. For a greedy person is an idolater, worshiping the things of this world.

6 Don't be fooled by those who try to excuse these sins, for the anger of God will fall on all who disobey him. 7 Don't participate in the things these people do. 8 For once you were full of darkness, but now you have light from the Lord. So live as people of light! 9 For this light within you produces only what is good and right and true.

10 Carefully determine what pleases the Lord. 11 Take no part in the worthless deeds of evil and darkness; instead, expose them. 12 It is shameful even to talk about the things that ungodly people do in secret. 13 But their evil intentions will be exposed when the light shines on them, 14 for the

light makes everything visible. This is why it is said,

"Awake, O sleeper,
rise up from the dead,
and Christ will give you light."

Living by the Spirit's Power
15 So be careful how you live. Don't live like fools, but like those who are wise. 16 Make the most of every opportunity in these evil days. 17 Don't act thoughtlessly, but understand what the Lord wants you to do. 18 Don't be drunk with wine, because that will ruin your life. Instead, be filled with the Holy Spirit, 19 singing psalms and hymns and spiritual songs among yourselves, and making music to the Lord in your hearts. 20 And give thanks for everything to God the Father in the name of our Lord Jesus Christ.

Spirit-Guided Relationships: Wives and Husbands
21 And further, submit to one another out of reverence for Christ.

22 For wives, this means submit to your husbands as to the Lord. 23 For a husband is the head of his wife as Christ is the head of the church. He is the Savior of his body, the church. 24 As the church submits to Christ, so you wives should submit to your husbands in everything.

25 For husbands, this means love your wives, just as Christ loved the church. He gave up his life for her 26 to make her holy and clean, washed by the cleansing of God's word. 27 He did this to present her to himself as a glorious church without a spot or wrinkle or any other blemish. Instead, she will be holy and without fault. 28 In the same way, husbands ought to love their wives as they love their own bodies. For a man who loves his wife actually shows love for himself. 29 No one hates his own body but feeds and cares for it, just as Christ cares for the church. 30 And we are members of his body.

31 As the Scriptures say, "A man leaves his father and mother and is joined to his wife, and the two are united into one." 32 This is a great mystery, but it is an illustration of the way Christ and the church are one. 33 So again I say, each man must love his wife as he loves himself, and the wife must respect her husband.

CHAPTER **6**
Children and Parents
Children, obey your parents because you belong to the Lord, for this is the right thing to do.

Key Verse "Put on all of God's armor so that you will be able to stand firm against all strategies of the devil. For we are not fighting against flesh-and-blood enemies, but against evil rulers and authorities of the unseen world."— EPHESIANS 6:11-12a

Read EPHESIANS 6:11-12a out loud. Then read it again. God gives us spiritual armor to protect us and make us stronger. Cool!

STAND Firm!

MAKE SOME ARMOR OF YOUR OWN!

1. Cut a big poster-board circle shield.

2. Cover the front of the shield with aluminum foil.

3. Use a permanent marker to write words from EPHESIANS 6:11-12a on your shield.

4. Cut a chenille wire in half, and tape it as a "handle" to the back.

Keep your shield in your room to remind you that with God's armor, we can stand firm against the devil. **Read EPHESIANS 6:13-17 to learn more!**

SEE HOW MANY REMINDERS OF GOD'S ARMOR YOU CAN COME UP WITH.

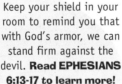

Write **"peace"** on a pair of shoelaces to remind you that you can put on the shoes of peace.

Read Philippians 4:13 to learn more about strength from God!

2"Honor your father and mother." This is the first commandment with a promise: 3If you honor your father and mother, "things will go well for you, and you will have a long life on the earth."

4Fathers, do not provoke your children to anger by the way you treat them. Rather, bring them up with the discipline and instruction that comes from the Lord.

Slaves and Masters

5Slaves, obey your earthly masters with deep respect and fear. Serve them sincerely as you would serve Christ. 6Try to please them all the time, not just when they are watching you. As slaves of Christ, do the will of God with all your heart. 7Work with enthusiasm, as though you were working for the Lord rather than for people. 8Remember that the Lord will reward each one of us for the good we do, whether we are slaves or free.

9Masters, treat your slaves in the same way. Don't threaten them; remember, you both have the same Master in heaven, and he has no favorites.

The Whole Armor of God

10A final word: Be strong in the Lord and in his mighty power. 11**Put on all of God's armor so that you will be able to stand firm against all strategies of the devil. 12For we are not fighting against flesh-and-blood enemies, but against evil rulers and authorities of the unseen world, against mighty powers in this dark world, and against evil spirits in the heavenly places.**

13Therefore, put on every piece of God's armor so you will be able to resist the enemy in the time of evil. Then after the battle you will still be standing firm. 14Stand your ground, putting on the belt of truth and the body armor of God's righteousness. 15For shoes, put on the peace that comes from the Good News so that you will be fully prepared. 16In addition to all of these, hold up the shield of faith to stop the fiery arrows of the devil. 17Put on salvation as your helmet, and take the sword of the Spirit, which is the word of God.

18Pray in the Spirit at all times and on every occasion. Stay alert and be persistent in your prayers for all believers everywhere.

19And pray for me, too. Ask God to give me the right words so I can boldly explain God's mysterious plan that the Good News is for Jews and Gentiles alike. 20I am in chains now, still preaching this message as God's ambassador. So pray that I will keep on speaking boldly for him, as I should.

Final Greetings

21 To bring you up to date, Tychicus will give you a full report about what I am doing and how I am getting along. He is a beloved brother and faithful helper in the Lord's work. 22 I have sent him to you for this very purpose—to let you know how we are doing and to encourage you.

23 Peace be with you, dear brothers and sisters, and may God the Father and the Lord Jesus Christ give you love with faithfulness. 24 May God's grace be eternally upon all who love our Lord Jesus Christ.

PHILIPPIANS A Joyful Letter

Look for **2** hidden messages in Philippians!

Philippians is the letter Paul wrote to the Christians in Philippi. It tells how to

- **GO FORWARD, EVEN WHEN YOU'RE TIRED**
- **HAVE PEACE, EVEN WHEN THINGS GO WRONG**
- **BE STRONG, EVEN WHEN YOU FEEL WEAK**
- **BE HAPPY, EVEN WHEN TIMES ARE TOUGH**

Dear Blabby

Q.: I'm worried I may fail math. I'm worried about my new school. I'm worried about everything! Please help. **A: Find out how to handle worry in Philippians 4:6.**

Amazing Feats

According to the Guinness World Records Web site, the longest time spent on a tightrope was 205 days! That's an amazing feat! But does it matter? You can do truly amazing things—things that matter and make a difference in people's lives. **Find out how by reading Philippians 4:13.**

The *Real* Hero

He's smarter than Einstein and stronger than Mr. Universe. Yet he was born in a lowly stable, and he lived a humble life. He's the Lord of lords, yet he lived on the earth as a man. **Who is it? Find out in Philippians 2:5-11!**

On Your Mark, Get Set, Go...and Go, and Keep Going!

Marathon runners may win a prize, or they might not. You're in a race, and your prize is way cooler than any ribbon. **Check out this special race in Philippians 3:13-14!**

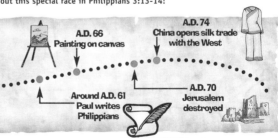

Timeline

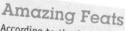

6/5 B.C. Jesus is born

A.D. 66 Painting on canvas

Around A.D. 61 Paul writes Philippians

A.D. 70 Jerusalem destroyed

A.D. 74 China opens silk trade with the West

The JESUS CONNECTION

You may already know that becoming a Christian doesn't make all of your problems go away. In fact, following Jesus can cause problems that you otherwise wouldn't have (like standing up for what's right). But God has given us everything we need to live for him. Jesus died on the cross for our sins so that, when we believe in him, we have a friendship with God that no one can take away! **No matter what happens, we can rejoice and praise God!**

CHAPTER **1**

Greetings from Paul

This letter is from Paul and Timothy, slaves of Christ Jesus.

I am writing to all of God's holy people in Philippi who belong to Christ Jesus, including the elders and deacons.

2May God our Father and the Lord Jesus Christ give you grace and peace.

Paul's Thanksgiving and Prayer

3Every time I think of you, I give thanks to my God. **4**Whenever I pray, I make my requests for all of you with joy, **5**for you have been my partners in spreading the Good News about Christ from the time you first heard it until now. **6**And I am certain that God, who began the good work within you, will continue his work until it is finally finished on the day when Christ Jesus returns.

7So it is right that I should feel as I do about all of you, for you have a special place in my heart. You share with me the special favor of God, both in my imprisonment and in defending and confirming the truth of the Good News. **8**God knows how much I love you and long for you with the tender compassion of Christ Jesus.

9I pray that your love will overflow more and more, and that you will keep on growing in knowledge and understanding. **10**For I want you to understand what really matters, so that you may live pure and blameless lives until the day of Christ's return. **11**May you always be filled with the fruit of your salvation—the righteous character produced in your life by Jesus Christ—for this will bring much glory and praise to God.

Paul's Joy That Christ Is Preached

12And I want you to know, my dear brothers and sisters, that everything that has happened to me here has helped to spread the Good News. **13**For everyone here, including the whole palace guard, knows that I am in chains because of Christ. **14**And because of my imprisonment, most of the believers here have gained confidence and boldly speak God's message without fear.

15It's true that some are preaching out of jealousy and rivalry. But others preach about Christ with pure motives. **16**They preach because they love me, for they know I have been appointed to defend the Good News. **17**Those others do not have pure motives as they preach about Christ. They preach with selfish ambition, not sincerely, intending to make my chains more painful to me. **18**But that doesn't matter. Whether their

motives are false or genuine, the message about Christ is being preached either way, so I rejoice. And I will continue to rejoice. **19**For I know that as you pray for me and the Spirit of Jesus Christ helps me, this will lead to my deliverance.

Paul's Life for Christ

20For I fully expect and hope that I will never be ashamed, but that I will continue to be bold for

Key Verse

"That at the name of Jesus every knee should bow, in heaven and on earth and under the earth, and every tongue confess that Jesus Christ is Lord, to the glory of God the Father."
—**PHILIPPIANS 2:10-11**

Move It!

Find a friend, and take turns reading PHILIPPIANS 2:10-11 out loud.

Then work together to make up motions to show the meaning of this verse.

HERE ARE A FEW IDEAS TO GET YOU STARTED.

Hug yourself when you say "Jesus" because Jesus loves us. **Drop to one knee** when you say "every knee should bow." **Wiggle your tongue** when you say "and every tongue confess."

ONCE YOU BOTH HAVE MADE UP MOTIONS, see if you can set this verse to music! Then put on a performance to teach the verse to someone else.

♪ WAY TO GO!

Christ, as I have been in the past. And I trust that my life will bring honor to Christ, whether I live or die. 21For to me, living means living for Christ, and dying is even better. 22But if I live, I can do more fruitful work for Christ. So I really don't know which is better. 23I'm torn between two desires: I long to go and be with Christ, which would be far better for me. 24But for your sakes, it is better that I continue to live.

25Knowing this, I am convinced that I will remain alive so I can continue to help all of you grow and experience the joy of your faith. 26And when I come to you again, you will have even more reason to take pride in Christ Jesus because of what he is doing through me.

Live as Citizens of Heaven

27Above all, you must live as citizens of heaven, conducting yourselves in a manner worthy of the Good News about Christ. Then, whether I come and see you again or only hear about you, I will know that you are standing together with one spirit and one purpose, fighting together for the faith, which is the Good News. 28Don't be intimidated in any way by your enemies. This will be a sign to them that they are going to be destroyed, but that you are going to be saved, even by God himself. 29For you have been given not only the privilege of trusting in Christ but also the privilege of suffering for him. 30We are in this struggle together. You have seen my struggle in the past, and you know that I am still in the midst of it.

CHAPTER **2**
Have the Attitude of Christ

Is there any encouragement from belonging to Christ? Any comfort from his love? Any fellowship together in the Spirit? Are your hearts tender and compassionate? 2Then make me truly happy by agreeing wholeheartedly with each other, loving one another, and working together with one mind and purpose.

3Don't be selfish; don't try to impress others. Be humble, thinking of others as better than yourselves. 4Don't look out only for your own interests, but take an interest in others, too.

5You must have the same attitude that Christ Jesus had.

6 Though he was God,
he did not think of equality with God
as something to cling to.
7 Instead, he gave up his divine privileges;
he took the humble position of a slave
and was born as a human being.

When he appeared in human form,
8   he humbled himself in obedience to God
and died a criminal's death on a cross.

9 Therefore, God elevated him to the place
of highest honor
and gave him the name above all
other names,
10**that at the name of Jesus every
knee should bow,
in heaven and on earth and
under the earth,**
11**and every tongue confess that
Jesus Christ is Lord,
to the glory of God the Father.**

Shine Brightly for Christ

12Dear friends, you always followed my instructions when I was with you. And now that I am away, it is even more important. Work hard to show the results of your salvation, obeying God with deep reverence and fear. 13For God is working in you, giving you the desire and the power to do what pleases him.

14Do everything without complaining and arguing, 15so that no one can criticize you. Live clean, innocent lives as children of God, shining like bright lights in a world full of crooked and perverse people. 16Hold firmly to the word of life; then, on the day of Christ's return, I will be proud that I did not run the race in vain and that my work was not useless. 17But I will rejoice even if I lose my life, pouring it out like a liquid offering to God, just like your faithful service is an offering to God. And I want all of you to share that joy. 18Yes, you should rejoice, and I will share your joy.

Paul Commends Timothy

19If the Lord Jesus is willing, I hope to send Timothy to you soon for a visit. Then he can cheer me up by telling me how you are getting along. 20I have no one else like Timothy, who genuinely cares about your welfare. 21All the others care only for themselves and not for what matters to Jesus Christ. 22But you know how Timothy has proved himself. Like a son with his father, he has served with me in preaching the Good News. 23I hope to send him to you just as soon as I find out what is going to happen to me here. 24And I have confidence from the Lord that I myself will come to see you soon.

Paul Commends Epaphroditus

25Meanwhile, I thought I should send Epaphroditus back to you. He is a true brother, co-worker, and fellow soldier. And he was your messenger to help me in my need. 26I am sending him because he has been longing to see you, and he was very distressed that you heard he was ill. 27And he certainly was ill; in fact, he almost died. But God had mercy on him—and also on me, so that I would not have one sorrow after another.

28So I am all the more anxious to send him back to you, for I know you will be glad to see him, and then I will not be so worried about you. 29Welcome him with Christian love and with great joy, and give him the honor that people like him deserve. 30For he risked his life for the work of Christ, and he was at the point of death while doing for me what you couldn't do from far away.

CHAPTER **3**
The Priceless Value of Knowing Christ

Whatever happens, my dear brothers and sisters, rejoice in the Lord. I never get tired of telling you these things, and I do it to safeguard your faith.

2Watch out for those dogs, those people who do evil, those mutilators who say you must be circumcised to be saved. 3For we who worship by the Spirit of God are the ones who are truly circumcised. We rely on what Christ Jesus has done for us. We put no confidence in human effort, 4though I could have confidence in my own effort if anyone could. Indeed, if others have reason for confidence in their own efforts, I have even more!

5I was circumcised when I was eight days old. I am a pure-blooded citizen of Israel and a member of the tribe of Benjamin—a real Hebrew if there ever was one! I was a member of the Pharisees, who demand the strictest obedience to the Jewish law. 6I was so zealous that I harshly persecuted the church. And as for righteousness, I obeyed the law without fault.

7I once thought these things were valuable, but now I consider them worthless because of what Christ has done. 8Yes, everything else is worthless when compared with the infinite value of knowing Christ Jesus my Lord. For his sake I have discarded everything else, counting it all as garbage, so that I could gain Christ 9and become one with him. I no longer count on my own righteousness through obeying the law; rather, I become righteous through faith in Christ. For God's way of making us right with himself depends on faith. 10I want to know Christ and experience the mighty power that raised him from the dead. I want to suffer with him, sharing in his death, 11so that one way or another I will experience the resurrection from the dead!

Pressing toward the Goal

12I don't mean to say that I have already achieved these things or that I have already reached perfection. But I press on to possess that perfection for which Christ Jesus first possessed me. 13No, dear brothers and sisters, I have not achieved it, but I focus on this one thing: Forgetting the past and looking forward to what lies ahead, 14I press on to reach the end of the race and receive the heavenly prize for which God, through Christ Jesus, is calling us.

15Let all who are spiritually mature agree on these things. If you disagree on some point, I believe God will make it plain to you. 16But we must hold on to the progress we have already made.

17Dear brothers and sisters, pattern your lives after mine, and learn from those who follow our example. 18For I have told you often before, and I say it again with tears in my eyes, that there are many whose conduct shows they are really enemies of the cross of Christ. 19They are headed for destruction. Their god is their appetite, they brag about shameful things, and they think only about this life here on earth. 20But we are citizens of heaven, where the Lord Jesus Christ lives. And we are eagerly waiting for him to return as our Savior. 21He will take our weak mortal bodies and change them into glorious bodies like his own, using the same power with which he will bring everything under his control.

CHAPTER **4**

Therefore, my dear brothers and sisters, stay true to the Lord. I love you and long to see you, dear friends, for you are my joy and the crown I receive for my work.

Words of Encouragement

2Now I appeal to Euodia and Syntyche. Please, because you belong to the Lord, settle your disagreement. 3And I ask you, my true partner, to help these two women, for they worked hard with me in telling others the Good News. They worked along with Clement and the rest of my co-workers, whose names are written in the Book of Life.

4Always be full of joy in the Lord. I say it again—rejoice! 5Let everyone see that you are considerate in all you do. Remember, the Lord is coming soon.

6Don't worry about anything; instead, pray about everything. Tell God what you need, and

Don't Worry, Be Happy

Got life? Then you've got worries! **Read PHILIPPIANS 4:6-7** to find a way to get rid of those worries!

When you pray instead of worrying, your worries will start to melt away. It's kind of like this!

LOOK OUT!
This is going to get messy!

You'll need:
- cornstarch
- water
- bowl
- spoon
- measuring spoons

1 Mix one heaping tablespoon of cornstarch with two teaspoons of water. (Hint: You may want to do this in the sink or over a piece of newspaper.)

2 Pick up the goo, and quickly move it around with your fingers.

3 Then set the goo ball in the center of your hand.

Want more reasons not to worry? Read Matthew 6:25-33!

Imagine that this goo is something you're worried about. The more we keep trying to "handle" our fears on our own, the more anxious we become. Now stop!

See how quickly your "worries" melt when you stop trying to "handle" your problems on your own?

COOL, HUH?

Think of one thing you're worried about today. Now pray—and quit worrying!

thank him for all he has done. 7 Then you will experience God's peace, which exceeds anything we can understand. His peace will guard your hearts and minds as you live in Christ Jesus.

8 And now, dear brothers and sisters, one final thing. Fix your thoughts on what is true, and honorable, and right, and pure, and lovely, and admirable. Think about things that are excellent and worthy of praise. 9 Keep putting into practice all you learned and received from me—everything you heard from me and saw me doing. Then the God of peace will be with you.

Paul's Thanks for Their Gifts

10 How I praise the Lord that you are concerned about me again. I know you have always been concerned for me, but you didn't have the chance to help me. 11 Not that I was ever in need, for I have learned how to be content with whatever I have. 12 I know how to live on almost nothing or with everything. I have learned the secret of living in every situation, whether it is with a full stomach or empty, with plenty or little. **13 For I can do everything through Christ, who gives me strength.** 14 Even so, you have done well to share with me in my present difficulty.

15 As you know, you Philippians were the only ones who gave me financial help when I first brought you the Good News and then traveled on from Macedonia. No other church did this. 16 Even when I was in Thessalonica you sent help more than once. 17 I don't say this because I want a gift from you. Rather, I want you to receive a reward for your kindness.

18 At the moment I have all I need—and more! I am generously supplied with the gifts you sent me with Epaphroditus. They are a sweet-smelling sacrifice that is acceptable and pleasing to God. 19 And this same God who takes care of me will supply all your needs from his glorious riches, which have been given to us in Christ Jesus.

20 Now all glory to God our Father forever and ever! Amen.

Paul's Final Greetings

21 Give my greetings to each of God's holy people—all who belong to Christ Jesus. The brothers who are with me send you their greetings. 22 And all the rest of God's people send you greetings, too, especially those in Caesar's household.

23 May the grace of the Lord Jesus Christ be with your spirit.

COLOSSIANS
Doing It God's Way

Look for **1** hidden message in Colossians!

Colossians is all about being connected to Jesus. It tells about
- **WHO JESUS REALLY IS**
- **WHAT JESUS REALLY DID**
- **WHERE SIN REALLY LEADS**
- **WHAT FOLLOWING JESUS REALLY MEANS**

Hidden Treasure

How would it feel to find a real treasure chest, break open the lock, and lift the lid? Guess what? There *is* a real treasure for you to find! **Read Colossians 2:2-3 to discover the treasure God has for you.**

Wanna Be a Star?

Wouldn't it be fun to be famous and sign autographs? As a Christian, you don't have to be in the spotlight. You're already being watched! **Find out who's watching in Colossians 4:5-6.**

Clear the Record

Imagine that you've committed a crime but the judge offers to take the punishment himself in your place. Would you take the offer? **Find God's offer for you in Colossians 2:13-15!**

Get Dressed!

Have you ever had a dream that you go to school still wearing your pajamas? Yikes! Better get dressed. **Read Colossians 3:14 to find out what clothes God wants you to wear.**

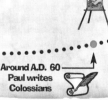

Timeline

6/5 B.C. Jesus is born

Around A.D. 60 Paul writes Colossians

A.D. 66 Painting on canvas

A.D. 70 Jerusalem destroyed

A.D. 74 China starts silk trade with the West

The JESUS CONNECTION

Being a Christian is all about having a relationship with God through Jesus. The whole point of Jesus' death and resurrection was so sinners could come to know God and live with him forever. You can't earn your way to heaven. And as long as you believe in Jesus, your sins don't ruin your relationship with God. We need to always try to do the right thing. But remember that being a Christian means being forgiven and accepted by God. **It's a gift, not something you can earn.**

CHAPTER **1**

Greetings from Paul

This letter is from Paul, chosen by the will of God to be an apostle of Christ Jesus, and from our brother Timothy.

2 We are writing to God's holy people in the city of Colosse, who are faithful brothers and sisters in Christ.

May God our Father give you grace and peace.

Paul's Thanksgiving and Prayer

3 We always pray for you, and we give thanks to God, the Father of our Lord Jesus Christ. 4 For we have heard of your faith in Christ Jesus and your love for all of God's people, 5 which come from your confident hope of what God has reserved for you in heaven. You have had this expectation ever since you first heard the truth of the Good News.

6 This same Good News that came to you is going out all over the world. It is bearing fruit everywhere by changing lives, just as it changed your lives from the day you first heard and understood the truth about God's wonderful grace.

7 You learned about the Good News from Epaphras, our beloved co-worker. He is Christ's faithful servant, and he is helping us on your behalf. 8 He has told us about the love for others that the Holy Spirit has given you.

9 So we have not stopped praying for you since we first heard about you. We ask God to give you complete knowledge of his will and to give you spiritual wisdom and understanding. 10 Then the way you live will always honor and please the Lord, and your lives will produce every kind of good fruit. All the while, you will grow as you learn to know God better and better.

11 We also pray that you will be strengthened with all his glorious power so you will have all the endurance and patience you need. May you be filled with joy, 12 always thanking the Father. He has enabled you to share in the inheritance that belongs to his people, who live in the light. 13 For he has rescued us from the kingdom of darkness and transferred us into the Kingdom of his dear Son, 14 who purchased our freedom and forgave our sins.

Christ Is Supreme

15 Christ is the visible image of the invisible God.
He existed before anything was created and is supreme over all creation,

16 for through him God created everything in the heavenly realms and on earth.
He made the things we can see and the things we can't see—
such as thrones, kingdoms, rulers, and authorities in the unseen world.
Everything was created through him and for him.
17 He existed before anything else, and he holds all creation together.
18 Christ is also the head of the church, which is his body.
He is the beginning, supreme over all who rise from the dead.
So he is first in everything.
19 For God in all his fullness was pleased to live in Christ,
20 and through him God reconciled everything to himself.
He made peace with everything in heaven and on earth
by means of Christ's blood on the cross.

21 This includes you who were once far away from God. You were his enemies, separated from him by your evil thoughts and actions. 22 Yet now he has reconciled you to himself through the death of Christ in his physical body. As a result, he has brought you into his own presence, and you are holy and blameless as you stand before him without a single fault.

23 But you must continue to believe this truth and stand firmly in it. Don't drift away from the assurance you received when you heard the Good News. The Good News has been preached all over the world, and I, Paul, have been appointed as God's servant to proclaim it.

Paul's Work for the Church

24 I am glad when I suffer for you in my body, for I am participating in the sufferings of Christ that continue for his body, the church. 25 God has given me the responsibility of serving his church by proclaiming his entire message to you. 26 This message was kept secret for centuries and generations past, but now it has been revealed to God's people. 27 For God wanted them to know that the riches and glory of Christ are for you Gentiles, too. And this is the secret: Christ lives in you. This gives you assurance of sharing his glory.

28 So we tell others about Christ, warning everyone and teaching everyone with all the wisdom God has given us. We want to present them to God, perfect in their relationship to Christ.

29That's why I work and struggle so hard, depending on Christ's mighty power that works within me.

CHAPTER **2**

I want you to know how much I have agonized for you and for the church at Laodicea, and for many other believers who have never met me personally. 2I want them to be encouraged and knit together by strong ties of love. I want them to have complete confidence that they understand God's mysterious plan, which is Christ himself. 3In him lie hidden all the treasures of wisdom and knowledge.

4I am telling you this so no one will deceive you with well-crafted arguments. 5For though I am far away from you, my heart is with you. And I rejoice that you are living as you should and that your faith in Christ is strong.

Freedom from Rules and New Life in Christ

6And now, just as you accepted Christ Jesus as your Lord, you must continue to follow him. 7Let your roots grow down into him, and let your lives be built on him. Then your faith will grow strong in the truth you were taught, and you will overflow with thankfulness.

8Don't let anyone capture you with empty philosophies and high-sounding nonsense that come from human thinking and from the spiritual powers of this world, rather than from Christ. 9For in Christ lives all the fullness of God in a human body. 10So you also are complete through your union with Christ, who is the head over every ruler and authority.

11When you came to Christ, you were "circumcised," but not by a physical procedure. Christ performed a spiritual circumcision—the cutting away of your sinful nature. 12For you were buried with Christ when you were baptized. And with him you were raised to new life because you trusted the mighty power of God, who raised Christ from the dead.

13You were dead because of your sins and because your sinful nature was not yet cut away. Then God made you alive with Christ, for he forgave all our sins. 14He canceled the record of the charges against us and took it away by nailing it to the cross. 15In this way, he disarmed the spiritual rulers and authorities. He shamed them publicly by his victory over them on the cross.

16So don't let anyone condemn you for what you eat or drink, or for not celebrating certain

"**Mirror, Mirror** on the wall, who represents Jesus to one and all?"

The answer? You!

When you believe in Jesus, you become his representative here on earth.

Read COLOSSIANS 3:17 for more on your mission!

Whatever you do or say, you can represent Jesus.

Make this mirror to remind you that people will be looking at you, so give a good impression of Jesus!

① Get an inexpensive pocket or hand mirror.

② Use colored permanent markers to write the words of COLOSSIANS 3:17 around the edge of the mirror.

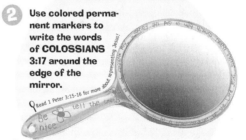

Read 1 Peter 3:15-16 for more about representing Jesus!

③ Decorate the handle or back of the mirror with words or pictures to remind you to represent Jesus in what you say and do!

holy days or new moon ceremonies or Sabbaths. 17For these rules are only shadows of the reality yet to come. And Christ himself is that reality. 18Don't let anyone condemn you by insisting on pious self-denial or the worship of angels, saying they have had visions about these things. Their sinful minds have made them proud, 19and they are not connected to Christ, the head of the body. For he holds the whole body together with its joints and ligaments, and it grows as God nourishes it.

20 You have died with Christ, and he has set you free from the spiritual powers of this world. So why do you keep on following the rules of the world, such as, 21 "Don't handle! Don't taste! Don't touch!"? 22 Such rules are mere human teachings about things that deteriorate as we use them. 23 These rules may seem wise because they require strong devotion, pious self-denial, and severe bodily discipline. But they provide no help in conquering a person's evil desires.

CHAPTER **3**
Living the New Life

Since you have been raised to new life with Christ, set your sights on the realities of heaven, where Christ sits in the place of honor at God's right hand. 2 Think about the things of heaven, not the things of earth. 3 For you died to this life, and your real life is hidden with Christ in God. 4 And when Christ, who is your life, is revealed to the whole world, you will share in all his glory.

5 So put to death the sinful, earthly things lurking within you. Have nothing to do with sexual immorality, impurity, lust, and evil desires. Don't be greedy, for a greedy person is an idolater, worshiping the things of this world. 6 Because of these sins, the anger of God is coming. 7 You used to do these things when your life was still part of this world. 8 But now is the time to get rid of anger, rage, malicious behavior, slander, and dirty language. 9 Don't lie to each other, for you have stripped off your old sinful nature and all its wicked deeds. 10 Put on your new nature, and be renewed as you learn to know your Creator and become like him. 11 In this new life, it doesn't matter if you are a Jew or a Gentile, circumcised or uncircumcised, barbaric, uncivilized, slave, or free. Christ is all that matters, and he lives in all of us.

12 Since God chose you to be the holy people he loves, you must clothe yourselves with tender-hearted mercy, kindness, humility, gentleness, and patience. 13 Make allowance for each other's faults, and forgive anyone who offends you. Remember, the Lord forgave you, so you must forgive others. 14 Above all, clothe yourselves with love, which binds us all together in perfect harmony. 15 And let the peace that comes from Christ rule in your hearts. For as members of one body you are called to live in peace. And always be thankful.

16 Let the message about Christ, in all its richness, fill your lives. Teach and counsel each other with all the wisdom he gives. Sing psalms and hymns and spiritual songs to God with thankful hearts. **17 And whatever you do or say, do it as a representative of the Lord Jesus, giving thanks through him to God the Father.**

Instructions for Christian Households

18 Wives, submit to your husbands, as is fitting for those who belong to the Lord.

19 Husbands, love your wives and never treat them harshly.

20 Children, always obey your parents, for this pleases the Lord. 21 Fathers, do not aggravate your children, or they will become discouraged.

22 Slaves, obey your earthly masters in everything you do. Try to please them all the time, not just when they are watching you. Serve them sincerely because of your reverent fear of the Lord. 23 Work willingly at whatever you do, as though you were working for the Lord rather than for people. 24 Remember that the Lord will give you an inheritance as your reward, and that the Master you are serving is Christ. 25 But if you do what is wrong, you will be paid back for the wrong you have done. For God has no favorites.

CHAPTER **4**

Masters, be just and fair to your slaves. Remember that you also have a Master—in heaven.

An Encouragement for Prayer

2 Devote yourselves to prayer with an alert mind and a thankful heart. 3 Pray for us, too, that God will give us many opportunities to speak about his mysterious plan concerning Christ. That is why I am here in chains. 4 Pray that I will proclaim this message as clearly as I should.

5 Live wisely among those who are not believers, and make the most of every opportunity. 6 Let your conversation be gracious and attractive so that you will have the right response for everyone.

Paul's Final Instructions and Greetings

7 Tychicus will give you a full report about how I am getting along. He is a beloved brother and faithful helper who serves with me in the Lord's work. 8 I have sent him to you for this very purpose—to let you know how we are doing and to encourage you. 9 I am also sending Onesimus, a faithful and beloved brother, one of your own people. He and Tychicus will tell you everything that's happening here.

10 Aristarchus, who is in prison with me, sends you his greetings, and so does Mark, Barnabas's cousin. As you were instructed before, make Mark welcome if he comes your way. 11 Jesus (the one we call Justus) also sends his greetings. These are the only Jewish believers among my co-workers; they are working with me here for the Kingdom of God. And what a comfort they have been!

12 Epaphras, a member of your own fellowship and a servant of Christ Jesus, sends you his greetings. He always prays earnestly for you, asking God to make you strong and perfect, fully confident that you are following the whole will of God. 13 I can assure you that he prays hard for you and also for the believers in Laodicea and Hierapolis.

14 Luke, the beloved doctor, sends his greetings, and so does Demas. 15 Please give my greetings to our brothers and sisters at Laodicea, and to Nympha and the church that meets in her house.

16 After you have read this letter, pass it on to the church at Laodicea so they can read it, too. And you should read the letter I wrote to them.

17 And say to Archippus, "Be sure to carry out the ministry the Lord gave you."

18 HERE IS MY GREETING IN MY OWN HANDWRITING—PAUL.

Remember my chains.

May God's grace be with you.

1 THESSALONIANS
Words of Comfort

Paul wrote a letter to the Christians in the young church he had founded in Thessalonica. That letter became this book in the Bible! Look for

- **A WARM WELCOME**
- **A REALLY GOOD REPORT**
- **A SURPRISE VISIT**
- **LESSONS FOR LIVING**

Hey, Quit Cryin'!

Funerals are sad in lots of ways. But there's something special about the funerals of believers. **Read all about it in 1 Thessalonians 4:13-18!**

Remember When...

Paul told some Christians to remember a cool thing that had happened to them. **Find out what it was in 1 Thessalonians 1:4-7.**

Life Lessons

How does God want you to live? Find out! **Read Paul's advice in 1 Thessalonians 5:12-22.**

How to live your life

"KNOCK!" "KNOCK!" "KNOCK!"

A Surprise Visit

There's a big day coming, and it might surprise you if you're not careful. **Read all about it in 1 Thessalonians 5:1-11.**

Timeline

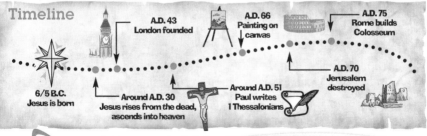

A.D. 43 London founded

A.D. 66 Painting on canvas

A.D. 75 Rome builds Colosseum

A.D. 70 Jerusalem destroyed

6/5 B.C. Jesus is born

Around A.D. 30 Jesus rises from the dead, ascends into heaven

Around A.D. 51 Paul writes 1 Thessalonians

The JESUS CONNECTION

Paul wrote to the Christians in Thessalonica to encourage them to remain strong in their faith in Jesus. He knew that it's not always easy to be a Christian—sometimes Christians are made fun of or even hurt for their beliefs. But Paul knew that believing in Jesus is the most important decision a person can ever make. **That fact was true for the Thessalonians, and it's still true for us today!**

Greetings from Paul

This letter is from Paul, Silas, and Timothy.

We are writing to the church in Thessalonica, to you who belong to God the Father and the Lord Jesus Christ.

May God give you grace and peace.

The Faith of the Thessalonian Believers

2 We always thank God for all of you and pray for you constantly. 3 As we pray to our God and Father about you, we think of your faithful work, your loving deeds, and the enduring hope you have because of our Lord Jesus Christ.

4 We know, dear brothers and sisters, that God loves you and has chosen you to be his own people. 5 For when we brought you the Good News, it was not only with words but also with power, for the Holy Spirit gave you full assurance that what we said was true. And you know of our concern for you from the way we lived when we were with you. 6 So you received the message with joy from the Holy Spirit in spite of the severe suffering it brought you. In this way, you imitated both us and the Lord. 7 As a result, you have become an example to all the believers in Greece—throughout both Macedonia and Achaia.

8 And now the word of the Lord is ringing out from you to people everywhere, even beyond Macedonia and Achaia, for wherever we go we find people telling us about your faith in God. We don't need to tell them about it, 9 for they keep talking about the wonderful welcome you gave us and how you turned away from idols to serve the living and true God. 10 And they speak of how you are looking forward to the coming of God's Son from heaven—Jesus, whom God raised from the dead. He is the one who has rescued us from the terrors of the coming judgment.

Paul Remembers His Visit

You yourselves know, dear brothers and sisters, that our visit to you was not a failure. 2 You know how badly we had been treated at Philippi just before we came to you and how much we suffered there. Yet our God gave us the courage to declare his Good News to you boldly, in spite of great opposition. 3 So you can see we were not preaching with any deceit or impure motives or trickery.

4 For we speak as messengers approved by God to be entrusted with the Good News. Our purpose is to please God, not people. He alone examines the motives of our hearts. 5 Never once did we try to win you with flattery, as you well know. And God is our witness that we were not pretending to be your friends just to get your money! 6 As for human praise, we have never sought it from you or anyone else.

7 As apostles of Christ we certainly had a right to make some demands of you, but instead we were like children among you. Or we were like a mother feeding and caring for her own children. 8 We loved you so much that we shared with you not only God's Good News but our own lives, too.

9 Don't you remember, dear brothers and sisters, how hard we worked among you? Night and day we toiled to earn a living so that we would not be a burden to any of you as we preached God's Good News to you. 10 You yourselves are our witnesses—and so is God—that we were devout and honest and faultless toward all of you believers. 11 And you know that we treated each of you as a father treats his own children. 12 We pleaded with you, encouraged you, and urged you to live your lives in a way that God would consider worthy. For he called you to share in his Kingdom and glory.

13 Therefore, we never stop thanking God that when you received his message from us, you didn't think of our words as mere human ideas. You accepted what we said as the very word of God—which, of course, it is. And this word continues to work in you who believe.

14 And then, dear brothers and sisters, you suffered persecution from your own countrymen. In this way, you imitated the believers in God's churches in Judea who, because of their belief in Christ Jesus, suffered from their own people, the Jews. 15 For some of the Jews killed the prophets, and some even killed the Lord Jesus. Now they have persecuted us, too. They fail to please God and work against all humanity 16 as they try to keep us from preaching the Good News of salvation to the Gentiles. By doing this, they continue to pile up their sins. But the anger of God has caught up with them at last.

Timothy's Good Report about the Church

17 Dear brothers and sisters, after we were separated from you for a little while (though our hearts never left you), we tried very hard to come back because of our intense longing to see you again. 18 We wanted very much to come to you, and I, Paul, tried again and again, but Satan prevented us. 19 After all, what gives us hope and joy,

and what will be our proud reward and crown as we stand before our Lord Jesus when he returns? It is you! ²⁰Yes, you are our pride and joy.

CHAPTER **3**

Finally, when we could stand it no longer, we decided to stay alone in Athens, ²and we sent Timothy to visit you. He is our brother and God's co-worker in proclaiming the Good News of Christ. We sent him to strengthen you, to encourage you in your faith, ³and to keep you from being shaken by the troubles you were going through. But you know that we are destined for such troubles. ⁴Even while we were with you, we warned you that troubles would soon come—and they did, as you well know. ⁵That is why, when I could bear it no longer, I sent Timothy to find out whether your faith was still strong. I was afraid that the tempter had gotten the best of you and that our work had been useless.

⁶But now Timothy has just returned, bringing us good news about your faith and love. He reports that you always remember our visit with joy and that you want to see us as much as we want to see you. ⁷So we have been greatly encouraged in the midst of our troubles and suffering, dear brothers and sisters, because you have remained strong in your faith. ⁸It gives us new life to know that you are standing firm in the Lord.

⁹How we thank God for you! Because of you we have great joy as we enter God's presence. ¹⁰Night and day we pray earnestly for you, asking God to let us see you again to fill the gaps in your faith.

¹¹May God our Father and our Lord Jesus bring us to you very soon. ¹²And may the Lord make your love for one another and for all people grow and overflow, just as our love for you overflows. ¹³May he, as a result, make your hearts strong, blameless, and holy as you stand before God our Father when our Lord Jesus comes again with all his holy people. Amen.

CHAPTER **4**
Live to Please God

Finally, dear brothers and sisters, we urge you in the name of the Lord Jesus to live in a way that pleases God, as we have taught you. You live this way already, and we encourage you to do so even more. ²For you remember what we taught you by the authority of the Lord Jesus.

³God's will is for you to be holy, so stay away from all sexual sin. ⁴Then each of you will control his own body and live in holiness and

FUN fact

The term *day of the Lord* is used in both the Old and New Testaments. It means the day Jesus will come back to earth to judge sin and set up his eternal kingdom.

No one knows exactly when that day will be. But we should be ready every day for Jesus to return! Are *you* ready?

If Jesus were to come back today, what would he find in your life?

Make a list of areas in your life that need work. Every day this week, pray about those areas, asking God to help you live so that you'll be ready for Jesus' return.

Update your list every month so your focus will stay on being ready!

honor—⁵not in lustful passion like the pagans who do not know God and his ways. ⁶Never harm or cheat a Christian brother in this matter by violating his wife, for the Lord avenges all such sins, as we have solemnly warned you before. ⁷God has called us to live holy lives, not impure lives. ⁸Therefore, anyone who refuses to live by these rules is not disobeying human teaching but is rejecting God, who gives his Holy Spirit to you.

⁹But we don't need to write to you about the importance of loving each other, for God himself has taught you to love one another. ¹⁰Indeed, you already show your love for all the believers throughout Macedonia. Even so, dear brothers and sisters, we urge you to love them even more.

¹¹Make it your goal to live a quiet life, minding your own business and working with your hands, just as we instructed you before. ¹²Then people who are not Christians will respect the way you live, and you will not need to depend on others.

The Hope of the Resurrection

13 And now, dear brothers and sisters, we want you to know what will happen to the believers who have died so you will not grieve like people who have no hope. 14 For since we believe that Jesus died and was raised to life again, we also believe that when Jesus returns, God will bring back with him the believers who have died.

15 We tell you this directly from the Lord: We who are still living when the Lord returns will not meet him ahead of those who have died. 16 For the Lord himself will come down from heaven with a commanding shout, with the voice of the archangel, and with the trumpet call of God. First, the Christians who have died will rise from their graves. 17 Then, together with them, we who are still alive and remain on the earth will be caught up in the clouds to meet the Lord in the air. Then we will be with the Lord forever. 18 So encourage each other with these words.

CHAPTER **5**

Now concerning how and when all this will happen, dear brothers and sisters, we don't really need to write you. 2 For you know quite well that the day of the Lord's return will come unexpectedly, like a thief in the night. 3 When people are saying, "Everything is peaceful and secure," then disaster will fall on them as suddenly as a pregnant woman's labor pains begin. And there will be no escape.

4 But you aren't in the dark about these things, dear brothers and sisters, and you won't be surprised when the day of the Lord comes like a thief. 5 For you are all children of the light and of the day; we don't belong to darkness and night. 6 So be on your guard, not asleep like the others. Stay alert and be clearheaded. 7 Night is the time when people sleep and drinkers get drunk. 8 But let us who live in the light be clearheaded, protected by the armor of faith and love, and wearing as our helmet the confidence of our salvation.

9 For God chose to save us through our Lord Jesus Christ, not to pour out his anger on us. 10 Christ died for us so that, whether we are dead or alive when he returns, we can live with him forever. 11 So encourage each other and build each other up, just as you are already doing.

Paul's Final Advice

12 Dear brothers and sisters, honor those who are your leaders in the Lord's work. They work hard among you and give you spiritual guidance. 13 Show them great respect and wholehearted love because of their work. And live peacefully with each other.

14 Brothers and sisters, we urge you to warn those who are lazy. Encourage those who are timid. Take tender care of those who are weak. Be patient with everyone.

15 See that no one pays back evil for evil, but always try to do good to each other and to all people.

16 Always be joyful. 17 Never stop praying. 18 Be thankful in all circumstances, for this is God's will for you who belong to Christ Jesus.

19 Do not stifle the Holy Spirit. 20 Do not scoff at prophecies, 21 but test everything that is said. Hold on to what is good. 22 Stay away from every kind of evil.

Paul's Final Greetings

23 Now may the God of peace make you holy in every way, and may your whole spirit and soul and body be kept blameless until our Lord Jesus Christ comes again. 24 God will make this happen, for he who calls you is faithful.

25 Dear brothers and sisters, pray for us.

26 Greet all the brothers and sisters with Christian love.

27 I command you in the name of the Lord to read this letter to all the brothers and sisters.

28 May the grace of our Lord Jesus Christ be with you.

2 THESSALONIANS A Call to Courage

Paul wrote a second letter to the Christians in Thessalonica. And *that* letter became *this* book in the Bible.

Look for

- **A PERSECUTION PROMISE**
- **TOUGH TALK ABOUT TIME**
- **A PLEA FOR PRAYER**
- **THE WISDOM OF WORK**

It's About Time

This. Then that. And this.

Paul said that certain events would take place before Jesus would come back to earth. **Read 2 Thessalonians 2:3-12 for the clues Paul gave.**

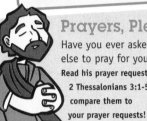

Prayers, Please

Have you ever asked someone else to pray for you? Paul did. **Read his prayer requests in 2 Thessalonians 3:1-5, and compare them to your prayer requests!**

Don't Be Fooled

Jesus is coming back! Really! But when? Some people were confused about when Jesus would return to earth, and *they* were confusing others. **Read how Paul set them straight in 2 Thessalonians 2:1-3.**

Get to Work!

Work? Me? Some Christians had it all wrong when it came to work. **Find out why in 2 Thessalonians 3:6-15.**

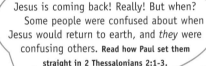

Timeline

A.D. 43 London founded	**A.D. 64** Fire burns much of Rome	**A.D. 66** Painting on canvas	**A.D. 75** Rome builds Colosseum

6/5 B.C. Jesus is born

Around A.D. 30 Jesus rises from the dead, ascends into heaven

Around A.D. 51 Paul writes 1 Thessalonians

Around A.D. 51 or 52 Paul writes 2 Thessalonians

The JESUS CONNECTION

As Christians, we know that Jesus will come back to earth some day. But we don't know exactly when that great day will be. The Christians in Thessalonica didn't know when Jesus would come back, either. Paul's advice to those Christians is good advice for us, too. **Don't listen to rumors; stand firm in your faith; pray for strength; tell others about Jesus; and live in a way that's pleasing to God.**

Greetings from Paul

This letter is from Paul, Silas, and Timothy.

We are writing to the church in Thessalonica, to you who belong to God our Father and the Lord Jesus Christ.

2 May God our Father and the Lord Jesus Christ give you grace and peace.

Encouragement during Persecution

3 Dear brothers and sisters, we can't help but thank God for you, because your faith is flourishing and your love for one another is growing. 4 We proudly tell God's other churches about your endurance and faithfulness in all the persecutions and hardships you are suffering. 5 And God will use this persecution to show his justice and to make you worthy of his Kingdom, for which you are suffering. 6 In his justice he will pay back those who persecute you.

7 And God will provide rest for you who are being persecuted and also for us when the Lord Jesus appears from heaven. He will come with his mighty angels, 8 in flaming fire, bringing judgment on those who don't know God and on those who refuse to obey the Good News of our Lord Jesus. 9 They will be punished with eternal destruction, forever separated from the Lord and from his glorious power. 10 When he comes on that day, he will receive glory from his holy people—praise from all who believe. And this includes you, for you believed what we told you about him.

11 So we keep on praying for you, asking our God to enable you to live a life worthy of his call. May he give you the power to accomplish all the good things your faith prompts you to do. 12 Then the name of our Lord Jesus will be honored because of the way you live, and you will be honored along with him. This is all made possible because of the grace of our God and Lord, Jesus Christ.

Events prior to the Lord's Second Coming

Now, dear brothers and sisters, let us clarify some things about the coming of our Lord Jesus Christ and how we will be gathered to meet him. 2 Don't be so easily shaken or alarmed by those who say that the day of the Lord has already begun. Don't believe them, even if they claim to have had a spiritual vision, a revelation, or a letter supposedly from us. 3 Don't be fooled by what they say. For that day will not come until there is a great rebellion against God and the man of lawlessness is revealed—the one who brings destruction. 4 He will exalt himself and defy everything that people call god and every object of worship. He will even sit in the temple of God, claiming that he himself is God.

5 Don't you remember that I told you about all this when I was with you? 6 And you know what is holding him back, for he can be revealed only when his time comes. 7 For this lawlessness is already at work secretly, and it will remain secret until the one who is holding it back steps out of the way. 8 Then the man of lawlessness will be revealed, but the Lord Jesus will kill him with the breath of his mouth and destroy him by the splendor of his coming.

9 This man will come to do the work of Satan with counterfeit power and signs and miracles. 10 He will use every kind of evil deception to fool those on their way to destruction, because they refuse to love and accept the truth that would save them. 11 So God will cause them to be greatly deceived, and they will believe these lies. 12 Then they will be condemned for enjoying evil rather than believing the truth.

Believers Should Stand Firm

13 As for us, we can't help but thank God for you, dear brothers and sisters loved by the Lord. We are always thankful that God chose you to be among the first to experience salvation—a salvation that came through the Spirit who makes you holy and through your belief in the truth. 14 He called you to salvation when we told you the Good News; now you can share in the glory of our Lord Jesus Christ.

15 With all these things in mind, dear brothers and sisters, stand firm and keep a strong grip on the teaching we passed on to you both in person and by letter.

16 Now may our Lord Jesus Christ himself and God our Father, who loved us and by his grace gave us eternal comfort and a wonderful hope, 17 comfort you and strengthen you in every good thing you do and say.

Paul's Request for Prayer

Finally, dear brothers and sisters, we ask you to pray for us. Pray that the Lord's message will spread rapidly and be honored wherever it goes, just as when it came to you. 2 Pray, too, that we will be rescued from wicked and evil people, for not everyone is a believer. 3 But the Lord is faithful; he will strengthen you and guard you from the evil one. 4And we are confident in the Lord that you are doing and will continue to do the things we commanded you. 5May the Lord lead your hearts into a full understanding and expression of the love of God and the patient endurance that comes from Christ.

An Exhortation to Proper Living

6And now, dear brothers and sisters, we give you this command in the name of our Lord Jesus Christ: Stay away from all believers who live idle lives and don't follow the tradition they received from us. 7For you know that you ought to imitate us. We were not idle when we were with you. 8We never accepted food from anyone without paying for it. We worked hard day and night so we would not be a burden to any of you. 9We certainly had the right to ask you to feed us, but we wanted to give you an example to follow. 10Even while we were with you, we gave you this command: "Those unwilling to work will not get to eat."

11Yet we hear that some of you are living idle lives, refusing to work and meddling in other people's business. 12We command such people and urge them in the name of the Lord Jesus Christ to settle down and work to earn their own living. 13As for the rest of you, dear brothers and sisters, never get tired of doing good.

14Take note of those who refuse to obey what we say in this letter. Stay away from them so they will be ashamed. 15Don't think of them as enemies, but warn them as you would a brother or sister.

Paul's Final Greetings

16Now may the Lord of peace himself give you his peace at all times and in every situation. The Lord be with you all.

17HERE IS MY GREETING IN MY OWN HAND-WRITING—PAUL. I DO THIS IN ALL MY LETTERS TO PROVE THEY ARE FROM ME.

18May the grace of our Lord Jesus Christ be with you all.

1 TiMoTHY A Letter to a Young Leader

Look for (**1**) hidden message in 1 Timothy!

Paul wrote a letter to his young friend Timothy, whom he had sent to lead the church in the city of Ephesus. Look for

- **CANDID CONFESSIONS**
- **GETTING RIGHT WITH GOD**
- **LEARNING TO LEAD**
- **MINDING YOUR MONEY**

True Confessions

Paul wasn't afraid to admit he had been wrong. In fact, the more he talked about it, the more thankful he was. Why? **Find out in 1 Timothy 1:12-17.**

BIBLE TIMES
I WAS WRONG!

Help Wanted

Think you have what it takes to be a leader? a church leader? Well, you'll have to meet certain standards. **Read 1 Timothy 3:1-13 to see what they are.**

One Way, OK?

GO GOD

There's only one way to get right with God, and Paul knew what it was. **You can discover it in 1 Timothy 2:1-6!**

True Riches?

News flash—money may be bad for your health! **Find out why in 1 Timothy 6:6-10.**

$ $ $ $ $

Timeline

A.D. 43 London founded

A.D. 66 Painting on canvas

A.D. 79 Mount Vesuvius erupts in Italy

6/5 B.C. Jesus is born

Around A.D. 30 Jesus rises from the dead, ascends into heaven

Around A.D. 51 Paul writes 1 Thessalonians

Around A.D. 64 Paul writes 1 Timothy

The **JESUS** CONNECTION

Paul told Timothy that, even though he was young, God could use Timothy in a big way. It doesn't matter how old you are or how long you've been a Christian—God has good works prepared for you to do. Take a lesson from Timothy. Listen to the advice of older, more experienced Christians; pray; and trust the Holy Spirit to help you. You can be an example and lead others to Jesus. **Who could ask for a better job?**

CHAPTER **1**

Greetings from Paul

This letter is from Paul, an apostle of Christ Jesus, appointed by the command of God our Savior and Christ Jesus, who gives us hope.

2I am writing to Timothy, my true son in the faith.

May God the Father and Christ Jesus our Lord give you grace, mercy, and peace.

Warnings against False Teachings

3When I left for Macedonia, I urged you to stay there in Ephesus and stop those whose teaching is contrary to the truth. 4Don't let them waste their time in endless discussion of myths and spiritual pedigrees. These things only lead to meaningless speculations, which don't help people live a life of faith in God.

5The purpose of my instruction is that all believers would be filled with love that comes from a pure heart, a clear conscience, and genuine faith. 6But some people have missed this whole point. They have turned away from these things and spend their time in meaningless discussions. 7They want to be known as teachers of the law of Moses, but they don't know what they are talking about, even though they speak so confidently.

8We know that the law is good when used correctly. 9For the law was not intended for people who do what is right. It is for people who are lawless and rebellious, who are ungodly and sinful, who consider nothing sacred and defile what is holy, who kill their father or mother or commit other murders. 10The law is for people who are sexually immoral, or who practice homosexuality, or are slave traders, liars, promise breakers, or who do anything else that contradicts the wholesome teaching 11that comes from the glorious Good News entrusted to me by our blessed God.

Paul's Gratitude for God's Mercy

12I thank Christ Jesus our Lord, who has given me strength to do his work. He considered me trustworthy and appointed me to serve him, 13even though I used to blaspheme the name of Christ. In my insolence, I persecuted his people. But God had mercy on me because I did it in ignorance and unbelief. 14Oh, how generous and gracious our Lord was! He filled me with the faith and love that come from Christ Jesus.

15This is a trustworthy saying, and everyone should accept it: "Christ Jesus came into the world to save sinners"—and I am the worst of them all. 16But God had mercy on me so that Christ Jesus could use me as a prime example of his great patience with even the worst sinners. Then others will realize that they, too, can believe in him and receive eternal life. 17All honor and glory to God forever and ever! He is the eternal King, the unseen one who never dies; he alone is God. Amen.

Timothy's Responsibility

18Timothy, my son, here are my instructions for you, based on the prophetic words spoken about you earlier. May they help you fight well in the Lord's battles. 19Cling to your faith in Christ, and keep your conscience clear. For some people have deliberately violated their consciences; as a result, their faith has been shipwrecked. 20Hymenaeus and Alexander are two examples. I threw them out and handed them over to Satan so they might learn not to blaspheme God.

CHAPTER **2**

Instructions about Worship

I urge you, first of all, to pray for all people. Ask God to help them; intercede on their behalf, and give thanks for them. 2Pray this way for kings and all who are in authority so that we can live peaceful and quiet lives marked by godliness and dignity. 3This is good and pleases God our Savior, 4who wants everyone to be saved and to understand the truth. **5For there is only one God and one Mediator who can reconcile God and humanity—the man Christ Jesus.** 6He gave his life to purchase freedom for everyone. This is the message God gave to the world at just the right time. 7And I have been chosen as a preacher and apostle to teach the Gentiles this message about faith and truth. I'm not exaggerating—just telling the truth.

8In every place of worship, I want men to pray with holy hands lifted up to God, free from anger and controversy.

9And I want women to be modest in their appearance. They should wear decent and appropriate clothing and not draw attention to themselves by the way they fix their hair or by wearing gold or pearls or expensive clothes. 10For women who claim to be devoted to God should make themselves attractive by the good things they do.

11Women should learn quietly and submissively. 12I do not let women teach men or have

Key Verse "For there is only one God and one Mediator who can reconcile God and humanity—the man Christ Jesus." —1 TIMOTHY 2:5

Need a Little Help?

Read 1 TIMOTHY 2:5 out loud a few times. Did you get stuck on some words?

First, there's *mediator*. A mediator is like a peacemaker. And to *reconcile* means to "make friendly again."

SINS	HOW TO GET RID OF SINS

On the left side of the chart, write three sins you've committed.

Now undo those sins. Can you? No way! But Jesus can! He's our mediator. When we believe in Jesus and tell God we're sorry for our sins, God forgives us, and it's like we never sinned.

Go back and write "Jesus" next to each sin in the chart. Then thank Jesus for being your mediator.

authority over them. Let them listen quietly. ¹³For God made Adam first, and afterward he made Eve. ¹⁴And it was not Adam who was deceived by Satan. The woman was deceived, and sin was the result. ¹⁵But women will be saved through childbearing, assuming they continue to live in faith, love, holiness, and modesty.

CHAPTER **3**
Leaders in the Church

This is a trustworthy saying: "If someone aspires to be an elder, he desires an honorable position." ²So an elder must be a man whose life is above reproach. He must be faithful to his wife. He must exercise self-control, live wisely, and have a good reputation. He must enjoy having guests in his home, and he must be able to teach. ³He must not be a heavy drinker or be violent. He must be gentle, not quarrelsome, and not love money. ⁴He must manage his own family well, having children who respect and obey him. ⁵For if a man cannot manage his own household, how can he take care of God's church?

⁶An elder must not be a new believer, because he might become proud, and the devil would cause him to fall. ⁷Also, people outside the church must speak well of him so that he will not be disgraced and fall into the devil's trap.

⁸In the same way, deacons must be well respected and have integrity. They must not be heavy drinkers or dishonest with money. ⁹They must be committed to the mystery of the faith now revealed and must live with a clear conscience. ¹⁰Before they are appointed as deacons, let them be closely examined. If they pass the test, then let them serve as deacons.

¹¹In the same way, their wives must be respected and must not slander others. They must exercise self-control and be faithful in everything they do.

¹²A deacon must be faithful to his wife, and he must manage his children and household well. ¹³Those who do well as deacons will be rewarded with respect from others and will have increased confidence in their faith in Christ Jesus.

The Truths of Our Faith

¹⁴I am writing these things to you now, even though I hope to be with you soon, ¹⁵so that if I

am delayed, you will know how people must conduct themselves in the household of God. This is the church of the living God, which is the pillar and foundation of the truth.

16 Without question, this is the great mystery of our faith:

Christ was revealed in a human body
and vindicated by the Spirit.
He was seen by angels
and announced to the nations.

Key Verse

"Don't let anyone think less of you because you are young. Be an example to all believers in what you say, in the way you live, in your love, your faith, and your purity." —1 TIMOTHY 4:12

GOOD Examples

Read 1 TIMOTHY 4:12 out loud to a friend. Then have your friend read it to you. Then read it together!

WOW! YOU CAN BE GREAT EXAMPLES!

Here's a way to get started.

Write **"speech," "life," "love," "faith,"** and **"purity"** on cards. Put the cards in a bag. With your friend, take turns picking a card and acting out a situation where you can be a good example of what's on the card.

Read more about being a good example in 2 Peter 1:10-11.

During the coming weeks, keep track of the ways you've been an example to others. **ASK GOD TO HELP YOU BE A GOOD EXAMPLE EVERY DAY!**

He was believed in throughout the world
and taken to heaven in glory.

CHAPTER **4**
Warnings against False Teachers

Now the Holy Spirit tells us clearly that in the last times some will turn away from the true faith; they will follow deceptive spirits and teachings that come from demons. 2 These people are hypocrites and liars, and their consciences are dead.

3 They will say it is wrong to be married and wrong to eat certain foods. But God created those foods to be eaten with thanks by faithful people who know the truth. 4 Since everything God created is good, we should not reject any of it but receive it with thanks. 5 For we know it is made acceptable by the word of God and prayer.

A Good Servant of Christ Jesus

6 If you explain these things to the brothers and sisters, Timothy, you will be a worthy servant of Christ Jesus, one who is nourished by the message of faith and the good teaching you have followed. 7 Do not waste time arguing over godless ideas and old wives' tales. Instead, train yourself to be godly. 8 "Physical training is good, but training for godliness is much better, promising benefits in this life and in the life to come." 9 This is a trustworthy saying, and everyone should accept it. 10 This is why we work hard and continue to struggle, for our hope is in the living God, who is the Savior of all people and particularly of all believers.

11 Teach these things and insist that everyone learn them. 12 **Don't let anyone think less of you because you are young. Be an example to all believers in what you say, in the way you live, in your love, your faith, and your purity.** 13 Until I get there, focus on reading the Scriptures to the church, encouraging the believers, and teaching them.

14 Do not neglect the spiritual gift you received through the prophecy spoken over you when the elders of the church laid their hands on you. 15 Give your complete attention to these matters. Throw yourself into your tasks so that everyone will see your progress. 16 Keep a close watch on how you live and on your teaching. Stay true to what is right for the sake of your own salvation and the salvation of those who hear you.

THE DISCIPLES' INNER CIRCLE *(former fishermen)*

Hi! Our names are Simon Peter, James, and John. Just so you don't get confused, I'm James. I'm writing this on behalf of the three of us. We're just simple fishermen. Well, that's what we were before we met Jesus! Since then we've been fishers-for-men. Jesus came by the lake where we were cleaning our fishing nets one day, and we dropped everything and followed him.

Want to know more about Jesus' calling of Peter, James, and John? Read the whole story in LUKE 5:1-11.

Peter was the most outspoken one among us and really became the leader of the whole batch. Peter made some bold statements, but he did his share of wrong things, just like the rest of us.

Speaking of mistakes, the one that John and I are most known for is based on our misunderstanding of how Jesus' kingdom was going to work. We thought he had come to earth to set up a new kingdom where he would rule right then and there, getting rid of all our enemies. Unfortunately, we acted on that mistaken notion and asked Jesus if we could be his right- and left-hand men! Not only was Jesus unhappy with us about that request, but so were the other disciples! Jesus made it clear that his kingdom was not going to be like that at all. He said if we wanted to be great, we had to be servants. Boy, that sure wasn't what we had in mind!

For one of Peter's bold and accurate statements, read MATTHEW 16:13-20. For one of his slightly misdirected bold statements, read MATTHEW 16:21-23.

Peter's biggest blunder was denying that he knew Jesus—not once, but three times—on the night Jesus was arrested. Jesus had predicted that Peter would deny him, but Peter never believed it would happen. When he realized what he had done, Peter was so sad and upset. But Jesus forgave him.

BLUNDERS OF YOUR OWN?

TURN THE PAGE TO FIND OUT MORE ABOUT THE REST OF THE DISCIPLES!

Do you know how to be forgiven?

Just believe in Jesus, admit the wrong things you've done, and ask for forgiveness.

Write on a slip of paper any sins you haven't asked forgiveness for. Then ask God to forgive you and to help you avoid those sins in the future. Then throw those sins in the wastebasket! **Why? Because you're forgiven! That's why.**

THE TWELVE (fishermen, tax collectors, regular guys)

We're "the Twelve," better known as Jesus' disciples or apostles.

Our lives were very different before Jesus called us to follow him. Some of us were commercial fishermen, and Matthew was a tax collector. We weren't a high-class bunch. Even Peter and John, who were kind of the leaders among us, were considered to be uneducated, ordinary men.

> You can find our names by reading MATTHEW 10:2-4; MARK 3:14-19; LUKE 6:13-16. (The lists are a little different. That's because some of us were known by two different names.)

One of our best-known but most-ashamed-of "feats" was how we deserted Jesus the night he was arrested. We had pretty much lived with Jesus for three years. We had heard him teach. We had seen him live a perfect, sinless life. We had seen him perform miracles. We had even heard him predict that he would die and then rise from the dead. But we still didn't get it.

And then Jesus rose from the dead. Even when we saw the empty tomb, we were confused; we *still* didn't get it. But Jesus didn't give up on us, even after that! He let us see that he was really alive, and then he forgave us. We were so excited about what had happened that we couldn't stop telling people about Jesus! And when the Holy Spirit came to us at Pentecost, God empowered us to spread the news about Jesus to many nations!

> What happened at Pentecost was really exciting! Read all about it in ACTS 2:1-47.

From that point on, we got it! So we spent the rest of our lives telling everyone we met about Jesus.

PRESSING ON

No, me!

I want to tell!

Do you ever find yourself embarrassed to be a Christian or afraid to speak up for your faith?
Read ACTS 4:1-31 and think about how you can stand up for Jesus in your life. Journal your thoughts and pray, asking God to help you be faithful to him. Then write a script of what you can tell others about Jesus. Practice your script with a friend, then commit to telling three other people about Jesus this week.
Then tell!

Oh, oh, me, me, me! Let me tell!!!

CHAPTER **5**
Advice about Widows, Elders, and Slaves

Never speak harshly to an older man, but appeal to him respectfully as you would to your own father. Talk to younger men as you would to your own brothers. 2Treat older women as you would your mother, and treat younger women with all purity as you would your own sisters.

3Take care of any widow who has no one else to care for her. 4But if she has children or grandchildren, their first responsibility is to show godliness at home and repay their parents by taking care of them. This is something that pleases God.

5Now a true widow, a woman who is truly alone in this world, has placed her hope in God. She prays night and day, asking God for his help. 6But the widow who lives only for pleasure is spiritually dead even while she lives. 7Give these instructions to the church so that no one will be open to criticism.

8But those who won't care for their relatives, especially those in their own household, have denied the true faith. Such people are worse than unbelievers.

9A widow who is put on the list for support must be a woman who is at least sixty years old and was faithful to her husband. 10She must be well respected by everyone because of the good she has done. Has she brought up her children well? Has she been kind to strangers and served other believers humbly? Has she helped those who are in trouble? Has she always been ready to do good?

11The younger widows should not be on the list, because their physical desires will overpower their devotion to Christ and they will want to remarry. 12Then they would be guilty of breaking their previous pledge. 13And if they are on the list, they will learn to be lazy and will spend their time gossiping from house to house, meddling in other people's business and talking about things they shouldn't. 14So I advise these younger widows to marry again, have children, and take care of their own homes. Then the enemy will not be able to say anything against them. 15For I am afraid that some of them have already gone astray and now follow Satan.

16If a woman who is a believer has relatives who are widows, she must take care of them and not put the responsibility on the church. Then the church can care for the widows who are truly alone.

17Elders who do their work well should be respected and paid well, especially those who work hard at both preaching and teaching. 18For the Scripture says, "You must not muzzle an ox to keep it from eating as it treads out the grain." And in another place, "Those who work deserve their pay!"

19Do not listen to an accusation against an elder unless it is confirmed by two or three witnesses. 20Those who sin should be reprimanded in front of the whole church; this will serve as a strong warning to others.

21I solemnly command you in the presence of God and Christ Jesus and the holy angels to obey these instructions without taking sides or showing favoritism to anyone.

22Never be in a hurry about appointing a church leader. Do not share in the sins of others. Keep yourself pure.

23Don't drink only water. You ought to drink a little wine for the sake of your stomach because you are sick so often.

24Remember, the sins of some people are obvious, leading them to certain judgment. But there are others whose sins will not be revealed until later. 25In the same way, the good deeds of some people are obvious. And the good deeds done in secret will someday come to light.

CHAPTER **6**

All slaves should show full respect for their masters so they will not bring shame on the name of God and his teaching. 2If the masters are believers, that is no excuse for being disrespectful. Those slaves should work all the harder because their efforts are helping other believers who are well loved.

False Teaching and True Riches

Teach these things, Timothy, and encourage everyone to obey them. 3Some people may contradict our teaching, but these are the wholesome teachings of the Lord Jesus Christ. These teachings promote a godly life. 4Anyone who teaches something different is arrogant and lacks understanding. Such a person has an unhealthy desire to quibble over the meaning of words. This stirs up arguments ending in jealousy, division, slander, and evil suspicions. 5These people always cause trouble. Their minds are corrupt, and they have turned their backs on the truth. To them, a show of godliness is just a way to become wealthy.

6Yet true godliness with contentment is itself great wealth. 7After all, we brought nothing with us when we came into the world, and we can't take anything with us when we leave it. [8]So if we have enough food and clothing, let us be content.

[9]But people who long to be rich fall into temptation and are trapped by many foolish and harmful desires that plunge them into ruin and destruction. [10]For the love of money is the root of all kinds of evil. And some people, craving money, have wandered from the true faith and pierced themselves with many sorrows.

Paul's Final Instructions

[11]But you, Timothy, are a man of God; so run from all these evil things. Pursue righteousness and a godly life, along with faith, love, perseverance, and gentleness. [12]Fight the good fight for the true faith. Hold tightly to the eternal life to which God has called you, which you have confessed so well before many witnesses. [13]And I charge you before God, who gives life to all, and before Christ Jesus, who gave a good testimony before Pontius Pilate, [14]that you obey this command without wavering. Then no one can find fault with you from now until our Lord Jesus Christ comes again. [15]For at just the right time Christ will be revealed from heaven by the blessed and only almighty God, the King of all kings and Lord of all lords. [16]He alone can never die, and he lives in light so brilliant that no human can approach him. No human eye has ever seen him, nor ever will. All honor and power to him forever! Amen.

[17]Teach those who are rich in this world not to be proud and not to trust in their money, which is so unreliable. Their trust should be in God, who richly gives us all we need for our enjoyment. [18]Tell them to use their money to do good. They should be rich in good works and generous to those in need, always being ready to share with others. [19]By doing this they will be storing up their treasure as a good foundation for the future so that they may experience true life.

[20]Timothy, guard what God has entrusted to you. Avoid godless, foolish discussions with those who oppose you with their so-called knowledge. [21]Some people have wandered from the faith by following such foolishness.

May God's grace be with you all.

2 TiMoTHY
Famous Last Words

Look for **1** hidden message in 2 Timothy!

Paul wrote his second letter to Timothy not long before he was put to death for his faith in Jesus. Look for

- **FLAMES OF FAITH**
- **A PURPOSEFUL PLAN**
- **USEFUL UTENSILS**
- **STEADFAST SCRIPTURE**

Fan the Flames

Was there a fire? You bet there was! Find out more in 2 Timothy 1:5-8.

Stand on Scripture

Times are bound to get tough. But if you believe in Jesus, God will see you through. You can count on it. Just read 2 Timothy 3:10-17!

Atten-*tion!*

Timothy was supposed to act like a soldier, but he wasn't in the army. He was supposed to act like an athlete, but he wasn't on a sports team. Huh? Read 2 Timothy 2:3-7 to clear things up!

Useful Utensils

Paul told Timothy he could be a fork. OK, not really. But he did say Timothy could be a utensil for God to use. Read all about it in 2 Timothy 2:20-21.

Timeline

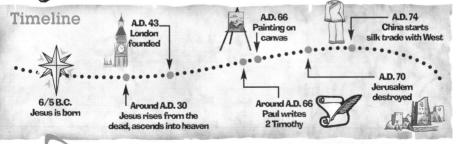

A.D. 43 London founded

A.D. 66 Painting on canvas

A.D. 74 China starts silk trade with West

6/5 B.C. Jesus is born

Around A.D. 30 Jesus rises from the dead, ascends into heaven

Around A.D. 66 Paul writes 2 Timothy

A.D. 70 Jerusalem destroyed

The JESUS CONNECTION

The book of 2 Timothy was the last letter Paul wrote before his death. He was alone in prison, writing to his young friend Timothy, who was a pastor of a church Paul had founded. He gave Timothy advice about standing firm in his faith, trusting the Bible, and telling others about Jesus. If you believe in Jesus, this letter is for you, too!

Greetings from Paul

This letter is from Paul, chosen by the will of God to be an apostle of Christ Jesus. I have been sent out to tell others about the life he has promised through faith in Christ Jesus.

²I am writing to Timothy, my dear son.

May God the Father and Christ Jesus our Lord give you grace, mercy, and peace.

Encouragement to Be Faithful

³Timothy, I thank God for you—the God I serve with a clear conscience, just as my ancestors did. Night and day I constantly remember you in my prayers. ⁴I long to see you again, for I remember your tears as we parted. And I will be filled with joy when we are together again.

⁵I remember your genuine faith, for you share the faith that first filled your grandmother Lois and your mother, Eunice. And I know that same faith continues strong in you. ⁶This is why I remind you to fan into flames the spiritual gift God gave you when I laid my hands on you. ⁷For God has not given us a spirit of fear and timidity, but of power, love, and self-discipline.

⁸So never be ashamed to tell others about our Lord. And don't be ashamed of me, either, even though I'm in prison for him. With the strength God gives you, be ready to suffer with me for the sake of the Good News. ⁹For God saved us and called us to live a holy life. He did this, not because we deserved it, but because that was his plan from before the beginning of time—to show us his grace through Christ Jesus. ¹⁰And now he has made all of this plain to us by the appearing of Christ Jesus, our Savior. He broke the power of death and illuminated the way to life and immortality through the Good News. ¹¹And God chose me to be a preacher, an apostle, and a teacher of this Good News.

¹²That is why I am suffering here in prison. But I am not ashamed of it, for I know the one in whom I trust, and I am sure that he is able to guard what I have entrusted to him until the day of his return.

¹³Hold on to the pattern of wholesome teaching you learned from me—a pattern shaped by the faith and love that you have in Christ Jesus. ¹⁴Through the power of the Holy Spirit who lives within us, carefully guard the precious truth that has been entrusted to you.

¹⁵As you know, everyone from the province of Asia has deserted me—even Phygelus and Hermogenes. ¹⁶May the Lord show special kindness to Onesiphorus and all his family because he often visited and encouraged me. He was never ashamed of me because I was in chains. ¹⁷When he came to Rome, he searched everywhere until he found me. ¹⁸May the Lord show him special kindness on the day of Christ's return. And you know very well how helpful he was in Ephesus.

A Good Soldier of Christ Jesus

Timothy, my dear son, be strong through the grace that God gives you in Christ Jesus. ²You have heard me teach things that have been confirmed by many reliable witnesses. Now teach these truths to other trustworthy people who will be able to pass them on to others.

³Endure suffering along with me, as a good soldier of Christ Jesus. ⁴Soldiers don't get tied up in the affairs of civilian life, for then they cannot please the officer who enlisted them. ⁵And athletes cannot win the prize unless they follow the rules. ⁶And hardworking farmers should be the first to enjoy the fruit of their labor. ⁷Think about what I am saying. The Lord will help you understand all these things.

⁸Always remember that Jesus Christ, a descendant of King David, was raised from the dead. This is the Good News I preach. ⁹And because I preach this Good News, I am suffering and have been chained like a criminal. But the word of God cannot be chained. ¹⁰So I am willing to endure anything if it will bring salvation and eternal glory in Christ Jesus to those God has chosen.

¹¹This is a trustworthy saying:

If we die with him,
we will also live with him.
¹² If we endure hardship,
we will reign with him.
If we deny him,
he will deny us.
¹³ **If we are unfaithful,
he remains faithful,
for he cannot deny who he is.**

¹⁴Remind everyone about these things, and command them in God's presence to stop fighting over words. Such arguments are useless, and they can ruin those who hear them.

An Approved Worker

¹⁵Work hard so you can present yourself to God and receive his approval. Be a good worker, one who does not need to be ashamed and who correctly explains the word of truth. ¹⁶Avoid

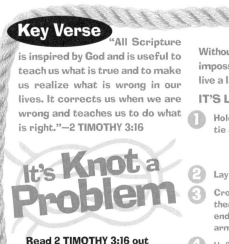

Key Verse

"All Scripture is inspired by God and is useful to teach us what is true and to make us realize what is wrong in our lives. It corrects us when we are wrong and teaches us to do what is right."—2 TIMOTHY 3:16

It's Knot a Problem

Read 2 TIMOTHY 3:16 out loud once or twice.

Then try writing the verse in your own words.

When you try to live your life without God's guidance, it seems impossible to make good decisions, just like it seems impossible to tie that knot. But the Bible teaches us to do what's right.

All Scripture points to one thing. Read what Jesus said in John 5:39!

You'll need a length of rope or clothesline. It should be at least a foot long.

Without God's Word, it's impossible to know how to live a life that pleases him.

IT'S LIKE THIS.

1. Hold one end of the rope in each hand, and tie a knot without letting go of the ends.

   Seems impossible, right? But there's a solution!

2. Lay the rope out straight on a table.

3. Cross your arms over your chest, then lean over and pick up the ends of the rope with your arms still crossed.

4. Unfold your arms.

THERE'S THE KNOT YOU WERE TRYING TO TIE!

How cool is that?

worthless, foolish talk that only leads to more godless behavior. ¹⁷This kind of talk spreads like cancer, as in the case of Hymenaeus and Philetus. ¹⁸They have left the path of truth, claiming that the resurrection of the dead has already occurred; in this way, they have turned some people away from the faith.

¹⁹But God's truth stands firm like a foundation stone with this inscription: "The LORD knows those who are his," and "All who belong to the LORD must turn away from evil."

²⁰In a wealthy home some utensils are made of gold and silver, and some are made of wood and clay. The expensive utensils are used for special occasions, and the cheap ones are for everyday use. ²¹If you keep yourself pure, you will be a special utensil for honorable use. Your life will be clean, and you will be ready for the Master to use you for every good work.

²²Run from anything that stimulates youthful lusts. Instead, pursue righteous living, faithfulness, love, and peace. Enjoy the companionship of those who call on the Lord with pure hearts.

²³Again I say, don't get involved in foolish, ignorant arguments that only start fights. ²⁴A servant of the Lord must not quarrel but must

be kind to everyone, be able to teach, and be patient with difficult people. ²⁵Gently instruct those who oppose the truth. Perhaps God will change those people's hearts, and they will learn the truth. ²⁶Then they will come to their senses and escape from the devil's trap. For they have been held captive by him to do whatever he wants.

CHAPTER 3

The Dangers of the Last Days

You should know this, Timothy, that in the last days there will be very difficult times. ²For people will love only themselves and their money. They will be boastful and proud, scoffing at God, disobedient to their parents, and ungrateful. They will consider nothing sacred. ³They will be unloving and unforgiving; they will slander others and have no self-control. They will be cruel and hate what is good. ⁴They will betray their friends, be reckless, be puffed up with pride, and love pleasure rather than God. ⁵They will act religious, but they will reject the power that could make them godly. Stay away from people like that!

⁶They are the kind who work their way into

people's homes and win the confidence of vulnerable women who are burdened with the guilt of sin and controlled by various desires. ⁷(Such women are forever following new teachings, but they are never able to understand the truth.) ⁸These teachers oppose the truth just as Jannes and Jambres opposed Moses. They have depraved minds and a counterfeit faith. ⁹But they won't get away with this for long. Someday everyone will recognize what fools they are, just as with Jannes and Jambres.

Paul's Charge to Timothy

¹⁰But you, Timothy, certainly know what I teach, and how I live, and what my purpose in life is. You know my faith, my patience, my love, and my endurance. ¹¹You know how much persecution and suffering I have endured. You know all about how I was persecuted in Antioch, Iconium, and Lystra—but the Lord rescued me from all of it. ¹²Yes, and everyone who wants to live a godly life in Christ Jesus will suffer persecution. ¹³But evil people and impostors will flourish. They will deceive others and will themselves be deceived.

¹⁴But you must remain faithful to the things you have been taught. You know they are true, for you know you can trust those who taught you. ¹⁵You have been taught the holy Scriptures from childhood, and they have given you the wisdom to receive the salvation that comes by trusting in Christ Jesus. **¹⁶All Scripture is inspired by God and is useful to teach us what is true and to make us realize what is wrong in our lives. It corrects us when we are wrong and teaches us to do what is right. ¹⁷God uses it to prepare and equip his people to do every good work.**

CHAPTER **4**

I solemnly urge you in the presence of God and Christ Jesus, who will someday judge the living and the dead when he appears to set up his Kingdom: ²Preach the word of God. Be prepared, whether the time is favorable or not. Patiently correct, rebuke, and encourage your people with good teaching.

³For a time is coming when people will no longer listen to sound and wholesome teaching. They will follow their own desires and will look for teachers who will tell them whatever their itching ears want to hear. ⁴They will reject the truth and chase after myths.

⁵But you should keep a clear mind in every situation. Don't be afraid of suffering for the Lord. Work at telling others the Good News, and fully carry out the ministry God has given you.

⁶As for me, my life has already been poured out as an offering to God. The time of my death is near. ⁷I have fought the good fight, I have finished the race, and I have remained faithful. ⁸And now the prize awaits me—the crown of righteousness, which the Lord, the righteous Judge, will give me on the day of his return. And the prize is not just for me but for all who eagerly look forward to his appearing.

Paul's Final Words

⁹Timothy, please come as soon as you can. ¹⁰Demas has deserted me because he loves the things of this life and has gone to Thessalonica. Crescens has gone to Galatia, and Titus has gone to Dalmatia. ¹¹Only Luke is with me. Bring Mark with you when you come, for he will be helpful to me in my ministry. ¹²I sent Tychicus to Ephesus. ¹³When you come, be sure to bring the coat I left with Carpus at Troas. Also bring my books, and especially my papers.

¹⁴Alexander the coppersmith did me much harm, but the Lord will judge him for what he has done. ¹⁵Be careful of him, for he fought against everything we said.

¹⁶The first time I was brought before the judge, no one came with me. Everyone abandoned me. May it not be counted against them. ¹⁷But the Lord stood with me and gave me strength so that I might preach the Good News in its entirety for all the Gentiles to hear. And he rescued me from certain death. ¹⁸Yes, and the Lord will deliver me from every evil attack and will bring me safely into his heavenly Kingdom. All glory to God forever and ever! Amen.

Paul's Final Greetings

¹⁹Give my greetings to Priscilla and Aquila and those living in the household of Onesiphorus. ²⁰Erastus stayed at Corinth, and I left Trophimus sick at Miletus.

²¹Do your best to get here before winter. Eubulus sends you greetings, and so do Pudens, Linus, Claudia, and all the brothers and sisters.

²²May the Lord be with your spirit. And may his grace be with all of you.

TiTUS How to Live Right

Look for **1** hidden message in Titus!

The book of Titus is a letter from Paul to a Gentile leader of the church named Titus. It tells about

- **THE GOOD LIFE**
- **GOOD LEADERS**
- **GOOD TEACHING**
- **AND DOING GOOD**

And the Winner Is...

The World Series. The Super Bowl. The Stanley Cup. Athletes who win those awards work hard to be the best.

But did you know there's an award you can receive that doesn't depend on you? **Check out Titus 3:5-6 to learn about God's amazing award!**

Instruction Manual

It really does matter how you live. **Find out why in Titus 2:1-8.**

CHURCH LEADER REQUIREMENTS

It's a Tough Job, But...

According to Paul, there are certain things a church leader should be—*and* shouldn't be. **Get the complete job description in Titus 1:5-9.**

It's a Jungle Out There

Have you ever been to camp? It can be hard to be away from home—in strange surroundings, with different people.

It's kind of like that for us as Christians. **Learn more in Titus 2:11-13.**

Timeline

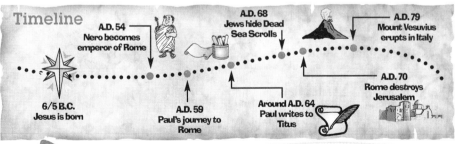

- **6/5 B.C.** Jesus is born
- **A.D. 54** Nero becomes emperor of Rome
- **A.D. 59** Paul's journey to Rome
- **Around A.D. 64** Paul writes to Titus
- **A.D. 68** Jews hide Dead Sea Scrolls
- **A.D. 70** Rome destroys Jerusalem
- **A.D. 79** Mount Vesuvius erupts in Italy

The JESUS CONNECTION

The world needs Jesus. And the people out there are going to have a tough time finding Jesus if his church is a big mess. If you're a Christian, the way you live and act affects what people think about Christianity. The Bible never tells us to be fake or judgmental. It does tell us to do the right thing so our behavior won't get in the way of others who are seeking Jesus. God wants to save *all* people because of his mercy, and he doesn't want our bad behavior getting in the way.

Titus 1 . . .

CHAPTER **1**

Greetings from Paul

This letter is from Paul, a slave of God and an apostle of Jesus Christ. I have been sent to proclaim faith to those God has chosen and to teach them to know the truth that shows them how to live godly lives. ²This truth gives them confidence that they have eternal life, which God—who does not lie—promised them before the world began. ³And now at just the right time he has revealed this message, which we announce to everyone. It is by the command of God our Savior that I have been entrusted with this work for him.

⁴I am writing to Titus, my true son in the faith that we share.

May God the Father and Christ Jesus our Savior give you grace and peace.

Titus's Work in Crete

⁵I left you on the island of Crete so you could complete our work there and appoint elders in each town as I instructed you. ⁶An elder must live a blameless life. He must be faithful to his wife, and his children must be believers who don't have a reputation for being wild or rebellious. ⁷For an elder must live a blameless life. He must not be arrogant or quick-tempered; he must not be a heavy drinker, violent, or dishonest with money.

⁸Rather, he must enjoy having guests in his home, and he must love what is good. He must live wisely and be just. He must live a devout and disciplined life. ⁹He must have a strong belief in the trustworthy message he was taught; then he will be able to encourage others with wholesome teaching and show those who oppose it where they are wrong.

¹⁰For there are many rebellious people who engage in useless talk and deceive others. This is especially true of those who insist on circumcision for salvation. ¹¹They must be silenced, because they are turning whole families away from the truth by their false teaching. And they do it only for money. ¹²Even one of their own men, a prophet from Crete, has said about them, "The people of Crete are all liars, cruel animals, and lazy gluttons." ¹³This is true. So reprimand them sternly to make them strong in the faith. ¹⁴They must stop listening to Jewish myths and the commands of people who have turned away from the truth.

¹⁵Everything is pure to those whose hearts are pure. But nothing is pure to those who are corrupt and unbelieving, because their minds

Key Verse "He saved us, not because of the righteous things we had done, but because of his mercy." —TITUS 3:5a

Read Titus 3:5a out loud. (The "a" means the first sentence in the verse.)

JESUS is like a life preserver because he saves us from drowning in sin.

AWESOME! God sent his Son, Jesus, to save us.

When someone is drowning, what does that person need? A life preserver!

Make this!

You'll need a rectangle of light-colored cloth (about 4x12 inches), a permanent marker, quilt batting or tissues, and colorful electrical tape.

1 Lay your fabric on a table, good side down. Place batting or tissues all along the center of the rectangle.

2 Roll the fabric around the batting and tape it into a long "snake."

3 Tape the ends together to form a life preserver.

4 Write the words of the verse around your life preserver.

Keep your life preserver to remind you that salvation is a free gift when you believe in Jesus!

FUN-fact

Be a TITUS Too!

Titus was leading the church on an island called Crete. It's a large island (3,190 square miles) in the Mediterranean Sea, and it was a Roman province at the time. Paul said that one of Crete's own prophets called the people there **"liars, cruel animals, and lazy gluttons."** A fun place? **NOT!** But that's where God called Titus to tell others about Jesus.

God doesn't want *you* to be lazy.

Write the name of someone you can tell about Jesus. Commit to telling that person about your faith this week. After you do, write the date below.

_____

WHO did you tell about Jesus?

_____

WHEN did you tell this person?

---

and consciences are corrupted. ¹⁶Such people claim they know God, but they deny him by the way they live. They are detestable and disobedient, worthless for doing anything good.

CHAPTER 2
Promote Right Teaching

As for you, Titus, promote the kind of living that reflects wholesome teaching. ²Teach the older men to exercise self-control, to be worthy of respect, and to live wisely. They must have sound faith and be filled with love and patience.

³Similarly, teach the older women to live in a way that honors God. They must not slander others or be heavy drinkers. Instead, they should teach others what is good. ⁴These older women must train the younger women to love their husbands and their children, ⁵to live wisely and be pure, to work in their homes, to do good, and to be submissive to their husbands. Then they will not bring shame on the word of God.

⁶In the same way, encourage the young men to live wisely. ⁷And you yourself must be an example to them by doing good works of every kind. Let everything you do reflect the integrity and seriousness of your teaching. ⁸Teach the truth so that your teaching can't be criticized. Then those who oppose us will be ashamed and have nothing bad to say about us.

⁹Slaves must always obey their masters and do their best to please them. They must not talk back ¹⁰or steal, but must show themselves to be entirely trustworthy and good. Then they will make the teaching about God our Savior attractive in every way.

¹¹For the grace of God has been revealed, bringing salvation to all people. ¹²And we are instructed to turn from godless living and sinful pleasures. We should live in this evil world with wisdom, righteousness, and devotion to God, ¹³while we look forward with hope to that wonderful day when the glory of our great God and Savior, Jesus Christ, will be revealed. ¹⁴He gave his life to free us from every kind of sin, to cleanse us, and to make us his very own people, totally committed to doing good deeds.

¹⁵You must teach these things and encourage the believers to do them. You have the authority to correct them when necessary, so don't let anyone disregard what you say.

CHAPTER 3
Do What Is Good

Remind the believers to submit to the government and its officers. They should be obedient, always ready to do what is good. ²They must not slander anyone and must avoid quarreling. Instead, they should be gentle and show true humility to everyone.

³Once we, too, were foolish and disobedient. We were misled and became slaves to many lusts and pleasures. Our lives were full of evil and envy, and we hated each other.

⁴But—"When God our Savior revealed his kindness and love, **⁵he saved us, not because of the righteous things we had done, but because of his mercy.** He washed away our sins, giving us a new birth and new life through the Holy Spirit. ⁶He generously poured out the Spirit upon us through Jesus Christ our Savior. ⁷Because of his grace he declared us righteous and gave us confidence that we will inherit eternal life." ⁸This is a trustworthy saying, and I want you to insist on these teachings so that all who trust in God will devote themselves to doing good. These teachings are good and beneficial for everyone.

⁹Do not get involved in foolish discussions about spiritual pedigrees or in quarrels and fights about obedience to Jewish laws. These things are useless and a waste of time. ¹⁰If people are causing divisions among you, give a first and second warning. After that, have nothing more to do with them. ¹¹For people like that have turned away from the truth, and their own sins condemn them.

Paul's Final Remarks and Greetings

¹²I am planning to send either Artemas or Tychicus to you. As soon as one of them arrives, do your best to meet me at Nicopolis, for I have decided to stay there for the winter. ¹³Do everything you can to help Zenas the lawyer and Apollos with their trip. See that they are given everything they need. ¹⁴Our people must learn to do good by meeting the urgent needs of others; then they will not be unproductive.

¹⁵Everybody here sends greetings. Please give my greetings to the believers—all who love us.

May God's grace be with you all.

PHiLEMON

Faith and Forgiveness

The book of Philemon is a letter Paul wrote to his friend Philemon. Look for

- **SOME FRIENDLY ADVICE**
- **A FRIEND IN NEED**
- **FAITH AND FRIENDSHIP**
- **FRIENDLY FORGIVENESS**

Many Thanks

There are probably many people and things in your life that you could say thank you for. Have you? **Look at Philemon 1:4-6 to see Paul's own personal thank-you words to a friend.**

S-o-o-o Refreshing

There are all sorts of ways we refresh ourselves. But what if your heart needs refreshing? **Read Philemon 1:7 to find one thing that can refresh our hearts.**

Dear Blabby

Q: Onesimus was my slave. I think he stole some stuff from me, then ran away. Well, he's on his way back, and I'm not sure what to do. My friend Paul sent me a letter asking me to...well, read it yourself. **A: It's in Philemon 1:8-19.**

Timeline

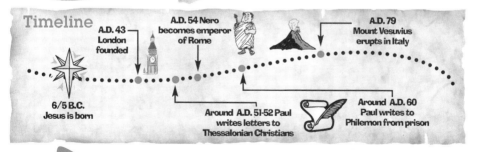

- **6/5 B.C.** Jesus is born
- **A.D. 43** London founded
- **A.D. 54 Nero** becomes emperor of Rome
- Around A.D. 51-52 Paul writes letters to Thessalonian Christians
- **A.D. 79** Mount Vesuvius erupts in Italy
- Around A.D. 60 Paul writes to Philemon from prison

The JESUS CONNECTION

Onesimus was a slave who ran away from his owner, Philemon. The laws of that day said that Onesimus could be killed for running away. But Paul asked Philemon to show forgiveness to Onesimus and love him like a brother. We're all kind of like Onesimus. Without Jesus, we're slaves to our sin and we deserve death away from God. **But if we believe in Jesus, he sets us free from our sin and welcomes us into God's family!**

Philemon · · ·

Greetings from Paul

This letter is from Paul, a prisoner for preaching the Good News about Christ Jesus, and from our brother Timothy.

I am writing to Philemon, our beloved co-worker, [2] and to our sister Apphia, and to our fellow soldier Archippus, and to the church that meets in your house.

[3] May God our Father and the Lord Jesus Christ give you grace and peace.

Paul's Thanksgiving and Prayer

[4] I always thank my God when I pray for you, Philemon, [5] because I keep hearing about your faith in the Lord Jesus and your love for all of God's people. [6] And I am praying that you will put into action the generosity that comes from your faith as you understand and experience all the good things we have in Christ. [7] Your love has given me much joy and comfort, my brother, for your kindness has often refreshed the hearts of God's people.

Paul's Appeal for Onesimus

[8] That is why I am boldly asking a favor of you. I could demand it in the name of Christ because it is the right thing for you to do. [9] But because of our love, I prefer simply to ask you. Consider this as a request from me—Paul, an old man and now also a prisoner for the sake of Christ Jesus.

[10] I appeal to you to show kindness to my child, Onesimus. I became his father in the faith while here in prison. [11] Onesimus hasn't been of much use to you in the past, but now he is very useful to both of us. [12] I am sending him back to you, and with him comes my own heart.

[13] I wanted to keep him here with me while I am in these chains for preaching the Good News, and he would have helped me on your behalf. [14] But I didn't want to do anything without your consent. I wanted you to help because you were willing, not because you were forced. [15] It seems you lost Onesimus for a little while so that you could have him back forever. [16] He is no longer like a slave to you. He is more than a slave, for he is a beloved brother, especially to me. Now he will mean much more to you, both as a man and as a brother in the Lord.

[17] So if you consider me your partner, welcome him as you would welcome me. [18] If he has wronged you in any way or owes you anything, charge it to me. [19] I, PAUL, WRITE THIS WITH MY OWN HAND: I WILL REPAY IT. AND I WON'T MENTION THAT YOU OWE ME YOUR VERY SOUL!

[20] Yes, my brother, please do me this favor for the Lord's sake. Give me this encouragement in Christ.

[21] I am confident as I write this letter that you will do what I ask and even more! [22] One more thing—please prepare a guest room for me, for I am hoping that God will answer your prayers and let me return to you soon.

Paul's Final Greetings

[23] Epaphras, my fellow prisoner in Christ Jesus, sends you his greetings. [24] So do Mark, Aristarchus, Demas, and Luke, my co-workers.

[25] May the grace of the Lord Jesus Christ be with your spirit.

HEBREWS
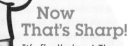
All About Jesus

Look for ①1 hidden message in Hebrews!

Hebrews tells how Jesus fulfills the Old Testament. It tells about
- **JESUS THE MESSIAH**
- **JESUS THE SON OF GOD**
- **JESUS THE SACRIFICE**
- **JESUS THE GREAT PRIEST**

Now That's Sharp!

It's finally here! The new Bible Blade, the sharpest knife in the drawer. It dices! It slices! It cuts to the heart of the matter—our relationship with God! **Learn more about this amazingly sharp blade in Hebrews 4:12.**

Guess Who's Coming to Dinner?

The people you meet aren't always what they seem. **Find out more about this mystery in Hebrews 13:2!**

Anchors Away!

Some of the largest ships in the world are held by anchors that weigh more than four tons! Even in the roughest water, that anchor can keep a huge ship from drifting away. **Read Hebrews 6:16-19 to discover how God is our anchor!**

Definite Definition

You can look up the word *faith* in the dictionary, but you'll never find *this* kind of definition! **Read God's definition of *faith* in Hebrews 11:1.**

Timeline

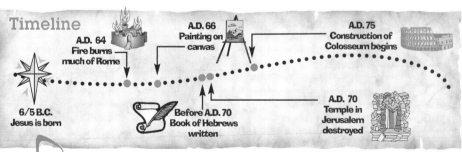

A.D. 64 Fire burns much of Rome

A.D. 66 Painting on canvas

A.D. 75 Construction of Colosseum begins

6/5 B.C. Jesus is born

Before A.D. 70 Book of Hebrews written

A.D. 70 Temple in Jerusalem destroyed

The JESUS CONNECTION

When Jesus came, he didn't throw out the Old Testament or the Jewish religion. Instead, he fulfilled it, or made it complete. Judaism (the religion of the Israelites) and all of the Old Testament point to Jesus. The book of Hebrews shows how Jesus is the promised Messiah who came to sacrifice himself for our sin. Jesus came to earth for you. **And you can live forever in heaven if you put your faith in Jesus.**

Jesus Christ Is God's Son

Long ago God spoke many times and in many ways to our ancestors through the prophets. ²And now in these final days, he has spoken to us through his Son. God promised everything to the Son as an inheritance, and through the Son he created the universe. ³The Son radiates God's own glory and expresses the very character of God, and he sustains everything by the mighty power of his command. When he had cleansed us from our sins, he sat down in the place of honor at the right hand of the majestic God in heaven. ⁴This shows that the Son is far greater than the angels, just as the name God gave him is greater than their names.

The Son Is Greater Than the Angels

⁵For God never said to any angel what he said to Jesus:

"You are my Son.
Today I have become your Father."

God also said,

"I will be his Father,
and he will be my Son."

⁶And when he brought his firstborn Son into the world, God said,

"Let all of God's angels worship him."

⁷Regarding the angels, he says,

"He sends his angels like the winds,
his servants like flames of fire."

⁸But to the Son he says,

"Your throne, O God, endures forever and ever.
You rule with a scepter of justice.
⁹ You love justice and hate evil.
Therefore, O God, your God has anointed you,
pouring out the oil of joy on you more than on anyone else."

¹⁰He also says to the Son,

"In the beginning, Lord, you laid the foundation of the earth
and made the heavens with your hands.
¹¹ They will perish, but you remain forever.
They will wear out like old clothing.
¹² You will fold them up like a cloak
and discard them like old clothing.
But you are always the same;
you will live forever."

¹³And God never said to any of the angels,

"Sit in the place of honor at my right hand
until I humble your enemies,
making them a footstool under your feet."

¹⁴Therefore, angels are only servants—spirits sent to care for people who will inherit salvation.

A Warning against Drifting Away

So we must listen very carefully to the truth we have heard, or we may drift away from it. ²For the message God delivered through angels has always stood firm, and every violation of the law and every act of disobedience was punished. ³So what makes us think we can escape if we ignore this great salvation that was first announced by the Lord Jesus himself and then delivered to us by those who heard him speak? ⁴And God confirmed the message by giving signs and wonders and various miracles and gifts of the Holy Spirit whenever he chose.

Jesus, the Man

⁵And furthermore, it is not angels who will control the future world we are talking about. ⁶For in one place the Scriptures say,

"What are mere mortals that you should think about them,
or a son of man that you should care for him?
⁷ Yet you made them only a little lower than the angels
and crowned them with glory and honor.
⁸ You gave them authority over all things."

Now when it says "all things," it means nothing is left out. But we have not yet seen all things put under their authority. ⁹What we do see is Jesus, who was given a position "a little lower than the angels"; and because he suffered death for us, he is now "crowned with glory and honor." Yes, by God's grace, Jesus tasted death for everyone. ¹⁰God, for whom and through whom everything was made, chose to bring many children into glory. And it was only right that he should make Jesus, through his suffering, a perfect leader, fit to bring them into their salvation.

¹¹So now Jesus and the ones he makes holy have the same Father. That is why Jesus is not ashamed to call them his brothers and sisters. ¹²For he said to God,

"I will proclaim your name to my brothers and sisters.

Hi, my name is

SAUL *(religious leader)*

Oh, the stories I could tell! First, you need to know who I really am. (I'm not King Saul of the Old Testament.) I'm sometimes known as Saul of Tarsus, since Tarsus is where I came from. But after I became a follower of Jesus, I became known as Paul. Before I met Jesus, I thought Christians were trying to change our Jewish faith with wrong teachings. So I was all about trying to stop them.

But Jesus stopped me in my tracks—literally! I was on my way to Damascus to nab some more Christians, when Jesus stopped me. A light from heaven shone down on me, and I heard a man's voice but couldn't see anyone! The voice said, "I am Jesus, the one you are persecuting." He told me to go into the city and wait.

When I stood up, I was blind! My friends led me into town, and I stayed there blind for three days. Then God sent a man named Ananias, a believer in Jesus, to restore my sight and get me started on the right path of telling others about Jesus.

God is amazing! Even though I had once tried to stop Christians, God changed my life and used me to spread the truth about Jesus. During my life I went on three big missionary trips. At God's direction and with his inspiration, I wrote a whole bunch of letters to people and churches, many of which are in this very Bible you're reading. I realized that nothing was more important than believing in Jesus!

For the whole startling story of Saul becoming a Christian, read ACTS 9:1-22.

CAN GOD USE YOU?

List the talents and abilities God has given you. Next to each talent, write a way you could use that talent to honor God. (Maybe you're a good listener, or maybe you encourage people. Those are talents too!) Every time you notice God using you, write the date on your paper. Let God use you in big—and little—ways!

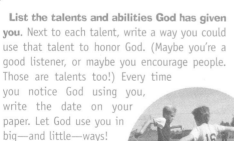

STEPHEN *(server of the poor)*

Not many people are known more for their death than for their life, but that's sure true for me! But hey, I'd like to talk a little bit about my life before I talk about my death!

I was a follower of Jesus from the early days of the church. More and more people were becoming Christians every day. At first, Jesus' disciples handled all the leadership. But soon they needed help.

> **Stephen gave quite a speech to the Jewish leaders! Read the whole thing in ACTS 7:1-53.**

They chose seven of us to help out so they could spend more time preaching. With God's power, I performed miracles that attracted people to Jesus. Unfortunately, they also attracted the attention of the Jewish leaders.

What came next was definitely not fun. When the leaders confronted me, God was with me. People even said that my face glowed like an angel when I answered them! At the end of my speech, I looked up toward heaven and I could actually see the glory of God, along with Jesus standing right beside God! When I told the Jewish leaders what I saw, I guess that was all they could take.

They dragged me out of the city and started throwing stones at me—a form of execution at the time. The stones hurt, but with God's help I was able to keep my focus on Jesus. Even as I was being killed, I asked God not to hold the people responsible for what they were doing to me.

> **What Stephen said when he was dying is similar to what Jesus said on the cross. Compare LUKE 23:34 with ACTS 7:60.**

I was the first Christian to die for his faith in Jesus, but my death was just one of many to come. I'm just thankful that I could stand up for Jesus!

WHERE DO YOU STAND?

Would you be able to stand up for your faith like Stephen?

ANSWER THESE QUESTIONS WITH A FRIEND:

What's the worst thing that could happen if you share your faith?

What's the hardest part about sharing your faith?

What's the worst thing that could happen if you DON'T share your faith?

Read over the answers you wrote, and then pray. Ask God to help you share your faith in Jesus, no matter what!

I will praise you among your
assembled people."

13 He also said,

"I will put my trust in him,"
that is, "I and the children God has given me."

14 Because God's children are human beings—made of flesh and blood—the Son also became flesh and blood. For only as a human being could he die, and only by dying could he break the power of the devil, who had the power of death. 15 Only in this way could he set free all who have lived their lives as slaves to the fear of dying.

16 We also know that the Son did not come to help angels; he came to help the descendants of Abraham. 17 Therefore, it was necessary for him to be made in every respect like us, his brothers and sisters, so that he could be our merciful and faithful High Priest before God. Then he could offer a sacrifice that would take away the sins of the people. 18 **Since he himself has gone through suffering and testing, he is able to help us when we are being tested.**

CHAPTER **3**
Jesus Is Greater Than Moses
And so, dear brothers and sisters who belong to God and are partners with those called to heaven, think carefully about this Jesus whom we declare to be God's messenger and High Priest. 2 For he was faithful to God, who appointed him, just as Moses served faithfully when he was entrusted with God's entire house.

3 But Jesus deserves far more glory than Moses, just as a person who builds a house deserves more praise than the house itself. 4 For every house has a builder, but the one who built everything is God.

5 Moses was certainly faithful in God's house as a servant. His work was an illustration of the truths God would reveal later. 6 But Christ, as the Son, is in charge of God's entire house. And we are God's house, if we keep our courage and remain confident in our hope in Christ.

7 That is why the Holy Spirit says,

"Today when you hear his voice,
8   don't harden your hearts
as Israel did when they rebelled,
    when they tested me in the wilderness.
9 There your ancestors tested and tried
    my patience,
even though they saw my miracles
    for forty years.

10 So I was angry with them, and I said,
'Their hearts always turn away from me.
They refuse to do what I tell them.'
11 So in my anger I took an oath:
'They will never enter my place of rest.'"

12 Be careful then, dear brothers and sisters. Make sure that your own hearts are not evil and unbelieving, turning you away from the living God. 13 You must warn each other every day, while it is still "today," so that none of you will be deceived by sin and hardened against God. 14 For if we are faithful to the end, trusting God just as firmly as when we first believed, we will share in all that belongs to Christ. 15 Remember what it says:

"Today when you hear his voice,
don't harden your hearts
as Israel did when they rebelled."

16 And who was it who rebelled against God, even though they heard his voice? Wasn't it the people Moses led out of Egypt? 17 And who made God angry for forty years? Wasn't it the people who sinned, whose corpses lay in the wilderness? 18 And to whom was God speaking when he took an oath that they would never enter his rest? Wasn't it the people who disobeyed him? 19 So we see that because of their unbelief they were not able to enter his rest.

CHAPTER **4**
Promised Rest for God's People
God's promise of entering his rest still stands, so we ought to tremble with fear that some of you might fail to experience it. 2 For this good news—that God has prepared this rest—has been announced to us just as it was to them. But it did them no good because they didn't share the faith of those who listened to God. 3 For only we who believe can enter his rest. As for the others, God said,

"In my anger I took an oath:
'They will never enter my place
    of rest,'"

even though this rest has been ready since he made the world. 4 We know it is ready because of the place in the Scriptures where it mentions the seventh day: "On the seventh day God rested from all his work." 5 But in the other passage God said, "They will never enter my place of rest."

6 So God's rest is there for people to enter, but those who first heard this good news failed to enter because they disobeyed God. 7 So God set

another time for entering his rest, and that time is today. God announced this through David much later in the words already quoted:

"Today when you hear his voice,
don't harden your hearts."

8Now if Joshua had succeeded in giving them this rest, God would not have spoken about another day of rest still to come. 9So there is a special rest still waiting for the people of God. 10For all who have entered into God's rest have rested from their labors, just as God did after creating the world. 11So let us do our best to enter that rest. But if we disobey God, as the people of Israel did, we will fall.

12For the word of God is alive and powerful. It is sharper than the sharpest two-edged sword, cutting between soul and spirit, between joint and marrow. It exposes our innermost thoughts and desires. 13Nothing in all creation is hidden from God. Everything is naked and exposed before his eyes, and he is the one to whom we are accountable.

Christ Is Our High Priest

14So then, since we have a great High Priest who has entered heaven, Jesus the Son of God, let us hold firmly to what we believe. 15This High Priest of ours understands our weaknesses, for he faced all of the same testings we do, yet he did not sin. 16**So let us come boldly to the throne of our gracious God. There we will receive his mercy, and we will find grace to help us when we need it most.**

CHAPTER 5
Every high priest is a man chosen to represent other people in their dealings with God. He presents their gifts to God and offers sacrifices for their sins. 2And he is able to deal gently with ignorant and wayward people because he himself is subject to the same weaknesses. 3That is why he must offer sacrifices for his own sins as well as theirs.

4And no one can become a high priest simply because he wants such an honor. He must be called by God for this work, just as Aaron was. 5That is why Christ did not honor himself by assuming he could become High Priest. No, he was chosen by God, who said to him,

"You are my Son.
Today I have become your Father."

6And in another passage God said to him,

"You are a priest forever in the order
of Melchizedek."

7While Jesus was here on earth, he offered prayers and pleadings, with a loud cry and tears, to the one who could rescue him from death. And God heard his prayers because of his deep reverence for God. 8Even though Jesus was God's Son, he learned obedience from the things he suffered. 9In this way, God qualified him as a perfect High Priest, and he became the source of eternal salvation for all those who obey him. 10And God designated him to be a High Priest in the order of Melchizedek.

A Call to Spiritual Growth

11There is much more we would like to say about this, but it is difficult to explain, especially since you are spiritually dull and don't seem to listen. 12You have been believers so long now that you ought to be teaching others. Instead, you need someone to teach you again the basic things about God's word. You are like babies who need milk and cannot eat solid food. 13For someone who lives on milk is still an infant and doesn't know how to do what is right. 14Solid food is for those who are mature, who through training have the skill to recognize the difference between right and wrong.

CHAPTER 6
So let us stop going over the basic teachings about Christ again and again. Let us go on instead and become mature in our understanding. Surely we don't need to start again with the fundamental importance of repenting from evil deeds and placing our faith in God. 2You don't need further instruction about baptisms, the laying on of hands, the resurrection of the dead, and eternal judgment. 3And so, God willing, we will move forward to further understanding.

4For it is impossible to bring back to repentance those who were once enlightened—those who have experienced the good things of heaven and shared in the Holy Spirit, 5who have tasted the goodness of the word of God and the power of the age to come—6and who then turn away from God. It is impossible to bring such people back to repentance; by rejecting the Son of God, they themselves are nailing him to the cross once again and holding him up to public shame.

7When the ground soaks up the falling rain and bears a good crop for the farmer, it has God's blessing. 8But if a field bears thorns and thistles,

Read HEBREWS 4:16. Then read it again until you can say it to someone else.

Coming boldly to God's throne means praying with complete confidence. Make this **Confidence Carryall** to remind you that you can pray boldly.

1. **Write the words of this verse on an empty container.**

2. **Decorate the container any way you want.**

3. **Think of things you're confident about. Write those things on slips of paper. (Can you ride a bike? tie your shoes? multiply? Write it down!)**

Look at all your confidence slips! Put your slips in your Confidence Carryall. Any time you feel shy about talking to God, open your Confidence Carryall.

THEN REMEMBER WHAT IT FEELS LIKE TO BE BOLD AND CONFIDENT.

it is useless. The farmer will soon condemn that field and burn it.

9 Dear friends, even though we are talking this way, we really don't believe it applies to you. We are confident that you are meant for better things, things that come with salvation. 10 For God is not unjust. He will not forget how hard you have worked for him and how you have shown your love to him by caring for other believers, as you still do. 11 Our great desire is that you will keep on loving others as long as life lasts, in order to make certain that what you hope for will come true. 12 Then you will not become spiritually dull and indifferent. Instead, you will follow the example of those who are going to inherit God's promises because of their faith and endurance.

God's Promises Bring Hope

13 For example, there was God's promise to Abraham. Since there was no one greater to swear by, God took an oath in his own name, saying:

14 "I will certainly bless you,
    and I will multiply your descendants
        beyond number."

15 Then Abraham waited patiently, and he received what God had promised.

16 Now when people take an oath, they call on someone greater than themselves to hold them to it. And without any question that oath is binding. 17 God also bound himself with an oath, so that those who received the promise could be perfectly sure that he would never change his mind. 18 So God has given both his promise and his oath. These two things are unchangeable because it is impossible for God to lie. Therefore, we who have fled to him for refuge can have great confidence as we hold to the hope that lies before us. 19 This hope is a strong and trustworthy anchor for our souls. It leads us through the curtain into God's inner sanctuary. 20 Jesus has already gone in there for us. He has become our eternal High Priest in the order of Melchizedek.

CHAPTER **7**
Melchizedek Is Greater Than Abraham

This Melchizedek was king of the city of Salem and also a priest of God Most High. When Abraham was returning home after winning a great battle against the kings, Melchizedek met him and blessed him. 2 Then Abraham took a tenth of all he had captured in battle and gave it to Melchizedek. The name Melchizedek means "king of justice," and king of Salem means "king of peace." ³There is no record of his father or mother or any of his ancestors—no beginning or end to his life. He remains a priest forever, resembling the Son of God.

⁴Consider then how great this Melchizedek was. Even Abraham, the great patriarch of Israel, recognized this by giving him a tenth of what he had taken in battle. ⁵Now the law of Moses required that the priests, who are descendants of Levi, must collect a tithe from the rest of the people of Israel, who are also descendants of Abraham. ⁶But Melchizedek, who was not a descendant of Levi, collected a tenth from Abraham. And Melchizedek placed a blessing upon Abraham, the one who had already received the promises of God. ⁷And without question, the person who has the power to give a blessing is greater than the one who is blessed.

⁸The priests who collect tithes are men who die, so Melchizedek is greater than they are, because we are told that he lives on. ⁹In addition, we might even say that these Levites—the ones who collect the tithe—paid a tithe to Melchizedek when their ancestor Abraham paid a tithe to him. ¹⁰For although Levi wasn't born yet, the seed from which he came was in Abraham's body when Melchizedek collected the tithe from him.

¹¹So if the priesthood of Levi, on which the law was based, could have achieved the perfection God intended, why did God need to establish a different priesthood, with a priest in the order of Melchizedek instead of the order of Levi and Aaron?

¹²And if the priesthood is changed, the law must also be changed to permit it. ¹³For the priest we are talking about belongs to a different tribe, whose members have never served at the altar as priests. ¹⁴What I mean is, our Lord came from the tribe of Judah, and Moses never mentioned priests coming from that tribe.

Jesus Is like Melchizedek

¹⁵This change has been made very clear since a different priest, who is like Melchizedek, has appeared. ¹⁶Jesus became a priest, not by meeting the physical requirement of belonging to the tribe of Levi, but by the power of a life that cannot be destroyed. ¹⁷And the psalmist pointed this out when he prophesied,

"You are a priest forever in the order of
    Melchizedek."

¹⁸Yes, the old requirement about the priesthood was set aside because it was weak and useless.

¹⁹For the law never made anything perfect. But now we have confidence in a better hope, through which we draw near to God.

²⁰This new system was established with a solemn oath. Aaron's descendants became priests without such an oath, ²¹but there was an oath regarding Jesus. For God said to him,

"The LORD has taken an oath and will not
    break his vow:
  'You are a priest forever.'"

²²Because of this oath, Jesus is the one who guarantees this better covenant with God.

²³There were many priests under the old system, for death prevented them from remaining in office. ²⁴But because Jesus lives forever, his priesthood lasts forever. ²⁵Therefore he is able, once and forever, to save those who come to God through him. He lives forever to intercede with God on their behalf.

²⁶He is the kind of high priest we need because he is holy and blameless, unstained by sin. He has been set apart from sinners and has been given the highest place of honor in heaven. ²⁷Unlike those other high priests, he does not need to offer sacrifices every day. They did this for their own sins first and then for the sins of the people. But Jesus did this once for all when he offered himself as the sacrifice for the people's sins. ²⁸The law appointed high priests who were limited by human weakness. But after the law was given, God appointed his Son with an oath, and his Son has been made the perfect High Priest forever.

CHAPTER **8**
Christ Is Our High Priest

Here is the main point: We have a High Priest who sat down in the place of honor beside the throne of the majestic God in heaven. ²There he ministers in the heavenly Tabernacle, the true place of worship that was built by the Lord and not by human hands.

³And since every high priest is required to offer gifts and sacrifices, our High Priest must make an offering, too. ⁴If he were here on earth, he would not even be a priest, since there already are priests who offer the gifts required by the law. ⁵They serve in a system of worship that is only a copy, a shadow of the real one in heaven. For when Moses was getting ready to build the Tabernacle, God gave him this warning: "Be sure that you make everything according to the pattern I have shown you here on the mountain."

⁶But now Jesus, our High Priest, has been

given a ministry that is far superior to the old priesthood, for he is the one who mediates for us a far better covenant with God, based on better promises.

⁷If the first covenant had been faultless, there would have been no need for a second covenant to replace it. ⁸But when God found fault with the people, he said:

"The day is coming, says the LORD,
  when I will make a new covenant
  with the people of Israel and Judah.
⁹ This covenant will not be like the one
  I made with their ancestors
when I took them by the hand
  and led them out of the land of Egypt.
They did not remain faithful to my
  covenant,
so I turned my back on them, says
  the LORD.
¹⁰ But this is the new covenant I will make
  with the people of Israel on that day,
  says the LORD:
I will put my laws in their minds,
  and I will write them on their hearts.
I will be their God,
  and they will be my people.
¹¹ And they will not need to teach their
  neighbors,
  nor will they need to teach their relatives,
  saying, 'You should know the LORD.'
For everyone, from the least to the greatest,
  will know me already.
¹² And I will forgive their wickedness,
  and I will never again remember
  their sins."

¹³When God speaks of a "new" covenant, it means he has made the first one obsolete. It is now out of date and will soon disappear.

CHAPTER **9**
Old Rules about Worship

That first covenant between God and Israel had regulations for worship and a place of worship here on earth. ²There were two rooms in that Tabernacle. In the first room were a lampstand, a table, and sacred loaves of bread on the table. This room was called the Holy Place. ³Then there was a curtain, and behind the curtain was the second room called the Most Holy Place. ⁴In that room were a gold incense altar and a wooden chest called the Ark of the Covenant, which was covered with gold on all sides. Inside the Ark were a gold jar containing manna, Aaron's staff that sprouted leaves, and the stone tablets of the covenant. ⁵Above the Ark were the cherubim of divine glory, whose wings stretched out over the Ark's cover, the place of atonement. But we cannot explain these things in detail now.

⁶When these things were all in place, the priests regularly entered the first room as they performed their religious duties. ⁷But only the high priest ever entered the Most Holy Place, and only once a year. And he always offered blood for his own sins and for the sins the people had committed in ignorance. ⁸By these regulations the Holy Spirit revealed that the entrance to the Most Holy Place was not freely open as long as the Tabernacle and the system it represented were still in use.

⁹This is an illustration pointing to the present time. For the gifts and sacrifices that the priests offer are not able to cleanse the consciences of the people who bring them. ¹⁰For that old system deals only with food and drink and various cleansing ceremonies—physical regulations that were in effect only until a better system could be established.

Christ Is the Perfect Sacrifice

¹¹So Christ has now become the High Priest over all the good things that have come. He has entered that greater, more perfect Tabernacle in heaven, which was not made by human hands and is not part of this created world. ¹²With his own blood—not the blood of goats and calves—he entered the Most Holy Place once for all time and secured our redemption forever.

¹³Under the old system, the blood of goats and bulls and the ashes of a young cow could cleanse people's bodies from ceremonial impurity. ¹⁴Just think how much more the blood of Christ will purify our consciences from sinful deeds so that we can worship the living God. For by the power of the eternal Spirit, Christ offered himself to God as a perfect sacrifice for our sins. ¹⁵That is why he is the one who mediates a new covenant between God and people, so that all who are called can receive the eternal inheritance God has promised them. For Christ died to set them free from the penalty of the sins they had committed under that first covenant.

¹⁶Now when someone leaves a will, it is necessary to prove that the person who made it is dead. ¹⁷The will goes into effect only after the person's death. While the person who made it is still alive, the will cannot be put into effect. ¹⁸That is why even the first covenant was put into effect with the blood of an animal. ¹⁹For

after Moses had read each of God's commandments to all the people, he took the blood of calves and goats, along with water, and sprinkled both the book of God's law and all the people, using hyssop branches and scarlet wool. ²⁰Then he said, "This blood confirms the covenant God has made with you." ²¹And in the same way, he sprinkled blood on the Tabernacle and on everything used for worship. ²²In fact, according to the law of Moses, nearly everything was purified with blood. For without the shedding of blood, there is no forgiveness.

²³That is why the Tabernacle and everything in it, which were copies of things in heaven, had to be purified by the blood of animals. But the real things in heaven had to be purified with far better sacrifices than the blood of animals.

²⁴For Christ did not enter into a holy place made with human hands, which was only a copy of the true one in heaven. He entered into heaven itself to appear now before God on our behalf. ²⁵And he did not enter heaven to offer himself again and again, like the high priest here on earth who enters the Most Holy Place year after year with the blood of an animal. ²⁶If that had been necessary, Christ would have had to die again and again, ever since the world began. But now, once for all time, he has appeared at the end of the age to remove sin by his own death as a sacrifice.

²⁷And just as each person is destined to die once and after that comes judgment, ²⁸so also Christ died once for all time as a sacrifice to take away the sins of many people. He will come again, not to deal with our sins, but to bring salvation to all who are eagerly waiting for him.

CHAPTER 10
Christ's Sacrifice Once for All

The old system under the law of Moses was only a shadow, a dim preview of the good things to come, not the good things themselves. The sacrifices under that system were repeated again and again, year after year, but they were never able to provide perfect cleansing for those who came to worship. ²If they could have provided perfect cleansing, the sacrifices would have stopped, for the worshipers would have been purified once for all time, and their feelings of guilt would have disappeared.

³But instead, those sacrifices actually reminded them of their sins year after year. ⁴For it is not possible for the blood of bulls and goats to take away sins. ⁵That is why, when Christ came into the world, he said to God,

"You did not want animal sacrifices
or sin offerings.
But you have given me a body to offer.
⁶ You were not pleased with burnt offerings
or other offerings for sin.
⁷ Then I said, 'Look, I have come to do your
will, O God—
as is written about me in the Scriptures.'"

⁸First, Christ said, "You did not want animal sacrifices or sin offerings or burnt offerings or other offerings for sin, nor were you pleased with them" (though they are required by the law of Moses). ⁹Then he said, "Look, I have come to do your will." He cancels the first covenant in order to put the second into effect. ¹⁰For God's will was for us to be made holy by the sacrifice of the body of Jesus Christ, once for all time.

¹¹Under the old covenant, the priest stands and ministers before the altar day after day, offering the same sacrifices again and again, which can never take away sins. ¹²But our High Priest offered himself to God as a single sacrifice for sins, good for all time. Then he sat down in the place of honor at God's right hand. ¹³There he waits until his enemies are humbled and made a footstool under his feet. ¹⁴For by that one offering he forever made perfect those who are being made holy.

¹⁵And the Holy Spirit also testifies that this is so. For he says,

¹⁶ "This is the new covenant I will make
with my people on that day, says the LORD:
I will put my laws in their hearts,
and I will write them on their minds."

¹⁷Then he says,

"I will never again remember
their sins and lawless deeds."

¹⁸And when sins have been forgiven, there is no need to offer any more sacrifices.

A Call to Persevere

¹⁹And so, dear brothers and sisters, we can boldly enter heaven's Most Holy Place because of the blood of Jesus. ²⁰By his death, Jesus opened a new and life-giving way through the curtain into the Most Holy Place. ²¹And since we have a great High Priest who rules over God's house, ²²let us go right into the presence of God with sincere hearts fully trusting him. For our guilty consciences have been sprinkled with Christ's blood to make us clean, and our bodies have been washed with pure water.

23 Let us hold tightly without wavering to the hope we affirm, for God can be trusted to keep his promise. **24 Let us think of ways to motivate one another to acts of love and good works. 25 And let us not neglect our meeting together, as some people do, but encourage one another, especially now that the day of his return is drawing near.**

26 Dear friends, if we deliberately continue sinning after we have received knowledge of the truth, there is no longer any sacrifice that will cover these sins. 27 There is only the terrible expectation of God's judgment and the raging fire that will consume his enemies. 28 For anyone who refused to obey the law of Moses was put to death without mercy on the testimony of two or three witnesses. 29 Just think how much worse the punishment will be for those who have trampled on the Son of God, and have treated the blood of the covenant, which made us holy, as if it were common and unholy, and have insulted and disdained the Holy Spirit who brings God's mercy to us. 30 For we know the one who said,

"I will take revenge.
I will pay them back."

He also said,

"The Lord will judge his own people."

31 It is a terrible thing to fall into the hands of the living God.

32 Think back on those early days when you first learned about Christ. Remember how you remained faithful even though it meant terrible suffering. 33 Sometimes you were exposed to public ridicule and were beaten, and sometimes you helped others who were suffering the same things. 34 You suffered along with those who were thrown into jail, and when all you owned was taken from you, you accepted it with joy. You knew there were better things waiting for you that will last forever.

35 So do not throw away this confident trust in the Lord. Remember the great reward it brings you! 36 Patient endurance is what you need now, so that you will continue to do God's will. Then you will receive all that he has promised.

37 "For in just a little while,
the Coming One will come and not delay.
38 And my righteous ones will live by faith.
But I will take no pleasure in anyone
who turns away."

Key Verse "Faith is the confidence that what we hope for will actually happen; it gives us assurance about things we cannot see."—HEBREWS 11:1

Faith is . . .

Read HEBREWS 11:1 out loud. We can't see God, but we see evidence of him all around us. It's like the wind. We can't see the wind, but we can see evidence of it when we see leaves blow and when we feel a breeze.

Make this windsock reminder that God is REAL!

1 Decorate one side of a sheet of construction paper to remind you of this verse.

2 Roll the paper into a cylinder, decorated side out. Tape the edges together.

3 Tape crepe paper strips to the inside of one end of the cylinder.

4 Punch two holes opposite each other at the other end of the cylinder. Thread yarn through the holes, and knot them to form a hanger.

Read James 2:17-18 to find out how to show your faith!

HANG YOUR WINDSOCK OUTSIDE. Every time you see it blowing in the wind, remember that even though we can't see God, we can know he's real!

39But we are not like those who turn away from God to their own destruction. We are the faithful ones, whose souls will be saved.

CHAPTER 11

Great Examples of Faith

Faith is the confidence that what we hope for will actually happen; it gives us assurance about things we cannot see. **2**Through their faith, the people in days of old earned a good reputation.

3By faith we understand that the entire universe was formed at God's command, that what we now see did not come from anything that can be seen.

4It was by faith that Abel brought a more acceptable offering to God than Cain did. Abel's offering gave evidence that he was a righteous man, and God showed his approval of his gifts. Although Abel is long dead, he still speaks to us by his example of faith.

5It was by faith that Enoch was taken up to heaven without dying—"he disappeared, because God took him." For before he was taken up, he was known as a person who pleased God. **6**And it is impossible to please God without faith. Anyone who wants to come to him must believe that God exists and that he rewards those who sincerely seek him.

7It was by faith that Noah built a large boat to save his family from the flood. He obeyed God, who warned him about things that had never happened before. By his faith Noah condemned the rest of the world, and he received the righteousness that comes by faith.

8It was by faith that Abraham obeyed when God called him to leave home and go to another land that God would give him as his inheritance. He went without knowing where he was going. **9**And even when he reached the land God promised him, he lived there by faith—for he was like a foreigner, living in tents. And so did Isaac and Jacob, who inherited the same promise. **10**Abraham was confidently looking forward to a city with eternal foundations, a city designed and built by God.

11It was by faith that even Sarah was able to have a child, though she was barren and was too old. She believed that God would keep his promise. **12**And so a whole nation came from this one man who was as good as dead—a nation with so many people that, like the stars in the sky and the sand on the seashore, there is no way to count them.

13All these people died still believing what God had promised them. They did not receive what was promised, but they saw it all from a distance and welcomed it. They agreed that they were foreigners and nomads here on earth. **14**Obviously people who say such things are looking forward to a country they can call their own. **15**If they had longed for the country they came from, they could have gone back. **16**But they were looking for a better place, a heavenly homeland. That is why God is not ashamed to be called their God, for he has prepared a city for them.

17It was by faith that Abraham offered Isaac as a sacrifice when God was testing him. Abraham, who had received God's promises, was ready to sacrifice his only son, Isaac, **18**even though God had told him, "Isaac is the son through whom your descendants will be counted." **19**Abraham reasoned that if Isaac died, God was able to bring him back to life again. And in a sense, Abraham did receive his son back from the dead.

20It was by faith that Isaac promised blessings for the future to his sons, Jacob and Esau.

21It was by faith that Jacob, when he was old and dying, blessed each of Joseph's sons and bowed in worship as he leaned on his staff.

22It was by faith that Joseph, when he was about to die, said confidently that the people of Israel would leave Egypt. He even commanded them to take his bones with them when they left.

23It was by faith that Moses' parents hid him for three months when he was born. They saw that God had given them an unusual child, and they were not afraid to disobey the king's command.

24It was by faith that Moses, when he grew up, refused to be called the son of Pharaoh's daughter. **25**He chose to share the oppression of God's people instead of enjoying the fleeting pleasures of sin. **26**He thought it was better to suffer for the sake of Christ than to own the treasures of Egypt, for he was looking ahead to his great reward. **27**It was by faith that Moses left the land of Egypt, not fearing the king's anger. He kept right on going because he kept his eyes on the one who is invisible. **28**It was by faith that Moses commanded the people of Israel to keep the Passover and to sprinkle blood on the doorposts so that the angel of death would not kill their firstborn sons.

29It was by faith that the people of Israel went right through the Red Sea as though they were on dry ground. But when the Egyptians tried to follow, they were all drowned.

30It was by faith that the people of Israel

marched around Jericho for seven days, and the walls came crashing down.

³¹It was by faith that Rahab the prostitute was not destroyed with the people in her city who refused to obey God. For she had given a friendly welcome to the spies.

³²How much more do I need to say? It would take too long to recount the stories of the faith of Gideon, Barak, Samson, Jephthah, David, Samuel, and all the prophets. ³³By faith these people overthrew kingdoms, ruled with justice, and received what God had promised them. They shut the mouths of lions, ³⁴quenched the flames of fire, and escaped death by the edge of the sword. Their weakness was turned to strength. They became strong in battle and put whole armies to flight. ³⁵Women received their loved ones back again from death.

But others were tortured, refusing to turn from God in order to be set free. They placed their hope in a better life after the resurrection. ³⁶Some were jeered at, and their backs were cut open with whips. Others were chained in prisons. ³⁷Some died by stoning, some were sawed in half, and others were killed with the sword. Some went about wearing skins of sheep and goats, destitute and oppressed and mistreated. ³⁸They were too good for this world, wandering over deserts and mountains, hiding in caves and holes in the ground.

³⁹All these people earned a good reputation because of their faith, yet none of them received all that God had promised. ⁴⁰For God had something better in mind for us, so that they would not reach perfection without us.

CHAPTER **12**
God's Discipline Proves His Love

Therefore, since we are surrounded by such a huge crowd of witnesses to the life of faith, let us strip off every weight that slows us down, especially the sin that so easily trips us up. And let us run with endurance the race God has set before us. ²We do this by keeping our eyes on Jesus, the champion who initiates and perfects our faith. Because of the joy awaiting him, he endured the cross, disregarding its shame. Now he is seated in the place of honor beside God's throne. ³Think of all the hostility he endured from sinful people; then you won't become weary and give up. ⁴After all, you have not yet given your lives in your struggle against sin.

⁵And have you forgotten the encouraging words God spoke to you as his children? He said,

"My child, don't make light of the LORD's discipline,
and don't give up when he corrects you.
⁶ For the LORD disciplines those he loves,
and he punishes each one he accepts as his child."

⁷As you endure this divine discipline, remember that God is treating you as his own children. Who ever heard of a child who is never disciplined by its father? ⁸If God doesn't discipline you as he does all of his children, it means that you are illegitimate and are not really his children at all. ⁹Since we respected our earthly fathers who disciplined us, shouldn't we submit even more to the discipline of the Father of our spirits, and live forever?

¹⁰For our earthly fathers disciplined us for a few years, doing the best they knew how. But God's discipline is always good for us, so that we might share in his holiness. ¹¹No discipline is enjoyable while it is happening—it's painful! But afterward there will be a peaceful harvest of right living for those who are trained in this way.

¹²So take a new grip with your tired hands and strengthen your weak knees. ¹³Mark out a straight path for your feet so that those who are weak and lame will not fall but become strong.

A Call to Listen to God

¹⁴Work at living in peace with everyone, and work at living a holy life, for those who are not holy will not see the Lord. ¹⁵Look after each other so that none of you fails to receive the grace of God. Watch out that no poisonous root of bitterness grows up to trouble you, corrupting many. ¹⁶Make sure that no one is immoral or godless like Esau, who traded his birthright as the firstborn son for a single meal. ¹⁷You know that afterward, when he wanted his father's blessing, he was rejected. It was too late for repentance, even though he begged with bitter tears.

¹⁸You have not come to a physical mountain, to a place of flaming fire, darkness, gloom, and whirlwind, as the Israelites did at Mount Sinai. ¹⁹For they heard an awesome trumpet blast and a voice so terrible that they begged God to stop speaking. ²⁰They staggered back under God's command: "If even an animal touches the mountain, it must be stoned to death." ²¹Moses himself was so frightened at the sight that he said, "I am terrified and trembling."

²²No, you have come to Mount Zion, to the city of the living God, the heavenly Jerusalem,

and to countless thousands of angels in a joyful gathering. 23 You have come to the assembly of God's firstborn children, whose names are written in heaven. You have come to God himself, who is the judge over all things. You have come to the spirits of the righteous ones in heaven who have now been made perfect. 24 You have come to Jesus, the one who mediates the new covenant between God and people, and to the sprinkled blood, which speaks of forgiveness instead of crying out for vengeance like the blood of Abel.

25 Be careful that you do not refuse to listen to the One who is speaking. For if the people of Israel did not escape when they refused to listen to Moses, the earthly messenger, we will certainly not escape if we reject the One who speaks to us from heaven! 26 When God spoke from Mount Sinai his voice shook the earth, but now he makes another promise: "Once again I will shake not only the earth but the heavens also." 27 This means that all of creation will be shaken and removed, so that only unshakable things will remain.

28 Since we are receiving a Kingdom that is unshakable, let us be thankful and please God by worshiping him with holy fear and awe. 29 For our God is a devouring fire.

CHAPTER **13**

Concluding Words

Keep on loving each other as brothers and sisters. 2 Don't forget to show hospitality to strangers, for some who have done this have entertained angels without realizing it! 3 Remember those in prison, as if you were there yourself. Remember also those being mistreated, as if you felt their pain in your own bodies.

4 Give honor to marriage, and remain faithful to one another in marriage. God will surely judge people who are immoral and those who commit adultery.

5 Don't love money; be satisfied with what you have. For God has said,

"I will never fail you.
I will never abandon you."

6 So we can say with confidence,

"The LORD is my helper,
so I will have no fear.
What can mere people do to me?"

7 Remember your leaders who taught you the word of God. Think of all the good that has come from their lives, and follow the example of their faith.

8 Jesus Christ is the same yesterday, today, and forever. 9 So do not be attracted by strange, new ideas. Your strength comes from God's grace, not from rules about food, which don't help those who follow them.

10 We have an altar from which the priests in the Tabernacle have no right to eat. 11 Under the old system, the high priest brought the blood of animals into the Holy Place as a sacrifice for sin, and the bodies of the animals were burned outside the camp. 12 So also Jesus suffered and died outside the city gates to make his people holy by means of his own blood. 13 So let us go out to him, outside the camp, and bear the disgrace he bore. 14 For this world is not our permanent home; we are looking forward to a home yet to come.

15 Therefore, let us offer through Jesus a continual sacrifice of praise to God, proclaiming our allegiance to his name. 16 And don't forget to do good and to share with those in need. These are the sacrifices that please God.

17 Obey your spiritual leaders, and do what they say. Their work is to watch over your souls, and they are accountable to God. Give them reason to do this with joy and not with sorrow. That would certainly not be for your benefit.

18 Pray for us, for our conscience is clear and we want to live honorably in everything we do. 19 And especially pray that I will be able to come back to you soon.

20 Now may the God of peace—
who brought up from the dead our
Lord Jesus,
the great Shepherd of the sheep,
and ratified an eternal covenant
with his blood—
21 may he equip you with all you need
for doing his will.
May he produce in you,
through the power of Jesus Christ,
every good thing that is pleasing to him.
All glory to him forever and ever! Amen.

22 I urge you, dear brothers and sisters, to pay attention to what I have written in this brief exhortation.

23 I want you to know that our brother Timothy has been released from jail. If he comes here soon, I will bring him with me to see you.

24 Greet all your leaders and all the believers there. The believers from Italy send you their greetings.

25 May God's grace be with you all.

JAMES
Encouraging Words

Look for (1) hidden message in James!

The book of James is all about putting our faith into action. It encourages us to

- **FURTHER OUR FAITH**
- **TURN FROM TEMPTATION**
- **TAME OUR TONGUES**
- **PATIENTLY PRAY**

Just Ask!

Want an A? Study! Want to become a good basketball player? Practice! But there's something that God will do *for* you, and all you have to do is ask! **Check it out in James 1:5.**

WiLd ThInG!

It's out of control! Even the most skilled animal tamers can't get this creature to behave. Don't let its small size fool you. Its power is huge!

If you dare, read James 3:2-10 to learn more about this beast.

Hats for Sale!

Picture a hat store—big hats, little hats, cowboy hats, sun hats.

But there's a special hat that's *not* for sale. You'll have to ask God about that hat. There's a special way to get it. **Look in James 1:12 to find out how.**

Rain or .... Shine

Is it raining in your life? The Bible says what to do! Is your life sunny? There's advice for that, too! **Read the Bible's advice for every kind of day in James 5:13!**

Timeline

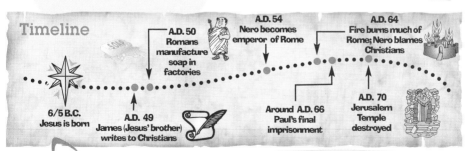

A.D. 50 Romans manufacture soap in factories

A.D. 54 Nero becomes emperor of Rome

A.D. 64 Fire burns much of Rome; Nero blames Christians

6/5 B.C. Jesus is born

A.D. 49 James (Jesus' brother) writes to Christians

Around A.D. 66 Paul's final imprisonment

A.D. 70 Jerusalem Temple destroyed

The JESUS CONNECTION

You can't get to heaven by doing good things. In fact, the only way to get to heaven is by having faith in Jesus. But if you believe in Jesus and he is Lord over your life, you're going to want to do things his way. The book of James encourages us to put our faith into practice. It's great to be saved. **It's even better to be saved and to spend our lives serving others!**

CHAPTER **1**
Greetings from James

This letter is from James, a slave of God and of the Lord Jesus Christ.

I am writing to the "twelve tribes"—Jewish believers scattered abroad.

Greetings!

Faith and Endurance

2 Dear brothers and sisters, when troubles come your way, consider it an opportunity for great joy. 3 For you know that when your faith is tested, your endurance has a chance to grow. 4 So let it grow, for when your endurance is fully developed, you will be perfect and complete, needing nothing.

5 If you need wisdom, ask our generous God, and he will give it to you. He will not rebuke you for asking. 6 But when you ask him, be sure that your faith is in God alone. Do not waver, for a person with divided loyalty is as unsettled as a wave of the sea that is blown and tossed by the wind. 7 Such people should not expect to receive anything from the Lord. 8 Their loyalty is divided between God and the world, and they are unstable in everything they do.

9 Believers who are poor have something to boast about, for God has honored them. 10 And those who are rich should boast that God has humbled them. They will fade away like a little flower in the field. 11 The hot sun rises and the grass withers; the little flower droops and falls, and its beauty fades away. In the same way, the rich will fade away with all of their achievements.

12 God blesses those who patiently endure testing and temptation. Afterward they will receive the crown of life that God has promised to those who love him. 13 And remember, when you are being tempted, do not say, "God is tempting me." God is never tempted to do wrong, and he never tempts anyone else. 14 Temptation comes from our own desires, which entice us and drag us away. 15 These desires give birth to sinful actions. And when sin is allowed to grow, it gives birth to death.

16 So don't be misled, my dear brothers and sisters. 17 Whatever is good and perfect comes down to us from God our Father, who created all the lights in the heavens. He never changes or casts a shifting shadow. 18 He chose to give birth to us by giving us his true word. And we, out of all creation, became his prized possession.

Listening and Doing

19 Understand this, my dear brothers and sisters: You must all be quick to listen, slow to speak, and slow to get angry. 20 Human anger does not produce the righteousness God desires. 21 So get rid of all the filth and evil in your lives, and humbly accept the word God has planted in your hearts, for it has the power to save your souls.

22 But don't just listen to God's word. You must do what it says. Otherwise, you are only fooling yourselves. 23 For if you listen to the word and don't obey, it is like glancing at your face in a mirror. 24 You see yourself, walk away, and forget what you look like. 25 But if you look carefully into the perfect law that sets you free, and if you do what it says and don't forget what you heard, then God will bless you for doing it.

26 If you claim to be religious but don't control your tongue, you are fooling yourself, and your religion is worthless. 27 Pure and genuine religion in the sight of God the Father means caring for orphans and widows in their distress and refusing to let the world corrupt you.

CHAPTER **2**
A Warning against Prejudice

My dear brothers and sisters, how can you claim to have faith in our glorious Lord Jesus Christ if you favor some people over others?

2 For example, suppose someone comes into your meeting dressed in fancy clothes and expensive jewelry, and another comes in who is poor and dressed in dirty clothes. 3 If you give special attention and a good seat to the rich person, but you say to the poor one, "You can stand over there, or else sit on the floor"—well, 4 doesn't this discrimination show that your judgments are guided by evil motives?

5 Listen to me, dear brothers and sisters. Hasn't God chosen the poor in this world to be rich in faith? Aren't they the ones who will inherit the Kingdom he promised to those who love him? 6 But you dishonor the poor! Isn't it the rich who oppress you and drag you into court? 7 Aren't they the ones who slander Jesus Christ, whose noble name you bear?

8 Yes indeed, it is good when you obey the royal law as found in the Scriptures: "Love your neighbor as yourself." 9 But if you favor some people over others, you are committing a sin. You are guilty of breaking the law.

10 For the person who keeps all of the laws except one is as guilty as a person who has broken all of God's laws. 11 For the same God who said,

"You must not commit adultery," also said, "You must not murder." So if you murder someone but do not commit adultery, you have still broken the law.

¹²So whatever you say or whatever you do, remember that you will be judged by the law that sets you free. ¹³There will be no mercy for those who have not shown mercy to others. But if you have been merciful, God will be merciful when he judges you.

Faith without Good Deeds Is Dead

¹⁴What good is it, dear brothers and sisters, if you say you have faith but don't show it by your actions? Can that kind of faith save anyone? ¹⁵Suppose you see a brother or sister who has no food or clothing, ¹⁶and you say, "Good-bye and have a good day; stay warm and eat well"—but then you don't give that person any food or clothing. What good does that do?

¹⁷So you see, faith by itself isn't enough. Unless it produces good deeds, it is dead and useless.

¹⁸Now someone may argue, "Some people have faith; others have good deeds." But I say, "How can you show me your faith if you don't have good deeds? I will show you my faith by my good deeds."

¹⁹You say you have faith, for you believe that there is one God. Good for you! Even the demons believe this, and they tremble in terror. ²⁰How foolish! Can't you see that faith without good deeds is useless?

²¹Don't you remember that our ancestor Abraham was shown to be right with God by his actions when he offered his son Isaac on the altar? ²²You see, his faith and his actions worked together. His actions made his faith complete. ²³And so it happened just as the Scriptures say: "Abraham believed God, and God counted him as righteous because of his faith." He was even called the friend of God. ²⁴So you see, we are shown to be right with God by what we do, not by faith alone.

²⁵Rahab the prostitute is another example. She was shown to be right with God by her actions when she hid those messengers and sent them safely away by a different road. ²⁶Just as the body is dead without breath, so also faith is dead without good works.

CHAPTER **3**
Controlling the Tongue

Dear brothers and sisters, not many of you should become teachers in the church, for we who teach will be judged more strictly. ²Indeed, we all make many mistakes. For if we could control our tongues, we would be perfect and could also control ourselves in every other way.

³We can make a large horse go wherever we want by means of a small bit in its mouth. ⁴And a small rudder makes a huge ship turn wherever

Have you ever had two friends with the same name? It can get confusing!

That's how it is with the three guys named **James** in the New Testament. Two of the original twelve disciples were named James. But it was probably Jesus' half brother James who wrote the book of James.

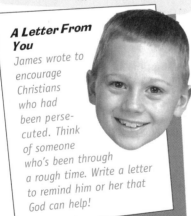

A Letter From You

James wrote to encourage Christians who had been persecuted. Think of someone who's been through a rough time. Write a letter to remind him or her that God can help!

the pilot chooses to go, even though the winds are strong. ⁵In the same way, the tongue is a small thing that makes grand speeches.

But a tiny spark can set a great forest on fire. ⁶And the tongue is a flame of fire. It is a whole world of wickedness, corrupting your entire body. It can set your whole life on fire, for it is set on fire by hell itself.

⁷People can tame all kinds of animals, birds, reptiles, and fish, ⁸but no one can tame the tongue. It is restless and evil, full of deadly poison. ⁹Sometimes it praises our Lord and Father, and sometimes it curses those who have been made in the image of God. ¹⁰And so blessing and cursing come pouring out of the same mouth. Surely, my brothers and sisters, this is not right! ¹¹Does a spring of water bubble out with both fresh water and bitter water? ¹²Does a fig tree produce olives, or a grapevine produce figs? No, and you can't draw fresh water from a salty spring.

True Wisdom Comes from God

¹³If you are wise and understand God's ways, prove it by living an honorable life, doing good works with the humility that comes from wisdom. ¹⁴But if you are bitterly jealous and there is selfish ambition in your heart, don't cover up the truth with boasting and lying. ¹⁵For jealousy and selfishness are not God's kind of wisdom. Such things are earthly, unspiritual, and demonic. ¹⁶For wherever there is jealousy and selfish ambition, there you will find disorder and evil of every kind.

¹⁷But the wisdom from above is first of all pure. It is also peace loving, gentle at all times, and willing to yield to others. It is full of mercy and good deeds. It shows no favoritism and is always sincere. ¹⁸And those who are peacemakers will plant seeds of peace and reap a harvest of righteousness.

CHAPTER **4**
Drawing Close to God

What is causing the quarrels and fights among you? Don't they come from the evil desires at war within you? ²You want what you don't have, so you scheme and kill to get it. You are jealous of what others have, but you can't get it, so you fight and wage war to take it away from them. Yet you don't have what you want because you don't ask God for it. ³And even when you ask, you don't get it because your motives are all wrong—you want only what will give you pleasure.

⁴You adulterers! Don't you realize that friendship with the world makes you an enemy of God?

I say it again: If you want to be a friend of the world, you make yourself an enemy of God. [5] What do you think the Scriptures mean when they say that the spirit God has placed within us is filled with envy? [6] But he gives us even more grace to stand against such evil desires. As the Scriptures say,

"God opposes the proud
but favors the humble."

[7] So humble yourselves before God. Resist the devil, and he will flee from you. [8] Come close to God, and God will come close to you. Wash your hands, you sinners; purify your hearts, for your loyalty is divided between God and the world. [9] Let there be tears for what you have done. Let there be sorrow and deep grief. Let there be sadness instead of laughter, and gloom instead of joy. [10] Humble yourselves before the Lord, and he will lift you up in honor.

Warning against Judging Others

[11] Don't speak evil against each other, dear brothers and sisters. If you criticize and judge each other, then you are criticizing and judging God's law. But your job is to obey the law, not to judge whether it applies to you. [12] God alone, who gave the law, is the Judge. He alone has the power to save or to destroy. So what right do you have to judge your neighbor?

Warning about Self-Confidence

[13] Look here, you who say, "Today or tomorrow we are going to a certain town and will stay there a year. We will do business there and make a profit." [14] How do you know what your life will be like tomorrow? Your life is like the morning fog—it's here a little while, then it's gone. [15] What you ought to say is, "If the Lord wants us to, we will live and do this or that." [16] Otherwise you are boasting about your own plans, and all such boasting is evil.

[17] Remember, it is sin to know what you ought to do and then not do it.

CHAPTER **5**
Warning to the Rich

Look here, you rich people: Weep and groan with anguish because of all the terrible troubles ahead of you. [2] Your wealth is rotting away, and your fine clothes are moth-eaten rags. [3] Your gold and silver have become worthless. The very wealth you were counting on will eat away your flesh like fire. This treasure you have accumulated will stand as evidence against you on the day of judgment. [4] For listen! Hear the cries of the field workers whom you have cheated of their pay. The wages you held back cry out against you. The cries of those who harvest your fields have reached the ears of the LORD of Heaven's Armies.

[5] You have spent your years on earth in luxury, satisfying your every desire. You have fattened yourselves for the day of slaughter. [6] You have condemned and killed innocent people, who do not resist you.

Patience and Endurance

[7] Dear brothers and sisters, be patient as you wait for the Lord's return. Consider the farmers who patiently wait for the rains in the fall and in the spring. They eagerly look for the valuable harvest to ripen. [8] You, too, must be patient. Take courage, for the coming of the Lord is near.

[9] Don't grumble about each other, brothers and sisters, or you will be judged. For look—the Judge is standing at the door!

[10] For examples of patience in suffering, dear brothers and sisters, look at the prophets who spoke in the name of the Lord. [11] We give great honor to those who endure under suffering. For instance, you know about Job, a man of great endurance. You can see how the Lord was kind to him at the end, for the Lord is full of tenderness and mercy.

[12] But most of all, my brothers and sisters, never take an oath, by heaven or earth or anything else. Just say a simple yes or no, so that you will not sin and be condemned.

The Power of Prayer

[13] Are any of you suffering hardships? You should pray. Are any of you happy? You should sing praises. [14] Are any of you sick? You should call for the elders of the church to come and pray over you, anointing you with oil in the name of the Lord. [15] Such a prayer offered in faith will heal the sick, and the Lord will make you well. And if you have committed any sins, you will be forgiven.

[16] **Confess your sins to each other and pray for each other so that you may be healed. The earnest prayer of a righteous person has great power and produces wonderful results.** [17] Elijah was as human as we are, and yet when he prayed earnestly that no rain would fall, none fell for three and a half years! [18] Then, when he prayed again, the sky sent down rain and the earth began to yield its crops.

Restore Wandering Believers

[19]My dear brothers and sisters, if someone among you wanders away from the truth and is brought back, [20]you can be sure that whoever brings the sinner back will save that person from death and bring about the forgiveness of many sins.

1 PETER Words of Encouragement

Look for **2** hidden messages in 1 Peter!

Peter wrote this letter to Christians who were suffering for their faith.
It tells about
- **FAITH AND FIRE**
- **PAIN AND PAYMENT**
- **CHRIST THE CORNERSTONE**
- **BEAUTIFUL BLESSINGS**

Feeding Time

Thirsty? Well, you should be! **Find out why—and for what—in 1 Peter 2:1-3!**

Construction Zone

God is a builder, but his construction project isn't like any other in the world. And you're part of it! **See for yourself in 1 Peter 2:4-6.**

You're Worth How Much?

Did you know that someone paid a price for you? A *huge* price? **Find out how much you're worth by reading 1 Peter 1:18-20.**

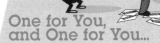

One for You, and One for You...

If someone insults you, what do you do? OK, let's rephrase that—what *should* you do? **The answer might surprise you. Check it out in 1 Peter 3:8-9!**

Timeline

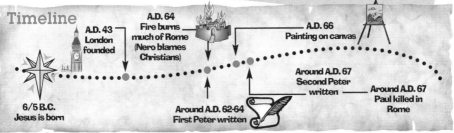

- **6/5 B.C.** Jesus is born
- **A.D. 43** London founded
- **A.D. 64** Fire burns much of Rome (Nero blames Christians)
- **Around A.D. 62-64** First Peter written
- **A.D. 66** Painting on canvas
- **Around A.D. 67** Second Peter written
- **Around A.D. 67** Paul killed in Rome

The JESUS CONNECTION

Peter knew what he was talking about when he encouraged other Christians. He himself had been beaten and jailed for being a Christian, and he was eventually killed for his faith. But Peter knew that faith in Jesus is the most important thing in life, and he had grown to the point that nothing could shake his faith in Jesus. **The next time you feel like it's hard to be a Christian, remember Peter and read this book again.**

CHAPTER **1**

Greetings from Peter

This letter is from Peter, an apostle of Jesus Christ.

I am writing to God's chosen people who are living as foreigners in the provinces of Pontus, Galatia, Cappadocia, Asia, and Bithynia. ²God the Father knew you and chose you long ago, and his Spirit has made you holy. As a result, you have obeyed him and have been cleansed by the blood of Jesus Christ.

May God give you more and more grace and peace.

The Hope of Eternal Life

³All praise to God, the Father of our Lord Jesus Christ. It is by his great mercy that we have been born again, because God raised Jesus Christ from the dead. Now we live with great expectation, ⁴and we have a priceless inheritance—an inheritance that is kept in heaven for you, pure and undefiled, beyond the reach of change and decay. ⁵And through your faith, God is protecting you by his power until you receive this salvation, which is ready to be revealed on the last day for all to see.

⁶So be truly glad. There is wonderful joy ahead, even though you have to endure many trials for a little while. ⁷These trials will show that your faith is genuine. It is being tested as fire tests and purifies gold—though your faith is far more precious than mere gold. So when your faith remains strong through many trials, it will bring you much praise and glory and honor on the day when Jesus Christ is revealed to the whole world.

⁸You love him even though you have never seen him. Though you do not see him now, you trust him; and you rejoice with a glorious, inexpressible joy. ⁹The reward for trusting him will be the salvation of your souls.

¹⁰This salvation was something even the prophets wanted to know more about when they prophesied about this gracious salvation prepared for you. ¹¹They wondered what time or situation the Spirit of Christ within them was talking about when he told them in advance about Christ's suffering and his great glory afterward.

Safe and SOUND

GUESS WHAT!
God has a priceless gift waiting for you.

Want to find out what it is?
JUST READ 1 PETER 1:3-6!

WOW! God is reserving the priceless gift of salvation for everyone who believes in Jesus. So make this reminder!

① On a colorful index card, write the words of 1 PETER 1:4, but substitute your name in the verse.

② Lay one sheet of clear Con-Tact paper on a table, sticky side up. Place your card in the center, and cover it with another sheet, sticky side down. Trim around the card.

③ Cut two posterboard stars the same size. In the center of each, cut a rectangle slightly smaller than the card.

④ Sandwich the card between the two star shapes, and glue the starry frame into place. Trim around the edges.

Hang your star reminder in your room so you can see it every day.

See how your card is kept safe between the clear sheets? That's how your gift of salvation is being kept safe for you in heaven!

12They were told that their messages were not for themselves, but for you. And now this Good News has been announced to you by those who preached in the power of the Holy Spirit sent from heaven. It is all so wonderful that even the angels are eagerly watching these things happen.

A Call to Holy Living

13So think clearly and exercise self-control. Look forward to the gracious salvation that will come to you when Jesus Christ is revealed to the world. 14So you must live as God's obedient children. Don't slip back into your old ways of living to satisfy your own desires. You didn't know any better then. 15But now you must be holy in everything you do, just as God who chose you is holy. 16For the Scriptures say, "You must be holy because I am holy."

17And remember that the heavenly Father to whom you pray has no favorites. He will judge or reward you according to what you do. So you must live in reverent fear of him during your time as "foreigners in the land." 18For you know that God paid a ransom to save you from the empty life you inherited from your ancestors. And the ransom he paid was not mere gold or silver. 19It was the precious blood of Christ, the sinless, spotless Lamb of God. 20God chose him as your ransom long before the world began, but he has now revealed him to you in these last days.

21Through Christ you have come to trust in God. And you have placed your faith and hope in God because he raised Christ from the dead and gave him great glory.

22You were cleansed from your sins when you obeyed the truth, so now you must show sincere love to each other as brothers and sisters. Love each other deeply with all your heart.

23For you have been born again, but not to a life that will quickly end. Your new life will last forever because it comes from the eternal, living word of God. 24As the Scriptures say,

"People are like grass;
      their beauty is like a flower in the field.
The grass withers and the flower fades.
25   But the word of the Lord remains forever."

And that word is the Good News that was preached to you.

CHAPTER **2**

So get rid of all evil behavior. Be done with all deceit, hypocrisy, jealousy, and all unkind speech. 2Like newborn babies, you must crave pure spiritual milk so that you will grow into a full experi-

FUN-fact What's the Church?

Did you know the Bible never mentions "church buildings," but the word *church* is mentioned more than 100 times? That's because the church isn't a building! The church is people!

After Jesus went back to heaven, God sent the Holy Spirit to live inside Jesus' followers. That's when the church began.

Wow—think about it! God's Holy Spirit is working in you to make you more like Jesus. And that's true of every other Christian.

Think of Christians you know and how you've seen God's presence in them. Then write a short note to each one, describing what you've seen. Mail or hand out the notes as an encouragement to the church!

ence of salvation. Cry out for this nourishment, 3now that you have had a taste of the Lord's kindness.

Living Stones for God's House

4You are coming to Christ, who is the living cornerstone of God's temple. He was rejected by people, but he was chosen by God for great honor.

5And you are living stones that God is building into his spiritual temple. What's more, you are his holy priests. Through the mediation of Jesus Christ, you offer spiritual sacrifices that please God. 6As the Scriptures say,

"I am placing a cornerstone in Jerusalem,
      chosen for great honor,
and anyone who trusts in him
      will never be disgraced."

7Yes, you who trust him recognize the honor God has given him. But for those who reject him,

"The stone that the builders rejected
      has now become the cornerstone."

8And,

"He is the stone that makes people stumble,
      the rock that makes them fall."

They stumble because they do not obey God's word, and so they meet the fate that was planned for them.

⁹But you are not like that, for you are a chosen people. You are royal priests, a holy nation, God's very own possession. As a result, you can show others the goodness of God, for he called you out of the darkness into his wonderful light.

10 "Once you had no identity as a people;
    now you are God's people.
Once you received no mercy;
    now you have received God's mercy."

¹¹Dear friends, I warn you as "temporary residents and foreigners" to keep away from worldly desires that wage war against your very souls. ¹²Be careful to live properly among your unbelieving neighbors. Then even if they accuse you of doing wrong, they will see your honorable behavior, and they will give honor to God when he judges the world.

Respecting People in Authority

¹³For the Lord's sake, respect all human authority—whether the king as head of state, ¹⁴or the officials he has appointed. For the king has sent them to punish those who do wrong and to honor those who do right.

¹⁵It is God's will that your honorable lives should silence those ignorant people who make foolish accusations against you. ¹⁶For you are free, yet you are God's slaves, so don't use your freedom as an excuse to do evil. ¹⁷Respect everyone, and love your Christian brothers and sisters. Fear God, and respect the king.

Slaves

¹⁸You who are slaves must accept the authority of your masters with all respect. Do what they tell you—not only if they are kind and reasonable, but even if they are cruel. ¹⁹For God is pleased with you when you do what you know is right and patiently endure unfair treatment. ²⁰Of course, you get no credit for being patient if you are beaten for doing wrong. But if you suffer for doing good and endure it patiently, God is pleased with you.

²¹For God called you to do good, even if it means suffering, just as Christ suffered for you. He is your example, and you must follow in his steps.

22 He never sinned,
    nor ever deceived anyone.
23 He did not retaliate when he was insulted,
    nor threaten revenge when he suffered.

Key Verse "Instead, you must worship Christ as Lord of your life. And if someone asks about your Christian hope, always be ready to explain it."—1 PETER 3:15

Have a PLAN

Grab a friend and take turns reading 1 PETER 3:15 out loud to each other.

Now, talk with your friend about how you can explain your faith in Jesus to others.

BE READY AT SCHOOL!

▶ Draw pictures of your favorite Bible stories on a book cover. Be ready to tell the stories to anyone who asks.

▶ Wrap a chenille wire around a pencil up to the eraser. Cut a small strip of poster board and write your favorite verse on it. Attach the verse to the pencil topper. Be ready to explain why it's your favorite verse.

you must worship Christ as the Lord of your life.

BE READY WITH YOUR FRIENDS!

▶ Use fabric paint and markers to create a faith T-shirt. Be ready to explain what you wrote and drew.

▶ Make invitations to your church. Keep them with you so you can invite friends to learn about God.

Read what Jesus said about sharing your faith in Matthew 28:18-20.

He left his case in the hands of God,
who always judges fairly.
24 He personally carried our sins
in his body on the cross
so that we can be dead to sin
and live for what is right.
By his wounds
you are healed.
25 Once you were like sheep
who wandered away.
But now you have turned to your Shepherd,
the Guardian of your souls.

Wives
In the same way, you wives must accept the authority of your husbands. Then, even if some refuse to obey the Good News, your godly lives will speak to them without any words. They will be won over 2by observing your pure and reverent lives.

3 Don't be concerned about the outward beauty of fancy hairstyles, expensive jewelry, or beautiful clothes. 4You should clothe yourselves instead with the beauty that comes from within, the unfading beauty of a gentle and quiet spirit, which is so precious to God. 5 This is how the holy women of old made themselves beautiful. They trusted God and accepted the authority of their husbands. 6 For instance, Sarah obeyed her husband, Abraham, and called him her master. You are her daughters when you do what is right without fear of what your husbands might do.

Husbands
7 In the same way, you husbands must give honor to your wives. Treat your wife with understanding as you live together. She may be weaker than you are, but she is your equal partner in God's gift of new life. Treat her as you should so your prayers will not be hindered.

All Christians
8 Finally, all of you should be of one mind. Sympathize with each other. Love each other as brothers and sisters. Be tenderhearted, and keep a humble attitude. 9 Don't repay evil for evil. Don't retaliate with insults when people insult you. Instead, pay them back with a blessing. That is what God has called you to do, and he will bless you for it. 10 For the Scriptures say,

"If you want to enjoy life
and see many happy days,

keep your tongue from speaking evil
and your lips from telling lies.
11 Turn away from evil and do good.
Search for peace, and work to maintain it.
12 The eyes of the Lord watch over those who
do right,
and his ears are open to their prayers.
But the Lord turns his face
against those who do evil."

Suffering for Doing Good
13 Now, who will want to harm you if you are eager to do good? 14But even if you suffer for doing what is right, God will reward you for it. So don't worry or be afraid of their threats. **15Instead, you must worship Christ as Lord of your life. And if someone asks about your Christian hope, always be ready to explain it.** 16 But do this in a gentle and respectful way. Keep your conscience clear. Then if people speak against you, they will be ashamed when they see what a good life you live because you belong to Christ. 17Remember, it is better to suffer for doing good, if that is what God wants, than to suffer for doing wrong!

18 Christ suffered for our sins once for all time. He never sinned, but he died for sinners to bring you safely home to God. He suffered physical death, but he was raised to life in the Spirit.

19 So he went and preached to the spirits in prison—20those who disobeyed God long ago when God waited patiently while Noah was building his boat. Only eight people were saved from drowning in that terrible flood. 21And that water is a picture of baptism, which now saves you, not by removing dirt from your body, but as a response to God from a clean conscience. It is effective because of the resurrection of Jesus Christ.

22Now Christ has gone to heaven. He is seated in the place of honor next to God, and all the angels and authorities and powers accept his authority.

CHAPTER 4

Living for God
So then, since Christ suffered physical pain, you must arm yourselves with the same attitude he had, and be ready to suffer, too. For if you have suffered physically for Christ, you have finished with sin. 2You won't spend the rest of your lives chasing your own desires, but you will be anxious to do the will of God. 3 You have had enough in the past of the evil things that godless people enjoy—their immorality and lust, their feasting and

No Pressure!

Read 1 PETER 5:7 a few times.

Sounds simple, huh? But is it?

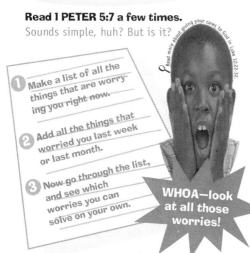

Read more about giving your cares to God in Luke 12:22-32

1. Make a list of all the things that are worrying you right now.

2. Add all the things that worried you last week or last month.

3. Now go through the list, and see which worries you can solve on your own.

WHOA—look at all those worries!

Most of the things we worry about are out of our control. So it makes perfect sense to give them to God! If you don't, this could happen to you.

Take a lump of clay, and form it into a person shape.

For each worry on your list, press down on your clay person's head a little.

What happened?

ALL THOSE WORRIES PRESSED YOUR PERSON FLAT!

DON'T LET THAT HAPPEN TO YOU!
Give your worries to God!

---

drunkenness and wild parties, and their terrible worship of idols.

4 Of course, your former friends are surprised when you no longer plunge into the flood of wild and destructive things they do. So they slander you. 5 But remember that they will have to face God, who will judge everyone, both the living and the dead. 6 That is why the Good News was preached to those who are now dead—so although they were destined to die like all people, they now live forever with God in the Spirit.

7 The end of the world is coming soon. Therefore, be earnest and disciplined in your prayers. 8 Most important of all, continue to show deep love for each other, for love covers a multitude of sins. 9 Cheerfully share your home with those who need a meal or a place to stay.

10 God has given each of you a gift from his great variety of spiritual gifts. Use them well to serve one another. 11 Do you have the gift of speaking? Then speak as though God himself were speaking through you. Do you have the gift of helping others? Do it with all the strength and energy that God supplies. Then everything you do will bring glory to God through Jesus Christ. All glory and power to him forever and ever! Amen.

Suffering for Being a Christian

12 Dear friends, don't be surprised at the fiery trials you are going through, as if something strange were happening to you. 13 Instead, be very glad—for these trials make you partners with Christ in his suffering, so that you will have the wonderful joy of seeing his glory when it is revealed to all the world.

14 So be happy when you are insulted for being a Christian, for then the glorious Spirit of God rests upon you. 15 If you suffer, however, it must not be for murder, stealing, making trouble, or prying into other people's affairs. 16 But it is no shame to suffer for being a Christian. Praise God for the privilege of being called by his name! 17 For the time has come for judgment, and it must begin with God's household. And if judgment begins with us, what terrible fate awaits those who have never obeyed God's Good News? 18 And also,

"If the righteous are barely saved,
what will happen to godless sinners?"

19 So if you are suffering in a manner that pleases God, keep on doing what is right, and trust your lives to the God who created you, for he will never fail you.

Advice for Elders and Young Men

And now, a word to you who are elders in the churches. I, too, am an elder and a witness to the sufferings of Christ. And I, too, will share in his glory when he is revealed to the whole world. As a fellow elder, I appeal to you: ²Care for the flock that God has entrusted to you. Watch over it willingly, not grudgingly—not for what you will get out of it, but because you are eager to serve God. ³Don't lord it over the people assigned to your care, but lead them by your own good example. ⁴And when the Great Shepherd appears, you will receive a crown of never-ending glory and honor.

⁵In the same way, you younger men must accept the authority of the elders. And all of you, serve each other in humility, for

"God opposes the proud
  but favors the humble."

⁶So humble yourselves under the mighty power of God, and at the right time he will lift you up in honor. **⁷Give all your worries and cares to God, for he cares about you.**

⁸Stay alert! Watch out for your great enemy, the devil. He prowls around like a roaring lion, looking for someone to devour. ⁹Stand firm against him, and be strong in your faith. Remember that your Christian brothers and sisters all over the world are going through the same kind of suffering you are.

¹⁰In his kindness God called you to share in his eternal glory by means of Christ Jesus. So after you have suffered a little while, he will restore, support, and strengthen you, and he will place you on a firm foundation. ¹¹All power to him forever! Amen.

Peter's Final Greetings

¹²I have written and sent this short letter to you with the help of Silas, whom I commend to you as a faithful brother. My purpose in writing is to encourage you and assure you that what you are experiencing is truly part of God's grace for you. Stand firm in this grace.

¹³Your sister church here in Babylon sends you greetings, and so does my son Mark. ¹⁴Greet each other with Christian love.

Peace be with all of you who are in Christ.

2 PETER

Words of Warning

Peter wrote this second letter to the early Christians not long before he was killed. He talked about

- **KNOWING GOD**
- **KNOWING THE BIBLE**
- **KNOWING TRUE FROM FALSE**
- **KNOWING HOW TO LIVE**

False Teachers bEwARe

Peter warned about people who would teach lies, instead of the truth, about Jesus. But watch out! Those false teachers are in for a nasty surprise.

Read more in 2 Peter 2:1-3.

LOVE

SELF CONTROL

FAITH

Growing Strong

Have you ever measured yourself on a growth chart to see how tall you were getting? Well, God gives you a growth chart in the Bible! **See how tall you are by reading 2 Peter 1:5-8.**

What's Taking Him So Long?

We know that Jesus will come back one day. But when? **Read 2 Peter 3:8-9 to see what Peter said about Jesus' return.**

Are You Ready?

Because Jesus is coming back, Peter tells us how we should be living our lives until that day. **Read his words for yourself in 2 Peter 3:11-15a.**

Timeline

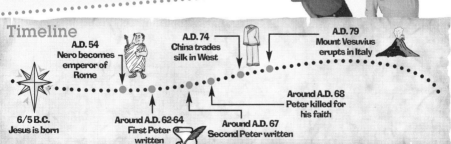

A.D. 54 Nero becomes emperor of Rome

A.D. 74 China trades silk in West

A.D. 79 Mount Vesuvius erupts in Italy

6/5 B.C. Jesus is born

Around A.D. 62-64 First Peter written

Around A.D. 67 Second Peter written

Around A.D. 68 Peter killed for his faith

The JESUS CONNECTION

The book of Second Peter gives great advice about how to keep your faith, even when times are tough. Peter knew that Christians would face hard times and temptations, but he urged us to keep our eyes on Jesus. **Faith in Jesus is all you need to be happy in this life, and to enjoy eternal life later in heaven.**

CHAPTER **1**

Greetings from Peter

This letter is from Simon Peter, a slave and apostle of Jesus Christ.

I am writing to you who share the same precious faith we have. This faith was given to you because of the justice and fairness of Jesus Christ, our God and Savior.

2May God give you more and more grace and peace as you grow in your knowledge of God and Jesus our Lord.

Growing in Faith

3**By his divine power, God has given us everything we need for living a godly life. We have received all of this by coming to know him, the one who called us to himself by means of his marvelous glory and excellence.** 4And because of his glory and excellence, he has given us great and precious promises. These are the promises that enable you to share his divine nature and escape the world's corruption caused by human desires.

5In view of all this, make every effort to respond to God's promises. Supplement your faith with a generous provision of moral excellence, and moral excellence with knowledge, 6and knowledge with self-control, and self-control with patient endurance, and patient endurance with godliness, 7and godliness with brotherly affection, and brotherly affection with love for everyone.

8The more you grow like this, the more productive and useful you will be in your knowledge of our Lord Jesus Christ. 9But those who fail to develop in this way are shortsighted or blind, forgetting that they have been cleansed from their old sins.

10So, dear brothers and sisters, work hard to prove that you really are among those God has called and chosen. Do these things, and you will never fall away. 11Then God will give you a grand entrance into the eternal Kingdom of our Lord and Savior Jesus Christ.

Paying Attention to Scripture

12Therefore, I will always remind you about these things—even though you already know them and are standing firm in the truth you have been taught. 13And it is only right that I should keep on reminding you as long as I live. 14For our Lord Jesus Christ has shown me that I must soon leave this earthly life, 15so I will work hard to make sure you always remember these things after I am gone.

16For we were not making up clever stories when we told you about the powerful coming of our Lord Jesus Christ. We saw his majestic splendor with our own eyes 17when he received honor and glory from God the Father. The voice from the majestic glory of God said to him, "This is my dearly loved Son, who brings me great joy." 18We ourselves heard that voice from heaven when we were with him on the holy mountain.

19Because of that experience, we have even greater confidence in the message proclaimed by the prophets. You must pay close attention to what they wrote, for their words are like a lamp shining in a dark place—until the Day dawns, and Christ the Morning Star shines in your hearts. 20Above all, you must realize that no prophecy in Scripture ever came from the prophet's own understanding, 21or from human initiative. No, those prophets were moved by the Holy Spirit, and they spoke from God.

CHAPTER **2**

The Danger of False Teachers

But there were also false prophets in Israel, just as there will be false teachers among you. They will cleverly teach destructive heresies and even deny the Master who bought them. In this way, they will bring sudden destruction on themselves. 2Many will follow their evil teaching and shameful immorality. And because of these teachers, the way of truth will be slandered. 3In their greed they will make up clever lies to get hold of your money. But God condemned them long ago, and their destruction will not be delayed.

4For God did not spare even the angels who sinned. He threw them into hell, in gloomy pits of darkness, where they are being held until the day of judgment. 5And God did not spare the ancient world—except for Noah and the seven others in his family. Noah warned the world of God's righteous judgment. So God protected Noah when he destroyed the world of ungodly people with a vast flood. 6Later, God condemned the cities of Sodom and Gomorrah and turned them into heaps of ashes. He made them an example of what will happen to ungodly people. 7But God also rescued Lot out of Sodom because he was a righteous man who was sick of the shameful immorality of the wicked people around him. 8Yes, Lot was a righteous man who was tormented in his soul by the wickedness he saw and heard day after day. 9So you see, the Lord knows how to rescue godly people from their trials, even while keeping the wicked under punishment until the day of final judgment. 10He is especially hard on those who follow their own twisted sexual desire, and who despise authority.

These people are proud and arrogant, daring even to scoff at supernatural beings without so much as trembling. 11But the angels, who are far greater in power and strength, do not dare to bring from the Lord a charge of blasphemy against those supernatural beings.

12These false teachers are like unthinking animals, creatures of instinct, born to be caught and destroyed. They scoff at things they do not understand, and like animals, they will be destroyed. 13Their destruction is their reward for the harm they have done. They love to indulge in evil pleasures in broad daylight. They are a disgrace and a stain among you. They delight in deception even as they eat with you in your fellowship meals. 14They commit adultery with their eyes, and their desire for sin is never satisfied. They lure unstable people into sin, and they are well trained in greed. They live under God's curse. 15They have wandered off the right road and followed the footsteps of Balaam son of Beor, who loved to earn money by doing wrong. 16But Balaam was stopped from his mad course when his donkey rebuked him with a human voice.

17These people are as useless as dried-up springs or as mist blown away by the wind. They are doomed to blackest darkness. 18They brag about themselves with empty, foolish boasting. With an appeal to twisted sexual desires, they lure back into sin those who have barely escaped from a lifestyle of deception. 19They promise freedom, but they themselves are slaves of sin and corruption. For you are a slave to whatever controls you. 20And when people escape from the wickedness of the world by knowing our Lord and Savior Jesus Christ and then get tangled up and enslaved by sin again, they are worse off than before. 21It would be better if they had never known the way to righteousness than to know it and then reject the command they were given to live a holy life. 22They prove the truth of this proverb: "A dog returns to its vomit." And another says, "A washed pig returns to the mud."

CHAPTER **3**
The Day of the Lord Is Coming
This is my second letter to you, dear friends, and in both of them I have tried to stimulate your wholesome thinking and refresh your memory.

2I want you to remember what the holy prophets said long ago and what our Lord and Savior commanded through your apostles.

3Most importantly, I want to remind you that in the last days scoffers will come, mocking the truth and following their own desires. 4They will say, "What happened to the promise that Jesus is coming again? From before the times of our ancestors, everything has remained the same since the world was first created."

5They deliberately forget that God made the heavens by the word of his command, and he brought the earth out from the water and surrounded it with water. 6Then he used the water to destroy the ancient world with a mighty flood. 7And by the same word, the present heavens and earth have been stored up for fire. They are being kept for the day of judgment, when ungodly people will be destroyed.

8But you must not forget this one thing, dear friends: A day is like a thousand years to the Lord, and a thousand years is like a day. **9The Lord isn't really being slow about his promise, as some people think. No, he is being patient for your sake. He does not want anyone to be destroyed, but wants everyone to repent.** 10But the day of the Lord will come as unexpectedly as a thief. Then the heavens will pass away with a terrible noise, and the very elements themselves will disappear in fire, and the earth and everything on it will be found to deserve judgment.

11Since everything around us is going to be destroyed like this, what holy and godly lives you should live, 12looking forward to the day of God and hurrying it along. On that day, he will set the heavens on fire, and the elements will melt away in the flames. 13But we are looking forward to the new heavens and new earth he has promised, a world filled with God's righteousness.

14And so, dear friends, while you are waiting for these things to happen, make every effort to be found living peaceful lives that are pure and blameless in his sight.

15And remember, the Lord's patience gives people time to be saved. This is what our beloved brother Paul also wrote to you with the wisdom God gave him—16speaking of these things in all of his letters. Some of his comments are hard to understand, and those who are ignorant and unstable have twisted his letters to mean something quite different, just as they do with other parts of Scripture. And this will result in their destruction.

Peter's Final Words

17I am warning you ahead of time, dear friends. Be on guard so that you will not be carried away by the errors of these wicked people and lose your own secure footing. 18Rather, you must grow in the grace and knowledge of our Lord and Savior Jesus Christ.

All glory to him, both now and forever! Amen.

1 JOHN A Love Letter

Look for **2** hidden messages in 1 John!

Blah, blah blah!
blah blah!

I ALWAYS help others. I'm good!

John wrote this letter to encourage Christians everywhere in their faith. It tells about

- **LIGHT AND DARK**
- **GOOD AND BAD**
- **TRUE AND FALSE**
- **LIFE AND DEATH**
- **LOVE AND MORE LOVE**

Yeah, right!

All Talk?

Maybe you've heard the expression, "Talk is cheap." Or how about, "Actions speak louder than words"? Well, the Bible says it best! **Check it out in 1 John 3:18. (Then follow that advice!)**

'Fess Up

Have you ever committed a sin and been afraid to admit it? Well, don't be afraid anymore! **Find out why in 1 John 1:8-9!**

True Love

What is love? *Real* love? Find out in 1 John 4:9-10!

FAMILY REUNION

Family Reunion

Welcome to the family! Whose family, you ask? **Find out in 1 John 3:1-2.**

Timeline

- **6/5 B.C.** Jesus is born
- **A.D. 1** Saddles first used in Europe
- **A.D. 43** London founded
- **A.D. 54** Nero becomes emperor of Rome
- **A.D. 70** Rome destroys Jerusalem
- **A.D. 79** Mount Vesuvius erupts in Italy
- **Around A.D. 85-90** First John written

The JESUS CONNECTION

This letter of John's is a real love story. It tells how much God loves us and how much we should love others. And right in the middle of all that love is Jesus, who loves us so much that he was willing to die on the cross for our sins. If we believe in him and confess our sins, God's love and light will shine on us forever. **It doesn't get any better than that!**

Introduction

We proclaim to you the one who existed from the beginning, whom we have heard and seen. We saw him with our own eyes and touched him with our own hands. He is the Word of life. ²This one who is life itself was revealed to us, and we have seen him. And now we testify and proclaim to you that he is the one who is eternal life. He was with the Father, and then he was revealed to us. ³We proclaim to you what we ourselves have actually seen and heard so that you may have fellowship with us. And our fellowship is with the Father and with his Son, Jesus Christ. ⁴We are writing these things so that you may fully share our joy.

Living in the Light

⁵This is the message we heard from Jesus and now declare to you: God is light, and there is no darkness in him at all. ⁶So we are lying if we say we have fellowship with God but go on living in spiritual darkness; we are not practicing the truth. ⁷But if we are living in the light, as God is in the light, then we have fellowship with each other, and the blood of Jesus, his Son, cleanses us from all sin.

⁸If we claim we have no sin, we are only fooling ourselves and not living in the truth. ⁹But if we confess our sins to him, he is faithful and just to forgive us our sins and to cleanse us from all wickedness. ¹⁰If we claim we have not sinned, we are calling God a liar and showing that his word has no place in our hearts.

My dear children, I am writing this to you so that you will not sin. But if anyone does sin, we have an advocate who pleads our case before the Father. He is Jesus Christ, the one who is truly righteous. ²He himself is the sacrifice that atones for our sins—and not only our sins but the sins of all the world.

³And we can be sure that we know him if we obey his commandments. ⁴If someone claims, "I know God," but doesn't obey God's commandments, that person is a liar and is not living in the truth. ⁵But those who obey God's word truly show how completely they love him. That is how we know we are living in him. ⁶Those who say they live in God should live their lives as Jesus did.

A New Commandment

⁷Dear friends, I am not writing a new commandment for you; rather it is an old one you have had from the very beginning. This old commandment—to love one another—is the same message you heard before. ⁸Yet it is also new. Jesus lived the truth of this commandment, and you also are living it. For the darkness is disappearing, and the true light is already shining.

⁹If anyone claims, "I am living in the light," but hates a Christian brother or sister, that person is still living in darkness. ¹⁰Anyone who loves another brother or sister is living in the light and does not cause others to stumble. ¹¹But anyone who hates another brother or sister is still living and walking in darkness. Such a person does not know the way to go, having been blinded by the darkness.

¹² I am writing to you who are God's children
    because your sins have been forgiven
        through Jesus.
¹³ I am writing to you who are mature
        in the faith
    because you know Christ, who existed
        from the beginning.
I am writing to you who are young
        in the faith
    because you have won your battle
        with the evil one.
¹⁴ I have written to you who are God's children
    because you know the Father.
I have written to you who are mature
        in the faith
    because you know Christ, who existed
        from the beginning.
I have written to you who are young
        in the faith
    because you are strong.
God's word lives in your hearts,
    and you have won your battle with
        the evil one.

Do Not Love This World

¹⁵Do not love this world nor the things it offers you, for when you love the world, you do not have the love of the Father in you. ¹⁶For the world offers only a craving for physical pleasure, a craving for everything we see, and pride in our achievements and possessions. These are not from the Father, but are from this world. ¹⁷And this world is fading away, along with everything that people crave. But anyone who does what pleases God will live forever.

Warning about Antichrists

18 Dear children, the last hour is here. You have heard that the Antichrist is coming, and already many such antichrists have appeared. From this we know that the last hour has come. 19 These people left our churches, but they never really belonged with us; otherwise they would have stayed with us. When they left, it proved that they did not belong with us.

20 But you are not like that, for the Holy One has given you his Spirit, and all of you know the truth. 21 So I am writing to you not because you don't know the truth but because you know the difference between truth and lies. 22 And who is a liar? Anyone who says that Jesus is not the Christ. Anyone who denies the Father and the Son is an antichrist. 23 Anyone who denies the Son doesn't have the Father, either. But anyone who acknowledges the Son has the Father also.

24 So you must remain faithful to what you have been taught from the beginning. If you do, you will remain in fellowship with the Son and with the Father. 25 And in this fellowship we enjoy the eternal life he promised us.

26 I am writing these things to warn you about those who want to lead you astray. 27 But you have received the Holy Spirit, and he lives within you, so you don't need anyone to teach you what is true. For the Spirit teaches you everything you need to know, and what he teaches is true—it is not a lie. So just as he has taught you, remain in fellowship with Christ.

Living as Children of God

28 And now, dear children, remain in fellowship with Christ so that when he returns, you will be full of courage and not shrink back from him in shame.

29 Since we know that Christ is righteous, we also know that all who do what is right are God's children.

CHAPTER **3**

See how very much our Father loves us, for he calls us his children, and that is what we are! But the people who belong to this world don't recognize that we are God's children because they don't know him. 2 Dear friends, we are already God's children, but he has not yet shown us what we will be like when Christ appears. But we do know that we will be like him, for we will see him as he really is. 3 And all who have this eager expectation will keep themselves pure, just as he is pure.

GOODBYE SINS!

Think of a sin you've committed.

Got one? OK, now undo it. Make it like it never happened.

Having trouble? Of course! We can't undo our sins. But God can! **Just read 1 JOHN 1:9.**

If we confess our sins to God and tell him we're sorry (and mean it!), he'll forgive us. We might have to deal with the consequences of our sins, but when God forgives a sin, it's gone!

THINK OF IT LIKE THIS:

① Use a highlighter to write on a coffee filter a sin you've committed.

② Now confess that sin to God and ask him to forgive you. Next, put a few drops of lemon juice on the writing, and watch as your "sin" disappears!

Read more about forgiveness in Romans 3:22!

The lemon juice made the writing disappear. When we confess our sins to God, he forgives us. He makes our sins completely disappear from his sight!

COOL!

Key Verse

"Dear friends, let us continue to love one another, for love comes from God. Anyone who loves is a child of God and knows God. But anyone who does not love does not know God, for God is love." —1 JOHN 4:7-8

GOD IS LOVE

For more about love, go to 1 Corinthians 13:4-7!

Read 1 JOHN 4:7-8 out loud a few times. Notice anything? Two words keep popping up. **God** and **love**.

When we show love to others, like this passage says to do, we're spreading God's love.

TRY THIS!

Write the words of 1 JOHN 4:7-8 around your heart!

1 Cut a heart out of white poster board. Mount it on a slightly bigger piece of colored poster board. Hang it on your wall.

2 Tear red construction paper into small pieces big enough to write on. Put the pieces in a bag or bowl near your poster.

3 Every time you show love to someone, write what you did on one of the paper pieces. Glue or tape the piece to the heart.

See how long it takes you to fill up the heart with loving actions!

GO SHOW GOD'S LOVE!

4 Everyone who sins is breaking God's law, for all sin is contrary to the law of God. 5 And you know that Jesus came to take away our sins, and there is no sin in him. 6 Anyone who continues to live in him will not sin. But anyone who keeps on sinning does not know him or understand who he is.

7 Dear children, don't let anyone deceive you about this: When people do what is right, it shows that they are righteous, even as Christ is righteous. 8 But when people keep on sinning, it shows that they belong to the devil, who has been sinning since the beginning. But the Son of God came to destroy the works of the devil. 9 Those who have been born into God's family do not make a practice of sinning, because God's life is in them. So they can't keep on sinning, because they are children of God. 10 So now we can tell who are children of God and who are children of the devil. Anyone who does not live righteously and does not love other believers does not belong to God.

Love One Another

11 This is the message you have heard from the beginning: We should love one another. 12 We must not be like Cain, who belonged to the evil one and killed his brother. And why did he kill him? Because Cain had been doing what was evil, and his brother had been doing what was righteous. 13 So don't be surprised, dear brothers and sisters, if the world hates you.

14 If we love our Christian brothers and sisters, it proves that we have passed from death to life. But a person who has no love is still dead. 15 Anyone who hates another brother or sister is really a murderer at heart. And you know that murderers don't have eternal life within them.

16 We know what real love is because Jesus gave up his life for us. So we also ought to give up our lives for our brothers and sisters. 17 If someone has enough money to live well and sees a brother or sister in need but shows no compassion—how can God's love be in that person?

18 Dear children, let's not merely say that we love each other; let us show the truth by our actions. 19 Our actions will show that we belong to the truth, so we will be confident when we stand before God. 20 Even if we feel guilty, God is greater than our feelings, and he knows everything.

21 Dear friends, if we don't feel guilty, we can come to God with bold confidence. 22 And we will receive from him whatever we ask because we obey him and do the things that please him.

23 And this is his commandment: We must believe in the name of his Son, Jesus Christ, and love one another, just as he commanded us. 24 Those who obey God's commandments remain in fellowship with him, and he with them. And we know he lives in us because the Spirit he gave us lives in us.

CHAPTER **4**
Discerning False Prophets

Dear friends, do not believe everyone who claims to speak by the Spirit. You must test them to see if the spirit they have comes from God. For there are many false prophets in the world. 2 This is how we know if they have the Spirit of God: If a person claiming to be a prophet acknowledges that Jesus Christ came in a real body, that person has the Spirit of God. 3 But if someone claims to be a prophet and does not acknowledge the truth about Jesus, that person is not from God. Such a person has the spirit of the Antichrist, which you heard is coming into the world and indeed is already here.

4 But you belong to God, my dear children. You have already won a victory over those people, because the Spirit who lives in you is greater than the spirit who lives in the world. 5 Those people belong to this world, so they speak from the world's viewpoint, and the world listens to them. 6 But we belong to God, and those who know God listen to us. If they do not belong to God, they do not listen to us. That is how we know if someone has the Spirit of truth or the spirit of deception.

Loving One Another

7 Dear friends, let us continue to love one another, for love comes from God. Anyone who loves is a child of God and knows God. 8 But anyone who does not love does not know God, for God is love.

9 God showed how much he loved us by sending his one and only Son into the world so that we might have eternal life through him. 10 This is real love—not that we loved God, but that he loved us and sent his Son as a sacrifice to take away our sins.

11 Dear friends, since God loved us that much, we surely ought to love each other. 12 No one has ever seen God. But if we love each other, God

lives in us, and his love is brought to full expression in us.

13 And God has given us his Spirit as proof that we live in him and he in us. 14 Furthermore, we have seen with our own eyes and now testify that the Father sent his Son to be the Savior of the world. 15 All who confess that Jesus is the Son of God have God living in them, and they live in God. 16 We know how much God loves us, and we have put our trust in his love.

God is love, and all who live in love live in God, and God lives in them. 17 And as we live in God, our love grows more perfect. So we will not be afraid on the day of judgment, but we can face him with confidence because we live like Jesus here in this world.

18 Such love has no fear, because perfect love expels all fear. If we are afraid, it is for fear of punishment, and this shows that we have not fully experienced his perfect love. 19 We love each other because he loved us first.

20 If someone says, "I love God," but hates a Christian brother or sister, that person is a liar; for if we don't love people we can see, how can we love God, whom we cannot see? 21 And he has given us this command: Those who love God must also love their Christian brothers and sisters.

CHAPTER **5**
Faith in the Son of God

Everyone who believes that Jesus is the Christ has become a child of God. And everyone who loves the Father loves his children, too. 2 We know we love God's children if we love God and obey his commandments. 3 Loving God means keeping his commandments, and his commandments are not burdensome. 4 For every child of God defeats this evil world, and we achieve this victory through our faith. 5 And who can win this battle against the world? Only those who believe that Jesus is the Son of God.

6 And Jesus Christ was revealed as God's Son by his baptism in water and by shedding his blood on the cross—not by water only, but by water and blood. And the Spirit, who is truth, confirms it with his testimony. 7 So we have these three witnesses—8 the Spirit, the water, and the blood—and all three agree. 9 Since we believe human testimony, surely we can believe the greater testimony that comes from God. And God has testified about his Son. 10 All who believe in the Son of God know in their hearts that this testimony is true. Those who don't

believe this are actually calling God a liar because they don't believe what God has testified about his Son.

[11]And this is what God has testified: He has given us eternal life, and this life is in his Son. **[12]Whoever has the Son has life; whoever does not have God's Son does not have life.**

Conclusion

[13]I have written this to you who believe in the name of the Son of God, so that you may know you have eternal life. [14]And we are confident that he hears us whenever we ask for anything that pleases him. [15]And since we know he hears us when we make our requests, we also know that he will give us what we ask for.

[16]If you see a Christian brother or sister sinning in a way that does not lead to death, you should pray, and God will give that person life. But there is a sin that leads to death, and I am not saying you should pray for those who commit it. [17]All wicked actions are sin, but not every sin leads to death.

[18]We know that God's children do not make a practice of sinning, for God's Son holds them securely, and the evil one cannot touch them. [19]We know that we are children of God and that the world around us is under the control of the evil one.

[20]And we know that the Son of God has come, and he has given us understanding so that we can know the true God. And now we live in fellowship with the true God because we live in fellowship with his Son, Jesus Christ. He is the only true God, and he is eternal life.

[21]Dear children, keep away from anything that might take God's place in your hearts.

2 JOHN
Words of Truth and Love

John wrote this letter to a friend and her family. Look for wisdom about

- **TRUTH AND LOVE**
- **WHY TO LOVE**
- **HOW TO LOVE**
- **WHO DOESN'T LOVE**

Don't Lose Your Way

If you stay on the path, one thing will happen. If you wander away, another thing will happen. What was John talking about? Find out for yourself in 2 John 1:9!

And Nothing But the Truth

John placed a lot of emphasis on truth. Not just on telling the truth, but on *the* truth. What truth was so important to John? Read 2 John 1:1-3.

Old Advice, New Advice

Different letter, same advice. Discover what John found worth repeating by reading 2 John 1:5-6.

A Bad Crowd

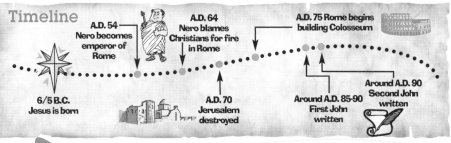

You've probably been told to stay away from the bad crowd, right? Well, John said the same thing way back in Bible times. Read 2 John 1:10-11 to find out who was in John's bad crowd.

Don't Listen to Them!

John warned his friends about listening to a certain type of person. And guess what? His advice applies to you, too! Find out who he was talking about in 2 John 1:7-8.

Timeline

- **6/5 B.C.** Jesus is born
- **A.D. 54** Nero becomes emperor of Rome
- **A.D. 64** Nero blames Christians for fire in Rome
- **A.D. 70** Jerusalem destroyed
- **A.D. 75** Rome begins building Colosseum
- **Around A.D. 85-90** First John written
- **Around A.D. 90** Second John written

The JESUS CONNECTION

John talks a lot about love. The Gospel of John, the three letters, and even the book of Revelation (yup, he wrote all of them) talk about the importance of love. Maybe that's because he had known Jesus personally and experienced his love firsthand. If *we* believe in Jesus, we can have a personal friendship with him and experience his love forever. What an awesome offer! Do you know him?

Greetings

This letter is from John, the elder.

I am writing to the chosen lady and to her children, whom I love in the truth—as does everyone else who knows the truth—²because the truth lives in us and will be with us forever.

³Grace, mercy, and peace, which come from God the Father and from Jesus Christ—the Son of the Father—will continue to be with us who live in truth and love.

Live in the Truth

⁴How happy I was to meet some of your children and find them living according to the truth, just as the Father commanded.

⁵I am writing to remind you, dear friends, that we should love one another. This is not a new commandment, but one we have had from the beginning. ⁶Love means doing what God has commanded us, and he has commanded us to love one another, just as you heard from the beginning.

⁷I say this because many deceivers have gone out into the world. They deny that Jesus Christ came in a real body. Such a person is a deceiver and an antichrist. ⁸Watch out that you do not lose what we have worked so hard to achieve. Be diligent so that you receive your full reward. ⁹Anyone who wanders away from this teaching has no relationship with God. But anyone who remains in the teaching of Christ has a relationship with both the Father and the Son.

¹⁰If anyone comes to your meeting and does not teach the truth about Christ, don't invite that person into your home or give any kind of encouragement. ¹¹Anyone who encourages such people becomes a partner in their evil work.

Conclusion

¹²I have much more to say to you, but I don't want to do it with paper and ink. For I hope to visit you soon and talk with you face to face. Then our joy will be complete.

¹³Greetings from the children of your sister, chosen by God.

3 JOHN — More Thoughts on Love

This third letter of John's, written to a dear friend, contains familiar themes. Look for
- **LESSONS ON LOVE**
- **TRAVELING TEACHERS**
- **EVIL EXAMPLES**

Happy News

Are you happy when your friends do well? Well, John was! **Read 3 John 1:3-4 to find what made him happy about his friends.**

Report Card

Gaius

Faithfulness	A
Truthfulness	A
Love	A
Worthiness	A

On the Road Again

Back in Bible times, teachers traveled from town to town to spread the good news about Jesus. That was their job. But what would they eat, and where would they stay? **Go to 3 John 1:5-8 for the answer!**

Body and Soul

As an apostle of Jesus, John *might* have been concerned only with his friend's spiritual health. Not so! **Read 3 John 1:2 to see what John wrote to his friend.**

A Good Example

What you do tells the world a lot about who you are, what you believe, and whether you know God or not. Don't believe it? **Read 3 John 1:11-12 to find out what John said about a friend of his.**

Timeline

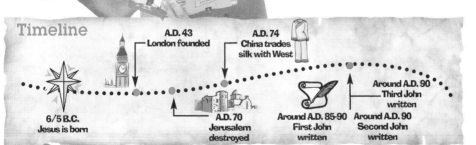

- 6/5 B.C. Jesus is born
- A.D. 43 — London founded
- A.D. 70 Jerusalem destroyed
- A.D. 74 — China trades silk with West
- Around A.D. 85-90 First John written
- Around A.D. 90 Second John written
- Around A.D. 90 — Third John written

The JESUS CONNECTION

Love one another. Be kind to one another. Follow Jesus. Stay away from evil. John talks about these things over and over. Why? Because he learned them from the Master himself. John knew that to love and follow Jesus were the most important things he could do in his life, and he wrote accordingly. **His words were true thousands of years ago, and they are still true for us today!**

3 John

Greetings

This letter is from John, the elder.

I am writing to Gaius, my dear friend, whom I love in the truth.

²Dear friend, I hope all is well with you and that you are as healthy in body as you are strong in spirit. ³Some of the traveling teachers recently returned and made me very happy by telling me about your faithfulness and that you are living according to the truth. ⁴I could have no greater joy than to hear that my children are following the truth.

Caring for the Lord's Workers

⁵Dear friend, you are being faithful to God when you care for the traveling teachers who pass through, even though they are strangers to you. ⁶They have told the church here of your loving friendship. Please continue providing for such teachers in a manner that pleases God. ⁷For they are traveling for the Lord, and they accept nothing from people who are not believers. ⁸So we ourselves should support them so that we can be their partners as they teach the truth.

⁹I wrote to the church about this, but Diotrephes, who loves to be the leader, refuses to have anything to do with us. ¹⁰When I come, I will report some of the things he is doing and the evil accusations he is making against us. Not only does he refuse to welcome the traveling teachers, he also tells others not to help them. And when they do help, he puts them out of the church.

¹¹Dear friend, don't let this bad example influence you. Follow only what is good. Remember that those who do good prove that they are God's children, and those who do evil prove that they do not know God.

¹²Everyone speaks highly of Demetrius, as does the truth itself. We ourselves can say the same for him, and you know we speak the truth.

Conclusion

¹³I have much more to say to you, but I don't want to write it with pen and ink. ¹⁴For I hope to see you soon, and then we will talk face to face.

¹⁵Peace be with you.

Your friends here send you their greetings. Please give my personal greetings to each of our friends there.

FUN-fact

Lots of Love

When people talk about love today, they don't always mean what the Bible means. Christian love is **a sacrificing and eternal love, a love that's modeled after God's love for us.**

WHO DO YOU LOVE?

Think of someone who isn't all that nice to you. God wants you to show his love to that person. Below, write at least two ways you could show love to that person.

_____

_____

Choose one of those ways, and do it! Ask God to help. Write how you think God felt when you showed love to that person.

date: _____

REMEMBER—by your love, others will know you're a follower of Jesus!

JUDE The Book of Unchanging Truth

Jude, the brother of Jesus and James, wrote this book to remind Christians to stay strong in their faith. It warns about
- **STINKING THINKING**
- **TERRIBLE TEACHERS**
- **FALSE FRIENDS**
- **OUR GREAT GOD**

Building Tips

You wouldn't want to build a house on a pile of wet noodles, would you? You have to start with a good foundation.

The same is true for you and your life. **Read Jude 1:17-20 to see what kind of foundation Jude recommends.**

Watch Out for Worms

You may think that what you're eating is good, but there could be worms hiding inside.

It's the same way with what you hear! Huh? Worms in words? **Read Jude 1:3-4 for the juicy report.**

SHOW MERCY

Bad NEWS Dudes

While You Wait

If you believe in Jesus, you're going to heaven! While you wait, there are some things you need to be doing. **Find out what they are in Jude 1:21-23!**

Stay away from them. They pretend to be nice and good, but they're sneaky, and they lie. **Who? Find out in Jude 1:12-13.**

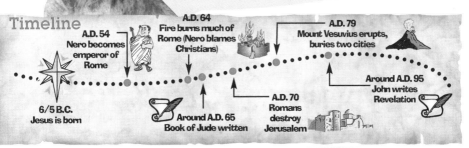

Timeline

A.D. 54 Nero becomes emperor of Rome

A.D. 64 Fire burns much of Rome (Nero blames Christians)

A.D. 79 Mount Vesuvius erupts, buries two cities

Around A.D. 95 John writes Revelation

6/5 B.C. Jesus is born

Around A.D. 65 Book of Jude written

A.D. 70 Romans destroy Jerusalem

The JESUS CONNECTION

Jesus said that he is "*the* way, *the* truth, and *the* life" and that he is the only way to God (John 14:6). The book of Jude warns us to watch out for false teachers who say otherwise. Ideas that take us away from Jesus are so incredibly dangerous because believing in Jesus is the only way we can be saved. It's OK to ask questions, and it's good to think things over, but guard your heart against any teaching that takes you away from Jesus. **Jesus made it clear that he is the only way to God!**

Jude ...

Greetings from Jude

This letter is from Jude, a slave of Jesus Christ and a brother of James.

I am writing to all who have been called by God the Father, who loves you and keeps you safe in the care of Jesus Christ.

2 May God give you more and more mercy, peace, and love.

The Danger of False Teachers

3 Dear friends, I had been eagerly planning to write to you about the salvation we all share. But now I find that I must write about something else, urging you to defend the faith that God has entrusted once for all time to his holy people. 4 I say this because some ungodly people have wormed their way into your churches, saying that God's marvelous grace allows us to live immoral lives. The condemnation of such people was recorded long ago, for they have denied our only Master and Lord, Jesus Christ.

5 So I want to remind you, though you already know these things, that Jesus first rescued the nation of Israel from Egypt, but later he destroyed those who did not remain faithful. 6 And I remind you of the angels who did not stay within the limits of authority God gave them but left the place where they belonged. God has kept them securely chained in prisons of darkness, waiting for the great day of judgment. 7 And don't forget Sodom and Gomorrah and their neighboring towns, which were filled with immorality and every kind of sexual perversion. Those cities were destroyed by fire and serve as a warning of the eternal fire of God's judgment.

8 In the same way, these people—who claim authority from their dreams—live immoral lives, defy authority, and scoff at supernatural beings. 9 But even Michael, one of the mightiest of the angels, did not dare accuse the devil of blasphemy, but simply said, "The Lord rebuke you!" (This took place when Michael was arguing with the devil about Moses' body.) 10 But these people scoff at things they do not understand. Like unthinking animals, they do whatever their instincts tell them, and so they bring about their own destruction. 11 What sorrow awaits them! For they follow in the footsteps of Cain, who killed his brother. Like Balaam, they deceive people for money. And like Korah, they perish in their rebellion.

12 When these people eat with you in your fellowship meals commemorating the Lord's love, they are like dangerous reefs that can shipwreck you. They are like shameless shepherds who care only for themselves. They are like clouds blowing over the land without giving any rain. They are like trees in autumn that are doubly dead, for they bear no fruit and have been pulled up by the roots. 13 They are like wild waves of the sea, churning up the foam of their shameful deeds. They are like wandering stars, doomed forever to blackest darkness.

14 Enoch, who lived in the seventh generation after Adam, prophesied about these people. He said, "Listen! The Lord is coming with countless thousands of his holy ones 15 to execute judgment on the people of the world. He will convict every person of all the ungodly things they have done and for all the insults that ungodly sinners have spoken against him."

16 These people are grumblers and complainers, living only to satisfy their desires. They brag loudly about themselves, and they flatter others to get what they want.

A Call to Remain Faithful

17 But you, my dear friends, must remember what the apostles of our Lord Jesus Christ said. 18 They told you that in the last times there would be scoffers whose purpose in life is to satisfy their ungodly desires. 19 These people are the ones who are creating divisions among you. They follow their natural instincts because they do not have God's Spirit in them.

20 But you, dear friends, must build each other up in your most holy faith, pray in the power of the Holy Spirit, 21 and await the mercy of our Lord Jesus Christ, who will bring you eternal life. In this way, you will keep yourselves safe in God's love.

22 And you must show mercy to those whose faith is wavering. 23 Rescue others by snatching them from the flames of judgment. Show mercy to still others, but do so with great caution, hating the sins that contaminate their lives.

A Prayer of Praise

24 Now all glory to God, who is able to keep you from falling away and will bring you with great joy into his glorious presence without a single fault. 25 All glory to him who alone is God, our Savior through Jesus Christ our Lord. All glory, majesty, power, and authority are his before all time, and in the present, and beyond all time! Amen.

REVELATION

THE END

Look for **2** hidden messages in Revelation!

Revelation reveals what will happen when Jesus comes back. It tells about
- **THE WAY CHURCHES SHOULD REALLY WORK**
- **THE POWER JESUS REALLY HAS**
- **THE HOME IN HEAVEN THAT'S REALLY WAITING FOR US**
- **THE VICTORY JESUS WILL REALLY HAVE**

IN THE BEGINNING

Always and Forever

Everything has a start and finish, right? Well, *almost* everything! Check out Revelation 1:8.

knock
knock

Knock, knock!
Who's there?
Dwayne.
Dwayne who?
Dwayne the bathtub!
I'm dwowning!

Knock-knock jokes are just plain silly. **Read Revelation 3:20 to learn about a knock-knock that's no joke!**

PTEWW!!!

THAT GOOD?

Hot or Cold, but Not Lukewarm!

Maybe you've been helping your dad shovel the walk. Your mom calls you in for a nice steamy cup of hot cocoa. You take a sip. Yuck! Lukewarm. **Jesus doesn't like things lukewarm either. Find out more in Revelation 3:15-16.**

No Contest

What if the best NFL team came to play a game with your football team? No contest, right? You'd know who was going to win and who would get crushed. Well, it's a lot like that between God and Satan and his henchmen. **See who crushes whom in Revelation 19:11–20:10!**

Dear Blabby

Q: I've heard about heaven and how long our time there is going to be—like forever, right? Well, I'm a little worried about what I'll do for such a long time. I'm afraid I might get bored.

A: No way! Read Revelation 7:9-15 to find out what we'll be doing with the angels in heaven!

It's Gonna Be Great!

Heaven's going to be so amazing! How amazing? Find out for yourself by reading Revelation 21:10-27.

The End

The bad guy gets caught, the hero gets the girl, and they ride off into the sunset. That's a standard ending, but here's a story that has the best ending of all. And it's not just a story—it's real!

Read Revelation 21:1-7 for the end of one story and the beginning of another!

THE END

Timeline

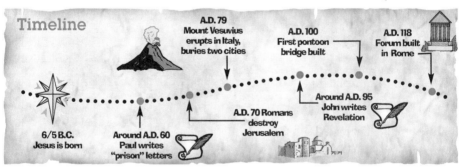

A.D. 79 Mount Vesuvius erupts in Italy, buries two cities

A.D. 100 First pontoon bridge built

A.D. 118 Forum built in Rome

Around A.D. 95 John writes Revelation

A.D. 70 Romans destroy Jerusalem

6/5 B.C. Jesus is born

Around A.D. 60 Paul writes "prison" letters

The JESUS CONNECTION

The book of Revelation shows who Jesus really is. The first time he came to earth, Jesus was humble and gave himself as a sacrifice for our sins. When Jesus comes back, he'll show all the world his full glory and power. Every knee will bow before Jesus. Either people will bow out of love and joy at seeing their King, or they'll bow out of fear and horror because they didn't follow Jesus when they had the chance. **The King of kings will return. And you can look forward to that day if you give your heart and life to Jesus today.**

CHAPTER 1

Prologue

This is a revelation from Jesus Christ, which God gave him to show his servants the events that must soon take place. He sent an angel to present this revelation to his servant John, ²who faithfully reported everything he saw. This is his report of the word of God and the testimony of Jesus Christ.

³God blesses the one who reads the words of this prophecy to the church, and he blesses all who listen to its message and obey what it says, for the time is near.

John's Greeting to the Seven Churches

⁴This letter is from John to the seven churches in the province of Asia.

Grace and peace to you from the one who is, who always was, and who is still to come; from the sevenfold Spirit before his throne; ⁵and from Jesus Christ. He is the faithful witness to these things, the first to rise from the dead, and the ruler of all the kings of the world.

All glory to him who loves us and has freed us from our sins by shedding his blood for us. ⁶He has made us a Kingdom of priests for God his Father. All glory and power to him forever and ever! Amen.

⁷ Look! He comes with the clouds of heaven.
And everyone will see him—
even those who pierced him.
And all the nations of the world
will mourn for him.
Yes! Amen!

⁸"I am the Alpha and the Omega— the beginning and the end," says the Lord God. "I am the one who is, who always was, and who is still to come—the Almighty One."

Vision of the Son of Man

⁹I, John, am your brother and your partner in suffering and in God's Kingdom and in the patient endurance to which Jesus calls us. I was exiled to the island of Patmos for preaching the word of God and for my testimony about Jesus. ¹⁰It was the Lord's Day, and I was worshiping in the Spirit. Suddenly, I heard behind me a loud voice like a trumpet blast. ¹¹It said, "Write in a book everything you see, and send it to the seven churches in the cities of Ephesus, Smyrna, Pergamum, Thyatira, Sardis, Philadelphia, and Laodicea."

¹²When I turned to see who was speaking to me, I saw seven gold lampstands. ¹³And standing in the middle of the lampstands was someone like the Son of Man. He was wearing a long robe with a gold sash across his chest. ¹⁴His head and his hair were white like wool, as white as snow. And his eyes were like flames of fire. ¹⁵His feet were like polished bronze refined in a furnace, and his voice thundered like mighty ocean waves. ¹⁶He held seven stars in his right hand, and a sharp two-edged sword came from his mouth. And his face was like the sun in all its brilliance.

¹⁷When I saw him, I fell at his feet as if I were dead. But he laid his right hand on me and said, "Don't be afraid! I am the First and the Last. ¹⁸I am the living one. I died, but look—I am alive forever and ever! And I hold the keys of death and the grave.

¹⁹"Write down what you have seen—both the things that are now happening and the things that will happen. ²⁰This is the meaning of the mystery of the seven stars you saw in my right hand and the seven gold lampstands: The seven stars are the angels of the seven churches, and the seven lampstands are the seven churches.

CHAPTER 2

The Message to the Church in Ephesus

"Write this letter to the angel of the church in Ephesus. This is the message from the one who holds the seven stars in his right hand, the one who walks among the seven gold lampstands:

²"I know all the things you do. I have seen your hard work and your patient endurance. I know you don't tolerate evil people. You have examined the claims of those who say they are apostles but are not. You have discovered they are liars. ³You have patiently suffered for me without quitting.

⁴"But I have this complaint against you. You don't love me or each other as you did at first! ⁵Look how far you have fallen! Turn back to me and do the works you did at first. If you don't repent, I will come and remove your lampstand from its place among the churches. ⁶But this is in your favor: You hate the evil deeds of the Nicolaitans, just as I do.

⁷"Anyone with ears to hear must listen to the Spirit and understand what he is saying to the churches. To everyone who is victorious I will give fruit from the tree of life in the paradise of God.

The Message to the Church in Smyrna

8"Write this letter to the angel of the church in Smyrna. This is the message from the one who is the First and the Last, who was dead but is now alive:

9"I know about your suffering and your poverty—but you are rich! I know the blasphemy of those opposing you. They say they are Jews, but they are not, because their synagogue belongs to Satan. 10Don't be afraid of what you are about to suffer. The devil will throw some of you into prison to test you. You will suffer for ten days. But if you remain faithful even when facing death, I will give you the crown of life.

11"Anyone with ears to hear must listen to the Spirit and understand what he is saying to the churches. Whoever is victorious will not be harmed by the second death.

The Message to the Church in Pergamum

12"Write this letter to the angel of the church in Pergamum. This is the message from the one with the sharp two-edged sword:

13"I know that you live in the city where Satan has his throne, yet you have remained loyal to me. You refused to deny me even when Antipas, my faithful witness, was martyred among you there in Satan's city.

14"But I have a few complaints against you. You tolerate some among you whose teaching is like that of Balaam, who showed Balak how to trip up the people of Israel. He taught them to sin by eating food offered to idols and by committing sexual sin. 15In a similar way, you have some Nicolaitans among you who follow the same teaching. 16Repent of your sin, or I will come to you suddenly and fight against them with the sword of my mouth.

17"Anyone with ears to hear must listen to the Spirit and understand what he is saying to the churches. To everyone who is victorious I will give some of the manna that has been hidden away in heaven. And I will give to each one a white stone, and on the stone will be engraved a new name that no one understands except the one who receives it.

The Message to the Church in Thyatira

18"Write this letter to the angel of the church in Thyatira. This is the message from the Son of God, whose eyes are like flames of fire, whose feet are like polished bronze:

19"I know all the things you do. I have seen your love, your faith, your service, and your patient endurance. And I can see your constant improvement in all these things.

20"But I have this complaint against you. You are permitting that woman—that Jezebel who calls herself a prophet—to lead my servants astray. She teaches them to commit sexual sin and to eat food offered to idols. 21I gave her time to repent, but she does not want to turn away from her immorality.

22"Therefore, I will throw her on a bed of suffering, and those who commit adultery with her will suffer greatly unless they repent and turn away from her evil deeds. 23I will strike her children dead. Then all the churches will know that I am the one who searches out the thoughts and intentions of every person. And I will give to each of you whatever you deserve.

24"But I also have a message for the rest of you in Thyatira who have not followed this false teaching ('deeper truths,' as they call them—depths of Satan, actually). I will ask nothing more of you 25except that you hold tightly to what you have until I come. 26To all who are victorious, who obey me to the very end,

To them I will give authority over all the nations.
27 They will rule the nations with an iron rod and smash them like clay pots.

28They will have the same authority I received from my Father, and I will also give them the morning star! 29"Anyone with ears to hear must listen to the Spirit and understand what he is saying to the churches.

CHAPTER **3**

The Message to the Church in Sardis

"Write this letter to the angel of the church in Sardis. This is the message from the one who has the sevenfold Spirit of God and the seven stars:

"I know all the things you do, and that you have a reputation for being alive—but you are dead. ²Wake up! Strengthen what little remains, for even what is left is almost dead. I find that your actions do not meet the requirements of my God. ³Go back to what you heard and believed at first; hold to it firmly. Repent and turn to me again. If you don't wake up, I will come to you suddenly, as unexpected as a thief.

⁴"Yet there are some in the church in Sardis who have not soiled their clothes with evil. They will walk with me in white, for they are worthy. ⁵All who are victorious will be clothed in white. I will never erase their names from the Book of Life, but I will announce before my Father and his angels that they are mine.

⁶"Anyone with ears to hear must listen to the Spirit and understand what he is saying to the churches.

The Message to the Church in Philadelphia

⁷"Write this letter to the angel of the church in Philadelphia.

This is the message from the one who is holy
and true,
the one who has the key of David.
What he opens, no one can close;
and what he closes, no one can open:

⁸"I know all the things you do, and I have opened a door for you that no one can close. You have little strength, yet you obeyed my word and did not deny me. ⁹Look, I will force those who belong to Satan's synagogue— those liars who say they are Jews but are not— to come and bow down at your feet. They will acknowledge that you are the ones I love.

¹⁰"Because you have obeyed my command to persevere, I will protect you from the great time of testing that will come upon the whole world to test those who belong to this world. ¹¹I am coming soon. Hold on to what you have, so that no one will take away your crown. ¹²All who are victorious will become pillars in the Temple of my God, and they will never have to leave it. And I will write on them the name of my God, and they will be citizens in the city of my God—the new Jerusalem that comes down from heaven from my God. And I will also write on them my new name.

¹³"Anyone with ears to hear must listen to the Spirit and understand what he is saying to the churches.

Jesus IS Knocking

The Bible says that someone is knocking at the door. Just read **REVELATION 3:20-21** to find out who!

Make this door hanger to remind you that Jesus is knocking at the door!

LOOK! I stand at the door and knock. If you hear my voice and open the door, I will come in, and we will share a meal together as friends.

1. Cut a 4x12-inch rectangle from poster board.

2. Cut two slits like a cross near one end of the rectangle. (But don't cut all the way to the edges.)

3. Now write the words of Revelation 3:20 on it to remind you that Jesus is knocking at the door!

AND GUESS WHAT?

JESUS IS KNOCKING ON EVERYBODY'S DOOR!

Make a whole bunch of door hangers with the words of **REVELATION 3:20** on them. Then hang them on every door at church. Or ask an adult to help you make a batch of cookies, then together deliver door hangers and little bags of cookies to all your neighbors.

The Message to the Church in Laodicea

14 "Write this letter to the angel of the church in Laodicea. This is the message from the one who is the Amen—the faithful and true witness, the beginning of God's new creation:

15 "I know all the things you do, that you are neither hot nor cold. I wish that you were one or the other! 16 But since you are like lukewarm water, neither hot nor cold, I will spit you out of my mouth! 17 You say, 'I am rich. I have everything I want. I don't need a thing!' And you don't realize that you are wretched and miserable and poor and blind and naked. 18 So I advise you to buy gold from me—gold that has been purified by fire. Then you will be rich. Also buy white garments from me so you will not be shamed by your nakedness, and ointment for your eyes so you will be able to see. 19 I correct and discipline everyone I love. So be diligent and turn from your indifference.

20 **"Look! I stand at the door and knock. If you hear my voice and open the door, I will come in, and we will share a meal together as friends.** 21 Those who are victorious will sit with me on my throne, just as I was victorious and sat with my Father on his throne.

22 "Anyone with ears to hear must listen to the Spirit and understand what he is saying to the churches."

CHAPTER 4

Worship in Heaven

Then as I looked, I saw a door standing open in heaven, and the same voice I had heard before spoke to me like a trumpet blast. The voice said, "Come up here, and I will show you what must happen after this." 2 And instantly I was in the Spirit, and I saw a throne in heaven and someone sitting on it. 3 The one sitting on the throne was as brilliant as gemstones—like jasper and carnelian. And the glow of an emerald circled his throne like a rainbow. 4 Twenty-four thrones surrounded him, and twenty-four elders sat on them. They were all clothed in white and had gold crowns on their heads. 5 From the throne came flashes of lightning and the rumble of thunder. And in front of the throne were seven torches with burning flames. This is the sevenfold Spirit of God. 6 In front of the throne was a shiny sea of glass, sparkling like crystal.

In the center and around the throne were four living beings, each covered with eyes, front and back. 7 The first of these living beings was like a lion; the second was like an ox; the third had a human face; and the fourth was like an eagle in flight. 8 Each of these living beings had six wings, and their wings were covered all over with eyes, inside and out. Day after day and night after night they keep on saying,

"Holy, holy, holy is the Lord God, the Almighty—
the one who always was, who is,
and who is still to come."

9 Whenever the living beings give glory and honor and thanks to the one sitting on the throne (the one who lives forever and ever), 10 the twenty-four elders fall down and worship the one sitting on the throne (the one who lives forever and ever). And they lay their crowns before the throne and say,

11 "You are worthy, O Lord our God,
to receive glory and honor and power.
For you created all things,
and they exist because you created
what you pleased."

CHAPTER 5

The Lamb Opens the Scroll

Then I saw a scroll in the right hand of the one who was sitting on the throne. There was writing on the inside and the outside of the scroll, and it was sealed with seven seals. 2 And I saw a strong angel, who shouted with a loud voice: "Who is worthy to break the seals on this scroll and open it?" 3 But no one in heaven or on earth or under the earth was able to open the scroll and read it.

4 Then I began to weep bitterly because no one was found worthy to open the scroll and read it. 5 But one of the twenty-four elders said to me, "Stop weeping! Look, the Lion of the tribe of Judah, the heir to David's throne, has won the victory. He is worthy to open the scroll and its seven seals."

6 Then I saw a Lamb that looked as if it had been slaughtered, but it was now standing between the throne and the four living beings and among the twenty-four elders. He had seven horns and seven eyes, which represent the sevenfold Spirit of God that is sent out into every part of the earth. 7 He stepped forward and took the scroll from the right hand of the one sitting on the throne. 8 And when he took the scroll, the four living beings and the twenty-four elders fell down before the Lamb. Each one had a harp, and

they held gold bowls filled with incense, which are the prayers of God's people. 9 And they sang a new song with these words:

"You are worthy to take the scroll
and break its seals and open it.
For you were slaughtered, and your blood
has ransomed people for God
from every tribe and language and people
and nation.
10 And you have caused them to become
a Kingdom of priests for our God.
And they will reign on the earth."

11 Then I looked again, and I heard the voices of thousands and millions of angels around the throne and of the living beings and the elders. 12 And they sang in a mighty chorus:

"Worthy is the Lamb who was slaughtered—
to receive power and riches
and wisdom and strength
and honor and glory and blessing."

13 And then I heard every creature in heaven and on earth and under the earth and in the sea. They sang:

"Blessing and honor and glory and power
belong to the one sitting on the throne
and to the Lamb forever and ever."

14 And the four living beings said, "Amen!" And the twenty-four elders fell down and worshiped the Lamb.

CHAPTER 6
The Lamb Breaks the First Six Seals

As I watched, the Lamb broke the first of the seven seals on the scroll. Then I heard one of the four living beings say with a voice like thunder, "Come!" 2 I looked up and saw a white horse standing there. Its rider carried a bow, and a crown was placed on his head. He rode out to win many battles and gain the victory.

3 When the Lamb broke the second seal, I heard the second living being say, "Come!" 4 Then another horse appeared, a red one. Its rider was given a mighty sword and the authority to take peace from the earth. And there was war and slaughter everywhere.

5 When the Lamb broke the third seal, I heard the third living being say, "Come!" I looked up and saw a black horse, and its rider was holding a pair of scales in his hand. 6 And I heard a voice from among the four living beings say, "A loaf of wheat bread or three loaves of barley will cost a day's pay. And don't waste the olive oil and wine."

7 When the Lamb broke the fourth seal, I heard the fourth living being say, "Come!" 8 I looked up and saw a horse whose color was pale green. Its rider was named Death, and his companion was the Grave. These two were given authority over one-fourth of the earth, to kill with the sword and famine and disease and wild animals.

9 When the Lamb broke the fifth seal, I saw under the altar the souls of all who had been martyred for the word of God and for being faithful in their testimony. 10 They shouted to the Lord and said, "O Sovereign Lord, holy and true, how long before you judge the people who belong to this world and avenge our blood for what they have done to us?" 11 Then a white robe was given to each of them. And they were told to rest a little longer until the full number of their brothers and sisters—their fellow servants of Jesus who were to be martyred—had joined them.

12 I watched as the Lamb broke the sixth seal, and there was a great earthquake. The sun became as dark as black cloth, and the moon became as red as blood. 13 Then the stars of the sky fell to the earth like green figs falling from a tree shaken by a strong wind. 14 The sky was rolled up like a scroll, and all of the mountains and islands were moved from their places.

15 Then everyone—the kings of the earth, the rulers, the generals, the wealthy, the powerful, and every slave and free person—all hid themselves in the caves and among the rocks of the mountains. 16 And they cried to the mountains and the rocks, "Fall on us and hide us from the face of the one who sits on the throne and from the wrath of the Lamb. 17 For the great day of their wrath has come, and who is able to survive?"

CHAPTER 7
God's People Will Be Preserved

Then I saw four angels standing at the four corners of the earth, holding back the four winds so they did not blow on the earth or the sea, or even on any tree. 2 And I saw another angel coming up from the east, carrying the seal of the living God. And he shouted to those four angels, who had been given power to harm land and sea, 3 "Wait! Don't harm the land or the sea or the trees until we have placed the seal of God on the foreheads of his servants."

4 And I heard how many were marked with the seal of God—144,000 were sealed from all the tribes of Israel:

Things will really be different in heaven! Read **REVELATION 7:16-17** to see how great things will be.

Then make this reminder that you won't need tissues when you get there!

1. Use fun wrapping paper to wrap an open box of tissues like a present.

2. Carefully cut the wrapping paper away from the opening for the tissues.

3. Write REVELATION 7:16-17 in your own words on a small card. Glue the card to the box.

There will be NO tears in heaven!

Read what Isaiah said about heaven in Isaiah 65:17-19. Sound familiar?

Give the box to someone else. Remind that person that in heaven there will be no more tears or sadness!

Then wrap a box for your family. The next time you reach for a tissue, remember that heaven will be a happy place!

Praise from the Great Crowd

9 After this I saw a vast crowd, too great to count, from every nation and tribe and people and language, standing in front of the throne and before the Lamb. They were clothed in white robes and held palm branches in their hands. 10 And they were shouting with a mighty shout,

"Salvation comes from our God
    who sits on the throne
    and from the Lamb!"

11 And all the angels were standing around the throne and around the elders and the four living beings. And they fell before the throne with their faces to the ground and worshiped God. 12 They sang,

"Amen! Blessing and glory and wisdom
    and thanksgiving and honor
and power and strength belong to our God
    forever and ever! Amen."

13 Then one of the twenty-four elders asked me, "Who are these who are clothed in white? Where did they come from?"

14 And I said to him, "Sir, you are the one who knows."

Then he said to me, "These are the ones who died in the great tribulation. They have washed their robes in the blood of the Lamb and made them white.

15 "That is why they stand in front
    of God's throne
    and serve him day and night
        in his Temple.
And he who sits on the throne
    will give them shelter.
16 They will never again be hungry or thirsty;
    they will never be scorched by the heat of
        the sun.
17 For the Lamb on the throne
    will be their Shepherd.
He will lead them to springs of
    life-giving water.
    And God will wipe every tear
        from their eyes."

CHAPTER **8**
The Lamb Breaks the Seventh Seal

When the Lamb broke the seventh seal on the scroll, there was silence throughout heaven for about half an hour. ²I saw the seven angels who stand before God, and they were given seven trumpets.

³Then another angel with a gold incense burner came and stood at the altar. And a great amount of incense was given to him to mix with the prayers of God's people as an offering on the gold altar before the throne. ⁴The smoke of the incense, mixed with the prayers of God's holy people, ascended up to God from the altar where the angel had poured them out. ⁵Then the angel filled the incense burner with fire from the altar and threw it down upon the earth; and thunder crashed, lightning flashed, and there was a terrible earthquake.

The First Four Trumpets
⁶Then the seven angels with the seven trumpets prepared to blow their mighty blasts.

⁷The first angel blew his trumpet, and hail and fire mixed with blood were thrown down on the earth. One-third of the earth was set on fire, one-third of the trees were burned, and all the green grass was burned.

⁸Then the second angel blew his trumpet, and a great mountain of fire was thrown into the sea. One-third of the water in the sea became blood, ⁹one-third of all things living in the sea died, and one-third of all the ships on the sea were destroyed.

¹⁰Then the third angel blew his trumpet, and a great star fell from the sky, burning like a torch. It fell on one-third of the rivers and on the springs of water. ¹¹The name of the star was Bitterness. It made one-third of the water bitter, and many people died from drinking the bitter water.

¹²Then the fourth angel blew his trumpet, and one-third of the sun was struck, and one-third of the moon, and one-third of the stars, and they became dark. And one-third of the day was dark, and also one-third of the night.

¹³Then I looked, and I heard a single eagle crying loudly as it flew through the air, "Terror, terror, terror to all who belong to this world because of what will happen when the last three angels blow their trumpets."

CHAPTER **9**
The Fifth Trumpet Brings the First Terror
Then the fifth angel blew his trumpet, and I saw a star that had fallen to earth from the sky, and he was given the key to the shaft of the bottomless pit. ²When he opened it, smoke poured out as though from a huge furnace, and the sunlight and air turned dark from the smoke.

³Then locusts came from the smoke and descended on the earth, and they were given power to sting like scorpions. ⁴They were told not to harm the grass or plants or trees, but only the people who did not have the seal of God on their foreheads. ⁵They were told not to kill them but to torture them for five months with pain like the pain of a scorpion sting. ⁶In those days people will seek death but will not find it. They will long to die, but death will flee from them!

⁷The locusts looked like horses prepared for battle. They had what looked like gold crowns on their heads, and their faces looked like human faces. ⁸They had hair like women's hair and teeth like the teeth of a lion. ⁹They wore armor made of iron, and their wings roared like an army of chariots rushing into battle. ¹⁰They had tails that stung like scorpions, and for five months they had the power to torment people. ¹¹Their king is the angel from the bottomless pit; his name in Hebrew is *Abaddon,* and in Greek, *Apollyon*—the Destroyer.

¹²The first terror is past, but look, two more terrors are coming!

The Sixth Trumpet Brings the Second Terror
¹³Then the sixth angel blew his trumpet, and I heard a voice speaking from the four horns of the gold altar that stands in the presence of God. ¹⁴And the voice said to the sixth angel who held the trumpet, "Release the four angels who are bound at the great Euphrates River." ¹⁵Then the four angels who had been prepared for this hour and day and month and year were turned loose to kill one-third of all the people on earth. ¹⁶I heard the size of their army, which was 200 million mounted troops.

¹⁷And in my vision, I saw the horses and the riders sitting on them. The riders wore armor that was fiery red and dark blue and yellow. The horses had heads like lions, and fire and smoke and burning sulfur billowed from their mouths. ¹⁸One-third of all the people on earth were killed by these three plagues—by the fire and smoke and burning sulfur that came from the mouths of the horses. ¹⁹Their power was in their mouths and in their tails. For their tails had heads like snakes, with the power to injure people.

²⁰But the people who did not die in these plagues still refused to repent of their evil deeds and turn to God. They continued to worship demons and idols made of gold, silver, bronze,

stone, and wood—idols that can neither see nor hear nor walk! [21] And they did not repent of their murders or their witchcraft or their sexual immorality or their thefts.

CHAPTER **10**

The Angel and the Small Scroll

Then I saw another mighty angel coming down from heaven, surrounded by a cloud, with a rainbow over his head. His face shone like the sun, and his feet were like pillars of fire. [2] And in his hand was a small scroll that had been opened. He stood with his right foot on the sea and his left foot on the land. [3] And he gave a great shout like the roar of a lion. And when he shouted, the seven thunders answered.

[4] When the seven thunders spoke, I was about to write. But I heard a voice from heaven saying, "Keep secret what the seven thunders said, and do not write it down."

[5] Then the angel I saw standing on the sea and on the land raised his right hand toward heaven. [6] He swore an oath in the name of the one who lives forever and ever, who created the heavens and everything in them, the earth and everything in it, and the sea and everything in it. He said, "There will be no more delay. [7] When the seventh angel blows his trumpet, God's mysterious plan will be fulfilled. It will happen just as he announced it to his servants the prophets."

[8] Then the voice from heaven spoke to me again: "Go and take the open scroll from the hand of the angel who is standing on the sea and on the land."

[9] So I went to the angel and told him to give me the small scroll. "Yes, take it and eat it," he said. "It will be sweet as honey in your mouth, but it will turn sour in your stomach!" [10] So I took the small scroll from the hand of the angel, and I ate it! It was sweet in my mouth, but when I swallowed it, it turned sour in my stomach.

[11] Then I was told, "You must prophesy again about many peoples, nations, languages, and kings."

CHAPTER **11**

The Two Witnesses

Then I was given a measuring stick, and I was told, "Go and measure the Temple of God and the altar, and count the number of worshipers. [2] But do not measure the outer courtyard, for it has been turned over to the nations. They will trample the holy city for 42 months. [3] And I will give power to my two witnesses, and they will be clothed in burlap and will prophesy during those 1,260 days."

[4] These two prophets are the two olive trees and the two lampstands that stand before the Lord of all the earth. [5] If anyone tries to harm them, fire flashes from their mouths and consumes their enemies. This is how anyone who tries to harm them must die. [6] They have power to shut the sky so that no rain will fall for as long as they prophesy. And they have the power to turn the rivers and oceans into blood, and to strike the earth with every kind of plague as often as they wish.

[7] When they complete their testimony, the beast that comes up out of the bottomless pit will declare war against them, and he will conquer them and kill them. [8] And their bodies will lie in the main street of Jerusalem, the city that is figuratively called "Sodom" and "Egypt," the city where their Lord was crucified. [9] And for three and a half days, all peoples, tribes, languages, and nations will stare at their bodies. No one will be allowed to bury them. [10] All the people who belong to this world will gloat over them and give presents to each other to celebrate the death of the two prophets who had tormented them.

[11] But after three and a half days, God breathed life into them, and they stood up! Terror struck all who were staring at them. [12] Then a loud voice from heaven called to the two prophets, "Come up here!" And they rose to heaven in a cloud as their enemies watched.

[13] At the same time there was a terrible earthquake that destroyed a tenth of the city. Seven thousand people died in that earthquake, and everyone else was terrified and gave glory to the God of heaven.

[14] The second terror is past, but look, the third terror is coming quickly.

The Seventh Trumpet Brings the Third Terror

[15] Then the seventh angel blew his trumpet, and there were loud voices shouting in heaven:

"The world has now become the Kingdom
of our Lord and of his Christ,
and he will reign forever and ever."

[16] The twenty-four elders sitting on their thrones before God fell with their faces to the ground and worshiped him. [17] And they said,

"We give thanks to you, Lord God, the
Almighty,
the one who is and who always was,
for now you have assumed your great power
and have begun to reign.

FUN-fact

Take a Number 12

There's something special about numbers in the Bible. Take the number **12**, for instance. Why do you think this number might be so important?

Here's why:

- the **12** sons of Jacob,
- the **12** tribes of Israel,
- the **12** apostles,
- the **12** gates of the New Jerusalem, and
- the tree of life bears **12** crops of fruit.

Pretty cool, right? See if you can find other numbers in the Bible that are mentioned often. You could ask your teacher or parents for sources. Below, write three cool facts you find about numbers in the Bible. (Here's a hint: 40 and 7 appear a lot.)

1. _____
2. _____
3. _____

18 The nations were filled with wrath,
but now the time of your wrath has come.
It is time to judge the dead
and reward your servants the prophets,
as well as your holy people,
and all who fear your name,
from the least to the greatest.
It is time to destroy
all who have caused destruction on
the earth."

19 Then, in heaven, the Temple of God was opened and the Ark of his covenant could be seen inside the Temple. Lightning flashed, thunder crashed and roared, and there was an earthquake and a terrible hailstorm.

CHAPTER **12**
The Woman and the Dragon
Then I witnessed in heaven an event of great significance. I saw a woman clothed with the sun, with the moon beneath her feet, and a crown of twelve stars on her head. 2 She was pregnant, and she cried out because of her labor pains and the agony of giving birth.

3 Then I witnessed in heaven another significant event. I saw a large red dragon with seven heads and ten horns, with seven crowns on his heads. 4 His tail swept away one-third of the stars in the sky, and he threw them to the earth. He stood in front of the woman as she was about to give birth, ready to devour her baby as soon as it was born.

5 She gave birth to a son who was to rule all nations with an iron rod. And her child was snatched away from the dragon and was caught up to God and to his throne. 6 And the woman fled into the wilderness, where God had prepared a place to care for her for 1,260 days.

7 Then there was war in heaven. Michael and his angels fought against the dragon and his angels. 8 And the dragon lost the battle, and he and his angels were forced out of heaven. 9 This great dragon—the ancient serpent called the devil, or Satan, the one deceiving the whole world—was thrown down to the earth with all his angels.

10 Then I heard a loud voice shouting across the heavens,

"It has come at last—
salvation and power
and the Kingdom of our God,
and the authority of his Christ.
For the accuser of our brothers and sisters
has been thrown down to earth—
the one who accuses them
before our God day and night.
11 And they have defeated him by the blood
of the Lamb
and by their testimony.
And they did not love their lives so much
that they were afraid to die.
12 Therefore, rejoice, O heavens!
And you who live in the heavens, rejoice!
But terror will come on the earth and
the sea,
for the devil has come down to you in
great anger,
knowing that he has little time."

13 When the dragon realized that he had been thrown down to the earth, he pursued the woman who had given birth to the male child. 14 But she was given two wings like those of a great eagle so she could fly to the place prepared for her in the wilderness. There she would be

cared for and protected from the dragon for a time, times, and half a time.

¹⁵Then the dragon tried to drown the woman with a flood of water that flowed from his mouth. ¹⁶But the earth helped her by opening its mouth and swallowing the river that gushed out from the mouth of the dragon. ¹⁷And the dragon was angry at the woman and declared war against the rest of her children—all who keep God's commandments and maintain their testimony for Jesus.

¹⁸Then the dragon took his stand on the shore beside the sea.

CHAPTER **13**
The Beast out of the Sea

Then I saw a beast rising up out of the sea. It had seven heads and ten horns, with ten crowns on its horns. And written on each head were names that blasphemed God. ²This beast looked like a leopard, but it had the feet of a bear and the mouth of a lion! And the dragon gave the beast his own power and throne and great authority.

³I saw that one of the heads of the beast seemed wounded beyond recovery—but the fatal wound was healed! The whole world marveled at this miracle and gave allegiance to the beast. ⁴They worshiped the dragon for giving the beast such power, and they also worshiped the beast. "Who is as great as the beast?" they exclaimed. "Who is able to fight against him?"

⁵Then the beast was allowed to speak great blasphemies against God. And he was given authority to do whatever he wanted for forty-two months. ⁶And he spoke terrible words of blasphemy against God, slandering his name and his dwelling—that is, those who dwell in heaven. ⁷And the beast was allowed to wage war against God's holy people and to conquer them. And he was given authority to rule over every tribe and people and language and nation. ⁸And all the people who belong to this world worshiped the beast. They are the ones whose names were not written in the Book of Life before the world was made—the Book that belongs to the Lamb who was slaughtered.

⁹ Anyone with ears to hear
   should listen and understand.
¹⁰ Anyone who is destined for prison
   will be taken to prison.
Anyone destined to die by the sword
   will die by the sword.

This means that God's holy people must endure persecution patiently and remain faithful.

The Beast out of the Earth

¹¹Then I saw another beast come up out of the earth. He had two horns like those of a lamb, but he spoke with the voice of a dragon. ¹²He exercised all the authority of the first beast. And he required all the earth and its people to worship the first beast, whose fatal wound had been healed. ¹³He did astounding miracles, even making fire flash down to earth from the sky while everyone was watching. ¹⁴And with all the miracles he was allowed to perform on behalf of the first beast, he deceived all the people who belong to this world. He ordered the people to make a great statue of the first beast, who was fatally wounded and then came back to life. ¹⁵He was then permitted to give life to this statue so that it could speak. Then the statue of the beast commanded that anyone refusing to worship it must die.

¹⁶He required everyone—small and great, rich and poor, free and slave—to be given a mark on the right hand or on the forehead. ¹⁷And no one could buy or sell anything without that mark, which was either the name of the beast or the number representing his name. ¹⁸Wisdom is needed here. Let the one with understanding solve the meaning of the number of the beast, for it is the number of a man. His number is 666.

CHAPTER **14**
The Lamb and the 144,000

Then I saw the Lamb standing on Mount Zion, and with him were 144,000 who had his name and his Father's name written on their foreheads. ²And I heard a sound from heaven like the roar of mighty ocean waves or the rolling of loud thunder. It was like the sound of many harpists playing together.

³This great choir sang a wonderful new song in front of the throne of God and before the four living beings and the twenty-four elders. No one could learn this song except the 144,000 who had been redeemed from the earth. ⁴They have kept themselves as pure as virgins, following the Lamb wherever he goes. They have been purchased from among the people on the earth as a special offering to God and to the Lamb. ⁵They have told no lies; they are without blame.

The Three Angels

⁶And I saw another angel flying through the sky, carrying the eternal Good News to proclaim to the people who belong to this world—to every nation, tribe, language, and people. ⁷"Fear God,"

BIBLE BIOS
Hear From the Heroes

ANGELS *(full-time servants and worshipers of God)*

Hi! I'm Michael! I'm one of God's leading angels, and I'm going to be speaking for all of us today. First, I want to get one thing straight. We are not humans who have died and gone to heaven. Let me repeat that: We are not humans who have died and gone to heaven! No matter how many TV shows and movies try to make you think that, don't buy it. We're separate beings, created by God, and actually we're a little higher than humans in the whole scheme of things.

We also are not pretty females with white robes and wings. The white robe idea comes from times when we appeared as humans. Though we are spirit beings, we sometimes need to take human form. But the Bible never records an angel appearing as a woman. And the wings thing? I'm not sure where that came from.

> **Want to check that out? Look at ZECHARIAH 4:11-13; LUKE 1:18-19; 2:8-11; and MATTHEW 28:2-6, just to name a few!**

We angels do lots of things: We worship God, we deliver God's messages to people, we follow God's direction to help people or watch over them. There are lots of us— no human really knows how many! But we all follow God's directions.

Well, I guess I should say all of us who are on God's side follow his directions. God created us all as good beings. But he didn't force us to follow him. So at one point, some of the angels decided to rebel and follow Satan's leadership. (Yes, he actually was one of us.) All of those angels rebelling against God were thrown out of heaven.

> **Do angels die, like humans do? Look at LUKE 20:34-36 for the answer!**

When Jesus lived as a human on earth, we appeared a lot. Angels appeared to Mary and Joseph to let them know Jesus was going to be born. Then we announced Jesus' birth to the shepherds in the fields. One of us told Joseph to take Jesus and Mary to Egypt to escape Herod's evil plan. Then after Jesus was tempted by Satan, we went and ministered to him. And it was a great day when we got to announce Jesus' resurrection at the tomb!

> **Did you know that angels have broken people out of jail? Read ACTS 5:17-20 and 12:5-11.**

It's a wonderful life, being an angel! And we look forward to joining humans in worshiping God for eternity!

WHERE'S MY ANGEL?

See what the Bible says about guardian angels in **PSALM 91:9-12**. Now, from what you've learned in this Bible Bio, draw a picture of a time you would like to have an angel watching over you. Then write a heading on the paper: "God sends angels to watch over me." Keep your drawing where it will remind you that God cares about you so much that he uses angels to look after you.

he shouted. "Give glory to him. For the time has come when he will sit as judge. Worship him who made the heavens, the earth, the sea, and all the springs of water."

8 Then another angel followed him through the sky, shouting, "Babylon is fallen—that great city is fallen—because she made all the nations of the world drink the wine of her passionate immorality."

9 Then a third angel followed them, shouting, "Anyone who worships the beast and his statue or who accepts his mark on the forehead or on the hand 10 must drink the wine of God's anger. It has been poured full strength into God's cup of wrath. And they will be tormented with fire and burning sulfur in the presence of the holy angels and the Lamb. 11 The smoke of their torment will rise forever and ever, and they will have no relief day or night, for they have worshiped the beast and his statue and have accepted the mark of his name."

12 This means that God's holy people must endure persecution patiently, obeying his commands and maintaining their faith in Jesus.

13 And I heard a voice from heaven saying, "Write this down: Blessed are those who die in the Lord from now on. Yes, says the Spirit, they are blessed indeed, for they will rest from their hard work; for their good deeds follow them!"

The Harvest of the Earth

14 Then I saw a white cloud, and seated on the cloud was someone like the Son of Man. He had a gold crown on his head and a sharp sickle in his hand.

15 Then another angel came from the Temple and shouted to the one sitting on the cloud, "Swing the sickle, for the time of harvest has come; the crop on earth is ripe." 16 So the one sitting on the cloud swung his sickle over the earth, and the whole earth was harvested.

17 After that, another angel came from the Temple in heaven, and he also had a sharp sickle. 18 Then another angel, who had power to destroy with fire, came from the altar. He shouted to the angel with the sharp sickle, "Swing your sickle now to gather the clusters of grapes from the vines of the earth, for they are ripe for judgment." 19 So the angel swung his sickle over the earth and loaded the grapes into the great winepress of God's wrath. 20 The grapes were trampled in the winepress outside the city, and blood flowed from the winepress in a stream about 180 miles long and as high as a horse's bridle.

CHAPTER 15

The Song of Moses and of the Lamb

Then I saw in heaven another marvelous event of great significance. Seven angels were holding the seven last plagues, which would bring God's wrath to completion. 2 I saw before me what seemed to be a glass sea mixed with fire. And on it stood all the people who had been victorious over the beast and his statue and the number representing his name. They were all holding harps that God had given them. 3 And they were singing the song of Moses, the servant of God, and the song of the Lamb:

"Great and marvelous are your works,
O Lord God, the Almighty.
Just and true are your ways,
O King of the nations.
4 Who will not fear you, Lord,
and glorify your name?
For you alone are holy.
All nations will come and worship
before you,
for your righteous deeds have
been revealed."

The Seven Bowls of the Seven Plagues

5 Then I looked and saw that the Temple in heaven, God's Tabernacle, was thrown wide open. 6 The seven angels who were holding the seven plagues came out of the Temple. They were clothed in spotless white linen with gold sashes across their chests. 7 Then one of the four living beings handed each of the seven angels a gold bowl filled with the wrath of God, who lives forever and ever. 8 The Temple was filled with smoke from God's glory and power. No one could enter the Temple until the seven angels had completed pouring out the seven plagues.

Then I heard a mighty voice from the Temple say to the seven angels, "Go your ways and pour out on the earth the seven bowls containing God's wrath."

2 So the first angel left the Temple and poured out his bowl on the earth, and horrible, malignant sores broke out on everyone who had the mark of the beast and who worshiped his statue.

3 Then the second angel poured out his bowl on the sea, and it became like the blood of a corpse. And everything in the sea died.

4 Then the third angel poured out his bowl on

FUN-fact

Alpha and Omega

The Bible says that God is the Alpha and Omega. (Alpha and omega are the first and last letters of the Greek alphabet.)

So it's natural that the first and last books of the Bible tell about the beginning and the end of the world. Look at this!

Ⓐ Genesis

Sun created

Satan gets his way

Sin enters the world

Tears shed because of sin

Ω Revelation

Sun not needed

Satan defeated

Sin thrown out of the world

No more tears, no more sin

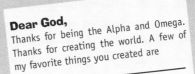

This prayer is already started. Fill in the endings for yourself!

Dear God,

Thanks for being the Alpha and Omega. Thanks for creating the world. A few of my favorite things you created are

_____

_____

I know that believing in Jesus is how I can get to heaven. This is how I feel about Jesus:

_____

_____

Thanks, God, for sending Jesus.

Love, _____

the rivers and springs, and they became blood. 5 And I heard the angel who had authority over all water saying,

"You are just, O Holy One, who is and
    who always was,
 because you have sent these judgments.
6 Since they shed the blood
    of your holy people and your prophets,
 you have given them blood to drink.
    It is their just reward."

7 And I heard a voice from the altar, saying,

"Yes, O Lord God, the Almighty,
    your judgments are true and just."

8 Then the fourth angel poured out his bowl on the sun, causing it to scorch everyone with its fire. 9 Everyone was burned by this blast of heat, and they cursed the name of God, who had control over all these plagues. They did not repent of their sins and turn to God and give him glory.

10 Then the fifth angel poured out his bowl on the throne of the beast, and his kingdom was plunged into darkness. His subjects ground their teeth in anguish, 11 and they cursed the God of heaven for their pains and sores. But they did not repent of their evil deeds and turn to God.

12 Then the sixth angel poured out his bowl on the great Euphrates River, and it dried up so that the kings from the east could march their armies toward the west without hindrance. 13 And I saw three evil spirits that looked like frogs leap from the mouths of the dragon, the beast, and the false prophet. 14 They are demonic spirits who work miracles and go out to all the rulers of the world to gather them for battle against the Lord on that great judgment day of God the Almighty.

15 "Look, I will come as unexpectedly as a thief! Blessed are all who are watching for me, who keep their clothing ready so they will not have to walk around naked and ashamed."

16 And the demonic spirits gathered all the rulers and their armies to a place with the Hebrew name *Armageddon*.

17 Then the seventh angel poured out his bowl into the air. And a mighty shout came from the throne in the Temple, saying, "It is finished!" 18 Then the thunder crashed and rolled, and

lightning flashed. And a great earthquake struck—the worst since people were placed on the earth. ¹⁹The great city of Babylon split into three sections, and the cities of many nations fell into heaps of rubble. So God remembered all of Babylon's sins, and he made her drink the cup that was filled with the wine of his fierce wrath. ²⁰And every island disappeared, and all the mountains were leveled. ²¹There was a terrible hailstorm, and hailstones weighing seventy-five pounds fell from the sky onto the people below. They cursed God because of the terrible plague of the hailstorm.

CHAPTER **17**
The Great Prostitute

One of the seven angels who had poured out the seven bowls came over and spoke to me. "Come with me," he said, "and I will show you the judgment that is going to come on the great prostitute, who rules over many waters. ²The kings of the world have committed adultery with her, and the people who belong to this world have been made drunk by the wine of her immorality."

³So the angel took me in the Spirit into the wilderness. There I saw a woman sitting on a scarlet beast that had seven heads and ten horns, and blasphemies against God were written all over it. ⁴The woman wore purple and scarlet clothing and beautiful jewelry made of gold and precious gems and pearls. In her hand she held a gold goblet full of obscenities and the impurities of her immorality. ⁵A mysterious name was written on her forehead: "Babylon the Great, Mother of All Prostitutes and Obscenities in the World." ⁶I could see that she was drunk—drunk with the blood of God's holy people who were witnesses for Jesus. I stared at her in complete amazement.

⁷"Why are you so amazed?" the angel asked. "I will tell you the mystery of this woman and of the beast with seven heads and ten horns on which she sits. ⁸The beast you saw was once alive but isn't now. And yet he will soon come up out of the bottomless pit and go to eternal destruction. And the people who belong to this world, whose names were not written in the Book of Life before the world was made, will be amazed at the reappearance of this beast who had died.

⁹"This calls for a mind with understanding: The seven heads of the beast represent the seven hills where the woman rules. They also represent seven kings. ¹⁰Five kings have already fallen, the sixth now reigns, and the seventh is yet to come, but his reign will be brief.

¹¹"The scarlet beast that was, but is no longer, is the eighth king. He is like the other seven, and he, too, is headed for destruction. ¹²The ten horns of the beast are ten kings who have not yet risen to power. They will be appointed to their kingdoms for one brief moment to reign with the beast. ¹³They will all agree to give him their power and authority. ¹⁴Together they will go to war against the Lamb, but the Lamb will defeat them because he is Lord of all lords and King of all kings. And his called and chosen and faithful ones will be with him."

¹⁵Then the angel said to me, "The waters where the prostitute is ruling represent masses of people of every nation and language. ¹⁶The scarlet

FUN-fact STAMP OF APPROVAL

APPROVED

Kings used to have a special way of sealing their letters. They'd roll them up and pour a small dab of wax on the edges to keep them rolled shut. Before the wax dried, they'd stamp it with a special seal. The seal looked kind of like a rubber stamp.

TRY THIS! Write a letter to a friend. Roll it up, and have an adult pour a small amount of candle wax from a lit candle onto your letter to keep the edges together. Press a stamper or a coin into the wax as a seal. (Don't forget to deliver your letter!)

STOP!! Before you read any further, go get an adult to help you light a candle!

Not that kind of seal!!!

This kind!

beast and his ten horns all hate the prostitute. They will strip her naked, eat her flesh, and burn her remains with fire. ¹⁷For God has put a plan into their minds, a plan that will carry out his purposes. They will agree to give their authority to the scarlet beast, and so the words of God will be fulfilled. ¹⁸And this woman you saw in your vision represents the great city that rules over the kings of the world."

The Fall of Babylon

After all this I saw another angel come down from heaven with great authority, and the earth grew bright with his splendor. ²He gave a mighty shout:

"Babylon is fallen—that great city is fallen!
    She has become a home for demons.
She is a hideout for every foul spirit,
    a hideout for every foul vulture
    and every foul and dreadful animal.
³ For all the nations have fallen
    because of the wine of her passionate
        immorality.
The kings of the world
    have committed adultery with her.
Because of her desires for extravagant luxury,
    the merchants of the world have
        grown rich."

⁴Then I heard another voice calling from heaven,

"Come away from her, my people.
    Do not take part in her sins,
    or you will be punished with her.
⁵ For her sins are piled as high as heaven,
    and God remembers her evil deeds.
⁶ Do to her as she has done to others.
    Double her penalty for all her evil deeds.
She brewed a cup of terror for others,
    so brew twice as much for her.
⁷ She glorified herself and lived in luxury,
    so match it now with torment and sorrow.
She boasted in her heart,
    'I am queen on my throne.
I am no helpless widow,
    and I have no reason to mourn.'
⁸ Therefore, these plagues will overtake
        her in a single day—
    death and mourning and famine.
She will be completely consumed by fire,
    for the Lord God who judges her is
        mighty."

⁹And the kings of the world who committed adultery with her and enjoyed her great luxury will mourn for her as they see the smoke rising from her charred remains. ¹⁰They will stand at a distance, terrified by her great torment. They will cry out,

"How terrible, how terrible for you,
    O Babylon, you great city!
In a single moment
    God's judgment came on you."

¹¹The merchants of the world will weep and mourn for her, for there is no one left to buy their goods. ¹²She bought great quantities of gold, silver, jewels, and pearls; fine linen, purple, silk, and scarlet cloth; things made of fragrant thyine wood, ivory goods, and objects made of expensive wood; and bronze, iron, and marble. ¹³She also bought cinnamon, spice, incense, myrrh, frankincense, wine, olive oil, fine flour, wheat, cattle, sheep, horses, chariots, and bodies—that is, human slaves.

¹⁴ "The fancy things you loved so much
    are gone," they cry.
"All your luxuries and splendor
    are gone forever,
    never to be yours again."

¹⁵The merchants who became wealthy by selling her these things will stand at a distance, terrified by her great torment. They will weep and cry out,

¹⁶ "How terrible, how terrible for that great city!
    She was clothed in finest purple and
        scarlet linens,
    decked out with gold and precious
        stones and pearls!
¹⁷ In a single moment
    all the wealth of the city is gone!"

And all the captains of the merchant ships and their passengers and sailors and crews will stand at a distance. ¹⁸They will cry out as they watch the smoke ascend, and they will say, "Where is there another city as great as this?" ¹⁹And they will weep and throw dust on their heads to show their grief. And they will cry out,

"How terrible, how terrible for that
        great city!
    The shipowners became wealthy
    by transporting her great wealth
        on the seas.
In a single moment it is all gone."

²⁰ Rejoice over her fate, O heaven
    and people of God and apostles
    and prophets!

For at last God has judged her
for your sakes.

²¹ Then a mighty angel picked up a boulder the size of a huge millstone. He threw it into the ocean and shouted,

"Just like this, the great city Babylon
will be thrown down with violence
and will never be found again.
²² The sound of harps, singers, flutes,
and trumpets
will never be heard in you again.
No craftsmen and no trades
will ever be found in you again.
The sound of the mill
will never be heard in you again.
²³ The light of a lamp
will never shine in you again.
The happy voices of brides and grooms
will never be heard in you again.
For your merchants were the greatest
in the world,
and you deceived the nations with your
sorceries.
²⁴ In your streets flowed the blood of the
prophets and of God's holy people
and the blood of people slaughtered all
over the world."

CHAPTER **19**
Songs of Victory in Heaven

After this, I heard what sounded like a vast crowd in heaven shouting,

"Praise the LORD!
Salvation and glory and power belong
to our God.
² His judgments are true and just.
He has punished the great prostitute
who corrupted the earth with her
immorality.
He has avenged the murder of his
servants."

³ And again their voices rang out:

"Praise the LORD!
The smoke from that city ascends forever
and ever!"

⁴ Then the twenty-four elders and the four living beings fell down and worshiped God, who was sitting on the throne. They cried out, "Amen! Praise the LORD!"

⁵ And from the throne came a voice that said,

"Praise our God,
all his servants,
all who fear him,
from the least to the greatest."

⁶ Then I heard again what sounded like the shout of a vast crowd or the roar of mighty ocean waves or the crash of loud thunder:

"Praise the LORD!
For the Lord our God, the Almighty, reigns.
⁷ Let us be glad and rejoice,
and let us give honor to him.
For the time has come for the wedding feast
of the Lamb,
and his bride has prepared herself.
⁸ She has been given the finest of pure white
linen to wear."
For the fine linen represents the good
deeds of God's holy people.

⁹ And the angel said to me, "Write this: Blessed are those who are invited to the wedding feast of the Lamb." And he added, "These are true words that come from God."

¹⁰ Then I fell down at his feet to worship him, but he said, "No, don't worship me. I am a servant of God, just like you and your brothers and sisters who testify about their faith in Jesus. Worship only God. For the essence of prophecy is to give a clear witness for Jesus."

The Rider on the White Horse

¹¹ Then I saw heaven opened, and a white horse was standing there. Its rider was named Faithful and True, for he judges fairly and wages a righteous war. ¹² His eyes were like flames of fire, and on his head were many crowns. A name was written on him that no one understood except himself. ¹³ He wore a robe dipped in blood, and his title was the Word of God. ¹⁴ The armies of heaven, dressed in the finest of pure white linen, followed him on white horses. ¹⁵ From his mouth came a sharp sword to strike down the nations. He will rule them with an iron rod. He will release the fierce wrath of God, the Almighty, like juice flowing from a winepress. ¹⁶ On his robe at his thigh was written this title: King of all kings and Lord of all lords.

¹⁷ Then I saw an angel standing in the sun, shouting to the vultures flying high in the sky: "Come! Gather together for the great banquet God has prepared. ¹⁸ Come and eat the flesh of kings, generals, and strong warriors; of horses and their riders; and of all humanity, both free and slave, small and great."

¹⁹ Then I saw the beast and the kings of the world and their armies gathered together to

fight against the one sitting on the horse and his army. ²⁰And the beast was captured, and with him the false prophet who did mighty miracles on behalf of the beast—miracles that deceived all who had accepted the mark of the beast and who worshiped his statue. Both the beast and his false prophet were thrown alive into the fiery lake of burning sulfur. ²¹Their entire army was killed by the sharp sword that came from the mouth of the one riding the white horse. And the vultures all gorged themselves on the dead bodies.

CHAPTER **20**

The Thousand Years

Then I saw an angel coming down from heaven with the key to the bottomless pit and a heavy chain in his hand. ²He seized the dragon—that old serpent, who is the devil, Satan—and bound him in chains for a thousand years. ³The angel threw him into the bottomless pit, which he then shut and locked so Satan could not deceive the nations anymore until the thousand years were finished. Afterward he must be released for a little while.

⁴Then I saw thrones, and the people sitting on them had been given the authority to judge. And I saw the souls of those who had been beheaded for their testimony about Jesus and for proclaiming the word of God. They had not worshiped the beast or his statue, nor accepted his mark on their forehead or their hands. They all came to life again, and they reigned with Christ for a thousand years.

⁵This is the first resurrection. (The rest of the dead did not come back to life until the thousand years had ended.) ⁶Blessed and holy are those who share in the first resurrection. For them the second death holds no power, but they will be priests of God and of Christ and will reign with him a thousand years.

The Defeat of Satan

⁷When the thousand years come to an end, Satan will be let out of his prison. ⁸He will go out to deceive the nations—called Gog and Magog—in every corner of the earth. He will gather them together for battle—a mighty army, as numberless as sand along the seashore. ⁹And I saw them as they went up on the broad plain of the earth and surrounded God's people and the beloved city. But fire from heaven came down on the attacking armies and consumed them.

¹⁰Then the devil, who had deceived them, was thrown into the fiery lake of burning sulfur,

Time to Celebrate!

We know that Jesus is coming back. And when he comes, boy, are things going to change!

Read **REVELATION 21:10-21** to get a glimpse of what the New Jerusalem will be like after Jesus has judged the world. Wow!

Have a New Jerusalem party to celebrate the beautiful place where Jesus will live with his followers forever!

1 Spread colored frosting on graham crackers, and use them to build a square city wall. Hold the walls together with more frosting.

2 Stick small candies to the walls as gems.

3 Serve apple juice to represent the streets of gold.

NOW CELEBRATE!

Before you eat, make sure everyone knows that the only way to live in the New Jerusalem is by believing in Jesus. Then celebrate because it's going to be a great day when Jesus comes back!

Bright Morning Star

Did you ever get up so early in the morning you could still see a bright star in the sky? That's a morning star.

Jesus calls himself the bright morning star—read it for yourself in **REVELATION 22:16**!

Make a star of your own to remind you that Jesus is coming back. Write **"REVELATION 22:16"** somewhere on your creation. Here are a few ideas to get you started.

Cut a star from a white doily, and glue it to a sheet of black paper.

Draw a star shape on dark paper. Glue bits of white paper or foil inside the star outline.

Use paper reinforcements or glitter glue to make your star on dark paper.

Make an edible morning star! Spread chocolate pudding on a small plate. Decorate a star-shaped cookie with sprinkles, then place it in your pudding "night sky."

USE YOUR MORNING STAR REMINDER TO TELL SOMEONE ELSE THAT JESUS IS COMING BACK.

Read Matthew 24:26-27 for more about Jesus' return.

joining the beast and the false prophet. There they will be tormented day and night forever and ever.

The Final Judgment

11And I saw a great white throne and the one sitting on it. The earth and sky fled from his presence, but they found no place to hide. **12**I saw the dead, both great and small, standing before God's throne. And the books were opened, including the Book of Life. And the dead were judged according to what they had done, as recorded in the books. **13**The sea gave up its dead, and death and the grave gave up their dead. And all were judged according to their deeds. **14**Then death and the grave were thrown into the lake of fire. This lake of fire is the second death. **15**And anyone whose name was not found recorded in the Book of Life was thrown into the lake of fire.

CHAPTER **21**
The New Jerusalem

Then I saw a new heaven and a new earth, for the old heaven and the old earth had disappeared. And the sea was also gone. **2**And I saw the holy city, the new Jerusalem, coming down from God out of heaven like a bride beautifully dressed for her husband.

3I heard a loud shout from the throne, saying, "Look, God's home is now among his people! He will live with them, and they will be his people. God himself will be with them. **4**He will wipe every tear from their eyes, and there will be no more death or sorrow or crying or pain. All these things are gone forever."

5And the one sitting on the throne said, "Look, I am making everything new!" And then he said to me, "Write this down, for what I tell you is trustworthy and true." **6**And he also said, "It is finished! I am the Alpha and the Omega—the Beginning and the End. To all who are thirsty I will give freely from the springs of the water of life. **7**All who are victorious will inherit all these blessings, and I will be their God, and they will be my children.

8"But cowards, unbelievers, the corrupt, murderers, the immoral, those who practice witchcraft, idol worshipers, and all liars—their fate is in the fiery lake of burning sulfur. This is the second death."

9Then one of the seven angels who held the seven bowls containing the seven last plagues came and said to me, "Come with me! I will show you the bride, the wife of the Lamb."

10So he took me in the Spirit to a great, high

mountain, and he showed me the holy city, Jerusalem, descending out of heaven from God. ¹¹It shone with the glory of God and sparkled like a precious stone—like jasper as clear as crystal. ¹²The city wall was broad and high, with twelve gates guarded by twelve angels. And the names of the twelve tribes of Israel were written on the gates. ¹³There were three gates on each side— east, north, south, and west. ¹⁴The wall of the city had twelve foundation stones, and on them were written the names of the twelve apostles of the Lamb.

¹⁵The angel who talked to me held in his hand a gold measuring stick to measure the city, its gates, and its wall. ¹⁶When he measured it, he found it was a square, as wide as it was long. In fact, its length and width and height were each 1,400 miles. ¹⁷Then he measured the walls and found them to be 216 feet thick (according to the human standard used by the angel).

¹⁸The wall was made of jasper, and the city was pure gold, as clear as glass. ¹⁹The wall of the city was built on foundation stones inlaid with twelve precious stones: the first was jasper, the second sapphire, the third agate, the fourth emerald, ²⁰the fifth onyx, the sixth carnelian, the seventh chrysolite, the eighth beryl, the ninth topaz, the tenth chrysoprase, the eleventh jacinth, the twelfth amethyst.

²¹The twelve gates were made of pearls—each gate from a single pearl! And the main street was pure gold, as clear as glass.

²²I saw no temple in the city, for the Lord God Almighty and the Lamb are its temple. ²³And the city has no need of sun or moon, for the glory of God illuminates the city, and the Lamb is its light. ²⁴The nations will walk in its light, and the kings of the world will enter the city in all their glory. ²⁵Its gates will never be closed at the end of day because there is no night there. ²⁶And all the nations will bring their glory and honor into the city. ²⁷Nothing evil will be allowed to enter, nor anyone who practices shameful idolatry and dishonesty—but only those whose names are written in the Lamb's Book of Life.

CHAPTER **22**

Then the angel showed me a river with the water of life, clear as crystal, flowing from the throne of God and of the Lamb. ²It flowed down the center of the main street. On each side of the river grew a tree of life, bearing twelve crops of fruit, with a fresh crop each month. The leaves were used for medicine to heal the nations. ³No longer will there be a curse upon any-

thing. For the throne of God and of the Lamb will be there, and his servants will worship him. ⁴And they will see his face, and his name will be written on their foreheads. ⁵And there will be no night there—no need for lamps or sun—for the Lord God will shine on them. And they will reign forever and ever.

⁶Then the angel said to me, "Everything you have heard and seen is trustworthy and true. The Lord God, who inspires his prophets, has sent his angel to tell his servants what will happen soon."

Jesus Is Coming

⁷"Look, I am coming soon! Blessed are those who obey the words of prophecy written in this book."

⁸I, John, am the one who heard and saw all these things. And when I heard and saw them, I fell down to worship at the feet of the angel who showed them to me. ⁹But he said, "No, don't worship me. I am a servant of God, just like you and your brothers the prophets, as well as all who obey what is written in this book. Worship only God!"

¹⁰Then he instructed me, "Do not seal up the prophetic words in this book, for the time is near. ¹¹Let the one who is doing harm continue to do harm; let the one who is vile continue to be vile; let the one who is righteous continue to live righteously; let the one who is holy continue to be holy."

¹²"Look, I am coming soon, bringing my reward with me to repay all people according to their deeds. ¹³I am the Alpha and the Omega, the First and the Last, the Beginning and the End."

¹⁴Blessed are those who wash their robes. They will be permitted to enter through the gates of the city and eat the fruit from the tree of life. ¹⁵Outside the city are the dogs—the sorcerers, the sexually immoral, the murderers, the idol worshipers, and all who love to live a lie.

¹⁶"I, Jesus, have sent my angel to give you this message for the churches. I am both the source of David and the heir to his throne. I am the bright morning star."

¹⁷The Spirit and the bride say, "Come." Let anyone who hears this say, "Come." Let anyone who is thirsty come. Let anyone who desires drink freely from the water of life. ¹⁸And I solemnly declare to everyone who hears the words of prophecy written in this book: If anyone adds anything to what is written here, God will add to

that person the plagues described in this book. [19] And if anyone removes any of the words from this book of prophecy, God will remove that person's share in the tree of life and in the holy city that are described in this book.

[20] He who is the faithful witness to all these things says, "Yes, I am coming soon!"

Amen! Come, Lord Jesus!

[21] May the grace of the Lord Jesus be with God's holy people.

Did You Know?

Frequently Asked Questions About the Bible

Note: This section of the New Testament uses references from the Old Testament to answer some questions. That's OK, because someday you'll be reading from a full Bible and be able to dive into the whole story!

Who wrote the Bible?

The Bible has more than 40 different authors and only one author! Sound confusing? Not really!

God is the one true author of Scripture. From Genesis to Revelation, it all comes from him. That's why we call it God's Word. Now here's the tricky part: God chose to use more than 40 different human authors to do the actual writing.

That's what it means when people say the Bible is "inspired by God." God inspired Moses, for example, to write the first five books of the Bible. That means he guided Moses along so that he wrote exactly what God wanted him to write. God did the same thing with prophets such as Isaiah, who wrote the book of Isaiah, and the Apostle Paul, who wrote 13 New Testament books. You get the idea.

Now take some time to look up these verses, which tell a little more about the Bible-writing process: **2 TIMOTHY 3:16** and **2 PETER 1:20-21**.

When was the Bible written?

How long do you think it would take you to read the whole Bible, cover to cover? Six months? A year? Two years? Well, that's nothing compared to how long it took to write the Bible.

It took more than 1,000 years to write the whole Bible! God inspired Moses to write the first five books of the Bible around 1400 B.C. (The book of Job might have been written even earlier than that!) The Apostle John wrote Revelation, the last book of the Bible, in the late first century A.D. That's close to 1,500 years later!

Why did it take so long? Think about it—the Bible covers a ton of history, from the creation of the world to the days when Jesus' disciples founded the church. The Bible kept growing and growing until the New Testament was finished.

And there's something really amazing about the Bible: It still speaks to us today. The Bible is the most important book you can ever read. It was written long ago, but it was written for you!

Why was the Bible written?

Let's let the Bible speak for itself. Here's what the Bible says about why it was written!

> Your word is a lamp to guide my feet and a light for my path.
>
> **PSALM 119:105**

> All Scripture is inspired by God and is useful to teach us what is true and to make us realize what is wrong in our lives. It corrects us when we are wrong and teaches us to do what is right. God uses it to prepare and equip his people to do every good work.
>
> **2 TIMOTHY 3:16-17**

> For the word of God is alive and powerful. It is sharper than the sharpest two-edged sword, cutting between soul and spirit, between joint and marrow. It exposes our innermost thoughts and desires.
>
> **HEBREWS 4:12**

God gave us his Word for lots of reasons, but the most important reason is so we can know him personally. The Bible shows us who God really is and what he's really like. The Bible shows us that God loves us so much that he made a way through his Son, Jesus, for us to spend forever with him in heaven.

And the Bible shows us how to live while we're here on earth. It guides us through our daily lives and shows us how to have Jesus as our forever friend, starting right now! The Bible shines the brightness of God's truth on our path.

What other book can do all those things? None! You got that right. The Bible's awesome!

Will God put new stories in the Bible?

Nope, that's all he wrote. Christians believe that God won't add anything new to the 66 books of the Bible we already have. There's no need. God's already told us all we need to know. The Bible tells us how the world and the human race got started, how sin entered God's perfect creation, how God made a plan to save sinful people, how God put that plan into action through Jesus, and how God will complete his plan when Jesus returns. That's the whole story from start to finish.

Our job is to study and obey God's perfect Word as we wait for Jesus to return. That day will be the start of a whole new, wonderful story—the story of eternity! The Bible gives us only hints of what eternity will be like (look at **REVELATION 21:3-4** for starters). But it's clear from those hints that you won't want to miss out on it!

Is all of the Bible true?

Absolutely! The Bible is the very Word of God, and God can't lie. He can't make mistakes either. You and I might be tempted to lie sometimes, but God never is. You and I might make mistakes sometimes, but God never does.

God is perfect, which means he never does anything wrong. He's given us his Word because he wants us to know the truth about some very important stuff—like who he is, how much he loves us, and how to get to heaven!

So when you open the Bible, you can rely on every word because, after all, it's God's Word!

Why does the Bible have two parts?

The Bible covers a big chunk of history, from the creation of the world and everything we see in it (including human beings like you and me) to the time just after Jesus was on earth. That's a lot of years!

Part of that time, God dealt mainly with the nation called Israel. The Old Testament is all about his dealings with Israel. The New Testament tells of a big turning point in history, when the focus shifted from the nation of Israel to the entire world.

What caused the shift? Jesus came and died on the cross for the sins of everyone. After he rose from the dead, Jesus sent his disciples out into the world to tell everyone about the Good News of salvation through faith in him. That triggered a chain reaction that hasn't stopped yet! In fact, the very reason that you're reading this Bible is because you're a part of what started way back then.

Tell someone about Jesus today and keep the chain reaction going!

Do all the promises and commands God gave to the Israelites apply to my life?

Hey, you're asking some good questions here!

Before we answer this one, go back and read the answer to question 6 again. (Thanks.) Some things that God said to the Israelites don't apply to us today. For example, Christians can eat pork if they want, but the Israelites couldn't because God wanted to set them apart from their neighbors. (Compare **DEUTERONOMY 14:8** with **MARK 7:19** and **ACTS 10:9-15**.)

On the other hand, there are lots of things that do still apply to us today. For example, Christians today shouldn't murder or steal or worship idols, just like the Ten Commandments and other parts of the Old Testament say.

How can you know what applies to you today? Ask yourself, Does the New Testament give Christians the same command or promise I'm finding in the Old Testament? (To find out, you'll need to do some detective work. Use the easy concordance that starts on page 1369, or ask your Sunday school teacher or another Christian for help.) If it does, then you know you need to obey that command or believe that promise.

For example, think about God's promise to create a new heaven and earth some day. Isaiah, an Old Testament book, says it (see **ISAIAH 65:17**), and so does 2 Peter, a New Testament book (see **2 PETER 3:13**). Since both the Old and New Testaments say it, you know that it's a promise that applies to you, just like it did to the Israelites.

There's a lot more to say on this subject, but you can start by practicing the kind of checking you just learned. (Hey, what are you waiting for?)

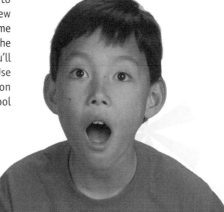

Does Jesus really want us to poke our eye out if it makes us sin?

Yikes! What Jesus said in MATTHEW 5:29-30 is a shocker. That's because Jesus wanted to shock people with those words! Sin is seriously bad news. It can ruin your life, and for those who never turn to Jesus to save them from their sins, it will cause them to go to hell when they die.

The problem is, people can get comfortable with sin. Any one of us can trick ourselves into believing sin isn't really that big a deal, right? Well, Jesus blows that idea right out of the water in these verses! Jesus' point is this: Don't get comfortable with sin in your life. Take radical steps to get rid of the sin and its cause because sin causes problems that are way worse than anything that could happen to your body. Jesus made his point in a way that gets our attention. The question is, Will we pay attention?

There are other places in the Bible where shocking or colorful language is used in a way that makes us say, "Huh?" Our job then is to understand the point. It's not always easy, but there are tools to help you, including some of the notes in this Bible. So keep reading, and keep asking God to help you understand his Word!

Does the Bible talk about things that haven't happened yet?

The Bible is full of prophecies—statements God made ahead of time before the events actually happened. Many of those prophecies have already come to pass.

For example, way back in Abraham's day, God told Abraham that future members of his family would live as slaves in a foreign land for four hundred years before God rescued them and brought them into the Promised Land (see GENESIS 15:13-16). Sure enough, decades later the Israelites became slaves in Egypt. And then God fulfilled his promise and delivered them into the Promised Land. (Read the book of JOSHUA for details!)

Other prophecies in the Old Testament were fulfilled when Jesus came. For example, God told the prophet Isaiah that the Messiah would be born of a virgin (see ISAIAH 7:14). Hundreds of years later, Jesus was born to a virgin named Mary (see MATTHEW 1:22-23). Pretty cool, right?

The Bible also talks about things that haven't happened yet. The main one is that Jesus will one day return to set up his kingdom (see MATTHEW 24:44; JOHN 14:2-4). The fact that we can look back and see so many prophecies that God fulfilled in the past gives us complete confidence that God will fulfill this and other prophecies for the future.

Look up these verses for some other prophecies that have yet to be fulfilled: 2 THESSALONIANS 2:1-12; REVELATION 20:1-15.

Why are there so many words that are hard to read in the Bible?

What do you mean? Don't tell me you find Maher-shalal-hash-baz (ISAIAH 8:1) hard to pronounce. Or what about Tahtim-hodshi (2 SAMUEL 24:6)? Piece of cake, right? (OK, just kidding.)

Sure, many words in the Bible are hard to pronounce and understand, especially names of people and places. That's because the Bible was written a long time ago in far away places. (Even today, people from other countries have different-sounding names for people, places, and things, don't they? Try Heilongjiang, the name of a province in China!)

There are other words in the Bible that might not be as difficult to pronounce, but they're still not familiar to us. We don't use the word *tabernacle* too much in everyday talk, but it's an important word in the Bible—it's the tent where God originally lived among the Israelites (see EXODUS 25:8).

Some other words seem strange to us because they come from other languages. The fifth book of the Bible, for instance, is called Deuteronomy. What does that mean? Actually it's Greek for "second" (*deuter-*) "law" (*nomos*). It's called that because in Deuteronomy Moses repeats much of the Law God gave him earlier on Mount Sinai.

Other words have big meanings that are hard to understand. For example, Jesus is called our mediator in 1 TIMOTHY 2:5. A mediator is someone who comes between two people who have a disagreement and works out a solution. God is deeply offended by sin, but Jesus took away our sin. He comes between God and us so we can have a friendly relationship again.

Even though you may stumble over the words once in a while, don't stop reading the Bible! Every time you open it, God is speaking to you.

Why are there so many different Bible versions?

The Bible wasn't originally written in English. In fact, different parts were written in different languages. Most of the Old Testament was written in ancient Hebrew. Small portions of the Old Testament were written in ancient Aramaic. The New Testament was originally written in ancient Greek. See a pattern?

God wants everyone in the world to read, understand, and believe the Bible. To meet this goal, people throughout the ages have translated the Bible into lots of different languages—English, Spanish, Chinese, French, Russian, and Arabic, to name a few. The list goes on and on. In some languages, the Bible has been translated more than once. That's because languages change over time. People don't speak and write English today the same way they did a hundred years ago, right? (Heard anybody say "Four score and seven years ago" lately?)

Bible translators have a special calling to make sure the Bible speaks as clearly to as many people as possible in every generation. That's the main reason there are so many different versions of the Bible.

Why is it so important to read the Bible?

Imagine setting off on a journey in a foreign land. If you didn't have a map, you'd probably get lost; you might even die. Or imagine trying to build a house without a plan in mind. Trying to live life without regularly reading the Bible is kind of like setting off on a journey with no map or trying to build a house with no blueprint.

The Bible helps us make good decisions and helps us know what is right and wrong. Most important of all, it teaches us to know God and tells us what to do if we want to spend eternity with him in heaven. God's given us a real treasure chest in the Bible. We'd be silly not to read it—a lot!

Many people try to read a little bit every single day. That's a smart plan! Others read it more, some less. The important thing to remember is that the more you read, study, and obey God's Word, the more you'll benefit from it. Because the Bible is a collection of smaller books, you can begin your reading at a lot of different places.

The Gospel of John is a good place to start to learn about Jesus. The book of Genesis tells about the creation of the world. And there are lots of places in Psalms, Proverbs, and the New Testament letters where even reading a verse or chapter a day really pays off! You could also use a plan that helps you read all the way through the Bible in one or two years. (There's a reading plan you can look at on page 1338!)

You've got tons of options. So start reading!

Some Other BIG Questions

Why can't I see God? How do we know God is real?

There are a number of things that we can't see, yet know they're real. We know the wind is real because we can feel it on our skin or because we can see it blow the leaves off a tree. Yet we can't technically see the wind.

Because God is a spirit, he's invisible unless he chooses to reveal himself in some way for some special occasion. (Look at these examples of God revealing himself in special ways: **EXODUS 3:4-6**; **1 KINGS 19:11-13**; **MATTHEW 3:16-17**.) Only a few people in history have met God in these ways. For the rest of us, there are other ways we can "know" God exists, even though we don't see him.

First, we know by faith that God exists. The Bible says he's real. So those who believe the Bible believe God is real. (Take a look at what **HEBREWS 11:6** says.) Second, we know God exists because of the impact he has on our lives. Just like we know the wind is real because we see what it does, we know God is real because he changes our lives. He lets us know when we do wrong. He comforts us when we're sad. He answers our prayers. And the list goes on and on. Those who have faith know that God is real because he really is active in their lives.

How old is God? What has God been doing for all that time?

Good luck trying to wrap your mind around this one! God has been around forever. It's impossible to say how old he is, because he had no beginning and will have no end. That means you can try to imagine the biggest number ever, and God would still be older than that. God is infinite. Everything else had a beginning.

The Bible doesn't tell us everything there is to know about God, including all that God has been doing for eternity. Even the biggest book in the world couldn't hold all there is to know about him. Many people spend their entire lives trying to learn all that the Bible has to teach about God, and even that is a tall order. Better get started!

Why does God let bad things happen?

People have wrestled with this question for a long, long time. In the Old Testament book of Job (possibly the oldest book in the Bible), the main character, Job, had a bunch of bad things happen to him one day. He wondered why God would allow such bad things to happen, but Job never lost trust in God. We don't always know why God allows hard things to happen.

Whatever happens, it's important to remember these truths: First, God is always in control. We never need to worry that bad things could happen without God allowing them to happen. And second, God always does what is right and good. Even when Christians suffer, we can know that God is using suffering for our benefit (see **ROMANS 8:28** and **2 CORINTHIANS 12:7-10**). Sometimes when we're suffering, we can feel like God has forgotten us. But that's impossible. God has promised never to leave us (see **HEBREWS 13:5**). And God keeps his promises!

How is Jesus different from other teachers?

Good question. There have been many people throughout history who've claimed to be prophets and teachers sent from God. Some were real, like the true prophets of the Old Testament. Others were fakers, like the false prophets of the Old Testament and those who've started their own religions.

Jesus is special because he's much more than just a teacher. He's the Son of God! He is God in human form. The entire Bible is about Jesus in one way or another. That's why Christians should have nothing to do with the writings and teachings of other religions. The Bible is all we need, and it's all we can trust because it alone comes from God.

Human beings were designed to know God. But because of sin, humans don't want to come to God on his terms. They want to make up their own way to live. So it's easy to see why so many other religions have sprung up throughout history. But that displeases God greatly. God's Word is true, so stay focused right there!

Why did Jesus have to die?

The Bible says that the penalty for sin is death (see **ROMANS 6:23**). That's real bad news because it also says that all people have sinned, including you and me (see **ROMANS 3:23**).

But there's some real good news too. God loved us enough to make a way for us sinners to be holy in his sight. It was a way that cost God a lot, because it meant sending Jesus, his only Son, to the world to take our punishment for us.

Jesus never sinned, but he allowed himself to be treated like a criminal by taking our sin upon himself and dying in our place on the cross. Three days later God raised Jesus from the dead so that now whoever believes in Jesus is pure and holy in God's sight.

The penalty for sin has been paid, and we can go to heaven because of that payment. That's good news—no, that's great news! (Hey, did you know that the word *gospel* means "good news"? You better believe it!)

What does it mean to be a Christian?

First of all, to be a Christian means that you know Jesus Christ as your personal Savior. You've realized that you are a sinner and that the only way to heaven is through faith in Jesus, who died on the cross to take the punishment for your sins. Knowing Jesus as your personal Savior means you'll spend eternity with him in heaven and have him as your best friend here on earth. Way to go!

But there's more to it than that. Being a Christian also means that we live our lives each day in a way that honors Jesus. A true Christian has Jesus living inside his or her heart (see COLOSSIANS 1:27). So a Christian can't just go on living as he or she feels like. Christians are supposed to love Jesus and grow in faith and obedience to him with each new day (see COLOSSIANS 3:1-17).

Sure, sometimes we mess up, but Jesus is always there to help us get back on the right path again. Sometimes obeying Jesus is hard. But God gives every Christian a special gift to help—the Holy Spirit. When you believe in Jesus, the Holy Spirit comes and changes your heart so that living for God is something you want to do, not something you have to do. Cool, huh?

Who is the Holy Spirit?

Like God the Father and Jesus, the Holy Spirit is God. Wait, does that mean there are three Gods? Nope! At the heart of the Christian faith is a giant mystery. (No, not the kind a detective solves. This mystery is a truth that's not easy for us humans to understand.) Here it is: There is only one God, but he has always existed as three persons—the Father, the Son (that's Jesus), and the Holy Spirit. Just like Jesus came to earth with a special purpose—to save us—the Holy Spirit has a special role. Actually he has a few.

Here are some important roles: The Holy Spirit shows people their sin so they'll believe in Jesus and be saved (see JOHN 16:8). He lives inside Christians (see ROMANS 8:9-11) and helps them live in a way that honors Jesus (see GALATIANS 5:22-24). The Holy Spirit living in us is God's seal of ownership on us. And the Holy Spirit gives us spiritual gifts that we can use to serve God. (Check out these lists of spiritual gifts: ROMANS 12:6-8; 1 CORINTHIANS 12:4-11; 1 PETER 4:10-11.) The Holy Spirit helps us pray, too, and reminds us of God's Word. What a helper!

Should I be afraid of demons? What are they?

Demons are angels who rebelled against God at the same time the devil, the prince of demons, rebelled. God threw them out of heaven but has permitted some of them to be active in the world until the time he has planned to banish them to hell. Demons can sometimes trouble people through temptation or other forms of harassment such as illness. That's why the Bible tells Christians to be ready by putting on the spiritual armor that God provides (see EPHESIANS 6:10-12).

It's important to remember that although demons try to work against God's plans, they are totally powerless against him. When Jesus was on earth, he cast out many demons from people, and when he died and rose again, he won the final victory over the devil and all fallen angels.

So Christians can be sure that God will protect them from harm by demons (see 1 JOHN 5:18). But we are called to be on guard against the temptations and suffering the devil and his helpers can trouble us with (see 1 PETER 5:8-9). So put on that spiritual armor—and don't be afraid, because Jesus has already won the battle!

Does God talk to us? How can I hear him?

Throughout the Bible, there are times God spoke out loud to people. (Moses heard God speak to him lots of times.) For most of us, though, God speaks mostly through his Word, the Bible. The Bible is so full of truth that we can find answers there to all of life's big questions.

Sometimes, though, God uses other ways to talk to us. God might send a wise person to give you the advice you need (see EXODUS 18:13-27). Or he might show you what to do by making other options impossible (see ACTS 16:6-10). Sometimes the Holy Spirit might put the right decision in your heart (see ROMANS 8:14, 16).

The most important thing to remember is that no matter how God communicates, his message will never go against the Bible. So if you get advice from someone, but that advice goes against what the Bible teaches, you can be sure that the advice didn't come from God.

Does God answer all our prayers?

God does always answer our prayers, but he doesn't always give us the answer we want. Suppose you really wanted to go away to summer camp one year. You prayed and prayed, but Dad and Mom decided they needed you to be at home to help the family. Did God answer your prayer? Yes, even though it wasn't the answer you wanted.

We should always remember that God is a lot smarter than we are. He knows the future, and he knows what's best for you. Next time you pray for something and God says no or not right now, thank him for knowing what's best for you. (The Apostle Paul did just that when God said no to him one time. See for yourself in 2 CORINTHIANS 12:7-9.)

Charts, Charts, Charts

God Uses Common People

God uses all sorts of people to do his work—people like you and me! Don't believe it? Just look at these people!

Person	Known As	Task	Bible Reference
JACOB	A LIAR	To father the Israelite nation	GENESIS 27
JOSEPH	A SLAVE	To save his family	GENESIS 39-47
MOSES	A SHEPHERD in exile (and a murderer)	To lead Israel out of bondage and into the Promised Land	EXODUS 3
GIDEON	A FARMER	To deliver Israel from Midian	JUDGES 6:11
HANNAH	A HOUSEWIFE	To be the mother of Samuel	1 SAMUEL 1
DAVID	A SHEPHERD BOY and youngest of the family	To be Israel's greatest king	1 SAMUEL 16
EZRA	A SCRIBE	To lead the return to Judah and to write some of the Bible	EZRA, NEHEMIAH
ESTHER	AN ORPHAN	To save her people from massacre	ESTHER
MARY	A PEASANT GIRL	To be the mother of Christ	LUKE 1:27-38
MATTHEW	A TAX COLLECTOR	To be an apostle and Gospel writer	MATTHEW 9:9
LUKE	A GREEK DOCTOR	To be a companion of Paul and a Gospel writer	COLOSSIANS 4:14
PETER	A FISHERMAN	To be an apostle, a leader of the church, and a writer of two New Testament letters	MATTHEW 4:18-20

Unsung Heroes in Acts

When we think of the success of the early church, we often think of the work of the apostles. But the church might have died if it hadn't been for some unsung heroes, men and women who through some small act helped move the church forward.

So read about these unsung heroes from the book of Acts, and then think of a way you can help others find out more about Jesus!

Bible Hero	Reference	Heroic Action
LAME BEGGAR	ACTS 3:9-10	After his healing, he praised God. As crowds gathered to see what happened, Peter used that opportunity to tell many about Jesus.
FIVE DEACONS	ACTS 6:2-5	Everyone knows Stephen, and many people know Philip, but there were five other men chosen to be deacons. Not only did they set the standard for service in the church, but their hard work gave the apostles more time to preach the gospel.
ANANIAS	ACTS 9:10-19	He had the responsibility of bringing Christ's love to Saul (Paul) after his conversion.
CORNELIUS	ACTS 10:30-35	He showed Peter that the gospel was for all people, Jews and Gentiles.
RHODA	ACTS 12:13-16	Her persistence brought Peter inside Mary's home, where the people could "see" the answers to their prayers.
JAMES	ACTS 15:13-21	He took command of the Jerusalem council and had the courage to make a decision that would affect millions of Gentiles over many generations.
LYDIA	ACTS 16:13-15	She invited Paul to her home, from where he led many to Christ.
JASON	ACTS 17:5-9	He risked his life for the gospel by letting Paul stay in his home. He stood up for what was right, even though he faced persecution for it.
PAUL'S NEPHEW	ACTS 23:16-24	He saved Paul's life by telling officials of a plot to murder Paul.
JULIUS	ACTS 27:1, 43	He spared Paul's life when the other soldiers wanted to kill him.

Simple Objects

God often uses simple, ordinary objects to accomplish his tasks in the world. They just need to be dedicated to him for his use. Look at these everyday objects from Bible times to see how God used them.

Then ask yourself: What do I have that God can use? Anything and everything is a possible "instrument" for him!

Object	Reference	Who used it?	How was it used?
SHEPHERD'S STAFF	EXODUS 4:2-4	MOSES	To work miracles before Pharaoh
RAM'S HORN	JOSHUA 6:3-5	JOSHUA	To flatten the walls of Jericho
FLEECE	JUDGES 6:36-40	GIDEON	To confirm what God wanted Gideon to do
HORNS, JARS, AND TORCHES	JUDGES 7:19-22	GIDEON	To defeat the Midianites
JAWBONE	JUDGES 15:15	SAMSON	To kill the enemy: 1,000 Philistines
SMALL STONE	1 SAMUEL 17:40	DAVID	To kill Goliath
OIL	2 KINGS 4:1-7	ELISHA	To show God's power to provide
RIVER	2 KINGS 5:9-14	ELISHA	To heal a man of leprosy
LINEN BELT	JEREMIAH 13:1-11	JEREMIAH	As an object lesson about God's wrath
POTTERY	JEREMIAH 18:1-10; 19:1-13	JEREMIAH	As an object lesson about God the creator
FOOD AND WATER	EZEKIEL 4:9-17	EZEKIEL	As an object lesson about judgment
FIVE LOAVES OF BREAD AND TWO FISH	MARK 6:30-44	JESUS	To feed a crowd of over 5,000 people

349

Systems of Sacrifice

You've probably heard the expression "Out with the old, in with the new." Well, that's exactly what happened to the way people made sacrifices to God after Jesus came on the scene. Jesus' life, death, and resurrection changed everything—for all time!

Jesus made the ultimate sacrifice by dying on the cross for our sins. Because he did, we no longer have to be afraid of God and worry about whether he'll forgive us for our sins or not. All we have to do is believe in Jesus. Then when we tell God we're sorry for a sin, he forgives us and wipes the sin away just like it never happened. And all because of Jesus!

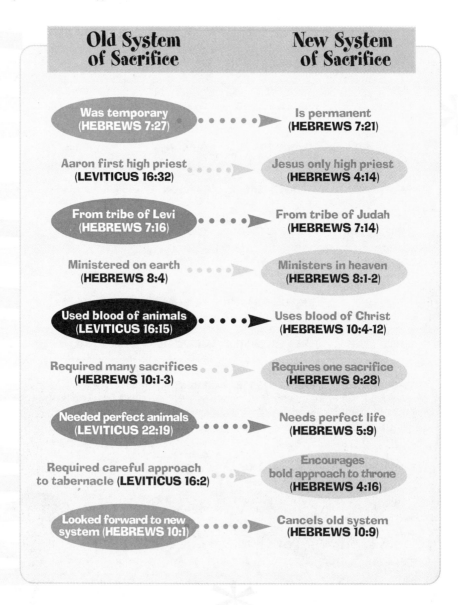

Old System of Sacrifice	New System of Sacrifice
Was temporary (HEBREWS 7:27)	Is permanent (HEBREWS 7:21)
Aaron first high priest (LEVITICUS 16:32)	Jesus only high priest (HEBREWS 4:14)
From tribe of Levi (HEBREWS 7:16)	From tribe of Judah (HEBREWS 7:14)
Ministered on earth (HEBREWS 8:4)	Ministers in heaven (HEBREWS 8:1-2)
Used blood of animals (LEVITICUS 16:15)	Uses blood of Christ (HEBREWS 10:4-12)
Required many sacrifices (HEBREWS 10:1-3)	Requires one sacrifice (HEBREWS 9:28)
Needed perfect animals (LEVITICUS 22:19)	Needs perfect life (HEBREWS 5:9)
Required careful approach to tabernacle (LEVITICUS 16:2)	Encourages bold approach to throne (HEBREWS 4:16)
Looked forward to new system (HEBREWS 10:1)	Cancels old system (HEBREWS 10:9)

The Offerings and Jesus

Here are the five key offerings the Israelites made to God. The Jews made those offerings to have their sins forgiven and to restore their friendship with God.

But Jesus changed everything! The death of Jesus made those sacrifices unnecessary. Because of Jesus' death and resurrection, we have a way for our sins to be completely forgiven and our friendship with God restored. What's the way? Believe in Jesus! (By the way, it's the *only* way.)

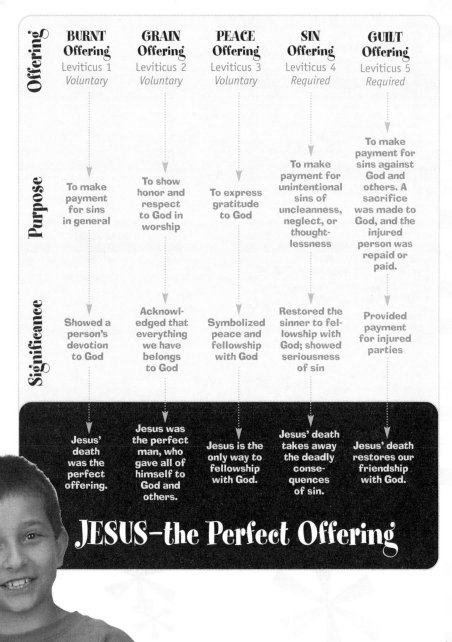

Offering	BURNT Offering Leviticus 1 *Voluntary*	GRAIN Offering Leviticus 2 *Voluntary*	PEACE Offering Leviticus 3 *Voluntary*	SIN Offering Leviticus 4 *Required*	GUILT Offering Leviticus 5 *Required*
Purpose	To make payment for sins in general	To show honor and respect to God in worship	To express gratitude to God	To make payment for unintentional sins of uncleanness, neglect, or thoughtlessness	To make payment for sins against God and others. A sacrifice was made to God, and the injured person was repaid or paid.
Significance	Showed a person's devotion to God	Acknowledged that everything we have belongs to God	Symbolized peace and fellowship with God	Restored the sinner to fellowship with God; showed seriousness of sin	Provided payment for injured parties
	Jesus' death was the perfect offering.	Jesus was the perfect man, who gave all of himself to God and others.	Jesus is the only way to fellowship with God.	Jesus' death takes away the deadly consequences of sin.	Jesus' death restores our friendship with God.

JESUS—the Perfect Offering

Jesus' Appearances After His Resurrection

The truth of Christianity rests on the Resurrection. Jesus died on the cross for our sins. Then he rose from the dead in a final victory over death and Satan.

The people who saw Jesus after he rose from the grave went on to turn the world upside down. (Most of them also died for being followers of Jesus.)

Here are people who saw Jesus after he rose from the grave.

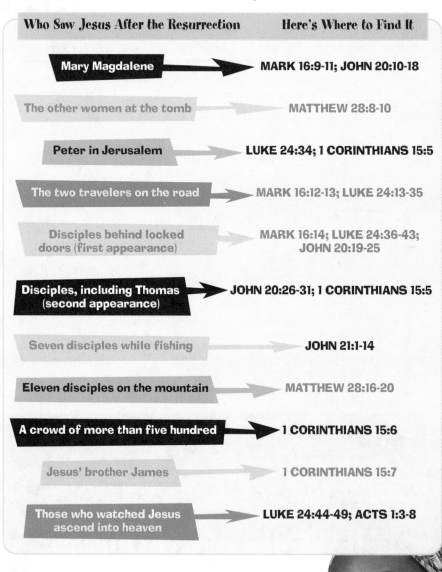

Who Saw Jesus After the Resurrection	Here's Where to Find It
Mary Magdalene	MARK 16:9-11; JOHN 20:10-18
The other women at the tomb	MATTHEW 28:8-10
Peter in Jerusalem	LUKE 24:34; 1 CORINTHIANS 15:5
The two travelers on the road	MARK 16:12-13; LUKE 24:13-35
Disciples behind locked doors (first appearance)	MARK 16:14; LUKE 24:36-43; JOHN 20:19-25
Disciples, including Thomas (second appearance)	JOHN 20:26-31; 1 CORINTHIANS 15:5
Seven disciples while fishing	JOHN 21:1-14
Eleven disciples on the mountain	MATTHEW 28:16-20
A crowd of more than five hundred	1 CORINTHIANS 15:6
Jesus' brother James	1 CORINTHIANS 15:7
Those who watched Jesus ascend into heaven	LUKE 24:44-49; ACTS 1:3-8

Jesus and the Ten Commandments

God gave his people the Ten Commandments to teach them how to live in a way that would please him. Jesus says he came not to cancel the laws but to fulfill them (see MATTHEW 5:17). Read this comparison between the Ten Commandments and what Jesus says!

The Ten Commandments said...   Jesus said...

The Ten Commandments said...	Jesus said...
Do not worship any other god but me. EXODUS 20:3	You must worship the LORD your God and serve only him. MATTHEW 4:10
Do not make idols of any kind, whether in the shape of birds or animals or fish. EXODUS 20:4	No one can serve two masters. LUKE 16:13
Do not misuse the name of the LORD your God. The LORD will not let you go unpunished if you misuse his name. EXODUS 20:7	Do not make any vows! Do not say, "By heaven!" because heaven is God's throne. MATTHEW 5:34
Remember to observe the Sabbath day by keeping it holy. EXODUS 20:8	The Sabbath was made to benefit people, and not people to benefit the Sabbath. So the Son of Man is Lord, even of the Sabbath! MARK 2:27-28
Honor your father and mother. Then you will live a long, full life in the land the LORD your God will give you. EXODUS 20:12	If you love your father or mother more than you love me, you are not worthy of being mine; or if you love your son or daughter more than me, you are not worthy of being mine. MATTHEW 10:37
Do not murder. EXODUS 20:13	If you are angry with someone, you are subject to judgment! If you call someone an idiot, you are in danger of being brought before the court. And if you curse someone, you are in danger of the fires of hell. MATTHEW 5:22
Do not commit adultery. EXODUS 20:14	Anyone who even looks at a woman with lust has already committed adultery with her in his heart. MATTHEW 5:28
Do not steal. EXODUS 20:15	If you are sued in court and your shirt is taken from you, give your coat, too. MATTHEW 5:40
Do not testify falsely against your neighbor. EXODUS 20:16	You must give an account on judgment day for every idle word you speak. MATTHEW 12:36
Do not covet your neighbor's house. Do not covet your neighbor's wife, male or female servant, ox or donkey, or anything else your neighbor owns. EXODUS 20:17	Guard against every kind of greed. Life is not measured by how much you own. LUKE 12:15

To Obey–Or Not

Here are a few examples of people in the Bible who didn't obey. Carefully read what each did about one of God's instructions and what happened as a result. Read it over, and then ask God to help you obey every day, every way! (And remember: If you believe in Jesus and really mean it when you tell God you're sorry for a sin, God forgives you and wipes that sin away!)

Who	God's Instruction	Disobedience	What Happened
ADAM AND EVE	Don't eat fruit from the tree of the knowledge of good and evil. (GENESIS 2:16-17)	Satan tempted them, and they ate. (GENESIS 3:1-6)	They were banished from the Garden of Eden; pain and death were inflicted on all humanity. (GENESIS 3:24; ROMANS 5:12)
NADAB AND ABIHU	Fire for the sacrifice must come from the proper source. (LEVITICUS 6:12-13)	They used a different kind of fire for their sacrifice. (LEVITICUS 10:1)	They were struck dead. (LEVITICUS 10:2)
MOSES	"Speak to the rock over there, and it will pour out its water." (NUMBERS 20:8)	He spoke to the rock, but also struck it with his staff. (NUMBERS 20:11)	He wasn't allowed to enter the Promised Land. (NUMBERS 20:12)
SAUL	Completely destroy the evil Amalekites. (1 SAMUEL 15:3)	He spared the king and kept some of the plunder. (1 SAMUEL 15:8-9)	God promised to end his reign. (1 SAMUEL 15:16-26)
UZZAH	Only a priest can touch the tabernacle's furnishings and articles. (NUMBERS 4:15)	He touched the ark of the covenant. (2 SAMUEL 6:6)	He died instantly. (2 SAMUEL 6:7)
UZZIAH	Only the priests can offer incense in the Temple or tabernacle sanctuary. (NUMBERS 16:39-40; 18:7)	He entered the sanctuary in the Temple, where only priests were allowed to go. (2 CHRONICLES 26:16-18)	He became a leper. (2 CHRONICLES 26:19)

The Beginning and the End

The Bible tells us about the beginning of the world and the end of the world. The story of the human race, from beginning to end—from our fall into sin to our redemption by Jesus and God's victory over evil—is all found in the Bible!

Look at this chart to see how the first and last books of the Bible compare.

Genesis	Revelation
THE SUN IS CREATED	THE SUN IS NOT NEEDED
SATAN IS VICTORIOUS	SATAN IS DEFEATED
SIN ENTERS THE HUMAN RACE	SIN IS BANISHED
PEOPLE RUN AND HIDE FROM GOD	PEOPLE ARE INVITED TO LIVE WITH GOD FOREVER
PEOPLE ARE CURSED	THE CURSE IS REMOVED
TEARS ARE SHED, WITH SORROW FOR SIN	NO MORE SIN, NO MORE TEARS OR SORROW
THE GARDEN AND EARTH ARE CURSED	GOD'S CITY IS GLORIFIED, THE EARTH IS MADE NEW
THE FRUIT FROM THE TREE OF LIFE IS NOT TO BE EATEN	GOD'S PEOPLE MAY EAT FROM THE TREE OF LIFE
PARADISE IS LOST	PARADISE IS REGAINED
PEOPLE ARE DOOMED TO DEATH	DEATH IS DEFEATED, BELIEVERS LIVE FOREVER WITH GOD

Where to Turn in My Bible

No matter what's happening in your life, the Bible can help! The Bible gives great advice—because it's God's advice. And he knows everything. God made you. He knows you. So it's natural that he would know how to solve your problems.

The next time you're upset, scared, or confused, let God help you. Read his words. Follow his advice. You'll be glad you did!

Here are a few ideas to get you started. Add your own favorite verses whenever you want. Pretty soon, you'll have your very own handy advice guide. Then you can start helping others follow God's good advice!

Where to Turn in My Bible When I Feel...

PROVERBS 15:1 • "A gentle answer..." ◀ • • • • • • • • • • **ANGRY**
19:11 • "Sensible people control..."
LUKE 6:27-30 • "But to you who are willing..."
6:31 • "Do to others..."
JOHN 13:34-35 • "So now I am giving you..."
EPHESIANS 4:26-27 • "And 'don't sin by...' "
4:31-32 • "Get rid of all bitterness..."
COLOSSIANS 3:8-10 • "But now is the time..."

JOSHUA 1:9 • "This is my command..." ◀ • • • • • • • • **AFRAID**
PSALM 46:10 • "Be still, and know..."
91:11 • "For he will order his angels..."
118:6 • "The LORD is for me..."
ISAIAH 41:10 • "Don't be afraid, for..."
ROMANS 8:28 • "And we know that God..."
EPHESIANS 6:11-12 • "Put on all of God's armor..."
JAMES 1:2-3 • "Dear brothers and sisters, when troubles come..."

ALONE
- JOSHUA 1:9 • "This is my command..."
- PSALM 139:1-6 • "O LORD, you have examined..."
- ISAIAH 41:10 • "Don't be afraid, for..."
- MATTHEW 28:20 • "Teach these new disciples..."
- PHILIPPIANS 4:13 • "For I can do everything through Christ..."

ANXIOUS
- PSALM 46:10 • "Be still, and know..."
- ISAIAH 40:31 • "But those who trust..."
- MATTHEW 6:25-26 • "That is why I tell you..."
- 6:33-34 • "Seek the Kingdom of God..."
- 11:28 • "Then Jesus said, 'Come to me...' "
- ROMANS 8:28 • "And we know that God..."
- PHILIPPIANS 4:6-7 • "Don't worry about anything..."
- 1 PETER 5:7 • "Give all your worries and cares..."

ASHAMED
- LUKE 15:10 • "In the same way..."
- JOHN 1:12 • "But to all who believed him..."
- 3:17-18 • "God sent his Son..."
- 2 CORINTHIANS 5:17 • "This means that anyone..."
- 1 JOHN 1:9 • "But if we confess our sins..."

DEPRESSED
- PSALM 34:19 • "The righteous person..."
- 46:10 • "Be still, and know..."
- JOHN 14:27 • "I am leaving you with a gift..."
- 16:33 • "I have told you..."
- PHILIPPIANS 4:6-7 • "Don't worry about anything..."

JEALOUS
- PSALM 37:8 • "Stop being angry..."
- PROVERBS 14:30 • "A peaceful heart..."
- 23:17-18 • "Don't envy sinners..."
- MATTHEW 6:19-21 • "Don't store up treasures here..."
- 1 CORINTHIANS 13:4-5 • "Love is patient..."
- JAMES 3:14-15 • "But if you are..."

TEMPTED
- MATTHEW 26:41 • "Keep watch and pray..."
- 1 CORINTHIANS 10:13 • "The temptations in your life..."
- GALATIANS 6:1 • "Dear brothers and sisters, if..."
- EPHESIANS 6:11-12 • "Put on all of God's armor..."
- HEBREWS 2:18 • "Since he himself has gone through..."

Where to Turn in My Bible When I Need...

PSALM 139:14 • "Thank you for making me..." ◄····· CONFIDENCE

MATTHEW 5:16 • "In the same way, let your..."

JOHN 15:5 • "Yes, I am the vine..."

2 CORINTHIANS 5:17 • "This means that anyone..."

EPHESIANS 6:11-12 • "Put on all of God's armor..."

PHILIPPIANS 4:13 • "For I can do everything through Christ..."

HEBREWS 4:16 • "So let us come boldly to the throne..."

MATTHEW 6:33-34 • "Seek the Kingdom of God..." ◄····· ENCOURAGEMENT

11:28 • "Then Jesus said, 'Come to me...' "

LUKE 11:9 • "And so I tell you, keep on asking..."

JOHN 1:12 • "But to all who believed him..."

ROMANS 8:28 • "And we know that God causes..."

PHILIPPIANS 4:6-7 • "Don't worry about anything..."

4:13 • "For I can do everything through Christ..."

1 THESSALONIANS 5:11 • "So encourage each other..."

2 CHRONICLES 7:14 • "Then if my people who are called ◄····· FORGIVENESS
by my name..."

NEHEMIAH 9:17b • "But you are a God of forgiveness..."

LUKE 6:9-13 • "Then Jesus said to his critics..."

6:31 • "Do to others..."

15:10 • "In the same way..."

JOHN 3:17-18 • "God sent his Son..."

COLOSSIANS 3:13 • "Make allowance for each other's faults..."

1 JOHN 1:9 • "But if we confess our sins..."

LUKE 6:27-30 • "But to you who are willing..." ◄····· TO FORGIVE SOMEONE ELSE

6:31 • "Do to others..."

1 CORINTHIANS 13:4-10 • "Love is patient and kind..."

EPHESIANS 4:32 • "Instead, be kind to each other..."

COLOSSIANS 3:13 • "Make allowance for each other's faults..."

HELP • • • • • • • • • • • • ➤ **PSALM 23** • "The Lord is my shepherd..."

121:1-2 • "I look up to the mountains..."

ISAIAH 40:31 • "But those who trust..."

41:10 • "Don't be afraid, for..."

LUKE 11:9 • "And so I tell you, keep on asking..."

JOHN 15:5 • "Yes, I am the vine..."

EPHESIANS 6:11-12 • "Put on all of God's armor..."

REVELATION 3:20 • "Look! I stand at the door and knock..."

TO OBEY • • • • • • ➤ **DEUTERONOMY 6:5-6** • "And you must love the Lord your God..."

MATTHEW 5:16 • "In the same way, let your..."

MARK 16:15 • "And then he told them, 'Go into all the world...' "

LUKE 6:31 • "Do to others..."

JOHN 13:34 • "So now I am giving you..."

14:15 • "If you love me, obey..."

ROMANS 12:1-2 • "And so, dear brothers and sisters..."

12:13 • "When God's people are in need..."

1 PETER 5:7 • "Give all your worries and cares..."

PATIENCE • • • • • • • • • • • • ➤ **PSALM 23** • "The Lord is my shepherd..."

37:7 • "Be still in the presence of the Lord..."

46:10 • "Be still, and know..."

MATTHEW 6:33-34 • "Seek the Kingdom of God..."

ROMANS 8:38-39 • "And I am convinced that nothing..."

GALATIANS 5:22 • "But the Holy Spirit produces this kind of fruit..."

WISDOM • • • • • • • • • • • ➤ **PROVERBS 1:7** • "Fear of the Lord is the foundation..."

10:14 • "Wise people treasure knowledge..."

JEREMIAH 33:3 • "Ask me and I will tell you..."

MATTHEW 6:19-21 • "Don't store up treasures here..."

JOHN 14:26 • "But when the Father sends the Advocate..."

EPHESIANS 6:11-12 • "Put on all of God's armor..."

JAMES 1:5 • "If you need wisdom, ask..."

Where to Turn in My Bible When...

PSALM 19:1 • "The heavens proclaim the glory..." ◄•••• **I HAVE DOUBTS ABOUT GOD**

46:10 • "Be still, and know..."

LUKE 21:33 • "Heaven and earth will disappear..."

JOHN 1:1 • "In the beginning the Word already..."

1:14 • "So the Word became human..."

3:16 • "For God loved the world so much..."

14:6 • "Jesus told him, 'I am the way...' "

20:31 • "But these are written so that you may continue to believe..."

HEBREWS 4:16 • "So let us come boldly to the throne..."

11:1 • "Faith is the confidence that what we hope for..."

1 JOHN 4:10 • "This is real love—not..."

DEUTERONOMY 6:5-6 • "And you must love the LORD your God..." ◄•• **I DON'T KNOW WHAT DECISION TO MAKE**

ISAIAH 40:8 • "The grass withers and the flowers..."

MATTHEW 19:19 • "Honor your father and mother..."

LUKE 6:31 • "Do to others..."

JOHN 14:26 • "But when the Father sends the Advocate..."

ROMANS 12:1-2 • "And so, dear brothers and sisters..."

GALATIANS 6:7 • "Don't be misled—you cannot mock..."

EPHESIANS 6:11-12 • "Put on all of God's armor..."

PHILIPPIANS 4:8 • "And now, dear brothers and sisters..."

JAMES 1:5 • "If you need wisdom, ask..."

PSALM 100:4 • "Enter his gates with thanksgiving..." ◄••• **I DON'T KNOW HOW TO PRAY**

118:1 • "Give thanks to the LORD, for..."

LUKE 6:27-30 • "But to you who are willing..."

11:9 • "And so I tell you, keep on asking..."

1 THESSALONIANS 5:16-18 • "Always be joyful..."

JOHN 3:16 • "For God loved the world so much..." ◄••• **I'M WORRIED ABOUT GOING TO HEAVEN**

3:17-18 • "God sent his Son..."

ROMANS 6:23 • "For the wages of sin is death..."

10:9 • "If you confess with your mouth..."

EPHESIANS 2:8-9 • "God saved you by his grace..."

1 JOHN 4:10 • "This is real love—not..."

5:12 • "Whoever has the Son has life..."

MY FRIENDS TALK BEHIND MY BACK

- **LUKE 6:31** • "Do to others..."
- **ROMANS 3:23** • "For everyone has sinned..."
- **EPHESIANS 4:32** • "Instead, be kind to each other..."
- **PHILIPPIANS 4:6-7** • "Don't worry about anything..."
- **COLOSSIANS 3:13** • "Make allowance for each other's faults..."
- **1 PETER 3:9** • "Don't repay evil for evil..."

I'M AFRAID TO SHARE MY FAITH

- **ISAIAH 55:10-11** • "The rain and snow..."
- **MATTHEW 5:15-16** • "No one lights a lamp and then puts it..."
- **28:19-20** • "Therefore, go and make disciples..."
- **ACTS 1:8** • "But you will receive power..."
- **ROMANS 1:16** • "For I am not ashamed of this Good News..."
- **2 CORINTHIANS 2:14-17** • "But thank God!..."
- **HEBREWS 11:6** • "And it is impossible to please God without..."
- **1 PETER 3:15** • "Instead, you must worship Christ..."
- **1 JOHN 3:18** • "Dear children, let's not merely say..."

MY PARENTS FIGHT

- **PSALM 23** • "The LORD is my shepherd..."
- **46:1** • "God is our refuge and strength..."
- **MATTHEW 6:33-34** • "Seek the Kingdom of God..."
- **11:28** • "Then Jesus said, 'Come to me...' "
- **PHILIPPIANS 4:6-7** • "Don't worry about anything..."
- **HEBREWS 4:16** • "So let us come boldly to the throne..."

Guess What!

There's a really cool tool you can use when you want to know more about any subject! It's called a concordance, and there's one at the back of this very Bible! It's like a dictionary of subjects and people, and it tells you where to look in the Bible for information.

Want to know more about angels? Prayer? David? Just look up the word or name!

It's a cool tool you'll use a lot!

Personal Bible Reading Plan

Introduction

We usually think of the Bible as one book. That's logical because it looks like one book, right? We also speak of the Bible as God's Word. That's because God wrote the Bible! (For more on that, go to the Frequently Asked Questions section on page 1273.)

When we read and study the Bible, we discover that it's actually an entire library between two covers. Not one book, but 66! Each book has its own style and qualities—but each book contributes to the message God wants to get across.

You know what else? Even though we use the word *book*, some parts of the Bible are actually letters (like Paul's letter to the Romans) or collections (like Psalms). Still, the Bible is one big message from God because it has one real Author—God! So you know it's worth reading. Here's a way to do it!

How This Plan Is Different

There are lots of plans to help you read through the Bible. You can start at page one and read straight through. Or you can get a flavor of the whole Bible by reading parts from it during a whole year. That's what this reading plan is all about.

Your mission, should you choose to accept it, is to read the best-known stories and important lessons. Some parts of the Bible offer so much help that you can read them every day. (Those are the Gospels, Psalms, and Proverbs.) One way or another, you need to read God's Word!

Before You Begin

You'll see that each day's reading has a title and a question. (Those questions will help you as you read—you can count on it.) And always pray before you read and ask God to help you understand, apply, and obey his Word. And remember, this is only the start of the great adventure of reading God's Word and getting to know him!

New Testament

You'll be reading different parts of the four Gospels
so you can get a good picture of Jesus' life.

LUKE 1:1-4; JOHN 1:1-18
Beginnings
Have you personally received
Jesus as your Savior and
become a child of God?

LUKE 1:5-25
The Angel and Zechariah
How would you react
to an angel's visit?

LUKE 1:26-56
Mary and Elizabeth
What gives you joy in your life?

LUKE 1:57-80
John the Baptist Is Born
When did you last say
thank you to your parents?

MATTHEW 1:1-25
A Family Tree
Which of these people have you
read about in the Old Testament?

LUKE 2:1-20
Jesus Is Born!
What does Christmas mean to you?

LUKE 2:21-39
Jesus' First Trip to Church
How would you react to
holding Jesus when he was a baby?

MATTHEW 2:1-12
Foreign Visitors
What gifts have you given Jesus?

MATTHEW 2:13-23
Escape and Return
How has knowing God brought
excitement into your life?

LUKE 2:41-52
Jesus in the Temple Again
What four words could summarize
what people might say you are like?

LUKE 4:1-13
Temptation
What are your most difficult
temptations? Compare them
to Jesus' temptations.

JOHN 1:19-34
John the Baptist and Jesus
Who do you talk to about Jesus?

JOHN 1:35-51
Jesus' First Disciples
How would someone know
that you believe in Jesus?

JOHN 2:1-25
Jesus and Surprises
How has Jesus surprised
you in your life?

JOHN 3:1-21
Jesus and Nicodemus
When did you first meet Jesus? How?

JOHN 3:22-36; LUKE 3:19-20
John Gets Into Trouble
When has knowing Jesus
ever gotten you into trouble?

JOHN 4:1-42
Jesus Changes a Town
In what ways has Jesus
affected your town?

JOHN 4:43-54
Jesus Preaching and Healing
Why do you believe in Jesus?

LUKE 4:16-30
Jesus Rejected
How would Jesus be received
in your church next Sunday?

MARK 1:16-39
Jesus Calls People to Follow
What things have you left
behind to follow Jesus?

LUKE 5:1-39
Miracles and Questions
How do Jesus' miracles
affect you today?

JOHN 5:1-47
Jesus Demonstrates
He Is God's Son
What is special to you
about Jesus?

MARK 2:23–3:19
Jesus and Disciples
How would Jesus treat
your personal traditions?

MATTHEW 5:1-16
Jesus Gives the Beatitudes
Which of these attitudes most needs
to be in your life today?

MATTHEW 5:17-30
Jesus on Law, Anger, and Lust
How do Jesus' views
compare with yours?

MATTHEW 5:31-48
Jesus on Relationships
What part of your life could be
most changed by these words?

MATTHEW 6:1-18
Jesus on Doing Good Things
How do your public and
private lives compare?

MATTHEW 6:19-34
Jesus on Money and Worry
In what ways are money and
worry related in your life?

MATTHEW 7:1-12
Jesus on Criticizing and Praying
Which one do you do the most? Why?

MATTHEW 7:13-29
How Jesus Looks at Us
What foundation is your life
built upon?

LUKE 7:1-17
Jesus and Foreigners
What is your attitude toward
foreigners? How can you
show them God's love?

MATTHEW 11:1-30
Jesus Describes John
How would you want Jesus
to summarize your life?

LUKE 7:36–8:3
Jesus and Women
How would you have fit into
the group that followed Jesus?

MATTHEW 12:22-50
Troubles for Jesus
When are you tempted to
have Jesus prove himself to you?

MARK 4:1-29

Jesus Seeks, Plants Seeds, and Weeds

What kind of soil is your life right now?

MATTHEW 13:24-43

More of Jesus' Parables

How concerned are you about whether people you know will go to heaven?

MATTHEW 13:44-52

Even More Parables

What does the Bible say the hidden treasure is?

LUKE 8:22-56

Jesus in Control

Which of these examples gives you the greatest comfort?

MATTHEW 9:27-38

The Concerns of Jesus

How do you picture Jesus caring for you?

MARK 6:1-13

Some Don't Listen; Some Need to Hear

How clear an idea do you have of what God wants you to do?

MATTHEW 10:16-42

Jesus Prepares His Disciples

In what ways do Jesus' words speak to your fears?

MARK 6:14-29

Herod Kills John the Baptist

How can you be like John the Baptist?

MATTHEW 14:13-36

Jesus: Miracle Worker, Water Walker, Healer

Would you have been more likely to step out with Peter or to stay in the boat? Why?

JOHN 6:22-40

Jesus Is the Bread From Heaven

How is Jesus "bread" to you?

JOHN 6:41-71

Jesus Is Criticized and Deserted

How do you react when you hear people make critical comments about Jesus?

MARK 7:1-37

Jesus Teaches About Purity

What would you like God to do to improve the purity of your life?

MATTHEW 15:32-16:12

Jesus Feeds and Warns

How do you evaluate what you hear?

MARK 8:22-9:1

Peter Identifies Jesus

In what ways have you come to understand Jesus better lately?

LUKE 9:28-45

Jesus Is Transfigured

Would you rather leave the world and be with Jesus or be with Jesus in the world?

MATTHEW 17:24-18:6

Who's the Greatest?

Does Jesus' teaching about who is the greatest surprise you? Why?

MARK 9:38-50

Who's on Our Side?

How do you respond to what other people believe?

MATTHEW 18:10-22

Jesus as He Teaches

How do you react to the failures of others?

MARK 11:20-33
Permission to Pray for Anything
How bold is your prayer life?

MATTHEW 21:28-46
Two Parables
Which son do you resemble most?

MATTHEW 22:1-14
Jesus Tells About the Wedding Feasts
How does it make you feel to know that God has invited you to his table?

LUKE 20:20-40
Jesus Answers Questions
How do you feel about living forever?

MARK 12:28-37
Questions Given and Taken
Who's one person who seems close to the Kingdom of God?

MATTHEW 23:1-39
Jesus: Warnings and Grieving
Which of these seven warnings most directly relates to your life?

LUKE 21:1-24
Jesus Talks About the Future
What kind of giving habits do you have?

LUKE 21:25-38
Jesus on Being Prepared
What does your schedule today say about your watchfulness?

MATTHEW 25:1-30
Parables About Being Prepared
Which of the people in these two stories do you identify most with?

MATTHEW 25:31-46
Jesus on the Final Judgment
What people in your life are you treating in ways you would want to treat Jesus?

LUKE 22:1-20
The Last Supper
What does the Lord's Supper mean to you?

JOHN 13:1-20
Jesus Washes His Disciples' Feet
What's the greatest service someone has done for you? How do you serve others?

JOHN 13:21-38
A Sad Prediction
How well do you feel Jesus knows you?

JOHN 14:1-14
Jesus Is the Way
How would you rate your present level of understanding of Jesus and his teachings?

JOHN 14:15-31
Jesus Promises the Comforter
How have you experienced the Holy Spirit?

JOHN 15:1-16
Jesus on the Vine and the Branches
What kind of fruit has God produced in you?

JOHN 15:17-16:4
Jesus Warns About Troubles
What have you learned recently about loving others?

JOHN 16:5-33
Jesus on the Holy Spirit and Prayers
How do these verses bring you peace?

JOHN 17:1-26
Jesus Prays
Whom did Jesus pray for?
Whom do you pray for?

MARK 14:27-31
A Broken Promise
When have you made a promise you couldn't keep?

JOHN 18:25-27
Jesus Betrayed
Have you ever felt like denying Jesus? What did you do?

MATTHEW 26:57-75
Trial and Denial
How has being a follower of Jesus complicated your life?

MATTHEW 27:1-10
Judas' Death
When you think of sin, what personal examples come to mind?

LUKE 23:1-12
Two Political Trials
In what ways has your family helped you to respond to Jesus?

MARK 15:6-24
Sentencing and Torture
Was there a time you chose to do the wrong thing on purpose? Why? What happened?

LUKE 23:32-49
Jesus Crucified
What do you feel when you read about the Crucifixion?

MATTHEW 27:57-66
Jesus' Body Laid in a Guarded Tomb
Why do you think people resist believing in Jesus?

JOHN 20:1-18
Jesus Is Alive!
What makes Easter an important celebration in your life?

MATTHEW 28:8-15
Reactions to the Resurrection
What would your first words to Jesus be if he appeared to you today?

LUKE 24:13-43
Appearances of Jesus
Would you recognize Jesus if you saw him today? How?

JOHN 20:24–21:14
More Appearances of Jesus
How has Jesus helped you with your doubts?

JOHN 21:15-25
Jesus Talks With Peter
What difference would it make to you to read these verses with your name in place of Peter's?

MATTHEW 28:16-20
Jesus Gives the Great Commission
What are you doing to obey Jesus?

LUKE 24:44-53
Jesus Says Farewell
How do you find Jesus opening your mind as you read the Bible?

ACTS 1:1-11
The Departure of Jesus
What one thing would you be sure to do if you knew Jesus were coming back today?

ACTS 1:12-26
First Things First
What's your idea of the right
amount of time for prayer?

ACTS 2:1-13
An Amazing Gift
What do you think is the main purpose of any gift God has given you?

ACTS 2:14-40
Peter's First Sermon
How would you put the main points of
this sermon into your own words?

ACTS 2:41-3:11
Daily Life in the Early Church
What part of these early days would
you have enjoyed the most?

ACTS 3:12-4:4
Peter's Second Sermon
If you were given three minutes
to tell the story of Jesus, what
would you say?

ACTS 4:5-22
Hostile Reactions
What excuses might you use to
keep from sharing your faith?

ACTS 4:23-37
Praying and Sharing
When was the last time you shared
something with someone else?

ACTS 5:1-16
Strange Events
How often are you tempted
to take God lightly?

ACTS 5:17-42
Arrested!
How do you react when
you're treated unfairly?

ACTS 6:1-15
Stephen: Special Servant
What are some ways you
could help out at church?

ACTS 7:1-29
History Review I
How familiar are you becoming
with the history of Christianity?

ACTS 7:30-60
History Review II
How would you want to be
more like Stephen?

ACTS 8:1-25
Benefits of Persecution
Which difficulties in your life has God
used to help you grow spiritually?

ACTS 8:26-40
Unexpected Appointment
What does your church
believe about baptism?

ACTS 9:1-19
Paul Meets Jesus
What unusual events has God
used to catch your attention?

ACTS 9:20-31
Paul's New Life
What are three ways that
Jesus has changed your life?

ACTS 9:32-42
God Uses Peter
This past week, what special ability
did you use to meet someone's need?

ACTS 10:1-23
Peter Sees a Lesson
What lessons has God had to
repeat in your life?

ACTS 21:1-17
Difficult Decision
What hard decisions do you
have to make right now?

ACTS 21:18-36
Paul in Jerusalem
How important is it to respect
what others think is right?

ACTS 21:37-22:29
Paul Speaks
What are some things God has
done for you that you could tell
people about?

ACTS 22:30-23:22
A Plan to Kill Paul
How well do you know your
rights as a citizen of your country?

ACTS 23:23-24:27
Paul in Prison
What would be harder for you,
the pressure or the prison?

ACTS 25:1-27
Paul Speaks to Festus
If Christianity were outlawed, what
evidence could be brought against
you to prove that you're a Christian?

ACTS 26:1-32
Paul Speaks to Agrippa
How comfortable are you in
explaining your faith?

ACTS 27:1-26
The Storm at Sea
What is your attitude when you
are going through difficulties
as part of a group?

ACTS 27:27-44
The Shipwreck
What scary times in your life
has God used to teach you?

ACTS 28:1-14
The Winter on Malta
How aware of God are you
in your everyday life?

ACTS 28:15-31
Paul in Rome
What would you like to be doing
when your time on earth is over?

ROMANS 5:1-11
Faith Brings Joy
When was the last time you thanked
God for all he's done for you?

ROMANS 8:1-18
Truly Free From Sin
In what ways do you struggle with
your sinful nature?

ROMANS 8:19-39
How God Loves
What things do you sometimes
feel might be able to separate
you from the love of Jesus?
Can they really?

ROMANS 12:1-21
Living Sacrifice
What act of sacrifice might
God allow you to do today?

1 CORINTHIANS 13:1-13
Real Love
Which quality of real love do you
most need to ask God to increase
in your life?

1 CORINTHIANS 15:1-20
The Basic Gospel
What parts of the gospel are really helpful to you in times of doubt or stress?

1 CORINTHIANS 15:42-58
Destiny!
How much are you looking forward
to all Jesus has planned for you?

2 CORINTHIANS 4:1-18
Weak Containers; Strong Contents
Who can you talk to about what you think this passage means?

GALATIANS 5:13-26
Two Radically Different Lives
Who is someone you need to love as you love yourself?

EPHESIANS 1:3-23
God's Action
What special things has God done for you that make you want to praise him?

EPHESIANS 2:1-22
God's Plan
How do you think that God can use your life for his purposes?

EPHESIANS 4:1-16
Picture of the Church
What is your role as part of the church?

EPHESIANS 6:10-20
Armor of God
Which of these weapons do you need to learn to use better?

PHILIPPIANS 2:1-18
The Mind of Jesus
In what ways would having Jesus' attitude help you face this day differently?

PHILIPPIANS 3:1-21
Learning Joy
What areas of your life could God be using to teach you joy?

COLOSSIANS 2:1-15
What We Have in Christ
How does your environment affect your relationship with Jesus?

COLOSSIANS 3:1-17
Christian Relationships
What do you think about heaven?

1 THESSALONIANS 1:1-10
Spiritual Reputation
How do you think others would describe your spiritual life?

1 THESSALONIANS 4:1-18
Living for God
What's one way you could obey God today?

2 THESSALONIANS 1:1-12
Encouragement
What other Christians could you encourage today?

2 THESSALONIANS 3:1-18
Final Requests
How could you help spread the news about Jesus?

1 TIMOTHY 4:1-16
Always Going Forward
Which of these positive commands need to be more important in your life?

1 TIMOTHY 6:3-21
A Friend's Final Words
How does your attitude toward money match Paul's advice?

2 TIMOTHY 1:1-18
The Importance of Examples
Who has been a good spiritual example for you? How can you thank him or her?

2 TIMOTHY 3:1-17
Last Days
How many of these characteristics are part of your world today?

TITUS 3:1-11; PHILEMON 1:4-7
Good Counsel
Which of these commands
apply directly to your life?

HEBREWS 10:19-39
The New Life
What do your prayer habits say about
the importance of faith in your life?

HEBREWS 11:1-40
A Review of Faith
How deep is your
commitment to Jesus?

HEBREWS 12:1-13
Our Turn
Which of these directions should you
follow more carefully to have a real
impact on your relationship with God?

JAMES 1:2-27
Tough Times, Happy People
What are you facing where you could
use the "James plan" right now?

JAMES 2:1-13
Valuing Other People
How do you treat others?

JAMES 3:1-12
Words as Weapons
How sharp would others
consider your tongue?

1 PETER 2:1-25
Living Stones
Which would you choose as
the biggest personal challenge
in these verses?

1 PETER 3:1-22
Relationships and Pain
How willing are you to carry
out your relationships God's way,
even when it's hard?

2 PETER 1:2-21
Knowing God
What would you say if someone asked
you what it means to know God?

1 JOHN 1:1-10
The Way of Forgiveness
What part does confessing
your sins play in your life?

1 JOHN 3:1-24
God Is Love
How can you tell if your
love is really growing?

1 JOHN 5:1-21
The Life God Gives
How do you know that you
have eternal life?

2 JOHN 1:4-6; 3 JOHN 1:5-8; JUDE 1:17-25
Family Matters
How often do you go out of your way
to meet the needs of other Christians?

REVELATION 1:1-20
Jesus the King
How would you describe
your mental picture of Jesus?

REVELATION 21:1-27
Everything Made New
What difference do you think
you will most notice between
the new world and the old?

REVELATION 22:1-21
Life in the New City
What makes you excited about heaven?

Family Devotions

HEY, LOOK!

Here are a whole bunch of devotions you can do with your family! You can even be the one to lead the devotions if you want. Each devotion has a box to check off when you're finished and a place to write who led the devotion. (You can write the date you did the devotion too. It'll be fun to look back later to see who did what when. Did that make sense?)

You might want to look at each devotion a few days before you plan to do it. That way, you'll have plenty of time to get the supplies you need.

SO ARE YOU READY?

Go call your family together and get started!

DISAPPEARING ACT

With your family, read and do the "Disappearing Act" activity found near **MATTHEW 2** (page 943). Take some time to let the whole family master the trick. (You might have to help one or both of your parents figure it out.) Then take turns making the saltshaker disappear while praying this prayer: "Thank you, God, for protecting Jesus. And thank you for protecting me." Then talk about these very salty questions:

- Why do you think God protected Jesus the way he did?
- What are some ways God protects people today?
- When has God protected our family?

Pray for God's continued protection for your family. Then commit to pray together for God's protection each morning before you start your day.

STANDING FIRM

With your family, read and do the "Standing Firm" activity found near **MATTHEW 4** (page 944). Make as many domes as you can. When they're dry, find a board, a large book, or a piece of sturdy cardboard, and lay it across the domes. Put the smallest person in your family on the board, and see if the domes hold. How many domes does it take? Can they support heavier family members? If it doesn't work, how many do you think you would need? Here are some questions to discuss while you share some gumdrops:

- What makes these domes so strong?
- What makes our family strong?
- How can being a strong family help us fight temptation?
- How can we do a better job of helping each other fight temptation?

Pray, asking God to strengthen your family and help you support each other in fighting temptation. Then pledge to ask each other how you are doing fighting temptation.

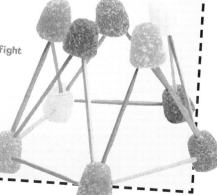

THE WAY TO PRAY

With your family, read and do "The Way to Pray" activity found near **MATTHEW 6** (page 947). Make a whole bunch of bags of trail mix. Write the five P's on them—the five basic ingredients of the Lord's Prayer. Then open one of the bags and share the trail mix while you talk about these questions:

👋 Why do you think Jesus thought it was important to teach us how to pray?

👋 Why are these five prayer "ingredients" so important?

👋 What ingredients do our family prayers need more of?

Use the five P's for a family prayer time. Then plan to give away your bags of trail mix. Deliver them to neighbors, friends, and people at church, and tell them about the Lord's Prayer!

MIRROR IMAGE

With your family, read and do the "Mirror Image" activity found near **MATTHEW 7:12a** (page 948). Then try mirroring each other with your whole bodies instead of just your hands. Challenging, huh? Instead of writing the verse on a sticky note, have fun as a family writing it on a mirror in your house. Do some fun decorating, too. Bathtub crayons work well. So does soap—especially if you have a few different colors. When your mirror masterpiece is complete, talk about these questions:

👋 What makes this simple verse so powerful?

👋 How would the world be different if everyone did what this verse says to do?

👋 How would our family be different if we always treated each other the way we want to be treated?

👋 How can our family do a better job of doing what Jesus asks us to do in this verse?

Pray together for God's help in following "the golden rule." Leave your mirror art up for a while. Every time you look in the mirror, remember to treat your family—and others—the way you want to be treated.

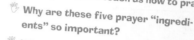

COMPLETE CONTROL

With your family, read and do the "Complete Control" activity found near **MATTHEW 8** (page 949). Instead of making your crosses into necklaces, hang all your crosses on one piece of string. Hang the crosses from the rearview mirror in your family car (they beat fuzzy dice), or hang them on the inside of the doorknob on your front door. Then use these questions for discussion:

🖐 What kinds of "storms" has our family faced?

🖐 How has Jesus shown us that he is in control of the storms in our lives?

🖐 How can knowing that Jesus is in control change the way we live?

Pray, asking God to help your family trust that Jesus is in control of the storms in your lives. Leave the crosses hanging for a while. Every time you leave the house or drive somewhere as a family, let the crosses remind you that Jesus is in control of your family's lives.

JESUS ATTRACTION

With your family, read and do the "Jesus Attraction" activity found near **MATTHEW 11:28** (page 952). Instead of gluing the cereal to a piece of construction paper, find a bigger piece of paper—or poster board—or tape pieces of construction paper together. Work together to glue the cereal and make your reminder of the verse. Then use more cereal to make pictures or symbols of yourselves around your reminder. When the glue is dry, spray the picture and hang it in your kitchen (maybe near the cupboard where you keep your cereal). When you're finished gluing and munching on cereal, discuss these questions:

🖐 When have you felt drawn to Jesus?

🖐 When has Jesus given you rest and peace?

🖐 How do we "come to Jesus"?

Pray together as a family, thanking Jesus for calling you to himself. Ask him to draw your family closer and closer to himself every day.

☐ WE DID THIS ONE. LED BY ....

PARADE OF PRAISE

With your family, read and do the "Parade of Praise" activity found near MATTHEW 21 (page 964). Then spend some time planning a family praise service. Each person should do one part of the service, using one of the ideas he or she came up with. Set a time and a place for the service. Don't forget to practice so you'll be able to do your best for Jesus! After you're finished planning, talk over these questions:

☝ Why do you think the people got so excited praising Jesus?

☝ When have you seen people get excited as they praise Jesus?

☝ Why does Jesus deserve our praise?

☝ How can our family praise Jesus at home?

Come together at your scheduled time and place for your family praise service. Praise Jesus together!

☐ WE DID THIS ONE. LED BY ....

WORTH THE EFFORT

With your family, read and do the "Worth the Effort" activity found near MATTHEW 28 (page 973). Make sure each person gets to try at least once. Then spend a little time talking about what it means to know Jesus and how a person can know Jesus. On your gum wrappers, write your own stories about what Jesus means in your lives. (Your little sister might need some help.) Then read your stories to each other. You just shared your faith! Talk about these questions:

☝ Why do we get so nervous about sharing our faith?

☝ Why does Jesus want us to share our faith in him?

☝ What's the best way to share our faith with others?

Pray together for boldness, honesty, and excitement in sharing your faith with other people. Then work on remembering your stories so you can share them!

GOOD SOIL

With your family, read and do the "Good Soil" activity found near **MARK 4** (page 980). Then work together to plant something you can keep either inside your home or outside. You might plant a tree or a vine in your yard or a houseplant in a pot in your kitchen. Or you might try starting a new plant by taking a clipping off a plant you already have. (If you don't have a green thumb, try a cactus!) As you plant, make sure you're using good soil that will help your plant to grow. Then gather around your plant and talk about these questions:

🖐 What kinds of things make a person's heart "good soil" for a growing relationship with God?

🖐 What kind of soil do we have in our family?

🖐 How can we become better soil?

Pray, asking God to use the plant as a reminder to be ready for a growing relationship with him. As you watch the plant grow over time (or slowly die if you don't take care of it), remember to keep the right kind of soil in your heart.

STAYIN' AFLOAT

With your family, read and do the "Stayin' Afloat" activity found near **MARK 6** (page 983). After you make your list of Jesus' miracles, add more miracles to your list—miracles your family has experienced and ones you've heard about from other people. You might even try an Internet search to find true stories of miracles God has done. Then discuss these questions:

🖐 What do you think the disciples thought when they saw Jesus walking on water?

🖐 What makes something a miracle?

🖐 Why do you think Jesus chose to do miracles while he was on earth?

🖐 Why do you think God sometimes chooses to do miracles today?

Pray for God to open your eyes to miracles in the world. Keep your list of miracles. Watch and listen for other miracles, and add them to the list. (And no, a clean room is not a miracle.)

AFTER YOU...

With your family, read and do the "After You..." activity found near **MARK 9:35b** (page 987). Then put each other first for one whole evening. For example, one person can let another person go first in picking a piece of pizza and another person can let someone else go first in choosing what to watch on television. Then come back to this page and discuss these questions:

- How did it feel to put others first?
- When was it hard? When was it easy?
- Why do you think Jesus wants us to put others first?
- What happens when we put others first?

Pray together, and have each person pray for someone else in the family. Don't stop being kind to each other just because the devotion is over! Keep putting each other first every day!

HEAD AND SHOULDERS, KNEES AND TOES

With your family, read and do the "Head and Shoulders, Knees and Toes" activity found near **MARK 10** (page 990). Then have family members choose their favorite of the five senses and do something together to enjoy that sense. You may want to enjoy tasting an ice-cream sundae, smelling the flowers in your backyard garden, or listening to your favorite music together.

- What's your favorite thing to see? touch? smell? feel? taste? hear?
- What would life be like if we didn't have these senses?
- What do your senses help you to do?
- What makes you most thankful when you think about how God has made you?

Have every person in your family say one thing about their senses that they enjoy. Keep going until everyone's mentioned at least three things. Then pray together, thanking God for giving us such wonderful ways of enjoying the world he created!

WE DID THIS ONE. LED BY ....

THE #1 COMMAND

With your family, read and do "The #1 Command" activity found near **MARK 12** (page 993). Have family members choose two things from their drawings to do this week: one thing to show love for God and one thing to show love for a friend. Tell each other what you're going to do and when you're planning to do these things. (Don't forget to follow through on your plans!) Next, discuss these questions:

- Why do you think the Bible tells us to love God with our heart and our mind and our soul and our strength?

- Why do you think love is so important to God?

- How can we, as a family, show love for God this week?

Together with your family, sing your favorite praise song to God, telling him how much you love him.

WE DID THIS ONE. LED BY ....

IS THAT POSSIBLE?

With your family, read and do the "Is That Possible?" activity found near **LUKE 1** (page 1002). In the margin of the Bible activity, let each person write one word to represent another "impossible" thing that your family's glad God did.

- What kinds of things are impossible for people to do? Why are some things impossible for people?

- How can it be that none of those things is impossible for God?

- God can do anything; how does that make you feel about God?

- How would you describe God's amazing abilities to someone who has never heard of him?

Make up a family cheer for God. Every night before dinner, shout your cheer to praise him because nothing is impossible for God!

ARMIES OF HEAVEN

With your family, read and do the "Armies of Heaven" activity found near **LUKE 2** (page 1004). Just think! With Jesus' birth, not only did one angel come, but a whole army of angels appeared! Just for fun, pretend that your family is the army of angels announcing Jesus' birth. Make up a melody for these words and sing them just the way you think the angels might have sung them.

> "Glory to God in highest heaven, and
> peace on earth to those with whom
> God is pleased."

Then discuss these questions together:

🖐 What do you think angels do all day?

🖐 What does the Bible say angels look like?
(Look at the angel bio on page 1263!)

🖐 Why do you think God uses angels?

Together, look through your Bible for other times God used angels to send messages. Then thank God for angels!

YOUNG AND OLD TOGETHER

With your family, read and do the "Young and Old Together" activity found near **LUKE 2** (page 1005). Next, tell each other about a time you've told someone outside of your family about Jesus. What happened?

🖐 What can we tell others about Jesus?

🖐 When is it hard to tell others about Jesus?

🖐 Why is it important to tell others about Jesus?

Have each family member choose an older person to talk to about Jesus. Pray for each other, asking God to help you tell about Jesus boldly.

WE DID THIS ONE. LED BY ·····························

GONE FISHIN'

With your family, read and do the "Gone Fishin'" activity found near **LUKE 5** (page 1009). Next, name each paper clip you "caught" with the name of someone you can tell about Jesus. You might want to cut small paper fish shapes, write the names on them, and hang the fish on your refrigerator to help you remember to tell them about Jesus. Then make sure you each tell one of those people about Jesus this week!

- 🖐 How was this activity like telling others about Jesus?
- 🖐 What does it mean to go "fishing" for people?
- 🖐 Who are you going to tell about Jesus?
- 🖐 What are you going to say about Jesus?

Pray together and ask God to help you all enjoy a good fishing trip this week!

☐ WE DID THIS ONE. LED BY ·····························

ANYTHING IS POSSIBLE

With your family, read and do the "Anything Is Possible" activity found near **LUKE 6** (page 1010). Then have each family member think of someone to be nice to, even though it may be hard. All of you can write in the margin of this activity the first name or initials of the person you thought of. Then answer these questions together:

- 🖐 When have you had a hard time being nice to someone who wasn't nice to you?
- 🖐 Why does God want us to love our enemies?
- 🖐 What happens when we love people who don't love us?

It can be hard to love people who don't love us. But we're showing God's love when we love our enemies. Pray for each other, and ask God to give you true love for others and to help you show that love every day.

☐ WE DID THIS ONE. LED BY ....

THE ADVENTURES OF SUPER SAMARITAN!

With your family, read and do "The Adventures of Super Samaritan!" activity found near **LUKE 10** (page 1017). After a few days of being Super Samaritans, write on your Super Samaritan badges the names of the people you helped. Talk about what else you can do to help others. Hang your badges in a place where they'll remind you to love your neighbors every day in every way! Then discuss these questions:

🖐 **Whose names did you write on your badges? What did you do to help those people?**

🖐 **How does it feel to help others?**

🖐 **Why does God want us to help others no matter what?**

🖐 **How does God help us?**

Tell each other about the best part of being a Super Samaritan. Then pray for each other, asking God to help you see more and more ways to help others.

☐ WE DID THIS ONE. LED BY ....

ASK, SEEK, KNOCK

With your family, read the "Ask, Seek, Knock" activity found near **LUKE 11:9** (page 1019). Assign specific "prayer tasks" from the list to specific family members. Every night at dinner, talk about how your prayer tasks are going. At the end of one week, discuss these questions:

🖐 **Which prayer tasks were easy? Were any hard? Why?**

🖐 **When is it hard for you to pray?**

🖐 **Why do you suppose God wants us to talk to him so much?**

🖐 **What happens when we pray?**

Keep the list of prayer requests someplace where you'll all see them—like on the breakfast table. Update the prayer request list often, and keep on praying for each other!

KID STUFF

With your family, read the "Kid Stuff" activity found near **LUKE 18** (page 1027). Have each family member make a heart paper. Show each other your papers and pictures, and talk about what it means to have the faith of a little child. As you're working, discuss these questions together:

- Why do you think God wants us to have faith like little children?

- Why do little kids trust God (and people) so much?

- Do you ever find it hard to trust God like that? Why?

- What could help our family remember to trust God more?

Display all of the pictures in a place that will remind your family to have "little kid" faith in God.

Jesus

CLEAN UP YOUR ACT

With your family, read and do the "Clean Up Your Act" activity found near **LUKE 19** (page 1030). What are some ways you've seen yourselves change since you decided to follow Jesus? Encourage family members to talk about the changes they've seen in themselves and in each other. Then discuss these questions:

- Do you always want to do the right thing? Why or why not?

- What would it be like to stop wanting to do the wrong thing?

- Why do you think believing in Jesus changes us so we want to do right?

Thank God for the way he's changing you day by day to be more like him. Pray together and praise God for his power to change your hearts.

☐ WE DID THIS ONE. LED BY . . . .

GIVE YOURSELF TO GOD!

With your family, read and do the "Give Yourself to God!" activity found near **LUKE 21** (page 1033). Show each other the cards you made, and tell why you decorated them the way you did. Then each pick one thing you'll do to give yourself to God this week. Tell each other what you're going to do—then do it! Encourage your family members all week to follow through too! During the week, discuss these questions:

- ✋ What do you think it means to give yourself to God?

- ✋ What are ways you've seen others give themselves to God?

- ✋ How do you think that giving yourself to God will change what you do and think?

- ✋ How can we encourage each other to keep giving ourselves to God?

Have each family member pray for another family member every day for the next several days. Ask God to help all of you give yourselves to God.

☐ WE DID THIS ONE. LED BY . . . .

THREE IN ONE

With your family, read and do the "Three in One" activity found near **JOHN 1:1-2** (page 1042). Talk about what each member of the Trinity means to your family. Then discuss these questions together:

- ✋ Who is Jesus?

- ✋ Why is it so important to believe that Jesus is God?

- ✋ How can we explain the Trinity to someone else?

Then invite a friend or neighbor over, and do the experiment for him or her. Use the experiment to explain the Trinity to your friend. Pray together, praising God for always existing. Then thank God for sending Jesus and the Holy Spirit into the world to teach us about him.

....

A WONDERFUL WEDDING

With your family, read and do the "A Wonderful Wedding" activity found near JOHN 2 (page 1043). Then enjoy glasses of grape juice together to celebrate Jesus' first miracle. While you're sipping your juice, see how many more of Jesus' miracles you can think of. (Look through this Bible for ideas!) Then discuss these questions:

- What makes what you just did with the volcano different from the miracles Jesus did?

- Why do you think Jesus did miracles when he was on earth?

- What do those miracles tell us about Jesus?

Jesus really can do anything! Pray together, thanking Jesus for having the power to do miracles.

....

GOD LOVES YOU!

With your family, read and do the "God Loves You!" activity found near JOHN 3:16 (page 1044). Then get a local phone book and look at all the names inside. Can you find some names that you know? What's the longest last name you can find? the funniest? the strangest?

God loves all those people as much as he loves each member of your family. Today, as you go about your business, look at each person you see and remember, God loves him (or her)! Then at dinner, discuss these questions:

- How did learning that God loves everyone change how you think about people?

- Sometimes we call the news about Jesus the Good News. Why is it such good news?

- What can our family do to make sure that others hear the Good News about Jesus?

Pick names from a phone book, and pray for them. Ask God to make sure those people understand how much he loves them. Then thank God for loving everyone.

LIVING WATER

With your family, read and do the "Living Water" activity found near **JOHN 4** (page 1047). Did you know that people can live only about three days without water? There are people right now who are very thirsty for the living water because they don't know about Jesus. As a family, talk about why people need to know about Jesus. Then discuss these questions as you share a pitcher of ice cold water:

🖐 What does it mean to say that Jesus is living water?

🖐 What would happen if people didn't drink water?

🖐 What happens when people don't know about Jesus, the "living water"?

🖐 Why is it important for us to tell people about Jesus?

🖐 What might happen if we don't tell others about Jesus?

Write your family's favorite idea for telling people about Jesus, and then make plans to do it!

ROLL AWAY THAT STONE!

With your family, read and do the "Roll Away That Stone!" activity found near **JOHN 11** (page 1055). Make sure each person gets a few turns to try the game. What's the family record for the number of times you caught the paper ball "stone" in the paper cup "tomb"? After you applaud the champion, discuss these questions together:

🖐 Why do you think Jesus raised Lazarus from the dead?

🖐 What do you suppose everyone thought after seeing what Jesus had done?

🖐 How does learning about this miracle help you believe in Jesus?

🖐 Do you think there's anything that Jesus can't do? Explain.

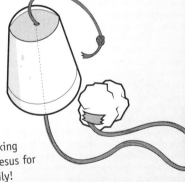

Jesus can do anything! Pray together, thanking Jesus for his awesome power. Then thank Jesus for using his awesome power to help your family!

SERVICE WITH A SMILE

With your family, read and do the "Service With a Smile" activity found near
JOHN 13 (page 1058). Grab a light-colored towel and some permanent markers.
Have family members write on the towel the name of someone they'd like to serve.
Let each person explain one way to serve the person named. Hang the towel in the
bathroom to remind you to follow through on your service ideas. Then
discuss these questions:

🖐 Why was Jesus willing to be a servant?

🖐 Why does Jesus want us to follow his example of servanthood?

🖐 What are ways our family members can serve each other?

🖐 How can we encourage each other to remember to be servants?

Remembering to serve others can be hard, so pray
together and ask God to remind you to be willing and
cheerful servants.

THE ONLY WAY

With your family, read and do "The Only Way" activity found near JOHN 14:6 (page
1060). Sign each other's pictures to show that you've all shown and explained them
to each other. Then say the verse aloud together several times, replacing the words
I and *me* with the word *Jesus*. (You'll need to use *is* instead of *am* too.) Say the
verse louder each time, and end with a great big cheer for God! Then relax and talk
about these questions:

🖐 Do you know many people who don't understand
who Jesus is and what he does?
How can you help?

🖐 What other ways can you think of to
explain this exciting fact?

🖐 Who will you tell next?

Collect the pictures, and put them in an
area of your house where guests visit.
Each time you have guests, show them
all the pictures your family made about
Jesus.

DON'T DOUBT

With your family, read and do the "Don't Doubt" activity found near **JOHN 20** (page 1066). Together, make a great big chart just like the one shown in the Bible, and brainstorm about things you know about Jesus. You can write all those things in the right column. Next, fill in the column at the left with situations when knowing each fact about God could help or comfort you. Then discuss these questions:

✋ Were you surprised at how much your family knows about God? Why or why not?

✋ Look at all the facts you wrote about God. What do they tell you about the one true God?

✋ How will knowing all these things about God help you when you're feeling bad or doubtful?

Together, look at the long list you came up with. Count all the things you know for sure about Jesus. Then pray together, thanking and praising God for being so big and powerful and loving that he can wipe all your doubts away. Hang your chart where you'll all see it often. Whenever you have doubts about God or your faith, check out your chart!

SAY AGAIN?

With your family, read and do the "Say Again?" activity found near **ACTS 2** (page 1072). Come up with a secret, made-up word that will be a signal in your family that God loves you. You can tell each other this word over the phone, in e-mails, or in notes you leave for each other as reminders of how much God loves you. If people ask you what your word means, you'll have a chance to tell them about Jesus! Then discuss these questions:

✋ Do you know anyone who speaks a different language than you do? Can you communicate very well with that person? Why or why not?

✋ Sometimes people go to a language school for many months to learn how to tell others about Jesus in a different language. Why is it so important to tell people all over the world about Jesus?

✋ What can you do to help people who speak other languages learn about Jesus?

Pray together, asking God to put opportunities in your path to tell others about Jesus. Ask God to give you the boldness and the love to tell everyone the Good News about Jesus!

HUH

WE DID THIS ONE, LED BY . . . .

HEROES OF THE FAITH

With your family, read and do the "Heroes of the Faith" activity from **ACTS 6** (page 1077). Have everyone in your family make a note. Then tell each other who you're sending your notes to and why. Pray together, thanking God for these wonderful examples of faithful living. Ask God to bless them for the help they've given you. Then discuss these questions:

- ✋ Why do you think the heroes that you recognized do what they do to serve God?
- ✋ What can you learn about following God from their examples?
- ✋ What does it take to be a hero of the faith?
- ✋ How can you be a hero of the faith to someone else?

Now pray again, asking God to help you be an extra faithful example to others every day.

WE DID THIS ONE, LED BY . . . .

REFLECTION OF LOVE

With your family, read and do the "Reflection of Love" activity from **ACTS 8** (page 1079). Next, shine the flashlight onto each person's head so that the light hits the top of his or her head. As each family member is treated to a turn in the spotlight, have that person name one way to reflect Jesus' love and light to others. You can keep going until you run out of ideas. Everyone should get at least two turns in the spotlight. Then talk about these questions:

- ✋ Who has reflected the light and love of Jesus to you?
- ✋ How does it feel to help shine Jesus' light into the world?
- ✋ What else can our family do to be a shiny reflection of Jesus?

Have each person pray for the person he or she wants to reflect Jesus' love to this week. Ask God to help you find a way to show those people Christlike love.

INSIDE OUT

With your family, read and do the "Inside Out" activity from **ACTS 9** (page 1080). While you're enjoying the bananas and chocolate sauce, talk about the different ways that God wants to change people. Write a few of your ideas right here in the margin. Then talk about these questions:

✋ When have you discovered that someone was different on the inside than on the outside?

✋ How has God changed the members of this family?

✋ How can our family be more open to God's changes in our lives?

Pray together, asking God to make each of you more and more like him on the inside. Thank God for the changes that he's already made in your family.

KNOCK, KNOCK

With your family, read and do the "Knock, Knock" activity found near **ACTS 12** (page 1085). On a sheet of paper, have everyone draw what he or she thinks heaven might look like. Then have everyone describe the drawings to each other.

After that, talk about these questions:

✋ Why do you think God rescued Peter from jail?

✋ Can you think of a time God helped your family out of a tight spot? Explain.

✋ Why does God rescue us when we're in trouble and can't help ourselves?

During the next week, choose one person to tell Peter's prison rescue story to and give that person your heavenly illustration to help him or her remember how God rescues us.

STAYIN' PUT

With your family, read and do the "Stayin' Put" activity found near **ACTS 16** (page 1089). Have everyone in your family take a close look at the penny you used in the activity. Notice the words "In God We Trust." Then have your family members each tell about a time they trusted God.

- ✋ What happens when you trust God, even if you're unsure of what might happen?
- ✋ Why do you think God wants us to trust him?
- ✋ Have you ever been afraid to trust God? Explain.
- ✋ How can we encourage each other to trust God more?

Give everyone in the family a penny to keep in his or her shoe during the coming week as a reminder to trust God. At the end of the week, talk about what it was like to trust God more. Then pray together and thank God for being trustworthy.

SHIPWRECKED!

With your family, read and do the "Shipwrecked!" activity found near **ACTS 27** (page 1102). Now pretend that, like Paul, your family has been shipwrecked on a deserted island. Get a piece of paper, and as a family, list five ways you'd try to send an SOS signal. Then answer these questions:

- ✋ How do signals alert other people that we need help?
- ✋ In what ways do you rely on your family to help?
- ✋ How does God help us when we're in trouble?
- ✋ How can we encourage each other to turn to God when we need help?

Now devise a secret family SOS signal (something like a secret handshake or code word) to use when someone needs help with a problem. Use your secret signal to help each other remember to turn to God for help.

EVERYONE HAS SINNED

With your family, read and do the "Everyone Has Sinned" activity found near ROMANS 3 (page 1110). On the bull's-eye target you drew, have everyone in your family write behaviors that do hit the target with God—the kind that make God smile! When everyone has written something, look at your list together and discuss these questions:

- Are there any other good behaviors we can think of? (If you think of more, go ahead and add them to your list.)
- Why is it important to act in ways that please God?
- Why do you think God has a high standard of behavior for us?
- How can we, as a family, act better toward one another?

Now have all the members of your family choose a behavior from the list that they'd like to improve on. Make a point during the next week to practice each good behavior at least once.

THE PIECES FIT!

With your family, read and do "The Pieces Fit!" activity found near ROMANS 8 (page 1116). Then have each family member choose a leftover piece of the puzzle. Have everyone think of a problem in his or her life right now that's frustrating or confusing and write the situation on the back of the puzzle piece. Then talk about these questions together:

- Why do you think God allows problems to come into our lives?
- Have you learned anything about yourself because of having to deal with a problem? Have you learned anything about God? Explain.
- Have you asked God to help you solve the problem you have? Why or why not?

Pray together, thanking God for seeing the "big picture" of our lives and asking for his guidance for each person's problem. Have everyone trade puzzle pieces. During the next week, pray daily for the person whose puzzle piece you have and for the problem he or she is facing.

WE DID THIS ONE. LED BY . . . .

LOVE ALL AROUND

With your family, read and do the "Love All Around" activity found near
1 CORINTHIANS 13 (page 1136). Using the ball you created, play this game. Form
a circle. Let the person wearing the most red start the game by bouncing the ball to
someone else in the circle. The person who catches the ball will look to see what
picture his or her right hand landed on. Then that person must "nominate" another
family member who's especially good at showing that kind of love,
and pass the ball to this person. Play the game until everyone
has had the ball at least twice. Then answer these questions together:

🖐 How many different ways can you think of to
   show love?

🖐 Why does God want us to love each other?

🖐 How does our family show love to each other?

During the next week, challenge each family member
to show love to another family member in a unique and
unexpected way.

☐ WE DID THIS ONE. LED BY . . . .

CHRIST IN ME

With your family, read and do the "Christ in Me" activity found near **GALATIANS 2**
(page 1154). Then take a field trip to your kitchen. Have everyone pick out two
favorite snacks or foods and put them on the kitchen table. Check the ingredients
of the food, and make a list of the foods that contain salt. Then talk about the following questions:

🖐 Which of your favorite foods are made with salt? Do any of your favorite
   sweets contain salt? Why do you think that is?

🖐 How do you think these foods would taste without salt?

🖐 How important is salt in our everyday lives? (Think about all the
   foods you eat during the day. How many of them contain salt?)

🖐 How is having Jesus in our lives like or unlike having salt in
   our food?

Just for fun, when preparing your next meal, choose one food,
such as green beans or mashed potatoes, and omit salt from the
recipe. Have your family eat the dish without salt and discuss the difference in taste. Then pray together, thanking God for sending Jesus into your lives!

FRUIT OF THE SPIRIT

With your family, read and do the "Fruit of the Spirit" activity found near **GALATIANS 5** (page 1158). Create a Fruit of the Spirit poster to remind your family of the qualities God's love produces in us. Across the top of a sheet of poster board, draw the fruits your family chose to represent the fruits of the Spirit. Under the drawings, write the quality each fruit represents. Hang the poster in a place where everyone will see it during the week. Then, whenever a family member demonstrates a fruit of the Spirit, write that person's name under the fruit on the poster. Right now, talk about these questions:

🖐 How does God create fruit of the Spirit in us?

🖐 Do you think one of these qualities is more important than the others? Why or why not?

🖐 Which fruits of the Spirit do you need to develop more?

During the next week, choose one fruit of the Spirit you'd like God to develop more in you. Practice that quality, and pray daily for God to help you grow more in that quality. At the end of the week, pray together and thank God for guiding you. Then pick another fruit and start over!

STAND FIRM!

With your family, read and do the "Stand Firm!" activity found near **EPHESIANS 6** (page 1166). Give each person a sheet of paper. Have each family member draw or cut out a piece of "armor" from the paper to represent the armor that God uses to protect us. Have each person write on the armor how he or she will use it to stand firm against the devil's tricks. Talk over these questions as you work:

🖐 Why does God protect us against evil?

🖐 How can you stand firm in circumstances where it's easy to do the wrong thing?

🖐 How can we as a family help each other stand firm?

🖐 How can we do a better job of relying on God's armor to help us make tough choices?

Each night, talk about the different temptations and choices each of you faced during the day. How did God's armor help you? Pray for each other, asking God to help you stand firm against temptation each day.

MOVE IT!

To do this activity, ask everyone except one person to leave the room. Have that person read and do the "Move It!" activity found near **PHILIPPIANS 2** (page 1171). That person should then choose a family member to come back into the room and then teach the second person the motions to the verse. The first person should leave the room as the one who has learned the motions chooses another family member. Repeat the process until everyone has learned the motions from a different person. Then gather everyone and do the motions together. Discuss these questions:

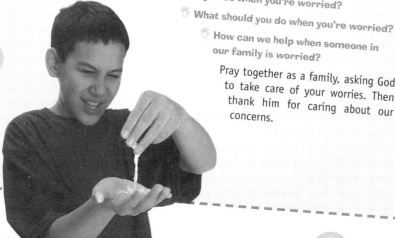

🖐 Was it easy or difficult to teach the motions to each other? Why?

🖐 Is it always easy to tell others about your faith? Explain.

🖐 Why is it important to pass on God's Word?

During the next week, have each family member share the Scripture with a friend. Next week, choose a different Scripture passage, and share some more!

DON'T WORRY, BE HAPPY

With your family, read and do the "Don't Worry, Be Happy" activity found near **PHILIPPIANS 4** (page 1173). Have people name one thing they're currently worried about and explain why they're worried. Then talk over these questions:

🖐 What kinds of things do you worry about?

🖐 What do you do when you're worried?

🖐 What should you do when you're worried?

🖐 How can we help when someone in our family is worried?

Pray together as a family, asking God to take care of your worries. Then thank him for caring about our concerns.

GOOD EXAMPLES

With your family, read and do the "Good Examples" activity found near 1 TIMOTHY 4 (page 1195). Then create a Good Examples chart for your family using poster board, tempera paint, and markers. Ask each family member—no matter how old or young—to make a handprint somewhere on the board. Write the person's name under each handprint. Talk about the ways each person is a good example, and write those ways around the person's handprint. As your poster dries, answer these questions together:

✋ How do you try to be a good example for others?

✋ How is Jesus a good example for us?

✋ Is being a good example important? Why or why not?

✋ What can you do this week to set a good example?

Devote the following week to setting good examples—especially in areas where you might be a little weak. Each night at dinner, compare notes on how each of you is doing. Pray for God's help as you strive to be good examples!

IT'S KNOT A PROBLEM

With your family, read and do the "It's Knot a Problem" activity found near 2 TIMOTHY 3 (page 1199). Then have everyone stand very close together and grab hands with two different people. When you give the signal, your family must work itself out of the "people knot" and into a circle without letting go of anyone's hands. No cheating! This may require stepping over legs, heads, and entire bodies! Once the knot is untied, sit down and relax! Then discuss these questions:

✋ Did you think your human knot could become a circle? Why or why not?

✋ How is that like facing problems in our lives that seem impossible to solve?

✋ How can we encourage each other to rely on God to help us with our problems?

Set the knotted rope you made in a place where you'll all see it this week. Every time you look at the rope, remember that God can solve all of your "impossible" problems!

WE DID THIS ONE. LED BY

LIFE PRESERVER

With your family, read and do the "Life Preserver" activity found near **TITUS 3** (page 1202). Then share Life Savers candies with your family. As everyone enjoys the candies, discuss the following questions:

🖐 **What is mercy?**

🖐 **When has someone in our family shown mercy?**

🖐 **When have you felt God's mercy?**

🖐 **Why does God show us mercy?**

Give each person five individually wrapped Life Savers candies, one to eat each day of the coming work or school week. As you eat each day's candy, focus on mercy. Remember that God shows mercy to us because he loves us, and try to pass God's love to someone else each day.

WE DID THIS ONE. LED BY

FAITH IS...

With your family, read and do the "Faith Is..." activity found near **HEBREWS 11:1** (page 1217). Then sit together near a window in your home. As you look outside, make a list together of the evidence of God that you see. When you finish your list, talk over these questions together:

🖐 **Why do you think God created such a beautiful world?**

🖐 **How does having faith in God help you every day?**

🖐 **How important is faith in God to our family?**

🖐 **When is it hard to have faith?**

Pray together, thanking God for all the beautiful "evidence" he gives us of his love and presence. Ask God to help the faith of your family grow. Then hang your list on the refrigerator to remind you that God is real!

GOT GOD?

With your family, read and do the "Got God?" activity found near **JAMES 1:5** (page 1223). Have you ever heard of tying string around a finger to help you remember something? Give it a try! Cut a five-inch piece of string or yarn for each family member. Take turns tying the yarn onto another family member's index finger. When everyone has a string tied to his or her finger, shout together, "Remember: Go to God first!" Then answer the following questions:

✋ When you're confused or facing a decision, who do you turn to first for help?

✋ Why does God want us to go to him for guidance?

✋ Why is God the very best source of wisdom?

Have family members tie their pieces of string to something they'll carry with them during the week—maybe a key chain, purse, or backpack. When you see the string this week, remember to go to God first!

GOODBYE SINS!

With your family, read and do the "Goodbye Sins!" activity found near **1 JOHN 1** (page 1241). Now cut the coffee filter into enough pieces for each person to have one. Have everyone think of a sin he or she committed recently and pray silently for God's forgiveness. (If someone's sin hurt a family member, have that person apologize and ask for forgiveness.) Then talk over these questions together:

✋ What does it mean to confess your sins?

✋ Why is it important to say you're sorry when you've sinned?

✋ Why does God want us to confess our sins, even when he already knows what they are?

✋ Why does God forgive us when we confess and are sorry for our sins?

✋ What should we do when someone apologizes to us? Why?

Because God forgives us, we should forgive each other. As a family, pray for God's forgiveness for your sins and for his help in forgiving others. Then close with a big family hug.

WE DID THIS ONE. LED BY . . . .

GOD IS LOVE

With your family, read and do the "God Is Love" activity found near 1 JOHN 4 (page 1242). Add pieces of white construction paper to the poster board heart whenever a family member "gets caught" showing love to someone else. To get started, have family members think of a time someone else in the family showed them love. Each person should write a few words about what happened on a small piece of white construction paper and attach the paper to the heart. Keep a jar of white construction paper pieces next to the heart. When the heart is full, you'll have a mosaic full of loving actions! After everyone has added a paper to the heart, discuss these questions:

✋ Why does God want us to show love to each other?

✋ How does God show he loves you?

✋ In what ways does our family demonstrate God's love?

Make plans to intentionally share God's love as a family over the next week. Invite another family to dinner, send a care package to a friend, or donate to a charity. (And don't forget to keep adding to your paper heart!)

WE DID THIS ONE. LED BY . . . .

JESUS IS KNOCKING

With your family, read and do the "Jesus Is Knocking" activity found near REVELATION 3 (page 1255). Have family members who believe in Jesus tell about the moment when they answered Jesus' knock and invited him into their hearts. As each person shares, have him or her answer the following questions:

✋ How did you know Jesus was knocking on the door of your heart?

✋ How did you feel when you answered Jesus' knock?

✋ How has Jesus made your life better?

✋ Why does Jesus want to be your forever friend?

✋ Why is opening the door to Jesus' knock the most important decision you'll ever make?

During the next week, set a family goal for each person in your family to tell one other person about Jesus. Pray together, asking God to help you have the courage to share your faith in Jesus this week!

TIME TO CELEBRATE!

With your family, read and do the "Time to Celebrate!" activity found near REVELATION 21 (page 1269). Using a sheet of poster board and markers or paint, have one person begin illustrating what he or she thinks it will be like when Jesus comes back. Set a timer for three minutes. At the end of three minutes, give the paper and art supplies to the next person to continue the illustration for another three minutes. Keep illustrating until every person has had a chance to draw or until the picture is complete. Then answer these questions:

🖐 How does knowing that God has such wonderful plans for his children make you feel?

🖐 How can we as a family prepare for Jesus' return?

🖐 How can our family help others get ready for Jesus' return?

Pray together, thanking God for the gift of Jesus and for the amazing things he has in store for us. Hang your poster somewhere in your house where you (and your guests!) can see it every day. Remember that Jesus is coming back! Hooray!

Dictionary/Concordance

It's a DICTIONARY!

It's a CONCORDANCE!

IT'S BOTH!

Actually, a concordance is very much like a dictionary. It's an alphabetical listing of important words you'll find in the *Hands-On Bible*. Just use it like you would a dictionary at school. Plus, it can tell you where in the Bible to find references to those words.

So, for example, if you want to know more about angels, just look up the word *angel* in this dictionary/concordance. This is what you'll find.

> **ANGEL**
> Matt 28:2 . . . an *a* of the Lord came down
> Luke 2:9 . . . an *a* of the Lord appeared
> 2 Cor 11:14 . . . disguises himself as an *a*
> Gal 1:8 . . . or even an *a* from heaven,

See? It's easy! You'll find this dictionary/concordance is a fun tool to use as you read more and more of God's Word.

Dictionary/Concordance . . .

A

ABANDON
Heb 13:5 . . . I will never *a* you.

ABRAHAM (ABRAM) Father of the nation of Israel (John 8:37-59); father of all people of faith (Rom 4; Heb 11); made covenant with the Lord (Gal 3:17-20; Heb 6:13); called to leave home (Acts 7:2-4; Heb 11:8-10); blessed by Melchizedek (Heb 7:1); faith counted as righteousness (Rom 4:3; Gal 3:6-9; Jas 2:21-23); circumcision commanded (Rom 4:9-12); given son (Isaac) by Sarah (Heb 11:11-12); offered Issac as test (Heb 11:17-19; Jas 2:21).

ACCEPTED
Luke 4:24 . . . no prophet is *a* in his own
John 1:12 . . . believed him and *a* him,
John 17:8 . . . They *a* it and know that
Gal 2:9 . . . they *a* Barnabas and me
Col 2:6 . . . just as you *a* Christ Jesus

ADAM First man (Rom 5:14; 1 Tim 2:13-14); son of God (Luke 3:38); sinned (Rom 5:12-21); died (1 Cor 15:22-49).

ADD
Matt 6:27 . . . worries *a* a single moment
Rev 22:18 . . . God will *a* to that person

ADOPT
Gal 4:5 . . . so that he could *a* us as
Eph 1:5 . . . decided in advance to *a* us

ADULTERY
Matt 5:27 . . . You must not commit *a*.

ADVICE
Rom 11:34 . . . enough to give him *a*?

ADVOCATE *see* (HOLY) SPIRIT
John 14:16 . . . will give you another *A*,
John 14:26 . . . the Father sends the *A*
John 15:26 . . . will send you the *A*—
1 Jn 2:1 . . . an *a* who pleads our case

ALIVE
Luke 24:23 . . . Jesus is *a*!
Acts 1:3 . . . ways that he was actually *a*.
Rev 2:8 . . . who was dead but is now *a*:

ALMIGHTY
Rev 4:8 . . . the *A*—the one who always was,
Rev 15:3 . . . O Lord God, the *A*.
Rev 19:6 . . . our God, the *A*, reigns.

ALTAR
Matt 5:23 . . . presenting a sacrifice at the *a*
Rev 6:9 . . . I saw under the *a* the souls

ALWAYS
Matt 28:20 . . . I am with you *a*, even to
John 12:8 . . . you will not *a* have me.
1 Pet 3:15 . . . *a* be ready to explain it.

AMAZED
Mark 7:37 . . . They were completely *a* and
Luke 2:33 . . . Jesus' parents were *a* at

ANGEL
Matt 28:2 . . . an *a* of the Lord came down
Luke 2:9 . . . an *a* of the Lord appeared
2 Cor 11:14 . . . disguises himself as an *a*
Gal 1:8 . . . or even an *a* from heaven,

ANGELS
Matt 4:6 . . . will order his *a* to protect

Heb 2:7 . . . a little lower than the *a*
Heb 13:2 . . . entertained *a* without

ANGER
Eph 4:26 . . . by letting *a* control you.
Jas 1:20 . . . Human *a* does not produce

ANTICHRIST
1 Jn 2:18 . . . heard that the *A* is coming,
1 Jn 4:3 . . . has the spirit of the *A*,

APPEARED
Luke 2:9 . . . angel of the Lord *a* among
Phil 2:7 . . . When he *a* in human form,

APPROVAL
John 6:27 . . . the seal of his *a*.
Rom 14:4 . . . will receive his *a*.
1 Cor 11:19 . . . you who have God's *a*
Heb 11:4 . . . God showed his *a* of his gifts.

ARGUE
Rom 14:1 . . . and don't *a* with them

ARMOR
Rom 13:12 . . . put on the shining *a*
Eph 6:11 . . . Put on all of God's *a*
Eph 6:13 . . . put on every piece of God's *a*
1 Thes 5:8 . . . protected by the *a* of faith

ARMS
Mark 10:16 . . . took the children in his *a*

ARMY
Rev 19:19 . . . the horse and his *a*.

ASHAMED
Mark 8:38 . . . If anyone is *a* of me
Rom 1:16 . . . I am not *a* of this Good News
2 Tim 1:8 . . . So never be *a* to tell others
2 Tim 2:15 . . . who does not need to be *a*

ATHLETE
1 Cor 9:27 . . . body like an *a*, training it

ATHLETES
1 Cor 9:25 . . . All *a* are disciplined
2 Tim 2:5 . . . *a* cannot win the prize unless

ATTITUDE
Phil 2:5 . . . have the same *a* that Christ
1 Pet 3:8 . . . keep a humble *a*.

AUTHORITY
Matt 28:18 . . . been given all *a* in heaven
John 5:22 . . . absolute *a* to judge,
Rom 13:1 . . . For all *a* comes from God,
1 Cor 15:24 . . . ruler and *a* and power.
Eph 1:22 . . . under the *a* of Christ
1 Tim 2:2 . . . all who are in *a* so that
1 Pet 5:5 . . . accept the *a* of the elders.

AWE *see also* FEAR, RESPECT, REVERENCE
Acts 2:43 . . . sense of *a* came over them
Heb 12:28 . . . holy fear and *a*.

B

BABIES
1 Cor 14:20 . . . Be innocent as *b* when
1 Pet 2:2 . . . Like newborn *b*, you must

BABY
Luke 1:44 . . . *b* in my womb jumped for
Luke 2:12 . . . find a *b* wrapped snugly

BAPTISM
Matt 3:16 . . . After his *b*, as Jesus came up
Rom 6:3 . . . joined with Christ Jesus in *b*,
Eph 4:5 . . . one Lord, one faith, one *b*,
1 Pet 3:21 . . . that water is a picture of *b*,

BAPTIZED
Mark 1:4 . . . that people should be *b*
Acts 1:5 . . . be *b* with the Holy Spirit.
Acts 2:41 . . . *b* and added to the church
Acts 8:12 . . . and women were *b*.
Acts 16:33 . . . were immediately *b*.
Acts 19:5 . . . *b* in the name of the Lord
1 Cor 10:2 . . . were *b* as followers

BEAUTIFUL
Rom 10:15 . . . How *b* are the feet of

BEAUTY
Jas 1:11 . . . and its *b* fades away.
1 Pet 3:4 . . . *b* of a gentle and quiet spirit,

BEGINNING
John 1:1 . . . In the *b* the Word already
Rev 21:6 . . . the *B* and the End.

BELIEVE
Mark 9:24 . . . I do *b*, but help me
Luke 24:25 . . . You find it so hard to *b*
John 4:41 . . . hear his message and *b*.
John 6:69 . . . We *b*, and we know you are
John 9:35 . . . asked, "Do you *b* in the Son
John 11:40 . . . see God's glory if you *b*?
John 16:30 . . . *b* that you came from God.
John 19:35 . . . so that you also can *b*.
Acts 16:31 . . . *B* in the Lord Jesus and
Acts 27:25 . . . For I *b* God.
Rom 3:25 . . . *b* that Jesus sacrificed his
Rom 10:9 . . . *b* in your heart that God
Rom 10:14 . . . unless they *b* in him?
Rom 14:23 . . . anything you *b* is not right,
Rom 16:26 . . . they too might *b* and obey
1 Cor 1:21 . . . to save those who *b*.
1 Thes 4:14 . . . For since we *b* that Jesus
Heb 11:6 . . . must *b* that God exists
1 Jn 5:10 . . . All who *b* in the Son

BELIEVED
Rom 4:3 . . . tell us, "Abraham *b* God,
1 Cor 15:2 . . . *b* something that was never
Gal 3:6 . . . same way, "Abraham *b* God,
Eph 2:8 . . . his grace when you *b*.

BELONG
Rom 12:5 . . . we all *b* to each other.
2 Cor 10:7 . . . who say they *b* to Christ
Gal 5:24 . . . Those who *b* to Christ
2 Tim 2:19 . . . All who *b* to the Lord

BETHLEHEM
Matt 2:1 . . . Jesus was born in *B* in Judea,
Matt 2:6 . . . you, O *B* in the land of Judah,

BIRTH
John 3:6 . . . Spirit gives *b* to spiritual life.
Titus 3:5 . . . giving us a new *b* and new life

BLAMELESS *see also* INTEGRITY
Phil 1:10 . . . live pure and *b* lives
Titus 1:6 . . . must live a *b* life.
2 Pet 3:14 . . . are pure and *b* in his sight.

BLESSED *see also* GLAD, HAPPY, JOY
Acts 20:35 . . . *b* to give than to receive.
Rev 22:7 . . . *B* are those who obey

Rev 22:14 . . . *B* are those who wash

BLESSES
Matt 5:3 . . . God *b* those who are poor
Matt 5:7 . . . God *b* those who are merciful,
Jas 1:12 . . . God *b* those who patiently

BLIND
Matt 11:5 . . . the *b* see, the lame walk,
Matt 15:14 . . . *b* guides leading the *b*,

BLOOD
Mark 14:24 . . . my *b*, which confirms the
John 6:53 . . . and drink his *b*, you cannot
1 Pet 1:19 . . . the precious *b* of Christ,
1 Jn 1:7 . . . the *b* of Jesus, his Son, cleanses
Rev 1:5 . . . by shedding his *b* for us.

BOAST *see also* PRIDE, PROUD
1 Cor 1:31 . . . *b*, *b* only about the Lord.
Jas 1:9 . . . poor have something to *b* about,

BODIES
1 Cor 15:44 . . . as spiritual *b*.
2 Cor 5:4 . . . so that these dying *b* will
Eph 5:28 . . . love their own *b*.

BODY
Matt 26:41 . . . willing, but the *b* is weak!
1 Cor 6:19 . . . that your *b* is the temple
1 Cor 11:24 . . . my *b*, which is given for
2 Cor 5:1 . . . eternal *b* made for us by God
Eph 1:23 . . . the church is his *b*;
Eph 5:30 . . . are members of his *b*.

BOLD
Phil 1:20 . . . continue to be *b* for Christ,

BOLDLY
Eph 3:12 . . . *b* and confidently into God's
Heb 4:16 . . . let us come *b* to the throne
Heb 10:19 . . . *b* enter heaven's Most Holy

BOLDNESS
Acts 4:13 . . . they saw the *b* of Peter

BOOK
Phil 4:3 . . . written in the *B* of Life.
Rev 3:5 . . . names from the *B* of Life,
Rev 21:27 . . . in the Lamb's *B* of Life.

BORN
John 3:3 . . . unless you are *b* again,
John 3:7 . . . You must be *b* again.
1 Pet 1:3 . . . we have been *b* again,
1 Pet 1:23 . . . you have been *b* again,

BOUGHT
1 Cor 6:20 . . . God *b* you with a high price.

BRANCH
John 15:4 . . . a *b* cannot produce fruit if

BRANCHES
John 15:5 . . . you are the *b*.

BREAD *see also* FOOD
Mark 14:22 . . . Jesus took some *b* and
John 6:48 . . . Yes, I am the *b* of life!
John 6:51 . . . I am the living *b*
1 Cor 10:16 . . . when we break the *b*,
1 Cor 11:23 . . . the Lord Jesus took some *b*

BRIDE
Rev 21:9 . . . the *b*, the wife of the Lamb.
Rev 22:17 . . . Spirit and the *b* say, "Come."

BUILD
Matt 16:18 . . . rock I will *b* my church,

Dictionary/Concordance . . .

Eph 4:12 . . . work and *b* up the church,
Jude 20 . . . must *b* each other up

BUILT
Eph 2:20 . . . *b* on the foundation of the
Col 2:7 . . . let your lives be *b* on him.

BURDEN
Matt 11:30 . . . the *b* I give you is light.
2 Cor 11:9 . . . a financial *b* to anyone.
2 Cor 12:14 . . . I will not be a *b* to you.
2 Thes 3:8 . . . so we would not be a *b*

BURIED
Rom 6:4 . . . we died and were *b* with Christ
1 Cor 15:4 . . . He was *b*, and he was raised
Col 2:12 . . . For you were *b* with Christ

BUSH
Mark 12:26 . . . story of the burning *b*?

CALF
Acts 7:41 . . . made an idol shaped like a *c*,

CALL
Mark 2:17 . . . I have come to *c* not those
Rom 10:12 . . . to all who *c* on him.
Rom 11:29 . . . *c* can never be withdrawn.
1 Cor 1:2 . . . *c* on the name of our Lord

CALLED
Rom 8:28 . . . *c* according to his purpose
1 Thes 4:7 . . . God has *c* us to live holy
1 Pet 3:9 . . . what God has *c* you to do,

CAMEL
Matt 23:24 . . . but you swallow a *c*!
Mark 10:25 . . . easier for a *c* to go through

CAPTIVE
Acts 8:23 . . . and are held *c* by sin.
2 Tim 2:26 . . . they have been held *c*

CAPTIVES
Luke 4:18 . . . that *c* will be released,

CARE
John 10:13 . . . really *c* about the sheep.
John 21:16 . . . Then take *c* of my sheep,
1 Tim 5:14 . . . take *c* of their own homes.
1 Pet 5:2 . . . *C* for the flock that God

CAREFUL
Eph 5:15 . . . So be *c* how you live.

CARRIED
1 Pet 2:24 . . . He personally *c* our sins

CELEBRATE
Luke 15:23 . . . We must *c* with a feast,
John 18:28 . . . to *c* the Passover.

CHAFF
Matt 3:12 . . . separate the *c* from the

CHARACTER
Rom 5:4 . . . develops strength of *c*,
1 Cor 15:33 . . . company corrupts good *c*.

CHEAT
Mark 10:19 . . . You must not *c* anyone.
1 Cor 6:8 . . . who do wrong and *c* even
1 Cor 6:10 . . . abusive, or *c* people—

CHEATED
1 Cor 6:7 . . . Why not let yourselves be *c*?

CHEEK
Matt 5:39 . . . slaps you on the right *c*,

CHEERFUL
Prov 15:30 . . . A *c* look brings joy
Prov 17:22 . . . A *c* heart is good medicine,

CHILD
Matt 1:23 . . . virgin will conceive a *c*!
1 Cor 13:11 . . . and reasoned as a *c*.
1 Jn 4:7 . . . who loves is a *c* of God

CHILDLIKE
Matt 11:25 . . . revealing them to the *c*.

CHILDREN
Matt 5:9 . . . they will be called the *c* of God.
Mark 10:14 . . . Let the *c* come to me.
Luke 18:15 . . . their little *c* to Jesus
John 1:12 . . . the right to become *c* of God.
Rom 9:26 . . . called '*c* of the living God.'
Gal 3:26 . . . you are all *c* of God
Eph 3:6 . . . riches inherited by God's *c*.
Eph 6:1 . . . *C*, obey your parents
Col 3:21 . . . do not aggravate your *c*,
1 Tim 3:4 . . . *c* who respect and obey him.
Heb 12:7 . . . treating you as his own *c*.

CHOSE
1 Cor 1:27 . . . *c* things that are powerless
Eph 1:4 . . . loved us and *c* us in Christ
Eph 1:11 . . . God, for he *c* us in advance,
2 Thes 2:13 . . . thankful that God *c* you
1 Pet 1:15 . . . as God who *c* you is holy.

CHOSEN
Matt 22:14 . . . are called, but few are *c*.
Mark 13:20 . . . for the sake of his *c* ones
Luke 23:35 . . . God's Messiah, the *C* One.
John 1:34 . . . that he is the *C* One of God.
1 Pet 2:9 . . . for you are a *c* people.
2 Pet 1:10 . . . God has called and *c*.

CHRISTIANS
Acts 11:26 . . . believers were first called *C*.
Gal 2:4 . . . some so-called *C*
1 Thes 4:12 . . . people who are not *C*

CHURCH
Matt 16:18 . . . this rock I will build my *c*,
Matt 18:17 . . . take your case to the *c*.
Acts 20:28 . . . shepherd God's flock—his *c*,
1 Cor 15:9 . . . way I persecuted God's *c*.
Eph 5:23 . . . Christ is the head of the *c*.
Col 1:24 . . . continue for his body, the *c*.

CLEANSE
2 Cor 7:1 . . . let us *c* ourselves from
Titus 2:14 . . . *c* us, and to make us his
1 Jn 1:9 . . . to *c* us from all wickedness.

CLOUDS
Mark 13:26 . . . coming on the *c* with great
1 Thes 4:17 . . . up in the *c* to meet the Lord
Rev 1:7 . . . comes with the *c* of heaven.

COINS
Mark 12:42 . . . dropped in two small *c*.
Luke 12:6 . . . sparrows—two copper *c*?

COMFORT
2 Cor 1:4 . . . so that we can *c* others.
2 Cor 1:6 . . . we will certainly *c* you.
2 Cor 2:7 . . . forgive and *c* him.
Col 4:11 . . . And what a *c* they have been!

COMMAND
John 15:14 . . . friends if you do what I *c*.
John 15:17 . . . my *c*: Love each other.

COMMANDED
1 Jn 3:23 . . . just as he *c* us.
2 Jn 4 . . . just as the Father *c*.

COMMANDMENTS
Matt 19:17 . . . eternal life, keep the *c*.
Mark 10:19 . . . you know the *c*:
Mark 12:28 . . . *c*, which is the most
Luke 18:20 . . . you know the *c*:
John 14:15 . . . If you love me, obey my *c*.
1 Jn 2:3 . . . know him if we obey his *c*.
1 Jn 3:24 . . . Those who obey God's *c*
Rev 12:17 . . . who keep God's *c* and

COMPASSION *see also* MERCY
Mark 6:34 . . . and he had *c* on them
Luke 15:20 . . . with love and *c*, he ran to

CONFESS
Rom 14:11 . . . every tongue will *c* and give
Phil 2:11 . . . and every tongue *c* that Jesus
Jas 5:16 . . . *C* your sins to each other
1 Jn 1:9 . . . But if we *c* our sins to him,

CONFESSED
Mark 1:5 . . . And when they *c* their sins,

CONFIDENCE
2 Cor 8:22 . . . of his great *c* in you.
Phil 1:14 . . . believers here have gained *c*
Phil 2:24 . . . And I have *c* from the Lord
Phil 3:4 . . . I could have *c* in my own
Col 2:2 . . . want them to have complete *c*
Titus 1:2 . . . This truth gives them *c*
Heb 11:1 . . . Faith is the *c* that what we

CONSCIENCE
Acts 24:16 . . . maintain a clear *c* before
1 Tim 1:5 . . . a clear *c*, and genuine faith.
1 Tim 1:19 . . . and keep your *c* clear.
1 Pet 3:16 . . . Keep your *c* clear.
1 Pet 3:21 . . . to God from a clean *c*.

CONTENT
Phil 4:11 . . . I have learned how to be *c*
1 Tim 6:8 . . . food and clothing, let us be *c*.

CONTROL
Rom 6:12 . . . Do not let sin *c*
Rom 8:6 . . . letting the Spirit *c* your mind
Rom 8:8 . . . still under the *c* of
Jas 1:26 . . . but don't *c* your tongue,
Jas 3:2 . . . could also *c* ourselves

CONVICT
John 7:51 . . . Is it legal to *c* a man
John 16:8 . . . he will *c* the world of
Jude 15 . . . He will *c* every person

CONVINCED
Rom 2:19 . . . are *c* that you are a guide
Rom 8:38 . . . I am *c* that nothing
Rom 14:14 . . . I know and am *c*
Rom 15:14 . . . I am fully *c*,
Phil 1:25 . . . I am *c* that I will

CORNERSTONE
Mark 12:10 . . . now become the *c*.
Acts 4:11 . . . now become the *c*.
Eph 2:20 . . . And the *c* is Christ
1 Pet 2:7 . . . now become the *c*.

CORRECT *see also* DISCIPLINE
2 Tim 4:2 . . . Patiently *c*, rebuke,
Titus 2:15 . . . the authority to *c* them

COUNSEL
Col 3:16 . . . Teach and *c* each other

COURAGE *see also* ENCOURAGE(D)
Mark 6:50 . . . Take *c*! I am here!
Acts 27:22 . . . But take *c*!
Heb 3:6 . . . if we keep our *c*
Jas 5:8 . . . Take *c*, for the coming
1 Jn 2:28 . . . be full of *c* and not shrink

COURAGEOUS *see also* ENCOURAGE(D)
1 Cor 16:13 . . . Be *c*.

COVENANT *see also* PROMISE
Luke 22:20 . . . new *c* between God and his
2 Cor 3:6 . . . under the new *c*,
Heb 9:15 . . . mediates a new *c* between
Heb 12:24 . . . new *c* between God and

COVET *see also* DESIRE
Rom 7:7 . . . You must not *c*.
Rom 13:9 . . . You must not *c*.

CREATED *see also* MADE
John 1:3 . . . *c* everything through him,
Rom 1:20 . . . since the world was *c*,
Rom 9:20 . . . the thing that was *c* say
Eph 2:10 . . . He has *c* us anew
Eph 4:24 . . . *c* to be like God—
Col 1:16 . . . Everything was *c* through him
1 Tim 4:3 . . . But God *c* those foods
Heb 9:11 . . . part of this *c* world.
1 Pet 4:19 . . . to the God who *c* you,
Rev 4:11 . . . For you *c* all things,
Rev 10:6 . . . who *c* the heavens

CREATION
Rom 8:19 . . . For all *c* is waiting
Rom 8:39 . . . nothing in all *c* will ever
Gal 6:15 . . . into a new *c*.
Col 1:17 . . . holds all *c* together.
Jas 1:18 . . . we, out of all *c*,
Rev 3:14 . . . of God's new *c*:

CREATOR
Rom 1:25 . . . instead of the *C* himself,
Eph 3:9 . . . the *C* of all things,
Eph 3:15 . . . the *C* of everything

CRITICISM
2 Cor 8:20 . . . guard against any *c*

CROSS
Mark 8:34 . . . take up your *c*,
Acts 2:23 . . . you nailed him to a *c*
Acts 5:30 . . . hanging him on a *c*.
1 Cor 1:18 . . . message of the *c* is
Gal 3:1 . . . death on the *c*.
Gal 6:12 . . . that the *c* of Christ alone
Col 1:20 . . . Christ's blood on the *c*.
Heb 12:2 . . . he endured the *c*,
1 Pet 2:24 . . . his body on the *c*

CROWN
Matt 27:29 . . . thorn branches into a *c*
Mark 15:17 . . . thorn branches into a *c*
John 19:2 . . . wove a *c* of thorns
John 19:5 . . . wearing the *c* of thorns
Phil 4:1 . . . and the *c* I receive
1 Thes 2:19 . . . our proud reward and *c*
Jas 1:12 . . . will receive the *c* of life

Dictionary/Concordance . . .

Rev 2:10 . . . will give you the *c* of life.
Rev 14:14 . . . He had a gold *c* on his head

CRUCIFIED
Mark 15:32 . . . who were *c* with Jesus
Mark 16:6 . . . who was *c*.
Luke 23:23 . . . demanding that Jesus be *c*,
Luke 23:33 . . . the criminals were also *c*—
Luke 24:20 . . . and they *c* him.
John 19:20 . . . place where Jesus was *c*
John 19:32 . . . the two men *c* with Jesus.
Rom 6:6 . . . were *c* with Christ
1 Cor 1:23 . . . preach that Christ was *c*,
1 Cor 2:8 . . . would not have *c*
Gal 5:24 . . . and *c* them there.
Rev 11:8 . . . where their Lord was *c*.

CRUCIFY
Mark 15:13 . . . *C* him!
John 19:6 . . . *C* him! *C* him!
John 19:10 . . . to release you or *c* you?

CURED
Matt 11:5 . . . the lepers are *c*,
John 5:10 . . . said to the man who was *c*,

DANCE
Mark 6:22 . . . a *d* that greatly pleased

DANGER
Rom 8:35 . . . or in *d*, or threatened

DARKEST
Ps 23:4 . . . walk through the *d* valley,

DARKNESS
Matt 4:16 . . . people who sat in *d*
Luke 23:44 . . . it was noon, and *d* fell
John 1:5 . . . light shines in the *d*,
John 3:19 . . . people loved the *d* more
John 12:35 . . . the *d* will not overtake
2 Cor 6:14 . . . can light live with *d*?
Eph 5:8 . . . once you were full of *d*,
Eph 5:11 . . . deeds of evil and *d*;
1 Pet 2:9 . . . called you out of the *d*
1 Jn 1:5 . . . there is no *d* in him at all.
1 Jn 2:9 . . . is still living in *d*.
Jude 6 . . . chained in prisons of *d*,

DAVID   King of Israel (United Kingdom); son
of Jesse, in the family line of Jesus (Matt 1:1;
Luke 3:32).

DAYS
Matt 24:38 . . . In those *d* before the
Acts 2:17 . . . 'In the last *d*,' God says,
2 Tim 3:1 . . . in the last *d* there will be
Heb 1:2 . . . now in these final *d*, he has
2 Pet 3:3 . . . in the last *d* scoffers will

DEAD
Luke 24:46 . . . rise from the *d* on the third
Eph 2:1 . . . Once you were *d* because of
Jas 2:17 . . . good deeds, it is *d* and useless.
1 Pet 2:24 . . . that we can be *d* to sin and
Rev 2:8 . . . Last, who was *d* but is now
Rev 20:12 . . . I saw the *d*, both great and

DEATH
Acts 2:24 . . . *d* could not keep him
Rom 5:12 . . . brought *d*, so *d* spread
Rom 6:23 . . . the wages of sin is *d*,

1 Cor 15:21 . . . see, just as *d* came into the
1 Cor 15:26 . . . enemy to be destroyed is *d*.
Gal 3:1 . . . the meaning of Jesus Christ's *d*
Heb 2:14 . . . the power of *d*.

DEBT
Matt 18:25 . . . to pay the *d*.
Matt 18:27 . . . and forgave his *d*.
Matt 18:30 . . . in prison until the *d* could

DECEIVED
2 Cor 11:3 . . . as Eve was *d* by the cunning
1 Tim 2:14 . . . The woman was *d*, and sin
2 Tim 3:13 . . . will themselves be *d*.
Heb 3:13 . . . you will be *d* by sin
Rev 20:10 . . . devil, who had *d* them, was

DEEDS *see also* WORK
Matt 5:16 . . . let your good *d* shine out for
2 Cor 9:9 . . . Their good *d* will be
Col 3:9 . . . all its wicked *d*.
Jas 2:20 . . . without good *d* is useless?

DEFEND
Phil 1:16 . . . been appointed to *d* the Good
Jude 3 . . . urging you to *d* the faith

DELIGHT
Mark 12:37 . . . to him with great *d*.

DEMONS
Matt 8:31 . . . So the *d* begged, "If you cast
Matt 9:34 . . . by the prince of *d*.
Matt 12:28 . . . if I am casting out *d* by the
Mark 1:34 . . . But because the *d* knew who
Mark 5:15 . . . by the legion of *d*.
Mark 9:38 . . . to cast out *d*, but we told
Mark 16:9 . . . cast out seven *d*.
Mark 16:17 . . . will cast out *d* in my name,
Luke 8:30 . . . with many *d*.
Luke 9:49 . . . to cast out *d*, but we told
Luke 10:17 . . . Lord, even the *d* obey us
Luke 11:20 . . . casting out *d* by the power
1 Tim 4:1 . . . come from *d*.

DEN
Matt 21:13 . . . into a *d* of thieves!
Mark 11:17 . . . into a *d* of thieves.

DENIED
Matt 26:70 . . . But Peter *d* it
John 18:25 . . . He *d* it, saying,
Jude 4 . . . they have *d* our only Master

DENY
Matt 26:35 . . . I will never *d* you!
Luke 22:34 . . . you will *d* three times
Acts 4:16 . . . We can't *d* that they
2 Tim 2:12 . . . *d* him, he will *d* us.
Titus 1:16 . . . *d* him by the way they live.
2 Pet 2:1 . . . and even *d* the Master who
Rev 3:8 . . . and did not *d* me.

DESIRE *see also* COVET
Mark 4:19 . . . wealth, and the *d* for
1 Cor 12:31 . . . earnestly *d* the most
1 Cor 14:1 . . . should also *d* the special
Phil 2:13 . . . you the *d* and the power

DESPISE
Matt 6:24 . . . to one and *d* the other.
Luke 16:13 . . . to one and *d* the other.
2 Pet 2:10 . . . and who *d* authority.

DESTROY *see also* DIE, PERISH
Matt 10:28 . . . God, who can *d* both soul
John 10:10 . . . and kill and *d*.

DESTROYED
1 Cor 15:26 . . . enemy to be *d* is death.
Heb 7:16 . . . that cannot be *d*.

DESTRUCTION
1 Cor 1:18 . . . are headed for *d*!
2 Thes 1:9 . . . punished with eternal *d*,

DICE
Matt 27:35 . . . by throwing *d*.

DIE *see also* DESTROY, PERISH
John 13:37 . . . I'm ready to *d* for you.
Rom 4:25 . . . handed over to *d* because of
Rom 5:8 . . . by sending Christ to *d* for us
Rom 14:8 . . . whether we live or *d*, we
1 Cor 9:15 . . . I would rather *d* than lose
1 Cor 15:32 . . . for tomorrow we *d*!
1 Cor 15:42 . . . in the ground when we *d*,
1 Cor 15:51 . . . will not all *d*, but we will
2 Tim 2:11 . . . saying: If we *d* with him,
Heb 9:27 . . . is destined to *d* once and

DIED
Luke 16:22 . . . The rich man also *d* and
Rom 5:6 . . . the right time and *d* for us
Rom 6:7 . . . For when we *d* with Christ we
Rom 6:10 . . . When he *d*, he *d* once
1 Cor 15:18 . . . all who have *d* believing in
2 Cor 5:15 . . . for Christ, who *d* and was
1 Thes 4:16 . . . who have *d* will rise from
1 Thes 5:10 . . . Christ *d* for us so
1 Pet 3:18 . . . sinned, but he *d* for sinners

DISAPPEAR
Matt 5:18 . . . until heaven and earth *d*,
Matt 24:35 . . . Heaven and earth will *d*,
Mark 13:31 . . . Heaven and earth will *d*,
Luke 16:17 . . . and earth to *d* than for the

DISASTER
1 Thes 5:3 . . . then *d* will fall on them

DISCIPLE
Luke 14:26 . . . cannot be my *d*.
Luke 14:33 . . . become my *d* without
John 13:23 . . . The *d* Jesus loved
John 21:7 . . . Then the *d* Jesus loved
John 21:20 . . . the *d* Jesus loved—

DISCIPLES
Matt 28:19 . . . go and make *d* of all the
Mark 16:20 . . . the *d* went everywhere and
John 8:31 . . . truly my *d* if you remain
John 13:5 . . . to wash the *d'* feet, drying
John 15:8 . . . are my true *d*.

DISCIPLINE *see also* CORRECT
1 Cor 9:27 . . . I *d* my body
Heb 12:5 . . . of the Lord's *d*, and don't
Heb 12:11 . . . No *d* is enjoyable

DISCIPLINES
Heb 12:6 . . . For the Lord *d* those he

DISCOURAGED *see also* COURAGE(OUS)
Col 3:21 . . . will become *d*.

DISEASE
Matt 9:35 . . . every kind of *d* and illness.
Matt 10:1 . . . every kind of *d* and illness.

DISGRACE
Matt 1:19 . . . did not want to *d* her
Acts 5:41 . . . worthy to suffer *d* for

DISHONEST
Luke 16:8 . . . to admire the *d* rascal for
Luke 16:10 . . . But if you are *d* in little

DISHONESTY
Rom 3:7 . . . sinner if my *d* highlights his
Rev 21:27 . . . idolatry and *d*—but only

DISOBEY
Rom 1:30 . . . and they *d* their parents.
Eph 5:6 . . . fall on all who *d* him.
Heb 4:11 . . . But if we *d* God, as the

DISOBEYED
Rom 5:19 . . . Because one person *d* God,
Heb 3:18 . . . the people who *d* him?
Heb 4:6 . . . enter because they *d* God.
1 Pet 3:20 . . . those who *d* God long ago

DIVISIONS
1 Cor 1:10 . . . there be no *d* in the church.
1 Cor 11:18 . . . that there are *d* among you
Titus 3:10 . . . are causing *d* among you,

DIVORCE
Matt 5:31 . . . A man can *d* his wife by
Matt 19:8 . . . Moses permitted *d* only as a
Mark 10:2 . . . be allowed to *d* his wife?

DIVORCES
Matt 5:32 . . . man who *d* his wife, unless
Mark 10:11 . . . Whoever *d* his wife and
Mark 10:12 . . . if a woman *d* her husband
Luke 16:18 . . . a man who *d* his wife and

DOOR
Matt 7:7 . . . the *d* will be opened to you.
Luke 13:24 . . . enter the narrow *d* to God's
Acts 14:27 . . . had opened the *d* of faith to
2 Cor 2:12 . . . opened a *d* of opportunity
Rev 3:20 . . . stand at the *d* and knock.

DOUBT
Matt 14:31 . . . Why did you *d* me?
Matt 21:21 . . . faith and don't *d*, you
Mark 11:23 . . . have no *d* in your heart.

DRUNK
Acts 2:15 . . . These people are not *d*, as

DRUNKARDS
1 Cor 6:10 . . . greedy people, or *d*, or are

DUST
Matt 10:14 . . . shake its *d* from your feet
1 Cor 15:47 . . . from the *d* of the earth,

EARNEST
Jas 5:16 . . . The *e* prayer of a righteous

EARTH
Matt 5:18 . . . until heaven and *e* disappear,
Matt 6:10 . . . your will be done on *e*,
Matt 28:18 . . . in heaven and on *e*.
Luke 2:14 . . . peace on *e* to those
Acts 4:24 . . . Creator of heaven and *e*,
2 Pet 3:13 . . . and new *e* he has promised,
Rev 21:1 . . . a new heaven and a new *e*,

Dictionary/Concordance

EAT
Matt 26:26 ... Take this and *e* it,
1 Cor 11:26 ... every time you *e* this bread

ELIJAH Powerful prophet in Israel (Northern Kingdom); proclaimed drought (Jas 5:17); performed miracles for widow (Luke 4:25); return prophesied and expected (Matt 11:14; Luke 1:17; John 1:25); compared to John the Baptist (Matt 17:9-13; Mark 9:9-13; Luke 1:17); appeared at Jesus' Transfiguration (Matt 17:1-8; Mark 9:1-8).

EMPTY
Luke 1:53 ... the rich away with *e* hands.
1 Pet 1:18 ... to save you from the *e* life
2 Pet 2:18 ... with *e*, foolish boasting.

ENCOURAGE *see also* COURAGE(OUS)
Rom 12:8 ... your gift is to *e* others,
Eph 6:22 ... how we are doing and to *e*
Col 4:8 ... how we are doing and to *e*
1 Thes 3:2 ... to strengthen you, to *e* you
1 Thes 5:11 ... So *e* each other
Titus 1:9 ... he will be able to *e* others
1 Pet 5:12 ... purpose in writing is to *e* you

ENCOURAGED
Acts 11:23 ... and he *e* the believers
Acts 20:1 ... sent for the believers and *e*
Rom 1:12 ... I also want to be *e* by yours.
2 Cor 7:6 ... *e* us by the arrival of Titus.
2 Cor 7:13 ... have been greatly *e* by this.
1 Thes 2:12 ... pleaded with you, *e* you,
1 Thes 3:7 ... we have been greatly *e* in the

END
Matt 24:13 ... one who endures to the *e*
Matt 24:14 ... and then the *e* will come.
1 Cor 15:24 ... After that the *e* will come,
Phil 3:14 ... press on to reach the *e* of
Rev 21:6 ... the Beginning and the *E*.
Rev 22:13 ... the Beginning and the *E*.

ENDURE
2 Cor 6:4 ... patiently *e* troubles and
2 Tim 2:3 ... *E* suffering along with me,
2 Tim 2:12 ... If we *e* hardship,
Heb 12:7 ... As you *e* this divine discipline,
Jas 1:12 ... who patiently *e* testing and
Jas 5:11 ... those who *e* under suffering.
1 Pet 2:19 ... patiently *e* unfair treatment.

ENEMIES
Matt 5:44 ... love your *e*!
Rom 5:10 ... while we were still his *e*,
Rom 12:20 ... If your *e* are hungry,
Phil 3:18 ... they are really *e* of the cross

ENEMY
Luke 10:19 ... over all the power of the *e*,
1 Cor 15:26 ... the last *e* to be destroyed
Jas 4:4 ... makes you an *e* of God?
1 Pet 5:8 ... Watch out for your great *e*,

ENTER
Matt 5:20 ... will never *e* the Kingdom
Matt 19:23 ... rich person to *e* the
Mark 9:43 ... *e* eternal life with only
Mark 10:23 ... for the rich to *e* the
Luke 13:24 ... Work hard to *e* the narrow
Luke 18:17 ... a child will never *e* it.
John 3:5 ... no one can *e* the Kingdom

ENVY *see also* JEALOUS(Y)
Mark 7:22 ... lustful desires, *e*, slander,
Rom 1:29 ... sin, greed, hate, *e*, murder,
Gal 5:21 ... *e*, drunkenness, wild parties,
Titus 3:3 ... full of evil and *e*, and we hated
Jas 4:5 ... within us is filled with *e*?

EQUIP
Eph 4:12 ... to *e* God's people to do
2 Tim 3:17 ... to prepare and *e* his people

ETERNAL *see also* FOREVER
Luke 10:25 ... should I do to inherit *e* life?
Luke 18:18 ... should I do to inherit *e* life?
John 3:16 ... not perish but have *e* life.
John 5:29 ... will rise to experience *e* life,
John 6:68 ... the words that give *e* life.
John 17:2 ... He gives *e* life
Rom 5:21 ... resulting in *e* life through
Rom 6:23 ... gift of God is *e* life
Rom 16:26 ... the *e* God has commanded,
Eph 3:11 ... This was his *e* plan,
Titus 3:7 ... we will inherit *e* life.
Heb 5:9 ... source of *e* salvation
Heb 9:15 ... *e* inheritance God has
Heb 13:20 ... an *e* covenant with his
1 Pet 1:23 ... from the *e*, living word
1 Pet 5:10 ... to share in his *e* glory
1 Jn 2:25 ... we enjoy the *e* life he
1 Jn 5:20 ... and he is *e* life.
Jude 21 ... who will bring you *e* life.

EVIL
Matt 6:13 ... rescue us from the *e* one.
Matt 15:19 ... from the heart come *e*
John 3:20 ... All who do *e* hate the light
John 17:15 ... them safe from the *e* one.
Rom 12:21 ... Don't let *e* conquer you,
1 Thes 5:15 ... no one pays back *e* for *e*,
1 Thes 5:22 ... away from every kind of *e*.
2 Thes 3:3 ... guard you from the *e* one.
1 Tim 6:10 ... the root of all kinds of *e*.
Heb 1:9 ... You love justice and hate *e*.
Jas 1:21 ... get rid of all the filth and *e*
1 Pet 3:9 ... Don't repay *e* for *e*.
1 Pet 3:11 ... Turn away from *e* and do
1 Jn 5:18 ... the *e* one cannot touch

EXALT *see also* HONOR
Luke 14:11 ... *e* themselves will be
2 Thes 2:4 ... He will *e* himself

EXAMINE
1 Cor 4:4 ... Lord himself who will *e*
1 Cor 11:28 ... you should *e* yourself

EXAMPLE
Heb 13:7 ... follow the *e* of their faith.
1 Pet 2:21 ... your *e*, and you must follow

EXCUSE
Rom 1:20 ... no *e* for not knowing God.
Rom 2:1 ... and you have no *e*!
Eph 5:6 ... who try to *e* these sins,
1 Pet 2:16 ... your freedom as an *e*.

EYE
Matt 5:38 ... An *e* for an *e*,
Matt 6:22 ... When your *e* is good,
1 Cor 2:9 ... when they say, "No *e* has seen,

EYES
Heb 12:2 ... by keeping our *e* on Jesus,
2 Pet 1:16 ... with our own *e*
Rev 21:4 ... wipe every tear from their *e*,

F

FACE
Luke 9:29 . . . appearance of his *f* was
2 Cor 3:7 . . . his *f* shone with the glory
Rev 1:16 . . . And his *f* was like the sun
Rev 22:4 . . . they will see his *f*,

FAIL
Luke 22:32 . . . faith should not *f*.
Heb 13:5 . . . I will never *f* you.
1 Pet 4:19 . . . he will never *f* you.

FAIR
Rom 3:25 . . . God was being *f* when he
Rom 3:26 . . . he himself is *f* and just,
Col 4:1 . . . be just and *f* to your slaves.

FAITH *see also* BELIEVE, TRUST
Matt 9:29 . . . Because of your *f*, it will
Matt 17:20 . . . *f* even as small as a mustard
Mark 5:34 . . . your *f* has made you well.
Luke 7:50 . . . Your *f* has saved you;
Luke 12:28 . . . Why do you have so little *f*?
Rom 3:28 . . . right with God through *f*
Rom 4:12 . . . same kind of *f* Abraham had
Rom 10:17 . . . So *f* comes from hearing,
1 Cor 13:13 . . . *f*, hope, and love—
Gal 3:24 . . . right with God through *f*.
Eph 4:5 . . . one Lord, one *f*, one baptism,
Eph 6:16 . . . hold up the shield of *f*
Phil 3:9 . . . righteous through *f* in
Heb 10:38 . . . will live by *f*.
Heb 12:2 . . . perfects our *f*.
Jas 2:14 . . . Can that kind of *f* save anyone?
Jas 2:26 . . . so also *f* is dead
Jas 5:15 . . . prayer offered in *f* will heal

FAITHFUL
1 Thes 5:24 . . . calls you is *f*.
2 Thes 3:3 . . . But the Lord is *f*; he will
2 Tim 4:7 . . . I have remained *f*.
Heb 2:17 . . . merciful and *f* High Priest
1 Jn 1:9 . . . to him, he is *f* and just to
Rev 17:14 . . . chosen and *f* ones will be

FAITHFULNESS
Gal 5:22 . . . kindness, goodness, *f*,
Eph 6:23 . . . give you love with *f*.
2 Thes 1:4 . . . your endurance and *f*
2 Tim 2:22 . . . pursue righteous living, *f*,

FALSE
Matt 24:11 . . . And many *f* prophets will
Mark 13:22 . . . For *f* messiahs and *f*
1 Jn 4:1 . . . many *f* prophets in the world.
Rev 20:10 . . . the beast and the *f* prophet.

FAMILY
Mark 3:25 . . . a *f* splintered by feuding
Gal 6:10 . . . to those in the *f* of faith.
Eph 2:19 . . . members of God's *f*.
1 Tim 3:4 . . . manage his own *f* well,
1 Jn 3:9 . . . been born into God's *f*

FASTING
Acts 13:2 . . . worshiping the Lord and *f*,
Acts 14:23 . . . prayer and *f*, they turned the

FATHER *see also* PARENTS
Matt 5:16 . . . will praise your heavenly *F*.
Matt 6:9 . . . Our *F* in heaven, may your
Matt 6:14 . . . heavenly *F* will forgive
Matt 11:27 . . . no one truly knows the *F*

Matt 16:27 . . . in the glory of his *F*
Matt 19:29 . . . or *f* or mother or children
Matt 23:9 . . . is your spiritual *F*.
Mark 7:10 . . . Honor your *f* and mother,
John 4:21 . . . you worship the *F* on this
John 5:17 . . . My *F* is always working,
John 5:20 . . . For the *F* loves the Son
John 6:44 . . . come to me unless the *F*
John 6:65 . . . unless the *F* gives them
John 10:38 . . . understand that the *F* is in
John 14:6 . . . to the *F* except through me.
John 14:21 . . . love me, my *F* will love
John 15:8 . . . brings great glory to my *F*.
John 20:17 . . . ascending to my *F* and
Rom 4:11 . . . Abraham is the spiritual *f*
Rom 8:15 . . . we call him, "Abba, *F*."
2 Cor 6:18 . . . I will be your *F*, and you
Eph 5:31 . . . man leaves his *f* and mother
Eph 6:2 . . . Honor your *f* and mother.
Phil 2:11 . . . to the glory of God the *F*.
Heb 12:7 . . . is never disciplined by its *f*?
1 Jn 1:3 . . . fellowship is with the *F* and
1 Jn 3:1 . . . See how very much our *F* loves
Rev 3:21 . . . with my *F* on his throne.

FATHERS
Eph 6:4 . . . *F*, do not provoke
Col 3:21 . . . *F*, do not aggravate
Heb 12:9 . . . earthly *f* who disciplined

FAVOR *see also* GRACE
Luke 2:40 . . . and God's *f* was on him.
Luke 2:52 . . . and in *f* with God
Luke 4:19 . . . time of the Lord's *f*
Rom 11:7 . . . have not found the *f* of God
Phil 1:7 . . . with me the special *f* of God,
Jas 2:9 . . . But if you *f* some people over

FAVORITES
Matt 22:16 . . . and don't play *f*.
Gal 2:6 . . . for God has no *f*.
Eph 6:9 . . . he has no *f*.
Col 3:25 . . . For God has no *f*.

FEAR *see also* AWE, REVERENCE
2 Cor 7:1 . . . because we *f* God.
Heb 13:6 . . . so I will have no *f*.
Rev 11:18 . . . all who *f* your name,

FEED
Matt 14:16 . . . you *f* them.
Matt 25:42 . . . and you didn't *f* me.
John 21:15 . . . Then *f* my lambs,
John 21:17 . . . Then *f* my sheep.
Rom 12:20 . . . enemies are hungry, *f*

FEET
Matt 10:14 . . . shake its dust from your *f*
Luke 24:39 . . . Look at my *f*.
John 13:5 . . . began to wash the disciples' *f*,
John 13:14 . . . wash each other's *f*.
Rom 16:20 . . . crush Satan under your *f*.
1 Cor 15:25 . . . his enemies beneath his *f*.
Heb 12:13 . . . a straight path for your *f*

FIELDS
Luke 2:8 . . . staying in the *f* nearby,
John 4:35 . . . The *f* are already ripe

FIGHT
1 Tim 6:12 . . . *F* the good *f*
2 Tim 4:7 . . . fought the good *f*,
Jas 4:2 . . . so you *f* and wage war

FILL
Acts 2:28 . . . you will *f* me with the joy
Rom 5:5 . . . Holy Spirit to *f* our hearts
Rom 15:13 . . . *f* you completely with joy
Col 3:16 . . . its richness, *f* your lives.

FIND
Matt 7:7 . . . seeking, and you will *f*.
Matt 10:39 . . . life for me, you will *f* it.

FINGER
Luke 16:24 . . . dip the tip of his *f* in water
John 8:6 . . . wrote in the dust with his *f*.

FIRE
Matt 3:11 . . . the Holy Spirit and with *f*.
Luke 3:16 . . . the Holy Spirit and with *f*.
Acts 2:3 . . . tongues of *f* appeared and

FIRST
Mark 9:35 . . . to be *f* must take last
1 Cor 15:45 . . . The *f* man, Adam,
Eph 6:2 . . . the *f* commandment with
1 Tim 2:13 . . . God made Adam *f*,
Heb 10:9 . . . He cancels the *f* covenant
1 Jn 4:19 . . . he loved us *f*.
Rev 22:13 . . . and the Omega, the *F* and the

FIRSTBORN
Heb 1:6 . . . his *f* Son into the world,

FISH
Matt 12:40 . . . in the belly of the great *f*
Mark 1:17 . . . how to *f* for people!
Mark 6:38 . . . loaves of bread and two *f*.

FLATTERY
1 Thes 2:5 . . . try to win you with *f*,

FLOOD
Matt 24:38 . . . days before the *f*,
2 Pet 2:5 . . . with a vast *f*.

FOLLOW
Matt 8:19 . . . I will *f* you wherever you go.
Matt 8:22 . . . *F* me now.
Matt 16:24 . . . take up your cross, and *f*
Matt 19:27 . . . given up everything to *f* you.
Mark 1:17 . . . Come, *f* me,
Luke 9:23 . . . your cross daily, and *f* me.
Luke 17:23 . . . go out and *f* them.
John 8:12 . . . If you *f* me, you won't have
John 10:4 . . . they *f* him because they know
John 12:26 . . . to be my disciple must *f* me,
John 21:19 . . . Jesus told him, "*F* me."
Gal 5:25 . . . *f* the Spirit's leading
Phil 3:17 . . . those who *f* our example.
1 Pet 2:21 . . . must *f* in his steps.

FOOD
Matt 6:11 . . . today the *f* we need,
Matt 6:25 . . . life more than *f*,
1 Tim 6:8 . . . have enough *f* and clothing,
Jas 2:15 . . . who has no *f* or clothing,

FOOL
1 Cor 3:18 . . . need to become a *f* to be

FOOLISH
1 Cor 1:18 . . . the cross is *f* to those who
1 Cor 1:27 . . . world considers *f* in order to
1 Cor 2:14 . . . It all sounds *f* to them
Eph 5:4 . . . Obscene stories, *f* talk,
1 Tim 6:20 . . . Avoid godless, *f* discussions
Titus 3:9 . . . Do not get involved in *f*

FOOLS
Rom 1:22 . . . became utter *f*.
Eph 5:15 . . . Don't live like *f*,
2 Tim 3:9 . . . recognize what *f* they are,

FOREIGNERS
Eph 2:19 . . . are no longer strangers and *f*.
1 Pet 1:1 . . . living as *f* in the provinces
1 Pet 2:11 . . . temporary residents and *f*

FOREVER *see also* ETERNAL
John 6:51 . . . eats this bread will live *f*;
1 Cor 13:13 . . . Three things will last *f*—
1 Thes 4:17 . . . will be with the Lord *f*.
Heb 7:24 . . . Jesus lives *f*,
Heb 13:8 . . . yesterday, today, and *f*.
1 Pet 1:25 . . . word of the Lord remains *f*.
1 Jn 2:17 . . . will live *f*.
Rev 22:5 . . . they will reign *f* and ever.

FORGAVE
Luke 7:42 . . . so he kindly *f* them both,
Eph 1:7 . . . and *f* our sins.
Col 1:14 . . . and *f* our sins.
Col 2:13 . . . with Christ, for he *f* all our

FORGET
Luke 12:6 . . . God does not *f* a single one
Rom 3:31 . . . we can *f* about the law?
Heb 13:16 . . . And don't *f* to do good
Jas 1:24 . . . walk away, and *f*
Jas 1:25 . . . and don't *f* what you heard,
2 Pet 3:8 . . . must not *f* this one thing,

FORGIVE *see also* COMPASSION, MERCY
Ps 79:9 . . . Save us and *f* our sins
Ps 86:5 . . . so good, so ready to *f*,
Isa 55:7 . . . for he will *f* generously.
Jer 31:34 . . . I will *f* their wickedness,
Dan 9:19 . . . O Lord, hear. O Lord, *f*.
Hos 14:2 . . . *F* all our sins and
Matt 6:12 . . . and *f* us our sins,
Matt 6:15 . . . if you refuse to *f* others,
Matt 9:6 . . . authority on earth to *f* sins.
Matt 26:28 . . . to *f* the sins of many.
Mark 2:7 . . . Only God can *f* sins!
Mark 11:25 . . . first *f* anyone you are
Luke 6:37 . . . *F* others, and you will be
Luke 17:4 . . . forgiveness, you must *f*.
Luke 23:34 . . . Father, *f* them,
1 Jn 1:9 . . . faithful and just to *f* us

FORGIVENESS
Luke 24:47 . . . There is *f* of sins for all
Acts 13:38 . . . this man Jesus there is *f*
Rom 5:15 . . . his gift of *f* to many
Heb 9:22 . . . of blood, there is no *f*.
Jas 5:20 . . . bring about the *f* of many

FORGIVING
Luke 7:49 . . . he goes around *f* sins?

FORMED *see also* CREATE(D), MAKE
Heb 11:3 . . . universe was *f* at God's

FREE
John 8:32 . . . the truth will set you *f*.
John 8:36 . . . sets you *f*, you are truly *f*.
Rom 6:7 . . . we were set *f* from the power
Rom 6:18 . . . you are *f* from your slavery
Jas 1:25 . . . the perfect law that sets you *f*,

FREEDOM
2 Cor 3:17 . . . there is *f*.
Gal 2:4 . . . take away the *f* we have in Christ

Gal 4:5 . . . sent him to buy *f* for us
Gal 5:13 . . . don't use your *f* to satisfy
Eph 1:7 . . . purchased our *f* with the blood
1 Pet 2:16 . . . don't use your *f* as an excuse

FRIEND
John 11:3 . . . Lord, your dear *f* is very sick.
Jas 2:23 . . . even called the *f* of God.
Jas 4:4 . . . want to be a *f* of the world,

FRIENDS
John 15:13 . . . one's life for one's *f*.
John 15:14 . . . You are my *f* if you do
John 15:15 . . . Now you are my *f*,

FRIENDSHIP
Rom 5:10 . . . since our *f* with God was
Jas 4:4 . . . realize that *f* with the world

FRUIT
Matt 3:10 . . . not produce good *f* will be
Matt 7:20 . . . can identify a tree by its *f*,
Matt 12:33 . . . is bad, its *f* will be bad.
John 15:2 . . . that doesn't produce *f*,
Gal 5:22 . . . produces this kind of *f*

FULFILL
John 18:9 . . . this to *f* his own statement:
John 19:28 . . . and to *f* Scripture he said,
Rom 3:31 . . . do we truly *f* the law.
Rom 13:8 . . . you will *f* the requirements
Eph 1:9 . . . plan to *f* his own good pleasure.

FULFILLED
Matt 2:15 . . . This *f* what the Lord had
Matt 13:35 . . . This *f* what God had spoken
Matt 27:9 . . . This *f* the prophecy of
Luke 24:44 . . . in the Psalms must be *f*.
Acts 1:16 . . . Scriptures had to be *f*

FURNACE
Matt 13:42 . . . throw them into the fiery *f*,

FUTURE
Rom 8:19 . . . waiting eagerly for that *f*

GATE
Matt 7:13 . . . only through the narrow *g*.
John 10:1 . . . going through the *g*,
John 10:2 . . . who enters through the *g*
John 10:7 . . . I am the *g* for the sheep.
John 10:9 . . . I am the *g*.
Rev 21:21 . . . each *g* from a single pearl!

GATES
Rev 21:21 . . . *g* were made of pearls—

GAVE
John 3:16 . . . he *g* his one and only Son,
Rom 8:32 . . . *g* him up for us all,
Gal 2:20 . . . loved me and *g* himself for me.
1 Tim 2:6 . . . He *g* his life

GENEROUS
2 Cor 9:6 . . . will get a *g* crop.
1 Tim 6:18 . . . *g* to those in need,

GENTILES *see also* NATIONS
Luke 21:24 . . . of the *G* comes to an end.
Acts 14:27 . . . faith to the *G*, too.
Acts 15:14 . . . God first visited the *G*
Acts 28:28 . . . also been offered to the *G*,

Rom 3:9 . . . all people, whether Jews or *G*,
Rom 3:29 . . . God of the *G*?
Rom 11:11 . . . available to the *G*.
Rom 15:9 . . . so that the *G* might give glory
Rom 15:27 . . . *G* received the spiritual
Gal 2:2 . . . preaching to the *G*.
Gal 3:8 . . . God would declare the *G* to be
Gal 3:14 . . . blessed the *G* with the same
Eph 3:8 . . . the privilege of telling the *G*

GENTLE
Matt 11:29 . . . am humble and *g* at heart,
1 Cor 4:21 . . . love and a *g* spirit?
Eph 4:2 . . . be humble and *g*. Be patient
Titus 3:2 . . . be *g* and show true humility
Jas 3:17 . . . *g* at all times,

GIFT
Rom 4:16 . . . given as a free *g*.
Rom 5:15 . . . and God's gracious *g*.
Rom 6:23 . . . free *g* of God is eternal
1 Cor 12:7 . . . A spiritual *g* is given
2 Cor 9:5 . . . I want it to be a willing *g*,
Gal 2:9 . . . recognized the *g* God had
Eph 2:8 . . . it is a *g* from God.
2 Tim 1:6 . . . the spiritual *g* God gave you
1 Pet 3:7 . . . equal partner in God's *g*

GIVE
Matt 7:11 . . . heavenly Father *g* good gifts
Matt 16:19 . . . And I will *g* you the keys
Luke 11:13 . . . know how to *g* good gifts to
John 14:27 . . . And the peace I *g* is a gift
Acts 20:35 . . . is more blessed to *g* than to
Rom 2:7 . . . He will *g* eternal life
Rom 12:8 . . . is giving, *g* generously.
2 Cor 9:7 . . . how much to *g*.
Eph 4:28 . . . and then *g* generously to

GIVEN
Luke 22:19 . . . body, which is *g* for you.
Acts 5:32 . . . Spirit, who is *g* by God
Rom 5:5 . . . because he has *g* us the Holy
1 Cor 11:24 . . . body, which is *g* for you.
Eph 4:7 . . . However, he has *g* each one of
1 Jn 4:13 . . . And God has *g* us his Spirit

GLAD *see also* HAPPY, JOY, REJOICE
Matt 5:12 . . . Be very *g*!
Acts 13:48 . . . they were very *g*
1 Cor 12:26 . . . the parts are *g*.
2 Cor 2:2 . . . will make me *g*?
Rev 19:7 . . . Let us be *g* and rejoice,

GLORY
Matt 16:27 . . . angels in the *g* of his Father
Matt 25:31 . . . comes in his *g*, and all the
Mark 13:26 . . . great power and *g*.
Luke 2:14 . . . *G* to God in highest heaven,
Luke 9:32 . . . they saw Jesus' *g* and the two
Rom 8:18 . . . compared to the *g* he will
Rom 9:4 . . . God revealed his *g* to them.
Rom 15:6 . . . giving praise and *g* to God,
Rom 16:27 . . . All *g* to the only
1 Cor 10:31 . . . all for the *g* of God.
Phil 4:20 . . . Now all *g* to God our
2 Tim 4:18 . . . All *g* to God forever
Heb 2:9 . . . crowned with *g* and honor.
1 Pet 5:4 . . . of never-ending *g* and honor.
Jude 25 . . . All *g*, majesty, power,
Rev 4:9 . . . beings give *g* and honor and
Rev 5:12 . . . honor and *g* and blessing.

Rev 21:11 . . . shone with the *g* of God and
Rev 21:23 . . . for the *g* of God
Rev 21:26 . . . will bring their *g* and honor

GODLY
Acts 22:12 . . . He was a *g* man, deeply
Gal 6:1 . . . you who are *g* should gently
1 Tim 6:3 . . . promote a *g* life.
2 Tim 3:12 . . . to live a *g* life in Christ
Titus 1:1 . . . how to live *g* lives.
2 Pet 2:9 . . . how to rescue *g* people from
2 Pet 3:11 . . . what holy and *g* lives you

GODS *see also* IDOL
Acts 19:26 . . . aren't really *g* at all.

GOLD
Matt 2:11 . . . gifts of *g*, frankincense,
Rev 3:18 . . . advise you to buy *g* from me—

GOOD *see also* NEWS
Matt 5:45 . . . evil and the *g*, and he sends
Matt 19:17 . . . One who is *g*.
Matt 25:21 . . . Well done, my *g* and
Mark 10:18 . . . God is truly *g*.
Luke 8:15 . . . seeds that fell on the *g* soil
John 10:11 . . . I am the *g* shepherd.
Rom 3:12 . . . No one does *g*, not a single
Rom 7:19 . . . do what is *g*, but I don't.
Rom 8:28 . . . together for the *g* of those
Rom 12:2 . . . you, which is *g* and pleasing
Rom 12:9 . . . Hold tightly to what is *g*.
Gal 6:9 . . . doing what is *g*.
Eph 2:10 . . . so we can do the *g* things he
Phil 1:6 . . . who began the *g* work within
1 Tim 4:4 . . . everything God created is *g*,
1 Tim 6:12 . . . Fight the *g* fight
2 Tim 3:17 . . . people to do every *g* work.
2 Tim 4:7 . . . I have fought the *g* fight,
Titus 3:8 . . . These teachings are *g*
Heb 10:24 . . . of love and *g* works.
Jas 2:8 . . . indeed, it is *g* when you obey

GOSSIP
2 Cor 12:20 . . . slander, *g*, arrogance,

GRACE *see also* FAVOR
Rom 11:5 . . . of God's *g*—his undeserved
1 Cor 3:10 . . . Because of God's *g* to me,
1 Cor 16:23 . . . May the *g* of the Lord
2 Cor 4:15 . . . And as God's *g* reaches more
2 Cor 9:14 . . . of the overflowing *g* God has
Gal 1:15 . . . by his marvelous *g*.
Gal 2:21 . . . do not treat the *g* of God as
Gal 5:4 . . . away from God's *g*.
Eph 1:7 . . . in kindness and *g* that he
Eph 2:8 . . . saved you by his *g* when you
Eph 3:2 . . . of extending his *g* to you
Eph 3:7 . . . By God's *g* and mighty
Phil 4:23 . . . May the *g* of the
2 Thes 2:16 . . . and by his *g* gave us eternal
1 Tim 1:2 . . . Lord give you *g*, mercy,
2 Tim 1:9 . . . show us his *g* through Christ
2 Tim 2:1 . . . strong through the *g* that God
Titus 2:11 . . . For the *g* of God has
Titus 3:7 . . . Because of his *g* he declared
Heb 4:16 . . . and we will find *g* to help us
Heb 13:9 . . . comes from God's *g*, not from
Heb 13:25 . . . May God's *g* be with you all.
Jas 4:6 . . . gives us even more *g* to stand
2 Pet 3:18 . . . grow in the *g* and knowledge
Rev 22:21 . . . May the *g* of the Lord

GREED
Rom 1:29 . . . of wickedness, sin, *g*, hate,
2 Pet 2:3 . . . In their *g* they will make up

GREEDY
1 Cor 6:10 . . . are thieves, or *g* people,
Eph 5:5 . . . For a *g* person is an
Col 3:5 . . . Don't be *g*,

GRIEF
John 16:20 . . . your *g* will suddenly turn

GRIEVE
1 Thes 4:13 . . . so you will not *g* like people

GROW
1 Cor 3:6 . . . God who made it *g*.
Phil 1:25 . . . all of you *g* and experience
Jas 1:15 . . . when sin is allowed to *g*,
2 Pet 3:18 . . . Rather, you must *g* in the

GRUMBLE
1 Cor 10:10 . . . And don't *g* as some
Jas 5:9 . . . Don't *g* about

GUARD
Phil 4:7 . . . His peace will *g* your hearts
2 Thes 3:3 . . . and *g* you from
2 Pet 3:17 . . . Be on *g* so that you

GUARDIAN
Gal 3:25 . . . the law as our *g*.
1 Pet 2:25 . . . your Shepherd, the *G* of your

GUIDE
John 16:13 . . . he will *g* you into all
Gal 5:16 . . . let the Holy Spirit *g* your lives.

GUILTY
Rom 3:19 . . . entire world is *g* before God.
1 Cor 11:27 . . . *g* of sinning against
1 Jn 3:20 . . . if we feel *g*, God is greater

H

HAIRS
Matt 10:30 . . . And the very *h* on your head

HAND
Matt 6:3 . . . don't let your left *h* know what
Matt 26:64 . . . at God's right *h* and coming
Mark 12:36 . . . at my right *h* until I humble
Acts 7:55 . . . at God's right *h*.
Heb 1:13 . . . at my right *h* until I humble

HANDS
Acts 6:6 . . . they laid their *h* on them.
Acts 8:18 . . . laid their *h* on people,
Acts 13:3 . . . men laid their *h* on them and
Acts 19:6 . . . Paul laid his *h* on them,
Acts 28:8 . . . and laying his *h* on him,
1 Thes 4:11 . . . working with your *h*,
1 Tim 2:8 . . . pray with holy *h* lifted up
1 Tim 4:14 . . . church laid their *h* on you.
2 Tim 1:6 . . . when I laid my *h* on you.

HAPPY *see also* GLAD, JOY, REJOICE
Rom 12:15 . . . Be *h* with those who are *h*,
Phil 2:2 . . . make me truly *h* by agreeing
Jas 5:13 . . . Are any of you *h*?

HARDENED
Matt 13:15 . . . hearts of these people are *h*,
John 12:40 . . . and *h* their hearts—
Eph 4:18 . . . their minds and *h* their hearts

HARMONY

Rom 12:16 . . . Live in *h* with each other.
Rom 14:19 . . . aim for *h* in the church
1 Cor 12:25 . . . This makes for *h*
2 Cor 6:15 . . . What *h* can there be
2 Cor 13:11 . . . Live in *h* and peace.
Col 3:14 . . . in perfect *h*.

HARVEST

Matt 9:37 . . . The *h* is great, but
John 4:35 . . . fields are already ripe for *h*.

HATE

Matt 5:43 . . . and *h* your enemy.
Luke 6:22 . . . when people *h* you
John 3:20 . . . All who do evil *h* the light
2 Tim 3:3 . . . be cruel and *h* what is good.
Heb 1:9 . . . You love justice and *h* evil.

HEAD

John 19:2 . . . thorns and put it on his *h*,
Eph 1:22 . . . and has made him *h* over all
Eph 5:23 . . . as Christ is the *h* of the
Rev 14:14 . . . He had a gold crown on his *h*
Rev 19:12 . . . on his *h* were many crowns.

HEAL

Matt 8:7 . . . will come and *h* him.
Luke 4:23 . . . Physician, *h* yourself
Luke 10:9 . . . *H* the sick,
Luke 14:3 . . . *h* people on the Sabbath
John 4:47 . . . to Capernaum to *h* his son,
John 12:40 . . . and have me *h* them.
Acts 28:27 . . . turn to me and let me *h*

HEALED

Matt 4:23 . . . And he *h* every kind
Matt 8:16 . . . and he *h* all the sick.
Matt 9:35 . . . he *h* every kind of disease
Matt 15:30 . . . Jesus, and he *h* them all.
Mark 1:34 . . . So Jesus *h* many people
Mark 3:2 . . . If he *h* the man's
Mark 3:10 . . . He had *h* many people
Mark 5:28 . . . touch his robe, I will be *h*.
Mark 6:56 . . . all who touched him were *h*.
Luke 4:40 . . . touch of his hand *h* every
Luke 8:50 . . . have faith, and she will be *h*.
Luke 14:4 . . . the sick man and *h* him
Luke 17:19 . . . Your faith has *h* you.
Luke 18:42 . . . Your faith has *h* you.
Acts 3:16 . . . this man was *h*—
Acts 4:9 . . . want to know how he was *h*?
Acts 4:14 . . . see the man who had been *h*
Acts 8:7 . . . or lame were *h*.
Acts 28:8 . . . laying his hands on him, he *h*
Jas 5:16 . . . so that you may be *h*.
1 Pet 2:24 . . . By his wounds you are *h*.

HEAR *see also* LISTEN

Matt 11:5 . . . cured, the deaf *h*, the dead
Matt 13:14 . . . When you *h* what I say,
Mark 4:12 . . . When they *h* what I say,
Luke 7:22 . . . cured, the deaf *h*, the dead
Acts 13:7 . . . he wanted to *h* the word of
Rom 10:14 . . . how can they *h* about him
1 Cor 12:17 . . . how would you *h*?
Heb 3:7 . . . Today when you *h* his voice,
Rev 3:20 . . . If you *h* my voice and

HEART

Matt 12:34 . . . whatever is in your *h*
Matt 15:19 . . . For from the *h* come evil
Matt 22:37 . . . God with all your *h*, all your

Mark 12:33 . . . love him with all my *h* and
Acts 1:24 . . . you know every *h*. Show us
Rom 2:29 . . . changed *h* seeks praise
Rom 10:9 . . . believe in your *h* that God
Eph 3:13 . . . don't lose *h* because of

HEAVEN

Matt 11:25 . . . Father, Lord of *h* and earth,
Rom 10:6 . . . go up to *h*' (to bring Christ
2 Cor 12:2 . . . to the third *h* fourteen years
Heb 9:24 . . . He entered into *h* itself to

HELL

Matt 5:22 . . . of the fires of *h*.
Matt 16:18 . . . all the powers of *h* will not
2 Pet 2:4 . . . threw them into *h*, in gloomy

HELP

Mark 9:24 . . . but *h* me overcome
Acts 16:9 . . . to Macedonia and *h* us!
Rom 12:13 . . . be ready to *h* them.
1 Cor 12:28 . . . those who can *h* others,
Gal 6:1 . . . and humbly *h* that person back
Phil 4:16 . . . you sent *h* more than once.
2 Tim 2:7 . . . Lord will *h* you understand

HELPER

Heb 13:6 . . . The Lord is my *h*, so I will

HELPLESS

Matt 9:36 . . . confused and *h*, like sheep
Rom 5:6 . . . were utterly *h*, Christ came

HIDDEN

Matt 13:35 . . . explain things *h* since the
Mark 4:22 . . . that is *h* will eventually be
1 Cor 2:7 . . . was previously *h*, even though
Col 3:3 . . . real life is *h* with Christ in

HOLY SPIRIT *see* ADVOCATE, SPIRIT

HOLY

Mark 1:24 . . . the *H* One sent from
Luke 1:35 . . . baby to be born will be *h*,
Rom 15:16 . . . made *h* by the *H* Spirit.
1 Cor 1:2 . . . be his own *h* people.
1 Cor 1:30 . . . made us pure and *h*,
2 Cor 5:5 . . . given us his *H* Spirit.
Eph 1:4 . . . in Christ to be *h* and without
Eph 2:21 . . . becoming a *h* temple for
Eph 4:24 . . . righteous and *h*.
Col 1:22 . . . and you are *h* and blameless
1 Thes 4:7 . . . called us to live *h* lives, not
1 Thes 5:23 . . . make you *h* in every
2 Tim 1:9 . . . called us to live a *h* life.
Heb 10:29 . . . which made us *h*, as if it
1 Pet 1:16 . . . You must be *h* because I am
Rev 3:7 . . . one who is *h* and true,
Rev 4:8 . . . on saying, "Holy, *h*, holy is

HOME *see also* HOUSE

Luke 19:9 . . . has come to this *h* today,
John 14:23 . . . make our *h* with each
Acts 16:15 . . . stay at my *h*.
Eph 3:17 . . . will make his *h* in your
1 Tim 5:4 . . . show godliness at *h*
1 Pet 4:9 . . . share your *h* with those who

HONEST

Matt 22:16 . . . we know how *h* you are.
1 Thes 2:10 . . . devout and *h* and faultless

HONEY

Rev 10:9 . . . be sweet as *h* in your mouth,

HONOR *see also* EXALT
Matt 15:4 . . . God says, '*H* your father and
Luke 14:8 . . . don't sit in the seat of *h*.
John 5:23 . . . that everyone will *h* the Son,
Rom 13:3 . . . and they will *h* you.
1 Cor 6:20 . . . So you must *h* God with your
Eph 1:20 . . . the place of *h* at God's right
Eph 6:2 . . . *H* your father
Col 1:10 . . . the way you live will always *h*
Heb 13:4 . . . Give *h* to marriage,
1 Pet 2:12 . . . they will give *h* to God when
1 Pet 3:7 . . . husbands must give *h* to
Rev 4:9 . . . give glory and *h* and thanks
Rev 19:7 . . . and let us give *h* to him.

HOPE
Rom 5:4 . . . our confident *h* of salvation.
Rom 8:20 . . . with eager *h*,
Rom 8:24 . . . don't need to *h* for it.
Rom 12:12 . . . our confident *h*.
Rom 15:4 . . . give us *h* and encouragement
Rom 15:13 . . . the source of *h*,
1 Cor 13:13 . . . faith, *h*, and love—
1 Cor 15:19 . . . And if our *h* in Christ is
Eph 2:12 . . . without God and without *h*.
1 Thes 1:3 . . . and the enduring *h* you have
1 Tim 4:10 . . . struggle, for our *h* is in the
Heb 10:23 . . . wavering to the *h* we affirm,
1 Pet 3:15 . . . your Christian *h*,

HOUSE *see also* HOME, TEMPLE
Matt 7:24 . . . who builds a *h* on solid rock.
Mark 11:17 . . . be called a *h* of prayer for
John 2:17 . . . for God's *h* will consume me.

HUMAN
John 1:14 . . . So the Word became *h*
John 2:24 . . . because he knew *h* nature.
John 8:15 . . . judge me by *h* standards,
Rom 6:19 . . . weakness of your *h* nature,
1 Cor 2:5 . . . trust not in *h* wisdom but in
2 Cor 3:3 . . . of stone, but on *h* hearts.
Col 2:9 . . . of God in a *h* body.
1 Thes 2:13 . . . words as mere *h* ideas.
Heb 7:28 . . . limited by *h* weakness.

HUMBLE
Matt 11:29 . . . I am *h* and gentle at
Matt 21:5 . . . He is *h*, riding on a
Eph 4:2 . . . Always be *h* and gentle.
Phil 2:3 . . . Be *h*, thinking of
Jas 4:6 . . . but favors the *h*.
Jas 4:10 . . . *H* yourselves before the Lord,
1 Pet 3:8 . . . and keep a *h* attitude.
1 Pet 5:6 . . . So *h* yourselves under

HUMILITY
Col 3:12 . . . kindness, *h*, gentleness,
Jas 3:13 . . . works with the *h* that comes
1 Pet 5:5 . . . each other in *h*, for "God

HUNGRY
Matt 25:35 . . . For I was *h*, and you fed me.
Luke 6:21 . . . you who are *h* now, for you
John 6:35 . . . never be *h* again.
Rom 12:20 . . . enemies are *h*, feed them.
Rev 7:16 . . . never again be *h* or thirsty;

HUSBAND
Rom 7:2 . . . binds her to her *h* as long as
2 Cor 11:2 . . . bride to one *h*—Christ.
Gal 4:27 . . . lives with her *h*!
Eph 5:23 . . . For a *h* is the head
1 Tim 5:9 . . . faithful to her *h*.

HYMNS
Eph 5:19 . . . psalms and *h* and spiritual

HYPOCRITE
Matt 7:5 . . . *H*! First get rid of the log

I

IDOL *see also* GODS
1 Cor 8:4 . . . an *i* is not really a god

IDOLS
Acts 15:20 . . . eating food offered to *i*,
Rom 1:23 . . . worshiped *i* made to look
1 Cor 6:9 . . . or who worship *i*, or commit
1 Cor 8:1 . . . has been offered to *i*.
Rev 2:14 . . . sin by eating food offered to *i*

IMAGE
Col 1:15 . . . Christ is the visible *i* of
Jas 3:9 . . . made in the *i* of God.

IMPOSSIBLE
Luke 1:37 . . . For nothing is *i* with God.
Heb 11:6 . . . it is *i* to please God

INFANTS
Matt 21:16 . . . and *i* to give you praise.
1 Cor 3:1 . . . were *i* in the Christian life.

INHERITANCE *see also* POSSESSION
Gal 4:30 . . . will not share the *i*
Eph 1:14 . . . give us the *i* he promised
Col 3:24 . . . give you an *i* as your reward,
Heb 9:15 . . . receive the eternal *i* God has

INNOCENT
Matt 27:4 . . . I have betrayed an *i* man.
Matt 27:24 . . . I am *i* of this man's blood.
Rom 16:18 . . . they deceive *i* people.

INSPIRED
2 Tim 3:16 . . . All Scripture is *i* by God

INSTRUCT
2 Tim 2:25 . . . Gently *i* those who oppose

INSTRUCTIONS
1 Tim 1:18 . . . here are my *i* for you,

INSULT
1 Pet 3:9 . . . insults when people *i* you.

INSULTED
1 Pet 2:23 . . . not retaliate when he was *i*,
1 Pet 4:14 . . . be happy when you are *i*

INTEGRITY
Titus 2:7 . . . you do reflect the *i*

INVISIBLE
Rom 1:20 . . . see his *i* qualities—
Col 1:15 . . . visible image of the *i* God.
Heb 11:27 . . . his eyes on the one who is *i*.

ISAAC Patriarch, son of Abraham; born (Acts 7:8); offered to God by Abraham (Heb 11:17-19); often mentioned in NT (Luke 3:34; Gal 4:28; Heb 11:9, 17-20; Jas 2:21).

J

JACOB Patriarch, son of Isaac, grandson of Abraham; younger twin son of Issac and Rebekah; often mentioned in NT (John 4:5-6, 12; Acts 7:8-15; Rom 9:13; Heb 11:20-21).

JAMES
1. One of the 12 disciples, brother of John, son of Zebedee (Matt 10:2; Mark 3:17); called by Jesus (Matt 4:21; Luke 5:10); zealous for the Lord (Luke 9:54); wanted honor (Mark 10:35-45); witnessed the Transfiguration (Matt 17:1-9; Mark 9:2-8; Luke 9:28-36); killed by Herod Agrippa I (Acts 12:2).
2. One of the 12 disciples, son of Alphaeus (Matt 10:3; Mark 3:18; Luke 6:15); called "the younger" (Mark 15:40).
3. Half-brother of Jesus (Matt 13:55; Mark 6:3; Luke 24:10; Gal 1:19; 2:9, 12; 1 Cor 15:7), brother of Jude (Jude 1); leader of Jerusalem Council (Acts 15:13; 21:18); with select group before Pentecost (Acts 1:13); wrote letter (Jas 1:1).
4. Father of the apostle Judas, not Iscariot (Luke 6:16).
5. Son of a certain Mary, perhaps the same as the "son of Alphaeus" (Matt 27:56).

JEALOUS *see also* ENVY, ZEAL
Rom 11:14 . . . *j* of what you Gentiles have,
1 Cor 13:4 . . . Love is not *j* or boastful
Gal 5:26 . . . provoke one another, or be *j*
Jas 3:14 . . . if you are bitterly *j* and there is

JEALOUSY
Rom 13:13 . . . or in quarreling and *j*.
Gal 5:20 . . . *j*, outbursts of anger,
1 Tim 6:4 . . . arguments ending in *j*,
1 Pet 2:1 . . . with all deceit, hypocrisy, *j*,

JERICHO
Luke 10:30 . . . trip from Jerusalem to *J*,
Heb 11:30 . . . around *J* for seven days,

JERUSALEM
Matt 20:18 . . . going up to *J*, where the Son
Luke 2:22 . . . parents took him to *J*
Luke 4:9 . . . Then the devil took him to *J*,
Acts 1:8 . . . about me everywhere—in *J*,
Rev 21:10 . . . he showed me the holy city, *J*,

JESUS Family line (Matt 1:1-17; Luke 3:23-38); birth announced (Matt 1:18-25; Luke 1:26-38); born in Bethlehem (Luke 2:1-20); circumcised and presented at Temple (Luke 2:21-40); visited by Magi (Matt 2:1-12); escape to and return from Egypt (Matt 2:13-23); amazed the Temple scholars (Luke 2:41-50); summary of youth (Luke 2:51-52); baptized by John (Matt 3:13-17; Mark 1:9-11; Luke 3:21-22; John 1:32-34); tempted by Satan (Matt 4:1-11; Mark 1:12-13; Luke 4:1-13); ministered in Galilee (Matt 4:12–18:35; Mark 1:14–9:50); transfigured on a mountain (Matt 17:1-13; Mark 9:2-13; Luke 9:28-36; 2 Pet 1:16-18); triumphal entry (Matt 21:1-11; Mark 11:1-11; Luke 19:28-44; John 12:12-19); the Last Supper (Matt 26:17-35; Mark 14:12-31; Luke 22:7-38; John 13–17); betrayed and tried (Matt 26:36–27:31; Mark 14:32–15:20; Luke 22:39–23:25; John 18:1–19:16); crucified, died, and was buried (Matt 27:32-66; Mark 15:21-47; Luke 23:26-56; John 19:17-42); rose again and appeared to followers (Matt 28; Mark 16; Luke 24; John 20–21; Acts 1:1-11; 7:55-56; 9:3-6; 1 Cor 15:1-8; Rev 1:1-20); ascended to heaven (Mark 16:19; Luke 24:50-53; John 1:51; Acts 1:9; Eph 4:8).

JEWS
Matt 2:2 . . . the newborn king of the *J*?
John 19:3 . . . Hail! King of the *J*!
Acts 20:21 . . . message for *J* and Greeks
1 Cor 9:20 . . . with the *J*, I lived like a Jew
1 Cor 12:13 . . . *J*, some are Gentiles,
Gal 2:8 . . . Peter as the apostle to the *J*
Eph 3:6 . . . Gentiles and *J* who believe

JOHN
1. The Baptist, son of Zechariah and Elizabeth (Luke 1:5-25, 57-80); called to prepare the way for the Messiah (Luke 3:1-6; John 1:19-28); called to preach and baptize (Matt 3:1-12; Mark 1:1-8); preached repentance (Luke 3:7-20); baptized Jesus (Matt 3:13-17; Luke 3:21-22); confirmed Jesus' ministry (Matt 3:11-12; Mark 1:7-8; Luke 3:15-18; John 3:22-36; 5:33); ministry compared to Elijah (Matt 11:11-19; Mark 9:11-13; Luke 7:24-35); arrested and beheaded by Herod Antipas (Matt 14:1-12; Mark 6:14-29; Luke 9:7-9).
2. One of the 12 disciples, brother of James, son of Zebedee (Matt 10:2; Mark 3:17); witnessed the Transfiguration (Matt 17:1-9; Mark 9:2-8; Luke 9:28-36); inner circle of Jesus' followers (Matt 17:1; Mark 5:37; 9:2; 13:3; Luke 8:51; 9:28; Gal 2:9); with Peter, healed a man and was arrested (Acts 3–4); with Peter, rebuked sorcerer (Acts 8:14-25); wrote fourth Gospel (John 13:23-25; *see also* 20:2; 21:20-25), letters of John (the "elder," 2 Jn 1; 3 Jn 1), and Revelation (the "servant," Rev 1:1, 9; 22:8).

JOY *see also* GLAD, HAPPY, REJOICE
Matt 2:10 . . . they were filled with *j*!
John 15:11 . . . you will be filled with my *j*.
John 16:20 . . . turn to wonderful *j*.
Acts 2:28 . . . you will fill me with the *j*
Acts 2:46 . . . their meals with great *j*
Acts 11:23 . . . filled with *j*,
Acts 13:52 . . . believers were filled with *j*
Gal 5:22 . . . fruit in our lives: love, *j*, peace,
Phil 4:1 . . . you are my *j* and the crown I
1 Thes 1:6 . . . received the message with *j*
1 Thes 2:19 . . . what gives us hope and *j*,
1 Thes 3:9 . . . we have great *j*
Jas 1:2 . . . it an opportunity for great *j*.
1 Jn 1:4 . . . you may fully share our *j*.

JUDEA
Matt 2:1 . . . was born in Bethlehem in *J*,
Luke 3:1 . . . Pilate was governor over *J*;
Acts 1:8 . . . throughout *J*, in Samaria,
1 Thes 2:14 . . . in God's churches in *J*

JUDGE
Matt 7:1 . . . Do not *j* others,
Matt 16:27 . . . will *j* all people according
John 5:22 . . . absolute authority to *j*,
John 5:27 . . . authority to *j* everyone
John 5:30 . . . I *j* as God tells me.
John 12:47 . . . not *j* those who hear me
Acts 7:35 . . . you a ruler and *j* over us?
Acts 10:42 . . . *j* of all—the living and
Rom 2:16 . . . Jesus, will *j* everyone's secret
2 Tim 4:1 . . . Jesus, who will someday *j*
Heb 10:30 . . . The Lord will *j* his own
Jas 4:12 . . . So what right do you have to *j*

1 Pet 1:17 ... He will *j* or reward you
Rev 14:7 ... he will sit as *j*.
Rev 20:4 ... given the authority to *j*.

JUST *see also* RIGHT, RIGHTEOUS
Matt 5:45 ... rain on the *j* and the unjust
1 Cor 11:1 ... imitate me, *j* as I imitate
1 Jn 1:9 ... he is faithful and *j* to forgive
Rev 15:3 ... *J* and true are your ways,
Rev 16:5 ... You are *j*, O Holy One,
Rev 16:7 ... your judgments are true and *j*.
Rev 19:2 ... His judgments are true and *j*.

JUSTICE *see also* RIGHTEOUSNESS
Matt 5:6 ... who hunger and thirst for *j*,
Matt 12:18 ... proclaim *j* to the nations.
Luke 11:42 ... you ignore *j* and the love of
Luke 18:3 ... Give me *j* in this dispute
Acts 17:31 ... *j* by the man
Rom 2:2 ... God, in his *j*, will punish
2 Thes 1:5 ... persecution to show his *j*
2 Thes 1:6 ... In his *j* he will pay back
Heb 1:8 ... You rule with a scepter of *j*.
Heb 11:33 ... ruled with *j*,

JUSTIFY *see also* RIGHT, RIGHTEOUS
Luke 10:29 ... wanted to *j* his actions,

KEEP *see also* GUARD, OBEY, PROTECT
Acts 2:24 ... death could not *k* him in its
Rom 10:3 ... by trying to *k* the law.
Rom 14:22 ... *k* it between yourself
1 Cor 1:8 ... He will *k* you strong
1 Cor 7:19 ... *k* God's commandments.
Eph 4:3 ... effort to *k* yourselves united
1 Tim 5:22 ... *K* yourself pure.
2 Tim 4:5 ... But you should *k* a clear mind
Jude 21 ... *k* yourselves safe in God's love.
Rev 12:17 ... *k* God's commandments

KEPT
John 17:6 ... and they have *k* your word.
Heb 11:27 ... going because he *k* his eyes
1 Pet 1:4 ... *k* in heaven for you, pure

KILL
Mark 10:34 ... flog him with a whip, and *k*
1 Tim 1:9 ... who *k* their father or mother

KINDNESS
Rom 2:4 ... his *k* is intended to turn you
Rom 3:24 ... with undeserved *k*, declares
Rom 12:8 ... gift for showing *k* to others,
2 Cor 6:1 ... marvelous gift of God's *k*
2 Cor 8:1 ... God in his *k* has done through
2 Cor 10:1 ... gentleness and *k* of Christ—
Gal 5:22 ... peace, patience, *k*, goodness,
Eph 2:7 ... his grace and *k* toward us,
Col 3:12 ... mercy, *k*, humility,
Titus 3:4 ... revealed his *k* and love,
1 Pet 2:3 ... of the Lord's *k*.

KINGDOM
Matt 3:2 ... for the *K* of Heaven is near.
Matt 5:10 ... right, for the *K* of Heaven is
Matt 6:10 ... May your *K* come soon.
Matt 7:21 ... will enter the *K* of Heaven.
Matt 18:4 ... greatest in the *K* of Heaven.
Matt 19:12 ... sake of the *K* of Heaven.
Matt 19:23 ... to enter the *K* of Heaven.

Matt 20:1 ... For the *K* of Heaven is
Mark 9:1 ... they see the *K* of God arrive
Luke 10:11 ... know this—the *K* of God is
Luke 12:31 ... Seek the *K* of God
Luke 13:18 ... What is the *K* of God like?
Luke 17:20 ... When will the *K* of God
Luke 23:42 ... come into your *K*.
John 3:3 ... you cannot see the *K* of God.
John 18:36 ... But my *K* is not of
1 Cor 6:10 ... will inherit the *K* of God.
1 Cor 15:24 ... will turn the *K* over to God
Gal 5:21 ... will not inherit the *K* of God.
Eph 5:5 ... will inherit the *K* of Christ

KNEE
Rom 14:11 ... every *k* will bend to me,
Phil 2:10 ... at the name of Jesus every *k*
Heb 12:12 ... strengthen your weak *k*.

KNELT
Matt 8:2 ... approached him and *k*
Matt 9:18 ... came and *k* before him.
Matt 17:14 ... came and *k* before Jesus
Matt 27:29 ... *k* before him in mockery
Acts 20:36 ... speaking, he *k* and prayed
Acts 21:5 ... There we *k*, prayed,

KNOCK
Rev 3:20 ... I stand at the door and *k*.

KNOW
Matt 6:3 ... don't let your left hand *k*
Mark 12:24 ... you don't *k* the Scriptures,
Luke 13:25 ... will reply, 'I don't *k*
Luke 23:34 ... they don't *k* what they are
John 3:11 ... what we *k* and have seen,
John 6:69 ... we *k* you are the Holy One
John 7:28 ... Yes, you *k* me, and you
John 8:32 ... And you will *k* the truth,
John 10:4 ... because they *k* his voice.
John 10:27 ... I *k* them, and they follow
Acts 1:24 ... O Lord, you *k* every heart.
Rom 1:19 ... They *k* the truth
Rom 12:16 ... And don't think you *k* it all!
1 Cor 2:11 ... no one can *k* God's thoughts
Phil 3:10 ... I want to *k* Christ and
Col 1:10 ... you learn to *k* God better and
Jas 4:17 ... it is sin to *k* what you ought
1 Pet 2:19 ... do what you *k* is right and
1 Jn 2:3 ... we can be sure that we *k* him
1 Jn 2:29 ... Since we *k* that Christ
1 Jn 3:1 ... they don't *k* him.
1 Jn 3:24 ... And we *k* he lives in us
1 Jn 4:8 ... does not *k* God, for God
1 Jn 5:15 ... And since we *k* he hears us
Rev 3:15 ... I *k* all the things you do,

KNOWLEDGE
Luke 11:52 ... the key to *k*
Rom 2:20 ... gives you complete *k*
2 Cor 2:14 ... to spread the *k* of Christ
Eph 1:17 ... grow in your *k* of God.
Eph 4:13 ... our faith and *k* of God's Son
Phil 1:9 ... will keep on growing in *k* and
Col 1:9 ... to give you complete *k* of his
Col 2:3 ... treasures of wisdom and *k*.
Heb 10:26 ... we have received *k* of the
2 Pet 1:5 ... and moral excellence with *k*,
2 Pet 1:8 ... *k* of our Lord Jesus Christ.
2 Pet 3:18 ... the grace and *k* of our Lord

L

LAID
Acts 6:6 . . . as they *l* their hands on them.
Acts 8:18 . . . the apostles *l* their hands on
1 Tim 4:14 . . . elders of the church *l* their

LAMB
Mark 14:12 . . . the Passover *l* is sacrificed,
John 1:29 . . . and said, "Look! The *L* of God
Acts 8:32 . . . And as a *l* is silent before
1 Pet 1:19 . . . sinless, spotless *L* of God.
Rev 5:6 . . . Then I saw a *L* that looked as
Rev 5:12 . . . Worthy is the *L* who was
Rev 7:14 . . . robes in the blood of the *L*
Rev 15:3 . . . the song of the *L*:
Rev 17:14 . . . to war against the *L*, but the
Rev 19:9 . . . to the wedding feast of the *L*.
Rev 21:23 . . . and the *L* is its light.

LAME
Matt 11:5 . . . blind see, the *l* walk,
Matt 15:31 . . . the *l* were walking,
Luke 14:21 . . . the blind, and the *l*.
Heb 12:13 . . . weak and *l* will not fall

LAMP
Matt 6:22 . . . Your eye is a *l* that
Luke 8:16 . . . No one lights a *l* and then

LAMPSTANDS
Rev 1:12 . . . I saw seven gold *l*.
Rev 1:20 . . . the seven gold *l*:

LANGUAGE
1 Cor 14:19 . . . in an unknown *l*.
Eph 4:29 . . . or abusive *l*. Let everything
Col 3:8 . . . slander, and dirty *l*.
Rev 7:9 . . . and tribe and people and *l*,

LAST
Acts 2:17 . . . In the *l* days,
1 Cor 15:52 . . . *l* trumpet is blown.
2 Tim 3:1 . . . that in the *l* days there will
2 Pet 3:3 . . . that in the *l* days scoffers
Jude 18 . . . you that in the *l* times there
Rev 1:17 . . . I am the First and the *L*.
Rev 22:13 . . . the First and the *L*,

LAUGHTER
Jas 4:9 . . . instead of *l*, and gloom

LAW *see also* INSTRUCTIONS
Matt 5:17 . . . to abolish the *l* of Moses or
Matt 22:40 . . . The entire *l* and all the
Mark 7:8 . . . ignore God's *l* and substitute
John 1:17 . . . For the *l* was given
Rom 2:15 . . . that God's *l* is written in
Rom 7:22 . . . I love God's *l* with all my
Rom 7:25 . . . I really want to obey God's *l*,
Rom 8:3 . . . did what the *l* could not do.
Rom 9:31 . . . with God by keeping the *l*,
1 Cor 9:9 . . . For the *l* of Moses
1 Cor 9:21 . . . I obey the *l* of Christ.
Gal 5:14 . . . the whole *l* can be summed
Gal 6:2 . . . this way obey the *l* of Christ.
Eph 2:15 . . . the system of *l* with its
Phil 3:6 . . . I obeyed the *l* without fault.
1 Tim 1:8 . . . know that the *l* is good when
Jas 1:25 . . . into the perfect *l* that sets
Jas 2:8 . . . obey the royal *l* as found in

LAZY
Rom 12:11 . . . Never be *l*, but work
1 Tim 5:13 . . . they will learn to be *l*

LEAD
Rom 6:22 . . . things that *l* to holiness and
Rev 7:17 . . . He will *l* them to

LEADER
Mark 10:43 . . . a *l* among you must be
Luke 22:26 . . . *l* should be like a servant.
3 Jn 9 . . . to be the *l*, refuses to have

LEARN
Col 1:10 . . . you *l* to know God
1 Tim 2:11 . . . Women should *l* quietly and

LED
Luke 4:1 . . . He was *l* by the Spirit
Acts 8:32 . . . He was *l* like a sheep
Rom 8:14 . . . all who are *l* by the Spirit

LEND
Luke 6:34 . . . Even sinners will *l* to other

LIAR
Rom 3:4 . . . everyone else is a *l*, God is true.
1 Jn 1:10 . . . calling God a *l* and showing
1 Jn 2:4 . . . that person is a *l* and is not
1 Jn 5:10 . . . calling God a *l* because they

LIE
Matt 5:11 . . . persecute you and *l*
Rom 1:25 . . . about God for a *l*.
Col 3:9 . . . Don't *l* to each other,

LIES
John 8:44 . . . the father of *l*.
Rom 3:13 . . . filled with *l*.
Eph 4:14 . . . to trick us with *l* so
Eph 4:25 . . . So stop telling *l*.
2 Thes 2:11 . . . they will believe these *l*.
1 Pet 3:10 . . . your lips from telling *l*.
2 Pet 2:3 . . . make up clever *l* to get
Rev 14:5 . . . They have told no *l*;

LIFE
Matt 7:14 . . . But the gateway to *l* is very
Matt 18:8 . . . to enter eternal *l* with only
Matt 20:28 . . . and to give his *l* as a ransom
Mark 8:35 . . . to hang on to your *l*,
Luke 6:9 . . . a day to save *l* or to destroy
Luke 9:24 . . . give up your *l* for my sake,
Luke 12:25 . . . single moment to your *l*?
John 1:4 . . . The Word gave *l* to everything
John 3:15 . . . will have eternal *l*.
John 5:24 . . . passed from death into *l*.
John 6:35 . . . I am the bread of *l*.
John 6:68 . . . the words that give eternal *l*.
John 10:10 . . . a rich and satisfying *l*.
John 14:6 . . . the truth, and the *l*.
Rom 5:10 . . . be saved through the *l* of his
Rom 6:23 . . . is eternal *l* through Christ
Rom 8:38 . . . death nor *l*, neither angels
2 Cor 3:6 . . . the Spirit gives *l*.
Phil 4:3 . . . written in the Book of *L*.
1 Pet 3:7 . . . God's gift of new *l*.
Rev 22:2 . . . a tree of *l*, bearing twelve
Rev 22:17 . . . from the water of *l*.
Rev 22:19 . . . in the tree of *l* and in the

LIGHT
Matt 5:14 . . . You are the *l* of the world—
Luke 2:32 . . . He is a *l* to reveal God to
Luke 11:33 . . . its *l* can be seen by all
John 1:4 . . . life brought *l* to everyone.
John 1:9 . . . who is the true *l*, who gives
John 3:21 . . . come to the *l* so others can

John 9:5 . . . I am the *l* of the world.
2 Cor 4:6 . . . said, "Let there be *l* in the
2 Cor 6:14 . . . can *l* live with darkness?
2 Cor 11:14 . . . as an angel of *l*.
1 Pet 2:9 . . . his wonderful *l*.
1 Jn 1:5 . . . God is *l*, and there is
1 Jn 1:7 . . . living in the *l*, as God is in
1 Jn 2:9 . . . I am living in the *l*,
Rev 21:23 . . . the Lamb is its *l*.

LIGHTNING
Matt 24:27 . . . For as the *l* flashes in the
Matt 28:3 . . . face shone like *l*, and his
Luke 10:18 . . . from heaven like *l*!
Rev 4:5 . . . came flashes of *l* and the

LION
1 Pet 5:8 . . . like a roaring *l*,
Rev 5:5 . . . Look, the *L* of the

LIPS
Matt 15:8 . . . honor me with their *l*,
Rom 3:13 . . . venom drips from their *l*.
1 Pet 3:10 . . . evil and your *l* from telling

LISTEN *see also* HEAR
Mark 9:7 . . . dearly loved Son. *L* to him.
John 10:27 . . . My sheep *l* to my
1 Tim 2:12 . . . Let them *l* quietly.
Jas 1:19 . . . be quick to *l*, slow to speak,
1 Jn 4:6 . . . they do not *l* to us.
Rev 1:3 . . . he blesses all who *l* to its
Rev 2:7 . . . to hear must *l* to the Spirit

LIVE
Matt 4:4 . . . People do not *l* by bread
John 14:19 . . . Since I *l*, you also will *l*.
Rom 13:13 . . . we must *l* decent lives
Rom 14:7 . . . we don't *l* for ourselves
2 Cor 5:7 . . . For we *l* by believing
2 Cor 6:16 . . . said: "I will *l* in them and
Gal 2:20 . . . no longer I who *l*, but Christ
Col 1:19 . . . was pleased to *l* in Christ,
1 Thes 4:11 . . . your goal to *l* a quiet life,
1 Thes 5:13 . . . And *l* peacefully with
1 Tim 2:2 . . . so that we can *l* peaceful and
1 Tim 4:16 . . . close watch on how you *l*
2 Tim 3:12 . . . who wants to *l* a godly life
Heb 10:38 . . . righteous ones will *l* by faith.
1 Pet 1:17 . . . So you must *l* in reverent

LOAVES
Mark 6:41 . . . took the five *l* and two fish,
Mark 8:6 . . . took the seven *l*, thanked God

LOCUSTS
Matt 3:4 . . . he ate *l* and wild honey.
Rev 9:3 . . . Then *l* came from

LOOK
Rom 14:10 . . . Why do you *l* down on
Phil 2:4 . . . Don't *l* out only
Jas 1:25 . . . But if you *l* carefully into

LOST
Luke 15:4 . . . and one of them gets *l*,
Luke 15:6 . . . I have found my *l* sheep.
Luke 15:9 . . . have found my *l* coin.
Luke 15:24 . . . He was *l*, but now he

LOVE
Matt 5:46 . . . If you *l* only those
Matt 6:24 . . . hate one and *l* the other;
Matt 10:37 . . . If you *l* your father or
Matt 19:19 . . . *L* your neighbor

Matt 22:37 . . . You must *l* the Lord your
Mark 10:21 . . . Jesus felt genuine *l* for him.
Luke 6:27 . . . I say, *l* your enemies!
John 5:42 . . . have God's *l* within you.
John 13:34 . . . *L* each other.
John 15:9 . . . Remain in my *l*.
John 15:13 . . . is no greater *l* than to lay
John 21:15 . . . do you *l* me more than
Rom 5:8 . . . showed his great *l* for us by
Rom 8:28 . . . of those who *l* God and are
Rom 8:35 . . . us from Christ's *l*?
Rom 8:39 . . . us from the *l* of God that is
Rom 13:10 . . . *L* does no wrong
1 Cor 13:13 . . . greatest of these is *l*.
Gal 5:22 . . . *l*, joy, peace,
Eph 3:18 . . . how deep his *l* is.
Eph 4:15 . . . the truth in *l*, growing in
1 Tim 6:10 . . . For the *l* of money is the
Heb 13:5 . . . Don't *l* money;
1 Pet 4:8 . . . for *l* covers a multitude
1 Jn 4:7 . . . for *l* comes from God.
1 Jn 4:16 . . . God is *l*, and all who
1 Jn 4:18 . . . perfect *l* expels all fear.

LOYALTY
Prov 19:22 . . . *L* makes a person

MADE *see also* CREATED
Matt 19:4 . . . *m* them male and female.
Matt 19:28 . . . when the world is *m* new
2 Cor 5:1 . . . an eternal body *m* for us by
Heb 4:3 . . . since he *m* the world.
Rev 13:8 . . . before the world was *m*—
Rev 14:7 . . . him who *m* the heavens,

MAJESTY
Jude 25 . . . All glory, *m*, power, and

MAKE
Matt 28:19 . . . *m* disciples of all
Heb 8:5 . . . you *m* everything according to

MAN
1 Cor 15:45 . . . The first *m*, Adam,
Eph 5:31 . . . A *m* leaves his father and
1 Tim 2:5 . . . the *m* Christ Jesus.

MANGER
Luke 2:7 . . . cloth and laid him in a *m*,
Luke 2:12 . . . strips of cloth, lying in a *m*.

MANNA
John 6:49 . . . Your ancestors ate *m* in the
Rev 2:17 . . . some of the *m* that has been

MARY
1. Mother of Jesus, the foretold virgin (Matt 1:16-25; Luke 1:26-38); psalmist of the Magnificat (Luke 1:46-56); gave birth in Bethlehem (Luke 2:5-20); at first sign (miracle) of Jesus (John 2:1-5); at the cross (John 19:25-27); in upper room after the ascension (Acts 1:14); Jesus assigned her care to John (John 19:25-27).
2. Mary Magdalene, former demoniac, supporter of Jesus (Luke 8:1-3); was at the cross and Jesus' burial (Matt 27:55-61; Mark 15:40-47; John 19:25); saw angel after resurrection (Matt 28:1-10; Mark 16:1-9; Luke 24:10); saw Jesus after resurrection (John 20:1-18).

3. Sister of Martha and Lazarus (Luke 10:38-42; John 11; 12:1-8).
4. Mother of James and Joseph (Matt 27:56; Mark 15:40, 47; 16:1).
5. Mother of John Mark (Acts 12:12).
6. A woman greeted by Paul in Rome (Rom 16:6).

MASTER
Rom 6:14 . . . Sin is no longer your *m*,
2 Tim 2:21 . . . ready for the *M* to use you
Jude 4 . . . denied our only *M* and Lord,

MASTERS
Matt 6:24 . . . No one can serve two *m*.

MATURE
1 Cor 14:20 . . . but be *m* in understanding
2 Cor 13:9 . . . that you will become *m*.
Eph 4:13 . . . we will be *m* in the Lord,
Phil 3:15 . . . all who are spiritually *m* agree
Heb 6:1 . . . *m* in our understanding.
1 Jn 2:13 . . . who are *m* in the faith

MERCIFUL
Matt 5:7 . . . God blesses those who are *m*,
Luke 1:54 . . . and remembered to be *m*.
Heb 2:17 . . . *m* and faithful High Priest
Jas 2:13 . . . God will be *m* when he judges

MERCY *see also* COMPASSION, FORGIVE
Matt 5:7 . . . for they will be shown *m*.
Matt 9:13 . . . I want you to show *m*,
Matt 18:33 . . . just as I had *m* on you?
Matt 23:23 . . . law—justice, *m*, and faith.
Rom 11:32 . . . have *m* on everyone.
2 Cor 4:1 . . . God in his *m* has given us
Gal 1:6 . . . through the loving *m* of Christ.
Eph 2:4 . . . But God is so rich in *m*, and
1 Tim 1:13 . . . But God had *m* on me
Titus 3:5 . . . but because of his *m*.
Heb 4:16 . . . we will receive his *m*,
Jas 3:17 . . . It is full of *m* and good
1 Pet 1:3 . . . by his great *m* that we
Jude 22 . . . show *m* to those whose faith

MESSENGER
Matt 11:10 . . . am sending my *m* ahead
2 Cor 12:7 . . . *m* from Satan to torment
Phil 2:25 . . . he was your *m* to help me
Heb 3:1 . . . to be God's *m* and High Priest.

MIGHTY
Eph 1:19 . . . This is the same *m* power
Eph 6:10 . . . with the Lord and in his *m*
Heb 1:3 . . . sustains everything by the *m*
1 Pet 5:6 . . . yourselves under the *m*

MILK
1 Cor 3:2 . . . feed you with *m*, not with
1 Pet 2:2 . . . must crave pure spiritual *m*

MIND
Mark 12:30 . . . all your soul, all your *m*,
Rom 8:6 . . . Spirit control your *m*
1 Cor 2:9 . . . heard, and no *m* has imagined
2 Tim 4:5 . . . clear *m* in every situation.

MINDS
Luke 24:45 . . . opened their *m*
2 Cor 4:4 . . . has blinded the *m* of those
Col 2:18 . . . sinful *m* have made them
Heb 8:10 . . . I will put my laws in their *m*,
Heb 10:16 . . . I will write them on their *m*.

MIRACLES
Matt 7:22 . . . and performed many *m*
Matt 13:54 . . . and the power to do *m*?
Mark 6:2 . . . power to perform such *m*?
Luke 19:37 . . . wonderful *m* they had seen.
Acts 2:22 . . . by doing powerful *m*,
Acts 8:13 . . . *m* Philip performed.
Acts 19:11 . . . to perform unusual *m*.
1 Cor 12:28 . . . those who do *m*, those who
2 Cor 12:12 . . . and *m* among you.
Gal 3:5 . . . Spirit and work *m* among you
Heb 2:4 . . . and various *m* and gifts of

MIRROR
1 Cor 13:12 . . . as in a cloudy *m*,
Jas 1:23 . . . glancing at your face in a *m*.

MONEY *see also* POSSESSIONS, TREASURE(S), WEALTH
Matt 6:24 . . . serve both God and *m*.
Luke 3:14 . . . Don't extort *m* or make false
Luke 16:13 . . . serve both God and *m*.
1 Tim 3:3 . . . and not love *m*
1 Tim 6:10 . . . love of *m* is the root of all
1 Tim 6:17 . . . and not to trust in their *m*,
1 Jn 3:17 . . . If someone has enough *m*

MORNING
2 Pet 1:19 . . . and Christ the *M* Star shines
Rev 2:28 . . . give them the *m* star!
Rev 22:16 . . . I am the bright *m* star.

MOSES
Deliverer of Israel from Egypt, Lawgiver, servant of God; "drawn out" of the Nile, raised in Pharaoh's house; killed an Egyptian and fled to Midian (Acts 7:24); Passover and the Exodus (1 Cor 10:2); song of salvation and praise (Rev 15:3); received the Law at Sinai (John 1:17; Heb 12:21); face glowed with the Lord's glory (2 Cor 3:13-15); died and was praised (Heb 3:2).

MOTHER *see also* PARENTS
Matt 10:37 . . . father or *m* more than you
Matt 12:48 . . . Who is my *m*?
Mark 10:19 . . . Honor your father and *m*.
John 19:27 . . . disciple, "Here is your *m*."
Eph 5:31 . . . A man leaves his father and *m*
Eph 6:2 . . . Honor your father and *m*.

MOTIVES
1 Cor 4:5 . . . will reveal our private *m*.
Phil 1:18 . . . Whether their *m* are false or
1 Thes 2:3 . . . with any deceit or impure *m*
1 Thes 2:4 . . . He alone examines the *m* of
Jas 4:3 . . . because your *m* are all wrong—

MOUNTAIN
Matt 17:20 . . . say to this *m*, 'Move
Mark 9:2 . . . led them up a high *m*
Mark 9:9 . . . went back down the *m*,
2 Pet 1:18 . . . with him on the holy *m*.

MOUTH
Matt 4:4 . . . word that comes from the *m*
Rom 10:9 . . . *m* that Jesus is Lord
Rev 2:16 . . . with the sword of my *m*.

MURDER
Matt 5:21 . . . If you commit *m*,
Rom 13:9 . . . You must not *m*.
Jas 2:11 . . . You must not *m*.

MUSIC
Eph 5:19 . . . and making *m* to the Lord

MYSTERY *see also* SECRET
1 Tim 3:9 . . . to the *m* of the faith
1 Tim 3:16 . . . the great *m* of our faith:
Rev 1:20 . . . the *m* of the seven stars

NAILED
Mark 15:24 . . . soldiers *n* him to the cross.
Acts 2:23 . . . you *n* him to a cross

NAILING
Col 2:14 . . . away by *n* it to the cross.
Heb 6:6 . . . are *n* him to the cross

NAME *see also* REPUTATION
Matt 1:21 . . . you are to *n* him Jesus,
Matt 24:5 . . . come in my *n*, claiming, 'I am
Matt 28:19 . . . baptizing them in the *n* of
Luke 11:2 . . . may your *n* be kept holy.
John 16:24 . . . Ask, using my *n*, and you
Acts 4:12 . . . no other *n* under heaven
Rom 10:13 . . . calls on the *n* of the Lord
Phil 2:9 . . . gave him the *n* above all
Phil 2:10 . . . that at the *n* of Jesus every
Jas 5:14 . . . with oil in the *n* of the Lord.
Rev 2:17 . . . stone will be engraved a new *n*
Rev 3:12 . . . write on them the *n*
Rev 20:15 . . . whose *n* was not found

NARROW
Matt 7:14 . . . the gateway to life is very *n*

NATIONS *see also* GENTILES
Matt 12:18 . . . proclaim justice to the *n*.
Matt 24:14 . . . so that all *n* will hear it;
Matt 28:19 . . . make disciples of all the *n*,
Mark 11:17 . . . house of prayer for all *n*,
Gal 3:8 . . . All *n* will be blessed through
Rev 21:24 . . . The *n* will walk in its light,
Rev 22:2 . . . for medicine to heal the *n*.

NEED
Matt 6:2 . . . give to someone in *n*,
Acts 2:45 . . . the money with those in *n*.
Acts 20:35 . . . you can help those in *n* by
Rom 12:13 . . . God's people are in *n*,
Eph 4:28 . . . give generously to others in *n*.
Phil 4:6 . . . Tell God what you *n*, and
Jas 1:5 . . . If you *n* wisdom, ask our

NEIGHBOR
Mark 12:31 . . . Love your *n* as yourself.
Luke 10:29 . . . And who is my *n*?
Rom 13:8 . . . If you love your *n*, you will
Gal 5:14 . . . Love your *n* as yourself.
Jas 2:8 . . . Love your *n* as yourself.

NEW
Mark 16:17 . . . will speak in *n* languages.
Luke 22:20 . . . cup is the *n* covenant
Rom 6:4 . . . we also may live *n* lives.
Rom 12:2 . . . you into a *n* person
1 Cor 11:25 . . . cup is the *n* covenant
2 Cor 3:6 . . . but under the *n* covenant,
2 Cor 5:17 . . . is gone; a *n* life has begun!
Gal 6:15 . . . into a *n* creation.
Eph 4:24 . . . Put on your *n* nature,
Heb 8:8 . . . when I will make a *n* covenant

Heb 9:15 . . . mediates a *n* covenant
Heb 12:24 . . . the *n* covenant
2 Pet 3:13 . . . new heavens and *n* earth he
Rev 2:17 . . . a *n* name that no one
Rev 21:1 . . . *n* heaven and a *n* earth,

NEWS
Mark 1:15 . . . sins and believe the Good *N*!
Acts 13:32 . . . to bring you this Good *N*.
Rom 1:16 . . . not ashamed of this Good *N*
Rom 10:17 . . . the Good *N* about Christ.
Rom 15:16 . . . I bring you the Good *N*
1 Cor 1:17 . . . to preach the Good *N*—
1 Cor 9:16 . . . preach the Good *N*!
1 Cor 9:23 . . . to spread the Good *N*
1 Cor 15:1 . . . the Good *N* I preached
2 Cor 4:4 . . . glorious light of the Good *N*.
2 Cor 11:7 . . . preaching God's Good *N*
Eph 6:15 . . . comes from the Good *N*
Col 1:5 . . . heard the truth of the Good *N*.
1 Thes 2:4 . . . entrusted with the Good *N*.
2 Thes 1:8 . . . obey the Good *N* of our Lord
2 Tim 1:10 . . . through the Good *N*.
2 Tim 4:5 . . . telling others the Good *N*,
Rev 14:6 . . . the eternal Good *N*

NIGHT
Rev 21:25 . . . there is no *n* there.

NOAH
Builder of great boat, survivor of the Flood (Matt 24:37-38; Luke 17:26-27; Heb 11:7; 1 Pet 3:20; 2 Pet 2:5).

OBEDIENT
Luke 2:51 . . . with them and was *o* to them.
Rom 16:19 . . . that you are *o* to the Lord.
2 Cor 9:13 . . . that you are *o* to the Good
1 Pet 1:14 . . . as God's *o* children.

OBEY
Matt 28:20 . . . to *o* all the commands
Luke 8:21 . . . hear God's word and *o* it.
John 3:36 . . . who doesn't *o* the Son
John 14:15 . . . *o* my commandments.
Acts 4:19 . . . to *o* you rather than him?
Acts 5:29 . . . We must *o* God rather than
Rom 6:17 . . . wholeheartedly *o* this
2 Cor 10:5 . . . teach them to *o* Christ.
Gal 3:10 . . . and *o* all the commands
Eph 2:2 . . . who refuse to *o* God.
Eph 6:1 . . . Children, *o* your parents
Rev 22:7 . . . Blessed are those who *o* the

OFFERING
Rom 15:26 . . . taken up an *o* for the poor
Phil 2:17 . . . faithful service is an *o*
Heb 10:11 . . . *o* the same sacrifices again
Heb 10:14 . . . that one *o* he forever made
Heb 11:4 . . . Abel's *o* gave evidence that he

OFFERINGS
Heb 10:5 . . . animal sacrifices or sin *o*.

OIL
Heb 1:9 . . . pouring out the *o* of joy

ORPHANS
John 14:18 . . . will not abandon you as *o*—
Jas 1:27 . . . caring for *o* and widows in

PAGANS
Matt 5:47 . . . Even *p* do that.
1 Cor 12:2 . . . when you were still *p*, you

PAID
1 Cor 7:23 . . . God *p* a high price for you,
1 Tim 5:17 . . . should be respected and *p*

PAIN
Heb 13:3 . . . as if you felt their *p* in your
Rev 21:4 . . . death or sorrow or crying or *p*.

PANIC
Mark 13:7 . . . threats of wars, but don't *p*.

PARABLES
Matt 13:35 . . . I will speak to you in *p*.
Luke 8:10 . . . I use *p* to teach the others

PARADISE
Luke 23:43 . . . you will be with me in *p*.
2 Cor 12:4 . . . that I was caught up to *p*

PARALYZED
Mark 2:3 . . . men arrived carrying a *p* man
Acts 9:33 . . . been *p* and bedridden

PARENTS
Rom 1:30 . . . and they disobey their *p*.
Eph 6:1 . . . Children, obey your *p*

PARTIES
Rom 13:13 . . . of wild *p* and drunkenness,
1 Pet 4:3 . . . and drunkenness and wild *p*,

PASSOVER
Mark 14:12 . . . *P* lamb is sacrificed,
Heb 11:28 . . . to keep the *P* and to sprinkle

PATH
Heb 12:13 . . . Mark out a straight *p*

PATIENCE
Rom 15:5 . . . May God, who gives this *p*
Gal 5:22 . . . joy, peace, *p*, kindness,
Col 1:11 . . . endurance and *p* you need.
Col 3:12 . . . humility, gentleness, and *p*.
2 Tim 3:10 . . . my faith, my *p*, my love,
Titus 2:2 . . . and be filled with love and *p*.
2 Pet 3:15 . . . Lord's *p* gives people time

PATIENT
Rom 12:12 . . . Be *p* in trouble,
1 Cor 4:12 . . . We are *p* with those who
1 Cor 13:4 . . . Love is *p* and kind.
1 Thes 5:14 . . . Be *p* with everyone.
Jas 5:8 . . . You, too, must be *p*.

PAUL Pharisee and Roman citizen (Acts 22:3); from city of Tarsus (Acts 9:11; Phil 3:5); became apostle (Gal 1) to the Gentiles (Rom 11:13); also known as "Saul" (Acts 7:58; 13:9); supported stoning of Stephen (Acts 8:1); attacked early Christians (Acts 8:1-3; 9:1-2; Gal 1:13); converted on road to Damascus (Acts 9:1-9; 22:6-16; 26:12-18); escaped over the wall in basket (Acts 9:23-25); saw visions in Arabia (Gal 1:17); with Barnabas in Antioch (Acts 11:22-26); sent to Jerusalem (Acts 11:27-30); first missionary journey (Acts 13–14); testified at Jerusalem Council (Acts 15:1-12); second missionary journey with Silas (Acts 15:36-18:22); third missionary journey (Acts 18:23-21:14); farewell to Ephesian elders (Acts 20:13-38); journey to Rome (Acts 21-28); arrived in Rome (Acts 28); his goal (Phil 3:7-15); last known written words of (2 Tim 4); intervened for returning slave (Phlm 8-22); wrote letters: Romans through Philemon.

PAY
Matt 22:17 . . . to *p* taxes to Caesar or not?
1 Tim 5:18 . . . who work deserve their *p*!

PEACE
Matt 5:9 . . . blesses those who work for *p*,
Mark 9:50 . . . live in *p* with each other.
Luke 1:79 . . . guide us to the path of *p*.
John 16:33 . . . you may have *p* in me.
Rom 5:1 . . . by faith, we have *p* with God
Rom 8:6 . . . your mind leads to life and *p*.
1 Cor 14:33 . . . God of disorder but of *p*,
Gal 5:22 . . . love, joy, *p*, patience,
Eph 2:14 . . . Christ himself has brought *p*
Eph 6:15 . . . put on the *p* that comes from
Phil 4:7 . . . experience God's *p*,
Heb 13:20 . . . the God of *p*—who brought
Jas 3:17 . . . It is also *p* loving, gentle
1 Pet 3:11 . . . Search for *p*, and work to

PEACEFUL
1 Thes 5:3 . . . Everything is *p* and secure,
1 Tim 2:2 . . . we can live *p* and quiet lives
Heb 12:11 . . . a *p* harvest of right living
2 Pet 3:14 . . . effort to be found living *p*

PENTECOST
Acts 2:1 . . . the day of *P* all the believers

PEOPLE
Matt 4:19 . . . show you how to fish for *p*!
Mark 8:27 . . . Who do *p* say I am?
Eph 1:14 . . . purchased us to be his own *p*.
2 Tim 3:17 . . . and equip his *p* to do every
Titus 2:11 . . . bringing salvation to all *p*.
Titus 2:14 . . . make us his very own *p*,
Heb 4:9 . . . waiting for the *p* of God.
1 Pet 2:9 . . . for you are a chosen *p*.
1 Pet 2:10 . . . now you are God's *p*.

PERFECT
Matt 5:48 . . . you are to be *p*, even as
John 17:23 . . . experience such *p* unity
Col 4:12 . . . God to make you strong and *p*,
Heb 5:9 . . . as a *p* High Priest,
Heb 9:11 . . . greater, more *p* Tabernacle
Heb 10:14 . . . he forever made *p* those
Jas 1:25 . . . look carefully into the *p* law
1 Jn 4:18 . . . because *p* love expels all fear.

PERFECTION
Phil 3:12 . . . I have already reached *p*.
Heb 7:11 . . . achieved the *p* God intended,
Heb 11:40 . . . not reach *p* without us.

PERISH *see also* DESTROY, DIE
John 3:16 . . . believes in him will not *p*
John 10:28 . . . they will never *p*.

PERSECUTED
Matt 5:10 . . . God blesses those who are *p*
Matt 5:12 . . . prophets were *p*
John 15:20 . . . Since they *p* me, naturally
Rom 8:35 . . . or are *p*, or hungry,
2 Thes 1:7 . . . for you who are being *p*

PERSEVERE *see also* ENDURE
Rev 3:10 . . . obeyed my command to *p*,

Dictionary/Concordance . . .

PETER Leader of the 12 disciples, also known as "Simon son of John" (John 21:17) and "Cephas" (John 1:42); called to "fish for people" (Mark 1:16-20; Matt 4:18-20; Luke 5:1-11; *see also* John 21:3); present at raising of the dead (Mark 5:37; Luke 8:51); walked on water (Mark 6:45-52; Matt 14:22-33; John 6:15-21); identified Jesus as the Christ (Mark 8:27-30; Matt 16:13-20; Luke 9:18-20; *see also* John 6:68-69); rebuked by Jesus for lack of heavenly perspective (Mark 8:32-33; Matt 16:21-23; *see also* John 13:6-11); witnessed the Transfiguration (Mark 9:1-13; Matt 16:28–17:8; Luke 9:28-36; 2 Pet 1:16-20); cut off ear of Malchus (Matt 26:51; Mark 14:47; Luke 22:50); denied Jesus—then wept (Mark 14:66-72; Matt 26:69-75; Luke 22:54-62; John 18:15-27); visited empty tomb (Luke 24:12; John 20:1-10; *see also* Matt 28:1-8); saw Jesus (Luke 24:34; 1 Cor 15:5); told by Jesus to shepherd his flock (John 21:15-19); in upper room before Pentecost (Acts 1:13); preached at Pentecost (Acts 2); performed miracles (Acts 3:1-10; 5:14-16; 9:32-43); preached at Temple (Acts 3:11-26); preached before Jewish high council (Acts 4:1-22); prophesied death of Ananias and Sapphira (Acts 5:1-11); preached again before Jewish high council (Acts 5:29-32); rebuked power seeker (Acts 8:14-25); healed sick (Acts 9:32-34); raised dead (Acts 9:36-43); introduced Gentiles to gospel (Acts 10–11); rescued by angel from prison (Acts 12:3-19); preached grace at Jerusalem Council (Acts 15); became pillar of the church (Gal 2:9); wrote letters (1 Pet 1:1; 2 Pet 1:1).

PHYSICAL
Col 1:22 . . . of Christ in his *p* body.
1 Tim 4:8 . . . *P* training is good, but

PIERCED
John 19:37 . . . look on the one they *p*.
Rev 1:7 . . . even those who *p* him.

PILLARS
Gal 2:9 . . . known as *p* of the church,
Rev 3:12 . . . victorious will become *p* in the

PLAN *see also* PURPOSE
Acts 7:44 . . . according to the *p* God had
Rom 16:25 . . . *p* kept secret from
Eph 3:9 . . . this mysterious *p* that God,
Eph 3:11 . . . This was his eternal *p*,
2 Tim 1:9 . . . *p* from before the beginning

PLANT
Matt 6:26 . . . They don't *p* or harvest or
Matt 13:3 . . . A farmer went out to *p* some
1 Cor 15:36 . . . it doesn't grow into a *p*
Jas 3:18 . . . will *p* seeds of peace

PLEASE
Rom 8:8 . . . sinful nature can never *p* God.
2 Cor 5:9 . . . our goal is to *p* him.
Gal 6:8 . . . live to *p* the Spirit will harvest
Col 1:10 . . . always honor and *p* the Lord,
1 Thes 2:4 . . . Our purpose is to *p* God,
Heb 11:6 . . . to *p* God without faith.
Heb 13:16 . . . sacrifices that *p* God.

PLEASURES
Luke 8:14 . . . by the cares and riches and *p*
Titus 2:12 . . . living and sinful *p*.

POOR
Matt 11:5 . . . is being preached to the *p*.
Matt 19:21 . . . and give the money to the *p*,
Mark 12:42 . . . Then a *p* widow came and
Luke 4:18 . . . to bring Good News to the *p*.
Luke 14:13 . . . Instead, invite the *p*, the
Rom 15:26 . . . an offering for the *p* among
2 Cor 8:9 . . . for your sakes he became *p*,
Jas 2:2 . . . another comes in who is *p*
Jas 2:6 . . . you dishonor the *p*!

POSSESSION *see also* INHERITANCE
1 Pet 2:9 . . . God's very own *p*.

POSSESSIONS *see also* MONEY, TREASURE(S), WEALTH
Matt 19:21 . . . sell all your *p* and
Mark 10:22 . . . for he had many *p*.

POSSIBLE
Matt 19:26 . . . with God everything is *p*.
Matt 26:39 . . . *p*, let this cup of suffering
Mark 9:23 . . . Anything is *p* if a person
Mark 10:27 . . . Everything is *p* with God.

POWER *see also* STRENGTH
Matt 22:29 . . . don't know the *p* of God.
Luke 4:14 . . . the Holy Spirit's *p*.
Acts 1:8 . . . receive *p* when the Holy Spirit
Rom 1:20 . . . his eternal *p* and divine
Rom 6:9 . . . Death no longer has any *p* over
Rom 15:13 . . . the *p* of the Holy Spirit.
1 Cor 1:18 . . . is the very *p* of God.
1 Cor 15:24 . . . ruler and authority and *p*.
2 Cor 4:7 . . . our great *p* is from God,
2 Cor 13:4 . . . now lives by the *p* of God.
Phil 3:10 . . . and experience the mighty *p*
2 Tim 1:7 . . . but of *p*, love, and
Rev 4:11 . . . receive glory and honor and *p*.
Rev 5:12 . . . receive *p* and riches and
Rev 19:1 . . . glory and *p* belong to our God.

PRAISE
Matt 5:16 . . . will *p* your heavenly Father.
Mark 11:9 . . . were shouting, "*P* God!
Eph 1:6 . . . we *p* God for the glorious
Rev 19:1 . . . heaven shouting, "*P* the Lord!

PRAY
Matt 6:5 . . . When you *p*, don't be like
Mark 11:24 . . . you can *p* for anything,
1 Cor 14:14 . . . For if I *p* in tongues,
2 Cor 13:9 . . . We *p* that you will become
Eph 1:18 . . . I *p* that your hearts will be
Eph 3:16 . . . I *p* that from his glorious,
Phil 4:6 . . . instead, *p* about everything.
1 Thes 1:3 . . . As we *p* to our God and
1 Tim 2:8 . . . to *p* with holy hands
Jas 5:13 . . . You should *p*.
Jas 5:16 . . . *p* for each other so that

PRAYER
Matt 11:25 . . . Jesus prayed this *p*:
John 17:9 . . . My *p* is not for the world,
Acts 1:14 . . . were constantly united in *p*,
Acts 4:31 . . . After this *p*, the meeting
Acts 6:4 . . . can spend our time in *p*
Acts 10:31 . . . your *p* has been heard,
Acts 13:3 . . . So after more fasting and *p*,
Col 4:2 . . . Devote yourselves to *p* with an

PREACH *see also* PROCLAIM, TEACH
Luke 9:60 . . . go and *p* about the Kingdom

Acts 5:42 . . . teach and *p* this message:
Acts 16:10 . . . to *p* the Good News
Rom 1:15 . . . to *p* the Good News.
2 Cor 4:5 . . . We *p* that Jesus Christ is Lord,
2 Cor 11:4 . . . Jesus than the one we *p*,
2 Tim 4:17 . . . might *p* the Good News

PREACHED
1 Cor 15:1 . . . Good News I *p* to you
Gal 1:8 . . . than the one we *p* to you.
Col 1:23 . . . Good News has been *p* all over
1 Pet 1:25 . . . Good News that was *p* to you.

PREPARE
John 14:2 . . . I am going to *p* a place

PRESENT
1 Cor 7:26 . . . Because of the *p* crisis,
Eph 5:27 . . . did this to *p* her to himself
2 Tim 2:15 . . . Work hard so you can *p*

PRETEND
Rom 12:9 . . . Don't just *p* to love

PRICE
1 Cor 6:20 . . . bought you with a high *p*.

PRIDE *see also* BOAST, PROUD
1 Jn 2:16 . . . *p* in our achievements and

PRIEST
Heb 5:6 . . . You are a *p* forever
Heb 6:20 . . . our eternal High *P*
Heb 8:1 . . . a High *P* who sat down

PRISON
Matt 25:36 . . . I was in *p*, and you visited
Heb 13:3 . . . Remember those in *p*,
Rev 20:7 . . . Satan will be let out of his *p*.

PRIZE
1 Cor 9:25 . . . we do it for an eternal *p*.
Phil 3:14 . . . heavenly *p* for which God,
2 Tim 2:5 . . . cannot win the *p* unless
2 Tim 4:8 . . . *p* awaits me—the crown

PROCLAIM *see also* PREACH
1 Jn 1:1 . . . *p* to you the one who existed

PROMISE *see also* COVENANT
Rom 4:20 . . . in believing God's *p*.
Heb 6:13 . . . God's *p* to Abraham.
Heb 10:23 . . . be trusted to keep his *p*.
Heb 11:11 . . . that God would keep his *p*.
2 Pet 3:4 . . . *p* that Jesus is coming again?
2 Pet 3:9 . . . being slow about his *p*,

PROMISES
Rom 9:4 . . . receiving his wonderful *p*.
Rom 15:4 . . . patiently for God's *p* to be
2 Cor 1:20 . . . God's *p* have been fulfilled
2 Cor 7:1 . . . Because we have these *p*,

PROPHECY
Matt 13:14 . . . fulfills the *p* of Isaiah
Acts 21:9 . . . who had the gift of *p*.
Acts 21:10 . . . who also had the gift of *p*,
1 Cor 13:2 . . . If I had the gift of *p*,
1 Cor 13:9 . . . gift of *p* reveals only part
1 Cor 14:6 . . . knowledge or *p* or teaching,
Rev 22:18 . . . words of *p* written in

PROPHETS
Matt 5:17 . . . or the writings of the *p*.
Matt 7:12 . . . in the law and the *p*.
2 Pet 1:21 . . . those *p* were moved by the
2 Pet 3:2 . . . what the holy *p* said long

PROTECT *see also* KEEP, OBEY, GUARD
John 17:11 . . . now *p* them by the power of
Rev 3:10 . . . I will *p* you from the great

PROUD *see also* BOAST, PRIDE
1 Cor 13:4 . . . not jealous or boastful or *p*
1 Tim 3:6 . . . he might become *p*,
1 Tim 6:17 . . . rich in this world not to be *p*
Jas 4:6 . . . God opposes the *p* but favors
1 Pet 5:5 . . . God opposes the *p* but favors

PROVIDE
2 Cor 9:8 . . . God will generously *p* all you
2 Cor 9:10 . . . he will *p* and increase your

PUNISH
Acts 7:7 . . . But I will *p* the nation

PURE *see also* HOLY
Matt 5:8 . . . those whose hearts are *p*,
Phil 4:8 . . . right, and *p*, and lovely,
1 Tim 5:22 . . . Keep yourself *p*.
2 Tim 2:21 . . . If you keep yourself *p*,
Titus 1:15 . . . Everything is *p* to those
Jas 1:27 . . . *P* and genuine religion
2 Pet 3:14 . . . are *p* and blameless

PURPOSE *see also* PLAN
Rom 8:28 . . . according to his *p* for them.
1 Cor 9:26 . . . I run with *p* in every step.
Phil 2:2 . . . together with one mind and *p*.

PURSUE
1 Tim 6:11 . . . *P* righteousness and a godly
2 Tim 2:22 . . . Instead, *p* righteous living,

QUARREL
1 Cor 3:3 . . . and *q* with each other.

QUIET
1 Thes 4:11 . . . to live a *q* life,
1 Tim 2:2 . . . peaceful and *q* lives marked

RACE
1 Cor 9:24 . . . that in a *r* everyone runs,
2 Tim 4:7 . . . I have finished the *r*,
Heb 12:1 . . . run with endurance the *r* God

RAIN
Matt 5:45 . . . and he sends *r* on the just
Jas 5:17 . . . earnestly that no *r* would fall,

RAISED
Luke 7:22 . . . the dead are *r* to life,
Acts 2:32 . . . God *r* Jesus from the dead,
Rom 1:4 . . . he was *r* from the dead
Rom 6:5 . . . will also be *r* to life
Rom 10:9 . . . God *r* him from the dead,
1 Cor 15:4 . . . he was *r* from the dead
Phil 3:10 . . . power that *r* him from
1 Thes 4:14 . . . died and was *r* to life
1 Pet 1:3 . . . because God *r* Jesus Christ

RANSOM
Matt 20:28 . . . life as a *r* for many.
Rev 5:9 . . . your blood has *r* people

READ
2 Cor 3:2 . . . everyone can *r* it and

REBELS
Luke 22:37 . . . was counted among the *r*.
Rom 11:30 . . . Gentiles were *r* against God,
Rom 13:2 . . . So anyone who *r* against

RECEIVE
Matt 19:17 . . . you want to *r* eternal life,
John 20:22 . . . said, "*R* the Holy Spirit.
Acts 1:8 . . . But you will *r* power when the
Acts 2:38 . . . Then you will *r* the gift of
1 Tim 1:16 . . . in him and *r* eternal life.
Rev 4:11 . . . our God, to *r* glory and honor

REIGNS
Rev 19:6 . . . Lord our God, the Almighty, *r*.

REJOICE *see also* GLAD, HAPPY, JOY
Luke 1:14 . . . and many will *r* at his birth,
1 Cor 13:6 . . . It does not *r* about injustice
Phil 2:18 . . . you should *r*, and I will
Phil 3:1 . . . and sisters, *r* in the Lord.
Phil 4:4 . . . I say it again—*r*!
Col 2:5 . . . I *r* that you are living as
Rev 19:7 . . . Let us be glad and *r*, and

REMAIN
John 15:9 . . . loved me. *R* in my love.
2 Tim 3:14 . . . But you must *r* faithful
Heb 13:4 . . . and *r* faithful to one another
1 Jn 2:27 . . . *r* in fellowship with Christ.

REMEMBER
Luke 22:19 . . . Do this to *r* me.
1 Cor 11:24 . . . Do this to *r* me.
Heb 8:12 . . . never again *r* their sins.
2 Pet 1:15 . . . you always *r* these things

RENEWED
Col 3:10 . . . be *r* as you learn to know

REPAY
1 Tim 5:4 . . . *r* their parents by taking
1 Pet 3:9 . . . Don't *r* evil for evil.

REPENT
Matt 3:2 . . . *R* of your sins and turn
Matt 4:17 . . . began to preach, "*R* of your
Acts 2:38 . . . you must *r* of your sins,
Acts 17:30 . . . everywhere to *r* of their sins
2 Pet 3:9 . . . but wants everyone to *r*.
Rev 2:5 . . . If you don't *r*, I will come

REPUTATION *see also* NAME
1 Tim 3:2 . . . wisely, and have a good *r*.

RESCUE *see also* RANSOM, SALVATION, SAVE
Matt 6:13 . . . but *r* us from the evil one.
2 Pet 2:9 . . . knows how to *r* godly people

RESCUES
Rom 11:26 . . . The one who *r* will come

RESIST
Jas 4:7 . . . *R* the devil, and he will flee

RESPECT
Eph 5:33 . . . the wife must *r* her husband.
1 Tim 3:4 . . . children who *r* and obey him.
Titus 2:2 . . . be worthy of *r*, and to live
1 Pet 2:17 . . . Fear God, and *r* the king.

RESPONSIBLE
Gal 6:5 . . . For we are each *r* for our own

REST *see also* SABBATH
Matt 11:28 . . . and I will give you *r*.
2 Thes 1:7 . . . God will provide *r* for you

RESTED
Heb 4:4 . . . seventh day God *r* from all

RESURRECTION *see also* RAISED, RISE
John 11:25 . . . I am the *r* and the life.
Acts 1:22 . . . as a witness of Jesus' *r*.
Acts 2:31 . . . speaking of the Messiah's *r*.
Acts 4:2 . . . there is a *r* of the dead.
Acts 4:33 . . . powerfully to the *r* of
Acts 17:32 . . . Paul speak about the *r* of
1 Cor 15:13 . . . if there is no *r* of the
1 Cor 15:42 . . . way with the *r* of the dead.
Phil 3:11 . . . experience the *r* from the
2 Tim 2:18 . . . claiming that the *r* of the
Heb 6:2 . . . of hands, the *r* of the dead,
Rev 20:5 . . . This is the first *r*.

REVELATION
Gal 1:12 . . . by direct *r* from Jesus
Rev 1:1 . . . This is a *r* from Jesus

REVENGE
Heb 10:30 . . . I will take *r*. I will

REVERENCE *see also* AWE, FEAR, RESPECT
Eph 5:21 . . . another out of *r* for Christ.
Heb 5:7 . . . of his deep *r* for God.

REWARD
Matt 5:12 . . . For a great *r* awaits you
Matt 6:18 . . . sees everything, will *r* you.
Luke 6:23 . . . For a great *r* awaits you
Luke 6:35 . . . your *r* from heaven will
Luke 14:14 . . . God will *r* you for
Eph 6:8 . . . the Lord will *r* each one
Phil 4:17 . . . you to receive a *r* for your
1 Thes 2:19 . . . be our proud *r* and crown
Heb 10:35 . . . the great *r* it brings you!
1 Pet 1:9 . . . The *r* for trusting him
Rev 11:18 . . . the dead and *r* your servants

RICH *see also* WEALTH
Matt 19:23 . . . hard for a *r* person to enter
Luke 1:53 . . . and sent the *r* away
Luke 6:24 . . . you who are *r*, for you
Luke 21:1 . . . watched the *r* people
2 Cor 8:9 . . . Though he was *r*, yet for
1 Tim 6:17 . . . those who are *r* in this world
Jas 1:10 . . . those who are *r* should boast
Jas 2:3 . . . seat to the *r* person, but you

RIGHT *see also* JUST
Matt 5:10 . . . for doing *r*, for the Kingdom
Acts 13:39 . . . is declared *r* with God—
Rom 1:17 . . . God makes us *r* in his sight.
Rom 5:1 . . . have been made *r* in God's
Gal 3:24 . . . could be made *r* with God
Phil 4:8 . . . honorable, and *r*, and pure,
2 Tim 3:16 . . . teaches us to do what is *r*.
1 Jn 2:29 . . . who do what is *r* are God's

RIGHTEOUS *see also* GODLY, INNOCENT, RIGHT
Rom 3:10 . . . No one is *r*—not even one.
Rom 4:3 . . . counted him as *r* because of
Titus 3:7 . . . he declared us *r* and gave us
Jas 5:16 . . . prayer of a *r* person has
1 Jn 2:1 . . . the one who is truly *r*.
1 Jn 3:7 . . . that they are *r*, even as

RIGHTEOUSNESS *see also* JUSTICE
Eph 6:14 . . . the body armor of God's *r*.
2 Tim 4:8 . . . the crown of *r*, which
Heb 11:7 . . . he received the *r* that comes
2 Pet 3:13 . . . filled with God's *r*.

RISE *see also* RAISED, RESURRECTION
Matt 27:63 . . . I will *r* from the dead.
Mark 8:31 . . . later he would *r* from the
Luke 18:33 . . . day he will *r* again.
John 5:29 . . . and they will *r* again.
John 20:9 . . . said Jesus must *r* from the
Acts 17:3 . . . must suffer and *r* from the
1 Thes 4:16 . . . have died will *r* from

RISEN *see also* RAISED, RESURRECTION
Matt 28:6 . . . He is *r* from the dead,
Mark 16:6 . . . He is *r* from the dead!
Luke 24:34 . . . The Lord has really *r*!

ROCK
Matt 7:24 . . . builds a house on solid *r*.
Matt 16:18 . . . upon this *r* I will build
Rom 9:33 . . . stumble, a *r* that makes them
1 Cor 10:4 . . . and that *r* was Christ.
1 Pet 2:8 . . . stumble, the *r* that makes

ROOT
1 Tim 6:10 . . . money is the *r* of all kinds

RUIN
1 Tim 6:9 . . . them into *r* and destruction.
2 Tim 2:14 . . . they can *r* those who hear

RULER
Matt 2:6 . . . for a *r* will come from
John 12:31 . . . when Satan, the *r* of this
Eph 1:21 . . . far above any *r* or authority
Rev 1:5 . . . and the *r* of all the kings

RUN
Phil 2:16 . . . that I did not *r* the race
1 Tim 6:11 . . . so *r* from all these evil
2 Tim 2:22 . . . *R* from anything that
Heb 12:1 . . . let us *r* with endurance

SABBATH *see also* REST
Matt 12:1 . . . some grainfields on the *S*.
Luke 13:10 . . . One *S* day as Jesus was

SACRIFICE
Rom 3:25 . . . Jesus as the *s* for sin.
Rom 12:1 . . . a living and holy *s*—the
Eph 5:2 . . . himself as a *s* for us,
Heb 9:28 . . . time as a *s* to take away
Heb 13:15 . . . Jesus a continual *s* of praise
1 Jn 4:10 . . . his Son as a *s* to take away

SACRIFICES
Matt 9:13 . . . to show mercy, not offer *s*.
Heb 7:27 . . . need to offer *s* every day.
Heb 13:16 . . . These are the *s* that please

SAFE
John 17:15 . . . keep them *s* from the evil

SALT
Matt 5:13 . . . You are the *s* of the earth.

SALVATION *see also* RESCUE, SAVE
Luke 1:77 . . . to find *s* through forgiveness
Luke 2:30 . . . I have seen your *s*,
Luke 21:28 . . . up, for your *s* is near!
John 4:22 . . . him, for *s* comes through the
Acts 13:26 . . . this message of *s* has been
Acts 13:47 . . . Gentiles, to bring *s* to the
Acts 28:28 . . . know that this *s* from God
Rom 11:11 . . . so God made *s* available to

2 Cor 7:10 . . . from sin and results in *s*.
Eph 6:17 . . . Put on *s* as your helmet,
Titus 2:11 . . . bringing *s* to all people.
Heb 2:3 . . . if we ignore this great *s* that
Heb 5:9 . . . source of eternal *s* for all
Heb 9:28 . . . but to bring *s* to all who
1 Pet 1:9 . . . will be the *s* of your souls.
Rev 7:10 . . . a mighty shout, "*S* comes from

SAMARITAN
Luke 10:33 . . . a despised *S* came along,
Luke 17:16 . . . man was a *S*.
John 4:5 . . . he came to the *S* village
John 4:7 . . . a *S* woman came to draw

SAMUEL Judge and prophet of Israel (Heb 11:32).

SANCTUARY *see also* TABERNACLE, TEMPLE
Heb 6:19 . . . curtain into God's inner *s*.

SARAH (SARAI) Wife of Abraham (Abram); was infertile (Rom 4:19); Isaac promised (Rom 9:9); example of faith (Heb 11:11).

SAVE *see* also RESCUE, SALVATION
Matt 1:21 . . . he will *s* his people
Luke 19:10 . . . seek and *s* those who are
John 12:47 . . . I have come to *s* the world
Rom 5:9 . . . he will certainly *s* us from
1 Tim 1:15 . . . the world to *s* sinners
Heb 7:25 . . . and forever, to *s* those who
Jas 5:20 . . . sinner back will *s* that person

SAVES
1 Cor 15:2 . . . this Good News that *s* you
Eph 1:13 . . . Good News that God *s* you.

SAVIOR
Luke 1:69 . . . He has sent us a mighty *S*
John 4:42 . . . he is indeed the *S* of the
1 Tim 4:10 . . . who is the *S* of all people
1 Jn 4:14 . . . Son to be the *S* of the world.

SCRIPTURE
2 Tim 3:16 . . . All *S* is inspired by God
2 Pet 1:20 . . . no prophecy in *S* ever came

SCRIPTURES
Matt 21:16 . . . Haven't you ever read the *S*?
Luke 24:27 . . . from all the *S* the things
Luke 24:45 . . . minds to understand the *S*.
John 2:22 . . . believed both the *S* and what
John 5:39 . . . You search the *S* because
John 7:42 . . . the *S* clearly state that
John 10:35 . . . you know that the *S* cannot
1 Tim 4:13 . . . focus on reading the *S* to
Heb 10:7 . . . written about me in the *S*.

SCROLL
Rev 6:14 . . . sky was rolled up like a *s*,

SEA
Matt 18:6 . . . in the depths of the *s*.
Jas 1:6 . . . wave of the *s* that is blown

SEARCH
1 Pet 3:11 . . . *S* for peace, and work

SECRET *see also* MYSTERY
Matt 10:26 . . . all that is *s* will be
Mark 4:22 . . . every *s* will be brought
Rom 2:16 . . . judge everyone's *s* life.
Rom 16:25 . . . a plan kept *s* from the
1 Cor 13:2 . . . all of God's *s* plans
1 Cor 14:25 . . . their *s* thoughts will be

1 Cor 15:51 . . . reveal to you a wonderful *s*.
Phil 4:12 . . . have learned the *s* of living
Col 1:26 . . . was kept *s* for centuries
Col 1:27 . . . the *s*: Christ lives in you.

SEED
Matt 13:31 . . . like a mustard *s* planted in
Matt 17:20 . . . as a mustard *s*, you could
1 Cor 3:6 . . . I planted the *s* in your
2 Cor 9:10 . . . one who provides *s* for

SEEK
Matt 6:33 . . . *S* the Kingdom of God above
Luke 19:10 . . . Son of Man came to *s* and
Heb 11:6 . . . those who sincerely *s* him.

SELF-CONTROL
Acts 24:25 . . . righteousness and *s* and the
Gal 5:23 . . . gentleness, and *s*. There is no
1 Tim 3:2 . . . must exercise *s*, live wisely,
1 Tim 3:11 . . . They must exercise *s* and be
1 Pet 1:13 . . . think clearly and exercise *s*.
2 Pet 1:6 . . . and knowledge with *s*, and

SELFISH
Matt 16:24 . . . turn from your *s* ways,
Luke 9:23 . . . turn from your *s* ways,
Gal 5:20 . . . of anger, *s* ambition,
Phil 1:17 . . . They preach with *s* ambition,
Jas 3:14 . . . and there is *s* ambition in
Jas 3:16 . . . is jealousy and *s* ambition,

SELL
Mark 10:21 . . . and *s* all your possessions
Rev 13:17 . . . could buy or *s* anything

SEND
Matt 9:38 . . . ask him to *s* more workers
1 Cor 1:17 . . . For Christ didn't *s* me to

SENT
Matt 10:40 . . . the Father who *s* me.
John 3:17 . . . God *s* his Son into the
Rom 8:3 . . . He *s* his own Son in a
Rom 10:15 . . . them without being *s*?
Gal 4:4 . . . time came, God *s* his Son,

SEPARATE
Rom 8:35 . . . Can anything ever *s* us

SEPARATED
Eph 2:14 . . . of hostility that *s* us.
Col 1:21 . . . were his enemies, *s* from him

SERPENT
2 Cor 11:3 . . . the cunning ways of the *s*.
Rev 12:9 . . . the ancient *s* called the devil,
Rev 20:2 . . . that old *s*, who is the devil,

SERVANT
Matt 20:26 . . . among you must be your *s*,
Luke 22:26 . . . leader should be like a *s*.
1 Tim 4:6 . . . be a worthy *s* of Christ

SERVE
Matt 4:10 . . . your God and *s* only him.
Matt 6:24 . . . No one can *s* two masters.
Matt 20:28 . . . served but to *s* others
Rom 12:7 . . . serving others, *s* them well.
Rom 12:11 . . . work hard and *s* the Lord
Rom 14:18 . . . If you *s* Christ with
1 Cor 16:18 . . . to all who *s* so well.
Gal 5:13 . . . freedom to *s* one another
1 Pet 5:5 . . . all of you, *s* each other

SHADOW
Heb 8:5 . . . only a copy, a *s* of the real
Heb 10:1 . . . was only a *s*, a dim preview

SHAME *see also* DISGRACE
1 Jn 2:28 . . . shrink back from him in *s*.

SHARE
Luke 3:11 . . . If you have food, *s* it with
Rom 8:17 . . . we must also *s* his suffering.
Rom 11:31 . . . they, too, will *s* in God's
1 Cor 12:13 . . . we all *s* the same Spirit.
2 Cor 9:8 . . . left over to *s* with others.
2 Thes 2:14 . . . you can *s* in the glory
1 Tim 6:18 . . . ready to *s* with others.
Heb 12:10 . . . we might *s* in his holiness.
Heb 13:16 . . . to *s* with those in need.
Rev 3:20 . . . and we will *s* a meal together

SHEEP
Matt 7:15 . . . disguised as harmless *s* but
Matt 9:36 . . . like *s* without a shepherd.
Matt 10:16 . . . you out as *s* among wolves.
Matt 12:11 . . . a *s* that fell into a well
Matt 25:32 . . . separates the *s* from the
John 10:3 . . . calls his own *s* by name
John 10:7 . . . I am the gate for the *s*.
John 10:15 . . . sacrifice my life for the *s*.
John 21:17 . . . Then feed my *s*.
1 Pet 2:25 . . . were like *s* who wandered

SHEPHERD
Matt 2:6 . . . will be the *s* for my people
Matt 9:36 . . . like sheep without a *s*.
John 10:11 . . . I am the good *s*.
Acts 20:28 . . . Feed and *s* God's flock—
Heb 13:20 . . . Jesus, the great *S* of the
Rev 7:17 . . . will be their *S*. He will lead

SHIELD
Eph 6:16 . . . hold up the *s* of faith

SHOULDERS
Luke 15:5 . . . carry it home on his *s*.

SHUT
Heb 11:33 . . . They *s* the mouths of lions,

SICK
Matt 9:12 . . . need a doctor—*s* people do.
Matt 10:8 . . . Heal the *s*, raise the dead,
Matt 25:36 . . . I was *s*, and you cared for
Mark 3:10 . . . all the *s* people eagerly
Jas 5:14 . . . Are any of you *s*?

SIGN
Matt 12:38 . . . a miraculous *s* to prove
Matt 24:3 . . . What *s* will signal your
Matt 24:30 . . . the *s* that the Son of Man
Luke 11:29 . . . them is the *s* of Jonah.
1 Cor 14:22 . . . in tongues is a *s*, not for

SILENT
Acts 8:32 . . . And as a lamb is *s* before
Acts 18:9 . . . Speak out! Don't be *s*!

SILVER
Matt 25:15 . . . two bags of *s* to another,
Matt 26:15 . . . gave him thirty pieces of *s*.
Luke 7:41 . . . 500 pieces of *s* to one
Acts 3:6 . . . don't have any *s* or gold
1 Cor 3:12 . . . materials—gold, *s*, jewels,

SIN
John 1:29 . . . takes away the *s* of the world!
John 8:11 . . . Go and *s* no more.

Rom 6:23 . . . the wages of *s* is death,
Heb 4:15 . . . we do, yet he did not *s*.
Heb 12:1 . . . the *s* that so easily trips
Jas 1:15 . . . when *s* is allowed to grow,
Jas 4:17 . . . is *s* to know what you ought
1 Jn 1:8 . . . claim we have no *s*, we are
1 Jn 2:1 . . . if anyone does *s*, we have
1 Jn 3:5 . . . there is no *s* in him.

SING
1 Cor 14:15 . . . I will also *s* in words
1 Cor 14:26 . . . one will *s*, another will
Col 3:16 . . . *S* psalms and hymns and

SINNER
Luke 5:8 . . . I'm too much of a *s* to be
Luke 15:7 . . . over one lost *s* who repents
Luke 18:13 . . . to me, for I am a *s*.
Jas 5:20 . . . whoever brings the *s* back

SINS
Matt 1:21 . . . save his people from their *s*.
Matt 6:12 . . . forgive us our *s*, as we
Matt 26:28 . . . to forgive the *s* of many.
Luke 5:24 . . . on earth to forgive *s*.
Acts 2:38 . . . repent of your *s*, turn to
1 Cor 15:3 . . . died for our *s*, just as
Gal 1:4 . . . gave his life for our *s*, just
Heb 9:28 . . . to take away the *s* of many
Heb 10:12 . . . sacrifice for *s*, good for all
Jas 5:16 . . . Confess your *s* to each other
1 Pet 2:24 . . . carried our *s* in his body
1 Pet 3:18 . . . suffered for our *s* once for
1 Jn 1:9 . . . to forgive us our *s* and to
1 Jn 3:5 . . . take away our *s*, and there is
Rev 1:5 . . . from our *s* by shedding his

SKY
Matt 24:29 . . . will fall from the *s*,
Rev 20:11 . . . The earth and *s* fled from

SLEEP
Rom 11:8 . . . has put them into a deep *s*.

SMOKE
Acts 2:19 . . . and fire and clouds of *s*.
Rev 9:2 . . . air turned dark from the *s*.
Rev 15:8 . . . filled with *s* from God's

SNAKE
John 3:14 . . . lifted up the bronze *s* on a

SNAKES
Matt 10:16 . . . as shrewd as *s* and harmless
Luke 3:7 . . . You brood of *s*! Who warned

SOLDIER
1 Cor 9:7 . . . What *s* has to pay his own
2 Tim 2:3 . . . a good *s* of Christ Jesus.

SOLOMON King of Israel (United Kingdom),
second son of David and Bathsheba; often
mentioned in NT (Matt 6:29; 12:42; Luke 11:31;
12:27; Acts 7:47).

SORROW
Eph 4:30 . . . do not bring *s* to God's Holy
Rev 21:4 . . . more death or *s* or crying

SORRY
Matt 15:32 . . . I feel *s* for these people.
Matt 20:34 . . . Jesus felt *s* for them and
Mark 8:2 . . . I feel *s* for these people.

SOUL
Matt 10:28 . . . can destroy both *s* and body
Matt 22:37 . . . all your heart, all your *s*,

Mark 8:37 . . . worth more than your *s*?
Mark 12:30 . . . heart, all your *s*, all your
Luke 16:23 . . . his *s* went to the place of

SPEAK
Matt 12:34 . . . men like you *s* what is good
Matt 15:18 . . . the words you *s* come from
1 Cor 14:2 . . . ability to *s* in tongues,
1 Cor 14:19 . . . I would rather *s* five
1 Pet 3:16 . . . if people *s* against you,

SPIRIT *see also* ADVOCATE
Matt 3:11 . . . baptize you with the Holy *S*
Matt 3:16 . . . and he saw the *S* of God
Matt 4:1 . . . was led by the *S* into the
Matt 28:19 . . . and the Son and the Holy *S*.
Mark 1:8 . . . baptize you with the Holy *S*!
Luke 1:35 . . . The Holy *S* will come upon
John 3:5 . . . born of water and the *S*.
John 6:63 . . . *S* alone gives eternal life.
John 14:26 . . . the Holy *S*—he will teach
John 16:13 . . . When the *S* of truth comes,
Acts 1:8 . . . when the Holy *S* comes
Acts 2:4 . . . as the Holy *S* gave them
Rom 8:5 . . . controlled by the Holy *S* think
Rom 8:26 . . . the Holy *S* prays for us
1 Cor 2:10 . . . For his *S* searches out
1 Cor 12:1 . . . abilities the *S* gives us.
1 Cor 12:13 . . . one body by one *S*, and we
1 Cor 14:1 . . . abilities the *S* gives—
Gal 3:2 . . . receive the Holy *S* by obeying
Gal 5:22 . . . But the Holy *S* produces this
Eph 4:4 . . . body and one *S*, just as you
Eph 6:17 . . . sword of the *S*, which is the
1 Thes 5:19 . . . Do not stifle the Holy *S*.
2 Tim 1:7 . . . not given us a *s* of fear
1 Pet 3:4 . . . gentle and quiet *s*, which

STAND
Rom 14:10 . . . all *s* before the judgment
1 Cor 10:13 . . . to be more than you can *s*.
2 Cor 5:10 . . . we must all *s* before Christ
Eph 6:14 . . . *S* your ground, putting on the
1 Pet 5:9 . . . *S* firm against him, and
Rev 3:20 . . . I *s* at the door and knock.

STAR
Matt 2:2 . . . We saw his *s* as it rose,
2 Pet 1:19 . . . the Morning *S* shines in
Rev 2:28 . . . also give them the morning *s*!
Rev 22:16 . . . I am the bright morning *s*.

STEAL
Matt 19:18 . . . You must not *s*.
Rom 13:9 . . . You must not *s*.

STEPS
1 Pet 2:21 . . . you must follow in his *s*.

STILL
Mark 4:39 . . . Silence! Be *s*!

STONE
Matt 7:9 . . . give them a *s* instead?
Matt 21:42 . . . *s* that the builders rejected
Mark 16:3 . . . roll away the *s* for us from
Luke 4:3 . . . change this *s* into a loaf of
John 8:7 . . . sinned throw the first *s*!

STOOD
2 Tim 4:17 . . . But the Lord *s* with me

STOP
Matt 19:14 . . . come to me. Don't *s* them!
Eph 6:16 . . . shield of faith to *s* the

STORM
Luke 8:24 . . . *s* stopped and all was calm!

STRANGER
Matt 25:35 . . . I was a *s*, and you invited
John 10:5 . . . They won't follow a *s*;

STRANGERS *see also* FOREIGNERS
1 Tim 5:10 . . . been kind to *s* and served
Heb 13:2 . . . to show hospitality to *s*, for

STRENGTH *see also* POWER
Mark 12:30 . . . your mind, and all your *s*.
Phil 4:13 . . . Christ, who gives me *s*.
Heb 13:9 . . . Your *s* comes from God's

STUBBORN
Rom 2:5 . . . because you are *s* and refuse

STUMBLE
Rom 9:33 . . . that makes people *s*,
Rom 14:13 . . . believer to *s* and fall.
1 Cor 8:9 . . . weaker conscience to *s*.
2 Cor 6:3 . . . no one will *s* because of us,
1 Jn 2:10 . . . does not cause others to *s*.

SUFFER
Mark 8:31 . . . Son of Man must *s* many
Luke 24:26 . . . would have to *s* all these
Luke 24:46 . . . Messiah would *s* and die
Rom 8:18 . . . Yet what we *s* now is nothing
2 Cor 1:5 . . . the more we *s* for Christ,
2 Cor 12:10 . . . troubles that I *s* for Christ.
Phil 3:10 . . . I want to *s* with him, sharing
Heb 11:26 . . . better to *s* for the sake
1 Pet 4:16 . . . is no shame to *s* for being

SUFFERING
Phil 1:29 . . . the privilege of *s* for him.
2 Thes 1:4 . . . and hardships you are *s*.
2 Tim 2:3 . . . Endure *s* along with me,
2 Tim 4:5 . . . afraid of *s* for the Lord.
Heb 2:10 . . . through his *s*, a perfect
Heb 2:18 . . . gone through *s* and testing,

SUN
Matt 17:2 . . . shone like the *s*, and his
Luke 23:45 . . . light from the *s* was gone.
Eph 4:26 . . . Don't let the *s* go down while
Rev 1:16 . . . was like the *s* in all its
Rev 21:23 . . . has no need of *s* or moon,

SWORD
Matt 26:52 . . . who use the *s* will die by
Luke 2:35 . . . a *s* will pierce your very
Eph 6:17 . . . take the *s* of the Spirit,
Heb 4:12 . . . sharpest two-edged *s*, cutting
Rev 1:16 . . . sharp two-edged *s* came

SYNAGOGUE
Luke 4:16 . . . to the *s* on the Sabbath
Acts 17:2 . . . he went to the *s* service,

T

TABERNACLE *see also* SANCTUARY
Heb 9:11 . . . more perfect *T* in heaven,

TABLETS
2 Cor 3:3 . . . carved not on *t* of stone,

TAME
Jas 3:8 . . . no one can *t* the tongue.

TEACH *see also* PREACH, PROCLAIM, TRAIN
Matt 11:29 . . . Let me *t* you, because
Luke 11:1 . . . Lord, *t* us to pray,
Luke 12:12 . . . Holy Spirit will *t* you
John 14:26 . . . he will *t* you everything
Rom 15:4 . . . Scriptures long ago to *t*
Rom 15:14 . . . you can *t* each other all
1 Cor 14:26 . . . another will *t*, another
1 Tim 3:2 . . . he must be able to *t*.
2 Tim 3:16 . . . is useful to *t* us what

TEACHER
Luke 6:40 . . . will become like the *t*.
John 13:14 . . . Lord and *T*, have washed
Rom 12:7 . . . If you are a *t*, teach well.

TEAR
Rev 7:17 . . . will wipe every *t* from their
Rev 21:4 . . . will wipe every *t* from their

TEMPLE *see also* SANCTUARY, TABERNACLE
Matt 27:51 . . . sanctuary of the *T* was torn
John 2:14 . . . the *T* area he saw merchants
Acts 5:20 . . . Go to the *T* and give the
1 Cor 3:16 . . . together are the *t* of God
1 Cor 6:19 . . . body is the *t* of the Holy
Rev 21:22 . . . and the Lamb are its *t*.

TEMPTATION
Matt 6:13 . . . don't let us yield to *t*,
Matt 26:41 . . . will not give in to *t*.
Luke 8:13 . . . fall away when they face *t*.
1 Cor 10:13 . . . not allow the *t* to be
Gal 6:1 . . . fall into the same *t* yourself.
1 Tim 6:9 . . . to be rich fall into *t* and
Jas 1:12 . . . endure testing and *t*.

TEMPTATIONS
Matt 18:7 . . . *T* are inevitable, but what
1 Cor 10:13 . . . The *t* in your life are

TEMPTED
Matt 4:1 . . . wilderness to be *t* there by
Luke 4:2 . . . where he was *t* by the devil
1 Cor 10:13 . . . When you are *t*, he will
Jas 1:13 . . . you are being *t*, do not say,

TEST
Luke 4:12 . . . You must not *t* the Lord your
1 Thes 5:21 . . . but *t* everything that is said.
1 Jn 4:1 . . . You must *t* them to see if

THANKFUL
Col 3:15 . . . And always be *t*.
Col 3:16 . . . to God with *t* hearts.
1 Thes 5:18 . . . Be *t* in all circumstances,
Heb 12:28 . . . let us be *t* and please God by

THANKS
Rom 1:21 . . . as God or even give him *t*.
1 Cor 11:24 . . . gave *t* to God for it.
Phil 1:3 . . . of you, I give *t* to my God.
1 Tim 2:1 . . . behalf, and give *t* for them.

THIEF
Rev 16:15 . . . as unexpectedly as a *t*!

THINK
Rom 11:20 . . . So don't *t* highly of
Phil 1:3 . . . Every time I *t* of you, I give
Phil 3:19 . . . they *t* only about this life
Heb 10:24 . . . Let us *t* of ways to motivate
1 Pet 1:13 . . . So *t* clearly and exercise

THIRSTY
Matt 25:35 . . . I was *t*, and you gave
John 4:14 . . . will never be *t* again.

Rom 12:20 ... If they are *t*, give them
Rev 7:16 ... never again be hungry or *t*;
Rev 22:17 ... Let anyone who is *t* come.

THORN
Matt 27:29 ... wove *t* branches into a
2 Cor 12:7 ... was given a *t* in my flesh,

THOUGHTS
Matt 15:19 ... heart come evil *t*, murder,
1 Cor 14:25 ... their secret *t* will be
Eph 4:23 ... renew your *t* and attitudes.
Rev 2:23 ... searches out the *t* and

THREE
Matt 12:40 ... *t* days and *t* nights,
Matt 18:20 ... where two or *t* gather
Matt 26:34 ... you will deny *t* times that
Mark 8:31 ... *t* days later he would rise

THRONE
Acts 7:49 ... Heaven is my *t*, and the
Heb 12:2 ... place of honor beside God's *t*.
Rev 3:21 ... sat with my Father on his *t*.
Rev 22:3 ... the *t* of God and of the Lamb

TIME
Luke 12:40 ... ready all the *t*, for the Son
John 4:53 ... was the very *t* Jesus had told
John 12:23 ... the *t* has come for the Son
Acts 18:5 ... spent all his *t* preaching
1 Cor 7:29 ... The *t* that remains is very
2 Cor 6:2 ... the "right *t*" is now.
Gal 6:9 ... just the right *t* we will reap
2 Tim 1:9 ... the beginning of *t*—to show
Heb 9:28 ... once for all *t* as a sacrifice
Heb 10:12 ... for sins, good for all *t*.

TIRED
Gal 6:9 ... let's not get *t* of doing what
2 Thes 3:13 ... never get *t* of doing good.
Heb 12:12 ... new grip with your *t* hands

TODAY
Matt 6:11 ... Give us *t* the food we
Luke 2:11 ... born *t* in Bethlehem,
Luke 23:43 ... I assure you, *t* you will
Heb 13:8 ... is the same yesterday, *t*, and

TOMORROW
Rom 8:38 ... our worries about *t*—not even

TONGUE
Rom 14:11 ... and every *t* will confess
Phil 2:11 ... and every *t* confess that
Jas 3:5 ... same way, the *t* is a small

TONGUES *see also* LANGUAGE
1 Cor 14:4 ... speaks in *t* is strengthened
1 Cor 14:5 ... all speak in *t*, but even
Jas 3:2 ... if we could control our *t*, we

TOUCHED
Matt 14:36 ... all who *t* him were healed.
Luke 8:45 ... "Who *t* me?" Jesus asked.
1 Jn 1:1 ... and *t* him with our own hands.

TRANSFORM
Rom 12:2 ... let God *t* you into a new

TRANSFORMED
Matt 17:2 ... appearance was *t* so that his
Mark 9:2 ... Jesus' appearance was *t*,
1 Cor 15:51 ... but we will all be *t*!

TRAP
Matt 16:23 ... are a dangerous *t* to me.
Matt 22:15 ... to plot how to *t* Jesus into

TRAPPED
1 Tim 6:9 ... temptation and are *t* by many

TREASURE
Matt 6:21 ... Wherever your *t* is, there the
Matt 13:44 ... Heaven is like a *t* that a man
Luke 12:33 ... will store up *t* for you in
2 Cor 4:7 ... jars containing this great *t*.

TREASURES *see also* MONEY, POSSESSIONS, WEALTH
Matt 6:19 ... Don't store up *t* here on
Eph 3:8 ... the endless *t* available to
Col 2:3 ... hidden all the *t* of wisdom

TRIALS
John 16:33 ... have many *t* and sorrows.
Rom 5:3 ... into problems and *t*, for we
1 Pet 1:7 ... through many *t*, it will bring
1 Pet 4:12 ... at the fiery *t* you are going

TRICK
2 Cor 4:2 ... We don't try to *t* anyone
Eph 4:14 ... people try to *t* us with lies

TROUBLE *see also* TEST, TRIALS
Matt 6:34 ... Today's *t* is enough
Luke 7:6 ... Lord, don't *t* yourself by

TRUE
Luke 16:11 ... the *t* riches of heaven?
Luke 18:31 ... Son of Man will come *t*.
John 1:9 ... one who is the *t* light,
John 4:23 ... *t* worshipers will worship
John 15:1 ... I am the *t* grapevine,
John 17:3 ... know you, the only *t* God,
Rom 15:8 ... God is *t* to the promises
Eph 5:9 ... is good and right and *t*.
Phil 4:1 ... stay *t* to the Lord.
Phil 4:8 ... thoughts on what is *t*,
1 Jn 5:20 ... He is the only *t* God,
Rev 19:9 ... These are *t* words that come
Rev 22:6 ... seen is trustworthy and *t*.

TRUMPET
Matt 24:31 ... blast of a *t*, and they will
1 Cor 15:52 ... when the last *t* is blown.
1 Thes 4:16 ... with the *t* call of God.

TRUST *see also* BELIEVE, FAITH
John 12:46 ... who put their *t* in me
John 14:1 ... in God, and *t* also in me.
Rom 15:13 ... peace because you *t* in
Eph 3:17 ... hearts as you *t* in him.
1 Tim 6:17 ... not to *t* in their money,
2 Tim 1:12 ... the one in whom I *t*,
Heb 2:13 ... will put my *t* in him,
1 Jn 4:16 ... have put our *t* in his love.

TRUTH
Luke 1:4 ... can be certain of the *t*
John 4:23 ... Father in spirit and in *t*.
John 7:18 ... him speaks *t*, not lies.
John 8:32 ... the *t* will set you free.
John 8:44 ... there is no *t* in him.
John 14:6 ... way, the *t*, and the life.
John 14:17 ... who leads into all *t*.
John 15:26 ... Advocate—the Spirit of *t*.
John 16:13 ... the Spirit of *t* comes,
John 17:17 ... your word, which is *t*.
John 18:37 ... to testify to the *t*.
Rom 2:8 ... to obey the *t* and instead
2 Cor 13:8 ... always stand for the *t*.
Eph 4:15 ... will speak the *t* in love,

Eph 6:14 . . . the belt of *t* and the body
2 Thes 2:10 . . . *t* that would save them.
2 Thes 2:12 . . . rather than believing the *t*.
2 Tim 2:15 . . . explains the word of *t*.
Heb 10:26 . . . received knowledge of the *t*,
1 Pet 1:22 . . . you obeyed the *t*, so now
1 Jn 1:8 . . . and not living in the *t*.
1 Jn 3:19 . . . belong to the *t*, so we

TWELVE
Matt 10:1 . . . Jesus called his *t* disciples
Rev 21:12 . . . names of the *t* tribes of
Rev 21:14 . . . names of the *t* apostles of
Rev 21:21 . . . The *t* gates were made of

U

UNBELIEF
Matt 13:58 . . . there because of their *u*.
Mark 6:6 . . . he was amazed at their *u*.
Mark 9:24 . . . help me overcome my *u*!
Mark 16:14 . . . them for their stubborn *u*
1 Tim 1:13 . . . it in ignorance and *u*.

UNDERSTAND
Luke 24:45 . . . minds to *u* the Scriptures.
Acts 8:30 . . . Do you *u* what you are
Rom 7:15 . . . I don't really *u* myself,
1 Cor 2:14 . . . and they can't *u* it,
Gal 1:11 . . . you to *u* that the gospel
Eph 5:17 . . . thoughtlessly, but *u* what
Phil 1:10 . . . want you to *u* what really
Phil 4:7 . . . exceeds anything we can *u*.
Col 2:2 . . . that they *u* God's mysterious
2 Tim 2:7 . . . will help you *u* all these
Heb 11:3 . . . By faith we *u* that the entire

V

VALUABLE
Matt 10:31 . . . you are more *v* to God

VALUE
Matt 13:46 . . . pearl of great *v*, he sold
Phil 3:8 . . . the infinite *v* of knowing

VICTORY
Rom 8:37 . . . overwhelming *v* is ours
1 Cor 15:54 . . . Death is swallowed up in *v*.

VIRGIN
Matt 1:18 . . . while she was still a *v*, she

VOICE
Mark 1:3 . . . He is a *v* shouting in the
John 10:3 . . . sheep recognize his *v* and
John 12:28 . . . a *v* spoke from heaven,
Rev 3:20 . . . If you hear my *v* and open

VOMIT
2 Pet 2:22 . . . A dog returns to its *v*.

W

WAGES
Rom 4:4 . . . their *w* are not a gift,
Rom 6:23 . . . For the *w* of sin is death,

WAIT
Rom 8:23 . . . We, too, *w* with eager hope

WALK
Mark 2:9 . . . pick up your mat, and *w*
John 8:12 . . . have to *w* in darkness,

WAR
Rev 12:7 . . . Then there was *w* in heaven.
Rev 19:11 . . . and wages a righteous *w*.

WARN
1 Thes 5:14 . . . urge you to *w* those who
Heb 3:13 . . . You must *w* each other

WASH *see also* BAPTIZED, CLEANSE
John 13:5 . . . he began to *w* the disciples'
John 13:10 . . . does not need to *w*, except
Jas 4:8 . . . *W* your hands, you sinners;

WATCH
Matt 24:42 . . . you, too, must keep *w*!
1 Pet 3:12 . . . eyes of the Lord *w* over

WATER
Matt 14:25 . . . them, walking on the *w*.
John 4:10 . . . would give you living *w*.
1 Jn 5:6 . . . his baptism in *w* and by
Rev 7:17 . . . springs of life-giving *w*.
Rev 21:6 . . . springs of the *w* of life.

WAY
Matt 3:3 . . . Prepare the *w* for the
Matt 3:8 . . . Prove by the *w* you live
Luke 7:27 . . . prepare your *w* before you.
John 14:6 . . . I am the *w*, the truth,
1 Cor 10:13 . . . will show you a *w* out
Col 1:10 . . . Then the *w* you live will

WEAK
Matt 26:41 . . . but the body is *w*!
1 Cor 9:22 . . . bring the *w* to Christ.
2 Cor 12:10 . . . For when I am *w*, then
1 Thes 5:14 . . . care of those who are *w*.

WEALTH *see also* MONEY, POSSESSIONS, TREASURE(S)
Luke 19:8 . . . give half my *w* to the poor,
1 Tim 6:6 . . . contentment is itself great *w*.

WEAPONS
Eccl 9:18 . . . have wisdom than *w* of war,

WEARY
Matt 11:28 . . . you who are *w* and carry
Heb 12:3 . . . won't become *w* and give up.

WEEP
Luke 6:21 . . . blesses you who *w* now,
Rom 12:15 . . . and *w* with those who *w*.

WHITE
Matt 28:3 . . . clothing was as *w* as snow.
Rev 1:14 . . . like wool, as *w* as snow.
Rev 19:11 . . . a *w* horse was standing

WIFE
Eph 5:33 . . . love his *w* as he loves

WILDERNESS
Matt 3:3 . . . the *w*, 'Prepare the way
Luke 5:16 . . . withdrew to the *w* for

WILL
Matt 6:10 . . . May your *w* be done on
Matt 7:21 . . . who actually do the *w*
Matt 18:14 . . . heavenly Father's *w* that
Matt 26:39 . . . want your *w* to be done,
Matt 26:42 . . . I drink it, your *w* be done.
John 6:38 . . . heaven to do the *w* of God
1 Thes 5:18 . . . this is God's *w* for you

Heb 13:21 . . . need for doing his *w*.
1 Pet 4:2 . . . to do the *w* of God.

WINE
John 2:3 . . . The *w* supply ran out
Eph 5:18 . . . Don't be drunk with *w*,

WINGS
Luke 13:34 . . . chicks beneath her *w*,
Rev 4:8 . . . living beings had six *w*,

WISDOM
Luke 2:52 . . . Jesus grew in *w* and in
Eph 1:17 . . . you spiritual *w* and insight
2 Tim 3:15 . . . given you the *w* to receive
Jas 1:5 . . . If you need *w*, ask our
Rev 5:12 . . . riches and *w* and strength

WISE
Matt 2:1 . . . some *w* men from eastern
Matt 11:25 . . . who think themselves *w*
Rom 3:11 . . . No one is truly *w*; no one
1 Cor 12:8 . . . ability to give *w* advice;
Jas 3:13 . . . If you are *w* and understand

WITHERS
1 Pet 1:24 . . . grass *w* and the flower

WITNESS
John 1:8 . . . simply a *w* to tell about

WOLVES
Matt 7:15 . . . but are really vicious *w*.
Matt 10:16 . . . you out as sheep among *w*.

WONDERFUL
Matt 21:15 . . . saw these *w* miracles
Acts 20:24 . . . News about the *w* grace of
Titus 2:13 . . . hope to that *w* day when

WORD
Matt 4:4 . . . by every *w* that comes
John 17:17 . . . teach them your *w*, which
2 Cor 2:17 . . . We preach the *w* of God
2 Cor 4:2 . . . or distort the *w* of God.
Eph 6:17 . . . which is the *w* of God.
Phil 2:16 . . . firmly to the *w* of life;
2 Tim 2:15 . . . explains the *w* of truth.
Heb 4:12 . . . For the *w* of God is
Heb 5:12 . . . things about God's *w*.
Jas 1:22 . . . listen to God's *w*.
1 Pet 1:23 . . . eternal, living *w* of God.

WORDS
Matt 24:35 . . . my *w* will never disappear.
John 6:68 . . . the *w* that give eternal life.
John 15:7 . . . and my *w* remain in you,
1 Cor 2:13 . . . do not use *w* that come
1 Cor 14:9 . . . to people in *w* they don't
Rev 22:19 . . . any of the *w* from this book

WORK *see also* DEEDS
Matt 6:28 . . . They don't *w* or make their
Luke 13:24 . . . W hard to enter the narrow
John 4:34 . . . and from finishing his *w*.
Acts 13:2 . . . for the special *w* to which

Acts 20:24 . . . finishing the *w* assigned
Rom 4:5 . . . not because of their *w*, but
Rom 8:28 . . . to *w* together for the good
Rom 12:11 . . . Never be lazy, but *w* hard
1 Cor 3:5 . . . the *w* the Lord gave us.
1 Cor 15:58 . . . Always *w* enthusiastically
Gal 6:4 . . . attention to your own *w*, for
Eph 4:16 . . . part does its own special *w*,
Eph 4:28 . . . your hands for good hard *w*,
Phil 1:6 . . . began the good *w* within you,
2 Thes 3:10 . . . unwilling to *w* will not

WORLD
John 1:29 . . . away the sin of the *w*!
John 3:16 . . . God loved the *w* so much
John 8:12 . . . I am the light of the *w*.
John 16:33 . . . I have overcome the *w*.
1 Cor 3:19 . . . of this *w* is foolishness
1 Jn 5:4 . . . defeats this evil *w*, and

WORRY
Matt 6:25 . . . I tell you not to *w* about
Phil 4:6 . . . Don't *w* about anything;

WORSHIP
Matt 2:2 . . . we have come to *w* him.
John 4:24 . . . *w* in spirit and in truth.
1 Cor 10:14 . . . flee from the *w* of idols.

WOUNDS
John 20:20 . . . he showed them the *w* in
1 Pet 2:24 . . . By his *w* you are healed.

WRONG
Rom 7:19 . . . don't want to do what is *w*,
Rom 12:9 . . . Hate what is *w*. Hold tightly
Rom 13:10 . . . Love does no *w* to others,
Rom 16:19 . . . to stay innocent of any *w*.
2 Tim 3:16 . . . make us realize what is *w*
Jas 1:13 . . . God is never tempted to do *w*,

YEARS
Luke 3:23 . . . about thirty *y* old when
2 Pet 3:8 . . . like a thousand *y* to the
Rev 20:2 . . . in chains for a thousand *y*.

YOKE
Matt 11:29 . . . Take my *y* upon you.

YOUNG
Acts 2:17 . . . Your *y* men will see visions,
Titus 2:6 . . . encourage the *y* men to live
1 Jn 2:13 . . . you who are *y* in the faith

ZEAL
Rom 10:2 . . . but it is misdirected *z*.

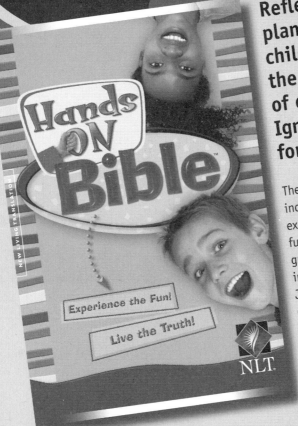